Policy Implementation
in Post-Mao China

STUDIES ON CHINA

A series of conference volumes sponsored by
the Joint Committee on Chinese Studies of the
American Council of Learned Societies and the
Social Science Research Council.

1. Origins of Chinese Civilization
edited by David N. Keightley,
University of California Press, 1982

2. Popular Chinese Literature and Performing Arts
in the People's Republic of China, 1949–1979
edited by Bonnie S. McDougall,
University of California Press, 1984

3. Class and Social Stratification in
Post-Revolution China
edited by James L. Watson
Cambridge University Press, 1984

4. Popular Culture in Late Imperial China
edited by David Johnson, Andrew J. Nathan, and Evelyn S. Rawski,
University of California Press, 1985

5. Kinship Organization in Late Imperial China, 1000–1940
edited by Patricia Buckley Ebrey and James L. Watson,
University of California Press, 1986

6. The Vitality of the Lyric Voice:
Shih Poetry from the Late Han to the T'ang
edited by Shuen-fu Lin and Stephen Owen,
Princeton University Press, 1986

7. Policy Implementation in Post-Mao China
edited by David M. Lampton,
University of California Press, 1987

Policy Implementation
in Post-Mao China

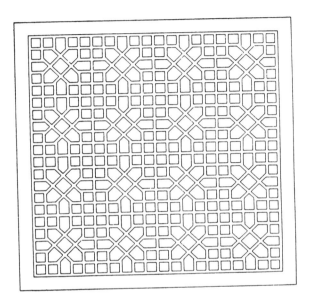

EDITED BY

David M. Lampton

UNIVERSITY OF CALIFORNIA PRESS

Berkeley · Los Angeles · London

This project was sponsored by the Joint Committee on Chinese Studies of the American Council of Learned Societies and the Social Science Research Council, with funds provided by the Andrew W. Mellon Foundation, the Ford Foundation, and the National Endowment for the Humanities.

University of California Press
Berkeley and Los Angeles, California
University of California Press, Ltd.
London, England
© 1987 by
The Regents of the University of California

Printed in the United States of America
1 2 3 4 5 6 7 8 9

Library of Congress Cataloging-in-Publication Data
Main entry under title:

Policy implementation in post-Mao China.

(Studies on China; 7)
Rev. papers from a conference held June 1983, Columbus, Ohio, sponsored by the Joint Committee on Chinese Studies of the American Council of Learned Societies and the Mershon Center of Ohio State University.
Includes index.
1. China—Politics and government—1976—
—Congresses.   I. Lampton, David M.
II. Joint Committee on Chinese Studies (U.S.)
III. Mershon Center for Education in National Security.   IV. Series.
DS779.16.P65   1987   320.951   85-23218
ISBN 0-520-05706-6 (alk. paper)

To those who had the vision to build a diversified infrastructure for the study of contemporary China. A call for this generation to maintain and improve the pillars of that edifice:

Archival resources in the West
Field and archival research in China
Language training in Taiwan
Research opportunities in Hong Kong

CONTENTS

TABLES

PREFACE

The June 1983 Columbus Conference and that gathering's revised papers, which constitute this volume, reflect the contributions of many individuals and organizations. Michel C. Oksenberg, then Chair of the Subcommittee on Political Science of the Joint Committee on Chinese Studies of the American Council of Learned Societies (ACLS) and the Social Science Research Council (SSRC), stimulated me to develop a conference proposal. My hope was to bring together scholars whose work was on the cutting edge of research on contemporary China and to provide a forum in which questions of comparative and disciplinary interest could be addressed.

Before the conference, during the meeting itself, and throughout the subsequent editorial process, I have received guidance and assistance from the following individuals: A. Doak Barnett, Thomas P. Bernstein, Richard Gunther, Harry Harding, Charles F. Hermann, Nicholas Lardy, John W. Lewis, Michel C. Oksenberg, Susan Shirk, and Peter Suttmeier. Special medals of commendation should be struck for Merilee Grindle and Randall Ripley, who repeatedly and with good humor challenged the conferees to extract from the China data the broader comparative implications. At the University of California Press, Gladys Castor edited the manuscript admirably and Rose Vekony moved it skillfully through to publication. To all I wish to express my gratitude.

Conferences need ideas as well as individuals and organizations willing to commit resources to their realization. In this enterprise I was blessed with the intellectual and material support of the two cosponsors (The Joint Committee and Ohio State University's Mershon Center), as well as that of the Department of Political Science and the East Asian Studies Program at Ohio State. I wish to thank Professor Charles F. Hermann, Director of the Mershon Center, and Carole Dale for their manifold exertions in both the pre- and postconference phases. Professor Chen Chung-min, Director of Ohio State University's East Asian Studies Program, and Sara Simpson also contributed mightily to the success of the meeting.

It is fitting that I single out two persons for special mention because they figured so centrally in all stages of the process leading to this volume: Dr. Jason Parker (American Council of Learned Societies) and Dr. Sophie Sa (Social Science Research Council). Both individuals have liberally contributed their knowledge of China and the China studies field to this and many other projects—our scholarly community owes them a great debt, and I wish to express our field's collective gratitude.

As I look back on the Columbus Conference and consider this volume that resulted from it, I have been struck with renewed force by the following observation: A community of scholars that defines itself in terms of a country of study must continually and self-consciously exert itself to ask questions that have meaning to the disciplines. Conversely, the disciplines must develop the conceptual tools and information to make the quest for general theory credible. The problem is simply this: How can we speak and contribute to our disciplines without becoming captives of them? This volume represents an effort to avoid both the Scylla of disciplinary irrelevance and the Charybdis of the addressing of issues that generate little interest or light among sinologists. In this enterprise, all of the people mentioned above sought to prevent me from running afoul of these hazards. It is for the reader to judge the success of those efforts.

David M. Lampton

PART I

Introduction

ONE

The Implementation Problem in Post-Mao China

David M. Lampton

An insider at the White House once told me that the image of the President of the United States as the captain of the ship of state, firmly in command at the helm, had but one defect—the wheel was not connected to the rudder!

In all organizations and polities there is a disjuncture between leadership intention, organizational behavior, and the actual results of action. One basic task confronting the public-policy analyst is to describe and explain the state's steering mechanism *and* the external forces that buffet the entire ship of state in the course of policy implementation. We need to understand the interrelationships among the *content* of policy, the institutional structures in which policy is implemented, and the wider sociopolitical *context* in which these structures and processes operate.[1]

This brings us to China. China's history since the mid-nineteenth century, and more particularly under its Communist leadership, has been that of a succession of contradictory efforts to produce economic and social change. Since Mao Zedong's death in September 1976 a new phase in the ongoing effort to modernize has been launched: "the four modernizations." In this latest modernization effort Deng Xiaoping and his allies intend to change the very structure and operation of China's rural and urban economy, overhaul aspects of the political and policy-making system, revitalize and reform the educational system, change the country's orientation toward (and role in) the global economy, and alter the nation's demographic trajectory. These efforts put in bold relief a question of universal concern: Is it possible for mass societies with their complex bureaucracies, in a matrix of global interdependency, to fix social purposes and proceed to implement them? At what social, economic, and political costs?

---

[1] Merilee S. Grindle, ed., *Politics and Policy Implementation in the Third World* (Princeton: Princeton University Press, 1980); also see James G. March and Johan P. Olson, "Organizing Political Life: What Administrative Reorganization Tells Us about Government," *American Political Science Review* 77, no. 2 (1983): 292.

The literature on policy implementation, as it pertains to states in both the industrialized and developing worlds, documents the difficulty in assuring congruence between policy intent and actual outcome. There also is agreement on the generic factors affecting policy implementation—the scope of affected interests, the characteristics of implementing agencies, the level of available resources and elite attention (commitment), the clarity and complexity of policy, the time span over which policy must be implemented, incentives for compliance, capacity to monitor policy implementation, and the relationship of implementors to clients.[2] Regrettably, however, the formal policy-implementation literature makes few references to Communist countries and none to China specifically.[3] China's sweeping objectives to produce politically directed change, in a setting in which central control and capacity to mobilize is sometimes impressive, offer the prospect of enriching the comparative literature on policy implementation.

THE IMPLEMENTATION APPROACH AS A WINDOW ON CHINESE POLITICS

The implementation literature does two things: First, it focuses attention on a particular phase of the policy process (the stage between the high politics of policy formulation and feedback once the effects of policies become apparent). Second, the approach identifies some generic variables that account for the difficulties policy makers in Beijing, Washington, Carthage, and Caesar's Rome have encountered in their efforts to assure that central directives are faithfully, efficiently, and predictably implemented by subordinates throughout the chain of influence—frequently there is no chain of *command*.

The implementation approach moves the level of analysis downward by viewing central politics in its interactive relationship with the multitude of subordinate functional and territorial entities. Moreover, the approach disaggregates "the Center" (*zhongyang*), making it clear that central authority in the national capital is itself highly fragmented. With Mao Zedong gone, greater foreign access to Chinese society at all levels, the proliferation of publications and statistics, and many Chinese voices speaking, what now strikes the observer is the diversity of the Chinese system and the tenuous

---

[2] Eugene Bardach, *The Implementation Game* (Cambridge: MIT Press, 1979); Helen Ingram, "Policy Implementation Through Bargaining," *Public Policy* 25, no. 4 (1977); Howard Leichter, *A Comparative Approach to Policy Analysis* (Cambridge: Cambridge University Press, 1979); Robert T. Nakamura and Frank Smallwood, *The Politics of Policy Implementation* (New York: St. Martin's Press, 1980); Jeffrey Pressman and Aaron Wildavsky, *Implementation* (Berkeley and Los Angeles: University of California Press, 1973); Randall Ripley and Grace Franklin, *Bureaucracy and Policy Implementation* (Homewood, Ill.: Dorsey Press, 1982); Walter Williams, *Studying Implementation: Methodological and Administrative Issues* (Chatham, N.J.: Chatham House Publisher, 1982).

[3] Karl W. Ryavec, *Implementation of Soviet Economic Reforms: Political, Organizational and Social Processes* (New York: Praeger, 1975).

hold that Beijing has over the hinterlands. It is precisely these circumstances of diversity, conflict, fragmented authority, and central policy that diverges from local reality, which the implementation approach is most useful in analyzing.

And herein lies the perspective's greatest danger. In fully acknowledging the many constraints Beijing faces, we must also remember that China has produced some changes that only a system with very great muscle could accomplish. The regime's draconian population policy has seemingly produced a birthrate which has dropped faster than that in any other very large less-developed country. Similarly, from 1957 until recently, the 800 million Chinese peasants were kept in collective agricultural units (communes), which demonstrably ran counter to their economic interests and predispositions. The Chinese state was able to depress the rate of population growth in urban areas considerably during the decade between the mid-1960s and the mid-1970s, with the mass deportation of urban youth to the countryside being but one of the methods employed.

In our fascination with the system's squeaky mechanism, a mechanism in which consultation, unresponsiveness, and miscommunication are conspicuous features, we must not forget that if power is the capacity to motivate people to do what they otherwise would not do, the Communists have produced a powerful system indeed.

THE ILLUSIVE CONCEPT OF IMPLEMENTATION "SUCCESS" AND "FAILURE"

Built into the very fabric of implementation analysis is the quest to identify factors that account for "successful" or, alternatively, "failed" policy implementation. There needs to be, it seems, a dependent variable (success or failure) that gives meaning to the search for explanatory factors. Yet, in the comparative literature and in the chapters that follow, there is no agreement concerning how one knows an implementation success or failure when one sees it. In the end, there are two very different concepts of success and failure, each of which has its own practical and conceptual drawbacks.

The first and most widely used definition of success presumes that congruence between the stated intention of policy makers (and formal policy documents) and actual policy outcomes signals success. If the makers promulgate policies designed to boost agricultural production, if those policies are put into effect, and if agricultural output rises, then such an implementation effort is declared successful (see chapter 9 in this volume). Logical as this reasoning may be, the attempt to link intention to outcome (and defining success as congruence between the two) has several generic defects.

For example, whose intentions does the analyst declare to be authoritative? Declarative policy frequently embodies diverse goals, thereby raising the question, Which goals are to be regarded as primary? Most policies are the result of coalitions, the members of which have come together for quite different reasons. One element of a coalition may come to see a previously agreed upon policy as a success, whereas another may soon come to view its continued implementation as increasingly disadvantageous. For instance, China's military leadership may have initially supported the liberalization of rural economic policy, partly in order to win peasant enthusiasm and boost the morale of its peasant recruits. However, as these rural reforms have been implemented (and rural incomes have jumped) it has become harder for the military to retain and recruit personnel.

This raises the related problem of unintended consequences flowing from policy implementation. Even if a policy indisputably achieves widely shared goals, these efforts may also have consequences that were unintended, the effects of which may lead some previous supporters to defect from the coalition. Sometimes the unintended consequences of policy can become the principal consequences. For example, the return to household production in China's countryside (along with increases in state commodity-purchase prices) has contributed to dramatic gains in agricultural output, with grain production rising 21.4 percent between 1978 and 1983 (while grain crops occupied progressively less arable land). Cotton output climbed 75.3 percent during the same period.[4] Predictably, peasant incomes (1978–1982) rose dramatically, with per capita income from the "collective" rising 58.2 percent and income from household sideline production rising 87.2 percent.[5]

However, the same policies that have boosted production have also simultaneously created incentives for families to maximize incomes by indiscriminately cutting trees (see chapter 8) and having more children (see chapter 10). Moreover, families have fewer incentives to maintain public works in the countryside, and there have been reports of increased rural illiteracy because some peasants have withdrawn children from school so they can labor in the fields. Similarly, higher state purchase prices for rural produce, while keeping urban consumer prices low, has saddled the national treasury with budget-busting subsidy expenditures. At what point, then, does one conclude that the implementation of one policy, taken in the context of its total effects, has succeeded or failed?

Judging implementation success by assessing the congruence between intention and outcome is further complicated by the "hidden agenda" problem. Frequently the principal objective of policy remains unspoken. For instance, if the criterion for judging the success of local elections in the post-Mao era is the institutionalization of democratic procedures, then, as McCormick

---

[4] *China Business Review*, January–February 1984, 52.

[5] Xue Muqiao, ed., *Zhongguo Jingji Nianjian*, 1983 (Almanac of China's Economy) (Beijing: Economic Management Magazine Press, 1983), III-42. Hereafter referred to as *Almanac 1983*.

shows in chapter 13, success has been limited indeed. However, if the principal purpose of elections was to remove or co-opt local cadres who might (or did) resist reform policies, then the implementation effort could be assessed more positively. The analyst must not confuse his or her goals with the actual objectives of the Chinese elite or confuse the elite's declared purposes with the totality of its actual aims.

The attempt to assess the congruence between intention and outcome is one method by which to gauge implementation success or failure. The procedural approach is another. Using such an approach, one does not become preoccupied with outcomes. Instead, one seeks to assess whether declarative policy was implemented efficiently and in ways consistent with the procedures called for in the policy document; if procedures were followed, it was successful by definition. This seemingly simple approach has precisely that virtue—simplicity; it avoids the problems of specifying intentionality and outcome.

UNIFYING THEMES

Policy implementation has been a central and self-conscious concern of the Chinese Communist elite since the Yanan days of the 1930s and 1940s. In April 1943, in "How to Be a Good Leader," Zhou Enlai explicitly dealt with the subject, saying that the implementation process must be consciously conceived and directed, elite attention and involvement must be sustained at a high level, program evaluation criteria must be explicit, and a monitoring system must be in place.[6] Zhou's analysis predates but closely parallels some of the central findings of contemporary policy analysis.

The Context: Institutional Structure and the Cycle of Reform

Mao, like Lenin before him in the Soviet Union, seized the "commanding heights" of the Chinese polity and economy and then fashioned institutions in the image of the Stalinist centrally planned bureaucratic system, a system with a number of features that are particularly salient to policy implementation. First, a comparatively high percentage of all social, economic, and political decisions are made centrally. The central decision-making apparatus is chronically overloaded. Feedback is slow, and therefore dysfunctional policies are continued for long periods before they are abruptly reversed.

Second, because the central authorities must monitor so many aspects of the economy and polity, they adopt simplistic performance indicators. Frequently these summary indicators produce micro economic and political behavior that is unanticipated. Furthermore, the multiplicity of performance

---

[6] Zhou Enlai, *Selected Works of Zhou Enlai*, vol. 1 (Beijing: Foreign Languages Press, 1981), 147.

objectives forces subordinate units and localities to emphasize a few objectives and ignore the rest. Both dynamics make unanticipated consequences and underachievement of objectives inevitable.

Third, the Party's monopoly over broad policy direction, and its ideological legitimization of this control, limits the inputs brought to bear on the formulation of policy. Subordinates become hesitant to speak out in the implementation process, preferring to wait until the failure is acknowledged by the Party itself. Fourth, because of Populist elements of the ideology, particularly under Mao, the bringing of the knowledge of experts to bear on policy was always in tension with the compulsion to seek legitimization in anti-intellectual behavior. In this setting, therefore, the subtle process of shaping (or sabotaging) implementation becomes the most effective avenue by which individuals, localities, and organizations can express their interests and shape policy to fit the peculiarities of their situations.

All of these features of the institutional system, and the pathologies and dissatisfactions to which they give rise, have created what Ed Hewett calls the "cycle of reform"—what others have called the "treadmill of reform."

> The frequency with which reform measures have been introduced in the Soviet Union and Eastern Europe testifies to the recurring dissatisfactions *leaders* have had with the traditional system. Indeed, it is the cycles of dissatisfaction within the leadership which drive reform cycles. . . . The implementation stage which follows is generally one of growing disappointment as old problems remain at least partially, if not totally, unresolved and new problems arise. Thus begins another cycle with growing concerns within the leadership about an interrelated set of problems, including many identified during the previous cycle.[7] (emphasis added)

In short, many of the implementation problems we see in the chapters to follow are endemic to centralized Leninist political and Stalinist bureaucratic systems. The reform measures analyzed in the chapters that follow were initiated by disaffected leaders facing widespread popular dissatisfaction. It remains to be seen whether these reforms accomplish more than past efforts in the Soviet Union, Eastern Europe, and, indeed, earlier efforts in the People's Republic itself have done.[8]

The Context: Tactics and Memory

If we wish to understand why certain reform efforts succeed while others flounder or spectacularly abort, we must consider the context, the random events occurring within it, the patterns of interpersonal relations, and elite

---

[7] Ed. A. Hewett, "Economic Reform in the Soviet Union and Eastern Europe" (Paper prepared for presentation at the Conference on "Reform of the Chinese Political Order," Wychmere Harbor Club and Hotel, Harwichport, Mass., June 18–24, 1984), 27–28.

[8] Harry Harding, *Organizing China* (Stanford: Stanford University Press, 1981), 32–86.

attention. Merely assessing the merits of the policy will get the analyst of politics little farther than it gets participants in the political process itself.

One recurrent theme throughout this volume is that a principal task of political leadership is to create an institutional and personnel context hospitable to the regime's specific policy initiatives. Since his "second coming" in late 1977, after a decade-long political exile dating from the earliest days of the Cultural Revolution, Deng Xiaoping has endeavored to reengineer both policy formulation and implementation structures and to replace the people who staff organization at all levels. As Clarke shows (chapter 2), Deng carefully and patiently oscillated between personnel changes that facilitated institutional alterations and institutional changes that facilitated further personnel shifts. Leadership attempts to modify the context must reinforce efforts to implement policies, and both efforts must be conceived as an integrated package.

Zweig in chapter 9 carries this theme one step further by showing how phased introduction of the agricultural responsibility system progressively changed the political context. The success of each small step created a hospitable setting for the next carefully crafted move during the period 1978–1983. Each alteration in the context facilitated in turn the next ratchet of policy content change. By this means, Deng and Zhao Ziyang effectively and progressively squeezed potentially recalcitrant middle-level rural cadres between the demands of a reform-minded elite and the desires of many peasants to return to household-managed production. Each year's increase in agricultural production made it increasingly difficult for opponents of household production to resist the next incremental step on the road to what has become the virtual emasculation of the entire commune system.

Deng and his allies not only have sought to change leaders and structures, they also have labored to introduce economic incentives that will encourage altered behavior. In chapter 12 Simon shows how the environment for scientific and technological development must be altered in order to provide both researchers and production units the incentives to innovate and utilize new technology. Providing profit incentives and creating consulting firms are two ways in which Beijing has tried to engineer an environment that will accomplish these goals. To conclude, as leaders design policies, not only must they keep in mind the environment in which these are to be implemented, but the environment itself must be modified to be receptive to the policy initiative.

Another theme that emerges from several of the following chapters is that the implementation context is perceptual to a substantial degree. Today's behavior is shaped by the "lessons" that different actors believe they have learned from the past. The record of past failures and successes produces present actions and attitudes that dramatically affect the way "new" policies will be implemented. Failure in any system can become cumulative, as can success. For instance, in chapter 4, which deals with Beijing's efforts to control the inflation of 1980, Solinger suggests that prior experience with uncontrollable inflation during the 1940s was one reason the elite and local implementors reacted (overreacted?) so decisively to a comparatively modest rate of price increase. Everyone recognized that this earlier episode had broken the political back of the Guomindang (Kuomintang). Vivid memories in the rural sector also affect the implementation of policy. Prior experience with poor quality medical care delivered in a mass campaign mode has augmented the already great reluctance of peasants to comply with demands for abortion and sterilization, as White suggests in chapter 10.

Policy Content

As important as the context in which policies are implemented is the *content* of the policies themselves. Some policies, by their very objectives and the means specified to achieve them, are difficult to implement. The content of post-Mao policies is strikingly different from that of the pre-1976 era.

Beijing is seeking direct control over a narrower range of economic and social activities than had Mao Zedong and, in many (but by no means all) areas of public policy, is trying to implement initiatives *indirectly* by manipulating individual and unit economic incentives. It should be underscored, however, that post-Mao leaders *have no intention* of reducing their control over the polity and economy. Rather, Mao's successors are endeavoring to control less and to control it better. These alterations should facilitate policy implementation while giving rise to new problems, as is evident in the chapters that follow.

Much of post-Mao policy deals with economic issues and is *deregulatory* in character. Deregulatory policies, by their nature, assume that policy should rely on its congruence with popular predisposition to assure implementation—bureaucratic or coercive mechanisms should only be necessary at the margins to prevent excesses, which would be widely recognized as such. In an important respect, these policies are designed to be self-implementing. In chapter 9 we see Beijing counting on peasant entrepreneurship to facilitate the implementation of the agricultural responsibility system, even in the face of the opposition of some local leaders. Scientists, Simon tells us, are encouraged to innovate, and factories are induced to use those innovations by providing economic incentives to both innovators and potential users. As Solinger explains, efforts to overhaul the commercial system have focused on introducing elements of the free market into the production and marketing systems. Ross shows in chapter 8 how Beijing has sought to improve forestry work by giving individuals ownership rights over some forested lands. Finally, Bachman in chapter 5 describes how the tax system is increasingly being viewed as a flexible means by which to structure incentives throughout the entire system.

The pathologies to which Mao Zedong's bureaucratic and mass campaign modes of policy implementation were vulnerable need not be catalogued here. However, in our Western enthusiasm for economic incentives and deregulation, it is prudent to observe that deregulatory policies produce at least three generic problems: unintended consequences, bureaucratic opposition from agencies whose role is diminished, and demands for further reform in a centrally planned economy with administratively set prices. With respect to the latter consequence, because deregulatory policies generally rely on economic incentives, and economic incentives are integrally related to prices, the logic of reform creates pressure to modify the rigid price system. Such modifications, however, run into a galaxy of bureaucratic, enterprise, and popular interests that have a stake in maintaining the benefits conferred on them by an "economically irrational" price system.

Interaction Among and Within Policies and Unanticipated Consequences
Much of the literature on policy implementation analyzes specific policies in isolation from other initiatives which may profoundly affect the fate of the particular policy under consideration. Because China has sought state-directed change in so many directions simultaneously, it provides a superb opportunity to observe the interaction among policies that may appear, at first blush, to have little relationship to one another. As was noted above, deregulatory policies frequently produce unintended consequences.

The Naughton and Fingar chapters reveal how the decision to decentralize some control over investment resources in the late 1970s (through retention of enterprise profit and other measures) made it *more* difficult for central planners to assure increased investment in energy and transport infrastructure, which also was a high central priority. Decentralization policies, designed to enhance local production incentives, simultaneously increased the capacity of localities to resist Beijing's sectoral investment priorities. More precisely, 83.3 percent of all capital construction investment in 1978 was *within* the national budget. By 1982 this percentage had fallen to 49.8 percent— 50.2 percent of all such investment was, by then, *"outside the budget."*[9] Aggregate expenditures have been contained only by the national authorities' holding down central spending while the localities continue to pursue their own priorities.

Other policy bundles have similar interrelationships. As Solinger demonstrates, central pleas to "enliven" the economy through the increased use of free markets, profit retention, and encouragement of household sideline production ran counter to concurrent regime efforts in 1980 to assure price stability by price freezes. The pursuit of one policy impeded realization of the other. Reinforcing the theme that policies in the urban sector frequently work at cross purposes, Lampton in chapter 6 shows how enterprises, now

[9] *Almanac 1983*, III-28.

eager to boost profits under the new profit-retention policies, resist increases in water and utility charges. Such fee increases would reduce the squandering of water, which the regime asserts is a major priority, particularly in North China.

The contradictions among policies are equally apparent in the rural sector. The interactive effects of the agricultural responsibility initiatives and the birth control campaign may be one of the most important events to occur in Chinese villages in the post-Mao era. As chapter 10 documents, the agricultural responsibility system, and the way in which contract land plots are allocated among villagers, provide economic incentives, which reinforce traditional peasant desires to have more male offspring. In addition, dismemberment of commune organizations made it more difficult to oversee the implementation of birth control policy just as the regime sought to monitor and enforce stricter regulations. As a result of all these and other demographic factors, the birthrate, which in 1979 was 17.8/1,000, had risen by 1982 to 21.1/1,000.[10] The 1983 birthrate was down slightly to "20 per thousand or less,"[11] according to Beijing. Though changes in birthrates reflect many factors, some of which are beyond the sway of public policy, today's household production system works at cross-purposes to the regime's efforts to curb population growth. Moreover, increased pressure to limit births, in the context of policies that make male offspring more desirable, has produced what appears to be an increased incidence of female infanticide.

Rural economic initiatives also have had adverse effects on the resource and conservation efforts of the regime. As chapters 6 and 8 show, a wave of deforestation followed implementation of the new agricultural policies and the reopening of rural free markets. Eager to augment their incomes quickly, peasants seized the opportunity afforded by access to free markets and other unregulated outlets for lumber. Trees were felled wherever they could be found. Similarly, now eager to expand the acreage under their family's control, peasants in some localities have encroached on waterways, floodplains, dikes, and every conceivable piece of unoccupied land, inflicting heavy, long-term ecological costs on the natural system.

Single policies also can embrace divergent goals and thereby create a situation in which the realization of one objective impedes realization of the other and produces unanticipated consequences as well. In chapter 11 Rosen shows how the policy of reestablishing key schools simultaneously embodied two contradictory goals: to raise the quality of college entrants *and* to help elevate the level of ordinary schools. Local administrators, however, focused on the easily measurable objective of increasing the percentage of their students who passed the college entrance examinations, for this became

[10] Ibid., III-5.
[11] *Beijing Review*, 1984, no. 13:10.

the best indicator of successful implementation. Success meant more money and better conditions for the schools. From this, it was but a small step to concentrating only on the most promising students and having schools compete for the best talent. In the end, the competitive dynamic created a setting in which each key school became reticent to help other institutions. Predictably, ordinary schools became intellectual backwaters with demoralized students and teachers. Even less promising students within the key schools themselves received less attention.

As a final example, Beijing's successful effort to stimulate agricultural production by raising its commodity purchase prices in 1979, and simultaneously trying to head off urban dissatisfaction by holding urban sales prices for food constant, has saddled the regime with enormous subsidy costs. In the three years 1979–1981,

> 41,600 million yuan were spent on keeping down the cost of grain, cooking oil, non staple foodstuffs and industrial products made with agricultural raw materials. These subsidies were paid to offset the increases in the state purchasing prices for farm produce and sideline products, which came into effect three years ago [1979] as part of an overall policy to boost agricultural production.[12]

Government subsidies designed to insulate urban residents from the full cost of consumption goods constituted about 22 percent of the total national budget in 1981.[13] For the years 1979–1981, 19.3 percent of all state revenue went to various food, rent, medical, and recreational subsidies.[14] In short, unless the regime is willing to pass costs directly on to consumers, greatly raise taxes, or print enormous quantities of money to finance debt, there are fiscal limits to how far the use of economic levers can go.

The interaction among policies and goal conflicts within policies are two reasons that the implementation process frequently produces unintended or unanticipated consequences. Another is what Naughton dubs an "implementation bias"; all central policies are bent to serve local purposes. As unintended consequences multiply, incentives to continue policy implementation may be reduced by both intraelite and popular friction. One alternative is to push reform further in the hope that more system change will reduce the contradictions.

Several chapters in this volume illustrate how the unanticipated or unintended consequences of policies create pressures to end or modify the implementation effort. As the negative effects of the unrestrained quest for entrance examination success became apparent, Rosen tells us, school administrators, teachers, and parents in ever larger numbers have come to oppose the key-

---

[12] *Beijing Review*, 1982, no. 43:7.

[13] Ibid., 6, and *Almanac 1983*, III-33.

[14] *Beijing Review*, 1982, no. 43:7. For more on subsidies, see Ma Hong, *New Strategy for China's Economy* (Beijing: New World Press, 1983), 16.

school policy. Bachman, for example, reveals how tax exemptions designed to stimulate the growth of rural small-scale industry achieved their goal, but did so at the expense of producing severe shortages of raw materials at some large-scale state-run enterprises. The new small-scale facilities consumed raw materials that previously had kept big urban factories going.

The Cellular Polity: "Systems," "Units," "Independent Kingdoms," and "Mothers-in-Law"

In interviews with Chinese bureaucrats, the preceding four words and phrases pepper conversation. They define the conceptual and organizational space in which all policies are implemented. The multiplicity of organizational and territorial players, their prerogatives, information flows, the way in which budgets are allocated and careers are structured—all impede the implementation of policies that cut broadly across China's territorial and organizational map. There are methods to overcome these barriers, but each approach inflicts its own costs. Certainly the Party, state, and military systems, stretching from Beijing to the lowest levels of Chinese society, are powerful integrative mechanisms, each of which periodically has shown impressive capacity to mobilize and focus activity. Simultaneously, however, the parallel nature of these vertical hierarchies provides opportunities for maneuver to localities and individuals. Conflicting signals from each hierarchy can reduce unified central control.

A. Doak Barnett pointed out more than a decade ago that China is divided into vertical, functionally defined "systems" (*xitong*): finance and trade, political/legal affairs, culture and education, agriculture, national defense, and industry.[15] While details of this structure have changed over time, the broad contours have endured. Personnel decisions, career paths, budgetary allocations, and information flows are all shaped by these functionally defined hierarchical systems. More precisely, careers generally occur within single systems. Budget shares among systems tend to remain relatively stable over time, reflecting an incremental budgetary process, as the Fingar, Naughton, and Lampton chapters discuss. Ministries in one system have little leeway to deal with (much less control) functionally related entities in other systems. Because information flows vertically within systems, and less easily horizontally across systems, coordination and efficiency are difficult to achieve.

The organizational environment for implementation also is shaped by the ubiquitous "unit" (*danwei*). Units encapsulate individuals and are the building blocks of ministries, commissions, and other complex organizations, which in turn are aggregated into the systems mentioned above. For the

---

[15] A. Doak Barnett, *Cadres, Bureaucracy and Political Power in China* (New York: Columbia University Press, 1967).

urbanite at least, the unit is not simply a place where one works, it is the individual's anchor in an otherwise boiling sea, the place where one acquires housing, scarce commodities, retirement benefits, health care, education, and, at times, a job for one's children. Most people spend their entire career in the same unit. All of this has two principal consequences: First, individuals within units become loathe to challenge leaders and colleagues with whom they will have to associate for the rest of their lives. Second, a siege mentality develops in which everyone in the unit comes to perceive that there is a collective interest in avoiding changes in routine or in financial allocations.

While some of the above observations apply to all organizations, in China the unit is responsible for so much, and has so few resources with which to discharge its obligations, that the costs of failure argue against risk-taking that, at most, could only marginally improve the unit's position. The probability of significantly enhancing the unit's position is usually low; the costs of failure are always high.

From the above it is not surprising that units and systems abhor having to rely on other entities and are reluctant to share resources with them. Chinese organizations and localities are in a perpetual quest to reduce their reliance on others. Although central authorities use the words "independent kingdom" (*duli wangguo*) as a term of reproach, it is the sacred objective of every unit and territorial jurisdiction to achieve precisely this freedom of action. With the rigidities of a Stalinist supply, personnel, information, planning, and budgetary system, and in the context of Mao Zedong's thirty-year injunction that all units should become self-reliant, it would be surprising if it were otherwise. Of all the possessions that a local official can have, sources of income outside the [national] budget (*yusuanwai*) are the most treasured. In providing local authorities with extrabudgetary sources of revenue in the late 1970s and early 1980s, Beijing has provided subordinates power and security, which they will be loathe to relinquish.

Leaders at all levels see themselves as subject to the conflicting demands of an entire galaxy of superiors—"too many mothers-in-law" (*po po duo*). For instance, chapter 6 shows that builders of the Gezhouba Dam on the Yangtze River had their project slowed by the Finance Ministry, the State Planning Commission, the Ministry of Machine Building, the Ministry of Communications, and the Ministry of Agriculture, Animal Husbandry, and Fisheries, to mention just a few of the agencies involved. Every organization sees itself enmeshed in a web of interdependency in which there are many who can delay and frustrate and few who can expedite. China is a rococo version of Pressman and Wildavsky's "complexity of joint action."[16]

These characteristics of organizational structure and life have a number of

[16] Pressman and Wildavsky, *Implementation*, 87–124.

consequences, some of which have been identified above. However, none is more important than the coping strategy which the Chinese have developed —"the study of relationships" (*guanxixue*).

> "The network of relationships" [*guanxihu*] is an expression of unhealthy tendencies, which is mainly characterized by the abnormal relations among some cadres who make use of and protect each other and take advantage of their power to seek private interests. It is a factionalist network with seeking private interests as their common goal. . . . What merits our attention is that some comrades are always fond of stressing the "study of relationships." They often establish contact with others at the expense of policies and principles or seek personal gains through the "network of relationships."[17]

Indeed, so tenacious are these networks that *Shanxi Daily* observed that "like grass," they "cannot be burned out by a prairie fire."[18]

In the section "Rational Legalism and Patrimonialism" in chapter 13, McCormick argues that

> The comprehensive character of Leninist organization inevitably generates extensive networks of informal relationships. The state demands that nearly all significant social interaction should occur within the bounds of its formal organization; there is very little "space" for an autonomous civil society to negotiate formal relationships on its own. On the other hand, the hierarchical and compartmentalized structure of official organization leaves many potentially practical or profitable relationships without official sanction or regulation. Administrators of formal bureaucratic authority perpetually find that official purposes cannot be accomplished within the confines of official organization. They find that they must negotiate informal relationships beyond the state's formal supervision, relationships that in turn open avenues for the pursuit of personal aims.

In the end, Party discipline aside, it is safest if policy makers at all levels assume that every policy directive will be distorted and transformed to serve the needs of these ubiquitous "associations." These networks, when mobilized by a cohesive central leadership on behalf of state purpose, can facilitate policy implementation. When various networks are mobilized by opposing elements of a fragmented elite, or by local authorities bent on resisting policy, effective implementation can become impossible and corruption almost inevitable.

The above features of Chinese society and politics make policies that require cross-unit or cross-jurisdictional cooperation much harder to implement than policies that do not. In the case studies which follow, those undertakings which have witnessed the greatest delay or divergence between

---

[17] Foreign Broadcast Information Service, *Daily Report: China* (hereafter *FBIS*), 1984, no. 71:T2–3; also no. 70:R1–3.
[18] *FBIS*, 1984, no. 70:R3.

intention and outcome have involved resource policy. Every functional and administrative jurisdiction is affected by resource policy. Resource issues activate multitudes of participants and generate high levels of conflict. Chapter 7 on the State Energy Commission shows how organizational and jurisdictional friction over energy availability and price have hamstrung efforts to conserve energy, change investment patterns, or alter energy prices to reflect scarcity values. Similarly, Lampton discusses how plans for the vast Three Gorges Dam Project affect so many jurisdictions and organizations that the project has been delayed for nearly three decades.

In China's fragmented and cellular setting, how do central authorities attempt to overcome centrifugal forces? Besides Party discipline, persistent efforts to imbue leaders at all levels with an integrated ideology that will make subordinates more responsive to central demands, and the use of market forces, all of which have been discussed above, two further mechanisms stand out in the chapters that follow: First, interagency forums are numerous and essential—commissions, "technical committees," and "work meetings" abound. At each level of the system there is an entire repertoire of interagency vehicles charged with hammering out policies acceptable to affected agencies and jurisdictions *and then* overseeing the implementation of agreed-upon policy. Second, the greatest ally that one can have in any implementation effort is leadership commitment, attention, and solidarity. In chapter 9 Zweig attributes the success of the implementation of agricultural responsibility policy to elite constancy and attention, noting that "the consistency of meetings and documents, sustained elite attention, and responsiveness to problems over such a long period of time was a rather remarkable feat and a key ingredient in the successful implementation." When problems arise in the implementation process, one can predict that leadership attention has been absent or that implementors have been receiving multiple (and contradictory) signals from a divided elite. In her study of rural birth control efforts (chapter 10), White discusses how local leadership attention has been diverted away from population policy by the opportunities which agricultural reforms offer cadres to increase their own incomes. At the national level, Fingar attributes the problems in implementing energy policy partially to the absence of an effective and powerful "champion." And Ross, in his contribution on the obligatory tree-planting campaign, reminds the reader that some policies can be symbolic, commanding little elite attention or commitment in the first place.

THE SYSTEM AND SYSTEM CHANGE IN THE POST-MAO ERA

How would one characterize the Chinese political system based on the following chapters? How has the system changed in the post-Mao era? Will those changes be sustained?

The System

The China that emerges from the essays that follow is one in which consensus-building and negotiation are central to the political process. While none of the contributors to this volume would deny the system's coercive aspect, these chapters, dealing as they do with policy issues, highlight a different face of the regime, the face of the haggler in a Chinese market.

Naughton tells us that "the approval of any individual investment project is the result of a long process of accommodation and negotiation between numerous power centers." Bachman shows how central authorities, in implementing the new policy of substituting taxes for profits, "compromised on contentious issues" with enterprises and localities which feared that the new tax system would diminish their revenues. Indeed, the Center's attempts to anticipate opposition and placate interests reduced the degree of change. McCormick reveals the negotiating aspects of candidate nomination at local levels.

The reader will also see a society in which the elite's policies of reform and rapid change conflict with the profoundly incremental processes characteristic of the economic and social system. As Fingar's chapter on energy policy explains, "core [budgetary] allocations remain relatively stable from year-to-year, producing intense competition for marginal increases in total supply and to effect minor shifts in core allotments." Although one should *not* overemphasize the incremental nature of the system, given some of the short-term changes in sectoral allocations that have occurred in the post-Mao period, there is a general expectation that the pattern of resource distribution should not, and will not, change dramatically from year to year. Moreover, with a large portion of budgets committed to recurrent and nondiscretionary items, the capacity of superiors to use the power of the purse is diminished further. As Rosen explains with respect to the Ministry of Education, "with over 90 percent of ministry funding going to recurrent expenses . . . the Ministry of Education has relatively few convenient financial levers with which to discipline districts or individual schools."

The following pages also lay bare a system in which central policies are always distorted in ways advantageous to implementors. Localities and units will always try to maximize the percentage of resource over which they can exercise discretion, and they will use these resources to minimize conflict in their unit or locality and maximize their independent authority. Cadres and citizens alike attempt to loot the state. Policies are threatening to the degree that they seek change; they become opportunities to the degree that they promise gain. Bachman reveals how tax exemptions were provided by local cadres in ways consistent with their interests. The needs of the central treasury were largely irrelevant to their calculus.

The final attribute of the Chinese political system which stands out below is the very limited capacity of central authorities to oversee how policy is being implemented or to assess the full range of its effects in a timely manner. The monitoring problem has a number of origins, one of which is the physical and human components of the communication system itself. Illiteracy is still a major problem, with 43.9 percent of persons aged 35–54 illiterate. And, illiteracy is generously defined as knowing less than 1,500 characters.[19] In addition to these structural problems, poor indicators of performance are frequently used, and information is distorted as it is passed up the administrative hierarchy.

Rosen provides an example of how the use of simplistic measures to assess performance can have negative effects. Originally, key-school policy had two objectives: to produce and identify the most promising students as quickly as possible for universities, and to raise the level of all schools through increasing cooperation between key and ordinary schools. However, it was easier to measure the "promotion rate" (who passed exams) than it was to measure the assistance that key schools provided to ordinary facilities. The former measure won out, to the great detriment of the majority of schools, which found morale sinking rapidly.

The monitoring system is a blunt instrument, not only because of the way in which it is calibrated, but also because it must rely on distorted information provided by cadres who know that the Center has limited capacity to verify lower-level reports independently. Bachman shows that the reestablishment of auditing organs to oversee tax collection is but a limited attempt to deal with the pervasive problem of tax fraud. White, in her analysis of the implementation of rural birth control policies, reveals a perverse convergence of interest between cadres and peasants, a convergence that diminishes the effectiveness of the policy. Cadres are anxious to preserve the facade of complying with birth quotas. Peasants are eager to have more children. Therefore, data that underreport births serve the interests of both parties.

Finally, some policies are impossible to implement meaningfully given the present monitoring system. As Lampton shows, water conservation policy cannot be enforced effectively when major consumers are not equipped with water meters to measure consumption. Similarly, Fingar asks, "How, for example, was one to determine the relative energy efficiency of different enterprises if one lacked even rudimentary data on consumption of fuel and power?"

System Change

The above description of the Chinese polity is incomplete in two important respects: First, it ignores the coercive face of state power. The security apparatus still is very much present. Because the chapters in this volume concentrate on other policy issues, this coercive aspect is obscured. Nonetheless, the

[19] *Beijing Review*, 1984, no. 14:22.

taproots of authoritarianism run deep in China. Second, the attributes identified above are presented as static snapshots of the system in the post-Mao
era. A central question remains: What are the directions of change and in
what fundamental respects is today's China different from its Maoist in-
carnation? If there have been changes, will they endure?

There have been four fundamental dimensions of change in the post-Mao
era. Of most importance has been the evolution of the leadership structure
from a personalistic regime with totalitarian pretensions into a "techno-
authoritarian" state,[20] one in which, however, interpersonal networks will
remain of great importance. A collective leadership structure is gradually
replacing a system in which the whims of a single individual assumed
monumental importance. The elite's ambitions to produce change also have
been narrowed, becoming largely a quest for economic growth. The "new
Maoist man," and all that "he" implied for social policy and the exercise of
state power, is an increasingly dim apparition.

The movement of the regime in the direction of "techno-authoritarian-
ism" has produced changes in recruitment criteria, though the actual effects
of these policy changes remain to be seen. Increased emphasis is being placed
on technical bases for recruitment into both Party and state structures.
Between late 1982 and mid-1983, the average age of provincial governors
and vice-governors dropped by almost eight years, and the number of
persons in these posts with college education rose by 26.6 percent. The number of cadres at the prefectural, county, municipal, and town levels with
college education rose 14 percent.[21] This change threatens at least two generations: the "lost" generation of the Cultural Revolution era and the elderly
revolutionary cadres whose claim to authority resides hardly at all in technical qualifications. The questions raised by these developments are profound.
Will the technocrats be able to consolidate their power? And will their ascen-
sion to authority widen the mass-elite gap and increase socioeconomic inequalities to the point that technocratic control is undermined? Finally, do
these recruitment changes reflect anything more than the fact that Beijing
now wants "competent conformists, not ill-qualified slogan chanters"?[22]

Second, China is increasingly being drawn into the international system
in ways that will have far-reaching effects on the economy and polity. One

[20] Edwin A. Winckler, "Protracted Implementation: Synthetic Fibers Under Systemic
Change" (Paper presented at Workshop on Policy Implementation in Post-Mao China, Columbus, Ohio, June 20–24, 1983).

[21] Christopher M. Clarke, "Reforming Institutions to Institutionalize Reforms" (Paper presented at the Panel on Strategies of Central-Regional Conflict During China's Year of Reform at
the 1984 Annual Meeting of the Association for Asian Studies, Washington, D.C., March 23–25,
1984), 18; see also Christopher M. Clarke, "China's Third Generation," *China Business Review*,
March–April, 1984, 36–38.

[22] Personal correspondence from Andrew Walder, Aug. 1, 1984.

measure of this change is to consider that in the early twentieth century the "Open Door Policy" was a euphemism describing Western attempts to open an unwilling China to commercial penetration. Today the "open policy" is used by Beijing to entice the West into increasing financial involvement in China's modernization effort. This change is also reflected more tangibly. Between 1978 and 1983 the number of travelers' entries into and exits from China rose four times. In 1983, 265,033 Japanese and 168,298 American tourists visited the People's Republic of China (PRC).[23] Even more dramatic: whereas in 1977 China's total foreign trade accounted for about 8.6 percent of gross national product, by 1983 it accounted for 12.1 percent.[24] Still modest, the growth in trade nevertheless reveals a significant trend toward increasing involvement in, and gradually increasing dependence upon, the global economy, though China's degree of dependence on the international economic system is still, overall, quite modest compared with other Third World and newly industrializing countries. World commodity prices and interest rates, as well as foreign tariff and technology transfer policies, all have assumed an importance to Beijing that was inconceivable while the Chairman lived.

A third fundamental aspect of change in the post-Mao era has been what Naughton calls the increased internalization of resources in production units and the control of discretionary finances by authorities, enterprises, and individuals. This internalization has been most dramatically symbolized by the fact that in 1982 more than half of all capital construction investment was being expended "outside of the budget." State planning, without control over a large category of expenditure, can become a chimera. Only the future will tell whether Beijing will be able to recapture control and, if it does, at what price to economic growth.

Finally, the loss of financial control is only part of the story. The attempt to make increasing numbers of entities responsible for their own profits and losses, if successful, will affect not only the central planning apparatus but also other pillars of the Stalinist institutional edifice, such as the personnel, police, propaganda, and price organs. For instance, since 1979 there has been an explosive growth in the number of self-published and self-financed newspapers in rural localities. Today more than four hundred provincial and county newspapers exist, "accounting for more than 50 percent of all newspapers published in the country." John Fitzgerald goes on to explain:

> Few of these local newspapers are entitled to the state subsidies enjoyed by the official CCP press, most being forced to subsist on revenue from sales alone. The appearance in some papers of sexual innuendo, risque pictures and other material. . . reflects their attempts to maintain or increase circulation to levels

---

[23] *FBIS*, 1984, no. 59:K19.
[24] *China Business Review*, January–February 1984, 52–53.

necessary for survival . . . the authorities must find themselves in a quandary
when faced with the task of eliminating vulgarity without dampening economic
recovery.[25]

To put the dilemma pithily, the logic of the marketplace is at variance with
the control needs of China's planners, police, propagandists, and central personnel organs.

At the most fundamental level, the post-Mao era has witnessed a change
in the Party's role. Under Mao the Party was mobilizer of the populace; mass
campaigns were a preferred mode of policy implementation. It is indicative
of much in today's China that in this volume only chapter 8 deals with a
mass campaign implementation effort. The question of paramount importance for the future is, Will these four pillars of a Stalinist Party state (the
planners, the price bureaucracy, the police, and the propagandists) try to
reassert their grip and, if they do, at what cost to China's modernization
effort?

FUTURE RESEARCH AGENDA

The exponential increase in publications and statistical series available
from and in China, combined with steady progress in obtaining limited
opportunities for social science field research in the People's Republic, make
possible an increasingly broad range of research projects. In addition, Hong
Kong will remain an important site for research. In each phase of the policy
process there are numerous opportunities for exploration. The chapters that
follow pose questions for future research and are examples of the creative
possibilities that exist.

The process of policy formulation remains an important subject for research.
Mao's death, the restoration of the Party Secretariat, the decline in the Politburo's role, new patterns of elite recruitment, the emergence of new policy
advisory bodies, the increased dispersion of budgetary resources, a limited
revival of legislative bodies, and China's increased involvement in the global
economy—all these have implications for how policy is made in China. Research is needed on each of these institutions and processes. At a more
exalted theoretical level, now may be a good time to reopen issues of the role
of interest-group-like activity in the policy process. With economic power
fragmented to some extent, with ideological inhibitions to self-interested
activity seemingly diminished, and with economic goals so prominent, the
case for interest group perspectives may be stronger than it has seemed in
the past.

Entire dimensions of the policy formulation process cry out for examination. For example: How is the Chinese budget made? What is the role of the

[25] *Far Eastern Economic Review*, April 5, 1984, 44.

Finance Ministry? Is incremental budgeting characteristic of China today? in the past? Do revenue-generating ministries have more power than non-revenue-generating organizations? If revenues are a mere artifact of the administered price system, do various political actors seek to change prices to conform to their interests? What is the process by which localities try to maximize their discretionary revenue by keeping categories of revenue outside of the budget? How do localities exert pressure at the Center in order to protect benefits they derive from subsidization? With rhetorical emphasis now being placed on the separation of Party and state responsibilities, what is the role of the Party in the evolution of state policy? Finally, certainly one of the notable characteristics of the post-Mao policy era has been the strong impulse toward reform. Why has the impulse toward reform seemingly been so much stronger in China than in the Soviet Union?

Implementing policy is a subject which the following chapters by no means exhaust. What is the role of provinces in adapting (distorting) central policy? What kinds of political resources do subprovincial (district, county, and township) units have to resist or shape policy? How are interlocality and interministerial ad hoc conflict-resolving bodies established and how do they operate? How do organizational ideologies affect the way in which specific ministries react to and implement central policy? Do past experiences with policy failure and success affect the policy implementation environment? What accounts for elite attention and concern with respect to the implementation of some policies and not others? If present policy has important deregulatory qualities, will this enhance, or diminish, effective central control? Is "controlling less, but controlling better" possible? Or is it a rhetorical fig leaf behind which a real diminution of central power will occur? How do interpersonal networks affect policy implementation? Does a change in these networks have specifiable consequences for the implementation of policy? How is corruption related to these networks and what are its implications for policy implementation? Finally, do different kinds of policies (e.g., Lowi's "regulatory," "distributive," and "redistributive") have different kinds of implementation problems? The range of system levels, functional organizations, and administrative units for which these questions may be asked is broad indeed.

Policy impact and performance evaluation is a research theme with broad vistas. In this area, as perhaps in no other, China's decision to rebuild its statistical monitoring system and to release comparatively large quantities of performance data (on everything from educational enrollments, manpower, health care, income, production, natural resources, to foreign trade, transport, capital construction, labor productivity, banking, and welfare) has provided scholars with unprecedented opportunities for research.

These data make it almost impossible to avoid asking central questions: Why has industrial labor productivity not risen much in the late 1970s and early 1980s, given new incentive policies? Why has arable land area, forested acreage, and the length of navigable waterways declined in the last thirty years? What will be the effect of great reductions in senior middle school enrollments on youth attitudes and urban-rural cultural gaps? What will the decline in the number of rural barefoot doctors mean for rural health care? What will be (and have been) the consequences of rapid increases in domestic cotton production on China's textile industry, domestic consumer prices, and world trade? Are present rates of increase in agricultural output sustainable at present levels of state investment in agriculture? How much nonstate investment is going into agriculture?

The questions posed above are just a sampling of the important themes waiting to be explored. A new generation of students has but to roll up its sleeves and get to work.

TWO

Changing the Context for
Policy Implementation:
Organizational and
Personnel Reform in
Post-Mao China

Christopher M. Clarke

CLASS STRUGGLE OR MODERNIZATION?

Within a few months in 1976, three of the last remaining founding fathers
of the People's Republic of China (PRC) passed into history. Zhou Enlai,
member of the Politburo of the Communist Party since 1927 and the only
premier of the PRC in its twenty-seven years, died in January. In July, Zhu
De, the founder of the People's Liberation Army (PLA) passed away; most
unsettling was the death of Mao Zedong on September 9. For more than
thirty years Mao had been the key factor in Chinese politics, decisively affecting the direction of economic, social, and foreign policy.

In more than a generational sense, the death of Mao marked a turning
point in China. Political discourse under Mao had been framed by the injunction to take "class struggle as the key link" and by his calls for selflessness and self-reliance. All political argument was constrained by these values.
China's domestic development and foreign relations bore the deep imprint of
Mao's quest, and the Chairman's approach to politics had brought China to
the brink of catastrophe by 1976. The economy was in shambles, society was
fragmented by petty partisanship, and the leadership was deeply divided.

Within months of Mao's death a comparatively centrist coalition in the
Politburo had formed, committed to the elimination of the faction that had

The author wishes to express his appreciation to the following conference participants for their
constructive comments on an earlier draft of this chapter: A. Doak Barnett, Merilee S. Grindle,
Harry Harding, John W. Lewis, Michel Oksenberg, and especially David M. Lampton. Of
course, none of them bears any responsibility for any errors remaining.

fomented the disastrous Cultural Revolution and determined to achieve stability in society and productivity in the economy. The two years after the purge of the "Gang of Four" were a time of stocktaking and soul searching in China. As the nature and extent of the country's problems became clearer, the touchstone of political discourse changed from class struggle to modernization.

In virtually every area of public policy and private life, the new Chinese leadership found that the decade of the Cultural Revolution had exacted tremendous costs. Macro-level management of the economy had led to an unresponsive, overly centralized bureaucratic system dominated by heavy industry. Unneeded goods were produced and stockpiled while consumer needs and desires were ignored. Irrational concentration on heavy industry was squeezing energy supplies at a time when the growth of energy output had slowed drastically. The single-minded pursuit of high output quotas in industry had led to the neglect of quality considerations, while the state pricing system ignored supply and demand.

As serious as these problems were, their effects could have been mitigated by the efforts of a disciplined, highly motivated work force led by competent and forceful managers. The Cultural Revolution, however, had destroyed discipline, removed incentive, and emasculated management. The situation was much the same in the countryside. Cropping patterns were determined by administrative fiat with little concern for the suitability of land, climate, and experience. Distribution and payment emphasized equality and undermined the farmer's incentive to increase output.

Beginning in 1977, but particularly after the Central Committee's Third Plenum in December 1978, the Chinese leadership attempted to implement policies to address these problems;[1] these initiatives are the subjects of the case studies to follow. The use of private plots for peasants was restored, rural markets reemerged, and beginning in 1978, various schemes of contract responsibility designed to close the gap between labor and remuneration were tried.[2] (See chapter 9.) Reinforcing these changes in the incentive structure in farming was a series of increases in the purchase price for a number of important agricultural commodities including grain, cotton, edible oil, and pigs. Thus, between 1978 and 1980 the Chinese peasant was given greater latitude to respond to demand, to enjoy the fruits of his labor, and to market or consume a larger portion of his produce.

An initially more cautious but similarly conceived series of reforms was

[1] See Richard Baum, ed., *China's Four Modernizations* (Boulder: Westview Press, 1980); A. Doak Barnett, *China's Economy in Global Perspective* (Washington: Brookings, 1981); Joint Economic Committee of the U.S. Congress, *China Under the Four Modernizations* (Washington, D.C.: U.S. Government Printing Office, Part 1, August 1982; Part 2, December 1982).

[2] Albert Keidel, "Incentive Farming," *China Business Review* (hereafter *CBR*), November–December 1983.

begun in industry.[3] Workers were, in theory, to be held responsible for the quality and quantity of their labor and were once again to see performance linked to remuneration in the form of bonuses and promotions. In late 1977 four out of ten Chinese workers were promoted to a higher wage grade, while another one-fifth received a wage increase. Once again, in 1979, about 40 percent of the work force received an upward salary adjustment. Factories and enterprises, too, were to function under a system of responsibility for profits and losses. Quality control and profitability were now supposed to determine the fate of plant managers and foremen. Factories that continued to operate at a loss or that produced substandard goods were to be merged with other factories, shifted to producing something else, or in extreme cases shut down altogether.

The government also attempted to reestablish the prestige of management by setting up training programs and providing bonuses for successful managers. Managers were given greater latitude in purchasing supplies and selling excess production. Talk began of replacing profit quotas, which must be remitted to the state, with taxes, a program that would leave more funds in the hands of management for renovation, technical upgrading, and incentive packages for labor. (See chapter 5.) And banks were to play a more aggressively entrepreneurial role in financing capital investment.

Even as the Chinese leadership in 1977–1978 began to look at ways to reform the economy, they began to realize that such reforms could not succeed without reform in other areas as well. First, the central leadership would have to build popular support for and confidence in the regime.[4] This meant the establishment of the rule of law and the repudiation of the arbitrary "patriarchal, feudal" system that had existed under Mao. (See chapter 13.)

China's leaders moved across a broad front to strengthen popular support. Elections for local office were to be held again; often there would be even more candidates than positions to be filled. A whole new body of law was promulgated, including criminal, civil, economic, and foreign trade law.[5] Those most responsible for the breakdown of law and order in the Cultural Revolution, including the Gang of Four, were tried and sentenced. The culmination of this process was a formal assessment in July 1981 of the

---

[3] See chapter 3 below. See also Susan Shirk, "The Politics of Economic Reform in China" (Paper delivered at the 1983 meeting of the American Political Science Association, Chicago, September 1–4, 1983); Barry Naughton, "The Profit System," Audrey Donnithorne, "Fiscal Relations," and Andrew Walder, "Rice Bowl Reforms," all in *CBR*, November–December 1983.

[4] Chen Yun in particular called reform of the Party's work-style a "matter of life and death," a sentiment later publicly echoed by Deng Xiaoping, Hu Yaobang, and others.

[5] See, e.g., *Law Annual Report of China 1982/3* (Hong Kong: Kingsway International Publications, Ltd., 1982), and Marianna Graham, "China's Major Trade and Investment Laws," *CBR*, September–October 1983, 30–33.

role of Mao Zedong in modern Chinese history and his responsibility for the decade of chaos.

Part and parcel of this appeal for the support of the *laobaixing* (commoners) was the removal of Party interference from the minutiae of daily existence and the depoliticization of everyday life. Spare-time hobbies were rehabilitated, including a renaissance of what not long before had been called "feudal culture" such as traditional opera, calligraphy, and martial arts. Political meetings were reduced in number, and religion was revived and sanctioned.[6] The division between Communist Party and state functions had always been fuzzy, but another attempt to define their respective roles was undertaken. Again, the Party was to provide policy guidance and supervision but was to stay out of routine administration.

Finally, for the reform of the economy to succeed, the regime found that it needed to address the problems of youth and intellectuals. Rustication of urban young people was stopped, and many youths "sent down" during the previous fifteen years were allowed to return home. Because state employment opportunities were inadequate to absorb school-leavers, never mind returning "sent down youth," cooperative and even individual employment was encouraged, particularly in service trades. At the same time, intellectuals were declared to be workers, who happened to work with their brains rather than with their hands. Attempts were made to redress their grievances, reestablish their prestige, and raise their standard of living. Between 1977 and 1981 hundreds of professional and academic societies and an equally large number of professional and technical journals were revived after a decade of dormancy. The leadership of the Chinese Academy of Sciences was turned over to scientists in mid-1981, an indication of the political leadership's desire to motivate intellectuals. Most important, thousands of ordinary intellectuals, some of whom had suffered more than two decades of humiliation and discrimination, were rehabilitated and reinstated, or compensated for past wrongs.

If economic reform depended on rebuilding popular confidence and support, it depended equally on maintaining a stable international environment in which minimal Chinese resources would have to be expended on goals other than modernization. The 1979 "punitive expedition" against Vietnam particularly sensitized China's leaders to the high costs to their development program of international tension and conflict.[7] As a result, with

---

[6] Accounts by several recent resident foreign diplomats and journalists give a feel for this liberalization. See, e.g., Roger Garside, *Coming Alive: China After Mao* (New York: Mentor Books, 1982); John Fraser, *The Chinese: Portrait of a People* (New York: Summit Books, 1980); and Jay and Linda Matthews, *One Billion: A China Chronicle* (New York: Random House, 1983).

[7] This became clear at the Third Session of the Fifth National People's Congress in September 1980. See Wang Bingqian, "Report on Financial Work," *Beijing Review* (hereafter *BR*), Sept. 29, 1980. See also Harlan Jencks, "China's 'Punitive' War on Vietnam: A Military Assessment," *Asian Survey*, July 1979, and Daniel Tretiak, "China's Vietnam War and Its Consequences," *China Quarterly*, December 1979.

the exception of the spurt in defense spending in 1979 after the Vietnam incursion, Chinese military expenditures have been held down, to the frustration of some in the Chinese military. China has also pursued an international policy that sought good relations with almost every country on the globe, with the exception of South Africa and Israel.[8]

As China began seriously to examine her modernization needs, the leadership found that Chinese industry, science, technology, and military capability were from one to two decades behind advanced world levels and falling farther behind at an ever increasing rate. Only the acquisition of foreign technology, and ultimately foreign management techniques and investment capital, would enable the Chinese to achieve the Four Modernizations.

MODIFYING THE CONTEXT IN POST-MAO CHINA

The architect of the Four Modernizations and the driving force behind the effort to shift China from a preoccupation with class struggle to a concentration on reform and economic development has been Deng Xiaoping.[9] Deng, twice purged by Chairman Mao, had earlier sketched out the program for modernization in 1973 and 1974.[10] The program was officially unveiled by Zhou Enlai at the Fourth National People's Congress in January 1975, but its enactment was postponed by Zhou's terminal illness and death, and by the struggle for succession to both Zhou and Mao. Upon his return to power in 1977, Deng again began forcefully to promote his program of reform.[11]

However, the successful implementation of any policy, including Deng's reforms, depends on the combination of the *content* of the policies and the *context* within which they are implemented.[12] Deng's strategy is built on one of the key themes of the essays in this volume. The ideological, institutional, and economic environment has to be supportive of the implementation of particular policies. One of the principal jobs of political leadership is to

[8] See, e.g., Carol Lee Hamrin, "China Reassesses the Superpowers," *Pacific Affairs* 56, no. 2 (Summer 1983).

[9] See *Deng Xiaoping Wenxuan* (Selected Works of Deng Xiaoping; hereafter *DXPWS*) (Beijing: Renmin Chubanshe, 1983).

[10] Purported texts of "On Some Problems in Accelerating Industrial Development," "On the General Program of Work for the Whole Party and the Whole Nation," and "On Some Problems in the Fields of Science and Technology," none of which has ever been officially released to the public, are found in Chi Hsin, *The Case of the Gang of Four* (Hong Kong: Cosmos Books, 1977).

[11] Much of the reform program is laid out in Liao Gailong, "The '1980 Reform' Program of China," in *Chi Shih Nien Tai* (The Seventies), translated in Foreign Broadcast Information Service, *Daily Report: China* (hereafter *FBIS*), Mar. 16, 1981. See also numerous articles in *DXPWS*.

[12] See especially Peter S. Cleaves, "Implementation Amidst Scarcity and Apathy: Political Power and Policy Design," and Merilee S. Grindle, "Policy Content and Context in Implementation," both in Merilee S. Grindle, ed., *Politics and Policy Implementation in the Third World* (Princeton: Princeton University Press, 1980).

reengineer the environment so that specific policies stand a chance of being effectively implemented.

Deng realized that he was trying to implement his initiatives in an inhospitable context. The ideological climate in 1977 was still dominated by "class struggle" and the "two whatevers."[13] Deng fought an ideological and psychological battle to "emancipate the mind" and encourage people to "seek truth from facts," in order to change this dimension of the context.[14] Another important aspect of the implementation context was institutional. As early as 1975 Deng tried to implement organizational reforms, but was stymied by the inertia of the bureaucracy and the opposition of key central leaders.[15] After the fall of the Gang of Four, Deng again set out to modify the institutional context within which his reform policies would be implemented. China's organizational system, which Deng characterized as "very unsuited to the needs of the four modernizations,"[16] suffered from "overstaffing, duplication of work, unclear responsibilities, too many unqualified personnel, failure to shoulder responsibility, and lack of spirit, knowledge and efficiency in work."[17]

These organizational problems stemmed from three related causes, one actuarial and two historical. At the time of Mao's death, China was being led and administered by the same generation of Communist Party leaders who had brought the revolution to victory in 1949. Now, three decades later, many of these individuals were too feeble, infirm, or senile to discharge their responsibilities. This problem was pervasive, extending down to the local level. To cite a few examples, in 1980 the Ministry of Coal had eleven known vice-ministers; at least three of these were inactive and "near retirement,"[18] and several others worked outside of Beijing as regional coal administrators. The Ministry of Metallurgical Industry had some twenty leaders of the rank of vice-minister or minister, many of them either inactive or working outside Beijing. The eighteen vice-premiers of the State Council in mid-1980 averaged almost sixty-eight years of age. Members of the Communist Party Politburo averaged more than seventy-one years, and the average age of the leaders of the Party's Military Affairs Commission exceeded seventy-seven years.

In addition to this actuarial cause of organizational ossification, two re-

---

[13] "'The Two Whatevers' Do Not Conform With Marxism," *DXPWS*, 35–36.

[14] "Emancipate the Mind, Seek Truth From Facts, Unite as One and Look Forward," *DXPWS*, 130–43.

[15] "Persist in the Party Line and Improve Work Methods," *DXPWS*, 238–47, especially 244–45.

[16] Ibid., 244.

[17] "Streamlining Institutions Is a Revolution," *DXPWS*, 351. See also "On the Reform of the System of Party and State Leadership," *DXPWS*, 280–302.

[18] See Kathryn Dewenter and Christopher M. Clarke, *China Business Manual 1981* (Washington, D.C.: National Council for US–China Trade, 1980), 27.

lated historical factors exacerbated bureaucratic inefficiency in the immediate post-Mao period. China's bureaucracy in the late 1970s was staffed by two sets of people. First were those who had survived the vicissitudes of political turmoil during the previous decade and those who had benefited from the discomfiture of others by being promoted during the Cultural Revolution. In addition, beginning in the early 1970s and accelerating after Deng's second rehabilitation in 1977, numerous victims of the Cultural Revolution were resurrected and reinstated in their previous positions. As a result, the bureaucracy was often double-staffed with sets of people who harbored mutual ill will and who found it difficult to work together.[19]

In addition to problems of overstaffing and poor interpersonal relations, the bureaucracy now faced a crisis of competence. By and large, those appointed and promoted during the Cultural Revolution achieved their positions based on political, not technical, criteria. With their political credentials now eroded, their legitimacy was seriously jeopardized. By contrast, those officials recently returned to power often found themselves ten years out of date with professional and technical aspects of their jobs. Moreover, many were cowed into indifference and indecision by the psychological trauma of their Cultural Revolution experiences. Consequently, many bureaucracies virtually ground to a halt, as one set of officials was technically and psychologically unprepared to take a leading role and the other set was politically undermined and alienated. Decisions were delayed, avoided, or pushed up the bureaucratic ladder. Top leaders complained that even routine government matters were constantly referred to vice-premiers for decision.[20]

At the same time that individual agencies were suffering from double-staffing and immobilism, the state, Party, and military sectors were all feeling the effects of the proliferation of agencies, which began in the early 1970s as the leadership began to rebuild the organizational structure destroyed during the Cultural Revolution. Although the exact status of many agencies before 1975 remains unclear, it appears that the radical attack on bureaucracy during the late 1960s had left the State Council with only 3 or 4 commissions and about 22 ministries.[21] Even after the Fourth National People's Congress reconstructed the State Council in January 1975, it was composed of only 3 commissions and 26 ministries. By 1980 the government apparatus encompassed 13 commissions, 38 ministries, and about 60 other agencies.[22] On the eve of the major government restructuring in the spring of 1982, the State Council was composed of 108 agencies, with 1,000 ministers and vice-

---

[19] See, e.g., *China Daily*, "Two Tasks to be Done," *FBIS*, Feb. 1, 1985, K2, and *DXPWS*, 245.

[20] See, e.g., Michel Oksenberg, "China's Economic Bureaucracy," *CBR*, May–June 1982.

[21] Christopher M. Clarke, "The Politics of Bureaucratic Reorganization in the People's Republic of China: The State Council, 1949–1979" (Ph.D. dissertation, Ohio State University, 1980), 420.

[22] See *CBR*, September–October 1980, 9.

ministers and 5,000 section and bureau chiefs.[23] Government bureaucrats and cadres at all levels were said to number as many as 600,000.[24] Thus, compounding the difficulties of obesity, ossification, and senility was the problem of lack of coordination among a proliferation of competing and over-lapping agencies.[25]

Organizations, however, are a combination of institutional patterns of behavior and individual human beings with interests, priorities, skills, backgrounds, and opinions. As Deng realized, reform of the structure would have to proceed along with, and in some cases await, removal of opponents, co-optation of neutral and still useful bureaucrats, and promotion of "good successors." As Deng said, time was running out:

> Now we are pressed for time. Things will become irremediable if we fail promptly and properly to solve this problem. . . . When a plenary session of the Central Committee is held five years from now, many comrades will have lost their working ability. It will be too late if the problem of successors is not considered until then.[26]

Thus, Deng would have to move quickly but carefully to engineer the transition of power to a generation of "younger, better educated, more technically competent, and more revolutionary" successors.

PARTY REFORM: THE FIRST STAGE, 1978–1980

Almost immediately upon resuming his positions as vice-premier, PLA chief of staff, and Party vice-chairman in mid-1977, Deng Xiaoping began to implement his strategy for organizational and personnel reform. His first accomplishment was the reestablishment of the Party's Organization Department and the appointment of his protégé, Hu Yaobang, as its director. Hu, with his control over the crucial agency in charge of personnel actions on Party and important state officials, became a major asset as Deng attempted to build support in the central leadership for his program. This function had been largely usurped during the Cultural Revolution by the Party's General Office under Mao's former bodyguard, Wang Dongxing. The Organization Department now was assigned to "redress unjust, false and wrong cases"[27] of Party members who had suffered during the Cultural Revolution and whose cases, by implication, had been overlooked or acquiesced in by Wang and the General Office. Over the next two years, thousands of former Party and

---

[23] See, e.g., "Hsin Wan Pao on Size of Central Bureaucracy," *FBIS*, Dec. 31, 1981, W4.

[24] See, e.g., "200,000 May Be Hit by Chinese Purge," *Christian Science Monitor*, Feb. 10, 1982.

[25] For a discussion of cross-bureau lack of cooperation, see Oksenberg, and also Nicholas H. Ludlow, "Who's the Boss?" *CBR*, January–February 1981.

[26] *DXPWS*, 244.

[27] *BR*, Aug. 30, 1982, 8.

state cadres were rehabilitated, their "labels" removed, and in many cases, their positions restored. These included a number of high-ranking victims of the Cultural Revolution and former allies of Deng Xiaoping, like Xi Zhong-xun, Yang Shangkun, An Ziwen, and Peng Zhen.

In February 1978 China convened the First Session of the Fifth National People's Congress, at which Premier Hua Guofeng unveiled a ten-year program for economic development. In the following few months it became obvious, if indeed it hadn't been obvious all along, that this program was overly ambitious and ill-conceived.[28] It also became clear that China's economic difficulties had deeper causes than could be accounted for by Hua's official explanation of past interference by the Gang of Four. Whether by Deng's design, Hua's ambition, or accident, Deng did not publicly become closely identified with this ill-starred economic program, though he was a key official in the leadership that approved it.

The leadership's concern over the status and direction of the Chinese economy grew throughout the year and was one of several major topics of discussion when the Party Central Committee convened its Third Plenum in December. This meeting, which marked a turning point in post-Mao China, repudiated the rapid-growth strategy and the concentration on heavy industry embodied in the ten-year program. Brought back from obscurity to direct a new economic policy was Chen Yun, long associated with balanced- and moderate-growth strategies. Under the First Five-Year Plan, Chen was China's most influential economic planner.[29] Pushed into the background by Mao for his opposition to the Great Leap Forward, Chen was brought back to guide the post-Leap recovery. He disappeared again during the Cultural Revolution and through most of the 1970s served only honorary and ceremonial functions. In 1978 he was made a Party vice-chairman and charged with guiding a new economic readjustment.

Chen was not only to give economic policy guidance, he was to chair a

[28] See, e.g., Robert Dernberger and David Fasenfast, "China's Post-Mao Economic Future," and Nicholas R. Lardy, "Recent Chinese Economic Performance and Prospects for the Ten-Year Plan," both in Joint Economic Committee of the U.S. Congress, *Chinese Economy Post-Mao* (Washington, D.C.: U.S. Government Printing Office, 1978), and Dernberger, "The Chinese Search for the Path of Self-Sustained Growth in the 1980's: An Assessment," in Joint Economic Committee, *China Under the Four Modernizations*.

[29] See especially Nicholas R. Lardy and Kenneth Lieberthal, eds., *Chen Yun's Strategy for China's Development: A Non-Maoist Alternative* (Armonk, N.Y.: M. E. Sharpe, 1983); Martin Weil, "Chen Yun," *CBR*, July–August 1981; Dorothy Solinger, "Economic Reform Via Reformulation in China: Where Do Rightist Ideas Come From?" *Asian Survey*, September 1981; Roderick MacFarquhar, *The Origins of the Cultural Revolution, Vol. 1: Contradictions Among the People, 1956–1957* (New York: Columbia University Press, 1974), and *Vol. 2: The Great Leap Forward, 1958–1960* (New York: Columbia University Press, 1983). See also *Chen Yun Wengao Xuanbian, 1949–1956 (Collection of Chen Yun's Manuscripts, 1949–1956)* (n.p.: Renmin Chubanshe, Neibu, June 1982).

newly established Party Central Discipline Inspection Commission. This agency was to investigate the reliability and performance of Party cadres at all levels and to weed out remnant leftists and opponents of the new reform program. Assisting Chen would be Commission Second Secretary Deng Yingchao, the widow of Zhou Enlai, and Third Secretary Hu Yaobang. Both Mme. Deng and Mr. Hu would join the Politburo, as would Wang Zhen, an old and highly respected cadre with long experience in military, state, and Party affairs. The Third Plenum also rehabilitated nine prominent Cultural Revolution victims, reelevating them to Central Committee membership. Implicitly, Hua's stewardship over Party affairs and the economy had been questioned, his opponents were controlling new and powerful political institutions, and the legitimacy of those who had displaced older cadres during the Cultural Revolution was threatened.

Part of the economic reassessment undertaken at the Third Plenum was an examination of agricultural policies. In line with measures adopted by the plenum, various areas in China spent the next year experimenting with methods of increasing the peasants' incentive, including increases in state investment, a rise in the purchase price of commodities, the return of private plots and rural fairs, and the installation of new systems of responsibility for production. (See chapter 9.) At the forefront of these experiments were the Party first secretaries of Sichuan and Anhui provinces, Zhao Ziyang and Wan Li, respectively. At the September 1979 Fourth Plenum, Zhao's success with reform was rewarded by his elevation to the Politburo, further weakening the position of Hua Guofeng and several other Politburo opponents of economic reform.

At the February 1980 Fifth Plenum, Deng Xiaoping achieved another major victory in his crusade for organizational and personnel reform. The Party reestablished a Central Secretariat, the organ which had served as Deng's principal base of power during the late 1950s. The Secretariat would take over day-to-day Party operations from the Politburo, where Deng's opponents remained strongest. The membership of the Secretariat, largely a centrist coalition, included Deng's supporters Wan Li and Hu Qiaomu but conspicuously excluded Hua Guofeng and his followers. The General Secretary would be Hu Yaobang, who, along with Zhao Ziyang, would join the Politburo Standing Committee. The Fifth Plenum also dismissed four of Hua's supporters from the Politburo—including Wang Dongxing—with two of them losing their jobs as vice-premiers as well.[30]

STATE RESTRUCTURING: 1979–1980

From early 1977 to early 1979, Deng Xiaoping concentrated his efforts for personnel and organizational reform on the top level of the Party, where

[30]They were Wang Dongxing, Wu De, Ji Dengkui, and Chen Xilian.

major policy decisions were made. Having achieved some preliminary gains in removing opponents and building new institutional bases for allies, he turned his attention in 1979 to the government structure where new policies —including the program of economic "readjustment and restructuring"— would have to be implemented. The existing government apparatus, set up at the February 1978 National People's Congress (NPC), was dominated by Cultural Revolution survivors led in the State Council by Hua Guofeng, Li Xiannian, and Yu Qiuli. None of the vice-premiers was a close associate of Deng, nor could any be considered a strong supporter of Deng's reform efforts.

As in the Party, Deng began to infiltrate his supporters and erode the positions of his opponents. In July 1979 the Second Session of the Fifth National People's Congress appointed three new vice-premiers, all bona fide economic and planning experts whose experience predated the Cultural Revolution. The senior was Chen Yun, who would chair a newly created State Financial and Economic Commission. This agency, which like the Party's Secretariat did not include Hua or his supporters, would serve as an inner cabinet, tasked with dismantling Hua's 1978 program and replacing it with the strategy of "readjustment, restructuring, consolidation, and improvement." Joining Chen Yun as vice-premiers would be his old ally Yao Yilin, an expert in commercial affairs, and Bo Yibo, China's chief industrial and construction administrator before the Cultural Revolution. While Chen, Yao, and Bo probably did not favor some of the more radical reforms advocated by Deng's advisers, they clearly approved of the gradual introduction of measures designed to improve management, raise living standards, and modernize industry. On certain issues, they served as key allies for Deng.[31]

The State Financial and Economic Commission was only one of several State Council commissions set up between 1979 and 1980 to oversee new reformist policies and to enforce coordination and discipline on fractious bureaucracies. In March 1979 a State Agricultural Commission was established to spread the "responsibility system" in the countryside and to coordinate the activities of various agencies administering the agricultural sector.[32] In July the State Council set up a Foreign Investment Control Commission and an Import-Export Commission to coordinate the functions of the growing number of foreign trade agencies and to supervise the expected influx of foreign investment capital. In February 1980 a State Machine Building Industry Commission (SMBIC) was created with Bo Yibo at the

---

[31] See Carol Lee Hamrin, "Competing 'Policy Packages' in Post-Mao China," *Asian Survey*, May 1984; Hamrin's chapter in the Joint Economic Committee, *The Chinese Economy in the Eighties* (forthcoming); and Dorothy Solinger, *Chinese Business Under Socialism* (Berkeley and Los Angeles: University of California Press, 1984).

[32] See Charles Y. Liu, "The State Agricultural Commission," *CBR*, January–February 1981. Much work remains to be done on the role and politics of these relatively short-lived commissions.

helm. The SMBIC was to break down the rigidly hierarchical machinery industries, to force parallel agencies to cooperate, to increase profitability and efficiency, to promote machinery exports, and to incorporate the military industry's idle capacity more closely into the civilian economy.[33]

By the spring of 1980, Deng's tactic of geriatrification in the top levels of the State Council had all but achieved its aim of bringing about a policy transformation and undermining the positions of the opponents of reform. In April the government announced that several older vice-premiers would soon step down in favor of younger people. Paving the way for this, the NPC Standing Committee appointed two new, dynamic vice-premiers—Zhao Ziyang and Wan Li—whose experience in pioneering agricultural and industrial reforms in the provinces would now be put to the national test.

The wave of reform in the State Council crested, at least temporarily, at the September 1980 Third Session of the Fifth National People's Congress.[34] The economic policies of the past again came under severe criticism, including denunciations of runaway spending on capital construction, overemphasis on heavy industry, and mismanagement of energy development policy. These criticisms were accompanied by the retirement, removal, or demotion of most of those responsible for the economy over the previous five years. Vice-Premier Li Xiannian, chief economic administrator for a decade and an opponent of many of Deng's reforms, retired from the State Council. Yu Qiuli was "demoted" from chairman of the State Planning Commission to head the newly formed and much less prestigious State Energy Commission.[35] (See chapter 7.) Most significant, Hua Guofeng was forced to step down as premier, maneuvered into an untenable position, with his policies discredited and his supporters removed or powerless. Replacing Hua as premier was Zhao Ziyang, with Wan Li functioning as "first" or executive vice-premier.[36]

[33] See, e.g., Fan Muhan, "A Discussion of the Present Task of Readjustment and Restructuring of the Machine-Building Industry," *Jingji Yanjiu* (Economic Research), Oct. 20, 1981, in Joint Publications Research Service (hereafter *JPRS*), no. 79586, *Economic Affairs*, no. 187, Dec. 3, 1981; Wu Ming, "Reorganizing and Restructuring Our Machine Building Industry," *Jingji Guanli* (Economic Management), in *JPRS*, no. 78905, *Economic Affairs*, no. 168, Sept. 3, 1981; and Ludlow, "Who's the Boss?" On exports of machinery, see "Vice Premier Bo Yibo on Promoting Exports," *FBIS*, Feb. 2, 1982, K10; "Bimonthly on Machinery Published in Hong Kong," *FBIS*, Feb. 11, 1982, and "Equimpex Factories Gear Up for Exports," *China Trader*, September 1981.

[34] The best account of the first four sessions of the Fifth NPC is Dorothy Solinger, "The Fifth National People's Congress and the Process of Policy Making: Reform, Readjustment, and the Opposition," *Asian Survey*, December 1982.

[35] That the management of the entire energy sector was under attack was made clear by the firing of petroleum minister Song Zhenming and the public humiliation of State Economic Commission Chairman Kang Shien—both protégés of Yu Qiuli—for the coverup of an earlier oil-rig disaster in the Bohai. The process of finding a replacement for Song was long and apparently politically heated.

[36] See Solinger, "The Fifth National People's Congress"; and Christopher M. Clarke, "Building China's New Leadership," *CBR*, November–December 1980.

REGAINING MOMENTUM: 1981

Originally it seemed that Deng expected to push his advantage by convening the Sixth Plenum of the Central Committee in late 1980, and that an agreement had been wrung out of Hua Guofeng to resign as Party chairman in return for keeping his name out of the trial of the Gang of Four.[37] However, the rumblings from delegates to the September NPC meeting gave warning that Deng's reforms were encountering serious local as well as national opposition. Decentralization had led to confusion, expansion of capital construction expenditures, large central budget deficits in 1979 and 1980, and inflation.[38] (See chapter 3.) Entrenched bureaucrats felt that their positions were threatened; enterprise managers were now expected to meet new and unfamiliar criteria of performance. Channels of authority, supply, and marketing were disrupted as they were being redrawn, and inflation for the first time in more than two decades was eating away at fixed incomes. (See chapter 4.) The military also was somewhat disaffected over its share of the budget and its treatment in the aftermath of its less-than-glorious incursion into Vietnam.

Not yet ready for the final showdown, the leadership postponed the full Central Committee plenum, convening instead a central work conference in December at which Chen Yun's suggestion to "slow down reforms and emphasize readjustment" was finally adopted.[39] Simultaneously, Hua Guofeng dug in his heels, refusing to resign as Party chairman, reportedly bolstered by Ye Jianying and other disgruntled PLA leaders. Taking a leaf from Ye's book, Hua apparently chose to absent himself from official public functions during the winter and early spring.[40]

In this context, the Party leadership debated the resolution on the contributions of Mao Zedong to the Chinese revolution, which was to be published on July 1, the Party's sixtieth anniversary. Some leaders, apparently including Hu Yaobang, were rumored to be demanding a very critical assessment. Others, reportedly led by Ye Jianying and fellow senior PLA officers, insisted on a more moderate approach. On April 10 General Huang Kecheng, permanent secretary of the Central Discipline Inspection Commission and a prominent focus of Mao's ire in 1959, used the PLA's newspaper

---

[37] See Liao Gailong (n. 11 above) and the numerous press reports at about that time, including Michael Parks, "China Party Chief May Be Replaced," *Los Angeles Times*, Dec. 2, 1980, and Takashi Oka, "Hua Sidelined After Losing Struggle," *Christian Science Monitor*, Dec. 24, 1980.

[38] Wang Bingqian, "Report on Financial Work," *BR*, Sept. 29, 1980, 11–23; Solinger, "The Fifth National People's Congress," 1258–62; and chapter 4 below.

[39] See Chen's speech as reported in *Cheng Ming* (Contending), translated in *FBIS*, Feb. 2, 1981.

[40] Ye apparently boycotted meetings by remaining in Guangzhou throughout the winter. See Takashi Oka, "China's Chairman Hua Won't Say Goodbye," *Christian Science Monitor*, Jan. 8, 1981. On Hua's absence, see Lowell Dittmer, "China in 1981," *Asian Survey*, January 1982. Hua may in fact have been undergoing "training" at the Higher Party School.

to publish a critique of Mao that fell far short of total negation, presaging the tone of the final Party document.[41] On the very day after Huang's article was published, Hua Guofeng reappeared in public, apparently reconciled to the fact that he had achieved the best bargain he could. He had not been implicated in the trial of the Gang of Four, Mao's good points would be declared to have outweighed his faults, and Hua would be allowed to step down without disgrace.

It now remained only to consummate the decision. On the eve of the Party's sixtieth anniversary, the Eleventh Central Committee held its sixth plenary session. Hua Guofeng was replaced as Party chairman by Hu Yaobang and demoted to the lowest of seven vice-chairmanships, and Premier Zhao became the third ranking vice-chairman. The cornerstone of opposition in the Party had finally been dug up.

THE YEAR OF CENTRAL RESTRUCTURING: 1982

Throughout 1981 there was a steady turnover of ministers and vice-ministers in the State Council as Deng, Hu, and Zhao looked for "younger, better educated, and more technically competent" cadres to lead the reform and readjustment program. In February and March twelve top agencies changed hands, including the ministries for the civilian machinery, textiles, and communications industries, and the capital construction and economic commissions. In September the ministries of foreign trade, light industry, railroads, and aviation industry got new leaders. However, the final plan for restructuring the State Council was revealed by Premier Zhao at the Fourth Session of the Fifth National People's Congress in December 1981. It would include "relatively important reductions in or mergings of State Council departments, accompanied by all possible cuts in staff and fairly big changes in leadership."[42]

Implementation of Zhao's plan to restructure the State Council began almost immediately after the NPC session closed. The process started with an intensive propaganda and mobilization campaign aimed at bringing social pressure on aged cadres to retire.[43] At the same time, the regime offered substantial positive inducements for compliance, with the implication being

---

[41] Text in *FBIS*, April 13, 1981.

[42] Text in *BR*, Dec. 21, 1981.

[43] See, e.g., the republication of Chen Yun's 1945 speech, "Tell the Truth, Don't Save Face," in *FBIS*, Jan. 5, 1982, K1–5. See also Xue Muduo, "Studying Lenin's Thoughts on the Simplification of Administrative Structure," in *Renmin Ribao* (People's Daily), Feb. 16, 1982, in *FBIS*, Jan. 22, 1982; "Personnel Readjustment Rally to be Held in January," in *FBIS*, Jan. 5, 1982, W4; report on high-level discussion forum in *FBIS*, Jan. 5, 1982, K5–8; and "Hu Yaobang Calls for Decisive Change," in *Ta Kung Pao* (Impartial News), in *FBIS*, Jan. 8, 1982, W2–4.

that these incentives might apply only to those who quickly and voluntarily stepped down.[44]

Many newly retired cadres would be made "advisers," subject to the "four no changes" policy under which their political status wouldn't change; their roles as senior cadres of their agencies would be preserved; they would still review documents and hear reports; and their privileges would be retained.[45] Retirement benefits would be positively generous, including full pay for life, plus a bonus of one yuan per month for every year worked since "joining the revolution"; retention of housing, vehicles, telephone, and other perquisites; yearly travel for "inspection trips" for higher cadres; and, in many cases, a one-grade promotion on retirement.[46] This, in addition to continued access to classified documents and to one's old office, and the right to attend meetings and receive briefings, seriously called into question the meaning of "retirement." When these benefits for "retiring" leaders are combined with an extensive "training" and reassignment program for staff who lose their jobs through reductions in force, the short-term economic savings were probably nonexistent.

Nevertheless, between March and May 1982 the State Council made major strides in streamlining and rejuvenating itself. The number of vice-premiers was reduced from 13 to 2, with a new position of State Councillor created for most of the outgoing vice-premiers. The number of State Council agencies was cut by almost half, while the number of ministers and vice-ministers was reduced from 505 to 167, and their average age lowered from sixty-four to fifty-eight. Thirty new ministers were appointed and only 11 were retained. Of the top ministerial leaders, more than half were now college educated, compared with 38 percent before the reform.[47]

Although the announced accomplishments probably masked significant continuities of both organizations and personnel, substantial progress appears to have been achieved at lower levels as well. Ministerial bureaus were cut by one-third, and the number of bureau directors was reduced by 43 percent. The average age of bureau directors was lowered by five years, to

[44] See, e.g., "Peking Journal Implies Purge of Party May Be in the Offing," *New York Times*, Feb. 6, 1982, and Takashi Oka, "China Warns Corrupt, Inept Officials of Possible Purge," *Christian Science Monitor*, Feb. 12, 1982. The article referred to is Zhang Yun, "Enhance Party Spirit, Strive for a Fundamental Turn for the Better in Party Spirit," *Hong Qi* (Red Flag), no. 3, Jan. 2, 1982, translated in *JPRS*, no. 80469, *Red Flag*, no. 3, Apr. 1, 1982.

[45] See "Veterans of 3rd Machine Building Ministry Resign," in *FBIS*, Jan. 19, 1982, K12–13. See also "Ta Kung Pao on Reform of PRC State Organs," in *FBIS*, Jan. 25, 1982, W1–2; Christopher Wren, "Official Shake-Up Reported in China," *New York Times*, Jan. 20, 1982; and "Bureau Cadres Yield Positions to Young," *FBIS*, Feb. 11, 1982.

[46] See Takashi Oka, "China's 'Administrative Revolution' Moves Forward," *Christian Science Monitor*, Mar. 4, 1982.

[47] See Christopher M. Clarke, "China's Organizational Revolution," *CBR*, July–August 1982.

fifty-four, and almost half of them had a college education, compared with 36 percent of their predecessors.[48]

Even more significant, the new State constitution, promulgated in May, established for the first time a statutory limit of two five-year terms for top government officials.[49] Moreover, under new State Council rules, ministers were expected to retire at age sixty-five and vice-ministers or department directors at sixty, under normal conditions. Although retirement regulations have yet to be uniformly implemented, substantial progress toward promoting younger, more expert cadres to top ministerial posts has been made. In addition, each ministry is now limited to between three and five cadres of vice-ministerial rank or higher, and each department to two or three directors and deputy directors.[50]

With the major top-level logjam broken at the Sixth Plenum in June 1981, the Party also began its restructuring. In May 1982 the Central Committee announced the consolidation and streamlining of its internal organs. Protégés or allies of Hu Yaobang or Deng Xiaoping took over the Central Committee's important General Office (Hu Qili), and its United Front Work Department (Yang Jingren), Propaganda Department (Deng Liqun), and Central Party School (Wang Zhen).[51]

The spring and summer months were occupied with selecting delegates to the Twelfth Party Congress and candidates for the new Central Committee. When the Congress finally convened in September, it became clear that although Deng's victory in the short term was not complete, he had set the stage for the long-term transition to "good successors."[52] Although Deng was able to force out several of his opponents at the Twelfth Congress and to achieve the promotion of a number of his supporters to the Politburo, he was unable to engineer a complete transition of power to a new generation.

[48] *China Daily*, Apr. 27, 1982. For the effects of this reform on two ministries, see "Good Results Noted in Newly Merged Ministries," *FBIS*, Mar. 10, 1982, K11–12; "Li Peng, Chen Muhua Comment on Restructuring," *FBIS*, Mar. 9, 1982, K9–10; Liu Jiancheng, "Organs Must Be Established on a Scientific and Rational Basis," *Guangming Ribao* (Enlightenment Daily), Mar. 28, 1982, in *FBIS*, Apr. 9, 1982, K2–5.

[49] Interestingly, the new Central Military Commission was not so limited. Detailed discussion of the constitution lies beyond the scope of this chapter. The text can be found in *China Daily* and *FBIS*, Apr. 28, 1982. See also Byron Weng, "Some Aspects of the 1982 Draft Constitution of the PRC," *China Quarterly*, September 1982, 492–506.

[50] "Restructuring State Council," *FBIS*, Mar. 8, 1982, K3. The State Planning and State Economic commissions were exempt from the limitations on senior leadership.

[51] "Streamlining of CCP Departments Continues," *FBIS*, May 17, 1982. Deng Liqun's later role in the 1983 "spiritual pollution" campaign should not obscure his early role as one of Deng's reform brain-trust along with Hu Qiaomu, Xue Muqiao, and others.

[52] See, e.g., Hong Yung Lee, "China's 12th Central Committee: Rehabilitated Cadres and Technocrats," *Asian Survey*, June 1983.

The structural changes embodied in the new Party constitution and the transformation of the Central Committee membership are the keys to Deng's success. With the abolition of the positions of Party chairman and vice-chairman, the Politburo has been pushed progressively to the background. The Secretariat, packed with reformers and moderates, now is the operational center of the Party and maintains control over the forty million members of the Chinese Communist Party (CCP). At the same time, the Party established a new Central Advisory Commission as a "half-way house" to retirement for aging cadres, and more than sixty elderly members and alternates of the Eleventh Central Committee were eased into this new body.

The Twelfth Congress dramatically altered the composition of the new Central Committee as well. Of the 210 full members elected, less than half held a membership on the Eleventh Central Committee. Best represented was the State Council, where organizational and personnel reform had progressed the farthest, with more than 50 members. The military's representation was down to about 40 from some 70 in the previous Central Committee. At the same time, at least 50 older military officers were "promoted" to the Advisory Commission, signaling the extensive changes in military leadership at all levels which would occur during the next year. Similarly, more than 30 top provincial leaders, including 7 first secretaries and 4 governors, were elected advisers, presaging the major provincial reorganization that took place in early 1983.[53]

The situation among alternate members was even more striking. Of 138 alternates, 115 were new. Only 18 were reelected from the previous list of alternates, and 6 full members were demoted.[54] In addition, more than two-thirds of the 348 members and alternates are under sixty years of age. Thus, based on available evidence, it appears that Deng Xiaoping was quite successful in achieving the promotion of a large number of "younger, better educated, more technically competent, and more revolutionary" successors to the Twelfth Central Committee.

[53] On the military, see Kan Wei, "Analysis of the New Central Committee and Advisory Commission," *Ta Kung Pao*, in *FBIS*, Sept. 14, 1982. On the provincial leadership, see "Analysis of the Personnel Elected to the 12th CCP Central Committee from the Provincial Level," *Issues and Studies*, January 1983. Hong Yung Lee's figures differ from those used here because he counts both full and alternate members in his categories. By his criteria the State Council now has some 73 members and alternates of the Central Committee, while military representation dropped from 92 in the Eleventh Central Committee to 73 in the Twelfth.

[54] Including Wang Dongxing. Kan Wei, "Many Special Features in List of Alternate Central Committee Members," *Ta Kung Pao*, FBIS, Sept. 17, 1982; "Personnel Selected at the 12th CCP National Congress," *Issues and Studies*, November 1982; Fang Hsueh-chun, "Analysis of the Personnel Selected at the 12th CCP National Congress," *Issues and Studies*, November 1982; and Lowell Dittmer, "The 12th Congress of the Communist Party of China," *China Quarterly*, March 1983.

THE SHAKEUP MOVES DOWN: 1983

Although the People's Liberation Army apparently was instrumental in bringing about the return of Deng Xiaoping in 1977, it quickly became frustrated and concerned with the direction in which Deng's reforms were moving.[55] The reforms made it harder to attract high-quality recruits, who increasingly had more attractive avenues for upward social and economic mobility. Similarly, Deng's reforms threatened the privileged position of military families, PLA veterans, and relatives of wounded or deceased soldiers and sailors. In the past, for example, demobilized veterans often found both employment and prestige as rural agricultural or political cadres. With the emasculation of the commune system, either these positions have been phased out or their power has been drastically curtailed. Likewise, families of active-duty or deceased military men formerly were awarded extra work points and benefits to compensate for the loss of family work-power. Such families now must often fend for themselves. These factors both reduced the PLA's ability to replace demobilized troops with high-quality recruits and disturbed the morale of active-duty personnel.

The military also has been dissatisfied with its share of the national budget, a share that fell from a high of 17.7 percent in 1977 to about 13.1 percent by 1984,[56] and with the deemphasis on industries from which it derives armaments. The Vietnam invasion graphically demonstrated the antiquated nature of much of China's equipment, and especially of its transportation and command-and-control systems. These are expensive items to modernize, and some PLA leaders have felt that insufficient effort was being devoted to the task.[57]

More important, some senior military leaders have been distressed at the turn away from the social and economic policies of the halcyon years when the PLA guided land reform, redistribution, and social equalization. For many of the old military commanders, this heritage, and the atmosphere of rural revolution and peasant cooperativism surrounding it, represents one of

[55] Much of the following is taken from Christopher M. Clarke, "Leadership Divisions," *CBR*, March–April 1981.

[56] See Christopher M. Clarke, "Defense Modernization," *CBR*, July–August 1984, 44. This represents only the publicly announced PLA budget, which is probably only about half of actual military expenditures. According to Ed Parris of the Defense Intelligence Agency, estimated real spending has hovered around 40 billion yuan per year since 1977 (except for 1979), representing a substantial decrease as a proportion of overall Chinese spending. See "Chinese Defense Expenditures, 1967–83," unpublished manuscript, autumn 1984.

[57] For evidence of disagreement, see Thomas W. Robinson, "Chinese Military Modernization in the 1980s," in Joint Economic Committee, *China Under the Four Modernizations, Part I*, and Christopher M. Clarke, "The Strategy and Politics of Modernizing China's Conventional Military Forces," unpublished manuscript, July 1984.

the two main reasons for the Communist Party's success in China's twentieth-century revolution. Also, some of China's military leaders are thought to be less than completely comfortable with China's economic and political dependence on the West. Some may favor an easing of Sino-Soviet tensions, and they are likely one force behind the policy of strategic independence.[58]

Deng's program for military reform was to consist of regularization, streamlining, and rejuvenation.[59] Regularization meant modernizing the PLA's training, equipment, logistics, and most important, its strategic and tactical thinking. This transformation into a modern, technically sophisticated army would necessitate a large-scale reduction in force, possibly including the demobilization of as many as one million soldiers.[60]

Success at military regularization and streamlining, however, would require the removal of many of the PLA's most senior and revered leaders and their replacement by younger, more technically trained commanders. This delicate task had to wait until high-level Party opposition to Deng's overall reform program had been rooted out or neutralized and until a reformist base of support in the Party and state bureaucracies had been assured. By late 1982 Deng was ready to force his reorganization of the PLA. The process began in September with the appointment of 43 top military leaders, including 6 of the 11 regional commanders, to the Party's Central Advisory Commission.[61] Within weeks, leaders of three regions had been changed, along with at least 170 senior officers. Progress in personnel changes at the top of the PLA, however, has continued to be a slow and difficult process.

Early in 1983 China took one of the first major steps in "regularizing" the armed forces, the establishment of a *state* Central Military Commission. The Commission is under the executive administration of five top advocates of the modernization of military doctrine, training, tactics, and leadership, and appears further to reduce the role of the old-line commanders who dominate the Party's Military Affairs Commission.

[58] Evidence on these points is largely circumstantial. However, Deng Xiaoping's repeated calls for the military to defer spending increases, support economic modernization, and streamline its forces indicate that substantial opposition to these policies may still exist. See, for example, "A Talk by Deng Xiaoping at the Third Plenary Session of the Central Advisory Commission on 22 October 1984," and "Armed Forces Must Serve National Construction (November 1, 1984)," in Deng's *Building Socialism With Chinese Characteristics* (Beijing: Renmin Chubanshe, 1984).

[59] *DXPWS*, numerous articles on military reform.

[60] See, e.g., Chief of Staff Yang Dezhi's call for a major reduction in force in the PLA in *China Daily*, Jan. 4, 1985, 1.

[61] Much of the following is taken from Christopher M. Clarke, "The Lean Machine," *CBR*, January–February 1983.

One of these technocrats is Minister of Defense Zhang Aiping.[62] Zhang, who has had one of the most impressive careers of any senior PLA leader, is the prototype of what China expects of future officers. He served as commander of China's first combined-forces operations in the mid-1950s and as vice-chairman of the National Defense Science and Technology Commission (NDSTC) in the 1960s, where he played a major role in the development of China's nuclear capability. By 1975 Zhang was chairman of NDSTC and supervised China's satellite, ICBM, and submarine-launched missile programs.

That all this military reorganization stimulated considerable hesitation and opposition is clear.[63] In March 1981 the army was forced to require all personnel to take a loyalty oath.[64] More than a year later, Deng fired the director of the PLA's General Political Department for not censoring an article in the army's newspaper which criticized the regime's reform policies.[65] Deng's first choice for a successor in that position—variously reported to be Secretariat member Chen Pixian or General Logistics Department Commissar Wang Ping—aroused opposition, forcing Deng to accept a compromise candidate more acceptable to the PLA, Yu Qiuli.[66] Nevertheless, throughout 1983 remnant "leftism" was still being denounced in the army,[67] and calls for a "shake-up" in the military persisted.[68]

Despite apparently continuing opposition, however, reform of both cen-

[62] The others are Chief of Staff Yang Dezhi, Director of the PLA General Political Department Yu Qiuli, Director of the PLA General Logistics Department Hong Xuezhi, and MAC/CMC Permanent Vice-Chairman Yang Shangkun.

[63] See, e.g., "PLA Deputies Boycott of NPC Discussion Defended," and "Ba Yi Radio Comments on PLA Spending Reduction, Possible Purge," both *Radio Ba Yi* (August First), various dates. However, this is a Soviet propaganda outlet. Nevertheless, the number of speeches and visits by top Party and military men to military units and to meetings to explain policy lends credence to the rumors of PLA dissatisfaction. See, e.g., "Yang Dezhi on Planned Reduction in Defense Spending," *Summary of World Broadcasts*, Sept. 30, 1980, C1/2, and "PLA's Yang Dezhi Gives Lecture to General Staff," in *FBIS*, Feb. 17, 1981, L1–2.

[64] See *Xinhua*, Mar. 2, 1981, "PLA General Staff Issues Mandatory Soldier's Oath," in *FBIS*, Mar. 3, 1981, L3–4.

[65] See Hai Feng, "Inside Story of CCP Propaganda Chief's Resignation," *Cheng Ming*, in *FBIS*, May 26, 1982.

[66] The report of Deng's nomination of Chen comes from a private interview by David M. Lampton. The report on Wang Ping is in Parris Chang, "PLA Factions and Leadership," unpublished manuscript, summer 1984.

[67] Li Desheng, "Continue to Eliminate 'Leftist' Ideological Influence, Strive to Create a New Phase of Armed Forces Building," in *FBIS*, Apr. 14, 1983.

[68] "PLA's Yu Qiuli Calls for 'Shake-Up' in Army," *FBIS*, July 26, 1983. Some other aspects of regularization include the restoration of military war games in September 1982 and the establishment of an armed police force to take over from the PLA the responsibility for guarding civilian facilities in the summer of 1983. Throughout 1984 the PLA underwent a campaign to "negate the Cultural Revolution" and to repudiate its role in supporting the left during that decade as part of the Party's rectification program.

tral and lower-level military units had continued. Details are sketchy, but existing reports indicate that during 1983 and 1984 as many as 9 of the 11 military regions and some 22 of the 28 military districts were reorganized.[69] In November 1984 Deng Xiaoping announced that "the question of making leading bodies [in the PLA] younger in average age was solved at and below the corps level in the last two years. But the question has not been solved at higher levels."[70] Less than two months later, forty senior general officers were retired from posts at or above the corps level and in Beijing headquarters units, apparently the first group to feel the effects of Deng's renewed push for retirement.[71]

At the same time that reform of the military structure was taking place, streamlining and rejuvenation were being pushed down through the provincial, prefectural, municipal, and county levels. Between December 1982 and May 1983, nearly one-third of the Party provincial first secretaries and all but 3 provincial governors were replaced. In all, nearly two-thirds of the country's top 1,400 provincial officials either retired or "retreated into the second line of leadership" as advisers.[72] In the process, provincial Party standing committees on average were reduced from 15 to 20 people to a nucleus of 4 to 6. The average age of top Party people seems to have been lowered from the sixties to the fifties; but most important, the average educational level was raised substantially, with many engineers and technicians taking on positions of political responsibility. Indeed, state and Party organs "stealing" educated teachers from schools and universities has become a problem for the educational system. In the provincial government apparatus, the number of organs was cut from about 70 to about 40, on average. Provincial government leaders in each province now typically number 6 where there were 12 or more before, and more than half of them are college edu-

[69] The Guangzhou and Nanjing regions were reportedly hardest hit, but the Chengdu, Lanzhou, and Wuhan regions also have new commanders. Michael Weisskopf reported that 1,000 officers from the PLA headquarters were retired along with 1,500 air force officers and 10,000 officers from the Beijing military district. See "China Tries to March its Antiquated Military into Modern Times," *Washington Post*, Oct. 31, 1983. This reorganization has also been pushed down to the corps level and below. See "PLA Readjusts Corps-Level Leading Bodies," *FBIS*, Oct. 4, 1983, K3–4.

[70] See Deng's "Armed Forces Must Serve National Construction."

[71] See Beijing, *Xinhua*, in English, "Senior PRC Army Officers Make Way for Younger Officers," *FBIS*, Dec. 31, 1984.

[72] For details, see Christopher M. Clarke, "The Shakeup Moves Down," *CBR*, September–October 1983; Li Shanzhi, "New Changes in Leading Bodies of Provincial CCP Committees," in *Banyuetan* (Fortnightly Chats), in *JPRS*, no. 83866, *Political, Sociological and Military Affairs* (hereafter *PSMA*), no. 437, July 11, 1983; and *Xinhua*, Mar. 26, 1983, in *FBIS*, Apr. 1, 1983, K1.

cated. Provincial government functionaries overall are said to have been reduced by some 30 percent.[73]

Throughout the summer and fall of 1983, this process was repeated at prefectural, county, and municipal levels. When completed, these reductions in force could affect as many as one million civilian cadres at all levels.[74] A central research task, however, is to measure the actual extent and impact of these alleged reductions.

DENG'S VISION FOR A BRAVE NEW WORLD: 1984 AND BEYOND

It appears that Deng Xiaoping and his reformist colleagues have achieved some significant successes in streamlining and rejuvenating the Party and state structures at all levels—they are beginning to see success in reorganizing the military. Extensive as the impact of these reforms may seem, however, what has gone before is dwarfed by what remains to be done. China has set for itself the ultimate test of its ability to put into power a new generation of "good successors." Between 1984 and 1986 the Communist Party must reassess the credentials, accomplishments, ideological standpoint, and political reliability of its almost forty million members.[75] Early estimates that as many as three to five million members would be asked to retire or resign, or be expelled, do not appear to have been borne out as of late 1984. Only a few of the most violent Cultural Revolution rebels have been singled out for removal, along with a few profiteers and other "economic criminals." In the process, however, the Party may also weed out a few aged and infirm or incompetent members.

Having struggled to remake the *context* within which their policies must be implemented, Deng and the reformers must then prove that the *content* of those policies provides the answers to China's problems. The long-term success of these policies will depend on three factors: First, the successors, led by Hu Yaobang and Zhao Ziyang, must assure a smooth transition of power as Deng Xiaoping, Chen Yun, and their generation pass from the scene. They must show skill at building leadership support and maintaining a strong coalition, not allowing the policy process to become polarized. So far, the signs are moderately encouraging.

Second, China will need a stable international environment in which to

[73] *Xinhua*, Aug. 4, 1983, in *FBIS*, Aug. 5, 1983, K22.

[74] E.g., Nei Monggol alone reported more than 159,000 Party, government, and mass organization cadres in 1981. Fu Tingcheng, "While Streamlining the Structure We Must Pay Attention to Administrative Legislation," in *Shijian* (Practice), Jan. 20, 1983, in *JPRS*, no. 83802, *PSMA*, no. 434, June 30, 1983.

[75] See text of decision of the Party Central Committee on Party consolidation and Communique of the Second Plenum of the Twelfth Central Committee, both in *FBIS*, Oct. 13, 1983, K2–18.

modernize. Military conflict or serious deterioration of relations with the industrialized world can only inhibit China's economic development. This means that China probably will continue to try to ease tensions with the Soviet Union while maintaining a strong economic relationship with the West and Japan, and that China's leaders will continue their attempt to pursue an "independent foreign policy."[76]

Finally, whether the reform policies have time enough to succeed in the long term will depend to a large extent on how successful they are in providing tangible economic benefits to large segments of the population in the mid and short range. After decades of hearing about the radical changes and improvements in Chinese society since 1949, we are now being told—often by the Chinese themselves—that in many respects little improvement has been felt by the average Chinese citizen since at least the mid-1950s.[77] Widening social and economic inequality among regions or social strata, even in the context of a generally rising standard of living, could force a drastic reassessment of the economic model of the Four Modernizations.[78]

The key to changing the life of the Chinese citizen lies partly in the economic realm and partly in the organizational realm. China's leaders must motivate peasants to produce, workers to labor, intellectuals to create, and managers and bureaucrats to perform their functions imaginatively and efficiently. These tasks can only be accomplished through an organizational structure that accurately transmits the leadership's policies to lower levels and translates them into appropriate and effective action. In a word, the results of the content of Deng's reform and modernization policies will continue to be held hostage to the context within which those policies are implemented. The chapters that follow deal with the implementation of specific policies so much affected by Deng's efforts to reengineer the personnel and organizational contexts discussed above.

[76] See, e.g., Donald Zagoria, "The Moscow-Beijing Detente," *Foreign Affairs*, Spring 1983; transcript of the McNeil-Lehrer Report: "U.S.–China Relations," April 7, 1983, no. 1964; Harry Harding, "Change and Continuity in Chinese Foreign Policy," and William E. Griffith, "Sino-Soviet Rapprochement," both in *Problems of Communism*, March–April 1983.

[77] See, e.g., William L. Parish and Martin King Whyte, *Village and Family in Contemporary China* (Chicago: University of Chicago Press, 1978); the accounts cited in note 6 above; Richard Bernstein, *From the Center of the Earth* (Boston: Little, Brown and Co., 1982); and *Statistical Yearbook of China, 1981* (Hong Kong: Economic Information and Agency, 1982).

[78] See David M. Lampton, "New 'Revolution' in China's Social Policy," *Problems of Communism*, September–December 1979; Werner Klatt, "The Staff of Life: Living Standards in China, 1977–1981," *China Quarterly*, Mar. 1983; Nicholas R. Lardy, "Subsidies," *CBR*, November–December 1983.

PART II

Planning and Economic Policy

THREE

The Decline of Central Control over Investment in Post-Mao China

Barry Naughton

The single most striking, consistent change in the Chinese economy since 1978 has been the decline in the proportion of total fixed investment that is controlled directly by the central government. Shifting central government priorities have caused other economic changes to be delayed, or at times reversed, but in each successive year the proportion and the absolute amount of investment resources controlled at local levels has increased.[1] Yet decentralization of investment in itself has never been a policy objective of the central government. On the contrary, the sustained increase in decentralized investment has occurred in the face of repeated adoption of annual economic plans that call for a *reduction* in the share of decentralized investment. This repeated failure to recentralize investment control has in turn jeopardized the attainment of objectives to which the regime is strongly committed, in particular the concentration of investment in energy and transportation de-

The author gratefully acknowledges assistance in developing the ideas presented in this chapter through discussions with William Byrd, David Lampton, Nicholas Lardy, and Wu Jinglian. The criticisms of participants at the SSRC–ACLS conference helped to reduce errors and inconsistencies and sharpen the presentation. Remaining errors are of course the sole responsibility of the author.

[1] The term "local" is used in this chapter to designate governmental and Party officials outside Beijing, including enterprise managers. In practice this refers to the governors of provinces and the mayors of large cities (or the appropriate Party secretaries); the vice-governors and vice-mayors in charge of the local planning commissions and industrial systems; and the various officials in charge of the different industrial bureaus. There are generally between six and ten industrial bureaus in a large city. Thus, as many as fifteen or twenty local leaders may be at the head of systems that dispose of significant resources. Individual enterprises may sometimes enjoy a high degree of autonomy in disposing of their investment resources (profit or depreciation funds), but this occurs because, for various reasons, some enterprises have substantial bargaining power within their "systems," and not because enterprises have independent authority.

velopment. This striking pattern raises important questions about the nature of central and local power in China: It suggests that the conflicting interests of central and local power holders may be as important as, or more important than, divisions among central government leaders in determining the fate of specific policy initiatives.

The decline in central government control over investment can best be seen by constructing a single measure, comparable across time, that divides total state fixed investment into central and local components. Existing Chinese statistical categories do not adequately fulfill this requirement, but it is possible to construct such a measure. In the first section of this chapter I shall present the results of this exercise. After quantifying the amount of realized fixed investment carried out under local auspices, I then examine the major local funding sources that finance this investment. From these figures we can see that local authorities have long been accustomed to disposing of a substantial share of investment resources, but that a dramatic increase in locally controlled funds in recent years has raised this share to historically unprecedented levels. Now awash with liquidity, local authorities compete aggressively with central planners for control of the material resources needed for investment.

In the next section I examine the relationship between the decentralization described earlier and the projections and objectives expressed by central planners. At the outset, the annual investment plan is compared with the realized quantities of investment in various categories reported at year-end. This comparison reveals that the local component of investment plans is persistently overfulfilled, while central investment generally conforms to the plan specifications. However, this is not the outcome of a single central government policy that envisages an appropriate division of resources between the Center and localities. Rather, the totals of central and local investment reflect the implementation of numerous individual policies, each of which addresses certain perceived needs, but each of which has in addition an effect on the division of investment resources between the Center and localities. Moreover, these policies are frequently in conflict, particularly in that each policy implies a different set of priorities for the use of investment resources. The consistent trend toward decentralization and the persistent overfulfillment of the decentralized investment plan reflect an "implementation bias" in the realization of numerous individual policies. A persistent characteristic of economic policy in the period 1979 through 1983 has been the presence of this implementation bias, which indicates the individual policies were consistently implemented in a way that incorporated a greater degree of local control over resources than was envisioned by the original policy.

This implementation bias has affected the realization of different government objectives in sharply differing ways. The Center has succeeded in rapidly redirecting investment into the production of consumer goods and into the construction of housing, but it has failed dramatically in directing investment into energy and transport. Beijing has had some success in reducing the overall level of investment, in order to release resources for consumption, but the expansion of local investment has greatly impeded progress in this area and has forced the government to pay a higher price for the progress made. Finally, government efforts to increase efficiency and responsiveness to consumer needs through economic reforms have been both helped and hindered by the trend toward greater local power.[2] In each of these cases, the creation of new decentralized funding sources has had a critical impact on the ability of economic planners to realize their goals, an impact greatly intensified by what appears to be a remarkable degree of inertia and unresponsiveness on the part of the existing investment allocation institutions in Beijing.

In the final section, I shall attempt to explain why local political power is so important in China today. Part of the answer lies in the fact that provincial Party secretaries form an identifiable interest group that defends local interests directly in Party councils in Beijing. Moreover, a careful analysis of the economic management system reveals that effective control over actual disposition of most resources lies with local-level managers, and that central planners simply do not have sufficient tools to control these local-level officials. Changes initiated since 1979 have further increased the autonomy of local levels, in spite of the attempt of central planners to introduce new control mechanisms. Finally, the ambiguous attitude of central leaders to the erosion of their control over investment is examined. These leaders know that an overly harsh recentralization would cripple the process of economic reform. As a result, they proceed gingerly, balancing their desire to decisively break out of China's energy-transport bottleneck against their desire to "enliven" the economy and their need to respect the power and position of numerous local power holders.

In this first section I account for the disposition of total fixed investment in units under state ownership.[3] Since 1978 the Chinese have regularly published data on state "capital construction." In other centrally planned economies, the category of capital construction accounts for virtually all fixed

[2] The complex relationship between economic reforms and the control of investment cannot be fully addressed here. See Barry Naughton, "False Starts and Second Wind: Financial Reforms in China's Industrial System," in Elizabeth Perry and Christine Wong, eds., *The Political Economy of Reform in Post-Mao China* (Cambridge: Harvard Contemporary China Series No. 2, 1985), 223–252. In general, the argument of this chapter leads to the conclusion that further reforms cannot be effective until after the overall scale of investment has been controlled.

[3] We therefore exclude from further consideration the following categories of fixed investment: urban collectives, rural collectives, and investment in private housing (predominantly in rural areas).

investment in the state-run economy, and during the 1950s this was true in China as well. However, since the mid-1960s capital construction in China has been a declining proportion of total fixed investment, and an increasing proportion has been provided through "replacement and reconstruction" (*gengxin gaizao*) investment.[4] The name "replacement and reconstruction" (hereafter abbreviated as RR) was first applied to a portion of investment in 1964 when central planners set up a separate funding category for small investments made in existing factories. The intention was to assure the timely replacement and technical upgrading of aging fixed assets in state factories, given that these needs were often neglected because of the pressing demands on investment resources created by the large demands of numerous new factories. Thus, RR investment was initially distinguished from capital construction on the basis of use, and both types of investment were dominated by state budgetary allocations.

Major changes in the Chinese budgetary system soon made this distinction obsolete. From 1967, enterprises under local jurisdiction were allowed to retain their depreciation allowances, and in 1971 this provision was extended to all state-run enterprises. With these changes depreciation retention replaced budgetary allocations as the major source of RR investment. In socialist accounting practices depreciation is considered part of the cost of industrial production, designed to account for the "using up" of a small proportion of fixed assets during the production process. In China before 1967, as in most centrally planned economies up to that time, this sum of money was subtracted by the enterprise from the revenues it received from the sale of its output and remitted to the central government budget alongside, but separate from, the profits and tax that the enterprise also remitted. As part of central budgetary revenues, this sum of money was an important source of government financing of investment. Once depreciation retention replaced budgetary allocations as the primary source of RR investment, control of these funds devolved upon local authorities. In theory enterprises decided how these funds were to be used, and in practice the local industrial bureaus and local governments that controlled the enterprises gained control over these funds. Enjoying a high degree of autonomy in the disposition of these funds, local authorities used them freely for expansion projects and new construction. Investigations of the actual use of RR funds during the 1970s have repeatedly indicated that as much as two-thirds of the amount spent was used for new or expanded construction.[5] The distinction between RR

[4] Synonyms are "funds for uncovering potential, innovation, and reconstruction" (*wagegai*), and "technological measures" (*jicuo*). These funds are the lineal descendants of the "Four Items" of small-scale investment allocations during the First Five-Year Plan.

[5] See, e.g., Ma Hong, "Implementing Technical Reform in Existing Enterprises Is a Strategic Task of China's Economic Development," *1982 Jingji Nianjian* (hereafter *JJNJ*), IV-30–32; State Construction Commission Economic Research Institute Investigation Group, "How to Do

TABLE 3.1   Central and Local Fixed Investment
(in billion yuan)

	1977	1978	1979	1980	1981	1982
Capital construction						
Central	31.2	41.7	41.3	34.9	25.2	27.7
Local	7.0	8.4	11.0	20.9	19.2	27.9
TOTALS	38.2	50.1	52.3	55.9	44.3	55.6
Replacement and Reconstruction (RR)						
Central	1.8	2.6	4.4	3.3	3.5	3.3
Local	14.7	14.1	13.2	15.4	18.9	25.7
TOTALS	16.6	16.8	17.6	18.7	22.5	29.0
Total fixed investment						
Central	33.0	44.4	45.7	38.2	28.7	31.0
Local	21.8	22.5	24.2	36.4	38.1	53.6
TOTALS	54.8	66.9	69.9	74.6	66.8	84.6
Percentage of total fixed investment						
under local control	40	34	35	49	58	63

SOURCE: Table 3.5 (Appendix). Figures are rounded and may not sum exactly. Capital construction figures are given according to the augmented definition used in Chinese statistical publications beginning in 1983. See text for definition of central and local.

investment and capital construction on the basis of *use* thus rapidly lost its meaning, and the true distinction between the two categories became one of *funding source*. However, by the late 1970s even this distinction became increasingly meaningless as the government resumed a program of significant budgetary allocations for RR investment, and as a host of new funding sources were introduced, which swelled the volume of both capital construction and RR investment. Therefore we must combine capital construction and RR investment into a single series for fixed investment in order to address the issues involved in control over investment.[6]

Table 3.1 presents a breakdown of both capital construction and RR investment, and thus total fixed investment, into central and local categories. It is based on a more detailed breakdown of investment, presented in the Appendix (table 3.5). A few words about the definitions used in constructing the central and local categories are in order. Central investment includes all investment funded through the central government budget. This includes

Technical Reform Work in Existing Enterprises Well," *Jingji Guanli* (hereafter *JJGL*) 2 (1982): 21–22; and Zuo Chuntai and Xiao Jie, *Caimao Jingji* (hereafter *CMJJ*) 5 (1983): 4–8.

[6]The most straightforward recounting of this history is Hu Jing and Wang Chengyao, *Caizheng* (hereafter *CZ*) 1 (1980): 17–19.

most of the capital construction arranged through foreign loans, the portion coordinated through the central budget (*tongjie tonghuan*). Local investment is composed of a consolidation of three accounting categories: investment arranged through "own funds" (*zichou zijin*); domestic bank loans; and foreign funds not coordinated through the central budget. The definitions slightly overstate the degree of local control over investment, for two reasons. While all domestic bank loans have been included as local investment, there is in fact a certain, relatively small proportion of domestic loans that is set aside for specific projects designated by the Central Planning Commission. This is unlikely to have been an important factor in most years, but there are some indications that in 1982 a special effort was made to designate such projects, and they may account for as much as 2 billion yuan in that year.[7] A similar caveat should apply to the small quantity of foreign funds used in RR investment (300 million yuan in 1982). Although all of these funds have been included in local investment, there is again a portion that is coordinated by central planners, as part of a special program of factory modernization in cooperation with Japanese manufacturers.[8] These exceptions do not materially affect the conclusions that are advanced below.[9]

Two striking facts emerge from an inspection of table 3.1. The first is that a fairly high degree of decentralization characterized fixed investment before the initiation of economic reforms. In 1977 fully 40 percent of fixed investment was controlled by local authorities, and the centralizing "technological leap forward" of 1978 reduced this percentage somewhat on the eve of China's reform era. The high degree of decentralization in 1977 is in fact the culmination of trends that began in 1970. According to the measure of local control used in table 3.1, the proportion of investment under local control jumped to 29 percent in 1971 and then grew steadily through 1977.[10] This trend primarily reflects the impact of full depreciation retention beginning in 1971. Second, since 1978 decentralized investment has grown steadily, both in absolute terms and as a proportion of total investment. The cutbacks in centralized investment in 1980 and 1981 were not matched by a corresponding reduction in decentralized investment, and the modest upturn in centralized investment in 1982 was overshadowed by the dramatic jump in decentralized investment in that year.

[7] Liu Hongru, *Jinrong Yanjiu* 3 (1982): 25.

[8] Masaki Yabuuchi, "New Rules for Reform of Chinese Enterprises," *JETRO China Newsletter* 46 (September–October 1982): 19; "Japanese Cooperation in China's Factory Modernization," *JETRO China Newsletter* 42 (January–February 1983): 22–23.

[9] The large majority of foreign funds used for RR investment are arranged locally, either in Shanghai or in the Special Economic Zones of Guangdong and Fujian. See Liang Xi, *1982 JJNJ*, V-286–87.

[10] Except for a slight dip in 1973. This measure can be calculated from the sources given for table 3.5 (Appendix).

A fuller understanding of the decentralization of investment control requires that we identify the major funding sources of local investment. Four decentralized funding sources dominate local investment: retained depreciation funds; retained profits; bank loans; and extrabudgetary income of local governments and nonprofit organizations.

1 Retained depreciation funds have been the largest source of decentralized investment since 1967, and in spite of the major changes in the investment management system since 1979, they have remained so to the present. A partial recentralization of depreciation funds took place in 1978, and it can be estimated that about 4 billion yuan worth of depreciation funds were drawn into the central government budget.[11] With the institution of the various expanded autonomy policies for enterprises in 1979, participating enterprises no longer had to remit this percentage of depreciation to the central budget. As these provisions have spread to most industrial enterprises, and as depreciation rates have been modestly raised, the total of retained depreciation has increased faster than the fixed capital stock (since 1978). Subtracting central government exactions from the total depreciation fund yields estimates of 18.3 billion yuan in 1980; 20 billion in 1981; and 22 billion in 1982.[12]

2 Retained profits have increased rapidly since 1978, when only a small portion (2.1 billion yuan) of total profits was retained in order to form "enterprise funds," used primarily for bonuses and collective welfare expenses. With the introduction of profit-sharing programs in 1979, and their rapid growth thereafter, and the institution of "profit contracting" (so-called industrial responsibility systems) in 1981, the total of retained profit has exploded. The following profits were retained by state-run enterprises for the years 1978–1982 (in billions of yuan): 2.1

[11] The provision was for 30 percent of the depreciation funds of large and medium enterprises (which account for the bulk of the capital stock) to be remitted to the central treasury. According to Zhang Jingfu's budget report in *Beijing Review*, 1979, no. 29 (July 20): 17, revenues grew 4.2 billion yuan less in "comparable items" than in total. Most of this difference would appear to be depreciation funds. See n. 12.

[12] Figures on the capital stock are available in the various Economic Yearbooks (1981, VI-8; 1982, VIII-8) and the 1983 *Tongji Zhaiyao* (hereafter *TJZY*), 10. Taking the capital stock at the end of the previous year as the relevant figure, 1980's capital stock is 489 billion; 1981, 531 billion; 1982, 577 billion. Applying the depreciation rate of 4.2 percent given in Qiao Rongzhong, *Jingji Wenti* 9 (1982): 19–24 (translated in Joint Publications Research Service, *Economic Affairs* [hereafter *JPRS, Ec.*], no. 303, 17), yields total depreciation. Funds in central government budget can be taken from the budget reports presented in *Beijing Review*, Sept. 29, 1980, 11, 16, 19, and May 31, 1982, 17. These are subtracted from the totals to derive the figures in the text. Note that we are not arguing that the enterprises themselves have autonomous control over these funds: on the contrary, local governments and industrial bureaus seem to have preponderant say in actual uses.

in 1978; 6.7 in 1979; 9.6 in 1980; 11.8 in 1981; and 17.0 in 1982. The total of the profits retained in 1979–1981 was 28.1 billion yuan, and has been shown as being derived from these channels: enterprise funds, 4.9; profit sharing, 14.2; profit-loss contracts, 7.0; and tax for profits, 2.0.[13]

Whereas all depreciation fund expenditures are directed at fixed investment, the same is not true for retained profits, which also fund individual bonuses and operating expenses of collective welfare undertakings (clinics, daycare, recreation centers). Based on a large sampling of the Chinese press, as well as interviews conducted in Wuhan in 1982, I estimate that 65 percent of retained profits are used for fixed investment. A relatively small proportion of this is for goods-producing capital: most has been spent on construction of workers' housing.[14] Application of the 65 percent ratio produces estimates of retained profits available for fixed investment of 6.2 billion yuan in 1980, 7.7 billion in 1981, and 11.1 billion in 1982.

3   Bank loans have also grown rapidly since 1978, but accounting for this growth is somewhat complicated by the large number of separate lending programs. The People's Bank of China (the central bank), the Bank of Construction (formerly a conduit for budgetary investments), and the Bank of China (primarily a foreign exchange bank) all currently make loans for fixed investment, and in addition local governments and local credit corporations (*xintuo gongsi*) participate in lending operations. Table 3.5 (Appendix) contains figures for the amount of realized investment financed by loans, but these figures may differ substantially from the amount of new credit made available in a given year, because of delays in actually spending money borrowed. Table 3.2 tabulates available information about bank credit extended in 1980 and 1981. The figures do not tally perfectly with the realized investment totals in table 3.5 (Appendix), and the 1981 total of credit extended substantially exceeds the figure for bank-financed completed investment in that year. Since the estimates presented in table 3.2 must

[13]Absolute figures are derived from these sources: for 1978 and 1979, Wang Bingqian, *JJGL* 11 (1982): 3; for 1982, Wang Bingqian, in BBC FE 7209/C2/3; for 1979–80, see below; for breakdown of channels from which profits were derived, Shen Jingnong and Tao Cengji, *1982 JJNJ*, V-322. Wang Meihan, *Caizheng Yanjiu* 1 (1983): 15, gives the proportion of total profits retained in the years 1979–1981. The figures for total profit given in *Ganjiang Jingji* 5 (1982): 17 are then used to calculate retained profit. The totals so derived tally closely with the figures given by Shen and Tao.

[14]See *Qiye Guanli* 2 (1981): 21–22, 25, for figures on 41 enterprises in Heilongjiang, 495 enterprises in Tianjin, and 342 enterprises in Beijing; *New China News Agency* 3 March 1980 in BBC FE/W1077/A/2 for 153 enterprises in Hubei; *Caiwu yu Kuaiji* 2 (1980): 5–6, for 10 enterprises in Shanghai; and Mu Rong et al., *Guangdong Jingji Diaocha* (Guangzhou: Guangdong People's Publishing House, 1981), 267, for 100 enterprises in Guangdong.

TABLE 3.2   Bank Loans Extended for Fixed Investment
(in billion yuan)

	1980	1981
1. People's Bank of China short- and medium-term equipment loans	5.1	5.3
2. Construction bank loans for capital construction		
in-budget	[1.4]	[2.5]
from deposits	0.6	2.48
3. Construction bank loans for RR investment	c. 2.0	3.75
4. Bank of China loans in domestic currency (*renminbi*)	0.4	0.8
TOTALS (excluding in-budget loans in brackets)	8.1	12.3

SOURCES: Row 1: 1982 *JJNJ*, V-328.
Row 2: 1982 *JJNJ*, V-344–45, gives the figures for in-budget loans in both years, and 1981 loans from deposits. Liu Lixin, *Jinrong Yanjiu* 3 (1982): 31, gives figures for total Bank of Construction loans for capital construction as 2.0 billion in 1980 and 4.9 billion in 1981. 1980 loans from deposits have been derived through subtraction.
Row 3: 1982 *JJNJ*, V-344–45, gives the figure for 1981 and says this represents "an increase of nearly 100% from 1980."
Row 4: 1982 *JJNJ*, V-341. The source gives only the total for both 1980 and 1981, which has been arbitrarily apportioned between the two years in the ratio 1 : 2.

be considered minimums, this result is striking. It may also explain part of the dramatic increase in bank-financed investment in 1982 as a result of delayed disbursements of bank credit made available in 1981.

4   Finally, additional fixed investment is financed through funds of local governments and nonprofit organizations. The estimation of this category is particularly problematic because no Chinese statistics account systematically for these funds. The recent concern with "extrabudgetary funds" (which include this category, as well as, inter alia, retained profits and depreciation) does provide some insight into the magnitude of funds involved. In 1980 earmarked funds of nonprofit organizations amounted to 8 billion yuan, and in addition local governments disposed of about 4 billion yuan in local surtaxes.[15] These fees and surtaxes are generally collected from users of public facilities and are devoted to operating expenses and investment in the particular sector involved. The largest single item is the "highway maintenance fund," collected from vehicle taxes, which amounted to 2.8 billion yuan in 1979, of which about 40 percent was spent for fixed investment.[16] If we assume that this 40 percent figure applies to the other items as well (many of which, such as urban utility surtaxes or

[15] Gu Baofu, *CMJJ* 4 (1982): 34.
[16] "China: Socialist Economic Development," A World Bank Country Report (Washington, D.C., 1983), 2:373.

TABLE 3.3   Total Local Funding Sources
(in billion yuan)

	1980	1981	1982
Depreciation	18.3	20.0	22.0
Retained profit	6.2	7.7	11.1
Domestic loans	8.1	12.3	[13.4]
Local government and nonprofit organizations	7.8	8.3	8.8
Foreign capital	[0.4]	[0.7]	[1.6]
TOTAL	40.8	49.0	57.9
Less bond purchases	—	−4.9	−2.2
REVISED TOTAL	40.8	44.1	55.7
Realized investment	36.4	38.0	53.3

SOURCE: See text. Figures in brackets are from the Appendix table, since independent estimates of available funds are lacking.

rural water-conservancy fees, are of a similar nature as the highway maintenance fund), this would provide a total of 4.8 billion available for fixed investment in 1980. If we assume that this category grew at about 10 percent per year in the following years, this would yield totals of 5.3 billion in 1981 and 5.8 billion in 1982. Though imprecise, these estimates can give us an idea of the orders of magnitude involved.

In addition to these earmarked financial resources, there are also the general reserve funds and standby resources of local governments (*jidong caili*). The magnitude of these funds depends directly on the provisions of the budgetary system: standby resources are left to the local governments both as a fixed sum and as the surplus remaining after they have fulfilled their revenue-raising targets. However, the budgetary system has been in such a constant state of change since 1980 that it is nearly impossible to estimate these funds. From an inspection of the various budget reports, the annual magnitude of these funds must vary between 1.5 billion and 6 billion yuan per year. I have therefore rather arbitrarily added 3 billion yuan annually to the quantity of investment funds available from local governments and nonprofit organizations.

In table 3.3, the various funding sources are tabulated and compared with the total of realized fixed investment funded through decentralized sources. It will be seen that the sum of funding sources significantly exceeds the realized investment. In 1981 this can be partially accounted for by the blockage of 3–4 billion yuan in bank accounts, accounts that may have been transferred to the compulsory purchase of treasury bonds (to the amount of 4.8 billion). In 1982 a further 2 billion yuan in treasury bonds was allocated to organized units. In spite of these measures, the total of funds available is significantly greater than realized investment, a relationship all the more striking in that our estimates of funding sources are clearly minimum estimates, and may omit smaller funding sources that are cumulatively significant. The surplus of funding sources over investment outlays shows up in two places. The first is that these funds finance a certain amount of inventory accumulation: between 18 and 19 billion yuan worth of inventories were so financed in the four years 1979–1982.[17] Part of this inventory accumulation may be a simple substitution of enterprise-owned funds for bank loans (which normally finance inventory accumulation); part may be an effort by the enterprises to hold their newfound wealth in material rather than financial assets. Second, bank accounts of enterprises and nonprofit organizations increased by 40 billion yuan (or 60 percent) from the end of 1979 to the end of 1982. This is not an unreasonable increase, considering that decentralized investment has more than doubled and industrial production increased by a little more than 20 percent, but it does indicate that local units retain substantial funds in reserve.

The importance of carrying over funds from previous periods is particularly clear in the case of depreciation funds, where we have some figures for earlier years. The surplus of depreciation funds, unused at year-end in the years 1976–1979, came successively to 6.5 billion, 7.9 billion, 6.2 billion, and "over 7" billion.[18] These funds are not forfeited if unused within the year drawn; as a result, they form a substantial quantity of enterprise "wealth," which is carried into future years.[19] In many enterprises the retained depreciation funds are simply lumped together with ordinary working capital, with no particular effort being made to keep the two funds separate. In these cases funds are only transferred to special bank accounts when expenditure on a specific project is imminent.[20]

It can be seen from table 3.3 that retained depreciation funds remain the largest source of local investment by a large margin. However, of the *increase* in local investment between 1979 and 1982 (an increase of 29 billion yuan, or

[17] Shen Shuigen, "Several Questions on the Reform of the System of Circulating Capital Management," *CMJJ* 9 (1983): 39–42.

[18] Hu Jing and Wang Chengyao, *Gongye Jingji Guanli Congkan* 3 (1980): 7; Wang Meihan, *Caizheng Yanjiu* 1 (1983): 15.

[19] Li Qiushi, *CZ* 4 (1981): 11. This can also be seen by examining the bank balance sheets published by the People's Bank of China. These reveal that enterprise deposits have increased 53 percent (24.9 billion yuan) between 1979 and 1982, while capital construction deposits (which include both budgetary allocations and earmarked deposits of enterprises) have increased 118 percent (15.4 billion yuan).

[20] Zhang Meilin, *Zhongguo Jinrong* 7 (1982): 17. At the same time, regular working capital is diverted to investment and then "repaid" from later depreciation funds. These sloppy accounting practices continue because it is in the enterprise's interests to offset interest-bearing loans for working capital with depreciation funds, which would earn substantially lower interest if placed in a bank deposit.

120 percent), the largest contributing factor has been bank loans, which increased 11 billion yuan, accounting for nearly 40 percent of the increase. The second most important source of increase has been profit retention, which contributed about 9 billion to the investment pool (assuming that a lower percentage of retained profits was used for fixed investment in 1979, since the program was instituted in the last quarter), accounting for a little over 30 percent of the increase. Increases in retained depreciation accounted for slightly over 20 percent of the increase, and increases in government and nonprofit organizations funds (though this is the weakest estimate) accounted for about 5 percent, as did foreign capital.

A corollary of the above figures is that the decentralization of investment is not the direct result of reforms of the industrial system. The central reform of the industrial system was the institution of profit-sharing in 6,600 enterprises at the end of 1979. It is estimated that the 5,700 of these enterprises included in calculations of local authorities retained 1.24 billion yuan more in 1980 than they would have received under the (prereform) "enterprise fund" system.[21] This amounts to about 3 percent of decentralized funds in 1980. Most of the local financial resources accrue to local power holders on the basis of administrative regulations, and very little is provided as part of the incentives for economically effective behavior. In particular, bank loans are rationed on the basis of administrative regions, not provided at market-clearing interest rates, and payback provisions are so flexible that they remain basically risk-free (and nearly costless, in spite of the interest charges they bear) to the enterprise.[22] The increase in local investment thus reflects a changed political environment, one in which local authorities are able to compete more effectively for resources *within* the bureaucracy.

The sustained, substantial increase in decentralized investment documented in the previous section has occurred in the face of repeated attempts by the central government to restrict (and in some years reduce) the total amount of investment and to decrease the proportion of investment carried out through decentralized channels. Early in each year, the government issues the economic plan expressing its intentions for the scale of fixed investment in the coming year. Figure 3.1 shows graphically the relationship between these intentions and the actual outcomes in each year for which we have data. While central budgetary investment has conformed closely to planned figures, decentralized investment has regularly exceeded

---

[21] *State Council Bulletin* 9 (1981): 271.

[22] This is so for a number of reasons. First, loans are repaid, not from the portion of profit retained by the enterprise, but from total profits *before* the enterprise's retention share has been calculated. Therefore, a large proportion of loan repayment is in fact borne by the government budget. In addition, in actual practice enterprises that run into difficulty with poor investments regularly enjoy tax remissions, which protect their interests.

FIGURE 3.1   Degree of Plan Fulfillment for Different Categories
of Investment

SOURCES: 1980: 1981 *JJNJ*, IV-9.
1981: 1982 *JJNJ*, V-297.
1982: 1983 *JJNJ*, III-82.
1983: The six-month figures for 1983 are calculated on the assumption that 34% of total investment
is normally completed in the first six months of the year. This was true in the 1950s (*Jihua Jingji*
6[1957]: 8), and in 1982 (*Tongji* 4[1982]: 47). In addition, budgetary investment in the first six
months of 1983 equaled 34% of the planned figure.

the plan. In 1980 "own-funds" capital construction *exceeded* the plan target
by 105 percent. The collapse of control which this implied, together with a
budget deficit that seemed to be spiraling out of control, caused planners to
drastically cut back 1981 investment plans in all sectors. By concentrating all
the political resources of the government on this issue, central planners were
able to reduce own-funds capital construction by 2 billion yuan, an amount
that left this category of investment 48 percent over target. Although we have
no figure for the RR investment plan for 1981 (if there was one), it is noteworthy that while every other component of investment declined in that year,
RR investment increased by almost 4 billion yuan, more than offsetting the
decline in own-funds capital construction. Finally, in 1982 and the first half
of 1983, while capital construction financed from local own-funds, and even
RR investment, came somewhat closer to the plan target (35 and 17 percent
over plan, respectively), bank loans shot out of control, overfulfilling the plan
by 106 percent. These figures do not take cognizance of the fact that in both
1981 and 1982 the plans were adjusted upward during the course of the year:
the figures cited are comparisons with the adjusted plans, so that results
diverged even more substantially from planners' initial intentions.

Central planners seem to be in the position of trying to compress an air-
filled balloon: no matter how hard they squeeze, the excess always bulges out

somewhere. Financial resources are switched between investment categories in order to protect investment projects to which local leaders are committed. Considering the sums of money at the disposal of local authorities, this result is hardly suprising. Restriction of outlays from various retained funds may even cause bank loans to increase, because increased deposits serve as credit funds for new bank loans. Why then do planners not simply reduce the total financial resources at local levels? In order to address this question, we need to consider the motives of central planners and their often conflicting objectives for the use of investment resources.

Since 1979 central planners have attempted to make three major changes in the disposition of fixed investment. The first change has been to control the overall volume of investment and reduce the proportion of national income that goes to investment. On balance, this objective has been obtained: The increase in national income since 1979 has gone almost entirely to increased consumption, while the total of all types of investment has remained approximately level. However, the failure to control local investment has meant that in order to obtain this objective, planners have been forced to absorb the full amount of investment cutbacks from central government investment. Even after the modest upturn in 1982, central government investment was 30 percent less than in 1978, while local investment had more than doubled. Moreover, this process has been accompanied by painful budgetary deficits, fears of inflation, and occasional spasmodic cutbacks in central government spending. The most dramatic such incident occurred in December 1980, when central planners, alarmed by persistent deficits and complaints about price rises, decreed massive cutbacks in all forms of investment, cutbacks which, as we have seen, were fully realized only in central investment (see chapter 4, which analyzes the events leading up to this incident).

In itself, a decline in central investment is not necessarily harmful nor inconsistent with the regime's objectives. But this decline has been accompanied by a failure to accomplish the second major change in investment structure sought by central planners: the concentration of investment in the development of energy and transportation. It has been widely recognized that energy, and its transport to industrial centers, is the crucial bottleneck in Chinese industrial production, with Chinese planners estimating that industrial production is as much as 30 percent below capacity solely because of energy shortages (see chapter 7). But new investments in energy production or transportation facilities generally require large, frequently interregional projects that only the central government is in a position to carry out.[23]

---

[23] This is not invariably the case, however. Local investment resources are so substantial that they can sometimes fund such large-scale projects. The province of Shandong recently completed a highway bridge over the Yellow River at Jinan financed predominantly from its own resources. Zhang Mingfa, *Gonglu* 8 (1982): 41, translated in *JPRS, Ec.*, no. 297, 59.

TABLE 3.4   Energy and Transportation Investment
(in billion yuan)

	1978	1979	1980	1981	1982
Capital construction					
Energy	11.4	11.0	11.4	9.1	10.1
	(22.7%)	(21.0%)	(20.6%)	(20.6%)	(18.3%)
Transportation	6.8	6.4	6.2	4.0	5.7
	(13.6%)	(12.2%)	(11.2%)	(9.1%)	(10.3%)
RR investment					
Energy	—	—	—	5.4	7.2
				(23.9%)	(24.7%)
Transportation	—	—	—	2.5	3.2
				(11.2%)	(10.9%)
Total fixed investment					
Energy	—	—	—	14.5	17.3
				(21.7%)	(20.5%)
Transportation	—	—	—	6.5	8.9
				(9.7%)	(10.5%)

SOURCE: Capital construction, 1983 *Tongji Zhaiyao*, 60–62. RR investment, "Report on Fulfillment of 1982 Plan," *Xinhua Yuebao* 4 (1983).

Table 3.4 shows trends since 1978 in investment in energy and transportation. Even after the upturn of 1982, capital construction investment in both energy and transport is lower, both absolutely and as a percentage of total capital construction, than in 1978. Since there has been a persistent upward cost drift during this period, real investment has declined even more.

Although there are no figures for the sectoral composition of RR investment prior to 1981, it can be seen that energy and transport investment in this category was quite substantial in both 1981 and 1982. This does not fundamentally change the reality that emerges from examining the capital construction figures alone, though, for two reasons. First, both energy and transportation are highly capital-intensive sectors, which generate large depreciation funds. However, these large funds reflect the technological reality that the rate of physical deterioration of assets in these sectors is quite high, and that large sums are necessary simply to maintain current levels of production. Depreciation rates in the petroleum industry of 9.8 percent annually are more than twice that of industry generally, but this high rate reflects the unavoidable need to promptly replace quickly deteriorating assets used in petroleum extraction.[24] RR investment worth 1.3 billion yuan was carried

[24] Liang Wensen and Tian Jianghai, *Shehui Zhuyi Guding Zichang Zaishengchan* (Beijing: China Social Sciences Publishing House, 1983), 219. Moreover, because the RR investment in energy

out at Daqing oilfield in 1982 (4.5 percent of total RR investment in the
nation), but this sum was necessary simply to maintain Daqing's production
without a significant decline.[25] In the transportation sector, a large part of
RR investment goes for the purchase of vehicles and boats, while the crucial
bottleneck lies in railroad carrying capacity.[26] Thus, in spite of the large sum
of money going to energy and transport sectors through RR investment, this
is unlikely to contribute much to the development of *new* energy resources.

A check on this assertion is provided by an examination of the figures for
new production capacity added annually in these sectors. Although annual
figures show substantial variation due to the "lumpiness" of large projects, a
clear downward trend is visible between 1978 and 1982 in coal, petroleum,
electric power, highways, and railroads (which completed only 34 km of new
track in 1981–1982). Only in port construction has the picture been radically different, with 20 million tons of new capacity added in 1982, an amount
greater than the total of the previous four years.[27] In addition to the creation of new capacity, energy conservation measures contribute to the effective
supply of energy, but the amount spent in this fashion does not appear to
have been large. Although there were plans to spend 1 billion yuan for conservation loans in 1981, only 200 million of such loans were subsequently
reported,[28] and most energy saving has come through closing egregiously
inefficient plants and reorienting production to light industry, which is far
less energy intensive. Overall, Chinese planners have failed dramatically in
their attempt to direct investment effectively toward energy and transportation.

While the decentralization of investment has created obstacles to the implementation of the first two objectives of planners, it has facilitated the third
objective, the channeling of more investment into housing and the production of consumer goods. The proportion of capital construction going into
housing has exploded; from only 7.8 percent in 1978 it surpassed 25 percent
in both 1981 and 1982.[29] Moreover, a major portion of current housing
construction, and nearly the entire amount of increase, comes from a single

and transport comes largely from depreciation funds, which are the slowest growing component
of decentralized investment, they are unlikely to have expanded rapidly enough to offset the
declines in capital construction investment.

[25] Daqing Petroleum Management Bureau, *Xinhua Yuebao* 4 (1983): 102. The coal mining
industry enjoys special treatment in the calculation of depreciation, with an allowance for resource depletion calculated on the basis of output, rather than on the basis of fixed assets.

[26] From mid-1979 to mid-1982, bank loans funded 1.3 billion yuan worth of vehicle and boat
purchases. Zhu Tianshun, *Zhongguo Jinrong* 22 (1982): 1–3, translated in *JPRS Ec.*, no. 303, 4–6.

[27] *TJZY*, 63.

[28] Zhao Haikuan, *CMJJ* 7 (1982): 56–57. Only 300 million in such loans were reported for the
period mid-1979 through mid-1982. See Zhu Tianshun above.

[29] *TJZY*, 60–62.

decentralized funding source: the program of enterprise profit retention. Retained profits have accounted for about 60 percent of urban housing constructed in recent years.[30] The proportion of investment going to light industries has also expanded rapidly since 1978, and most of this increase has been implemented through the medium of a decentralization in investment control, in this case through the expanded program of bank lending. From mid-1979 to mid-1982 the People's Bank of China extended 8.9 billion yuan in loans to consumer goods industries, an amount more than twice state budgetary investment in the same category.[31] Although in some cases this rapid expansion has led to inefficient duplicate investment, the overall objective of rapidly expanding production of consumer goods, and especially consumer durables, has been rapidly achieved.

The decentralization of investment resources by itself cannot explain the failure to concentrate resources in energy and transport development, for we are left to ask why the central government has not concentrated the resources left to it more dramatically in these key sectors. To this question there can be no simple answer, but it appears that both economic and institutional factors constrain the ability of the Center to concentrate resources through the unwieldy central allocation process. In the first place, Beijing's flexibility is severely limited by the massive commitment of resources to hundreds of half-completed projects throughout the country. The large number of projects under construction is in part a reflection of erratic changes in investment policy since 1975, and in part a reflection of chronic overinvestment and dispersal of resources into too many projects; naturally this reduces the Center's ability to begin new projects in the current period without sustaining serious losses. There were 1,624 active large-scale investment projects at the end of 1978, and this total was reduced to 663 at the end of 1981. Of the net reduction of nearly 1,000 projects, only 289 were completed; almost 900 projects have been postponed or abandoned, at incalculable cost (200 new projects were begun).[32] At the same time, Chinese planners have paid repeated heavy costs for hastily conceived and poorly designed investment projects in the past. These painful lessons have no doubt induced them to move deliberately in the development of a new program of energy and transport development.

Yet in spite of these constraining factors, the minimal shift of investment to identified priority sectors raises serious questions about the degree of responsiveness of the Center's investment allocation mechanisms. The degree

[30]Xie Minggan, *1982 JJNJ*, V-42. In Liaoning, which has been a leader in encouraging individual investment in housing, the percentage figures were state enterprises 55; collective enterprises 10; individuals 5; and budgetary investment 30. Liaoning Provincial Service of December 29, 1982, translated in *JPRS, Ec.*, no. 311.

[31]Zhu Tianshun (n. 26 above).

[32]Kang Zhixin, *1982 JJNJ*, V-298.

of bureaucratic inertia appears to be high, and the difficulties of dividing resources between competing demands seems to be very great. We noted above that the category of RR investment was initially created in order to protect an important category of investment from being whittled away by the competing demands of numerous new investment projects. There can be no doubt that the annual process of allocation of investment resources by the State Planning Commission is a protracted and contentious process, with each ministry (and province) pushing its own claims and attempting to expand and protect its share of total resources.[33] Demands for new projects inevitably outrun the supply of investment goods, and there is no recognized standard for arbitrating claims. Long-term price rigidity and attendant price distortions make it impossible to judge projects in different sectors on the basis of profitability, and though in theory planners can rely on shortage signals to identify priority sectors, in practice there are so many shortage sectors that balancing claims on this basis must be particularly difficult. Besides energy and transport, current shortfalls are serious in the supply of high-grade metals, building materials, dyestuffs, and chemical fertilizers.

We can speculate that in this situation actual allocation decisions are determined largely by the influence that different Beijing-based bureaucracies can bring to bear, and by various ad hoc sharing arrangements. In the face of overall cutbacks, bureaucracies may find their entire raison d'être threatened and muster all their influence to preserve a few key projects. Ministers struggle to protect their power bases and keep subordinates busy; in order to succeed in this struggle, they must insure that at least their share of the total investment is not too drastically reduced. Though we know little about how this process works in practice, we may get a hint of it from the outcome of the highly contested allocation of resources to continue the Baoshan steel mill. Xue Muqiao has written: "In order to guarantee the construction of the first stage of the Baoshan Steel Mill, almost the entire quantity of investment allocated by the state to the Metallurgy Ministry has been taken up, and there is no money left for technical upgrading of nearly a score of large and medium sized steel mills which desperately need it."[34] This would appear to indicate that the Metallurgy Ministry is able to defend a certain share of total investment, which is relatively firm. Allocations are made not so much to individual projects as to bureaucratic systems. The meager results obtained in intensifying energy investment appears to indicate that the shifting of resources between these bureaucratic systems is particularly difficult for central planners.

Similar power-sharing arrangements have often been used to explain the

[33] An illuminating general discussion of this process, with specific reference to Hungary, is provided in Janos Kornai, *Economics of Shortage* (Amsterdam: North-Holland, 1981).
[34] Xue Muqiao, *Jinrong Yanjiu* 6 (1981): 4.

remarkable long-term stability of investment structure in the Soviet Union, but even in the Soviet Union planners were capable of redirecting investment in the late 1970s in response to clearly perceived problems.[35] Chinese planners, on the other hand, seem to be forced to content themselves with relatively small increments in the amount of investment directed to bottleneck sectors. While this "incrementalism" may be a general phenomenon in bureaucratic decision-making,[36] it appears to be extreme in China. China has undoubtedly forgone substantial increased output in the 1980s because of the failure to expand effective energy supplies in a timely fashion, and this suggests that the rigidity of the Chinese allocation process is a serious impediment to accelerated and more efficient economic growth.

Evidence of bureaucratic rigidity also suggests an important motivation for investment decentralization. We noted above that the successes achieved in redirecting investment toward housing and consumer goods production were directly linked to the creation of new, decentralized funding sources. In fact, the redirection of investment has been successfully accomplished *only* in those cases where a new funding mechanism has been created. In the case of expanded bank lending, the new funding mechanism has been accompanied by the creation of what is, in effect, a new bureaucratic organization as well, for the banking system has been dramatically expanded in recent years, and many of the new personnel are employed in kinds of credit activity which had not been part of the bank's operation in previous years. In the case of housing investment, of course, the Center has been able to rely on the self-interest of enterprises to expand this category of investment.

At the beginning of 1983, central planners created another new funding mechanism. Henceforth a special levy is to be made specifically for the creation of an "energy and transportation development fund." Ten percent of all extrabudgetary funds, which includes all of the funding sources we have discussed above (with the exception of depreciation in energy producing sectors), is to be remitted directly to this fund, under the control of the central budgetary authorities.[37] This fund has the dual advantage of reducing decentralized investment funds while simultaneously creating "new" financial resources for priority sectors outside the standard investment allocation framework. It should be noted that this special fund accounts for the totality of the increase in projected budgetary revenues in 1983.[38] Whether this new

---

[35] See the discussion of this issue in Myron Rush, "The Soviet Policy Favoring Arms over Investment since 1975," in U.S. Congress Joint Economic Committee, ed., *Soviet Economy in the 1980s: Problems and Prospects* (Washington, D.C.: Government Printing Office, 1982), 324–25, and related articles in the same volume.

[36] See Aaron Wildavsky, *The Politics of The Budgetary Process* (Boston: Little, Brown, 1964).

[37] Wang Bingqian, "Report on the 1982 State Budget and Draft 1983 Budget," translated in BBC FE/7209/C2/4–5.

[38] Ibid.

funding mechanism will successfully direct investment into energy development remains to be seen. If the implementation bias identified above persists, we can expect that local levels will be able to defend a portion of their funding sources, and the central government will raise less money for energy development than it currently intends.

Central planners have been notably unsuccessful in their attempt to control local investment, and they appear to have had only marginally greater success in redirecting resources that are nominally under their direct control. Fragmented power, based on the control of resources within discrete organizational systems, seems to be a pervasive characteristic of the Chinese system. Planners do seem to be able to restrict the total volume of investment under their direct control, and this enables them to realize some of their objectives by freeing up resources for consumption and for investment in increased consumption in the immediate future. In these cases, the self-interest of enterprises and local bureaucracies can be rapidly brought into play by the central government; in cases where such a clear interest does not exist, the institutional rigidity of the system seriously constrains effective redeployment of resources. But institutional rigidities cannot explain the phenomenon of increased local control of investment, because we have seen that localities have rapidly and consistently been able to expand their investment share over the past several years. We must therefore seek further explanations in the characteristics of the Chinese political system and economic management system as these have evolved over the past several years.

We know very little about the relationship between central and local power holders in China, yet there can be no doubt that this is a crucial aspect of decision-making and that it directly influences the way decisions are implemented. In this section I examine briefly the balance in political power between the Center and localities; the concrete aspects of the economic system which affect the distribution of economic power; and finally the new rules that affect decision-making in the current reform period and that tilt the balance of power toward the localities.

The division of power between the national capital and local officials has been a contentious issue in China for centuries. Although in theory the power of the emperor was absolute, in practice his control was limited by the sheer expanse of the empire and by a bureaucracy in which local officials were expected to take the interests of the people to heart and protect them from unfair exactions by the central government. Local bureaucrats who could defend or curtail existing taxation levels were regularly exalted as model officials in the dynastic histories,[39] and this political ethic survives in China

---

[39] Ho Ping-ti, *Studies on the Population of China, 1368–1953* (Cambridge: Harvard University Press, 1959), 33. See also the entertaining account of bureaucratic paralysis included in Ray Huang, *1587: A Year of No Significance* (Cambridge: Harvard University Press, 1982).

today. A good bureaucrat is one who can protect his subordinates, insure them an adequate supply of resources, and vigorously advocate their interests at the next higher level of government. The history of China since 1949 reveals hundreds of cases of local officials who have been criticized for taking this local advocacy to an extreme and sacrificing national goals for "departmental self-interest" (*benwei zhuyi*) and the construction of local "independent kingdoms." These criticisms have not noticeably reduced the incidence of this particular "deviation."

In addition to acting as advocates of local interests on an individual basis, provincial Party secretaries, in particular, also have a strong collective voice in central government decisions. A large number of provincial Party secretaries are represented in the Central Committee of the Communist Party, and it is well known that the late Chairman Mao successfully appealed to this group on several occasions when he found himself outvoted by his colleagues at the Center. Control of investment resources is always an important issue in central government decisions. In particular, the control of depreciation funds was a contentious issue as early as 1976. During the early part of that year, while Deng Xiaoping was in charge of central government work, a decision was made to recentralize a portion of depreciation funds (then, as now, the largest component of local investment funds). Later in that year Deng Xiaoping was purged, and at a Central Work conference in June the recentralization decision was reversed. In a situation where (remarkably like the present) a drastic cutback in total investment had become necessary, a bitter struggle took place over the allocation of these cuts.[40] In this struggle the "Gang of Four" took the side of local power holders and for a time prevailed. After the fall of the Gang of Four, a modest recentralization was put through in 1978, only to be largely reversed by the new decentralizing measures that are the topic of this essay. Thus, one explanation for the inability of the Center to control local investment is simply that local power holders are a potent political force, whose influence on the composition of the central leadership cannot be ignored, least of all by the central leadership itself.

As a result, local power holders have had a tremendous impact on the evolution of economic policy in recent years. A few examples will serve to illustrate this point. In 1980 a new budgetary system was introduced which gave each level of government (county, municipal, or provincial) control over the profits of industrial enterprises subordinate to that level. This reform was supposed to be accompanied by the return of several thousand larger enterprises to direct central government subordination, but in practice the second part of this reform remained largely unimplemented. Local governments got greater operational autonomy without having to sacrifice any of their rev-

---

[40] Partial insight into this struggle is provided in Allen S. Whiting, "Domestic Politics and Foreign Trade in the PRC, 1971–1976" (Ann Arbor: Michigan Papers in Chinese Studies, no. 36, 1979). The "Gang of Four" advocated reducing foreign-plant imports as an alternative to reducing local investment.

enue sources.[41] Similarly, it has been central government policy for several
years to reduce the number of wholesale commercial organs because in past
years these organs had been set up in each administrative region, creating
unnecessary duplication of facilities. But "this suggestion has been completely unrealizable, mainly because it influences the financial income of the
localities."[42] Such cases might be interpreted to mean that local governments
are opposed to economic reforms, but such is not the case. When the central
government introduced a program of profit retention in 1979, this was meant
to be an experimental program instituted at a small number of enterprises in
each province. By the end of that year, 1,600 enterprises were participating,
and the central government announced that the number should not increase.
Yet, within a few months it was acknowledged that 6,600 enterprises were
now participating and that these were the largest and most profitable enterprises, accounting for a majority of profits and output.[43] Local industrial
officials recognized that profit retention meant more resources under their
direct control, and they moved rapidly to take advantage of this opportunity.
Thus implementation bias is not simply a matter of control over investment;
it influences the whole range of decisions made in Beijing. Local interests
consistently deflect central government decisions toward their own interests.

However, returning to the question of investment control, we find that
besides the substantial political presence that local authorities have in Beijing, effective central direction of investment is impeded by the lack of sufficient control mechanisms that reach down to local levels. As a result, local
control is increased by the simple reality of weak supervision of local activity.
What tools does the Center dispose of in its effort to restrain local investment?
Before 1978 central government control was purely financial; there was *no*
plan for RR investment, and the capital construction plan was not comprehensive. Only by regulating the amount of funds available to the lower levels
could the Center affect the total decentralized investment. Since during this
period the great bulk of RR investment was provided through retained
depreciation, and the total amount of depreciation available is known in
advance, it was at least theoretically possible for the state to plan investment
taking this sum of local financing into consideration.[44] However, the proliferation of funding sources that has taken place since 1979 has made such control

[41] Zhu Fulin, "Some Opinions on the Reform of Our Nation's Budgetary System in the Past
Several Years," *CZ* 2 (1983): 17.
[42] Xue Muqiao, *CMJJ* 8 (1982): 1–3.
[43] *Renmin Ribao*, Jan. 2, 1981, 1.
[44] There is little evidence that planning in fact took systematic account of these decentralized
funds during the pre-1978 period. Capital construction plans were promulgated with "gaps"
that were supposed to mobilize local investment to complete projects, but this was apparently
done in an entirely unsystematic way. In addition, slack enterprise accounting during this
period allowed the diversion of substantial funds to investment purposes through a quasi-legal
process of padding production costs.

impossible. While we have listed the main categories of decentralized investment funds above, each of these is composed of different subcategories, including special depreciation programs, numerous lending programs, and various uses of local government funds. One source lists twelve different funding sources in 1980.[45] The central government has been making a large effort to determine the volume of these funding sources retrospectively, and has not come close to forecasting future values. Given the proliferation of funding sources, the rather clumsy attempts by the state to reduce the total volume of financial resources have not succeeded. In 1981 the state issued bonds, froze bank accounts, and levied a compulsory "loan" from local governments. Although this had some effect in restraining the growth of decentralized investment, it apparently had negative effects as well, since the impounding of funds blocked progress on some important state projects.[46]

In the absence of effective financial controls on decentralized investment, the state has attempted to restrict such investment through increasingly strict administrative and planning controls. In 1978 and 1979 the government decreed that funds for RR investment should be managed through the Bank of Construction. Compliance was slow, and as of the end of 1979 only a small proportion of such funds were so managed.[47] Beginning in 1981 the government began to require that large RR projects be integrated into the planning process. Projects with a value over 1 million yuan were to be reported to the State Planning Commission, with smaller projects reported to the provincial and municipal planning commissions.[48] Also in 1981, the State Council required that all capital construction investments be included in the unified plan of the state and appropriated under Bank of Construction supervision.[49] These were not regulations aimed at increasing compliance to existing procedures, but were rather attempts to provide a modicum of centralized direction of total investment for the first time in many years. In 1982 the state took its first steps toward bringing RR investment together with capital construction investment into a single fixed investment plan, and at the same time attempted to set some regional limits for housing construction and similar outlays from enterprise collective welfare funds.[50] Finally, in 1983

---

[45] Zhai Zhibin et al., *CZ* 8 (1980): 23. Other sources have mentioned as many as thirty different funding sources.

[46] A number of statements appearing in late 1981 indicated that "some projects had been inappropriately cut back" during the contraction of the early part of the year.

[47] By the end of 1979, only 4.5 billion yuan worth of RR funds had been so managed. Zong Wen, *CZ* 12 (1980): 25. The relevant document is *Zhongfa* (1978), no. 102.

[48] *State Council Bulletin* 7 (1980): 207.

[49] State Council Directive, February 3, 1981. Translated in Foreign Broadcast Information Service (*FBIS*), Feb. 5, 1981, L6–7.

[50] Interviews conducted in Wuhan, April–May 1982. These efforts did not succeed in preventing a 20.4 percent increase in housing construction during the year. *Jingji Ribao*, March 5, 1983, 2, translated in *FBIS*, Mar. 18, 1983, K-20.

the Planning Commission, for the first time, set a full system of regional quotas for total fixed investment, including both capital construction and RR investment. Reportedly, these quotas also included a separate quota for housing construction. In addition, the 1983 regulations included, for the first time, an enforcement mechanism. A 30 percent surcharge—payable into the specialized fund for energy and transportation projects mentioned above— was to be exacted on all projects above the quota.[51]

It will be difficult for central authorities to impose this penalty. If a given province, for example, reports total investment of 10 percent over their quota, central authorities will have to determine which of the projects in that province are responsible for exceeding the target figure. Keeping in mind that the Center does not possess budgets or breakdowns for individual projects, but has simply imposed an arbitrary quota on the entire province, the selection of the "guilty" projects will be difficult. This difficulty will be especially clear if we consider the way investment projects are approved at the local level. Chinese sources have repeatedly referred to the multiplicity of authority relations to which an enterprise is subject, a condition they describe as having "too many mothers-in-law." This situation inevitably means that the approval of any individual investment project is the result of a long process of accommodation and negotiation between numerous power centers. A partial list of these power centers would include the local planning commission, construction commission, finance bureau, bank, and material supply companies,[52] in addition to the industrial bureau that directly supervises the enterprise. Since this approval may represent a complex set of mutual obligations and trade-offs for these agencies, central demands for a reduction in the number of projects has an impact on every aspect of the local structure of coordination. The Center has no single chain of command to compel all these agencies to follow its priorities, and the multiplicity of local decision-makers makes it still more difficult to determine who is responsible for any given decision. This is especially true in the frequent case where different funding sources are "blended" in a single investment project. Ultimately the Center has little choice but to hold the top authority—the local Party secretary—responsible for these choices. But since local Party secretaries are responsible for many types of activity, the resort to criticism or demotion of Party secretaries who preside over investment excesses is no easy matter. It is an especially difficult problem when, as must frequently be the case, the locales that exceed their investment quotas are also the

[51] *Xinhua* release of January 12, 1983, translated in *FBIS*, January 21, 1983, K-9. This source refers only to capital construction investment, but it is clear from other sources that the new control figures are designed to include RR investment as well.

[52] This list is drawn from Zhang Zhongmin et al., *Jiben Jianshe Jingji* (Beijing: Finance and Economics Publishing House, 1982), 52.

locales that are turning in especially good performances in accelerating economic growth.

Thus, while the Center has moved steadily during the last five years to strengthen its data-collection and planning capabilities, it still does not possess adequate tools for directly controlling the volume of total investment. A glance at figure 3.1 reveals that in the first half of 1983, after the establishment for the first time of a comprehensive investment plan, the Center was just as far as before from being able to ensure compliance with its directives. Moreover, the trends during the past five years have been somewhat paradoxical: at a time when Beijing was advocating the increased use of "economic levers" (price and tax policy) to control economic activity, the failure to control local investment was actually pushing planners to develop an increased administrative planning ability in the attempt to supplement earlier, inadequate, reliance on financial control. And yet, given the extreme dispersal of financial resources, the Center's ability to collect information and promulgate plans has not yielded the kind of direct control that one might ordinarily expect from a "centrally planned" economy. In mid-1983 planners resorted to a type of control that resembles a "campaign" strategy more than a set of administrative controls. On the heels of a joint central government and central Party committee meeting at the end of June devoted to the problem of investment control, the media were full of exhortations to reduce local investment, and special work conferences were convened in each province, directed to eliminate investment projects and pare down the total investment in each locality. We can expect that such a campaign strategy will attain some temporary results (particularly since it involves the mobilization of the Party hierarchy as well as governmental authority relations). But such campaigns cannot be sustained indefinitely, and in the absence of changes in the underlying structure of investment control, the problems are sure to reassert themselves. The Center will probably exert some control over investment in the last half of 1983, but the problems examined in this chapter will continue to be major issues in China's economic policy in 1984 and beyond.

Recent changes in the economic management system have actually reinforced the ability of local organs to act independently (thus conforming to their increased disposition of financial resources). In recent years, the economic system has evolved toward an increasing "internalization" of the resources needed to plan production. By "internalization" I mean that the resources related to production and investment are increasingly controlled within local administrative hierarchies. Financially, profits are increasingly held within industrial hierarchies for a period of time before they are remitted to the state treasury. As the central government set profit quotas for individual ministries and province-level industrial bureaus, these organs gained control over the day-to-day disposition of enterprise revenues, subject only to their ultimate obligation to remit a sum of profit on a quarterly or an annual basis. Previously these profits were remitted to the tax office of the Ministry of Finance wherever the enterprise was located.[53] At the same time, the Material Supply system has been reorganized in a way that places primary responsibility for supplemental materials allocation with material supply companies organized on a provincial basis.[54] This increases local control over the materials needed to carry out investment projects. Last but not least, the changes in the budgetary system initiated in 1980, besides increasing financial resources in local hands, dramatically reduced the amount of direct supervision over spending items which the central government could exert. Local governments are authorized to shift funds between different expenditure items, subject only to their responsibility to fulfill certain broadly defined tasks. These institutional changes mean that local governments and industrial systems are in some senses genuinely autonomous. They do not *depend* on the central government for any of their critical resources; all they need is *permission* to use them. Not surprisingly, when such permission is not forthcoming, the temptation to proceed without permission is very strong.

The above institutional facts lead us to a simple conclusion. The Center simply does not possess adequate tools to directly control local investment. Within the economic management system, neither financial supervision nor administrative planning directives offer central planners the option of effective control of local investment. The lack of effective institutions is the proximate explanation of the Center's failure to control local investment. But the Center's lack of tools to guide local investment in a measured fashion still leaves a larger question: Why does the Center not simply change the "rules of the game" in drastic fashion to reduce the total of resources under local control?

Partial answers to this question are provided by the factors discussed above. The substantial political power of local interests requires central authorities to move slowly and carefully in expropriating resources that local interests have grown accustomed to controlling. Moreover, the central elite is concerned, not solely with reducing local investment, but rather with carrying through a whole range of objectives relating to the structure of investment, and some of these have been carried out through the medium of investment decentralization. Furthermore, central planners are aware that the rigid and cumbersome central allocation process cannot be relied on to be sufficiently responsive to central planners' priorities either. But there is little doubt that if central planners chose to mobilize the full weight of political authority available to them—including the appeal to Party disci-

[53] Chen Zixin, *CZ* 8 (1982): 28–29. It should be noted that this process was furthered by central government regulations directing ministries and industrial bureaus to adjust funds between enterprises in order to compensate those hurt by plan reductions. See *State Council Bulletin* 14 (1981): 442.

[54] Wang Jinfu and Zhang Baozhu, *CMJJ* 8 (1982): 58.

pline—they could rapidly reduce the financial and material sources of local control over investment. Yet they do not choose to do so.

Ultimately this is because central leaders do not view a recentralized system as a viable option for the future. Economic reform remains an ambiguous concept in China, and steps in that direction have been halting and sometimes ineffectual. Yet the concept of a reformed economic system, in which a large range of economic decision-making takes place in a decentralized fashion and in response to rationalized incentives, remains the primary goal of the current Chinese leadership. The recommitment to economic reform which occurred at the beginning of 1983, in the face of the problems outlined above and the need to deal with them on an emergency basis, should provide strong support for this view.[55] Massive recentralization would cause an enormous setback to the prospects of real economic reforms and would vitiate the tentative results so far attained.

Each of the decentralized financial sources outlined above is *intended* to serve as an incentive to move the economic system toward more rational decision-making. This is most obvious in the case of profit retention, but it is also true for bank loans and depreciation retention. Bank loans, bearing interest and payback requirements, are intended to introduce rational economic calculation into investment decisions. Depreciation retention is intended to serve as a source for the technical upgrading of fixed assets and to serve as an alternative to the duplication of production facilities at a low technological level. None of these programs actually provides at present the type of incentives which central leaders intend. The incentive effects of profit retention are vitiated by irrational pricing structures, incomplete capital charges (though this is improving), and most significant, continued institutional bargaining over "fair" levels of retained profits. Bank loans are repaid on terms that are excessively concessionary (and often involve reductions in tax or profit delivery responsibilities), while interest rates remain too low. Finally, retained depreciation funds continue to be used for new and expanded investment projects, in the absence of real incentives to use these funds for technical upgrading. Thus, as reform measures, all of these mechanisms are inadequate and incomplete. But the current leadership sees the future task as the improvement of the incentive environment in which these mechanisms operate, rather than as a wholesale scaling back of any of the programs.

As these programs have been instituted thus far, they all share a common drawback. All these programs release resources to lower levels without accompanying them with appropriate responsibilities or adequate incentives for efficient use. As a result, decentralization of resources takes place, rather

---

[55] This recommitment is evident in the adoption of the "tax for profit" scheme for enterprises, as well as in the burst of pro-reform propaganda which swept the media in early 1983. For examples, see the dispatches translated in *FBIS* Mar. 17, 1983, K-15, and Jan. 20, 1983, K-9.

than decentralization of the right to use resources in economically productive areas. Local authorities naturally welcome the decentralization of resources, and since control over resources remains close to costless, they fight to control as large a quantity of resources as possible. Local authorities are pragmatists; they seek to expand their control of resources through whatever means is available. This leads them sometimes to support "reforms" (in the case of profit retention), and sometimes to oppose "reforms" (such as those in the commercial system, or by resisting economically effective charges on capital). Particularly in a country as poor as China, pragmatism means effective defense of local interests.

The central leadership, on the other hand, is motivated by a vision of a reformed economic system, even though that vision is often vague and ill-defined. Well aware of the problems and costs incurred because of the previous economic management system, central planners are unwilling to take measures that would reinstate a highly centralized system and perpetuate the problems of past years. They have shown themselves willing to accept a dramatic decline in their own control over investment resources in the pursuit of the elusive goal of "reform." The struggle between Center and locality for control over investment resources thus remains fundamentally unequal because the Center fights with one hand tied behind its back. In this situation the vigorous advocacy of local "pragmatists" deflects the outcome of a wide range of economic policies toward their interests, and the ultimate outcome of these myriad processes is a steady erosion of Beijing's ability to direct the economy.

In the long run, this trend cannot persist. It is inconceivable that China's central planners will abandon their attempts to direct China's development and simply allow either local officials or pure market forces to determine China's economic future. For the future, there are two, and only two, possible outcomes. First, central planners can continue to proceed with an effective reform program that will make local levels genuinely accountable for their use of resources. This will be a difficult and contentious process, involving technical grasp of economic principles, as well as considerable political skill. Price reforms must be instituted and combined with effective charges for all fixed capital; bargaining over responsibilities for profit and tax remittance must be replaced by firm, clear, automatic obligations; and local levels must face genuine penalties for inefficient and wasteful use of resources.[56]

---

[56] The importance of the "tax for profit" schemes advanced since early 1983 is their move in this direction, even though the initial advance is relatively modest. The "tax for profit" schemes are designed to ultimately incorporate fixed capital charges in all enterprises (currently only a portion are so covered), and to introduce a much greater degree of automaticity to enterprise contributions to the budgetary authorities. If, in addition, the recalculations of profit retention ratios reduces total quantities of retained profit, this is an additional advantage, so far as central planners are concerned. Previous schemes, and in particular the "profit contracting" or "indus-

These changes will be resisted by local authorities, who are loathe to be made responsible for decisions they now make with little accountability. The other possible outcome is simply that the Center will curtail programs of decentralization and insist on its ultimate authority to direct economic activity. Thus, the ultimate question is whether China will proceed with an economic reform program or retreat to a centralized planning system, albeit one characterized by higher levels of technical proficiency than in the past. In order to proceed down the path to further economic reforms, the central authorities must persuade local authorities to accept greater accountability—and greater risk— in their disposition of investment resources. The future path of the Chinese economy will be largely determined by the degree of success that reformers in Beijing have in overcoming the pragmatic bureaucratic politics of local leaders in the provinces, cities, and counties of China.

---

trial responsibility system," relied on ad hoc negotiation of profit delivery responsibilities between enterprises and their supervisory bodies. In practice, this did not impose on enterprises serious penalties for nonfulfillment of their targets. An illuminating example of how the "profit contracting" system worked out in practice in Gu Fuwen, *CZ* 8 (1982): 26–27. Of 260 state-run enterprises in Yantai *diqu* in Shandong, only 2 were penalized for not meeting their targets, even though nonfulfillment was pervasive.

Appendix

TABLE 3.5   Total Fixed Investment in State-run Units
(in billion yuan)

	1977	1978	1979	1980	1981	1982
Capital construction						
budgetary from domestic funds	31.2	41.7	38.5	30.0	22.3	23.3
budgetary from foreign funds	0	0	2.8	4.9	2.9	4.4
non-budgetary foreign funds	0	0	0	0.4	0.6	1.3
domestic bank loans	0	0	0.5	4.1	4.5	7.3
local "own-funds"	7.0	8.4	10.5	16.4	14.1	19.3
TOTALS	38.2	50.1	52.3	55.9	44.3	55.6
Replacement and Reconstruction (RR)						
budgetary allocations	1.8	2.6	4.4	3.3	3.5	3.3
local "own-funds"	13.8	13.0	11.2	10.8	14.2	19.0
domestic bank loans	0.9	1.1	2.0	4.6	4.6	6.4
foreign funds	0	0	0	0	0.1	0.3
TOTALS	16.6	16.8	17.6	18.7	22.5	29.0

NOTE: Figures are rounded and do not sum exactly.

All Chinese capital construction figures were augmented beginning in 1982 by the addition of a previously undisclosed sum of central government investment, presumably representing construction for military and civil defense purposes. Current statistical publications incorporate this adjustment retrospectively, and the figures in this table have been adjusted to take account of these changes. This has meant dividing the new component equally between 1976 and 1977, since specific data are not yet available for those two years. For all other years, Chinese sources give the exact figure of increase and show that it should be included with budgetary investment. Figures for 1977 and 1978 are from the 1981 Statistical Yearbook, 295, with the above adjustment incorporated on the basis of figures in *TJZY*, 58–64. In addition, foreign funds and domestic bank loans are assumed to be zero. Figures for 1979 and 1980 are from 1981 *JJNJ*, IV-9; 1981 figures are from 1982 *JJNJ*, V-297; and 1982 figures from 1983 *JJNJ*, III-82. All these figures have been corrected on the basis of *TJZY*, 58–64, and in particular an inconsistency in the definition of budgetary investment which is incorporated in the 1981 Statistical Yearbook, 295, has been corrected. The proportion of foreign funds not arranged through the budget is given in 1983 *JJNJ*, III-82, and these figures demonstrate that the division of capital construction into budgetary and nonbudgetary components in *TJZY*, 58–64, appropriately excludes these funds from budgetary investment in those years. This last source is then used to derive the amount of nonbudgetary foreign funds invested in 1980.

All figures for Replacement and Reconstruction investment are from the 1983 Statistical Yearbook, 360. It should be noted that Chinese statistics for RR investment before 1981 are based on retrospective reconstruction, and cannot claim anything like the degree of accuracy attained by capital construction figures. Moreover, for certain years the figures given in the 1983 Statistical Yearbook (which are incongruously given to the nearest million) contrast fairly sharply with earlier figures available in Chinese sources. In particular, the figure for 1979 has been revised downward by 2.5 billion yuan, and the figure for 1980 revised downward by 4.2 billion yuan. No explanation for these changes is available. These figures should clearly be taken as no more than rough estimates, but it is unlikely that we will ever have any better figures.

FOUR

The 1980 Inflation and the
Politics of Price Control
in the PRC

Dorothy J. Solinger

INTRODUCTION

On December 7, 1980, for the second time in only eight months, China's
State Council issued a circular mandating that prices be brought under control. This second notice, one product of a more general policy of austerity and
retrenchment promulgated at that point, claimed to be aimed at organizing
the further implementation of the earlier directive, in the face of what were
termed "rather serious cases of increasing prices at will, inflating prices in
disguised ways and driving up negotiated prices in the market"; and in response to "resentment among the broad masses."[1]

A whole set of measures—including terminating basic construction projects, borrowing from the surpluses of the local governments, selling government bonds to state-run enterprises, tightening bank credit, and reducing
various state expenditures—were instituted as part of an overall effort to
eliminate a state budgetary deficit. That 12.7 billion yuan deficit, the major
source of concern, was said to fuel the inflation. This chapter focuses on just
one aspect of that larger effort. It investigates the attempt to use price
controls to halt rising prices; and its time frame is the period immediately
surrounding the December 1980 circular. Thus, it examines one policy
cycle, centered around a mounting concern over the 1980 inflation as the year
progressed, and ending as the endeavor to check inflation was proclaimed
concluded in March 1981. Although this did not end price problems, total

I appreciate the suggestions for revision made in writing by David M. Lampton and Nicholas
Lardy, and those made orally by Michel Oksenberg. Thanks also to Barry Naughton for discussing some of the more economically oriented dimensions of the subject with me. I don't claim to
have followed all of my critics' advice, but I made an effort to respond to it where I could.

[1] For the text of the price-control circular, see Foreign Broadcast Information Service (FBIS),
Dec. 9, 1980, L14–16.

retail price inflation dropped from 6 percent in 1980 to 2.4 percent in 1981 and down to 1.9 percent in 1982 according to official accounts.[2]

In tracing the history of this policy, this chapter will make a more general observation about the nature of policy implementation in China, one that goes beyond the case at hand. To anticipate the argument, many of the features of the policy process in "democratic," "open," and "federalist" types of political systems are found in China as well, particularly for a policy of price control, albeit in somewhat altered form. Thus, the accommodating nature of democratic governments (with their dispersion of power, independence of participants, complex bureaucracy, limitations on central control, bargaining and coalition-building, and the profusion of actors and points of access), and the responsiveness imposed by elections in "open" systems (as opposed to the oft-remarked ineffectiveness of interest groups in authoritarian regimes),[3] actually do less to explain the relative ease or difficulty of carrying out price policy in one form of state as against another than is commonly assumed.

For, as this study will illustrate, many of these same traits characterize the socialist system as well. In the case of other traits less clearly present in socialist contexts—such as accountability to powerful constituents and accommodation with forceful interest groups—voluntary elite behavior can certainly have similar effects. The price-freeze policy in 1980 is a particularly apt one for examining the forms of interaction between state and society that often mark the process of implementation in the People's Republic of China (PRC).

Obviously, socialist systems lack the elections, the largely autonomous interest groups, and the governmental subunits with legally sanctioned local powers characteristic of Western-style democracies. Still, there are certain structural properties—functional analogues, perhaps—of socialist systems that may dispose them to operate in ways similar to democratic states. Thus, while socialist elites are not seeking to maximize the votes they receive,[4] they may nonetheless choose to design policies that will appeal to distinct social

---

[2] Inflation figures are in *Beijing Review (BR)*, 1983, no. 36:19.

[3] These features of democratic government are noted in John Case, *Understanding Inflation* (Harmondsworth: Penguin Books, 1982), 189; of federal systems, in Jeffrey L. Pressman and Aaron Wildavsky, *Implementation* (Berkeley and Los Angeles: University of California Press, 1979), 109 and 161; and Randall B. Ripley and Grace A. Franklin, *Bureaucracy and Policy Implementation* (Homewood, Ill.: Dorsey Press, 1982), 58, 59, 85, 188, 189; and of open and authoritarian systems, in Merilee S. Grindle, ed., *Politics and Policy Implementation in the Third World* (Princeton: Princeton University Press, 1980), 14, 16, 284.

[4] On this theme, see Michael J. Mumper and Eric M. Uslaner, "The Bucks Stop Here: The Politics of Inflation in the United States," in Richard Medley, ed., *The Politics of Inflation: A Comparative Analysis* (New York: Pergamon Press, 1982), 109; also, Edward R. Tufte, *Political Control of the Economy* (Princeton: Princeton University Press, 1978); and William Nordhaus, "The Political Business Cycle," *Review of Economic Studies* 42 (April 1975), 169–191.

groups for other reasons. Though politicians in China do not necessarily directly owe their position to the pleasure of "the masses" or of specific interest groups, they do need to take likely mass reactions into account when they speak for particular initiatives, or else risk lack of cooperation with their programs from below. Much of the implicit comparison made between democratic and socialist political systems rests on incomplete understanding of the possibilities and the range of inclinations among different rulers in socialist states.

Moreover, the absence in socialist states of definite terms of office ratified by the populace may mean that their elites are particularly conscious of a need to promote policies that succeed in the eyes of their fellow politicians, since it is they who decide a leader's political longevity. For this reason, intra-elite disagreements may be of special significance in such systems. In the end, this may produce as much complexity in policy implementation as exists in the "open" systems, especially as the contending factions of socialist elites may switch the content of key programs frequently and at will.

Other features of socialist systems also tend to weaken the power of central elites to see their initiatives through to completion as envisioned. Most important, within the state and Party bureaucracy, each functional and geographic unit and level has missions and motives of its own.[5] In the case of an economic policy, such as price control, the state plan and its targets do much to structure and inform the definition and the pattern of interest and alliance formation and thus the response of state offices and enterprises to governmental orders.

Taken as a whole, then, analysts of democratic federal systems need to revise some implicit model of omnipotence in socialist, supposedly unitary states against which they measure the subjects of their own study. Policy implementation is hard in disparate contexts, aggravated as much in China as in the United States by elite policy conflict, varying social groups, each with its own concerns, a bureaucracy split by a range of interests and corresponding reasons for resistance and, consequently, by disorganization. The facts of the plan, state ownership, the one-party system, and largely meaningless elections simply mold these features in distinctive ways in the different systems.

The discussion that follows will highlight the ways the issue of inflation in China in 1980 activated this conflict, these concerns, and these interests. It will also analyze the manner in which pertinent elites, social groups, and bureaucratic units handled these controversies in the course of policy implementation, and how their strategies affected that implementation.

[5] See Michel Oksenberg, "Economic Policy-Making in China: Summer 1981," *China Quarterly* *(CQ)*, no. 90 (1982), 182, 187, 192. See also chapter 6 in this volume.

THE ISSUE: CHINA'S 1980 INFLATION IN COMPARATIVE PERSPECTIVE

Comparative Analyses of Inflation: A Framework

Comparative explanations for inflation, especially inflation in democratic systems, put emphasis on the interaction between groups making claims on the state, on the one hand, and the weakness inherent in the modern democratic state, on the other.[6] The typical paradigm stresses a "fragmentation of domestic and international society into increasingly numerous economic and political power centers, and increasing friction among centers," which place "so many demands on public agencies that government expenditures have outpaced tax revenues."

In this account, state monetary systems are forced to create new money in response to these demands "for additional credit to restore, maintain, or increase [the separate centers'] shares of national and world income."[7] Thus, social demands create deficits, to which states respond by issuing currency, which then in turn forces prices up. This essay will return to this argument when it considers the Chinese case.

Other authors emphasize the fact that inflation represents governments' attempts to defuse, resolve, or contain a distributional struggle over shares in modern democratic society as, in the course of seeking support, incumbent regimes try to raise the incomes of various groups, thereby appearing to be giving out more than they have.[8] Such currying of popular forces is the result, in one political scientist's view, of the impotence of the contemporary state in the face of electoral competition, the coalescence of groups into inflationary coalitions, and the involvement of special interests in the making of policy.[9] One sociologist sees the "bourgeois state" as being particularly unable to regulate the organized interests that populate democracies, with inflation as the outcome.[10]

Once price rises have thereby been set in motion, a second feature of modern, democratic society is credited with contributing to the tendency of such inflation to "feed itself."[11] Here analysts stress the absence of consensus

[6]The following discussion draws on analyses offered in Case, *Understanding Inflation*; Fred Hirsch and H. Goldthorpe, eds., *The Political Economy of Inflation* (Cambridge: Harvard University Press, 1978), especially the articles by Maier, Portes, Brittan, Goldthorpe, Crouch, Anderson, and Hirsch; Richard Medley, ed., *Politics of Inflation*, especially articles by Lindberg, Mumper and Uslaner, Medley, and Pothier; Lester C. Thurow, *The Zero-Sum Society: Distribution and the Possibilities for Economic Change* (New York: Basic Books, 1980); and John G. Gurley, "The Elusive Strength of Capitalism," *Stanford Magazine* 11, no. 1 (1983).

[7]Gurley, 21.

[8]See Thurow, 46, and Chase, 189.

[9]Malcolm Anderson, "Power and Inflation," in Hirsch and Goldthorpe, 240.

[10]Colin Crouch, "Inflation and the Political Organization of Economic Interests," in Hirsch and Goldthorpe, 237.

[11]Case, 34.

in such societies today, and a concomitant reluctance of competing groups to cooperate to solve the problems, either with each other or with the state.[12]

Instead, each group proceeds in the face of inflation to attempt in a selfish way to anticipate the likelihood of continued inflation. In this process of "mental indexation," each helps to push the inflation onto a spiraling, self-generating course. As one observer put it, "In all countries we see a gradual movement toward indexation as each individual attempts to secure his economic standing in the future by betting on continued inflation."[13] Thus:

> Each competing interest under inflationary conditions seeks in effect to *monetize the assets* it controls, whether by means of commodity currency keyed to agricultural products thereby stabilizing the income of farmers, control of interest rates on the part of banks, or index of wages that would make labor time the unit of value. Rapid inflation involves the search for constant income shares and thus the attempted coinage of each group's respective scarce goods.[14]
> (Emphasis added to call attention to this term, which will be used below)

Drawing together these several explanations, we find that a few key elements constitute their largely sociological perspective on the dynamics of inflation: group claims; weak government; and multiple, independent, uncoordinated, and often antagonistic and self-serving actors. While this explanation for inflation was derived from democratic systems, the Chinese data can be read to show that there is nothing inherent in this socialist system to prevent it from manifesting similar behaviors, and for similar reasons.

The Chinese Case

The Chinese inflation of 1980 was the effect, not of democratic interest groups pressuring a weak regime garnering votes, but of a structurally different process with comparable dynamics. Typical pictures of Communist countries existing in more or less steady states emphasize their repressed inflation (as evidenced by queues and rationing), their "centralised pluralism" (as seen in "passive" pressures from below, such as threats to riot), or the "diffused" disobedience of their workers, who can only lobby through unwillingness to work harder or to raise productivity.[15] Such analyses focus

---

[12] Fred Hirsch, "The Ideological Underlay of Inflation," in Hirsch and Goldthorpe, 276.

[13] Hirsch, 270; see also John T. Pothier, "The Political Causes and Effects of Argentine Inflation," in Medley, *Politics of Inflation*, 205; and Richard Medley, "Introduction," in Medley, p. ix.

[14] Charles S. Maier, "The Politics of Inflation in the Twentieth Century," in Hirsch and Goldthorpe, 41.

[15] P. J. D. Wiles, *Communist International Economics* (Oxford: Basil Blackwell, 1963), chap. 3, "Inflation and the Soviet-Type Economy," 52; Alec Nove, *Political Economy and Soviet Socialism* (London: George Allen and Unwin, 1979), chap. 11, "Inflation in Communist Countries," 189; and Richard Portes, "Inflation under Central Planning," in Hirsch and Goldthorpe, 82.

on the weakness of interest groups as against the vastly more powerful state, a model akin to the one used by Grindle in describing her paradigmatic "closed system."[16]

But China in 1980 was not a socialist state maintaining a status quo. The political process there then was one best understood in light of the politics of succession described by Bunce in her study of public policy during periods of elite turnover.[17] At such junctures, she holds, new elites foster platforms geared to garner mass support, as they strive to shore up their authority and promote their values.

After a period of muted intra-elite debate and power struggle in the first years after 1976, by the late 1970s the more reform-minded members of the Chinese leadership were well enough ensconced in power to begin to enact initiatives in light of their own preferences (productivity, stability). (See chapter 2 for more detail.) The ensuing reform efforts entailed courting a range of social groups by responding to their perceived material demands.

By presenting the different groups—workers, managers, peasants, intellectuals, formerly disgraced cadres—with a package of material benefits, the new elite by its own choice in effect set in motion a process whereby the Chinese political economy came to resemble what Wiles has termed a "semi-decentralized STE [Soviet-type economy]." In such systems, microeconomic freedom[s] of economic subunits have been increased, thereby loosening the power of the command economy and its directives.[18] (See chapter 3 for examples of this.)

The particular significance of the moment at which the December 1980 anti-inflation directive was issued lies in the fact that it was then that the new leadership came to a consensus that the special difficulties of this type of consumer strategy had to be somehow addressed. It had become clear to virtually all key central politicians that the "reform" programs of decentralization and of satisfying the economic interests of large groups among the populace—the sorts of programs that typically put inflation under way in any sort of state—had produced a singularly problematic outcome under conditions of state ownership. For in such a context the state has not only to cope with the usual difficulties of managing a national budget; it has as well to manage the entire set of repercussive effects arising from heightened demand.

Thus, deficits ensued as increases in consumption and investment drained the state budget. For under the Chinese system, capital construction appropriations, wage bills for state employees, payments for state procurement of

[16] Grindle, ed., *Politics and Policy Implementation*, 16 and 284–85.

[17] See Valerie Bunce, *Do New Leaders Make a Difference? Executive Succession and Public Policy under Capitalism and Socialism* (Princeton: Princeton University Press, 1981), 164–69; see also pp. 28–31.

[18] Wiles, 53–54.

agricultural products, and subsidies for urban consumers are all directly or indirectly included in this budget.[19]

Probably the two most expensive reforms instituted by the post-Mao leadership after 1976 were, first, a series of three wage revisions (in 1977, 1978, and 1979),[20] and, second, an average increase of 22 percent in the purchase prices paid by the state to the peasants for eighteen key crops, carried out in summer 1979. One analyst accurately observed that, because "the urban working class and its cadres had provided most of the activists and many of the victims of the Cultural Revolution . . . it was only natural that the post-Mao leadership should try, as one of its first measures, to give some inducement to these citizens to accept the new order."[21] Oksenberg notes that the increases in rural procurement prices had been supported by a broad coalition which favored elevating peasant income.[22]

By the end of 1981 a total of more than 140 billion yuan had been expended in various forms of state subsidies: 44.2 billion to cover increased purchase prices for farm and sideline products; 30 billion for the rise in urban wages and salaries of workers and staff and for financing the newly reinstated bonus system; 10.5 billion to bring about the employment of 26 million urban residents; 15.2 billion to build housing for urban workers and staff; and other expenditures to allow for tax cuts or exemptions for the rural areas plus increased price subsidies for imported goods.[23] Already by the autumn of 1980 economist Xue Muqiao was able to announce that over 14 billion had been spent on wage increases and bonuses, while the annual subsidy for farm products was 20 billion yuan.[24] Chapter 6 addresses the subsidy issue as well.

The new leadership also instituted economic decentralization measures designed to loosen up the centrally planned economy. Key among these were permission given to free-market patrons and to state trade agencies to negotiate over prices for a large number of agricultural products, once state targets had been met, and to industrial managers to set negotiated prices for any output exceeding their targets and to sell such products on their own; a profit-retention scheme whereby firms could allocate extra funds for capital construction largely at their own discretion; and measures that enabled local

[19] Nai-ruenn Chen, "China's Inflation, 1979–82: A Quantitative Estimate" (draft), 34.

[20] For analyses of the wage reforms, see Susan L. Shirk, "Recent Chinese Labor Policies and the Transformation of Industrial Organization in China," *CQ*, no. 88 (1981): 575–93; Ch'en Ting-chung, "The Pay Raise Program in Mainland China," *Issues and Studies (I & S)* 14, no. 2 (1978): 1–11; Wang Hsiao-hsien, "Wage Adjustments in Communist China," *I & S* 14, no. 2 (1978): 12–21; and Ch'en Po-wen, "Rising Prices and Wages in Mainland China: An Analysis," *I & S* 16, no. 2 (1980): 30–45.

[21] W. Klatt, "The Staff of Life: Living Standards in China, 1977–81," *CQ*, no. 93 (1983): 20.

[22] Oksenberg, "Economic Policy-Making in China," 190.

[23] *FBIS*, Dec. 14, 1982, K16.

[24] *FBIS*, Sept. 9, 1980, L23, L25, and Feb. 4, 1981, L11.

governments to exercise greater control over a set of miscellaneous extra-budgetary funds.[25] This "marketeer"-oriented[26] leadership of late 1978 and 1979 expected this packet of incentives to arouse the enthusiasm of the ben-eficiaries and ultimately to spark more productivity in the total economy. However, besides the inflationary results of these policies, other unantici-pated consequences occurred as well. For instance, wage boosts tended to *increase* worker strife and elicited little enhancement in productivity.

In addition, the millions of unemployed youths who were allowed to re-turn to the cities (and who consumed but at first did not produce); the 1979 Vietnam military venture; the "foreign leap forward" of 1977 and 1978 with its whole plant purchases (which in the words of a Chinese critic "far ex-ceeded the limits of national power"); and the rectification of "unjust court cases, frame-ups, wrong verdicts," which involved granting various sorts of refunds, subsidies, and compensation to targets of the Cultural Revolution—these also contributed to the inflation by draining the state treasury in this period.[27] Finally, increased autonomy granted to the state bank enabled it to make more loans to the now more independent enterprises and local governments.[28]

In order to finance the deficit, government overdrafts amounting to 21.8 billion yuan in 1979 and 1980 led to a substantial expansion of the money supply. New money was created in those two years at a rate of more than three times the rate of the growth of gross domestic product (GDP) at current prices, and outpaced real GDP growth by more than four times in 1979 and almost eight times in 1980. All of this led, in the leadership's understanding, if not immediately into price increases, at least into the formation of excess purchasing power with its implicit pressure on prices.[29]

[25] On the effects of negotiated prices, see "Food Price Increases in Mainland China," *I & S* 15, no. 12 (1979): 7; "Inflation," *China News Analysis (CNA)*, no. 1178 (April 11, 1980); and Bruce Reynolds, "The Chinese Economy in 1980: Death of Reform?" in *China Briefing, 1981*, ed. Robert B. Oxnam and Richard C. Bush (Boulder: Westview, 1981), 50–51; on the behavior of firms under the stimulus of reform and the effects of this, see Kang Chao, "Economic Readjust-ment in Mainland China," *I & S* 17, no. 11 (1981): 30; and on the reforms involving giving greater powers to the localities and the provinces and what happened as a result, see Martin Weil, "The Sixth 5-Year Plan," *China Business Review* (March–April 1983), 23–24.

[26] See Dorothy J. Solinger, *Chinese Business Under Socialism* (Berkeley and Los Angeles: University of California Press, 1984), especially chap. 2.

[27] *FBIS*, Aug. 6, 1982, K13, in a speech on inflation by Luo Gengmo, adviser to the China Prices Society.

[28] Katherine H. Y. Huang Hsiao, "Money and Banking in the People's Republic of China: Recent Developments," *CQ*, no. 91 (1982): 473.

[29] Robert Delfs, "The High Cost of Stable Prices," *Far Eastern Economic Review (FEER)*, March 12, 1982, 84. Also, Hsiao, 473, notes that to finance the 1980 deficit, the budget borrowed 8 billion yuan from the People's Bank, and that the Bank had to increase currency supply by a similar magnitude to cover the borrowing. According to Ma Hong, in *New Strategy for China's Economy*, trans. Yang Lin (Beijing: New World Press, 1983), social purchasing power increased by 20 billion yuan in 1980, more than twice the annual average over the years 1970–1978.

Aside from the overissuance of currency to pay off deficits, two features of the socialist economy in China put additional pressure on the financial system. One of these has to do with the plan and its effect on state-run economic units; the other concerns the management of the state budget. The plan is important because it dictates output, sales, and purchase targets to industrial, commercial, and agricultural enterprises. The continued existence of these norms in tandem with the recent incentive policies (raises based in part on performance, plus a new right to retain a portion of extraquota earnings) gave economic actors in factories and shops a motive to tamper with state-set prices. For raising prices could enable them to surpass state-set profit and sales volume targets, which would in turn increase their personal incentive packages from the state.

In the countryside, the ability of farmers and their units to fetch higher prices for their goods (through "negotiated prices" paid at free markets and by state purchasers) apparently led many to sell to the highest bidder even before their state-delivery targets were met. One result was a shortage of state-priced goods, which then *forced* consumers to the free markets and thus worked to drive the total price index up even further. Here the coexistence of two forms of economic system made for a kind of competition between private and state sectors in which the state sector, with its lower purchase prices, often lost out.[30]

The other feature of the Chinese system that complicates the management of inflation is the state budget. Any increase in one type of state-set price eventually must affect a whole range of other such prices, because of the all-encompassing nature of that budget.[31] For instance, when agricultural purchase prices were raised in 1979, the state did not immediately raise consumer prices for these products, but spent 20 billion yuan to subsidize the difference between state purchase and retail sales prices.

Eventually, however, the elite realized that these subsidies were too expensive for the state to bear, and it became necessary to raise consumer prices for eight major nonstaple food items (in November 1979). But at the same time the state also gave monthly income supplements of five yuan to each state employee. Nove notes that subsidization of this nature is typical of socialist states; as Xue Muqiao put it, "A good agricultural harvest not only means increases in the supply of raw materials for our light industry, in the output of light industry and in revenues, but also means more subsidies from the state, thus reducing the state's revenues."[32] Moreover, because some of

---

[30] Liu Zhuofu, "How to View the Question of Current Market Prices," *Hong Qi* (Red Flag), no. 1, 1982, 34.

[31] A good account of the interconnectedness of individual state budgetary decisions can be found in an article by Xue Muqiao in *FBIS*, Sept. 9, 1980, L25. See also Liu, 33–36; and Xu Yi and Chen Baosen, "On the Necessity and Possibility of Stabilizing Prices," *Social Sciences in China*, no. 3 (1981), 124.

[32] Nove, *Political Economy*, 187–88; for Xue's remark, see *FBIS*, Sept. 9, 1980, L25.

the agricultural products whose purchase prices were raised serve as raw materials for industrial enterprises, some factories were caught with rising costs. This, in turn, generated industry demands that the sales prices of their goods be raised.

Thus, for most price changes, the elite felt obliged to pay out yet more money to offset their effects. Or, where the elite did not do so, those responsible for economic activity began to employ various sorts of semi-licit and illegal measures, which amounted to what the Chinese press terms "disguised" price hiking (mixing shoddy materials with good, shortweighting, false packaging, etc.).

The statistical result of these various processes in 1980 was, according to officially published reckoning, that the general index of retail prices (a measure calculated by the weighted averages of state-set list prices, negotiated prices, and free market prices and the index of living costs) rose by 6 percent. Within that index, the retail list-price index of state-owned commerce (equal to about 90 percent of the total volume of retail sales) went up by 4.4 percent; the negotiated price index, by 10.6 percent; and urban and rural fair prices, by 2 percent.[33] It is worth reiterating that, although these prices may not appear alarming when compared with recent inflation in the United States (much less that in Israel or Argentina), they induced near panic in an elite that had itself come to power in the wake of the preceding regime's inability to achieve price stability.

List-price increases may be attributed in part to the increase in purchase prices for farm produce of 7.1 percent in 1980 and to climatic difficulties that reduced the output of vegetables (problems claimed to be solved by the middle of 1983). The rise in negotiated prices can be explained by industrial enterprises, state purchasing units, and state-owned shops illicitly expanding the scope of commodities traded at bargained prices or driving up the price level of negotiated price goods beyond the range of fluctuation permitted by the state. And prices on the free market, higher than those set by the state to begin with, increased, especially for scarce and popular nonstaple foodstuffs such as vegetables, eggs, aquatic products, fish, and fruit, for several reasons. Principal among these reasons were that these prices rose in competition with the new, higher state-set purchase prices; that shortages of list-price commodities occurred in state shops (as a result of the freedom given peasants to trade on free markets), thereby forcing consumers into the free market; and that speculators captured control of local markets and then pushed up the prices there.

In sum, several elements combined to produce the 1980 inflation in China that forms the backdrop for this chapter. These included multiple group claims as well as explicit leadership decisions. The resulting expenditures

---

[33] BR, 1983, no. 35:19 and 24; Liu, "Current Market Prices."

threw the budget into deficit and this was, in turn, financed by printing money. While the excess money fed inflation (as elsewhere), the problem was exacerbated in the Chinese case by constraints associated with the presence of a state plan (with its fixed prices, sales targets, and rationed goods) and an omnibus-type state budget.

FORMULATION

To the outside world, the announcement on December 7 that strict price controls were to be enforced throughout the Chinese economy was somewhat shocking. For the previous year and a half, news out of China had portrayed an economy that was loosening up, becoming liberalized, even capitalistic. Moreover, the Third Session of the Fifth National People's Congress, which had been held in Beijing only three months before, had been heralded in the West as being an extension of this new pro-market thrust.

In fact, however, a close reading of the Chinese press over the three or so months preceding the meeting's convocation shows that this was a time of intense elite debate.[34] Although the specific deliberations that led to the decision to retrench (of which price control policy was one prong) were not published, it is nevertheless possible to discern the debate's contours from the open media.

First, before all the statistics were in, some leaders queried whether there was in fact inflation and a significant deficit. Then, as more data became available, the focus of attention shifted slightly, as doubters asked whether something needed to be done about it. Even when inflation had been determined to be a significant issue and the price control decision was published in December, debate then focused on why it had occurred, an inquiry that had implications for the entire reformist program. For, since a dominant theme in the elite's analysis of the problem was that the subsidies, purchase-price increases, wage raises, and decentralization schemes of the reform program had caused the inflation, the price-control policy presented critics of that program with a justification for taking "reform" as a scapegoat.

These debates, however, are different from those that also occur in the West, in two crucial respects: First, because the overwhelming bulk of economic activity in China is controlled centrally in the state plan and the omnibus budget, major issues of macro-economic management came within the purview of the central elite. These leaders do have it in their power, should they so desire, to rearrange the entire national economy. Cognizant of this potential for change, Party leaders pitch their debate at a higher, more en-

[34] See Dorothy J. Solinger, "The Fifth National People's Congress and the Process of Policy-making: Reform, Readjustment, and the Opposition," *Asian Survey* 22, no. 12 (December 1982): 1238–75.

compassing level of discussion, as they disagree about whether to "reform" (through decentralization and market-type levers) or "readjust" (through more centralization and administrative intervention) the total economy.

Second, important subthemes in the larger discussion, such as whether competition is good or bad, how much autonomy (if any) to allow firms, and how much free market activity should be permitted, are issues that do not arise so centrally in a capitalist setting. In 1980 China, however, such basic disagreements formed the backdrop for the debate.

As was mentioned at the outset of this chapter, a price-control directive had already been issued earlier in the year, in April,[35] and it was followed by price investigations and other measures throughout the provinces in the next month or so. But over the summer, especially from July through September, virtually all available local reports spoke of "flexible" economic policies, enlivening the market, and loosening controls, omitting mention of price problems.

A few scattered broadcasts, however, betrayed the fact that at least some members of the central elite were mulling over the issue. In late August the publication *Banyue tan* took note of a few lines from Chen Yun's speech to the Eighth Party Congress (1956), including the one in which he had made the point "Do not fear if prices rise to a certain extent."[36] Apparently forces in favor of allowing more flexible prices to register supply and demand and so to stimulate higher productivity (which had been the gist of Chen's then twenty-four-year-old argument) were borrowing his name to legitimate this position in a new setting.

A few days thereafter, economist Xue Muqiao, a strong proponent of market-type policies, made a similar observation. "Because the public felt secure and the market was brisk," he noted, savings deposits by the populace, by state-owned enterprises, and by local financing departments had all increased substantially. Thus, he went on, whatever financial deficit there might be did "not cause a big increase in the issue of paper money and did not seriously affect our economic life."[37] At this point, drawing on the data then at hand, Xue was not yet worried about deficits, excess purchasing power, or the upward drift of prices.

The Third Session of the Fifth National People's Congress was held just at this point. There major speakers took different tacks in dealing with—or ignoring—the question of inflation. Yao Yilin, the newly named head of the State Planning Commission, gave one of the keynote addresses and, as a deputy from Shanxi pointed out,[38] did not even mention the problem.[39]

---

[35] The text of this is in *Renmin ribao* (People's Daily) (*RMRB*), Apr. 26, 1980, 1–2, and in translation in *FBIS*, Apr. 28, 1980, L1–4.

[36] *FBIS*, Aug. 27, 1980, L9.

[37] *FBIS*, Sept. 2, 1980, L17.

[38] *FBIS*, Sept. 24, 1980, L13.

[39] Yao's speech is in *BR*, no. 38 (1980), 30–43.

Wang Bingqian, the Minister of Finance, at that point voiced agreement with the position Xue had taken in the press, as he explained that "China's financial deficit last year did not cause any big increase in the issue of paper money, nor did it bring serious difficulties to the economy."[40]

Two other speakers at the same meeting, however, saw the matter differently. Peng Zhen, in his capacity as Vice-Chairman of the Standing Committee of the NPC, delivered a report in which he revealed that some members of his committee had been complaining about rising prices and the excessive issuance of bonuses by some areas. According to Peng, these committee members were demanding that tighter price control be implemented. In addition, Liu Zhuofu, then director of the State Price Bureau, expressed particular concern about the price rises and advocated that the "main task" ought to be that of strengthening price control.[41]

Following the session, these differences of opinion were not immediately resolved. For instance, in early October, the General Administrative Bureau of Industry and Commerce (GABIC), in conjunction with the customs administration, issued a set of penalties for smuggling and profiteering, "for the sake of socialist economic order," and urged mass cooperation with the public security organs in carrying out their order.[42]

By way of contrast, on October 15 Xue Muqiao published an article in the magazine *Economic Management* in which he again decreed (as he had in August) that there would be no danger of price rises, provided the state controlled the issuance of currency and regulated prices in accord with the law of value.[43] Xue's caveat here (especially its second half) marks his statement more as a somewhat veiled plea for price reform than as a description of the actual price situation then existing in China.

Meanwhile, the State Council continued to approve proposals for economic reform, first authorizing a report, in early September, by the State Economic Commission on the expansion of enterprise autonomy, and then, at the end of October, passing a set of regulations permitting "socialist competition."[44] Such measures encouraged the very sort of behavior that would later be linked to inflation.

It was sometime in October, however, that a turnaround occurred within one group of decision makers, and it seems that a consensus on behalf of "readjustment" or retrenchment, at least for the near future, began to

[40] *FBIS*, Sept. 2, 1980, L20.

[41] Peng's report is in *BR*, 1980, no. 39 (see 29). For Liu's statement, see *FBIS*, Sept. 11, 1980, L17. *FBIS* translated his name as Liu Zhongfu, but it is actually Zhuofu. Liu was replaced in 1982 by Cheng Zhiping.

[42] *FBIS*, Oct. 9, 1980, L8–9.

[43] This article, in *Jingji Guanli* (Economic Management), no. 10 (1980), X-3 to X-8, is summarized by Xinhua (not totally in accord with the spirit of the original) in *FBIS*, Oct. 20, 1980, L9–10.

[44] These reports are in *FBIS*, Sept. 9, 1980, L27–29, and *RMRB*, Oct. 30, 1980, 1 (translated in *FBIS*, Oct. 30, 1980, L12–15), respectively.

emerge at that time. In his government work report of December 1981, Premier Zhao Ziyang made public the fact that a year before, after the Third Session of the NPC had closed in early September 1980, the State Council had "made a further comprehensive analysis of the economic situation and identified some major problems calling for immediate solution."[45] These meetings, Zhao told his audience, had occurred in October and November.

Translated radio broadcasts of this period suggest that a Financial Work Forum, held October 17–27, may have been the key turning point.[46] This meeting, convened by the Ministry of Finance, decisively endorsed the theme of readjustment and thereby put retrenchment on the agenda. Henceforth, the news release from the forum directed that in addition to the usual effort to increase output and revenues, the main tasks were to control expenditures, reduce deficits, promote readjustment, maintain economic stability, and achieve a balance between expenditures and revenue.

Political stability and unity were now beginning to take precedence over economic incentives as the way to win the hearts of the people. For the broadcast closed with this message: "Without balanced revenue, there can be no economic stability, and without economic stability, it will be impossible to have political stability and unity." Presumably some combination of new economic data and political discussion had convinced Finance Minister Wang that his perceptions of financial health voiced at the NPC meeting the month before had been in error.

Some sources suggest, though, that a few key actors and bodies were a bit slow in toeing the line. For example, the *People's Daily* of November 6 carried a Commentator's article in which the author charged some localities and departments, and "especially some leading comrades," with having devoted "relatively more energy to stressing long-term planning and reform of the system, while paying insufficient attention to readjustment."[47] Meanwhile, at the end of November, the State Council issued an order on bringing the circulation of money under control and sent out work teams to try to enforce this order.[48]

But on November 8 Yao Yilin gave an interview to a delegation of Japanese economic journalists, in which he spoke about how China is "now at a stage of protecting free competition, in order to make our business efficient and vital as part of our efforts for economic modernization."[49] Yao also seems to have displayed reluctance about readjustment at a meeting of directors of supply and marketing cooperatives which he addressed at about the same time. The news release from that meeting (and presumably his

[45] This report is in *FBIS*, Dec. 16, 1981, K1–35.
[46] This is reported in *FBIS*, Oct. 31, 1980, L3–4.
[47] Translated in *FBIS*, Nov. 10, 1980, L14.
[48] In *FBIS*, Nov. 28, 1980, L21–22.
[49] In *FBIS*, Nov. 10, 1980, L5–6.

address to it, though he was not quoted) decreed the work of the co-ops then to be to "stimulate the rural market, provided that efforts are made to effectively readjust the national economy and basically maintain stable prices."[50] This command to "maintain" a condition of stability evidences a lower degree of concern about the price situation than others were already exhibiting. The meeting also called for "vigorous and steady reform of the co-op system," *and for putting even more products into the category of those whose price could be negotiated.* Once again reform and fluctuating prices were being tied together.

By the end of November, however, the domestic-trade bureaucracy, of which the co-ops are one part, seems to have fallen in line with the thrust toward austerity. It endorsed the new pro-readjustment anti-reform direction, as the All-China Federation of Supply and Marketing Cooperatives, the Ministry of Commerce, and the Bureau of Commodity Prices joined forces in releasing a circular on price control in the catering and service trades.[51] This document preceded by about a week the formal State Council announcement of the overall price freeze on December 7.

In tandem with this apparent central-level disagreement about the extent of inflation and how to deal with it, translated radio broadcasts from a number of provinces suggest that local politicians similarly disagreed. By December, however, almost all gradually began to fall into line with the directive to control prices, and with the new campaign for retrenchment of which the freeze was a central part.

For instance, Anhui province, a province that championed reform (no doubt because of its having been led by now Vice-Premier Wan Li during the period when he was first promoting the new reform policies), was one locality in which disagreement was obvious. In one report from mid-September favoring flexible economic policies, "some comrades, mainly leading ones," were chastised for being "always unsure about such experiments and adaptations. . . . There are some leading organs and business departments concerned which have even restricted and censured efforts at flexibility," it charged.[52] Anhui was one of the last to hold onto the reform policies until nearly the end of November, directing its localities to "go on with reform," even on the eve of the official shutdown of this policy.[53]

Another particularly interesting case is that of Heilongjiang province, where on one day, October 29, Harbin Radio and *Harbin Daily*, on the one side, and *Heilongjiang Daily*, on the other, issued statements bearing diametrically opposed stances on economic matters. In Harbin the Municipal Industry and Commerce Administrative Bureau and the Municipal Public Secur-

[50] *FBIS*, Nov. 14, 1980, L1. The meeting was held from October 23 to November 9, so that most of it followed the finance forum.
[51] *FBIS*, Dec. 1, 1980, L43–44.
[52] *FBIS*, Sept. 19, 1980, O1–2.
[53] *FBIS*, Nov. 20, 1980, O1–2.

ity Bureau put forward a harsh directive on strengthening market controls, promising punishment to individuals or units in violation. But in the Heilongjiang paper, an editorial appears on further emancipating minds and speeding up reform of the system. "Some cadres," it complained, "are too cautious about initiating reforms. All localities should be determined in enacting reforms and bold in undertaking innovations."[54]

About a week later, after the climate at the Center had clearly begun to harden against reforms, a telephone conference was held in Heilongjiang. There the message was to halt price hikes. As it ordered all localities to strengthen leadership over the current tendency of increasing prices, it leveled an attack on the reform faction, castigating "some units" which, "having unhealthy ideas about management . . . pay attention only to en-livening markets and totally ignore price stability."[55] Here again it appears that reform-type policies of liberalization were viewed by the elite as being antithetical to price control.

Yet one more example of intraprovincial debate comes from Jilin, where the provincial daily still called for reforms in the middle of November. Here the pro-reform group still controlled the local media, and was able to use it to publicize the fact that "the work of economic reforms has not progressed satisfactorily in our province, . . . [this is] mainly because concerned depart-ments at the provincial, prefectural and county levels failed to recognize the significance of economic reforms and did not boldly implement them. They argue that policies are decided by the higher authorities and they will act when told to do so."[56] This quotation is provocative because of its hint that conservative groups may be linked to like-minded officials above them.

One theme that appeared in several provincial broadcasts, notably those from Shanxi, Heilongjiang, and Liaoning, but that was *not* present in avail-able translated central-level newscasts, was the fact that "the masses are complaining" over prices.[57] Commentators characterized the populace as "very unhappy and worried"; "most unhappy that certain prices [those for fruit, vegetables, eggs, and pork] have risen"; and "very sensitive . . . strongly objecting." How these people demonstrated their displeasure is not described. But the fact that authorities closer to consumers than policy makers in the capital made this displeasure known suggests a lobbying on behalf of constituents not commonly associated with socialist systems.

Three conclusions can be drawn from these doubtlessly incomplete data: First, there was certainly disagreement in central policy-making councils as late as September as to the existence of inflation in China and about how

[54] Reports of these are in *FBIS*, Oct. 30, 1980, S1–2.
[55] *FBIS*, Nov. 7, 1980, S1.
[56] *FBIS*, Nov. 13, 1980, S1.
[57] See *FBIS*, Sept. 24, L13, Nov. 7, S1, and Nov. 17, S4, respectively.

serious it was. At this point some officials were still attempting to hold onto the reform initiative, with its market incentives, fluctuating prices, and enterprise autonomy despite evidence of price instability. Second, to judge from which units issued what sort of directives in this period, and from the statements of their leading officials, it looks as if the State Price Bureau, the General Administrative Bureau of Industry and Commerce, the Customs Administration, and the public security organs all stood on the side of clamping down on what their bureaucrats viewed as problems in the marketplace.

On the other side, it seems that the State Council, the State Economic Commission, the State Planning Commission, and the commercial bureaucracy (of which the All-China Federation of Supply and Marketing Cooperatives appears at one juncture) were all reluctant to abandon reform. The Ministry of Finance, undoubtedly key in decisions of this sort, began from a position in support of reform (to judge from Minister Wang's remarks at the September NPC meeting), but switched into being an advocate of readjustment by late October, perhaps after having been convinced by some new data.

And third, there is evidence of a political process at the lower levels that included the voicing of divergent views over the relative priorities to be attached to price control versus reform. Materials from the media suggest that at least some locally based bureaucrats looked for signs from on high about how to behave; others were willing to speak out for the masses they governed, whether for purposes of their own or in order to articulate demands that have no institutional outlet in socialist China. These elements—central leadership debate, division within and among provinces, bureaucratically based differences, and the reactions of social groups—all influenced the implementation of price control policy.

IMPLEMENTATION

The Directive on Price Control of December 7, 1980

The directive on prices issued by the State Council on December 7, 1980, in effect decreed a general freeze. It demanded that at retail outlets in all parts of the country, all commodities, manufactured goods, or farm produce whose prices were set by the state must be sold at state-fixed prices; that at all urban markets (even at small towns below the county level), all commodities purchased at negotiated prices must henceforth be sold at their retail prices as of December 7, 1980; and that even for the less essential, more plentiful agricultural products of the third category, maximum prices in negotiated purchases were to be fixed by local governments, while for no other goods could such bargaining take place at all.

This order, especially when viewed in conjunction with several other pertinent documents, contains elements that were to complicate the course of its implementation. First, there is some evidence that even after a decision was reached to enforce a price freeze, some leadership differences persisted. A review of the previous, April 1980, directive on prices will put these differences into context.

For one thing, though proclaimed as a means of further implementing the April 1980 guideline on strengthening prices and curtailing willful price increases, the December document was a more severe measure. The April directive had called for a halt to the raising of state-set prices and for an adjustment of any "unjustified" price rises that had not been approved. Moreover, the spring order had merely set limits on the types of goods for which prices could be negotiated. In December, however, the prices of even those items for which bargaining had been allowed were now to be frozen at their December 7 levels, and no bargaining was to be allowed for means of production. Moreover, controls were now put on the varieties of industrial goods for daily use that could be placed in the negotiated-price category. Also, this was the first time that the local governments were to set maximum negotiated prices for third-category rural produce.

More interesting, however, is the fact that just about a month after the December regulations were issued another set appeared in mid-January 1981.[58] This second set, a State Council directive to "Strengthen Market Control and Crack Down on Speculation, Profiteering, and Smuggling," was more akin to the April order than to the one that had been issued just a few weeks earlier. Like the April directive, and unlike the one in December, this one praised the achievements of the December 1978 Third Plenum of the Eleventh Central Committee and the economic reforms that had been instituted in its wake. (See chapter 2 for more background.) It had, according to the April and January orders, invigorated the economy and greatly developed production.

And furthermore, while the December command had the essentially conservative goals of stabilizing the economy, ensuring a stable livelihood for the people, and guaranteeing the smooth progress of socialist construction, by January the authors of the new rules sought "to further develop production, enliven the economy and effectively maintain the order of the socialist economy." Not only was the motive of achieving stable conditions listed first in December and last in January, but the January document began its list with reform-oriented objectives that were not even mentioned in December.

Another hint of leadership differences may be found in contrasting the December directive with the *People's Daily* editorial calling for its enforcement.[59] Actually more similar to the January directive than to the Decem-

---

[58] *FBIS*, Jan. 16, 1980, L7–9.

[59] That editorial is translated in *FBIS*, Dec. 19, 1980, L23–25, and appeared on p. 1 of the newspaper on December 8.

ber guidelines themselves, this document praises the "series of effective measures" (i.e., the reforms-and-incentives package outlined earlier in this chapter) taken since the Third Plenum "to increase the real income of the majority of the people and improve their livelihood." The editorial goes on to endorse market regulation and its recent increasingly important role in the national economy. Also, it attributes any problems, not to reforms themselves, but, like the April and January measures, to "some areas, departments, and units [which had not] followed state regulations," and which had not instituted necessary control over the prices of negotiated-price commodities. Apparently, those in support of reform essayed to disconnect analyses of that program from the assessment of price problems, in the face of critics who linked the two. And finally, this editorial even went so far as to commend the policy of negotiating purchases and sales, claiming that it had been responsible for the more rapid development of production as well as for the mobilization of the enthusiasm of the peasants and handicraft workers.

Documentary analysis also once again reveals the firmer stance of the General Administrative Bureau of Industry and Commerce (GABIC), apparently the principal organ (with its subordinate units in the localities) charged with the implementation of the December directive. On December 10 that body issued a directive to its lower-level departments specifying what actions should be taken to enforce the State Council regulations.[60] Where the State Council had said that management over trade fairs should be strengthened, it had also called for a continued invigoration of this trade; also, it never mentioned the concept of speculation. The GABIC, however, only spoke of tightening control and stabilizing prices in the fairs, saying nothing about invigoration; and it commanded that speculative acts, such as illegally reselling and hoarding goods, be curbed.

The task of local governments and administrative offices trying to interpret these various pieces of paper was further complicated in three ways. Besides their having to choose which document expressed "real policy," local officials also had to figure out how to reconcile conflicting elements in the State Council's order itself. For instance, how could a locality encourage and invigorate fair trade while freezing even negotiated prices? How, too, could state commercial units manage to fulfill their planned targets for purchase of goods for the state while free market trade was to continue to be lively? And how could industrial units and urban shops not hike their prices while their own costs were now elevated as they produced and sold items made from raw materials whose purchase prices had been raised by the state the year before?

---

[60] *FBIS*, Dec. 12, 1980, L8–9. See Robert E. Lutz, "The General Administration for the Control of Industry and Commerce," *China Business Review*, March–April 1983, 25–29, which lists the regulation of markets as the most important function of this agency. According to Lutz each of the Bureau's provincial and municipal bureaus is staffed with about one hundred persons; and there are offices of the Bureau at county and town levels as well.

Also, a number of aspects of implementation were left up to local governments to handle, such as the drawing up of a list of goods whose purchase and sales price could be negotiated; the setting of the maximum prices for negotiated-price goods among rural products of the third category; and the determining of seasonal price differentials for fresh and live produce. But in what spirit should these tasks be carried out? Nothing in the regulations, especially when combined with the other documents then in the air, could have provided clear guidance. And for a third complication, even in the seemingly crucial area of how to affix penalties to particular infractions, nothing whatever was specified anywhere.

Thus, the framework for implementation was set by a directive, along with two companion pieces, that showed signs of leadership and bureaucratic differences in standpoint. Moreover, these documents embodied principles in conflict with the normal responsibilities of the local-level implementing units, and they left key dimensions of the work of realizing the directive open for local interpretation. From the start, then, there was wide latitude for differences in implementation. Objectives were unclear, standards for assessing goal achievement were murky, and any indication of the permissible means of assuring compliance was entirely absent from the directives.

Continuing Leadership Differences

Once implementation began, these features of the initial authorizing process began to play themselves out more fully. The most basic contradiction in leadership circles, one that had been alive already for more than a year by late 1980, was the closely related one over assigning priorities as between reform and readjustment.[61] That this controversy continued is indicated in an article that appeared in a December issue of the *People's Daily:*

> Are we now to make restructuring [reform of] the economic management system the crux of implementation of the eight-character policy? Some comrades are proposing exactly this. They feel that without thoroughly restructuring the management system, readjustment cannot be smoothly carried out, so now it is necessary, first of all, to act to restructure the economic system. This view is divorced from current Chinese realities. It . . . does not perceive the other aspect to the situation, namely, that when there is a serious imbalance in proportional relationships, conditions are not such that large-scale, across-the-board reforms to the system of management can be carried out.[62]

This fundamental conflict had significant implications for the inflation issue. Since those promoting restructuring (reform) obviously believed that the reforms had been beneficial to the economy, they were necessarily opposed to the other group of leaders who "say that the reforms have turned

---

[61] See Solinger (1982), n. 34 above.
[62] *RMRB*, December 5, 1980, 5, translated in *FBIS*, Dec. 29, 1980, L35.

out to be a mess, and that that is why there are potential dangers" (in the economy, that is, the deficit, inflation, imbalances). But, according to Yao Yilin in January, such views are incorrect, since "the basic cause of the deficit is overstretched capital construction." According to a Hong Kong paper, he went on to point out that "imbalances in the national economy have existed for a long time and were not caused by reforms. Our industrial and agricultural production could not have increased so much if we had not carried out the reforms."[63]

As for inflation itself, one source recounted the existence of two different views as to why it had occurred, and again these are in accord with the more general split over reform versus readjustment. The first, attributed to Minister of Finance Wang Bingqian, pointed to the reform's policies of wage increases and of raising the state purchase prices paid to the peasants for their produce, along with the costs of the Vietnam War, as causing the mounting prices.[64] Such a position was present as well in the speech of Chen Yun at the December Party Work Conference that authorized the across-the-board retrenchment.[65] In essence it finds fault with the incentives strategies of the pro-reform group.

The other opinion on inflation's causes coincides with that of Yao Yilin cited above, and with Premier Zhao Ziyang's speech at the same December 1980 work conference where Chen Yun spoke.[66] This second view puts the blame not on reform but on disproportions in the economy and on the overextended scale of construction. In that analysis, the state's limited financial resources and credit had been wasted on unnecessary heavy industrial capital construction, straining the budget and, presumably, limiting investment funds available for light industry and consumer goods, so that market

[63] In Hong Kong *Wen Wei Po*, Jan. 31, 1981, translated in *FBIS*, Feb. 3, 1981, U1–2. Following the same lines, Xinhua reported on January 16 and January 18, 1981 (translated in *FBIS*, Jan. 21, 1981, L20–21), that

> the main reason deficits appeared was that while we were taking measures to increase the income of the people in cities and the countryside and raise their purchasing power, we failed to promptly curtail the overextended front of our capital construction. As a result, the total of our accumulation and consumption exceeded our national income; our expenditures for capital construction and other sectors exceeded our revenues.

[64] Xiao Cheng, "Why Did the Economic Reforms Shift from Being Urgent to Following a Circuitous Route?" *Zheng Ming (ZM)*, no. 41 (March 1981), 48. According to Oksenberg, "Economic Policy-Making," 191, the Ministry of Finance had not been intimately involved in the late 1978 deliberations on raising agricultural purchase prices.

[65] Chen's speech (along with those of Deng, Zhao Ziyang, and Li Xiannian) is summarized and translated from *ZM*, no. 40 (1981), in *FBIS*, Feb. 2, 1981, U1–15. Chen emphasized "mistakes in reform," that "we cannot afford high wages and commodity prices," and that it is "wrong to stress economic laws alone."

[66] Zhao pinpointed the "major cause" of the troubles as being that "we did not grasp readjustment in industry," speaking as well of "the high accumulation rate," "huge investments," "high targets," and "serious dislocations." See *FBIS*, Feb. 2, 1981, U10.

supplies were not synchronous with the people's newly expanded purchasing power.

Yet another dimension of this disagreement surfaced in an article in a 1981 issue of the English-language journal *Social Sciences in China*.[67] Its authors held that stable prices, not incentives, would be the most effective way of encouraging productivity among workers, using this to justify the price-freeze policy. As they put it, "The stabilization of prices is vital to preserving the political situation of unity and stability and will help encourage the enthusiasm of the workers and peasants in production. In view of this, we think it is necessary to persist in the policy of stabilizing commodity prices." Against this view, economist Xue Muqiao brought forward yet one more aspect of the general debate when he addressed a meeting on reform in mid-March 1981:

> Some comrades hold that readjustment is to ensure a fiscal balance between income and expenditure, control the issue of currency and stabilize commodity prices in the markets. Speaking of this year, this is indeed a major task and is a very difficult task. However, in the long-term view, this is not the ultimate goal of our readjustment. Isn't it true that in the 10 years of catastrophe the fiscal income and expenditure was generally balanced, there was no inflation, and commodity prices were more stable? However, at that time, there was a serious disproportion in the national economy. We had suppressed the people's daily life to ensure such a balance.[68]

Thus, although the central elite was able to unite in an effort to effect a price freeze by early December 1980, the temporary consensus around that move was rent with fissures below the surface. To judge from the available sources, it seems that productivity and stability were not goals equally valued by all members of the leadership. Some, notably Zhao Ziyang, Yao Yilin, and Xue Muqiao, put reform and productivity in first place. Others, Wang Bingqian and Chen Yun, preferred to emphasize balance, readjustment, and stability, and it seems probable that the second group was the main force behind the crackdown on prices. One reason for variations in local-level implementation, then, was that provincial politicians probably reacted differently to these signs of elite discord. How much variety was there in implementation?

Provincial Variations

Provincial broadcasts reveal that a range of means was adopted in the different provincial-level units to curb inflation in the wake of the December 7 price-freeze directive. These included everything from Hunan's vigorous

---

[67] Xu and Chen (n. 31 above), 125.

[68] *FBIS*, Mar. 23, 1981, L3–7 (originally in *Gongren Ribao* [Worker's Daily] on March 13). This statement is on L5.

organizing of some ninety-two inspection teams at the several levels of administration throughout the province to Zhejiang's mild "mutual and sample inspections on the basis of self-inspection." Liaoning called an emergency mobilization meeting; Xinjiang had the top economic units organize departments to study the list of negotiated-price goods and then publicly announce the results, while stores were told to mark price tags clearly and to post their price lists.[69]

Taking monitored news releases as the basis, four provincial-level units stand out for the extreme nature of their reactions. Sichuan and Shanghai were unusual in their near neglect of the directive altogether and their continued optimism about the market.[70] Tibet and Beijing were notable for their harsh and almost panicky responses.[71]

Sichuan, Zhao Ziyang's base of reform, was alone among the provinces in mentioning the importance of the directive for achieving the four modernizations. Also, in its provincial paper's editorial accompanying its notice, it, like the *People's Daily* editorial, praised the policy of negotiating prices, asserting that the aim of straightening out prices was to make market readjustment serve to develop the economy and improve the people's livelihood. Furthermore, the Sichuan directive said nothing either about involving the masses in inspection work[72] or about penalties for violations. Both omissions differentiated Sichuan's order from the national one and from those issued in most other places.

Similarly, Shanghai's notices praised the lively market and mandated

[69] For Hunan, see *FBIS*, Dec. 24, 1980, P5; for Zhejiang, see the same day, O9; Liaoning is in *FBIS*, Dec. 18, 1980, S2; and Xinjiang is on Dec. 24, 1980, T3.

[70] For Sichuan, see *FBIS*, Dec. 18, 1980, Q1; for Shanghai, see Dec. 17, O3, and Dec. 24, O5, O7–8.

[71] Tibet has reports in *FBIS*, Dec. 16, 1980, Q3–4, on Dec. 18, O3, and on Feb. 25, 1981, Q4–5; Beijing has information on Dec. 16, 1980, L25 and R1, on Dec. 17, R1, and on Jan. 28, 1981, R2, and Jan. 30, 1981, R1–2.

[72] Two different documents tell us why it is considered crucial to involve the masses in price inspection work. First is an *RMRB* editorial of April 26, 1980, explicating the April price-control order, which, as translated in *FBIS*, Apr. 28, L6, says:

> We should know that, extremely resentful of arbitrary and covert price increases, the people will be very glad to take part in price inspections. However, this valuable enthusiasm on the part of the masses of people has not been given any of the attention it deserves, which is why a number of mass inspection units remain a formality.

Then, the *RMRB*, Dec. 10, 1980, editorial accompanying the December directive says, as translated in *FBIS*, Dec. 19, L25:

> Some enterprises have ingenious ways of handling price-inspection groups sent down by higher authorities. When the inspection group arrives, the prices become reasonable, no commodities are sold underweight and service is improved. Once they leave, the old practice resumes. Just as the masses say: "Once the inspection group is gone, 'shaobing' becomes smaller and 'youcha' becomes thinner." It is quite obvious that this method of duping inspection groups will never work with mass price-inspectors, since they live among the traders and have regular contacts with them. Again in this sense, mass inspection is more effective.

mainly the use of propaganda, ideological education, and study by officials. As in Sichuan, no mention was made about punishments. Here too the masses were not to be included in inspection teams (though they were given the weak-sounding "right to report"). In fact, in Shanghai the local office of the elsewhere rigorous General Administrative Bureau of Industry and Commerce was at that point paying attention only to rearranging the markets' locations within the city the better to enliven the economy, and setting up permanent marketplaces for peddlers.

In contrast, in Beijing a Municipal Price Control leadership group was immediately constituted, under the direction of five of the city's vice-mayors. Specific punitive measures closely pegged to the violation committed were quickly announced, including fines of up to 500 yuan to be imposed on units, wage deductions and bonus revocations for individuals, and confiscations and suspensions of business for shops engaging in serious infractions. Local newspapers solicited letters describing price gouging and published the state-set prices for daily necessities. Also, local groups were formed in all city districts, suburban counties, and bureaus to check up on prices. At one point the public security office was charged with handling violators, and the masses were encouraged to expose and report offenders.

In Tibet illicit activities not reported in the monitored media from other locations seem to have made the situation especially tense (or else local officials chose to emphasize activities that might have been going on elsewhere but which were attracting less public concern in other places for whatever reason). Apparently, people were coming to the Autonomous Region from other areas in order to buy up local specialties, such as musk, Chinese caterpillar fungus, pilose antler, and other precious Chinese medicines, wool, ox hair and hide, cultural relics, jewels, gold, silver, and foreign currency, and then either reselling them at a killing or allegedly "practicing medicine." Difficulties were also associated with exchange of foreign-made goods at small markets along Tibet's international borders.

In response to this situation, the local government decreed in an emergency circular that all units were to carry out examinations of the market "at all times." As in Beijing, confiscations were to be made when irregularities were uncovered, and both cadres and masses were urged to "strike at speculation, profiteering and smuggling activities in coordination with the industry and commerce administrative departments [that is, the local offices of the GABIC], the customs, the tax departments and the public security organizations."

Another interesting aspect of the provincial reports, especially in light of the internal cleavages within the provinces noted above, is the delay and hedging that seems present in the broadcasts from Heilongjiang and Anhui. It appears that just about all of the other provinces had managed to respond to the directive from the capital in the first two and a half weeks after it was issued (i.e., by December 24). Heilongjiang, by comparison, dragged its feet—only convening a conference of prefectural and municipal price bureau directors for five days starting January 15.[73] The five regulations passed there omitted mention of penalties or mass involvement in supervisory work.

In the case of Anhui, although a meeting was held for directors of industrial and commercial bureaus as early as December 16, its communique, like that of Shanghai, made a point of noting "the lively economic situation since the convocation of the 3d Plenary Session of the 11th CCP Central Committee." And here again, as in Sichuan and Shanghai, there was no recitation of any punishments and not even a word about inspection teams.[74] Anhui had provided a springboard for the reformer Wan Li, as had Sichuan province for Zhao Ziyang. It is probably no accident that both Sichuan and Anhui were not very responsive to price control efforts.

Another point of differentiation concerned a January 15 State Council directive banning smuggling, speculation, and profiteering. Only a few provinces, in particular Hunan and Tibet, picked this up.[75] This finding is consistent with Hunan's continued allegiance to the leftism of Mao Zedong and Hua Guofeng at this point; Tibet's attention to the interdicted practices may have been linked to particular problems in the unique marketplaces of that province-level unit.

At the end of January a Readjustment Office was set up under the State Council to exercise leadership over the readjustment program, aimed mainly at devoting more resources to the development of light industry and less to heavy.[76] This office, led by pro-reform leaders Wan Li and Yao Yilin, ordered lower-level governments to establish corresponding offices to be headed by vice-governors responsible for planning. Some provinces—in particular, Hebei, Anhui, and Sichuan—took this opportunity to concentrate their energies there, and if one may judge from the subsequent absence of price-related reports in the translated broadcasts in these places, essentially stopped working on the problem of the markets.[77] Anhui and Sichuan's liberal approach to their local economies has already been noted; in the case of Hebei, it is probably relevant that its leaders issued their response to the December 7 directive relatively late (on January 1), and that its contents were comparatively mild, as Anhui and Sichuan's had also been.[78]

These variations in implementation may well point to a relatively wide

[73] See the short report in *FBIS*, Jan. 28, 1981, S2.
[74] Anhui's news is reported in *FBIS*, Dec. 23, O1.
[75] Hunan's report is in *FBIS*, Feb. 5, 1980, P5; Tibet's is in Feb. 3, Q5 and Feb. 25, Q4.
[76] See *FBIS*, Feb. 3, 1981, U1.
[77] For Anhui, see *FBIS*, Mar. 3, 1981, O1, and Mar. 19, O1; for Hebei, see Feb. 27, 1981, R1; and for Sichuan, see Jan. 29, 1981, Q2–4 (i.e., a report on stressing readjustment *before* the formation of the central-level office was even announced).
[78] *FBIS*, Jan. 9, 1981, R1–2.

degree of discretion enjoyed by local officials. A reality of diversity underlies a facade of uniformity. Regarding the origins of these divergences among provinces, I have suggested that they may be traced to alliances between local leaders and central ones (as in Anhui, Hunan, and Sichuan), to the balance of local factions (in Heilongjiang), and to particular local conditions (in Tibet) in the various cases noted here. However, the absence of the ballot box, and the fluidity of politicians' tenure in office, may mean that in some ways implementation may be more complicated and more uncertain here than it is in democracies. In the Chinese system, uncertainty among elites breeds uncertainty and circumspection among subordinates. This, in turn, can produce divergences in implementation or nonimplementation.

The Structure of Bureaucratic Interests, Responses, and Coalitions

Implementation also reflected the pattern of bureaucratic interests. Here some insights from the literature on implementation in federal, democratic systems—particularly that pertaining to policies categorized by Ripley and Franklin as being of the "protective regulatory" type—help to explain the outcomes.[79] Specifically, these authors argue that at the stage of implementation, those affected by regulatory policies fight or try to capture the regulators. But the picture must be modified in the Chinese case, both because it has a socialist, that is, a state-owned and state-run economy, and also because of the addition to this economy of certain protomarket features in the late 1970s. The fundamental contradiction created by this hybrid system grows from the mixed goals of its designers, that is, in the clash between stability (or control) and productivity. Different leaders place different relative weights on these goals.

Concretely, since the state budget must cover nearly all costs in the Chinese economy, some leaders are most concerned about the stability of prices of the goods and services in it. For, once the prices of some commodities are permitted to rise, those of others are inevitably affected. Other leaders, however, also cognizant of their responsibility for all economic activity within the nation, focus upon generating productivity. They believe this is best done through incentives, as they push up the state's overall bill in the process.

The structure of interest and coalition-formation and of support for and resistance to price control is best understood in light of this underlying contradiction. For the fact of state ownership dictates one set of responsibilities, while the new market-like elements in the economy dictate yet another.

---

[79] See Ripley and Franklin, *Bureaucracy and Policy Implementation* (n. 3 above), especially 74 and 191. They defined such policies as those that are "designed to protect the public by setting conditions under which various private activities can occur." In China, the activities of state-run shops and factories are not private activities; still, as they work to protect their own interests their behavior resembles that of private actors in a capitalist system.

Thus, while the plan demands that targets for state-managed sales and profits be met, and that prices for key commodities be those set by the state, market initiatives inspire competition, cost-cutting, and even speculation. Often the state is "victim."

The effort to achieve price control under these conditions was rendered even more problematic by the opportunities afforded by the essentially two-tiered price system that existed in China in 1980 (and continues today), whereby state-set prices are often lower than the prices available through negotiating. In order to understand how these structural dimensions of the economy affected the interests of units engaged in price-control work (those of the regulators as well as those of the regulated), Oksenberg's concept of agency "mission" (see chapter 6) provides some guidance. That is, as he put it, "major problems are perceived through the lens of organizational responsibilities."[80]

Indeed, throughout the months immediately following the issuance of the price-freeze directive (December 1980 through March 1981), one group of departments particularly concerned itself with ensuring that prices be brought under control, by various means. These were, in addition to the General Administrative Bureau of Industry and Commerce and the public security units noted above, the Ministry of Finance, the People's Bank, and the pricing bureaucracy. The support of these units for this effort is of course not unexpected, given their mission to guarantee the correspondence between state expenditures and its revenues and to attempt to maintain a well-controlled socialist monetary system.

In early January, for example, the *Finance and Trade Journal* called for strict controls on the money supply, saying that an excessive supply of money by the Bank of China had led to price rises over the past few months. More than two months later, the deputy director of the Financial Science Institute under the Ministry of Finance, complaining about the deficit, took an anti-incentives stance, claiming that "things have not changed for the better since the Third Plenum" and that "because of the increase in workers' wages and the prices of farm products, state revenues fell short."[81]

Also in early January the People's Bank held a meeting for presidents of its various branches, at which a decision was made to tighten controls over credit and currency issuance, in order to help stabilize prices. The Bank's approach, to work through a withdrawal of surplus currency from circulation and a control over credit outlays, suggests which side of the issue it stood on.[82] The obvious interest of the pricing units was noted above in Liu Zhuofu's early attempt to draw attention to the problem of inflation at the Third Session of the NPC meeting in September 1980. The usual situation of

---

[80] Oksenberg, "Economic Policy-Making," 181–82.

[81] In *FBIS*, Jan. 8, 1981, L22, and Mar. 30, 1981, U4, respectively.

[82] *FBIS*, Jan. 8, 1981, L23.

its agents in the field is illustrated by this remark in a *People's Daily* article from early January, which shows the opposition between them and the local business units: "Some time ago, some units and departments set their own prices by their own efforts. When the pricing department interfered, some people regarded the interference as a 'stumbling block' to enlivening the economy."[83]

It appears to me that the Ministry of Commerce was less concerned than these bureaucracies about inflation. One indication is the fact that it issued only one public document in conjunction with the drive—and that was actually prior to the December 7 directive. As was mentioned earlier, on November 29 the ministry, along with the All-China Federation of Supply and Marketing Cooperatives and the State Price Bureau, sent down a joint circular calling on lower-level units to "strengthen price control" in the catering and service trades (but not actually freezing prices).[84] The implementation of the December 7 directive was given instead to the GABIC to manage, as was noted above.

Additional evidence comes from the fact that the one act of the ministry during the months investigated here was to hold a discussion meeting for directors of commercial departments and bureaus at the end of March 1981.[85] The assessment that forum made of the market and work in the market in 1980 is conspicuously at variance with the theme of readjustment and retrenchment that characterized the price-control decision, as the following quotation from its press release makes clear:

> Directors . . . reviewed the work in 1980. They used encouraging facts from all places to show that the market as a whole has rarely been so brisk since the founding of new China, thanks to the implementation of the line, principles and policies since the 3d Plenary Session of the 11th CCP Central Committee. They felt that it had been easy to bring about this excellent market situation.

The concept of organizational "mission" directs attention to the fact that this ministry is charged with drafting and executing sales and purchase plans in trade and with managing inventories. It could be that those running this bureaucracy consider fostering an active market more important than observing the strictures of price stability. The ministry's officials may appreciate the activity of the free market and its fluctuating prices in helping to achieve a balance between supply and demand. Relatedly, in dealing with the private sector over several decades, the commercial officials in the capital have consistently been notably more liberal than their cadres in the field.[86]

---

[83] *RMRB*, January 5, 1981, in *FBIS*, Jan. 9, L12.

[84] See n. 51 above.

[85] See the press release in *FBIS*, Mar. 30, 1981, L1–2.

[86] A conversation with Terry Sicular helped me in this analysis. For evidence on the Ministry's historical role vis-à-vis the private sector, see Solinger (1984), n. 26 above, especially chap. 4.

Although the policy-making echelons of the financial and banking bureaucracies—combined with the administration of commerce and industry and the public security units, plus all those responsible for price control at all levels—formed a coalition in favor of control, the commercial bureaucracy seems (as often in the past) to have stood on the side of the lower-level business, trade, and industrial firms in the state-run sector, who were the regulatees. These firms acted to expand the scope of commodities that could be sold at negotiated prices; sold commodities meant for planned supply (rationed goods that bear state-fixed prices) at negotiated, higher prices; carried out large-scale negotiated purchases and sales before fulfilling their procurement and allocation plan; went to production sites and factories for direct purchases, inducing a competitive bidding that produced shortages in the state sector; and used negotiated-price commodities to compete with fixed-price commodities by mixing the two in selling.[87]

Their motives are clear: they wanted to make profits and to obtain bonuses and to hold onto customers and their own previous monopolies.[88] In larger terms, the introduction of market-type elements into the state-planned economy provided opportunities to circumvent price control. This was especially so given the continued existence of low-priced goods where state-fixed prices still applied. Moreover, these opportunities really had to be snatched if firms were to meet their traditional and unchanged norms of making profits to be turned over to the state, given the new competition from individual and collective enterprises, given also the fact that the prices of many raw materials used in industry had risen, and since rural purchase prices were higher than selling prices for certain commodities (a condition that affected commercial units responsible for sales and purchases). In addition, the wage increases of 1979 were tied to performance in meeting state targets, a factor that probably influenced the effort of those in shops to try harder than before to be sure to turn in high earnings.[89] In short, one part of the bureaucracy was trying to hold prices down, whereas other decisions had provided incentives that made efforts to circumvent price control almost inevitable.

Probably the most instructive of the broadcasts on the price-control campaign are those about persecution of commodity-price workers. Several news reports between December and the end of March made references to harassment suffered by those who attempted to enforce the freeze, such as being transferred from their posts as price workers, being denied bonuses, and

---

[87] These behaviors are noted in many places. For a few examples, see *FBIS*, Apr. 28, 1980, L5, Dec. 19, L24, and Dec. 24, 1980, O3.

[88] *FBIS*, Nov. 13, 1980, S1, Dec. 19, 1980, L25, and Mar. 31, 1981, L22, to cite only three of many such references.

[89] See *CNA*, no. 1178 (1980): 1, 3, and 5; and Ch'en Po-wen, "Rising Prices and Wages" (n. 20 above), 33, 36, and 40–41 for discussion of these points.

coming under attack. The case of Pan Xianrong, who was serving as a commodity clerk of the Gongxian County Food Company in Yibin prefecture,
Sichuan, as of 1980, is instructive.[90]

In this case, Pan was persecuted for trying to bring a local (subcounty)-
level food-company manager into line for repeatedly violating the government price policy, as he "arbitrarily" raised the price of meat. Despite Pan's
efforts at appeal, he found that neither the County Party Committee nor its
Discipline Inspection Committee, nor even the County Finance and Trade
Department, was willing to carry out the Prefectural Party Discipline Committee's instructions to county units that Pan's rights be respected. Even the
Provincial Commodity Price Committee, Pan's ultimate superior, was unable to enforce its will in this or in similar cases.

The fact that a food company manager would try to counter the efforts of a
price worker is understandable, given the analysis above. What is more surprising at first glance is the fact that units usually thought of as favoring
controls—a party discipline inspection committee and a finance organ—
should collude with the food-company manager. Perhaps the regulatees were
able to capture—or at least make common cause with—these local units
because of the heightened freedoms given local governments to control extrabudgetary funds in 1979–1980. For among the funds in this category are
commercial surtaxes, profits from collective enterprises, and fees for administering free markets,[91] all of which are larger when business is more brisk
and profits earned by all sorts of marketing agencies are higher.

Here once again, then, is a case where units within the state sector are
confronted with conflicting tasks—to observe price controls while invigorating the local economy. The implementation of the freeze was shot through
with this contradiction, one that put a set of bureaus typically charged with
enforcing the state plan and its tight money against local-level business units.
But this was also a contradiction that set upper-level enforcing agents against
regulated localities, sometimes making for unexpected bedmates at the county echelon. Incentives were being provided subordinate levels *not* to comply.

Social Groups

There are two dimensions to the effect that the inflation of 1980 had on
various social groups; the analysis of both extends the understandings borrowed from the federal/democratic systems-implementation literature. First
of all, as was noted earlier, leaders of a socialist state, just as those in any
other sort of system, may *choose* to court particular social groups, even in the

[90] *FBIS*, Jan. 13, 1981, L6–7. There is another reference to persecution of price workers—and
about those who protect and cover up for offenders—in *FBIS*, Feb. 9, 1981, L19.
[91] Weil, "The Sixth 5-Year Plan" (n. 25 above), 23.

absence of elections and even without being actively lobbied or otherwise directly pressured by the groups themselves. In China in 1977–1979 the new post-Mao elite chose to court producers, and it did so through bestowing material benefits on them.

That the government recognized the effects of its policies in this regard is apparent in many provincial income surveys taken in 1980–1981, which over and over again state openly that certain groups have done better than others in the wake of the recent economic changes and the concomitant price increases. Material from the Sichuan and Guangdong surveys are illustrative, with the Sichuan survey admitting that

> the income from salary of most staff and workers in the cultural, educational and health departments and in the institutional bodies, is lower than that of the staff and workers in other lines of work. . . . Conditions are even worse for those staff and workers whose salaries have not been readjusted for years and for those families with many family members, few of whom are employed. Due to the rise of prices, their actual income has decreased, and their lives are rather difficult.[92]

Since part of the salary increases of recent years has been, at least in intent, pegged to work performance (this was especially the case for the third set of raises), the bias in the cities has been not just in favor of producers but particularly toward the most skilled of the state-employed workers, especially those in factories.[93]

The Guangdong study similarly shows that total average monthly income among state workers there is higher than the average for the rest of the country. This is so because, in addition to foreign remittances and the presence of overseas Chinese in Guangdong, salaries are higher, the employment rate is higher, and the dependency rate (of unemployed family members upon those with jobs) is lower.[94]

Official sources suggest one direct way in which the policies of economic liberalization—and the inflation that accompanied it—has led to differences in consumption related to the income polarization noted in such surveys. With the encouragement given to free markets and the instituting of negotiated prices, the state has been unable to purchase from peasants adequate quantities of certain goods to be sold at list prices. Consequently, "the masses" have been forced to buy nonstaple food products at negotiated and free-market prices, which are typically higher than the state-set list ones. For example, vegetables, eggs, and aquatic products are in short supply in state shops, and these items, more expensive when sold at the fairs, "meet the different consumer demands of the people, especially those with higher

[92] *FBIS*, Feb. 11, 1981, Q4.
[93] See n. 23 above.
[94] *FBIS*, Feb. 12, 1981, P1.

incomes."[95] It seems from such statements that those with less disposable income, for whatever reason—because of the sector in which they are employed, or because they are members of families with high dependency rates, in the cities; or because they belong to families with too few able-bodied laborers in relation to the number of mouths to feed in the countryside—may find many of the good things on the free markets beyond their reach, while there is at the same time nowhere else to obtain more ordinary necessities.

The new leadership's deliberate effort to encourage producers has also meant in effect that it first acted to co-opt those groups by passing what turned out to be inflationary measures, but then had to (try to) pull back when it found that many of the producers it was courting were also consumers, as this criticism of "some [probably rather numerous] persons" reveals:

> Some persons consider only the interests of their own departments or enterprises and one-sidedly seek higher prices for the commodities they produce or sell; but they want stable prices for the raw materials and the daily necessities they use and will complain about any hikes of these prices. They hardly know that when they hike prices, they cannot prevent others from following suit.[96]

This quotation illustrates well the second dimension of the impact of inflation on social groups in China in recent years. The reaction of affected groups here has been no different from the "mental indexation" that occurs in democratic contexts when each group bets on continued inflation and thereby pushes that inflation onto a self-generating course. Thus, though a consensus existed in 1980 China that a problem—inflation—existed, a factor which some students of implementation maintain should ease the way toward a solution,[97] in the case of inflation, affected groups sought to "monetize" their "assets," or to attempt in effect to trade in on the scarce goods under their own control. This in turn made irrelevant that particular consensus for purposes of implementation.

This image of groups monetizing assets is an apt one for understanding the behavior of various sectors within the populace which were all trying to shore up their incomes. Peasants with a surplus of popular produce made ready use of the free market, some undoubtedly acquiescing as procurers "illegally buy up state-controlled commodities for resale at high profits," as "state-operated and collective units go to production sources for purchasing, causing prices to rise . . . ," and as "some illegally purchase rural and sideline products intended for planned procurement and then smuggle them to other localities."[98]

---

[95] *BR*, no. 35 (1980), 23–24, and Liu, "Current Market Prices" (n. 30 above), 34, contain this information.

[96] *FBIS*, Jan. 12, 1981, L10.

[97] Ripley and Franklin, *Bureaucracy and Policy Implementation* (n. 3 above), 85.

[98] *FBIS*, Feb. 17, 1981, Q2; Dec. 19, 1980, L24; and Jan. 14, 1981, Q1.

Meanwhile, state retailers and private-sector peddlers, besides carrying on these activities in the countryside, bought up commodities from state-operated stores at negotiated prices (thereby enabling state shopworkers to monetize their assets, the state-priced goods) at several times higher than the state list prices; while others with a skill for trade as their asset (and perhaps some capital from who-knows-what source) acted as secondhand dealers, engaging in wholesaling by buying directly from factories; or even set up shops to speculate on price fluctuations.[99] Shopkeepers, in addition to colluding with these merchants, drew on their own assets, the goods under their control, to try to squeeze out higher profits. This they did by such timeworn methods as short-weighting, mixing inferior with higher-quality goods, adulteration, switching trademarks, and, as one report put it, "dishing up new forms and other foul means for inflating prices."[100]

Workers were reported to have engaged in strikes during this period, but no details were given.[101] However, some credibility is lent such rumors by the fact that workers definitely did strike in Hangzhou for higher wages in 1975, as some in other cities joined in pleas for wage increases and threatened to walk out if their demands were rejected.[102] There has been speculation that the December 1980 clampdown on prices was at least in part inspired by a fear of Polish-type incidents.[103]

As for groups with rather more authority, state cadres and active-duty soldiers dealt in power where they could, as is apparent in a broadcast from Hunan, which called for handling severely any such people who participated in speculation or used their power of office to practice favoritism and gain profits.[104] And factory managers used the new enterprise autonomy guidelines to jack up prices, and put part of the profits thereby gained into bonus funds. Several broadcasts suggest the possibility that managers did this in part to strengthen their own positions as enterprise leaders, now under threat from worker congresses holding the power of election.[105] Managers, then, had as

[99] *FBIS*, Jan. 14, 1981, Q2; Mar. 27, 1981, S2; and Jan. 14, 1981, Q1.

[100] *FBIS*, Dec. 19, 1980, L25.

[101] *FBIS*, Mar. 20, 1981, L1–2.

[102] Wang Hsiao-hsien, "Wage Adjustments" (n. 20 above), 12–18.

[103] According to an Agence France Presse report in *FBIS*, Mar. 20, 1981, L2, in several Chinese cities calls went out for setting up independent trade unions similar to those in Poland. This AFP report is based on remarks by Chinese trade union officials to a visiting French delegation.

[104] *FBIS*, Feb. 5, 1981, P6.

[105] On this theme, see *FBIS*, Mar. 23, 1981, O3: "A few enterprise leaders are imbued with serious individualism. They do not hesitate to violate party discipline and state law so they can recklessly award bonuses to buy popular support as a steppingstone in their official career." And, finally, Mar. 11, 1981, L15:

... many comrades have regarded bonuses as something to help workers solve their difficulties in everyday life. They even think that awarding more bonuses or more allowances will leave everyone satisfied with the leadership. Therefore the phenomenon of awarding bonuses has assumed very serious proportions. This has made for a greater outlay, a larger deficit and higher commodity prices.

their asset the enterprise profit-retention fund, which they now controlled and sought to use in expanding their own power, leading to a cost-push style of inflationary process as they did so.

Thus, social groups in China in 1980–1981 did not require lobbyists or interest associations with clout in order to complicate the quieting of inflationary pressures, once these pressures were set in motion by the regime. These social sectors were quite capable of "mentally indexing" their incomes, as they perceived that the costs of their staples would probably continue to escalate for some time to come.

Overall, then, the implementation of the price-freeze policy of December 1980 had several traits that likened it to implementation in democratic, federal, and even capitalist contexts: It was complicated by a lack of total consensus in leadership councils; it was marked by variations at the lower administrative levels; its implementing bureaucratic agencies had disparate missions to fulfill, and, as with regulatory policies elsewhere, those regulated attempted to escape the regulation; social groups made claims in whatever manner they were able to do so; and some central policies worked at cross-purposes to others. *The difference here is that for the Chinese case, the state plan was central in structuring the play of interests.* The omnibus state budget had to cope with the bill, as private-sectoral traders won competitions with state cadres, and as state cadres took advantage of the new market mechanism to deprive the state.

EVALUATION

The termination of the campaign to enforce the price freeze does not appear to have been the result of the "success" of that campaign. Indeed, there is little evidence that this mass-movement effort at checking inflation bore much fruit. Beijing City did announce on January 29 that it had solved its own municipal problem of price hikes in only one month's time.[106] The local authorities attributed this achievement to the shock type of tactics employed there—the "thousands of officials and deputies . . . calling at shops . . . to ask about prices," the documents issued to retailers, the newspaper columns, the fines and confiscations. But no other city made a similar claim. In fact, even after the national-level proclamation went out stating that prices had been brought under control and stabilized in mid-March (thanks, it said, to the "vigilance of the local governments" and to the fourteen central-level special teams sent throughout the country to carry out public criticism and fines),[107] at least three provinces continued to call for efforts to bring prices down.[108]

[106] *FBIS*, Jan. 30, 1981, R1–2.

[107] *FBIS*, Mar. 18, 1981, L7.

[108] See *FBIS*, Mar. 19, O19 (Anhui), Mar. 23, Q3–4 (Yunnan), and Mar. 27, S1–2 (Liaoning).

Also, although the official statistics do show that the rate of inflation went down in 1981 (the given rates were 5.8 percent for 1979, 6 percent for 1980, 2.4 percent for 1981, and only 1.9 percent in 1982), Nai-ruenn Chen has estimated that total inflationary pressure (both open and repressed) may have been more like 4.7 percent in 1979, 8.4 percent in 1980, and as high as 12.2 percent in 1981.[109] The high figure for 1981 represents the fact that repressed inflation may have risen to 9.6 percent in that year.

These ambiguities (especially when combined with the material on difficulties and variations in implementation recounted above) suggest to me first of all that the price-freeze policy may have succeeded under the near-terror tactics in the capital, but that it was probably not so efficacious elsewhere. And, second, they leave open the very real possibility that to the extent that inflation was ameliorated on a national scale, it was probably more the result of other, macro-type policies being instituted simultaneously than it was the effect of checkups by unpopular and harassed price workers.

James O'Connor, in *The Fiscal Crisis of the State*, speaking of the advanced capitalist state, lists three ways that the state may essay to keep costs down and thereby alleviate fiscal crisis. These are (1) to deflate the economy as a whole by engineering a managed recession; (2) to introduce and enforce wage and price controls; and (3) to cooperate with monopoly capital to increase productivity in both the private and state sectors.[110]

The essence of the first strategy is to reduce aggregate demand and sales, which in turn creates unused productive capacity, among other things. The available evidence from radio broadcasts from China during this period indicates that for the first few months after the price-control document was issued, that is, from January until mid-March, the thrust of policy was in the direction of installing just such a "managed recession." The leadership then in command opted for a program of fiscal and monetary policies aimed at removing surplus funds from state enterprises and local governments; tightening currency and credit; encouraging savings; forcing treasury bond sales on the localities and state firms; and reducing state expenditures, in particular those for capital construction, national defense, and administrative costs.[111]

[109] Chen, "China's Inflation" (n. 19 above), 20, 28.

[110] James O'Connor, *The Fiscal Crisis of the State* (New York: St. Martin's Press, 1973), especially 47–51.

[111] See Hsiao, "Money and Banking" (n. 28 above), 474; Chen, "China's Inflation," 35–37; Robert Delfs, "Carry on Tinkering," *FEER*, Dec. 11, 1981, 65–66; *FBIS*, Jan. 23, 1981, L1, Feb. 11, L2–3, Mar. 9, L33, and Mar. 11, L12. Aside from these austerity measures, the regime also used foreign loans as a way out of its difficulties. Another dimension of this "managed recession" was a policy of "slamming on the brakes" toward capital construction carried on outside the state plan. And, according to a chart in Xue Muqiao, *Wo guo guomin jingji di tiaozheng he gaige* (Our Country's National Economy's Readjustment and Reform) (Beijing: People's Publishing Co., 1982), 94, heavy industry exhibited negative growth in the first three quarters of 1981 (−8.7 percent, −7.8 percent, and −6.4 percent, respectively).

By mid-March, however, on the very day that the price-control campaign was decreed to be concluded, a socialist version of O'Connor's third strategy became policy: to battle fiscal crisis through *stimulating*, not restraining, the national economy. On that day a national forum on the structural reform of industrial management was held, and a statement was issued that efforts should now be placed on reforms. The method suggested was to continue with experiments in expanding the power of enterprises (though the December 1980 Party Work Conference had stipulated that there would be no further extension of that reform for the future); and to "push light industry forward" in the near future, concentrating mainly on increasing the production of consumer goods,[112] no doubt to soak up surplus funds in the hands of consumers. This line had been a minor theme since at least mid-January,[113] but it received full sanction in March, when a *People's Daily* editorial endorsed the approach of concentrating on consumer goods production. Its statement followed the analysis of Xue Muqiao that, as was noted above,[114] had appeared in the previous day's *Worker's Daily*, in saying that

> economic construction must always be developed gradually and cannot seek a balance in financial expenditure and revenue through reducing the scale of capital construction every year. The improvement of financial revenue should not merely rely on balancing expenditure and revenue. In that case, what is the basic solution? It is to develop production and extensively open up new routes to earn income.[115]

At the same time (on March 13), the State Council had a special conference to discuss plans for increasing the production of light industrial products, which was personally presided over by Zhao Ziyang, Wan Li, and Yao Yilin, all champions of the reform strategy with which this third of O'Connor's methods is most closely linked.[116]

It seems, then, that the mandated denouement of the price-freeze campaign came about, not because the policy itself had already succeeded, but because a more general policy of radical retrenchment had had some initial effect. That larger program's promise apparently was sufficient to enable the reformers once again to haul out their own program, one that stressed recovery through growth, not through stringency.

But, whether the ultimate cure used for the Chinese economy in 1980–1981 was O'Connor's first or third method, that is, whether it was fiscal and monetary controls or market initiatives, neither one of these tactics is the more typical communist/socialist solution of simply freezing prices and

---

[112] *FBIS*, Mar. 18, 1981, L8.
[113] An article in *RMRB*, Jan. 15, 1981, 4, not in *FBIS* until Feb. 3, L21.
[114] See n. 68 above.
[115] *RMRB*, editorial, Mar. 14, 1981, in *FBIS*, Mar. 31, L9–11.
[116] *FBIS*, Mar. 30, 1981, U1–2.

wages. Such a turn to strategies more akin to those used in capitalist states was predicted by Wiles some fifteen years ago as being the path likely to be chosen by semi-decentralized Soviet-type economies of the future.[117]

For, he reasoned, as micro-economic freedoms grow, macro-targets should lose much of their legal force. As he put it, "Then the macro-volume of activity will be the *ex post* sum of all micro-contracts, and the government's principal lever on these latter will be fiscal and monetary policy, much as in a pure ME [market economy]." And interestingly, around the time that these decisions were being made, a Chinese economist, Dai Yuanchen, in fact used the West as a model, pointing out in the journal *Economic Research* that Western nations in the 1970s and 1980s were adopting retrenchment policies involving high interest rates and the control of the monetary supply to halt inflation.[118]

CONCLUSION

The murky relationship between program effectiveness, leadership evaluation, and termination of this essentially mass movement type of effort to bring the problem of price hikes under control is clarified in several ways by the various lines of analysis presented in this chapter. For one thing, the elite disagreement specified here—about the seriousness of the problem, and about first whether and then how to handle it—suggests that the problem was not necessarily really licked when (as I surmise) a different group within the leadership (Zhao, Wan, Yao, informed by Xue) managed to bring their own approach to the fore in mid-March, thereby eclipsing that of Chen Yun and Wang Bingqian. Then inflation fighting through mass effort had to be labeled completed in order to justify choosing a new tactic for attacking the larger issue of fiscal crisis. Just as MacFarquhar noted in relation to the conclusion of the Great Leap Forward in 1961, "When a totally new policy is adopted, it is often smoke-screened by claims for success of the policy that is being abandoned."[119]

Second, the interprovincial differences in problem definition and implementation style outlined briefly above—probably growing in part, I have argued, from local politicians' awareness of the imperfect consensus at the top and their own links to particular central elites, in part from factional disputes within the separate provinces, and in part from specific local conditions—raises significant doubt about any overall success in price-freeze work, as was announced to have occurred nationally in only three months'

---

[117] Wiles, *Communist International Economics*, 54.

[118] Discussed in Delfs (December 11, 1981), 66.

[119] Roderick MacFarquhar, *The Origins of the Cultural Revolution*, vol. 2: *The Great Leap Forward, 1958–1960* (New York: Columbia University Press, 1983), 326.

time. Individual provincial broadcasts of continuing price problems made *after* that national-level announcement further vitiate the claim.

And, finally, the essentially protective or defensive behavior of local-level implementing firms and of social groups, with firms trying to fulfill norms and groups attempting to monetize assets, poses questions about how genuine the program's success in monitoring the freeze in the localities might have been had it not been for the more authoritative retrenchment initiated almost in tandem.

Most of these insights draw directly on the implementation literature written by students of democratic, federal, even capitalist systems. In China as in these other contexts, coalitions are formed, power is relatively dispersed, and difficulties of implementation are connected to problems in central-level control. Moreover, the modern state in China as elsewhere must necessarily pay attention to competing group claims in some manner, and this leads to complexities in carrying out economic policies that touch people's daily lives.

FIVE

Implementing Chinese
Tax Policy

David Bachman

INTRODUCTION

"The power to tax is the power to destroy."—*Chief Justice John Marshall*

"What follows the abolition of taxes and levies is the abolition of the state."
—*Marx and Engels*

The extraction of societal resources by a regime is one of the most fundamental tasks of any state, with some scholars arguing that the history of
the development of the state is inextricably linked with the development of
taxation.[1] Yet, with few exceptions, political scientists have ignored the
inherently important question of resource extraction.[2]

However, taxation has received substantial attention from economists
and legal scholars. The more political aspects of taxation, on the other hand,
have received almost no attention, despite its generally redistributive
character.[3] Resources are taken from society and used by the state. However,
most discussions of state finance focus on how this revenue is allocated
through the budgetary process and how expenditures are used. But the
actual process of taking resources from society is fraught with political issues.
How do states ensure that taxes are paid? What units of government are
involved in the taxation process? What resources do they possess? How can

[1] See Gabriel Ardant, "Financial Policies and Economic Infrastructures of Modern States
and Nations," and Rudolf Braun, "Taxation, Sociopolitical Structure, and State-Building:
Great Britain and Brandenburg Prussia," both in *The Formation of National States in Western
Europe*, ed. Charles Tilly (Princeton: Princeton University Press, 1975), 164–242 and 243–327,
respectively.

[2] For example, in the seventh of the Social Science Research Council's Studies in Political
Development, Leonard Binder et al., *Crises and Sequences in Political Development* (Princeton:
Princeton University Press, 1971), the words "tax" and "taxation" do not appear in the text.

[3] The *locus classicus* of discussions of distributive, redistributive, and regulatory policies is
Theodore Lowi, "American Business, Public Policy, Case Studies, and Political Theory," *World
Politics* 16 no. 4 (July 1964): 685–714.

taxpayers influence tax policy and the collection of taxes? What strategies do taxpayers use to evade taxation, and why do they choose to violate the law?

These questions are important because the extraction of resources is a precondition for the implementation of all other government programs. Moreover, taxes affect incentives. The imposition of taxes and fees has distinct consequences for production and consumption. States deliberately manipulate tax rates in order to stimulate or deter certain activities.

This chapter addresses several aspects of the question of how the Chinese government has dealt with the issue of taxation, particularly since 1978. I first discuss the conventional wisdom on finances and taxation in poor countries and suggest some reasons why China diverges from these generalizations. This is followed by a brief introduction to the nature and functions of Chinese taxation. The heart of this essay focuses on two facets of Chinese taxation. The first of these is a discussion of the "substituting taxes for profit" reform that was launched in 1983. This is potentially the most important change in Chinese tax policy since 1949. The other area of investigation concerns the implementation of existing tax policies. I conclude with general comments on the nature of taxation and policy implementation in post-Mao China.

FINANCES AND TAXATION IN POOR COUNTRIES AND HOW CHINA IS DIFFERENT

The financial and planning systems in poor countries have a number of characteristics.[4] First, taxes are collected yearly, if they are successfully collected at all; therefore, the amount of money in the state treasury varies greatly over the course of the year. Second, the lack of competent officials and adequate information systems prevents decision makers from making timely and appropriate decisions—or even knowing how much money is in the state treasury. Third, because of the above factors, budgets are remade throughout the course of the fiscal year, as priorities and the danger of depleting the state treasury change. Fourth, to protect themselves against these changes, government agencies attempt to develop autonomous guaranteed sources of finance, thereby weakening central financial authority. Fifth, because of the preceding attributes, budgetary politics is unending; uncertainty is continuous, thereby degrading economic performance. Sixth, political leaders frequently turn to planning; for a variety of reasons, however, planning is no more satisfactory than the budgetary process, and the politics of planning loses out to the politics of the budget.

---

[4]The following is a summary of some of the major arguments of Naomi Caiden and Aaron Wildavsky, *Planning and Budgeting in Poor Countries* (New York: John Wiley and Sons, 1974). See also, Alex Radian (a student of Wildavsky's), *Resource Mobilization in Poor Countries* (New Brunswick: Transaction Books, 1980).

The amount of taxes and other funds obtained by governments in poor countries is in the 10–15 percent range of gross national product; developed countries double this percentage. The major constraints on and opportunities for obtaining more financial resources are not economic, experts agree. Politics determines how much is supposed to be extracted and by what means. Implementation processes determine the extent to which policy goals are achieved. Implementation is, in turn, determined by the interplay of administrative capabilities and the complexity of the tasks to be undertaken. Partial implementation is the rule, and in poor countries the level of tax evasion reaches colossal dimensions.

Tax collection involves identifying and locating taxpayers, assessing their taxes, collecting their taxes, and enforcing tax laws. Because of limited organizational resources, the above steps cannot be fulfilled effectively unless the great majority of taxpayers voluntarily comply with the tax laws.

Limitations on information, expertise, and the number of personnel are severe in tax departments, forcing auditors, revenue collectors, and enforcement officials to compromise. Auditors examine the books just thoroughly enough to convince themselves that the person or company being audited is in arrears in his tax payments. But lacking time, the auditor reaches a partial settlement with the taxpayer, thereby reinforcing the tendency of the taxpayer not to meet his full tax obligation. Tax collectors are responsible for ensuring the collection from an impossibly large group of taxpayers; their records are incomplete and fail to show who owes what; and many taxpayers have failed to register altogether. They develop coping mechanisms to ensure that they meet their collection quota, but this is at the expense of thoroughness. Enforcement officials find that it is hard enough to identify tax law violators, much less prepare a case against them. Prosecution involves lengthy proceedings, further hindering their ability to collect taxes; thus, few are prosecuted.

All difficulties with the implementation of tax policy are compounded by the distribution of wealth in less developed countries. Frequently a small upper class holds the bulk of national wealth, which generally is protected by political power. A tax policy designed to mobilize resources would logically concentrate on those with the most income. However, the political and economic power of the rich prevents this from happening in most cases. Tax officials usually have no choice but to concentrate attention on less exalted taxpayers.

The nature of China's economic and political system is significantly different from the composite presented above. First, most Chinese enterprises are state or collectively owned, and the banking system is state owned. Because of state control of the banking system, taxes (theoretically) can be collected by merely transferring monies from one bank account to another, though subterfuges exist in this system as well. Moreover, because of state ownership, most taxes are collected, not from society, but from elements of the state itself.

China is also a planned economy. While the planning process in China is "coarse, fragmented, and non-consistent,"[5] the procedures of planning have insured that planners have played an extremely important role in allocational decisions. Planners control real resources in China, which is not the case with other Third World nations. Financial officials in China have less control over resources than do their counterparts in other developing nations. Part of the reason for this is political and part procedural. The type of balanced, careful growth often associated with financial officials in all countries has been largely anathema to the Chinese Communist Party (CCP) and to planning-heavy industrial interests in China. The "financial viewpoint" has often been criticized.[6] The procedural weakness of financial officials stems from the fact that in China plans are drawn up first, and budgets are drawn up on the basis of these plans;[7] production and investment have been more important to Chinese leaders than finance. Budgetary politics has been subordinate to the politics of planning.

Moreover, taxation is only one means of resource extraction in China. While the proportion of government revenues accounted for by taxes exceeded 60 percent in 1982, other methods of extracting resources are important. Profits from state enterprises are remitted to the state treasury (akin to a 100 percent profits tax). Agricultural procurement sales at concessionary prices have been another key extractive measure.

China's tax system differs significantly from that in other poor countries. The principal tax in China is the industrial and commercial tax, similar to the Soviet turnover tax. This is an indirect levy, assessed at the point of sale on the production or commercial unit. It is collected frequently, sometimes even daily. Until 1980 there were no individual income taxes in China, and the share of individual income tax as a percentage of all taxes collected today

[5] Barry Naughton, "Economic Reforms and Decentralization: China's Problematic Materials Allocation System" (Paper presented to the California Regional Seminar on Chinese Studies, Berkeley, Calif., April 6, 1984), 5.

[6] On the weak position of the financial officials, see David M. Bachman, *Chen Yun and the Chinese Political System* (Berkeley: Center for Chinese Studies Research Monograph No. 29, 1985). In "To Leap Forward: Chinese Policy-making, 1956–1957" (Ph.D. dissertation, Stanford University, 1984) I discuss the reasons for this Party–planner coalition and demonstrate how the planners established many of the programs that are associated with the Maoist Great Leap Forward. See also Robert F. Dernberger, "The Chinese Search for the Path of Self-Sustained Growth in the 1980's: An Assessment," *China under the Four Modernizations, Selected Papers Submitted to the Joint Economic Committee, Congress of the United States*, Part 1 (Washington, D.C.: Government Printing Office, 1982), 19–76, especially 33–72.

[7] This was the case in 1956, and there is no evidence that this has changed. See Zhou Enlai, "Report on the Proposals for the Second Five-Year Plan for the Development of the National Economy," in *Eighth National Congress of the Communist Party of China (Documents)* (Beijing: Foreign Languages Press, 1981), 295.

is minuscule, being levied only on those who earn over 800 yuan a month (approximately $275).

The political structure of the People's Republic of China further reveals the differences between the conventional wisdom and Chinese reality. Unguided mobilization of social forces (interest articulation and aggregation) for particularistic goals is illegitimate. Interest groups comparable to those in democratic societies do not exist. Policy options are the products of governmental organizations or CCP departments. This does not mean that there are no intragovernmental disputes, or that bargaining does not take place within the political system, but it does mean that there are fewer political factors inhibiting the implementation of tax policy than in other types of poor countries.

Because of these differences, the performance of the Chinese state in extracting resources from society has been comparable to that of developed capitalist societies. Until 1980 government revenue as a percentage of national income was in the 30 percent range. Since 1980 this figure has dropped to about 26 percent.[8] Unfortunately, China does not publish figures on its gross national product. However, the World Bank calculates (after being given extensive access to Chinese figures) that Chinese GNP was 391.24 billion yuan in 1979. In that year, state revenues were 110.3 billion yuan, almost 27 percent of GNP.[9]

It might be argued that since the state plays a much larger role in economic activity in socialist states, the ratio of revenue to national income should be higher than in poor capitalist economies, or even higher than is the case in developed capitalist states. However, the ratios presented in table 5.1 significantly understate extraction in China because the revenue figures exclude extrabudgetary funds, which are revenues of local governments in China. (See chapter 3.) In 1982 they totaled 65 billion yuan; these revenues are in addition to the 112 billion yuan in the state budget.[10] Nonetheless, compared to the Soviet Union (where in 1973 revenues were almost 56 percent of national income),[11] China's performance suggests that there is still a gap

[8] Data for these calculations come from the State Statistical Bureau, People's Republic of China, compiler, *Statistical Yearbook of China 1981* (Hong Kong: Economic Information and Agency, 1982), 20 and 403; "Communique on Fulfillment of China's 1982 National Economic Plan," *Beijing Review*, 1983, no. 19 (May 9): II; and Wang Bingqian, "Report on the Final State Accounts for 1982," in Foreign Broadcast Information Service, Daily Report: China (*FBIS*), June 24, 1983, K12.

[9] The World Bank, *China: Socialist Economic Development*, Annex A (Washington, D.C.: The World Bank, 1981), 47, and *Statistical Yearbook 1981*, 403.

[10] The source for the 1982 extrabudgetary figure is Zhao Ziyang, "Report on the Work of the Government," *FBIS*, June 23, 1983, K12. On extrabudgetary funds generally, see chapter 3 in this volume.

[11] Alec Nove, *The Soviet Economic System*, 2d ed. (London: George Allen and Unwin, 1980), 234. Nove notes that there are also extrabudgetary revenues in the Soviet Union, but he does not provide figures (see 235–37).

TABLE 5.1   Revenue as a Percentage of National Income
in China (selected years)

Year	National income (billion yuan)	Revenue (billion yuan)	Percentage
1952	58.9	18.37	31.2
1957	90.8	31.02	34.1
1962	92.4	31.36	33.9
1965	138.7	47.33	34.9
1978	301.0	112.10	37.2
1979	335.0	110.30	32.9
1980	366.7	108.50	29.5
1981	388.7	106.40	26.5
1982	424.7 (estimated)	112.90	26.5

SOURCES: *Statistical Yearbook of China, 1981*, for all figures prior to 1982, 20 and 403. 1982 national income figure from "Communique of the Statistical Bureau," in *Beijing Review*, 1983, no. 19 (May 9): II. Revenue figure from Wang Bingqian, "Report on Final Accounts for 1982," *FBIS*, June 24, 1983, K12.

between potential and realized revenues. Although more revenues could be extracted, a look at the performance of other Third World countries suggests that China's performance is impressive. In comparison, in 1971 India's ratio of tax to GNP was 14 percent, Indonesia's was 10 percent, and South Korea's was 15 percent.[12] China's performance is better because the nature of the Chinese political-economic system has made it easier for the PRC (compared to other poor countries) to tax.

THE CHINESE TAXATION SYSTEM

China's Tax Policies

In 1950–1951 China had a preliminary tax system with twenty-three individual taxes. These included various taxes on commerce, industry, real estate, salt, agriculture, and customs. Although these taxes and other extractive policies generated enough revenue for the government to balance the budget by 1952, the variety of tax categories and kinds of taxes, coupled with the fragile nature of the PRC's administrative apparatus in the early 1950s, led to many problems of implementation.

With the beginning of the First Five-Year Plan in 1953, the twenty-three taxes of 1950 were combined into fifteen taxes, and several individual levies were grouped together to facilitate implementation. During the period 1950–1956 taxes provided revenue and were also a means by which private ownership was restricted (through onerous, even confiscatory taxation).

[12] Figures cited in Radian, *Resource Mobilization*, 14 (n. 4 above).

With the Socialist Transformation of the economy in 1955–1956, private enterprises were effectively taken over by the state. Taxes designed to control private enterprise were no longer appropriate, and the simplification of 1953 remained difficult to administer.

In 1958 the Chinese reorganized the tax system again. The fifteen taxes were combined into ten. The unified industrial and commercial tax came into existence, and the industrial and commercial income tax took on its final form. The former, a turnover tax, was the only tax that applied to state-owned industrial and commercial enterprises not producing salt or engaged in foreign trade. The industrial and commercial income tax was assessed on collectively owned enterprises. Collective enterprises also had to pay the unified industrial and commercial tax.

In 1972–1973 the tax structure was further simplified and rates were readjusted. Motives for this change are obscure. After the simplification, only the industrial and commercial tax (ICT), the industrial and commercial income tax (ICIT), customs duties, and the agricultural tax remained as major tax categories. Recent Chinese commentaries have noted that this combined so many different activities into basic categories that taxation lost its "leverage role,"[13] that is, taxation only gathered revenue; it lost its ability to serve as an incentive.

Thus, on the eve of the Third Plenum of the Eleventh Central Committee in December 1978, when Deng Xiaoping fully consolidated his position (see chapter 2), there were only three major taxes in China: the ICT, the ICIT, and the agricultural tax. The amount of revenue produced by the ICT dwarfed the other two. A quick survey of the ICT and the ICIT follows.

The Industrial and Commercial Tax (ICT)

The 1958 unified industrial and commercial tax combined the separate commodity tax, commodity circulation tax, the business tax, and the stamp tax.[14] All units engaged in industry, purchase of agricultural products, importing, retailing, communications and transportation, and other services were subject to the ICT. The tax was assessed at the time of sale or transfer of possession. Tax rates ranged from 2.5 percent of sales price to 69 percent. Consumer goods, particularly nonessential products, were assessed at high

---

[13] Zhang Hua, "A Discussion of the Role of Tax Revenues in the New Period," *Caizheng* (Finance; hereafter *CZ*), 1980, no. 4 (April), in Joint Publications Research Service (*JPRS*), no. 76760, Nov. 5, 1980, *Economic Affairs* (*EA*), no. 95, 48–52 (see 50–51).

[14] Texts of the Unified Industrial and Commercial Tax and the Detailed Rules on the Unified and Commercial Tax are found in Owen D. Nee, Franklin Chu, and Michael Mosher, eds., *Commercial, Business, and Trade Laws: The People's Republic of China* (Dobbs Ferry: Oceana Publications, 1982), J73–94 and J95–110, respectively. Text of the 1972 version of the ICT is found in *Chengzhen Feinongye Geti Jingji Fagui Xuanbian* (Selected Collection of Laws and Regulations on Urban Nonagricultural Private Enterprise) (Beijing: Gongren Chubanshe, 1982), 32–41.

rates (30–69 percent), and heavy industrial products at lower rates (5–15 percent). Nonetheless, taxes on heavy industrial products were assessed at significantly higher rates than was the case in the Soviet Union, where the turnover tax on heavy industrial products is in the 0.5–1.0 percent range.[15] There is no clear reason why this is so.

Local tax authorities were to set time limits for the handing over of taxes. Tax exemptions, reductions, and increases had to be approved by the State Council for items under "national jurisdiction." Items under "provincial jurisdiction" could have rates increased, lowered, or exempted by authorities at the provincial level.

The 1972 regulations were a reformulation of the tax rates. The maximum rate was reduced to 66 percent, and the minimum rate was raised to 3 percent, with monthly payments mandated. The State Council and the Ministry of Finance were again given responsibility for tax rates and exemptions at the national level, and units at the provincial level were responsible for items under local control. Provincial-level units were also given the authority to lower or exempt taxes on commune, brigade, and team industries, in accordance with national policies. Although the 1972 regulations do not say so, another source states that the real estate tax, the vehicle- and ship-licensing tax, and the slaughter tax were incorporated into the 1972 version of the ICT.[16] One of the significant aspects of this incorporation was that these three taxes were previously collected and used by local authorities. Thus, this tax policy may reflect increasing financial centralization. On balance, however, the 1972 version of the ICT was only a marginal change from the 1958 regulations.

The Industrial and Commercial Income Tax (ICIT)

All enterprises were required to pay the ICIT as originally formulated in 1950.[17] However, state-owned enterprises were exempted from this tax, and the statutory inclusion of this exemption was the major change made in 1958 when the ICIT reached its final form. Privately owned, collective, and individual enterprises were the real targets of the ICIT. Only marginal amendments have been made over the last thirty years.[18]

---

[15] See Alec Nove, *The Soviet Economy*, 2d ed. rev. (New York: Praeger, 1972), 113. See also Franklyn D. Holzman, *Soviet Taxation* (Cambridge: Harvard University Press, 1955), 307.

[16] See Zhang Hua, "Role of Tax Revenues." See also Guo Hongde, Wang Wending, and Han Shaochu, "The Reform of the Industrial and Commercial Tax System Must Be Geared to the Four Modernizations," *Jingji Guanli* (Economic Management; hereafter *JJGL*), 1980, no. 3 (March), in *JPRS*, no. 75978, July 2, 1980, *EA*, no. 67, 34–41; and Liu Zhicheng, "On the Reform of the Industrial and Commercial Tax System of Our Country," *JJGL*, 1980, no. 9 (September), in *JPRS*, no. 77142, Jan. 9, 1981, *EA*, no. 107, 88–95.

[17] Text found in Nee, Chu, and Mosher, *Commercial, Business, Trade Laws*, J110–125.

[18] See Richard Pomp, Timothy A. Gelatt, and Stanley S. Surrey, "The Evolving Tax System of the People's Republic of China," *Texas International Law Review* 16, no. 1 (Winter 1981): 11–78, esp. 32–38.

Enterprises were assessed a tax on gross business receipts or earnings. A twenty-one-category tax ranged from a rate of 5.75 percent assessed on income of less than 300 yuan to a tax of 34.5 percent on income over 10,000 yuan. In addition, local authorities were given the right to impose a surtax of 10–100 percent. Especially profitable enterprises could be charged even higher surtaxes. These surtaxes have been an important source of discretionary funds for the localities.

THE ROLE OF TAXATION IN THE ECONOMY

Taxes as a percentage of government revenue have varied tremendously over the course of PRC history. Unfortunately, figures for tax collection are not available for the years 1960 to 1977. The following discussion reveals what is known about taxation's role in the Chinese economy.

Besides taxes, the other major mechanism of resource extraction has been the remission of enterprise profits to the state treasury. Although data are lacking, taxation apparently was originally the major source of revenue, but began to decline thereafter. Since the death of Mao Zedong, taxes have once again become the principal source of government revenue. In the early post-liberation years, taxes were about 70 percent of all government revenues. Just prior to the Great Leap Forward, this figure had fallen to about 50 percent. In 1959 (a time of great statistical manipulation) available figures show that taxes had fallen to less than 40 percent of government revenue.[19] Since 1978 the role of taxation has grown, with taxes accounting for 62 percent of all revenues in 1982. With the switch over to the system of substituting taxes for the remission of enterprise profits, which began in 1983, the share of taxation as a portion of total revenue is more than 81 percent.[20]

The only recent information giving relatively complete data on the percentage of tax revenue by each type of tax is for 1979.[21] In that year, taxes accounted for half of government income. Of total tax revenue, industrial and commercial taxes accounted for 78.5 percent; industrial and commercial income taxes, 8.3 percent; customs duties, 5.5 percent; agricultural taxes, 5.4 percent; salt tax, 1.8 percent; and other taxes, 0.5 percent. The industrial and commercial tax is by far the most important tax.

Table 5.2 reveals that total tax revenues in 1982 came to 62 percent of all revenue, or 70 billion yuan. Most of this was generated by the ICT. Since this is a turnover tax, the ratio of total taxes to the total value of the gross value of industrial and agricultural output (829.1 billion yuan) and commer-

[19] George Ecklund, *Taxation in Communist China, 1950–1959* (Washington, D.C.: Central Intelligence Agency, CIA/RR ER 61–32, 1961), 10.

[20] Calculated from the figures provided in "'Text' of Finance Minister's Report to the NPC," *FBIS*, June 4, 1984, K1–10; see K1.

[21] Wang Chengyao, "1979 Tax Revenue," in *1980 Yearbook of the Great Encyclopedia of China*, in *JPRS*, no. 78774, Aug. 18, 1981, *EA*, no. 164, 30.

TABLE 5.2   Changing Composition of Revenue Sources
over Time (percentage of total revenue)

	1952	1957	1965	1978	1981	1982
Enterprise revenues	31.2	46.5	55.8	51.0	32.6	—
Industrial profits	11.7	19.1	45.7	39.3	38.6	26.0[a]
Taxes (total)	53.2	49.9	43.2	46.3	59.1	62.0
ICT	33.5	36.5	35.0	40.3	50.6	—
Agriculture	14.7	9.6	5.4	2.5	2.6	—
Debts and borrowing	5.3	2.3	0	0.2	5.7	—

SOURCES: All figures except 1982: *Statistical Yearbook of China 1981*, 404; 1982: Wang Bingqian, "Report on Final Accounts for 1982," *FBIS*, June 24, 1983, K12. The Chinese do not explain these categories. Enterprise revenue likely includes profits, depreciation, and other funds from enterprises, both commercial and industrial. No explanation is offered for why industrial profits in 1981 were larger than total enterprise revenues. This may represent subsidies provided by the government to enterprises.
[a] Profits from all enterprises.

cial sales (262.25 billion yuan) should give a rough idea of the tax burden in China.[22] Apparently all taxes are only 8.4 percent of the total gross industrial and agricultural output and commercial sales, seemingly not a very heavy burden, though analysis of the situation elsewhere is required.

To summarize, the role of taxation in China's economy has fluctuated. However, the ICT and enterprise profits have provided a very large proportion of Chinese revenue since 1965, somewhere between 80 and 90 percent. The share of revenue provided by taxes (particularly the ICT) has been growing, while the share of enterprise profits handed over to the state has declined. With the implementation of a tax to partially replace profit remission, enterprise taxation will be the most important source of government revenue.

THE TAX BUREAUCRACY

The Ministry of Finance supervises tax affairs.[23] The General Taxation Department of the Ministry of Finance is relatively independent and is the unit most concerned with taxation. However, agricultural taxation is handled by the Finance Ministry's Agricultural Tax Office, which lacks the independence of the General Tax Bureau. The agricultural tax is collected by

[22] Figures are from Wang Bingqian, "Report," K12, and "Communique," II, III, and VIII (see n. 8 above).
[23] This section draws on *Guojia Shuishou* (National Taxation) (Beijing: Zhongguo Caizheng Jingji Chubanshe, 1979); Li Cha (Richard Diao), *Zhonggong Shuishou Zhidu* (Taxation System of Communist China) (Hong Kong: Union Research Institute, 1969); Audrey Donnithorne, *China's Economic System* (New York: Praeger, 1967), chaps. 13 and 14; and Pomp et al., "Evolving Tax System."

local units of the Ministries of Commerce and Food when compulsory sales are made. For the ICT and other taxes, the People's Bank of China actually receives tax monies.

Tax bureaus exist at the provincial and county levels. Under each county are a number of tax offices.[24] In 1980–1981 there were 170,000 tax cadres throughout China. In 1982–1983, another 80,000–110,000 personnel were recruited as part of the preparations for substituting taxes for profit.[25] A pilot population census in Wuxi, Jiangsu, on June 30, 1980, revealed that there were 137 tax collectors, 780 personnel engaged in financial business, 3,049 active in statistical work, and 8,582 accountants; this was in a city of 759,000.[26] The number and quality of tax collectors is obviously inadequate. For example, an investigation of 2,215 tax cadres in the forty-seven county tax bureaus in Liaoning province revealed that 1,137 cadres were "unfamiliar" with tax work. The same investigation demonstrated the lack of personnel as well. Beipiao county in Liaoning had eight agricultural tax collection stations under it. This work absorbed all the time of the cadres, and no one was available to collect taxes on market transactions, real estate taxes, and the slaughter tax. There were 200 industrial and commercial enterprises in Beipiao. The amount of work created by these enterprises normally required 20 full-time tax personnel. However, the county had only 6–7 cadres available to work on these enterprises.[27]

Nationally the picture is the same. A review of financial and accounting personnel in 1,200 enterprises produced the following results: 7 percent of the personnel in question had graduated from finance and accounting colleges, 15 percent from middle school; 30 percent had short-term training; and 48 percent had no specialized training in finance and accounting. Moreover, most of the educated personnel were over fifty years old and would be retiring relatively soon.[28] In rural areas there was frequently only one tax collector for several communes, containing tens of thousands of households. To collect as little as a tenth of a yuan, a tax collector had to travel from his office to a household and back several times. Some tax collectors were barely literate.[29]

[24] Li Cha, 69; Wu Xijin, "A Red Flag on the Taxation Front," *CZ*, 1981, no. 5 (May): 11, 16; and Li Weihua, "No Procedures, No People to Collect Taxes," *Zhongguo Caimao Bao* (China Finance and Trade Newspaper, hereafter *ZGCMB*), Apr. 11, 1981, 1.

[25] Liu Zhicheng, "1980 Taxation Work," in *1981 Zhongguo Jingji Nianjian* (1981 Economic Yearbook of China) (Beijing: Jingji Guanli Zazhi Chubanshe, 1981), IV, 157. On recent recruitment, see Xinhua News Agency, English Language Service, dispatch no. 031633, dated March 16, 1983, entitled "80,000 Tax Workers to Help Institute New Taxation System."

[26] *Statistical Yearbook 1981*, 103 and 95 (n. 8 above).

[27] Li Weihua, "No Procedures."

[28] Lu Peijian, "Vigorously Raise the Professional Level of Financial and Accounting Personnel," *Caiwu yu Kuaiji* (Financial Affairs and Accounting, hereafter *CWYKJ*), 1979, no. 2, in *JPRS*, no. 74161, Sept. 17, 1979, *EA*, no. 13, 1–5.

[29] Li Jiangjing, "Difficulties in the Work of Us Rural Tax Collectors," *CZ*, 1981, no. 10 (October), in *JPRS*, no. 79556, December 1, 1981, *EA*, no. 186, 12–13.

During the decade of the Cultural Revolution, tax departments had been reduced in size, and the number of tax offices had been cut. After the Third Plenum in 1978 tax departments were restored to their 1965 size, but the shortage of tax personnel was a "conspicuous problem." For instance, in 1981–1982 it was discovered that 40,000 units had not paid their taxes in a "long time." In some places, rural fair taxes, commune and brigade enterprise ICT, and so forth, were not collected. The number of tax cadres was insufficient to meet the demands of tax reform, policy studies, foreign tax work, and collecting taxes. Only one-third of all tax cadres were considered to be qualified, and many of the qualified were elderly. Problems were most acute at the basic or field level. In response, the State Council authorized an increase in the number of tax personnel.[30]

Given that one of the hallmarks of CCP rule in China is the extension of control systems in all basic social organizations, the apparent deliberate weakening of the tax system seems out of place. However, the radicalism of the Cultural Revolution, with its attack on "staff" functions, its antipathy to rules and regulations that were perceived as impeding mass mobilization and the realization of the "creative energy of the masses," partially explain the decline of the tax bureaucracy. Factory managers and their superiors in the production ministries may have tacitly approved the weakening of the tax organizations; it removed one more source of external control, since financial officials were denied the right to be stationed within enterprises. Moreover, given that people who engaged in the finance and trade system in China were looked on as the most conservative of officials even before the Cultural Revolution, it was unlikely that anyone stood up for the interests of this system and its tax departments during the Cultural Revolution. Finally, during the decade of the Cultural Revolution, taxes were still collected without too much difficulty, and resources were mobilized for state purposes. The tax system still produced revenue, and budgets were roughly in balance. There was no pressing need to change the situation as long as demands to increase investment and consumption were limited. After 1976 both investment and consumption did increase, forcing the state to be more concerned about the operation of the tax bureaucracy, as the state faced massive budget shortfalls.

The supervisory process was defective—there was virtually no auditing. Until 1979 there had never been an auditing body in Shanghai.[31] Only in 1982 did the new constitution of the PRC formally establish an auditing organ.[32]

---

[30] Commentator, "Reinforce and Develop Well a Contingent of Tax Revenue Cadres," *Renmin Ribao* (People's Daily, hereafter *RMRB*), July 14, 1982, in *FBIS*, July 29, 1982, K13–14.

[31] "Shanghai Municipal Financial Organization Established Auditing Agency," *Jiefang Ribao* (Liberation Daily), in *JPRS*, no. 73955, Aug. 3, 1979, *EA*, no. 5, 97–98.

[32] On auditing bodies, see Yao Meiyan, "Proposal for the Establishment of Auditing Organs," *CWYKJ*, 1981, no. 9 (September), *JPRS*, no. 79762, December 30, 1981, *EA*, no. 193, 14–17; "Further on Establishing State Auditing Organs," *FBIS*, May 11, 1982, K16–17; and *Constitution of the People's Republic of China*, Article 91, in *Beijing Review*, 1982, no. 52 (Dec. 27): 24.

Yet staffing of this body started only in mid-1983, and reports of its activities have been scarce. Moreover, financial supervisory systems, both within enterprises and from above, are extremely weak. Cultural Revolution policies severely weakened financial and accounting mechanisms within enterprises.[33] Regarding vertical supervision, there were only 3,500 financial supervisory cadres in all of China in August 1981—a 100 percent increase from 1979.[34] Only in 1982 did the State Council reauthorize the stationing of Ministry of Finance personnel in enterprises, a practice only started in 1962 and suspended by the Cultural Revolution.[35] The PRC launched its first ever national inspection and verification of financial revenues and expenditures in 1979, thirty years after the CCP came to power.[36]

Finally, in assessing implementation problems, the complexity of the tasks facing tax cadres should also be considered. China's taxpayers of various sorts exceed 2 million in number.[37] These units are subject to different types of taxes, to various tax categories, and to multiple tax rates. Tax liabilities range from trivial amounts to tens of millions of yuan. In short, even with a larger, more competent corps of tax officials and a more institutionalized supervision and auditing system, China's tax collectors face an arduous task.

In sum, the tax administration system is weak and cadres are insufficient in number and quality to meet their assigned responsibilities. Paradoxically, however, I have already shown that China is much better at extracting resources than are other poor countries. In the next section, we will move from considerations of the general attributes of the taxation system in China to specific cases of policy implementation.

IMPLEMENTING CHINESE TAX POLICIES

Two areas of tax policy and administration will be considered: one is the most significant change in Chinese tax policy since 1949, the institution of the "substituting taxes for profit," or *li gai shui* (LGS) reform. This case permits me to examine the interests of different actors in implementing Chinese tax policy, to study the experience in moving from pilot projects to

[33] Andrew Walder, "Some Ironies of the Maoist Legacy in Industry," in *The Transition to Socialism in China*, ed. Mark Selden and Victor Lippit (Armonk: M. E. Sharpe, Inc, 1982), 215–37, esp. 228–34.

[34] "Uphold Financial and Economic Discipline, Check Unhealthy Tendencies," *ZGCMB*, August 1, 1981, in *JPRS*, no. 78978, Sept. 15, 1981, *EA*, no. 172, 28–29.

[35] "Circular of the State Council on Approving and Circulating the Report of the Ministry of Finance and Restoring the System of Stationing Financial Personnel in State Owned Industrial Enterprises," in *Zhonghua Renmin Gongheguo Guowuyuan Gongbao* (Gazette of the State Council of the People's Republic of China, hereafter *Gongbao*), 1982, no. 10 (July 10): 456.

[36] "State Council on Improving Financial Management," *FBIS*, July 28, 1980, L8–9.

[37] Liu Zhicheng, "Strengthen the Management and Develop the Role of Taxation," *Caimao Jingji* (Finance and Trade Economics), 1982, no. 1, in *JPRS*, no. 80512, Apr. 7, 1982, *EA* no. 218, 85–92.

nationwide implementation in China, and to understand how the policy-making process can hinder implementation. The second case is at once less dramatic than the case of substituting taxes for profits, and perhaps more typical of policy implementation in China in general. This case will concentrate on the collection of existing taxes in the post-Mao period. I will show that, paradoxically, tax quotas have been continuously exceeded since the late 1970s, while tax evasion has been epidemic at the same time. The state has responded rather predictably, launching campaigns against this criminal behavior.

Chinese industrial taxation reforms, of which substituting taxes for profit (hereafter referred to as LGS) was the most important, grew out of the perceived problems of the industrial and commercial tax (ICT) and the system whereby enterprises handed all their profits over to the state. The ICT (turnover tax) was the only levy paid by state-owned industrial enterprises, as was explained above.

There were many problems with the ICT;[38] foremost among them was that it provided no incentives for enterprise efficiency. The ICT, coupled with administratively determined prices, assured that there was no linkage between enterprise profits and management practices. Under the ICT, differing factor endowments, rates of raw-material utilization, and rates of fixed and floating capital utilization did not affect tax liability. Sometimes low taxes on irrationally high-priced products led to high enterprise profits (e.g., petrochemicals). Conversely, tax and price factors made it very difficult for state-run coal mines to turn a profit, no matter how well managed.

The ICT also encouraged enterprise autarky. If several enterprises cooperated to produce parts for a final product, each enterprise was assessed the ICT on each part. This raised the price of the finished good. However, if one factory built the entire item by itself, it was subject to only one tax. This further degraded efficiency and discouraged cooperation and specialization.

The system where state-owned enterprises handed over all their profits to the state was also rife with disadvantages. Since enterprises received no reward for efficient operation, there was little reason to maximize profits. By providing enterprises with all the fixed and working capital they needed in exchange for all profits, managerial concern with efficiency was further undermined, and factories hoarded scarce resources and capital goods as a hedge against the rigidities of the central investment and supply systems, and

---

[38] Problems with the ICT are discussed in Wang Chengyao, "Give Full Play to the Role of Taxation as an Economic Lever," *RMRB*, Nov. 7, 1980, in *FBIS*, Nov. 26, 1980, L14–17; Yi Hongren, "Bring Taxation into Play as an Economic Lever," *JJGL*, 1979, no. 9, in *JPRS*, no. 74921, Jan. 14, 1980, *EA*, no. 36, 21–26; and Luo Jingfen, "The Reform of the Tax Price and Taxation System Is an Important Link in the Reform of the Economic System," *JJGL*, 1980, no. 9, in *JPRS*, no. 76987, Dec. 20, 1980, *EA*, no. 103. Many more articles, making the same points, could be cited here.

in order to assure the capacity to meet the state quotas. Because there was no price for capital, it was squandered. There were no sanctions against losing enterprises.

To overcome these ill effects, Chinese economists and officials proposed replacing or supplementing the ICT and profit-remission system with numerous other taxes, including a value added tax, a tax on fixed assets and floating capital, a land use tax, a resources tax, and a regulating tax (on excess profits resulting from artificially high sales prices).[39] With respect to the profit-remission system, the Chinese have tried both a profit-retention system and substituting taxes for profit remission. We will now consider the specifics of the LGS reform, which was supposed to address many if not all of these problems.

SUBSTITUTING TAXES FOR PROFITS

The Context

The LGS was launched nation wide because of perceived failings in two previous reforms launched by the Center to improve enterprise efficiency. These were the use of a profit-retention system in industrial enterprises and the system of contracting profit-delivery quotas. The profit-retention system had been initiated in late 1978; by 1983, 80 percent of all state-owned enterprises were under this system. Enterprises were allowed to retain a certain percentage of their profits, usually after they had fulfilled a certain quota of profit handed over. By the end of 1982, enterprises had retained more than 42 billion yuan of profit (a sum almost exactly the same as the total budget deficit for these years). Although this had some beneficial effects on enterprise management, there also were significant problems. Funds retained by enterprises increased faster than did overall profits or profits handed over to the state. It was difficult to set profit-retention rates because of differences between trades and enterprises. Enterprises negotiated long and hard for the best possible retention rates. Because the rates were to be fixed for several years, this system was unresponsive to changing economic conditions. Thus, the profit-retention system led to a decline in state revenues, enterprises were still not responsible for their losses, and fixed assets still came from the state.[40] Finally, the availability of these retained profits at the enterprise level

[39] Many of these proposals are discussed in Renmin Daxue (People's University), compiler, *Caizheng Jinrong* (Finance and Banking; this source is a clipping service on materials originally in specialized journals), in various issues.

[40] Some of the beneficial aspects of industrial reform, including profit retention, are discussed in William Byrd, "Enterprise Level Reforms in Chinese State Owned Industry," *American Economic Review* 73, no. 2 (May 1983): 329–32. Some of the problems are mentioned in Tian Jiyun, "State Run Enterprises' Switch from Profits Delivery System to Taxation Is a Major Reform in the Economic Management System," *Hongqi* (Red Flag), 1983, no. 7 (April 1), in *JPRS*, no.

helped fuel the problems of excess capital construction and bonus expenditures.[41]

The system of contracting profit-delivery quotas received a great deal of attention in 1982 and was based on experiments at Beijing's Shoudu Iron and Steel Company. Under this scheme, enterprises guaranteed that they would provide financial authorities with a profit target that had been mutually agreed upon. Any extra profit would be retained by the enterprise for its own use. While the system worked well at Shoudu, elsewhere remissions to the state were too low and enterprises had too large a share of the profits. It was extremely difficult to arrive at an equitable figure.[42] These problems were the impetus for the LGS reform.

Perhaps more important than the specific failings of these two reform efforts was a general change in the viewpoint of top Chinese leaders. In late 1978 and early 1979, when the profit-retention system was widely popularized, Chinese leaders concentrated on reforming the economy. Almost anything was considered if it served the vaguely defined rubric of reform. These policies served to enliven the economy and changed the way enterprise managers behaved—at the cost of the largest budget deficit in the PRC's history in 1979 and another very large deficit in 1980. In response, Chinese leaders emphasized restoring financial balance. They did not totally abandon reform policies, but they became more aware of their costs.[43] Given the massive investment requirements of the Sixth Five-Year Plan (1981–1985), these revenue short-falls could not be tolerated (see chapter 3). At the same time, the inflationary effects of the reforms and the deficits were a cause for concern (see chapter 4). Either the goals for the plan would have to be scaled back, to

83736, June 22, 1983, translations from *Red Flag*, 40–49; and Wang Bingqian, "We Must Properly Carry out the Work of Substituting Tax Payment for Profit Delivery," *CZ*, 1983, no. 5, in *JPRS*, no. 84356, Sept. 19, 1983, *EA*, no. 383, 54–60. Many other articles made the same points.

[41] See chapter 3 this volume and Andrew G. Walder, "Wage Reform and the Web of Factory Interests" (Paper delivered at the Joint ACLS-SSRC Workshop on Policy Implementation in Post-Mao China, Columbus, Ohio, June 1983).

[42] On the system at Shoudu, see Li Haibo, "Shoudu Steel—A Success Story," *Beijing Review*, 1983, no. 16 (Apr. 11): 19–25. On difficulties of arriving at a reasonable contract figure, see Liu Zhicheng, "Problems Concerning the Substitution of Tax for Profit Delivery of State Owned Enterprises," *Jingji Yanjiu*, 1983, no. 7, in *JPRS*, no. 84404, Sept. 26, 1983, *EA*, no. 387, 36; and Wang Chengbai and Su Linxiang, "Briefly Discuss Profit Contracting and Substituting Taxes for Profits by State Run Enterprises," *Ningxia Ribao* (Ningxia Daily), June 23, 1983, in *JPRS*, no. 84429, Sept. 28, 1983, *EA*, no. 388, 19–20.

[43] On the evolving view of the leadership, see generally, David Bachman, "Differing Visions of China's Post-Mao Economy: The Ideas of Chen Yun, Deng Xiaoping, and Zhao Ziyang," *Asian Survey* 26, no. 3 (March 1986); Dorothy J. Solinger, "The Fifth National People's Congress and the Process of Policy Making: Reform, Readjustment, and the Opposition," *Asian Survey* 22, no. 12 (December 1982): 1238–75; and Barry Naughton, "The Profit System," *China Business Review* 10, no. 6 (November–December 1983): 14–18.

avoid even greater deficit financing (with the concomitant danger of inflation), or central revenues would have to be increased. The fact that retained
profits or contracted profits had grown rapidly, without a significant increase
in productivity and economic efficiency, did not go unnoticed. Chinese leaders were seeking to develop a tax system that would both increase state
revenues and stimulate factory managers to improve economic efficiency. In
1983, LGS was put forward as the policy that could successfully achieve
these goals.

Policy Content

Under LGS as it was formalized in 1983, 55 percent of the profits of large
and medium-sized state-owned industrial enterprises were to be collected as
a tax. The remaining profit was shared between the state and the enterprise
by one of four methods: a progressive profit-sharing rate, a fixed rate, a regulating tax on anticipated profits, and a fixed delivery quota (only mining
enterprises were allowed to use this last method). Once the rates were set,
they were to remain unchanged for three years. The enterprises' share of the
profit was to be distributed among five funds: a new-product development
fund; a production development fund; a reserve fund; a workers' welfare
fund; and a workers' award fund. The sum of the first three funds was to be
at least 60 percent of retained profits. Small state enterprises were to pay
taxes on their profits according to an eight-grade progressive scale, and they
were to receive no more funds from the state—they were responsible for their
own profits and losses.[44]

Commentaries on the LGS reform noted many advantages to this policy.
It would increase state revenue and simultaneously promote economic
efficiency in enterprises. By making enterprises solely responsible for their
profits and losses, it would make factories self-financing. In addition, it
would sever the bonds between enterprises and local governments. Local governments would no longer receive the profits from locally owned enterprises.
Instead, the Center and the localities would each receive different categories
of taxes. It was made clear that the Center would control those taxes which
were to yield the most revenue while the localities would only gain control
over minor levies, such as the real estate tax.[45] In short, LGS was part of
a recentralization of fiscal power initiated by a Center that feared for its
revenues, was wary of local power, and was disappointed that economic
efficiency had failed to respond to the earlier initiatives.

The 1983 regulations on the LGS were much more conservative than were
various LGS experimental measures that preceded nationwide implementa-

---

[44] See "Trial Procedures for State Enterprises' Taxation," *FBIS*, May 5, 1983, K4–8.

[45] This is extensively discussed in Tian Jiyun, 43–44 (n. 40 above), and many other articles
on LGS.

tion. How and why the experiences of the test points were rejected in favor of the 1983 policy is unknown, although I will suggest some reasons for this after we consider the experience of these earlier tests. It is important to keep in mind a theme that runs throughout this volume—one hallmark of the post-Mao era has been how rapidly implementors have identified problems and modified behavior to ameliorate them. Under Mao, the "feedback circuits" in the implementation mechanism were frequently blocked.

Experiments with LGS started in 1979, although production units under the General Rear Services Department of the People's Liberation Army switched from handing over profits to paying the Industrial and Commercial Income Tax (the only state-owned plants to do so) in early 1976.[46] By late 1980 more than 400 plants were engaged in these reforms, which were exempted from the cutbacks brought about by economic readjustment.[47] However, by late 1982 there were still only about the same number of plants engaged in this reform.[48] Certainly, there was no upsurge in the number of units trying out LGS on the eve of its becoming national policy.

There were five major areas where LGS was tested. These were among commercial units in Sichuan; by units under the Shanghai Light Industrial Machine Corporation; in Liuzhou municipality, Guangxi province; in Guanghua county, Hebei province; and in scattered units nation wide under the aegis of the Ministry of Finance.[49]

Most of these experiments not only included LGS (or an income tax) but were a comprehensive reform of the ways that enterprises paid funds to the state and financed their internal operations. Most fundamentally, enterprises were to be self-financing after these reforms were instituted. Thus, the system that the Ministry of Finance tried out in various places throughout China called for enterprises to carry out an LGS system that saw enterprises paying three different taxes and two fees (a resource tax, an income-regulating tax,

---

[46] "Circular of the Ministry of Finance of the People's Republic of China and the General Rear Services Department of the People's Liberation Army on Industrial Factories Run by the Military Switching from Handing over Profits to Paying Industrial and Commercial Income Taxes," in *Caizheng Jinrong Guizhang Zhidu Xuanbian, 1976* (Selected Collection of Rules, Regulations, and Systems of Finance and Banking for 1976) (Beijing: Caizheng Jingji Chubanshe, 1978), 156.

[47] Zhao Ziyang, "Guanyu Tiaozheng Guomin Jingjide Jige Wenti" (Several Problems in Readjusting the National Economy), in *San Zhong Quanhui Yilai Zhongyao Wenxian Xuanbian* (Selected Important Documents since the Third Plenum) (Changchun: Renmin Chubanshe, 1982), 618.

[48] Zhao Ziyang, "Report on the Sixth Five Year Plan," in *Fifth Session of the Fifth National People's Congress* (Beijing: Foreign Languages Press, 1983), 173–74.

[49] Information in the following paragraphs comes from the following sources: Sichuan Provincial Finance Department, "Benefits and Problems from Trial 'Substitution of Payment of Taxes for Profits,'" *Shangye Kuaiji* (Commercial Accounting), 1981, no. 9, in *JPRS*, no. 7982, *EA*, no. 196, Jan. 12, 1982, 49–56; "The Shanghai Municipal Light Industrial Machinery Corporation

an income tax, and fees on fixed and floating capital). In Sichuan, three taxes were levied: the industrial and commercial tax, a fixed-assets tax, and an income tax. In Shanghai, a "five tax, two fee" system was tried out (industrial and commercial tax, income-regulating tax, land use tax, licensing tax, income tax, and fees on fixed and floating capital). In the Liuzhou experiments, administered by the Ministry of Finance, value added taxes, materials taxes, an income-regulating tax, an income tax, and fees on capital were assessed. Tax rates also varied among experimental areas.

In all the experiments, enterprise profits and efficiency increased, as did state income, after these new forms were tried out. In most of the test-point enterprises, the system of assuming full responsibility for profits and losses was in effect (the exception was Sichuan). It is impossible to assess whether a Chinese trial point is an average unit chosen to truly try out a new policy or whether it is an advanced unit or model used to demonstrate the superiority of a policy proposed by particular state leaders. In any event, in the course of implementation, problems surfaced, and these were addressed most frankly in the experiments in Sichuan.

First was the difficulty of fixing proper tax rates, and this was a problem in all the test areas. In Sichuan, many rates were so high that many enterprises had no after-tax profits. Another problem in Sichuan was that there was no regulating tax. There were great disparities in enterprise profits because of the price system, the sizes of the enterprises, and the line of business in which each firm was engaged. Enterprise per capita profit retention ranged from a high of 1,200 yuan to a low of 84 yuan. Even greatly improved management by firms at the lower end of this spectrum could not bridge this gap, and those enterprises at the higher end had little incentive to continue to improve.

A third problem concerned the relationship between the enterprise and local government. Under the previous system of commercial management in Sichuan, county authorities collected and paid taxes and handed in profits for commercial units under their control, keeping a share of the profit for themselves. Under LGS, enterprises paid taxes directly to the treasury. Although county authorities might still receive some funds through the sys-

Tries out Substituting Taxes for Profits, which in a Preliminary Way, Demonstrates Superiority," *1981 Gongye Jingying Guanli Jingyan Xuanbian* (Selected Edition of Industrial Enterprise Management Experiences in 1981) (Beijing: Renmin Chubanshe, 1981), 205–10; *Caizheng Jinrong*, 1981, no. 4, 31–34; Niu Licheng and Tu Zhizhong, "On Investigation of Guanghua County's Small State-Owned Enterprises Paying Income Tax and Being Responsible for Their Own Profits and Losses," *CZ*, 1981, no. 11, 16–18; and "Ministry Issues Circular on Tax on State Revenues," *FBIS*, Nov. 12, 1980, L1–2. General analyses of the LGS experiments or discussions of the differences between experiments are found in *Caizheng Jinrong*, 1981, no. 3:37–44, and no. 6: 7–20, and Wang Wending and Han Shaochu, "On Levying Income Taxes on State Enterprises," *JJGL*, 1981, no. 5, in *JPRS*, no. 78511, *EA*, no. 150, July 15, 1981, 24–29.

tem of revenue sharing by Center and province, the link between the enterprise and the county bureau was broken. Because county authorities no longer received funds from the test points, they discriminated against them in the allocation of goods, and may have demanded kickbacks in exchange for supplying the trial enterprises with the desired commodities.[50]

Thus, the various forms of the LGS as tried out in the period 1980–1982 did provide more revenue to the state, and enterprise economic performance was improved. However, there were several serious problems. These concerned the setting of tax rates, the effect of different factor endowments and the price system on enterprise earnings, and questions of the relationship between the enterprise and the locality. Nonetheless, at the Fifth Session of the Fifth National People's Congress in December 1982, Premier Zhao Ziyang called for expansion of LGS, noting that the experiments with LGS had yielded "fairly satisfactory" results.

> Therefore, this reform should be affirmed as a positive measure. Such reform should, however, be carried out step by step on the merits of each case. There should be two steps for big and medium state enterprises. The first step to be started in the period of the Sixth Five Year Plan, provides for both taxation and profit sharing, that is to say, a certain proportion of an enterprise's profit is paid to the state as income tax and local tax, while the remainder is divided appropriately and in different forms between the state and the enterprise. The second step provides for the collection, when the price system has in the main become appropriate, of a progressive income tax in accordance with the amount of profit.[51]

Despite Zhao's cautious endorsement of this policy and calls to go slow, by April 1983 almost all state-owned enterprises in China were to switch from paying taxes to the LGS system, effective June 1, with taxes calculated from January 1, 1983.[52]

It is important to note that the LGS system that was instituted in 1983 was much less comprehensive, and marked much less of a fundamental change than had the experiments just described—it was more cautious. Under the 1983 measures, the profit-retention system would not disappear entirely. The other taxes associated with the LGS test units were not mentioned in the 1983 regulations. Large and medium-sized enterprises were not responsible for their profits and losses. The 1983 version of LGS was to be merely the first step in a thorough change in relations between state and enterprise. In fact, LGS in 1983 was more an extension of the previous profit-retention system than it was a new policy initiative.

Many of the criticisms of the profit-retention and contract system apply

[50] See especially Sichuan Provincial Finance Department, "Benefits and Problems."
[51] See Zhao Ziyang, "Report," 173–174.
[52] See note 44 above.

also to the 1983 LGS reform. It was made clear that under LGS the revenues retained by enterprises would be about the same as under profit retention.[53] Consequently, LGS was unlikely to stimulate new enterprise initiatives, nor was it likely that the enterprises could afford to take on any new responsibilities under LGS—they would have no more resources at their disposal. State revenue was also unlikely to increase dramatically. Moreover, bargaining over most profit-retention rates (after the 55 percent profit tax was collected) remained. If the rates are to be set for three years under LGS, how did this make LGS any more adaptable to changing economic conditions than was the case under profit retention? Large and medium-sized state-owned enterprises were still not fully responsible for their profits and losses.

One final potential problem with LGS is that once it becomes institutionalized, it is likely to deter meaningful price reform. After LGS has gone into effect, enterprise profits, based on irrational prices, will account for at least 75 percent and perhaps as much as 90 percent of all government revenue in China. Could the Chinese government afford to overhaul its price system when so much of its revenue was based on this irrational system? Past experience leads me to be less than optimistic about the Chinese government's ability to correctly anticipate the revenue effects of the price changes. For example, the leadership seems to have misjudged the effects that the change in agricultural procurement prices would have in 1979. These miscalculations contributed to the record budget deficit in that year. LGS may, then, inhibit real reform or, if prices are changed, cause tremendous budgetary problems. Recently, at the Third Plenum of the Twelfth Party Congress, the Party held that price reform was vital to the reform of the economy; but the actual process of changing prices has yet to get under way, and it remains to be seen how meaningful price reform will be.[54]

But there remain three respects in which LGS is a major departure, promising the possibility of major change in the economic system. First, small state-owned enterprises are now fully responsible for their profits and losses, and have totally switched to paying taxes instead of handing over their profits. Even without price reform, these enterprises are now much more independent of the state than they were heretofore. The other two major aspects of change brought about by LGS concern enterprise relations with localities' revenue flows. Statements about LGS suggest that the new system will significantly change industrial and financial administration in these two areas. I will shortly discuss these two areas, but first we will consider why the test-point experience and the 1983 regulations were so different.

[53] See, for example, "Beijing Tax Experiment Shows Economic Results," *China Daily*, Jan. 27, 1983, in *JPRS*, no. 82858, Feb. 15, 1983, *EA*, no. 311, 8; "Financial Official Interviewed on New Tax System," *FBIS*, May 3, 1983, K7–14; and Wang Bingqian, n. 40 above.

[54] See "Decision of the Central Committee of the Communist Party of China on the Reform of the Economic Structure," *Beijing Review*, 1984, no. 44 (Oct. 29): I–XVI.

The phenomenon of one type of pilot-project reforms being replaced by another policy when attempts are made to extend the reforms to the entire country is not unusual.[55] Pilot projects are often nurtured in something of a hothouse environment. But such an environment cannot be replicated when the reform is implemented nation wide. It might be argued that the LGS test points were relatively successful because the leadership allowed them to be successful. They "provided a protective environment and supported it against the inroads of the established bureaucracy."[56] When extending the pilot project leaders ask themselves, not what is the optimal way of carrying out LGS, but what is the most politically and bureaucratically feasible way. This often results in a trade-off between quantity and quality.[57]

Chinese leaders continued to face the growing problems with the profit-retention and contract system and the Center's weak control over resources, with the consequences already enumerated. It thus became a question of doing something that appeared to satisfy the existing problem rather than developing an optimal solution. (The same grasping at easily available remedies appears in chapter 8.) Because the complex LGS experiments required many more resources to implement, central leaders deferred extending these reforms. Rather, they agreed on a simplified LGS policy that did not require significant amounts of personnel retraining. Moreover, as put into practice, the 1983 LGS regulations had only a limited impact on participants who might have mixed feelings about the reform—fewer interests were offended. Thus, Chinese leaders were under pressure to do something quickly that would stop and, it was hoped, reverse the Center's loss of revenue. They could not wait for the ideal LGS system to be spread gradually.

Implementation of LGS and Affected Interests

By late March 1984 there had been no article in the Chinese press describing how much more money had been turned into the state treasury because of the LGS system. Reports did note that state tax and profit quotas had been overfulfilled, but the increases over the previous year and the degree of target overfulfillment were not extraordinary. Therefore, LGS thus far has not marked a significant change in the Chinese fiscal system. At best, it is only a partial reform; at worst, it marks no real change at all. I will argue that this result stems from weaknesses in the Chinese policy-making process, the way implementation responsibility was assigned, and most especially from the divergent interests of implementors.

With respect to the policy process, three things are important: First, as often happens in Chinese politics, the leadership oversold the benefits of

---

[55] Gerald E. Sussman, "The Pilot Project and the Choice of an Implementing Strategy: Community Development in India," in Merilee S. Grindle, ed., *Politics and Policy Implementation in the Third World* (Princeton: Princeton University Press, 1980), 103–22.

[56] Sussman, 115.

[57] This paraphrases Sussman, 115.

LGS. As is shown in chapter 13, the Chinese state retains great power when it launches implementation campaigns. Nonetheless, the Center must create both a consensus on the utility of such a policy and a sense of urgency that only this policy will deal with critical problems. Predictably, leaders overstate the importance and benefits of the new policy, arguing that it is a bigger break with the past than it often is. In a sense, then, the failure of LGS is a reflection of the undue expectations aroused by the propaganda that accompanied the launching of this reform.[58]

Second, in an effort to win approval for LGS, central leaders apparently compromised on contentious issues. The Center made two fateful agreements that have checked the more revolutionary implications of LGS, at least so far. Beijing stated that enterprises would retain about the same amount of money under LGS as they had retained under profit retention.[59] It also announced that there would be no change in the distribution of central-local finances.[60] In other words, to overcome the (potential) resistance of key local interests (factory managers and local officials), the Center agreed that the redistributive dimensions of LGS would be minimal.

Finally, other reforms were occurring simultaneously, and many of these either complicated the implementation of LGS or directly undermined some of the goals associated with it. In particular, reforms were under way to strengthen the role of the county in economic decision making, and central policy continued to encourage the formation of industrial corporations and other forms of combination. The former effort weakened enterprise independence and autonomy and stipulated that counties should receive a share of enterprise-retained profits. County officials were not eager to implement an LGS reform that would have reduced their revenues. Enterprises might be less responsive to profit-making opportunities if they know that the county is going to take a significant share of their earnings.[61] The latter reform made it difficult to determine how profits should be distributed within new corporations. Should all profits go to the corporation as a single entity? a specific branch? the company that earned the profit? Or should some go to the corporate headquarters and some to particular plants? If so, what percentage should go to each?[62]

In addition to weaknesses in the policy-making process which contributed

---

[58] On this aspect of Chinese policy making, see Gordon Bennett, *Yundong: Mass Campaigns in Chinese Communist Leadership* (Berkeley: Center for Chinese Studies Research Monograph No. 12, 1976); Charles P. Cell, *Revolution at Work* (New York: Academic Press, 1977); and Lucian Pye, *The Dynamics of Chinese Politics* (Cambridge: Oelgeschlager, Gunn and Hain, 1981).

[59] See note 53 above.

[60] See "Financial Official," K12 (n. 53 above).

[61] Y. Y. Kueh, "Economic Reform at the 'Xian' Level," *China Quarterly*, no. 96 (December 1983), 665–88.

[62] "Put Pressures on Enterprises and Vitalize Them," *RMRB*, March 19, 1983, 2, in *JPRS*, no. 83527, May 23, 1983, *EA*, no. 343, 19–25, and Thomas H. Pyle, "Reforming Chinese Management," *China Business Review* 8, no. 3 (May–June 1981): 7–19, esp. 18–19.

to the failure of LGS, the structure of responsibilities in implementing this reform also limited its effectiveness. As was noted previously, the Finance Ministry's General Tax Office was responsible for overseeing taxation. However, jurisdiction of the LGS policy was placed under the control of the Industrial and Communications Finance Department of the Ministry of Finance (presumably because LGS replaced profit remissions, which had been the previous task of this office).[63] But while this bureau, and the Ministry of Finance generally, is responsible for financial affairs, enterprises are responsible for actually paying taxes. The weaknesses of intra-enterprise financial staffing and procedures was discussed above. Only recently has the Ministry of Finance recovered the right to assign its own personnel to enterprises, and only since late 1983 has a state auditing body been established.

Moreover, factory managers have few incentives to devote any great attention to tax matters as long as the enterprise is not responsible for its own profits and losses. If the manager can still obtain capital from the state at no cost, there are few incentives for him to increase efficiency. As it is now, handing over taxes is just one of many tasks facing managers, and it is not one of their top priorities. As long as the manager does not grossly violate tax regulations, his performance of this duty will have no effect on his chances for advancement. Additionally, the fact that LGS funnels money through the Ministry of Finance provides a disincentive for factory managers. Under the profit-retention system, money was channeled through the industrial ministries that directly supervised the work of the enterprise. This redirecting of financial flows may tend to weaken the political and economic support that the ministries provided their subordinate production units. Indeed, this re-direction of financial flows is one of the most important reasons for the LGS system, but one that is seldom discussed, for obvious political reasons.

This last point brings up the interests of those who might be negatively affected by the LGS reform. What are the specific conflicts of interest that lead managers and local officials to oppose LGS in its more ambitious form? Unfortunately, there have been surprisingly few studies of factory managers in China, and certainly none that match the pathbreaking work on managers in the Soviet Union.[64] However, because of the many similarities between the Soviet economy and the Chinese economy, it seems safe to assume (until studies prove otherwise) that Chinese managers behave much like their Soviet counterparts. The most important target for managers is that of gross value of output, a tendency which the Chinese have themselves noted. All other targets, with the possible exception of enterprise profit quotas, pale in

---

[63] See Xinhua dispatch (n. 25 above).

[64] See in particular, Joseph Berliner, *Factory and Manager in the U.S.S.R.* (Cambridge: Harvard University Press, 1957). Of use on China are the writings of Andrew Walder. See his "Rice Bowl Reforms," *China Business Review* 10, no. 6 (November–December 1983): 18–21.

significance to the gross output targets. Managers will frequently violate the law to meet this target—they hoard resources of all kinds to meet quotas. Slack in the system is the key guarantee for managers if they are to fulfill their output target consistently. They will appeal to the ministry that supervises their factory for aid and will call on the ministry to provide the necessary clout to see that key raw materials are received. Managers are evaluated by the ministry on the basis of their ability to surpass the gross-output target. The ministry is engaged in production, not in finance, and cares little about tax payments. Its claim for more resources in state budgetary decision making is based on how well it fulfills its production targets. Criteria of success, even of rationality, in the Chinese (or Soviet) system is task oriented.[65]

Any effort to move away from the gross value of output target or attempts to increase economic efficiency are threats to the manager and the well-entrenched coping mechanisms that have evolved since the groundwork of the Chinese planned economy was laid. LGS potentially threatens the manager's world in several ways: First, if the state tries to use LGS to extract more resources, it reduces the manager's slack. LGS also means that financial targets will become more important than they were before, and central reformers argue that enterprise financial targets should be as important (if not more so) than gross value of output.[66] From the manager's perspective, LGS must be resisted. And scattered media accounts suggest that this is exactly what happened,[67] at least before the Center promised that with LGS enterprises would end up with about the same amount of money as they did under profit retention.

Turning to the consideration of the interests of local officials,[68] for which there is also a paucity of information, since 1970 and particularly since about 1978 there has been a tremendous decentralization of authority and re-

---

[65] T. H. Rigby, "A Conceptual Approach to Authority, Power and Policy in the Soviet Union," in Rigby et al., eds., *Authority, Power and Policy in the USSR* (New York: St. Martin's Press, 1980), 9–31.

[66] This has long been a complaint of one of China's foremost economists, Sun Yefang. See his *Shehuizhuyi Jingjide Ruogan Lilun Wenti* (Certain Theoretical Problems of Socialist Economics) (Beijing: Renmin Chubanshe, 1979).

[67] See Sichuan Provincial Finance Dept. (n. 49 above); "Put Pressures on Enterprises" (n. 62 above); Hao Zhen, Zuo Linshu, and Wang Zhiliang, "The State Must Get the Bigger Share, but the Enterprises Must Also Receive Benefit," *JJGL*, 1983, no. 5, in *JPRS*, no. 83917, July 18, 1983, *EA*, no. 365, 36–39. And Tian Jiyun quotes managers saying how hard they must work under LGS: see Tian Jiyun, "Some Questions of Understanding Concerning State-run Enterprises Adopting the Practice of 'Replacing Delivery of Profits with Payment of Taxes,'" *RMRB*, Feb. 7, 1983, in *JPRS*, no. 83123, Mar. 23, 1983, *EA*, no. 321, 4–11 (Tian's name is misspelled in *JPRS*). See also Yong Wenyuan, Wei Kefu, and Zhou Kaida, "Responding to Several Questions about the Substitution of Tax Payment for Profit Delivery," *Jiefang Ribao*, June 8, 1983, in *JPRS*, no. 84156, Aug. 19, 1983, *EA*, no. 374, 55–60.

[68] Again the Soviet case is relevant; see Jerry Hough, *The Soviet Prefects* (Cambridge: Harvard University Press, 1969).

sources in the Chinese political system.[69] As chapter 3 details, local authorities responded with an orgy of capital construction. For local governments, as for enterprises, the "iron law of autarky" applies: whenever possible do not depend on anyone else in a planned economy. Locally built and run industry provides revenues and independence, which local leaders greatly value. They also desire a situation in which resources are not tightly controlled and under which they have a great deal of freedom of maneuver. In this way they can build up their localities.

They resist policies that may take resources away from them. They oppose full autonomy being granted to enterprises because this reduces their financial income and diminishes patronage potential. The LGS reform has clearly threatened the financial position of the counties. A responsible official in the Ministry of Finance, in discussing the LGS regulations, noted that they should have no effect on the distribution of central-local finances. But he stated:

> What requires explanation is the fact that in handling the profits of county-run industries and enterprises, the county originally shared its profits or financial liabilities with the state. From now on county-run industries and enterprises must also pay taxes or deliver profits in accordance with the regulations on changing the profit delivery system to the taxation system. Therefore, this practice will adversely affect the original financial benefits to the counties. It has been decided that this issue wll be solved in other ways. . . . Specific measures should be worked out by [the provincial level units] themselves.[70]

At the very least, counties are going to lose revenues from this reform, and it appears that provinces will have to compensate counties for this decline. Whether provincial leaders will go along is not clear.

What is certain is that the Center had to promise that central-local financial relations would remain stable if LGS was to become policy. Given Beijing's motivating concern over budget deficits, these concessions to factories and localities must have been painful. More needs to be learned about the process by which local leaders and factory managers were able to block what was originally held to be a critical objective of the LGS reform: its ability to increase central revenues. On this issue, as so many others, the Chinese political system is fragmented, as chapter 6 argues.

The central leadership is clearly aware that gains under the first stage of

[69] See Christine Wong, "The Local Industrial Sector in Post-Mao Reforms" (mimeograph), October 1983 (copy in author's possession); Naughton, "Economic Reforms" (n. 5 above); David Bachman, "Local Interests and Problems of Reform in Post-Mao China" (mimeograph), November 1981; and "More Consciously Carry out the Line of the Third Plenary Session of the Eleventh Central Committee," *RMRB*, Feb. 16, 1981, in *FBIS*, Feb. 18, 1981, L3.
[70] See n. 44 above.

LGS have been less than was hoped or expected. Vice-Premier Tian Jiyun, Zhao Ziyang's right-hand man and the leading proponent of LGS, conceded that the first stage of LGS was not significantly different from profit retention. This contradicted both his own earlier statements and numerous articles written in the first half of 1983. Consequently, Tian called for the rapid implementation of the second-stage version of LGS; he stated that this should occur even before the price system is changed. In this manner he may have conceded the point that if the second stage of LGS was dependent on price reform, the second stage might never be reached.[71]

Tian's statement on quickly moving to the second stage can be read in two ways. The first is that the initial stage of LGS has been implemented well, and that the time is ripe to push this reform to fruition. The process of changing prices will be so complicated and time-consuming that it is better to go on with the reform of the tax system than to wait, possibly forever, for price reform. Results may be less than optimal without price reform, but the results of a full-blown LGS system will still be better than not having it. The other interpretation, and the better one in this writer's view, is that LGS has not been particularly successful. Tian's recognition that LGS in its first stage was not much different from profit retention meant that many of the goals the state wanted to achieve through LGS have yet to be achieved. This is particularly true for severing the links between enterprises and the localities and centralizing government revenues. Tian's proposal should be read as an argument for further reform to break through the barriers of existing interests to revamp the industrial-management system and the financial system. Without further and immediate efforts to smash the web of interests that inhibit change, LGS will not produce desired results. However, if LGS in its first stage is not yielding good results because of local and enterprise opposition, it is not clear how further reform measures can be carried out in the face of this opposition. At present, the fate of LGS, as a major reform or as just incremental tinkering, is very much in doubt. Nonetheless, Chinese leaders began to implement the second stage of the LGS reform in late 1984.

COLLECTING OLD TAXES

Evaluating the effectiveness of the tax system in China is a classic case of whether the glass of water is half full or half empty. The Chinese press is replete with stories of widespread tax evasion, of taxes being in arrears, and of other forms of financial indiscipline. Given the above-mentioned quality of Chinese tax cadres, this is hardly suprising. However, for the last three years

---

[71] Huang Changliu and Zhu Minzhi, "An Interview with Tian Jiyun," *Liaowang* (Observation Post), 1983, no. 9, in *FBIS*, Oct. 26, 1983, K10–14.

for which data are available, 1980–1982, the tax departments have overfulfilled the quota for the ICT and the general tax target;[72] whether this simply reflects low tax quotas is an interesting question. Despite problems with the bureaucracy, the system still muddles through. It has been the drop in enterprise profits flowing to the state and the state's expanded expenditures that have caused China's financial difficulties. Tax departments cannot be held responsible for these policy problems. I will now consider the causes of tax evasion in China and the measures adopted in an attempt to cut tax evasions and other financial violations.

The Context

The Chinese leadership has tried to enliven the economy, as was noted in the section on the LGS. One of the key methods for doing this was to decentralize a great deal of power and resources to the lower level and to give localities the right to grant tax deferments or exemptions. Many of the leakages in the revenue system stem from these policies or from ambiguities inherent in them. However, most problems were the result of deliberate violations of financial rules and regulations. The basic reason for tax and financial violations was the activity of Party cadres and local officials. Local leaders have been accused of setting themselves above national laws and regulations and arbitrarily reducing or exempting their units from taxation. Some leaders ordered tax cadres to halt tax collections. In other cases, taxes were levied or reduced through the method of the "secretary's signature" (i.e., local Party secretaries determined the rate of taxation they felt was appropriate for the area they governed). Local authorities did not pay much attention to tax work. Some cadres felt that taxes should be "working capital" or "emergency financial resources" for the localities. Some regarded taxation as the "expropriation of the workers' profit by the state." Enterprise managers used the profit-retention system to avoid taxation. Through accounting dodges, they "squeezed taxes and dug up profits." Leading cadres were charged with not supporting tax cadres and with aiding those who violated the law. Cadres were denounced for featherbedding, falsifying records, exploiting loopholes, cultivating "relations," setting up independent kingdoms and economic blockades, and engaging in bribery and graft. Some leaders felt that taxes stifled economic reforms, limited the ability of local leaders to promote the people's livelihood, and hindered effective decentralization. When tax cadres reported financial or tax violations, local leaders encouraged the masses to blockade tax buildings and seal their gates. There were frequent reports of reprisals and physical assaults on honest tax collectors. When tax cadres

---

[72] For 1980, see "1980 Taxes up," *JPRS*, no. 77571, Mar. 12, 1981, *EA*, no. 119, 12; for 1981, "Industrial and Commercial Tax Revenue up," *JPRS*, no. 79807, Jan. 6, 1982, *EA*, no. 194, 50; and for 1982, "Industrial and Commercial Tax Revenue," *JPRS*, no. 82822, Feb. 8, 1983, *EA*, no. 309, 85.

reported tax and financial violations to the upper levels, it sometimes took higher-level cadres years to respond to the reports of the tax cadres.[73]

How extensive are tax evasions and violations of financial discipline? Although the full extent of tax evasion is unknown (and unknowable), from late 1980 to early 1982 a total of 2.5 billion yuan of financial violations had been recovered by the state; this did not include the 1.3 billion yuan of tax evasions uncovered.[74] By the end of 1982, 3.8 billion yuan of taxes were in arrears, an increase of 11.3 percent over 1981.[75] In Inner Mongolia, "the total amount of money involved in financial violations amounted to one-fourth of the region's annual financial revenue."[76] It was estimated that 40 percent of Shanghai's state-owned and collective enterprises evaded taxes.[77] In Qinghai 57 percent of all enterprises were guilty of tax evasion or fraud.[78] In Liaoning a survey of 2,617 enterprises revealed that 1,311 had evaded tax payments.[79] In ten provinces 47 percent of all enterprises and 63 percent of all supply and marketing co-ops inspected had violated financial discipline. Many small enterprises, it appears, are beyond the reach of the revenue men.

Most of this was attributed to a lack of understanding of the law and to negligence, but fraud and deliberate evasion also were present.[80] Wang Bing-

---

[73] See for example, "Strict Enforcement of Tax Law Urged," *CWYKJ*, 1979, no. 3, in *JPRS*, no. 74003, Aug. 7, 1979, *EA*, no. 7, 9–10; "Anhui Provincial Financial Conference," in *JPRS*, no. 74050, Aug. 21, 1979, *EA*, no. 9, 20; Ning Zhuansheng, "The Need for Strict Adherence to Tax Laws," *Nanfang Ribao* (Southern Daily), June 20, 1980, in *JPRS*, no. 76323, Aug. 28, 1980, *EA*, no. 79, 35–37; "Strengthen the Concept of Taking the Whole Situation into Account and Safeguard Financial and Economic Discipline," *Gongren Ribao* (Workers Daily), Dec. 2, 1980, in *JPRS*, no. 77198, Jan. 19, 1983, *EA*, no. 110, 42–43 (an unconvincing rebuttal to this article is found in *JPRS*, no. 77876, Apr. 20, 1981, *EA*, no. 131, 8–10); "Strictly Enforce Tax Laws, Safeguard State Revenue," *ZGCMB*, May 5, 1981, in *JPRS*, no. 78550, July 20, 1981, *EA*, no. 151, 24–27; Bao Youde and Pei Shian, "Our Views on the Real Duties of Finance and Tax Specialists in the New Situation," *CZ*, 1981, no. 7, in *JPRS*, no. 78872, Aug. 31, 1981, *EA*, no. 166, 10–12; Tan Limin, "The Need to Strictly Enforce Financial and Economic Discipline and Rectify Improper Practices," *ZGCMB*, Oct. 27, 1981, in *JPRS*, no. 79826, Jan. 8, 1982, *EA*, no. 195, 56–59; "Renmin Ribao Commentator's Article," *FBIS*, Aug. 18, 1980, L10–11; Liu Pinghai, "Taxation Work Should Receive Appropriate Support," *CZ*, 1981, no. 6 (June): 19–20; "All Excuses for Retaining State Tax Revenues Are Wrong," *ZGCMB*, Sept. 17, 1981, 1; "Taxation Evasion Problems in Yunnan Reported," *FBIS*, Aug. 4, 1981, Q3; Wang Bingqian, "It Is Absolutely Impermissible to Retaliate against and Persecute Financial and Accounting Personnel," *Gongren Ribao*, Jan. 27, 1983, in *FBIS*, Feb. 4, 1983, K5–6.

[74] "Enterprises Make Gains in Financial Inspections," *FBIS*, Mar. 8, 1982, K13.

[75] "Strengthen Taxation Work, Ensure Accomplishment of Annual Revenue," *Jingji Ribao*, Feb. 24, 1983, in *JPRS*, no. 83210, Apr. 6, 1983, *EA*, no. 326, 25–27.

[76] "Nei Monggol Reduces Financial Discipline Violations," *FBIS*, Apr. 20, 1981, R3–4.

[77] "Strictly Abide by Tax Laws," *FBIS*, July 30, 1981, O4.

[78] "Qinghai Tax Evasion," *JPRS*, no. 78946, Sept. 3, 1981, *EA*, no. 170, 57.

[79] "Tax Evasion in Liaoning Reported," *FBIS*, Sept. 4, 1981, S2.

[80] Liu Zhicheng, "Strengthen the Management" (n. 37 above).

qian, the Minister of Finance, described the extent of financial inspections in 1982 in his speech to the First Session of the Sixth National People's Congress in June 1983:

> In 1982 the nationwide check-up on the financial work of enterprises continued. Many cases of breaches of financial and economic discipline were exposed in various localities and departments over the past year and more. They were dealt with properly, and about 2.3 billion yuan were recovered and turned over to the state treasury. A nationwide tax registration and check-up on application of tax policy were carried out, and this further strengthened tax control. Statistics show that 4.2 million taxpayers registered in 1982, and that 253,000 longtime tax evaders were discovered and made to pay taxes in arrears.[81]

Tax evasion and financial indiscipline were obviously a major problem.

Policy Content

In late 1980, Chinese leaders, especially in the financial departments, were increasingly worried by disappearing revenues and growing expenditures. In November 1980 the State Council issued a circular on year-end financial work, demanding a step-up in revenue collection and a check-up on profit and tax submissions.[82] In May 1981 the General Tax Department announced a two-month inspection to crack down on tax evasions and defaults.[83] Immediately after this two-month period was over (during which 580 million yuan of back taxes were discovered), Wang Bingqian called for an additional two months of investigation.[84]

The basic method of these inspections was for enterprises to carry out the "three selfs": self-examination, self-assessment, and self-handing-in of back taxes. (The three selfs had been tried during the Great Leap Forward and led to a great decline in tax revenues because there was no follow-up by financial officials; that was not the case in the 1980s.) The populace was promised rewards for revealing tax cheats, and the masses were to be mobilized during these check-ups. Leniency was promised for those enterprises (and their leaders) that paid back what they owed. Tax officials then audited something like a quarter of all self-assessed enterprises and often discovered many additional abuses. During the second two-month period of investigation, many more audits were carried out. By 1981 the Procuracy had begun to prosecute

---

[81] Wang Bingqian, "Report," K12 (n. 8 above).

[82] "State Council Circular on Year-end Financial Work," *FBIS*, Nov. 5, 1980, L2–4.

[83] "Announcement of the General Tax Department of the Ministry of Finance of the People's Republic of China," *CZ*, 1981, no. 5 (May): 10.

[84] "Speech by Minister of Finance Wang Bingqian," *CZ*, 1981, no. 9 (September): 1–4; and "Finance Minister Wang Bingqian on Tax Work," *FBIS*, July 24, 1981, K9.

or become involved in the investigation of more than 1,000 cases of tax evasion under Article 121 of the Criminal Code.[85]

In December 1981 the State Council ordered still another audit, this time focusing on large and medium enterprises. Two hundred central cadres, including vice-ministers, were sent down in work teams to take part in inspections.[86] By late 1981 and early 1982, few factory managers could have had any doubts about the Center's commitment to a crack down on financial abuses. Moreover, by early 1982 violations of tax laws and economic discipline began to be seen as violations of Party discipline and as economic crimes.[87] In May 1982 (after a major campaign against economic crime from January through April 1982) the State Council approved a Ministry of Finance document calling for yet another round of financial inspections.[88] Further campaigns to inspect finances and taxes continued throughout 1983.[89]

The effect of these campaigns has been multifaceted. As with all campaigns, the mere fact that it is launched raises the importance of the issue being addressed. Finance and tax cadres and factory officials were particularly affected. These campaigns encourage tax officials to audit enterprises enthusiastically. Factory managers were aware of these campaigns and the support given to financial inspectors to audit the books of enterprises. It became more difficult for tax evasion to occur. In addition, the state has also been building a more stable, less ad hoc system of financial and tax control while the campaigns continue. The fledgling State Auditing Commission has been in existence since September 1983. Since its founding, it has uncovered over 300 million yuan of irregularities after inspecting about 1,250 enterprises. This organization, as it develops and matures, can provide the professional underpinning to the shock campaigns designed to uncover tax abuses.[90]

Clearly, the Center has been able to make its concern about financial irregularities known to enterprises at all levels. Beijing has demonstrated the capacity to plug some of the loopholes in the revenue system, at least as long as the pressure is applied; how many remain is unknown. But in its efforts to assure adequate revenues, the Center possesses an additional advantage

[85] "Procuratorates Prosecute Tax Evasion Cases," *FBIS*, Nov. 16, 1981, K12–13.

[86] "State Council Circular on Enterprise Audits," *FBIS*, Dec. 18, 1981, K27–28.

[87] See, for example, "Sichuan Ribao on Financial, Economic Discipline," *FBIS*, Feb. 26, 1982, Q1–2.

[88] See *Gongbao*, 1982, no. 10 (July 10): 459–67; and "State Council Views Financial Inspectors," *FBIS*, May 27, 1982, K3–4.

[89] On continued financial inspections, see *Gongbao*, 1983, no. 22 (Dec. 20): 1012–15.

[90] On the auditing bodies, see "Auditing Administration Uncovers Irregularities," *FBIS*, Mar. 19, 1984, K20; and "CPC, State Leaders Attend Conference on Auditing," *FBIS*, Mar. 20, 1984, K10–11.

in the fact that Chinese industry is so concentrated that financial and tax inspectors need only focus on a relatively small number of large enterprises. If the financial and tax conditions of these enterprises are satisfactory, the state is almost guaranteed that revenue quotas will be fulfilled. For example, there are 1,020 enterprises in China that each hand in more than 10 million yuan of taxes and profits a year; they produce 31.2 percent of the gross value of industrial output and 51.7 percent of all profits and taxes. Of these 1,020, there are 369 that each have profits and taxes of 30 million yuan per year; they account for 22.5 percent of gross output and 41.4 percent of all profits and taxes.[91] Once work in these enterprises is done well, financial authorities can gradually extend the scope of their supervision to include more enterprises. In this manner, the capacity of financial inspection will be gradually increased, and tax evasion and financial irregularities should become less of a concern for the leadership.

Assessing whether the Chinese tax system "works" is a complex question, the answer to which depends on the criteria of assessment. Tax quotas have been consistently met and exceeded, and China extracts many more resources from its economic system than do other Third World nations. This success may depend on the fact that a relatively small number of factories provide the bulk of state revenue. Yet, the tax system has been a drag on economic efficiency, and there have been widespread cases of tax evasion. Through rather traditional means (i.e., through the use of campaigns) the state retains the capacity to plug some of the holes in the revenue system. However, the state has been noticeably less successful in its attempts to reform the tax system so that it plays a useful role in creating incentives for efficiency. The Chinese political system, on the issue of taxation, appears capable of muddling along at a level many other countries might envy, but it confronts the same problems they face in trying to achieve fundamental tax reform.

CONCLUSION

This essay has revealed that there are a number of unusual aspects to resource extraction in China, the Chinese tax system, and the implementation of tax policy. Despite weaknesses in the tax and finance bureaucracy, China has been able to extract a much higher proportion of resources from the economy than have other Third World nations, approaching that of developed capitalist nations. The turnover tax and state ownership, among other factors, compensate for many of the weaknesses of its own bureaucracy and those found in other states. Indeed, over the past thirty-odd years, the

---

[91] "Economic Commission Circular on Large Enterprises," *FBIS*, Nov. 11, 1982, K12–14.

Chinese have extracted prodigious sums for investment. In this basic sense, the resource-extraction system in China has been highly successful.

But tax policy has also contributed to economic inefficiency. Cooperation and specialization is discouraged by the tax system. The industrial and commercial tax contributes to the emphasis on production quantity instead of quality. Taxes have not been consciously employed to encourage managers to increase profit and efficiency. Moreover, in recent years, tax evasion has been omnipresent. The extraction of resources has fallen behind the system's needs. In short, the Chinese extraction system has been effective in mobilizing resources for state building purposes, though this is less so today than it was in the 1950s or 1960s.

Since the late 1970s Chinese leaders have been increasingly aware of these shortcomings. The two case studies discussed above shed light on some of their expectations on how the tax system should be improved and reformed. They also provide insights on the implementation process in China.

In the case of LGS, a potentially significant reform appears to have been deflated (at least temporarily) in the course of policy formulation and implementation. The principal reason was the resistance of factory managers and local officials to the redistribution of resources originally embodied in the experimental points. How their resistance came to the attention of the central leadership is unknown. Nonetheless, the Center elected to compromise and guarantee that in the most crucial respects the institution of the LGS would not fundamentally affect the interests of these two concerned groups. Consequently, the LGS system has been widely implemented. Now that the basic procedures associated with the LGS are in place, can the Center push on to the next stage of the LGS policy, which may truly bring about a redistribution of resources? This does not appear likely, but as is shown in chapters 2 and 9, substantial elite attention, concern, and leadership will be required if policy is to be implemented effectively.

Tax reform is difficult under the best of circumstances—its redistributive effects assure this. Rather than directly challenge interests that are vigorously opposed to tax reform, most political systems compromise with those interests and attempt to reach an accommodation. The case discussed above suggests that such a result occurred in China in 1983 also. However, such compromise perpetuates problems of the past.

The other case examined suggests that the state still retains a substantial capacity to see that its concerns are addressed by local officials. To reverse the trend of increasing tax and financial indiscipline, the leadership has launched a series of campaigns to uncover these abuses and recover lost revenue. Impressive results have been obtained by these campaigns. The Center's commitment to controlling these abuses has been clearly communicated to all segments of the political system, and the state has established institutions and adopted policies that should serve to consolidate these gains. This, then, signifies a case of successful Leninist implementation, as Barrett McCormick calls it.

But the specifics that contributed to this success should not be overlooked. First, it took the repeated launching of campaigns to convince enterprise officials that Beijing was serious about cracking down on financial abuses. Second, because such abuses were clearly illegal, factory and lower-level cadres did not have a legitimate ground on which to oppose this policy. They may have tried to resist implementation and cover up their activities, but the fact that independent financial officials are in charge of implementing these financial check-ups weakens their ability to oppose policy. Resistance to the policy may in fact encourage closer scrutiny. Third, these campaigns were not implementing new policies; on the contrary, they were used to ensure that policies on the books were in fact receiving due attention. Finally, the goals of and procedures used to implement these campaigns were straightforward and simple and did not require the development of new or complex standard operating procedures, unlike the case with LGS. The question remains, however, whether a real, permanent change of behavior has been induced by these campaigns, or whether, once the campaigns stop, tax evasion will become as widespread as it has been.

The above two cases show that the Chinese political system finds it easier to implement policies that are simple, require no major change of procedures, are not redistributive, and provide no legitimate basis of opposition. Policies that are innovative, complicated, and redistributive may be very difficult to implement. This conclusion is not very surprising, and it is likely to hold for all political systems. The interesting question that remains unanswered is whether the strengths of the Chinese state can be mobilized to ensure that even redistributive policies can be implemented effectively. If the central leadership can agree on the necessity of such mobilization, this is possible, but only if the leadership places redistributive issues at the very top of the political agenda and defers action in other policy realms. Such an occurrence is unlikely but not impossible.

It might be asked what structural changes in the Chinese political and economic system must be made if taxation policy is to be better implemented in the future. Several suggest themselves from these case studies. First, the Center has to establish a clearer vision of what a reformed Chinese political and economic system will look like. Once this is done, policy conflicts such as the one between LGS and the strengthening of the economic role of counties can be more easily avoided. Tax reform is more likely to come about if the central leadership decides on a system of true enterprise autonomy (though tax evasion may increase in this event). Second, the leadership can manipulate incentives for enterprises and factory managers to fulfill tax quotas. If the importance of tax targets is heightened, tax performance is likely to be improved. Third, further efforts must be made to strengthen the professional abilities of financial, accounting, and tax personnel, and incentives for them must be enhanced—they might even be promised a share of all financial violations they uncover. Fourth, tax policies should be kept as simple as possible. Finally, instead of overdramatizing the effects of reform policies, the Center might try to underplay new initiatives. In this way, opposition might not be galvanized as quickly, nor as effectively, as was the case with LGS. To be sure, this might slow implementation, but it might also allow real reforms to become established in the Chinese economy.

PART III

Resource Policy

SIX

Water:
Challenge to a Fragmented
Political System

David M. Lampton

China's serious water problems of today will become increasingly burden-some constraints in the future unless remedial efforts are undertaken now. In simply describing these difficulties, one learns much about the system that generates them. However, the political system is important not just as a "source" of some of these problems, it is important also because it must fashion and implement "solutions" to them. Water politics revolves around the twin issues of who gets water (and its derivative resources) when there is not enough, and who must take it when there is too much. During floods one must find a place to put literally cubic miles of excess water. Coping with floods and droughts and allocating scarce derivative resources are matters in which the political system, its values, and its processes stand out in bold relief. Water, because it crosses administrative boundaries, forces different organizations and administrative units to do what they most abhor—deal with each other. The intersection of dynamic problems and static organizations is a superb vantage point from which to view any political system, particularly China's.

The questions this article addresses are simply these: What are China's water problems? What general characteristics of the political system affect its capacity to fashion appropriate responses? And what specific problems have

The field research for this paper was conducted in the People's Republic of China during November 1980 and August–December 1982. I would like to thank the Committee on Scholarly Communication with the People's Republic of China and Ohio State University for support-ing my research in Hubei and Beijing. Also, I would like to collectively thank the many Chinese colleagues at the Yangtze River Valley Planning Office, the four dam sites I visited in Hubei, Wuhan University, the Wuhan Institute of Hydrology and Electric Power, the Ministry of Water Conservancy and Electric Power, the State Planning Commission, The Ministry of Urban Construction and Environmental Protection, and the Machine Building Ministry. I, however, am responsible for any possible errors of fact or interpretation.

the Chinese had in implementing those policies in one particular context—the Yangtze Basin? To develop a plan is frequently less difficult than effectively translating those objectives into a reality that even approximates initial intention.

THE CHALLENGES

Some Chinese already are arguing that the "water crisis" is bigger than the country's widely acknowledged energy woes. Using water consumption and output value ratios for Tianjin, for instance, they argue that each 10 billion yuan increase (1 U.S. dollar equals about 3.0 yuan) in output value nationally will require four new reservoirs, each with a capacity of 100 million cubic meters of water.[1] To feed future growth, reservoirs must be started now. Even today, water shortages in selected areas of North China have produced partial plant shutdowns. Insufficient river flows, in at least one instance, have temporarily halted shipments in and out of a large critical production facility. In central China (Henan and Hubei provinces, for example), large areas that existent reservoirs were designed to irrigate remain unirrigated because of shortages. Planned economic growth, combined with inevitable population increases, can only exacerbate these problems. As one Chinese commentator put it, "The excessive density of the population has given rise to ever sharper contradictions between supply and demand, where water resources are concerned."[2] It is estimated that industrial water consumption in the year 2000 will be three to four times higher than today's.[3]

One must acknowledge the important achievements of the Chinese to date. Irrigated acreage embraces about 48 percent of all cultivated land, and from 1949 to 1980 more than 86,000 small, medium, and large-scale reservoirs, and 160,000 km of dikes, embankments, and seawalls, were built or renovated.[4] There have been no breaches in the dikes along the Yellow River since 1949 (though there has been some intentional diversion), and the damage caused by floods along the Yangtze River (such as the crests in 1954, 1981, and 1983) has been reduced by numerous diversion, storage, and drainage projects. Waterlogged acreage has been reduced significantly since

[1] *Zhongguo Shuili* (China Water Conservancy, hereafter *CWC*), 1981, no. 4:7.

[2] Foreign Broadcast Information Service, *Daily Report: China* (hereafter *FBIS*), 1981, no. 227:K5. Vice-Premier Wan Li delivered a speech in February in which he said, "The thing that will affect future construction in North China is neither the problem of energy nor the problem of human resources.... The deciding factor for economic development in North China is water."*FBIS*, 1983, no. 98:R1.

[3] *FBIS*, 1983, no. 200:K14.

[4] *CWC*, 1982, no. 3 in file 64; also *FBIS*, 1981, no. 126:K60; also *CWC*, 1981, no. 3 in file 13; *CWC*, 1982, no. 1:4.

1949.[5] In looking to the uncertain future, then, one should not forget the accomplishments of the past.

To ensure a sufficient supply of water for human use and economic growth, at least five interlocking problems must be addressed: flood control, land use and encroachment, erosion and pollution, interregional water transfers, and water conservation and utilization.

Flood Control

The Yangtze floods in 1981 and 1983 reminded both outside observers and the Chinese elite what the peasant who lives along major rivers never forgets: floods can inflict staggering losses. Even flood control efforts, however, contain within themselves a contradiction. As rivers become "safer," people build in more exposed areas so that potential economic losses can increase with flood control efforts. The higher agricultural yields become, and the more factory construction that occurs along inland waterways, the greater are the potential economic losses. Land use rules must accompany flood control development, and as we shall see, they have *not* done so. The floods of the future could inflict economic losses far in excess of those of the past.

Moreover, the flood control standard along China's main inland water system, the Yangtze, still is comparatively low. Most stretches now are able to withstand floods with a frequency of only 10–20 years.[6] If a flood like that of 1954 were to hit the Yangtze Basin, Chinese planners estimate that as many as 7 million persons could be displaced and economic losses could reach 20 billion yuan. The much smaller and regionally localized Yangtze flood of 1981, according to Chinese figures, caused 2 billion yuan in direct economic losses and left 1.13 million persons homeless; 2,600 factories were wiped out, 98,000 hectares of farmland were covered with debris, and 340,000 mu (1 mu equals .0667 hectares) of reclaimed land simply was swept away. In the floods of July 1983 about 70,000 homes and more than 290 factories were flooded in Wuhan; 80 counties and 8 million persons were affected in Sichuan province, with estimated income losses there of 200 million yuan. Extensive inundation also hit Hunan, Anhui, and Jiangxi provinces at the same time.

Along the Yellow River also, the situation is worrisome. With the silt-laden water inexorably raising the stream bed, literally interminable and costly dike-raising projects are required. During the period 1950–1978, the stream bed rose about two meters in the lower reaches, and until water and

[5] *FBIS*, 1981, no. 126:K60.

[6] The following sources provided the information in this section on flood control: *CWC*, 1981, no. 2:33, no. 4:7; 1982, no. 1:5 and 20, no. 3:4 and 5; *China Reconstructs*, December 1981, 7; *Washington Post*, Sept. 8, 1981, A17; *FBIS*, 1982, no. 91:Q2, no. 232:K3; 1983, no. 131:P1, no. 152:Q1 and T2; *Ren Min Chang Jiang* (People's Yangtze River), 1980, no. 5:15–22.

soil conservation in the upper and middle reaches is effectively carried out, this process will continue; Chinese hydrologists even now predict that a Yellow River water level such as that of 1958 would create "a grave situation." Moreover, in Shaanxi province it was revealed in late 1983 that there were "142 unsafe reservoirs." China's other principal rivers present problems too, with major floods having occurred along the Sung-Liao system in 1960, the Hai in 1963, and the Huai in 1954 and 1975. Bluntly, the meteorological clock is ticking; the potential remedies are enormously costly and require long lead times to complete.

Looking at the Yangtze River Basin alone, many of China's flood control planners argue that the most cost effective strategy is to build a high storage dam in the Three Gorges of western Hubei province. This would back water all the way up to Sichuan's major city of Chongqing, a project so grand that it even caught Mao Zedong's poetic sense in 1956—he wrote a poem entitled "Swimming." Cost estimates by different Chinese authorities vary widely, ranging from a high estimate of between 40 and 50 billion yuan to a low of 12.5 billion, including the costs of population displacement. No matter what the figure, it would constitute a very large chunk of China's capital-construction budget. To provide some perspective: planned budgetary allocations for capital construction in the draft 1983 national budget are 36.18 billion yuan. Every day that the Three Gorges project is delayed, costs and population displacements presumably grow.

Because of the displacement, land, and capital costs, some persons in the State Planning Commission's Office of Agriculture, Forestry, and Water Conservancy (as well as representatives of other ministries who fear that such large allocations to one project will dry up funds that might otherwise be available to them) argue that, instead of the Three Gorges project, emphasis should be placed on dikes, which, they assert, would be cheaper, would occupy less agricultural land, and would employ China's abundant manual labor. The Yangtze River Valley Planning Office, on the other hand, vigorously disputes this contention, pointing to the increasing danger of ever higher dikes, the mammoth quantities of earth and stone that would need to be moved in order to appreciably enhance flood control standards, and the structural weakness of the foundations of some of the basin's most strategic dikes. Sichuan province also prefers a different approach, arguing that it would be better to build a series of smaller storage dams upstream rather than one gigantic project at its eastern border, which would inundate large tracts of the province's most valuable real estate.

Information I have indicates that Beijing in the mid-1980s decided to launch the Three Gorges project late in the decade, despite the fact that *major* design and financial details still have not been resolved. It remains to be seen if the project is launched. If it is, it is unlikely that the construction schedule of fifteen years can even be approximated. China's experience of long construction times at other big projects (more below) suggests that a fifteen-year plan is exceedingly optimistic. And what will happen along the Yangtze in the interim?

Land Use and Encroachment

Land is, arguably, China's most precious resource. An expanding population, increasing industrial and urban sprawl, a housing boom in the country-side, erosion and desertification, and the inundation of large tracts of farm-land by reservoir projects, cumulatively have produced a decline in China's net stock of agricultural land. Though some outside observers assert that peasants are "hiding" land from the authorities, as peasants have done for eons, the government is genuinely alarmed. A *Beijing Review* article noted in 1982:

> China's farmland covered 111.33 million hectares in 1957, but it dropped to 99.33 [million] hectares in 1977. However, this figure includes 17 million hect-ares of farmland reclaimed from wasteland during this period, so the country actually lost 29 million hectares of farmland during those 20 years, an area equal to the total area of farmland of Shandong, Hebei, Henan and Heilong-jiang Provinces in 1979.[7]

Now that household incomes are most directly linked to household entre-preneurship, peasants are trying to secure land wherever and however possi-ble. Rising peasant incomes have set off a housing boom that requires land. In river basin and lake areas, this land hunger takes the form of filling, or otherwise encroaching upon, lakes, ponds, and rivers, as well as building on dikes and in diversion areas. Factories and enterprises, eager to expand, have built in areas that are vulnerable to flash floods and inundation; this obvious-ly escalates potential flood losses.

In the central Yangtze River region, the surface area of Hunan province's Dongting Lake has declined from 4,350 km² to 2,740 km² during the last three decades.[8] Although not all of this is due to peasant encroachment (siltation from upstream erosion also is very important), this decline is exceedingly worrisome. It reduces the potential of aquatic production, it further constricts inland navigation, and, most important, it diminishes the capacity of the middle reaches of the Yangtze River to safely store flood waters. This critical equalizing function of the middle-reaches lakes has been recognized since *at least* the Ming dynasty (A.D. 1368–1644). As Dongting's surface area (and the surface area of lakes throughout China) diminishes, more diversion or storage capacity must be built simply to replace what nature initially provided. Responding to this problem, the State Council

---

[7] *Beijing Review* (*BR*), 1982, no. 29:6.
[8] *CWC*, 1981, no. 2:32; see also 1982, no. 3.

DAVID M. LAMPTON

recently declared that it is necessary to "protect lakes in order to regulate surface runoffs and achieve an ecological balance. . . . No unit is allowed to seize land or water surface area."[9] Clearly, though, this policy of restraint is working against the combined momentum of an expanding rural population and economic policies designed to maximize rural production incentives—an unintended side effect has become a major policy problem.

Effective zoning is almost nonexistent. One interviewee recounted the perversity of the growth process. In one Hubei county, the state built a new storage and irrigation reservoir. In the belief that they could now depend on the state project for water, local peasants filled in about 70 percent of their ponds, trying to expand their land area.[10] In a huge irony of enormous consequence, it is as if the Chinese government were taxing and conscripting peasants to dig reservoirs by day, only to have them steal into the night and fill them in. One recent account observed, "The crux of the land problem is the lack of unified scientific control. Scientific land control includes legislation, investigation, planning, registration, statistics, and approval and supervision for its use."[11]

A similar perverse process has been occurring with respect to inland navigation. While it universally is conceded that inland waterway transport is a cheaper way to move bulk freight, the period 1965–1979 witnessed over a 30 percent *decline* in the length of China's navigable waterways.[12] From 1961 to 1982 the length of navigable waterways in the nation dropped from 170,000 km to 108,000 km, a 37 percent *decline*; as a result of these declines in navigable waterways, "the share of freight volume carried on inland waters dropped from 14 percent in 1957 to 7 percent in 1981." The length of navigable waterways in central China's Hubei province declined annually, and partly as a result, the volume of water-borne freight dropped from 56 percent of the total volume of road and water freight in 1957 to 37 percent in 1979.

Why is this occurring? Chinese interviewees and documentary evidence converge on the following factors: Dam construction has paid insufficient heed to the needs of navigation; factory construction frequently has obstructed smaller tributaries; erosion has caused extensive siltation of stream beds; and insufficient funds have been provided for channel maintenance, much less improvement.

Railroads have received a much larger share of capital construction investment than has inland-river development, despite the fact that investment per unit of water-borne freight capacity is less than one-half that needed to

[9] *FBIS*, 1982, no. 117:K18.

[10] Interview no. 3, WIWCEP (Wuhan Institute of Water Conservancy and Electric Power), 1982.

[11] *FBIS*, 1983, no. 150:K22.

[12] The figures in this paragraph are drawn from the following sources: *China Economic Yearbook*, 1981, VI-18; *FBIS*, 1983, no. 20 (Jan. 28): K20; *Economic Research Reference Materials* (unpublished document), 1981, no. 51:50.

create equivalent rail capacity. Moreover, railroads occupy extensive tracts of farmland.[13] At precisely the time that China's leaders are seeking to conserve farmland, a process of river deterioration is under way, in no small part due to poor land-use policies, weak enforcement of what guidelines there are, and suboptimal investment patterns. Many, but by no means all, of these problems are political in origin; therefore, solutions must be sought within the political system.

Erosion and Pollution

The current drive to accelerate economic growth has created tremendous pressures on the forests and on water quality. Present policies that increase household incentives to produce new sources of income have created additional pressures manifest in what *Beijing Review* describes as the "wanton felling of forests and destruction of other natural resources."[14] China's former minister of forestry, Yong Wentao, made the surprising admission in 1981 that "the degree of destruction [of forests in the upper reaches of the Yangtze Basin] became more serious since the founding of new China."[15] In 1979, by its own account China ranked 120th in the world in the percentage of its land area covered by forest (12.7 percent), and one-sixth of the country's land area now is classified as eroded.[16] Immediately after 1949 approximately 19 percent of Sichuan province's land area was forest covered; by 1982 this figure had declined to 13.3 percent. Even more dramatically, Sichuan's Wusheng county, hard hit by floods in 1981, had 10,000 hectares of forested area in the 1950s; during the 1966–1976 era (we now are told), this was reduced to 56 hectares. Situated upstream, these problem areas in Sichuan inevitably will affect the entire basin.

In the Yangtze Basin, erosion is serious, with the heavy silt load (there is some debate about whether or not the silt load is increasing) reducing lake surface areas, obstructing inland navigation, shortening the useful life of hydraulic projects, and further diminishing the absorptive capacity of upstream areas. Topsoil is being washed from where it is needed to where it is a problem. Against this background, Sichuan's former first Party secretary, Tan Qilong, flatly stated in the Party's theoretical journal, *Red Flag*, that "the 1981 Sichuan flood, which caused disastrous damage to vast areas of the province, was brought about by the drastic reduction of forest land in northern Sichuan."[17] Although there is debate over the degree to which deforestation was responsible for the 1981 Yangtze River floods (with Sichuan

[13] *Economic Research Reference Materials*, 1981, no. 51:47.

[14] *BR*, 1982, no. 25 (June 21): 9.

[15] *FBIS*, 1981, no. 186:K20.

[16] The figures in this paragraph are drawn from the following sources: *Current Events Information Handbook, Xinhua, 1981*, 101; *BR*, 1983, no. 17:22; *FBIS*, 1982, no. 91:Q2; *BR*, 1981, no. 36:8.

[17] Sources for this paragraph are *FBIS*, 1983, no. 9 (Jan. 13): Q1–2; 1982, no. 121:K11; 1983, no. 198:T1.

province and the Ministry of Forestry asserting that the disaster proves that more forestry investment is required and the Ministry of Water Conservancy and Electric Power countering that the inundation shows that more storage dams are essential), all parties concede that erosion is an increasingly grave problem. The Yellow River's erosion problems are even more serious (as was mentioned above), with silting in the river's middle and lower reaches threatening the security of vast downstream areas. In Gansu province, 2 million mu of forest and grass are damaged yearly by fuel acquisition, and there is a yearly decline in the net stock of forested area. "In the end, people have to go in for extensive cultivation; and a vicious cycle is formed when the more land they reclaim, the poorer they become; the poorer they become, the more wasteland they reclaim."

The test for judging the commitment of China's leaders in dealing with the erosion problem will be whether or not forestry investment climbs, whether or not forests can, in the words of Tan Qilong, be closed off for a few years, and whether or not lumber imports rise in order to give forests a respite from cutting.[18]

Pollution, while serious, is a subject about which only limited information is available. According to figures from the Chinese Ministry of Water Conservancy and Electric Power, in the early 1970s the nation discharged 40 million tons of polluted water daily; by 1979 that daily discharge rate had climbed to 72.58 million tons, an increase of over 80 percent.[19] Put another way, "for every 14 cubic meters of natural water available to China, one cubic meter was untreated wastewater." Industrial waste accounted for about four-fifths of the 1979 discharge. In a recent scientific gathering to discuss Lake Taihu in the lower Yangtze Valley, the link between industrial growth and water pollution was made explicit. "The irrational distribution of industry, for instance, has resulted in environmental pollution and damage to its (Lake Taihu's) aquatic resources"; in reference to Hubei's Lake Honghu, a recent survey "showed it to be one of the few unpolluted large inland lakes on the middle and lower reaches of the Changjiang (Yangtze) River." Indeed, an official 1979 survey found that *all* of China's major rivers are seriously polluted. Groundwater purity also has become a problem, with the Chinese acknowledging that groundwater in some urban areas is already being contaminated, in some cases severely.

In China as elsewhere, one set of policy objectives will frequently conflict with another. The drive to increase coal and other industrial output, for instance, has led to mining and refining practices that contribute to the deterioration of water purity. In speaking about a nearby ore-dressing plant in

---

[18] *FBIS*, 1983, no. 9 (Jan. 13): Q1; 1981, no. 186:K20.

[19] Sources for this paragraph are *CWC*, 1982, no. 2:19; Vaclav Smil, "Rivers of Waste," *China Business Review*, July–August 1983, 18; *BR*, 1982, no. 46:5–6.

Shanxi province, people in Yuxian county complained that it was ruining their water supply and destroying their reservoir: "It discharges 70–80 tons of tailings a day and contaminates the mountain spring flowing into the reservoir. In the past few years, over two-thirds of the storage capacity has been filled with silt. Further, the 200,000 fish we stocked the reservoir with all died because of the pollution."[20] Another article summed up the interlocking soil and water problems: "For the sake of temporary or local benefit, the people would not hesitate to build obstructions in rivers and streams, disrupt the water system, reclaim land from the rivers to build farms, [and] indiscriminately discharge mining waste."[21] The long-term effect of these practices is great, but the ability of the system to enforce control or invest necessary capital to correct the problems is in doubt. In asking what impedes the system's ability to effectively respond, one penetrates to the heart of the Chinese political-economic system, a topic to which we shall soon return.

Interregional Water Transfers

On the average, China's northern and northwestern provinces receive 500 or less millimeters of rain annually; the Yangtze Basin receives a mean annual precipitation of 1,100 millimeters.[22] Stated differently, the water available per capita in the Yangtze Basin is more than four times greater than that available per capita to residents of the Yellow River Basin. Each mu of cultivated land in the Yangtze Basin has more than nine times as much water available to it as does each mu of cultivated land in the Yellow River Basin. Also, a much greater percentage of the Yellow River's runoff is already stored in large and medium-sized reservoirs (84 percent) than is the case in the Yangtze Basin, where only 9.1 percent of the runoff is captured. In the ten years prior to 1983, flow on the Yellow River was cut eight times (in one case for nearly twenty days), affecting not only agriculture but also transport and industry, which rely upon the river.

Imprecise groundwater estimates suggest that North China's Huai, Yellow, and Hai River plain has only about 10 percent of China's estimated total primary reserves of groundwater. The water table is dropping throughout North China, and more wells frequently do not produce more water. Particularly during the repeated droughts of the 1970s and early 1980s in the arid North, some factories have had to operate well below capacity for lack of water. Irrigated acreage is below planned levels in many areas. Water is so scarce that one production unit with excess water sold its surplus to another

---

[20] *BR*, 1983, no. 5:26.

[21] *FBIS*, 1982, no. 91:Q2.

[22] Sources for this section are Interview File no. 2; *CWC*, 1982, no. 1:4 and 9; *Dili Zhishi* (Geographical Knowledge), 1982, no. 8:3; *CWC*, 1981, no. 2:52; no. 3, file 46; no. 4:47; *FBIS*, 1983, no. 170:K4; YRVPO (Yangtze River Valley Planning Office) interview no. 4 (2–5); interview, Ministry of WCEP, Nov. 4, 1982 (8).

"dry" unit for thirty times the price at which that water had been purchased from the water department. And yet, despite these present shortages, the regime is counting on economic expansion in North and West China to help meet its ambitious economic objectives for the year 2000.

There is some debate about whether there really is a water shortage in North China. Some geologists argue that more groundwater may be available than estimates indicate. Some agriculturalists assert that new irrigation techniques would save a great deal of water. Both foreign and domestic experts agree that the waste of water is staggering. Nonetheless, in light of the basic meteorological facts of life in the North, and the requirements that future growth will place on already strained supplies, experts in the Ministry of Water Conservancy and Electric Power believe that the only long-term solution to the basic regional imbalance is to move water northward from the Yangtze Basin. Other ministries fear that a project of this scope would siphon away investment that they need.

The plan to divert Yangtze water north is important in yet another respect. If additional water is not injected into the arid system in North and Northwestern China, intraregional conflict between upstream areas in the Yellow River Basin and those downstream in the urban and industrial areas of the North China Plain will increase. Areas in the West, such as Gansu province, desperately need to pump more water from the Yellow River system; growing areas downstream (e.g., Tianjin, which now is dependent to some degree on Yellow River water) want to minimize the upstream "take" so that they have as much left for themselves as possible. Even in 1958 the "contradiction" was clear to the Ministry of Water Conservancy; a growing upstream West, a growing downstream East, with the water take of each lessening the growth possibilities of the other. Today, the problems of China's West are serious. Areas of Gansu province, for instance, are in a vicious cycle of drought, leading to overcultivation, which produces desertification. In one Gansu county, during the period 1951–1955 the yearly average water supply was 1,360 cubic meters per capita. In the period 1971–1975 that average volume had fallen to 238 cubic meters per capita.

Given the importance of water to economic growth, combined with the desire to minimize intraregional conflict, the central authorities have been considering building a very large project (or projects) to move Yangtze water northward. Two possible routes have been under serious consideration, with a third (the "Western Line" along the Yalong River) an unlikely choice. The proposed "Central Route" would run from northwest Hubei province (Danjiangkou Reservoir, and ultimately the Three Gorges if the high dam is built there) past Zhengzhou, across the Yellow River, and up to the vicinity of Beijing. As envisioned, this project would be entirely gravity flow, with no pumping required. Significant tunneling would be needed. The proposed "Eastern Route" would run from the Yangtze River near Yangzhou up through portions of the Grand Canal to Jining, in Shandong province, and up to Tianjin when phase two is completed. The authorities recently settled on the Grand Canal route, though the matter probably is still being hotly debated.

The Yangtze River Valley Planning Office believes that the Central Route is preferable because its long-term operating costs would be lower and it fits in with its plans (or hopes) to raise the height of the Danjiangkou Dam and to build the Three Gorges Project. That is, the Planning Office wants to raise the height of Danjiangkou Dam, thereby enlarging the reservoir's capacity in order to supply more water for movement northward and to help meet the *initial* irrigation objectives of the Danjiangkou project. Even more dramatically, the Yangtze River Valley Planning Office wants the "Central Line" to ultimately draw its water from the Three Gorges Project. Provinces along the proposed "Central Route," particularly Hubei and Henan, want this route selected so that they can boost their irrigated acreage.

However, advocates of the "Eastern Route" have a case which even the Yangtze River Valley Planning Office candidly expected to prevail. Initial investment in the "Eastern Route" would be about one-third less than the "Central Line"; it would be somewhat faster to build; it would move more water; it would occupy less agricultural land; the Ministry of Communications (responsible for shipping) prefers the "Eastern Line"; and the provinces along this path, of course, want access to the water that would flow through their domains. On the minus side, however, the "Eastern Line" would require extensive pumping and would, therefore, consume a large quantity of electricity, producing permanently higher operating costs. The estimated cost of the "Eastern Route" is around 4 billion yuan. Considering the population displacement, the cost, technical complexities, and the welter of divergent interests, this project will likely continue to be debated and take longer to construct than anyone currently expects. Therefore, it does not appear as though North China's thirst will soon be quenched. In the short term, the regime will be left trying to conserve water and divert available supplies from the Luan River and other streams on the North China Plain itself.

Water Conservation and Water Utilization

In light of the above discussion concerning the North and Northwest's water shortage and the high cost of long-term solutions, it is not surprising that China's leaders have focused on the immediate need to conserve what water there is. Because waste is so substantial, this may be the one area in which comparatively rapid progress could be made.

Water, whether for agricultural, industrial, or household use, is underpriced. Water, like grain, housing, and urban medical care, is sold at prices below the cost of production. China's entire economic system is a web of subsidies and multi-tiered prices, which gives large sectors of the populace a perceived vested interest in perpetuating the inefficiencies of the present. Agricultural water is priced lowest, industrial water is in the middle, and household water is priced dearest. Underpricing water, like underpricing any commodity, encourages utilization that would not occur if the price were higher. One report from the Ministry of Water Conservancy and Electric Power asserts that Chinese industry reuses only 10 percent of its water, whereas the comparable figure for industries in the developed countries is 70 percent.[23]

Although Chinese water-pricing systems are of Byzantine complexity, one analysis by the Municipal Water Bureau of Beijing estimates that from 1966 to 1981 it received two *li* (one *li* equals 1/1,000 yuan) per cubic meter of water when the true cost of production was twenty-one *li* per cubic meter. In turn, because water revenues have been low, maintenance of the pipe system, water treatment facilities, and reservoirs has been neglected. Major maintenance projects require separate capital construction appropriations, which may or may not be forthcoming. Almost certainly such appropriations are not timely. Pipe leakage and resultant waste and contamination are serious problems. Ironically, large-scale waste coexists with a severe water shortage in North China. Even with low water fees, the water bills of many industrial units are in arrears, and collection has been difficult. Again showing how one policy affects another, enterprises that are increasingly being judged by their profitability vigorously oppose any increase in water rates to correct these problems. Until they can change the price of the goods they sell, factories and other enterprises do not want higher prices, which they are unable to pass along to someone else. A change in water prices would set off a chain reaction throughout the economy, as would a change in the price of any basic commodity. Policies designed to accelerate economic growth (by encouraging enterprise profitability) clash with the objectives and needs of a sound water-price policy. Finally, many consumers still do not have metered service; it is not even known how much water they use.

Waste not only is seen in direct physical loss, it also is evident in forgone opportunities due to mismanagement. For instance, fish production in state reservoirs, particularly in large reservoirs, is comparatively low. Fish production in one large-scale reservoir I visited was 2,721 *jin* (1 *jin* equals ½ kilogram) per square kilometer of lake surface area each year. In another, smaller county-run reservoir that I visited in southern Hubei province, fish production was about 20,000 *jin* for each square kilometer per year. The reasons for this wide disparity in productivity are many. Large reservoirs with hydroelectric plants lose a lot of fish through escape; there is a con-

[23] Sources for the information in this section are *FBIS*, 1982, no. 110:K12; *CWC*, 1981, no. 3:45–46; 1982, no. 3; field trip (FT) interviews: Danjiangkou, no. 3(1); Qing Shan, no. 11 (1).

tradiction between irrigation and pisciculture; reservoir security tends to
be poor; and illegal fishing, "bombing," "shooting," and "poisoning" are
significant problems. However, another important reason for the low productivity in big reservoirs is that they tend to straddle a multitude of local
jurisdictions. Each jurisdiction is reluctant to stock fish that another jurisdiction might take. When I suggested to interviewees that unified management of these large reservoirs might be a way to deal with this "free rider"
problem, they thought this would be very difficult to achieve because of the
inability to secure cooperation among competing local jurisdictions and because of difficulties in enforcement.

THE POLITICAL SYSTEM: FORMULATION AND IMPLEMENTATION OF POLICY AT THE MACRO LEVEL

The political-economic system not only is the "source" of some of China's
water problems, it also is the mechanism that must fashion and implement
"solutions" to them. What basic characteristics of the political-economic system affect whether or not timely and appropriate policies are developed,
adopted, and effectively implemented? Is the political system the problem or
the solution?

At least five fundamental attributes of the political system work against
the expeditious development and effective implementation of long-range
water (and other) policies. First, the political process with respect to these
sorts of distributive political issues is one of consensus building. The few at the
top generally do *not* choose to unilaterally impose their solutions on large
subordinate bureaucracies and territorial units. Instead, there is an elaborate
process of consultation and negotiation among bureaucratic and territorial
units and between administrative levels. This process can last for decades,
literally, because those at the top frequently have insufficient information to
decide unilaterally and they therefore request information and recommendations from below. The various bureaucracies respond with what Mao Zedong
called "washouts" (deluges) of information, so multiplying the options that
the top is immobilized by the range of choice. Even once a decision is made,
compliance cannot be taken for granted. Therefore, China's leaders seek
to have subordinates achieve a consensus, which they then can approve. Of
course, coercion is not absent from the entire process—eventually some
people will lose their homes, some jurisdictions will be inundated, and
some officials will lose their jobs. But coercive resources are limited and
therefore conserved. Consensus becomes the option of first resort.

This quest for consensus manifests itself in several ways. In budgetary
policy, there is an expectation at all levels that each territorial and
bureaucratic unit should receive roughly the same share of the budgetary
pie that it received previously. The absolute monetary amount may change

with economic and budgetary circumstance, but there is a baseline expectation that relative shares of the budget should not change dramatically.[24] Each superior unit allocates budget shares to subordinate units on a predetermined and apparently stable formula. Some changes in budgetary priorities have indeed occurred (witness the important shift in investment toward light industry and away from heavy industry), but these are exceptions to the rule. Moreover, such decisions require the expenditure of enormous political capital, and they tend to be short-term departures that gravitate back toward the original division of resources. Concisely, there is an ethic of budgetary "live and let live" that makes it hard to change priorities. All the budgetary fighting occurs at the margin, with the assumption being that most basic categories of expenditure will remain in a rather stable relationship to one another. Assuming that this is an accurate reflection of how resources are divided, it suggests that any significant reorientation of the budget in favor of water conservancy will be most difficult to achieve, even *if* water problems assume more importance on the elite's agenda. In China, as in Japan, budgeting functions to minimize conflict, and it is nonprogrammatic, all rhetoric about synoptic planning aside.[25]

The Chinese system is a complex hierarchy of territorial units. Leaders of superordinate territorial units are reluctant to impose severe costs on subordinate levels. Consequently, in water policy, where the effect of *any* decision to take, divert, impound, or allocate water or its derivative products inevitably affects a multitude of territorial units, one finds policy and projects slowed down by the need to build a consensus among the affected units. In the case of large-scale projects such as the Three Gorges Project or Danjiangkou Reservoir (of which more below), these consensus-building efforts actually become protracted negotiations with detailed understandings as to who must take how many displaced persons; who gets how much water and electrical power; what the priorities among irrigation, flood control, and electric-power generation are to be; and how net beneficiaries are to compensate net losers.

I have suggested that China's present and long-range water problems re quire gigantic responses. By their very nature, though, projects of this scale will cross many territorial and functional boundaries, thereby requiring an extensive negotiation process. For instance, the proposed Three Gorges reservoir, if built to the 200-meter level, would partially inundate about twenty-two counties.[26] It is amazing, if one has an exaggerated sense of Beijing's capacity to impose a solution, to hear water planners and project managers explain, with some exasperation, that projects have been stalled owing

[24] Interview, Ministry of Water Conservancy and Electric Power, Nov. 4, 1982 (6); also interview with State Planning Commission, Beijing.

[25] John Creighton Campbell, *Contemporary Japanese Budget Politics* (Berkeley and Los Angeles: University of California Press, 1980), 272–73.

[26] *People's Yangtze River*, 1979, no. 4:14.

to the opposition of this or that county, special district, or province. And as the negotiation process drags on, costs in terms of displacements and investment rise, making it still more difficult to achieve consensus. Mao Zedong's impatience with the process was well founded, and that is why several of China's biggest water projects were launched as a result of the Chairman having bypassed much of the bureaucracy. Mao, in the end, was a confrontational leader in a system that gravitates toward consensus.

What one finds in China, I believe, is a system in which every territorial unit, bureaucratic organization, and individual has very inadequate resources to accomplish assigned tasks. Consequently, it simply is not seen as "just" or "fair" to take resources away from already impoverished entities. You could call this the budgetary "iron rice bowl" ethic.

In the end, achieving a consensus can be facilitated through at least two noncoercive mechanisms: money (difficult to use habitually because of economic constraints) and crisis—the sudden recognition that a critical problem exists or is looming and that procrastination cannot persist. As Lester Ross has recently pointed out in his cogent analysis of the 1981 Yangtze flood, that disaster brought forestry and soil conservation work to the Center's attention in a way that mere bureaucratic entreaties could not. Disaster in China, as elsewhere, commands elite attention.

A second systemic attribute works against water planning. China's need for investment capital to fuel growth is endless. This money must be raised internally (from profitable enterprises or taxation) or from abroad. Those ministries and enterprises that generate rapid returns on investment are more attractive sites for further investment than are ministries and enterprises that generate fewer revenues and have comparatively slow "capital circulation" times. This, of course, does not reflect economic efficiency as much as it is an artifact of centrally fixed prices. The result has been that water-resource investment appears not to have been among the most attractive investment alternatives available to central planners. It remains to be seen whether the 1982 merger of the Ministry of Water Conservancy with the comparatively "profitable" Ministry of Electric Power will enhance the attractiveness of investment in this area.

Another aspect of the investment dilemma is that nonelectric-power water projects generally have low returns, require large capital expenditures, and take a long time to complete. These are just the types of projects that require an active central authority capable of extraction. Localities tend to put investment into projects that produce returns more rapidly. In the post-1978 period, however, central control over total investment monies has declined. Prior to 1979 *state planned investment* occupied about 80 percent of total capital construction investment. In 1980 this proportion dropped to 62.5 percent; in 1981 it declined further to 56.8 percent; and by 1982 it was 49.8 percent. Investment *outside of the budget* correspondingly swelled, not only making it harder for the Center to focus adequate resources on key projects but also making it more difficult for Beijing to assure that its projects would have adequate materials or skilled manpower even once they were launched.[27]

Third, the planning process is flawed and riven with division. Water planners in the Ministry of Water Conservancy and Electric Power, in organs such as the Yangtze River Valley Planning Office, frequently are viewed as spokesmen for flood control interests by other ministries and, indeed, by the electric power interest within the ministry itself. Although water planners claim to represent the general social interest, they are distrusted by the Ministry of Communications and electric power interests, particularly those committed to thermal power. These other organizations tend to believe that their missions are continually subordinated to the priorities of the flood control people. This leads to protracted discussions between the Ministry of Water Conservancy and Electric Power and other agencies and territorial units about priorities and, indeed, even what standards of comparison should be employed in establishing project priorities.

Each organization and unit has its own ideology, sense of mission, and priorities, which are sacred to it. Each believes that its objectives truly embody the general welfare. Each organization is afraid that it will not be adequately consulted and that its interests will be ignored. In order to resolve these sorts of conflicts as they apply to specific projects, the Chinese leadership repeatedly has had to resort to creating ad hoc interministerial groups to forge compromises. Such organs were established to build Gezhouba Dam and to evaluate proposals for the diversion of Yangtze water northward (as we shall see below).

Moreover, poor planning practices in the past, such as "simultaneous survey, design, and construction" (*san bian*), have resulted in projects having to be abandoned after the start of construction or having to be suspended for long periods in order to cope with unanticipated problems. This, in turn, has resulted in protracted construction times, cost overruns, and projects that, once finished, are not up to initial specifications. This was the case at both the Danjiangkou and Gezhouba dam projects (as we shall see shortly).

The planning process is defective in several other respects. Capital still is not seen as just another commodity. Planners, therefore, are reluctant to calculate the "interest costs" of investment. The Ministry of Water Conservancy and Electric Power *may* be particularly reticent to calculate interest because the capital requirements of its projects are large and because construction times have tended to be extremely long. Gezhouba will have taken about twenty years to build when it is completed. The result of not attaching a price to capital, however, has been that it has been wasted. Moreover, water conservancy planners are construction-oriented engineers. There has

[27] *FBIS*, 1983, no. 140:K17 and K3–5.

been less concern with financial planning than design planning. The Ministry acknowledges that the dominance of engineers, and the absence of social science and management training, has been one major reason for this.[28] Simply put, few persons in the planning process have asked how the maximum financial return can be extracted from every project.

The absence of an agreed-upon mode of cost-benefit analysis in the planning process also is a serious obstacle. Skewed domestic prices for such basic commodities as coal make balanced cost-benefit analysis difficult, even though planners at the Yangtze River Valley Planning Office said that they do an *economic analysis* of projects using *international prices*.[29] For instance, the underpricing of coal makes it difficult to judge the relative "costs" of thermal versus hydroelectrical power plants. Moreover, the Chinese whom I interviewed were very reluctant to even attempt to assess broader "social costs," such as coal emissions and mining accidents, as part of a comprehensive cost-benefit analysis process. In the absence of a widely accepted method of comparative analysis, bureaucratic wrangling is protracted, with each bureaucracy building partial arguments consistent with its preferred policy. And central decision-makers find it hard to choose from among all of the competing investment alternatives. With all this background noise of competing bureaucracies, central decision-makers are forced to rely on essentially political criteria for choice.

Finally—although this is less of a problem in key projects than ordinary undertakings—basic construction materials (wood, steel, and concrete) have been allocated to projects on the basis that each increment of capital construction investment is allocated a fixed quantity of each of these materials. Obviously, because different projects may need quite different proportions of these materials, shortages and surpluses are endemic to the entire construction process. Because materials shortages can stop a project dead in the water, project managers habitually ask for more investment than they need, and they hoard materials, thereby further aggravating the shortage of both capital and materials. In turn, these caches of materials become a resource that feeds corruption. As the Chinese explain it, "a few enterprises deliberately exaggerate estimate(s) of funds, demand excessive raw materials, and rope in and corrupt cadres who are responsible for contracting the construction of some projects."[30]

Tackling the water problems identified above will be inhibited by a fourth characteristic of the system: there is a web of subsidies and differential prices which creates constituencies that will resist any change of the status quo detrimental to their interests. The Chinese are just beginning to reveal the

---

[28] *CWC*, 1982, no. 3:26.
[29] YRVPO interview no. 6, Oct. 5, 1982 (1).
[30] *FBIS*, 1983, no. 162:K9.

enormity of the subsidy system they have created. A significant portion of
China's budgetary expenditure is being consumed by these subsidies. The
grain and cooking-oil subsidy (28.8 billion yuan from 1979 to 1981) is just
the best-known example. In 1983, for instance, Vice-Premier Yao Yilin
announced that in order to compensate for increases in cotton textile prices,
"subsidies of 100 million yuan will be granted to China's poorest areas in an
effort to balance the adverse effects scheduled increases for cotton textiles
might produce on living standards."[31]

And so it is with water—water is selling far below its cost of production,
as we observed above. Consequently, existent water systems decay, water is
wasted amidst a shortage in the North, and capital is not accumulated to
meet future repair and expansion needs. Yet, to raise the price to industry
and agriculture would set off a domino effect of price changes throughout the
economy.

When we turn to electricity we find that the subsidy arrangements are
complex. In Gansu province, for instance, some particularly arid areas at
high elevations use large quantities of electricity to drive their irrigation
pumps. These areas purchase electricity at a highly subsidized price, which
can be as low as one-sixth the nonsubsidized selling price. At this lower price,
electricity costs per mu constitute about 5 percent of the farmer's per mu
output value.[32] If the price were raised to a nonsubsidized level, electricity
costs per mu would constitute about 30 percent of the output value per mu.
The price of electricity is a critical matter for these areas, and they, predictably, resist efforts to change it. Similarly, small hydroelectric plants have
received political guarantees that the power grids will purchase their excess
electricity at comparatively high prices, even when the grid does not need the
power. The result has been that the grids (particularly in the South) have
had, on occasion, to curtail production at larger and more efficient generating plants so that they can purchase the output from the smaller and less
efficient generators. These electrical revenues have provided localities that
own and operate small hydroelectric facilities—areas such as Chong Yang
county in Hubei province—with very significant resources which *they can
control*. These revenues provide localities with some capability to accomplish
their own objectives, and they will fight to keep control of these funds.

What are the implications of all this subsidization? First, it means that
creating more economic efficiency is not simply a technical problem, it is a
political minefield. To propose changing the subsidy patterns is to propose
redistributing the benefits of society. Second, gradual change will be difficult
to produce because a change in the price of one commodity will reverberate
throughout the economy. Price changes will produce both wage demands
and budgetary demands.

[31] *FBIS*, 1983, no. 13:K9.
[32] *CWC*, 1981, no. 4:49.

The final attribute of the system which affects its ability to deal with long-range water problems is that in China, as everywhere else, the objectives of one policy frequently conflict with others. For instance, the drive for enterprise profitability makes managers resistant to costly pollution-control requirements. Managers in China like utility rate increases about as much as their capitalist counterparts abroad. Good forestry policy, controlled land use, and maintenance of collective irrigation projects run headlong into the perceived self-interests of peasants whose entrepreneurial instincts have recently been aroused. And finally, the drive by planners to accumulate investment capital leads them to invest in undertakings with a comparatively high return. The Chinese system, then, like systems elsewhere, tends to lurch from crisis to crisis. The needs of the present tend to overwhelm those of the future.

THE POLITICAL SYSTEM: IMPLEMENTATION AT THE MICRO LEVEL

Above I have outlined the scope and magnitude of China's water problems, analysed how the system "creates" some of these difficulties, and discussed how the nature of the system constrains the policy responses. However, this volume focuses on policy implementation: it assumes that there *is* a policy and that the problem is translating the vision into reality. Although frequently there is *no* water policy, sometimes there is. And, as one would predict, there frequently is little congruence between intention and outcome. Below we shall briefly identify the cascade of specific factors that can sabotage, distort, delay, and (occasionally) facilitate the implementation of effective water policy. Why in China, as in the United States, can one summarize the "implementation problem" as follows: "After a policy mandate is agreed to, authorized, and adopted, there is underachievement of stated objectives..., delay, and excessive financial cost?"[33] In trying to answer this question, I shall examine two projects in the Yangtze Basin.

In the year that the Communists came to power, floods along the Yangtze River (Changjiang) were serious. Flood control became a principal objective, and for good reason. The Yangtze drainage basin embraces 20 percent of China's land area and one-third of the nation's population. It touches all or part of 18 provinces, municipalities, and autonomous regions, and 684 counties and cities. The basin has 40 percent of China's total hydroelectrical generating potential, and a large percentage of the nation's total volume of inland waterway freight moves on its rivers. Finally, about 40 percent of China's total grain production comes from the basin.

Because of the frequency of major floods along the Changjiang in the pre-Communist era (1860, 1870, 1896, 1931, 1935, and 1949), and the staggering casualties and property losses that resulted, the Ministry of Water Conser-

---

[33] Eugene Bardach, *The Implementation Game* (Cambridge: MIT Press, 1979), 3.

vancy, and its subordinate planning organ called the Yangtze River Water Conservancy Commission (Changjiang Shuili Weiyuanhui), was ordered to develop plans to increase the basin's flood resistance. The immediate task was to protect the major cities of the middle and lower reaches, urban areas like Shashi and Wuhan. For instance, in the 1931 flood, more than 50 million mu of agricultural fields were inundated, there were 30 million "disaster stricken people," and parts of Wuhan were under water for three months.[34]

In 1951 Chairman Mao Zedong personally approved the Yangtze River Water Conservancy Commission's plans for a Jingjiang Flood Diversion Project. The following year, this 921 km² diversion area was built in seventy-five days—300,000 people were mobilized in the effort during the period from March to May. This diversion area had a simple purpose: to retain excess floodwaters which the 182 km Jingjiang dike could not handle. This strategic dike protects the middle Yangtze city of Shashi and the even more populated regions of the Jianghan Plain (Wuhan) to the east.

This project was completed none too soon. Two years later (1954), the diversion area was used three times in a single season and helped spare the city of Shashi and the downstream metropolis of Wuhan catastrophic losses. Even with the diversion of the floodwaters, however, the Jingjiang Dike itself had to be intentionally breached in two places. This resulted in enormous losses: 2.5 million mu (313,490 hectares) were inundated because of intentional diversions alone. Nineteen million persons suffered losses in the 1954 flood, and the Beijing–Canton Railroad was cut for a hundred days.

The diversion of water was an exceedingly costly stopgap measure. A long-term plan had to be developed to first tame the river's flood potential and then guide the basin's development to utilize its rich power, irrigation, fishery, and transport resources.

Even before the 1954 flood, and indeed before Liberation, some engineers had argued that the most cost-effective way to control floods in the middle and lower reaches of the Yangtze was to build a high dam in the Three Gorges (San Xia) above Yichang. In 1951 "the Center" (Zhongyang) ordered the Ministry of Water Conservancy to initiate research on such a project, despite the fact that "some comrades" wanted to "eliminate the idea."[35] However, because of budgetary and technical constraints, not much was done. In September 1954, at the First Session of the First National People's Congress in Beijing, Zhou Enlai called for comprehensive Yangtze River Basin planning. In the wake of the flood, protection of the middle and lower reaches was to be the plan's primary objective. This meant building retention reservoirs, increasing discharge capacities, raising dikes, and

[34] YRVPO interviews no. 1 (6) and no. 3 (1–2, 4) provided information for this and the following two paragraphs.

[35] Sources for this paragraph are *CWC*, 1956, no. 5:9 and 14–15; also YRVPO interview no. 1 (1).

expanding diversion area. While multiple use was a consideration, the needs of irrigation, electric power generation, navigation, and fishing were secondary concerns, particularly in the Ministry of Water Conservancy and the Yangtze River Water Conservancy Commission.

Despite the mandate to develop a comprehensive, multi-use, basin-wide plan, the Ministry of Water Conservancy found that difficult to do because of financial, data, and personnel constraints. Moreover, needed authority was fragmented among many new ministries in the state structure, and the Yangtze River Commission was itself weak. The Commission was divided into three branches: one each for the river's upper, middle, and lower reaches. All together, the Commission had only somewhat more than 1,000 personnel.[36] In an attempt to strengthen the planning effort, in 1956 the Yangtze River Valley Planning Office was formed (Changjiang Liuyu Guihua Bangongshi), with its headquarters still in Hankou (Wuhan), as had been the case with the commission it replaced. Lin Yishan, a close personal friend of Mao Zedong's, was placed in charge (where he stayed until 1982), and the organization's staff and responsibilities grew. Indeed, in about June 1956, Lin gave Mao a report (*huibao*) about development potential in the basin and the prospects for a high dam in the Three Gorges area.

In the period between the founding of the Planning Office (Changban) and the March 1958 Chengdu Conference, the Yangtze planners worked closely with the Ministry of Fuels, industrial ministries, the Ministry of Communications (responsible for inland waterway transportation), the Bureau of Water Products, the Academy of Sciences, and the Ministry of Water Conservancy to draft a basin-wide flood control and development plan. Indeed, prior to the Cultural Revolution, the Ministry of Communications had a large contingent of its personnel in residence at Changban. During this period, Changban's Lin Yishan reported (*huibao*) to Premier Zhou in 1957, 1958, and 1959, giving him progress reports on plan development. Parenthetically, the staff at Changban believes that Zhou was particularly "concerned" (*guanxin*) with their work, and they are quick to point out that Changban remained virtually untouched during the Cultural Revolution, a fact they attribute to Zhou's support. Finally, on March 30, 1958, Mao personally visited the Three Gorges to inspect possible sites of any future high dam project—he was in the company of Lin Yishan.

At the Chengdu Conference, a meeting in which decentralization, mass movements in agriculture, and opposition to "bourgeois intellectuals" were all watchwords, a basic outline plan for the comprehensive development of the Yangtze Basin was adopted. The plan's key features were these: to build a high dam in the Three Gorges in order to protect the middle and lower

[36]The information in the rest of this section is derived from YRVPO interviews no. 1 (1–2 and 6) and no. 4 (8); also interview B_2 (1).

reaches; to move Yangtze water to the North China Plain; to develop an extensive north-south inland-waterway network; and to promote comprehensive resource utilization, particularly irrigation and hydroelectric generation. The "plan" was a virtual "wish list" of dam and canal projects strewn across a map, which was published in early 1959.

Implementing the plan meant first formulating a set of project priorities, doing feasibility studies, choosing among contending alternatives, and then building selected projects. As we shall see, *implementing a policy at one level becomes a problem of policy formulation at another.* Moreover, the entire implementation process is more riddled with politics than is the initial process of plan formulation. It is one thing to create a "plan" that leaves out very little; it is another to decide what to do first and carry that to completion. In the inimitable words of one interviewee, there is "a difference between paper military strategies and actual combat." Below, I shall briefly recount the vagaries of two plan projects.

The Han River's Danjiangkou Project

The Han River joins with the Changjiang at Hankou (Wuhan). The river drains 174,000 km², and as the stream flows southward its water volume increases while its peak discharge capacity *diminishes*. Wuhan and the heavily populated Jianghan Plain, lying as they do at the confluence of the Han and Yangtze rivers, are in a treacherous position during the flood season. The 1935 Han River flood, which breached dikes in fourteen places,[37] inundated between 6.4 and 6.7 million mu of farmland (about 446,890 hectares), the "disaster stricken population" was 3.7 million, and the number of persons drowned was 80,000. From 1931 to 1948 the river flooded substantially once every two years, and dikes were breached during twelve of those eighteen years.

Given the threat posed by the Han River, as early as 1952 the Yangtze River Water Conservancy Commission began to repair and strengthen dikes, and in 1955–1956 the Dujiatai Diversion area was built in the vicinity of Wuhan. However, all of this did not fundamentally alter the river's basic character, and planners began to design a large storage dam about 330 kilometers upstream from Wuhan. The site was to be at the confluence of the Han and Dan rivers. The structure's initially designed height was to be 175 meters (above sea level). The dam was designed to handle about 80 percent of the lower Han's flood problems. The resulting reservoir would straddle (equally) the Hubei-Henan provincial boundary, large tracts of parched fields in both provinces could be irrigated, and hydropower could be supplied to electricity-short industry in Wuhan and (to a lesser extent) Zhengzhou. About all of this, there was little debate. Both the Hubei and Henan

---

[37] Figures in this paragraph are from YRVPO interview no. 4 (6) and FT interview no. 2 (2).

provincial governments supported the concept, adequate raw materials were available locally, and the site was generally good.

Project construction, however, went through a series of tortuous stages:

1. From September 1, 1958, to December 26, 1959, the earthen diversion dam was built. This was accomplished almost entirely by manual labor, with 100,000 people mobilized from sixteen surrounding counties—all of this done at the fever pitch of the Great Leap Forward. Communications and transport in the area were largely absent, there was no housing for the workers, and in the words of one interviewee, conditions were "very harsh" (*hen xingku*).[38]

2. From December 26, 1959, to March 1962, they commenced actual construction. This process was semi-mechanized, some communications by then had been installed, and some housing was available.

3. During the period from March 1962, to December 1964, construction was stopped entirely. The principal reasons for the halt were inadequate preconstruction planning and an infrastructure too primitive to support the effort once it was under way. The project was approved by Mao Zedong *before* the planners were ready to go. Once construction was under way, builders ran into technical problems with cement quality, with one respondent reporting that some of the concrete had big "holes."[39] According to the same informant, some of the concrete had to have new reinforcing added. Consequently, the project engineers apparently became worried that the dam's foundation might not be able to support a structure of the initially designed height. Moreover, planners thought that the structure (as designed) would not adequately discharge silt; they wanted to stop work and redesign that aspect of the project.

Economic considerations also were important. The Soviets had pulled out advisers from China in August 1960, and Beijing was repaying large outstanding obligations with Moscow as soon as possible. This, combined with the post–Great Leap "Three Hard Years" and the resulting precipitous decline in state revenues, literally dried up investment capital.[40] Moreover, the costs of persons dislocated by the project (*yimin fei*) were greater than was expected; in the end, they constituted between 28 and 30 percent of total project costs. The higher the dam was to be built, the greater would be the inundation and the higher these displacement costs. As a result, during the construction delay, planners and provincial officials considered alternative dam heights of 140, 152, 162, and the original 175 meters.

4. In December 1964 construction on the concrete portion of the dam was resumed and continued until November 1967, when filling of the reservoir

[38] FT interview no. 2 (3).
[39] Interview B_1 (2–3).
[40] Sources for this paragraph are FT interviews no. 2 (3) and no. 4 (2); also interview B_1 (2).

commenced. Only in 1965, though, was a revised dam-height approved for 152 meters (with a water level of 145).[41] However, the Hubei and Henan provincial governments were not satisfied—they wanted a 162-meter dam because it would have more utility for them. In 1966 the dam was approved for 162 meters, *but* it was agreed that the water level would stay at the 145-meter level until the problem of displaced persons could be resolved and paid for. In predictable political fashion, the provinces and planners got the higher dam, and local opponents to inundation (more below) and those concerned about financing got the lower water level, at least temporarily!

In addition to the concrete dam, earthen dams to the left and right of the center structure had to be built. Earth moving for these began in 1966 and lasted until 1970. However, this work was considerably slowed by the Cultural Revolution (1967–1969), as the following earth-moving figures attest:[42] In 1966, .62 million cubic meters of earth were moved; in 1967, .50 million; in 1968, .20 million; and in 1969, .37 million—a precipitous decline in the four-year period. In addition to the slower pace of work, "the quality of inspection was wrecked" (*pohuaile*) during this period. Some substandard materials were used. As a consequence, the earthen dam had some "weak spots," which were being repaired at considerable expense (5.3 million yuan) in 1982. Problems with the earthen dam, according to one interviewee, slowed construction time by an estimated one to two years.

By October 1973 all six power generators had been installed (though some electricity had been generated as early as 1968), and on February 24, 1974, *People's Daily* announced that the project had been completed. It had taken somewhat over fourteen years. By 1973 the water level was 155 meters, and in 1974 it reached 157 meters.

Many of the factors that impeded project implementation are self-evident from the chronology provided. Two factors, however, call for supplementary discussion: Why was the project so impetuously approved? And what role did local opposition and the problems of dislocated persons play in the delays?

Addressing the first question, interviewees agreed that starting construction in the fall of 1958 had been premature, both in terms of detailed planning and supporting infrastructure.[43] When asked why the project had been launched so prematurely, interviewees pointed to two factors: provincial pressure from Hubei and Henan (which needed the power, water, and flood protection to meet their ambitious economic goals), and Mao Zedong's mobilizational proclivities—what one informant called the "more, better, and faster mentality." Henan province, with Wu Zhipu at the provincial

[41] FT interview no. 2 (3).

[42] The source for this paragraph is FT interview no. 4 (4).

[43] Sources for this paragraph are FT interview no. 2 (7) and YRVPO interview no. 4 (8).

helm, was on the cutting edge of Great Leap mobilizational policy. In the words of one engineer, Hubei and Henan provinces were very "active" (*jiji de*). What appears to have happened is that planners simply were ignored (or chose to remain quiet). They presumably were loathe to confront two provinces eager to launch a project and a Chairman who embraced it because it promoted his vision of radically transforming the Chinese economy.

Once the project was under way, one very nettlesome problem was displaced persons: how to pay for them, where to put them, and how to deal with the local opposition. This entire bundle of issues was embodied in the question of dam height. If the water level was 157 meters (dam height 162), then the reservoir surface area would be about 813 km^2.[44] This water level created about 356,000 displaced persons, according to *central* figures, and 390,000 according to *local* figures. Parenthetically, the disparity between central and local estimates reveals a core aspect of project politics. Localities always adopt high estimates of damage and low projections of project benefit in order to extract the most favorable terms from higher authorities. The Center and unaffected localities have the opposite incentives. Were the dam built to the initially designed height of 175 meters (with a water level of 170), the reservoir surface area would expand to 1,000 km^2, thereby creating *about* 100,000–200,000 *additional* displaced persons. Keeping the dam height at 162 meters would save about 20 percent of total project costs. And, in the process, local opposition would be reduced.

Local opposition took a number of forms: First, protracted negotiations between Hubei and Henan provinces occurred, and in the end Hubei agreed to take 80,000 of Henan's displaced persons and to resettle them in Hubei.[45] One informant asserted that there was a written agreement between Hubei and Henan specifying the distribution of displaced persons, water, and electrical power.[46] Predictably, moving residents of the Henan plains to hilly areas in Hubei made neither the refugees nor the now disrupted Hubei communities happy. Moreover, all of this created conflict between cadres in the dislocated communities and the "old cadres" in the areas which now had to absorb them.

When asked why Hubei agreed to assume this burden, interviewees replied that Henan was poor, the plight of their displaced persons was worse, and "Henan's benefits from the reservoir were not as great."[47] One engineer identified four things that caused friction in the resettlement process: (1) People were moved from their "ancestral homes" (*lao jia*). (2) There was

---

[44] Sources for this paragraph are YRVPO interview no. 4 (7–8) and FT interview no. 4 (4–5).

[45] FT interview no. 4 (4).

[46] Interview B$_1$ (2).

[47] Sources for this paragraph are FT interview no. 4 (5), interview B$_1$ (2), and YRVPO interview no. 4 (8). Land requisitioning is a recurrent problem. See *FBIS*, 1983, no. 152:K8, and no. 131:R6–7.

uncertainty whether to move families, production teams, or entire production brigades and communes—where does one "put" them? (3) Hubei's economy and agriculture were different from Henan's. (4) "In fact, frequently people get land that is not as good as they had before." As a result, many people who had been moved out returned to their previous home area and squatted on land that had not yet been flooded. As one travels across the reservoir today, one sees people literally clinging to bits of land that will vanish if the water rises another meter. One exasperated informant simply summarized the whole dilemma as *hen kunnan* ("very difficult").

Noncompliance and opposition by local officials must be considered also.[48] Local opposition was clear and vocal in the Danjiangkou case. First, Jun Xian, a county town in Hubei with a long and illustrious history, fought to preserve its county seat and cultural relics. (Cultural relics costs finally came to around 250,000 yuan.)[49] Even when Jun Xian "lost" the battle to save its county seat, its government headquarters was moved about 30 km to behind the safety of the dam itself. From this sanctuary, the county seat administers what is left of its county and opposes raising the water level still further to the 170-meter level, as the planners wish. Such a move would inundate what remains of the county's domain. Also in Hubei, Yun Xian opposes further raising of the water level, as does Henan's Zhechuan Xian. At the special district level, Xiangyang Special District (SD) in Hubei and Nanyang SD in Henan oppose further inundation. One informant explained that the Henan provincial government was in favor of raising the water level further because of the benefits for the province as a whole, but it was unable to persuade the immediately affected localities. Superiors, it seems, somehow felt it unfair to bludgeon local communities into accepting their own territorial demise. The Chinese really would rather persuade subordinates than compel them.

Also to be considered is the fact that the planners and the Ministry of Water Conservancy and Electric Power do not determine how much compensation dislocated people will receive, they do not control the distribution of these resources, and they play little role in the implementation of resettlement plans. Instead, local officials implement resettlement plans with centrally supplied resources, the level of which is determined in Beijing.[50] Consequently, there is no way for planners (or Beijing) to assure that funds are used for intended purposes. Moreover, small localities do not have the expertise to handle many of the inevitable difficulties. Moving people from one territorial jurisdiction to another further degrades the process.

[48] The opposition of local officials to capital construction projects often hampers progress. For example, see *FBIS*, 1983, no. 186:P1.

[49] FT interview no. 4 (2).

[50] Sources for this paragraph are YRVPO interview no. 3 (9); *CWC*, 1981, no. 2:32; *People's Yangtze River*, 1979, no. 4:13–17.

Finally, once displaced persons programs have been mishandled in an area, the resistance of everyone who might be moved in the future increases.

These difficulties have led China's water planners and bureaucrats to recognize the need to reduce inundation and population displacements.[51] The problem is, of course, that only big projects will fundamentally reduce some of the principal hydrological threats and maximize development potential. The longer the delay, the higher become the economic and political costs and the less likely is action.

The Gezhouba Dam Project

As was noted above, the Three Gorges High Dam Project (San Xia) was the centerpiece of the 1958 basin development plan. However, the project's huge capital requirements, Chinese uncertainty as to whether they could technically accomplish something that big (given problems at Danjiangkou and elsewhere), the financial and political problems associated with the Leap and its aftermath, and the subsequent Cultural Revolution, all conspired to shelve plans for San Xia throughout the 1950s and 1960s. By the late 1960s, however, with Mao seemingly in control in the capital, the state ministerial structure in a near shambles, and provincial and military power at a high point, Hubei province began to promote the idea of a dam across the Yangtze at Yichang.[52] The initial 1958 basin plan had called for the Three Gorges High Dam to be built *first* and a smaller reregulating dam below it *later*. However, Hubei was starved for electric power, and the provincial government pushed the Ministry of Water Conservancy and Mao for approval of the reregulating dam first.

As nearly as I was able to reconstruct from interviews, Hubei submitted its proposal to Mao, *through* the Ministry of Water Conservancy (not Changban).[53] Changban could *not* stop this proposal from being submitted, because the proposed project was entirely within Hubei province, and in addition, the entire planning process was "very chaotic" (*hen luan*). In Beijing, the Ministry (perhaps out of fear of saying no?) sent the proposal on to Mao for his consideration. Flawed as the project was, he approved it! This may be a classic instance of every subordinate kicking a problem to his superior, hoping that each superior would kill the idea. While the experts at Changban had done extensive design and survey work for the Three Gorges Project, they had not done such extensive preparatory work for a dam at Yichang (Gezhouba, as it soon was to become known). So, when construction commenced on December 26, 1970 (Mao's birthday), Changban and the

---

[51] For example, see *CWC*, 1981, no. 2:31–33 and 38.

[52] Sources for this paragraph are YRVPO interview no. 6 (6); FT interview no. 7 (1–2); also YRVPO interview no. 4 (11).

[53] Sources for this paragraph are YRVPO interview no. 4 (11) and FT interview no. 7 (1).

dam builders had to undertake survey, design, and construction work *simultaneously* (*san bian*).

During the 1970–1973 period, the planners at Changban were not in charge of the building and design process, as they would be later.[54] Instead, a "headquarters" (*zhihuibu*) was set up to guide the effort, composed of representatives from Hubei province, the Ministry of Water Conservancy, the Ministry of Electric Power, Changban, the People's Liberation Army Construction Corps, and other unspecified organizations. The dam was a committee project in the worst sense of the word. The PLA, at this time, played down expertise; unruly civilian workers further aggravated problems.

Although interviewees were not exceedingly specific about the precise problems, in November 1972 Premier Zhou Enlai ordered a halt to construction, a pause that lasted until October 1974.[55] The principal reasons for the halt were to change important features of the dam design *and* to overhaul the management of the entire construction project. More specifically, a series of technical and design problems called for attention, difficulties that arose because there had been "inadequate preparation" (*meiyou hao junbei*). First, as at Danjiangkou, they were having problems assuring the quality of the concrete; some had to be ripped out. Additionally, sediment discharge was insufficient, and more discharge bays were added in the revised design. As well, elaborate silt-guiding embankments were incorporated into the design. Not to be overlooked, the Ministry of Communications was worried about lock capacity (apparently there was only one lock in the initial plan), lock-silting problems, and silting in the port of Yichang. The Ministry of Communications was pushing for a halt in construction until these problems could be resolved. Of course, these alterations boosted costs above the initial 1970 estimate, though I never succeeded in securing precise figures on this. The 1974 revised cost of the project was 3,556,000,000 yuan.

Parenthetically, even once construction resumed in late 1974, further changes would be made. For instance, the 1974 revised design for the dam's second phase called for a six-bay sluice, and this subsequently was changed to nine. Likewise, the 1974 revised design called for fewer electrical generators than are now to be installed.[56] Both changes were made in 1978, and naturally this further escalated costs. The only *estimate* I was given for final project cost was 4,500,000,000 yuan.

All of the problems that led to the halt in 1972–1974 reflected, of course, fundamental management problems. In 1972 Premier Zhou ordered the establishment of an interministerial body named the Technical Committee

---

[54] Sources for this paragraph are YRVPO interview no. 6 (6) and interview B₁ (3).

[55] Sources for this paragraph are FT interview no. 7 (1–2); also YRVPO interviews no. 4 (9 and 11) and no. 6 (6–7); also interview B₁ (3).

[56] Sources for this paragraph are FT interview no. 7 (4–5); YRVPO interview no. 6 (7); FT interview no. 6 (2).

(Jishu Weiyuanhui),[57] and the head of Changban, Lin Yishan, was placed in charge. The Committee reported *directly* to the State Council, and consisted of ranking political and technical people from several ministries: Communications, the Ministry of Water Conservancy, the Ministry of Electric Power, the State Planning Commission, Hubei province, Machine Building, the State Capital Construction Commission, the Gezhouba Construction Bureau, and *perhaps* Agriculture and Forestry, though my interviewees differed on this point. As well, a professor from Qinghua University attended meetings, though he was not a member.

The Committee's purpose was to provide a forum in which technical experts and ministry bureaucrats could "harmonize" (*xie tiao*) the different perspectives and then secure top-level approval expeditiously.[58] In a revealing article, Lin Yishan said that a project like Gezhouba involves many ministries and that "all relationships are complex."[59] Lin said that several principles were followed in the Committee's deliberations, among which were these: (1) On major "strategic decisions," unified opinion had to be achieved among all Committee members. (2) Prior to each plenary Committee meeting, technical people at the bureau level met for discussions, and after the issues were clarified there, they would be presented to the entire Committee, which would *first* "understand deeply" *and then* express attitudes.

With the design changes made and the Technical Committee functioning, construction resumed in October 1974. As was indicated above, additional alterations have been made since then. In 1982–1983, there still was debate about whether a third lock (the Number One Lock) would be built or postponed until some future date. Also, at that time there still was no firm date for project completion; estimates were lengthening, with the best guess being 1990.[60]

Throughout the entire process of design and construction, bureaucratic wrangling between the Ministry of Communications and the Ministry of Water Conservancy has occurred. Communications wanted as much lock capacity as possible, as a hedge against breakdowns and in order to handle future freight volumes. The Ministry of Water Conservancy and Electric Power, on the other hand, resisted these demands as excessive. The greater the dam's lock capacity, the greater the project cost and the greater the decline in electrical generating potential.[61] Moreover, because *all* project investment is charged against the primary use, the Ministry of Communica-

---

[57] Sources for this paragraph are *CWC*, 1981, no. 2:3; YRVPO interview no. 6 (5); FT interview no. 7 (5); interview B_1 (1).

[58] YRVPO interview no. 6 (5).

[59] *CWC*, 1981, no. 2:3.

[60] Interview B_2 (2); YRVPO interview no. 6 (7); also FT interview no. 6 (3).

[61] Sources for this paragraph are FT interviews no. 7 (5) and no. 6 (3); *FBIS*, 1981, no. 126:K58; *BR*, 1981, no. 35:22.

tions was in effect making demands for which it did not have to pay. Similar
bureaucratic pulling and hauling has been evident between the Ministry of
Water Conservancy and Electric Power and the Agriculture and Forestry
Ministry. The latter demanded that a fishway be installed at the dam so that
sturgeon could travel to their spawning grounds in Sichuan province. This
would increase costs further, and predictably, this suggestion has been resisted. One engineer half jokingly said that you cannot train fish to use a
fishway anyhow.

Another factor that has more recently affected costs has been inflation and
rising labor costs.[62] For instance, the post-1976 wage changes and bonuses
have driven up wage expenditures (*gongrenfei*) about 30–35 percent (one
estimate is as high as 40 percent) over what had been forecast earlier. How
far project investment goes, then, is not simply a question of managerial
efficiency—it is also a function of decisions made in Beijing and global economic trends. The degree to which Beijing is responsive to workers' wage
demands, and inflationary trends at home and abroad, will all affect the
implementation of major projects. The more integrated China becomes
into the world economy, the more this will be true.

Interdependencies among ministries was also another source of delay and
frustration. Gezhouba required enormous machinery and a large quantity of
parts from the Ministry of Machine Building (e.g., generators, lifts, doors,
cranes, hydraulics, and so on). Frequently, work was slowed in order to wait
for items that had not arrived. In an interview at the Ministry of Machine
Building, I asked about this. Here is an excerpt from my notes of that
discussion.

> Mr. xxx readily conceded that it had been a problem and he said that, in fact,
> they had sent their minister to the dam several times to solve problems. Also,
> he said, they have sent their people several times to Gezhouba and Gezhouba
> wasn't ready for them. Sometimes they (MMB) have had to warehouse gener-
> ators and sometimes the dam is ahead of them. "It is hard to synchronize,
> sometimes we are ahead and they are behind and sometimes we are behind and
> they are ahead." For instance, last year . . . the Minister of Water Conservancy
> went to Gezhouba "to overcome a dangerous situation." The problems were
> solved so fast that the Ministry of Machine Building was not ready and they
> were behind in their deliveries to Gezhouba by about one month. "This is a
> common phenomenon to have a delay in supplies."[63]

A final factor that has affected project implementation has been changes
in labor productivity.[64] The labor productivity figures for Gezhouba

---

[62] Sources for this paragraph are FT interview no. 7 (4); YRVPO interview no. 4 (10); interview B$_2$ (3).

[63] Interview M$_1$ (13).

[64] Labor productivity, in this case, is defined as the yuan figure that results from dividing the
total yearly number of workers and staff into the total value of the capital construction item
"erection and installation" (*jianzhu anzhuang*). FT interview no. 7 (4).

supplied by the Ministry of Water Conservancy's publication *China Water Conservancy* (no. 2, 1981, 14), demonstrate changes over time:

Years:

1971	1972	1973	1974	1975	1976	1977	1978	1979	1980

Amount in yuan:

925	1,304	1,814	1,557	2,660	2,707	3,992	6,051	5,020	4,845

Predictably, there is a large increase in labor productivity in the "post–Gang of Four" era. When I asked why this change occurred, I was told there were three reasons: (1) In the early years, most of the construction was earth work, which is of low value. (2) In the later years, the high-value equipment was installed and the project was more mechanized. (3) There had been poor management early on.[65]

By way of conclusion, one factor that was enormously important at Danjiangkou played a small role at Gezhouba—displaced persons. Because Gezhouba's reservoir is small, "only" 23,400 persons were displaced and 13,900 mu were inundated.[66] Moreover, in handling these people, lessons were learned from Danjiangkou. New housing was built in the vicinity of Yichang, close to where the people had lived before. Although their new land was not as good as what they had before, it seemed clear that the scale and intensity of displaced persons problems were much less at Gezhouba than had been the case at Danjiangkou.[67] This suggests, as the Chinese have themselves observed, that if projects are to be smoothly implemented, their planners would be well advised to minimize the negative impact on surrounding communities.

An Overview of Implementation

The cases analyzed above reveal several broader features of the Chinese political system and contribute to the understanding of the implementation process. "The implementation problem" in China arises from the combined effects of several factors: As Pressman and Wildavsky found in Oakland, California, interdependence and complexity ("the complexity of joint action"), the existence of multiple "clearance points," greatly reduces the probability of effective implementation.[68] In China, with its bureaucratic tradition and a centrally planned economy, a great percentage of social decisions must be processed by the political system. Moreover, the Chinese polity's capacity to handle them is less than that of other, higher-resource systems. Concisely, China's political system is overloaded.

[65] YRVPO interview no. 6 (8).

[66] *A Brief Introduction to the Yangtze River's Gezhouba Water Conservancy Project*, 9; also FT interview no. 7 (4).

[67] FT interview no. 7 (4).

[68] Jeffrey Pressman and Aaron Wildavsky, *Implementation* (Berkeley and Los Angeles: University of California Press, 1973).

At the same time that political authorities are asked to decide too much, they generally lack the kind of information needed to inform technical decisions. Too, there is a dearth of financial resources to win the compliance of subordinates. Even when resources are available, they may not be provided to the people with an incentive to spend them in approved or helpful ways, as was the case with giving local officials control of resettlement funds. And frequently, personnel are insufficiently skilled to effectively implement decisions once they have been made.

Perhaps even more fundamental, any implementation process is embedded within a culture. Chinese culture values consensus, discussion, and persuasion; all of this takes time. In a very basic way, the Chinese are process-oriented, rather than result-oriented. Moreover, the Chinese officials and managers with whom I dealt all seemed loathe to impose large economic costs on citizens and subordinates, who are just barely hanging on in any case. This is *not* to say that the state's iron fist never delivers any blows—it does. But, with most issues, most of the time, efforts to secure consensus are extensive.

This predisposition toward consensus, in turn, interacts with the most basic social structural entity above the family—"the unit" (*danwei*). Organizations and subordinates have their prerogatives, and this can be a genuine obstacle to securing compliance. Organizations in China are not simply places where one works, they are one's life in terms of housing, education for children, recreation, and association. There is the well-founded expectation that one will have to spend one's entire life in "the unit." Predictably, therefore, organizational memories are long, organizational ideologies are strong, and organizational resistance to change is greater in China than is the case in organizationally more fluid settings. With so little expectation of mobility and such well-defined organizational ideologies, "unitism" creates a feudalism of self-protecting entities that are only partially responsive to the Center and only occasionally inclined to cooperate with other units in the implementation of complex projects.

Because water policy and water projects affect almost everyone to some extent, and because the life-giving fluid blithely cuts across territorial and functional lines of administration, every issue of water politics energizes a broad range of units. In formulating and implementing water policy, one is dealing with an open-ended process in which both territorial and functional units at great distance from the immediate project site will perceive great stakes and seek to shape the outcome in a way favorable to them. In any political system, when there is a profusion of political participants with different views and intense commitments, the going will be slow at best.

Given all of the centrifugal forces identified above, what factors can facilitate more effective implementation? What centripetal forces can we identify? First, economic and political resources must be concentrated so that they can be effectively used to win compliance in the highest priority cases. Second, if a project is to be carried to fruition in the Chinese setting, key members of the elite must take a visible, protracted, and forceful interest. At strategic junctures, it will be they, and only they, who can overcome snags, as Premier Zhou Enlai's role in the Gezhouba project clearly shows. Third, decision-making bodies (like Gezhouba's Technical Committee), which are interministerial in nature, are essential. Finally, crises, painful as they are, frequently are essential in order to elevate the importance of a particular policy sufficiently to win sustained elite attention, resources, and popular compliance.

In the final analysis, whether a policy will be effectively implemented is a question of whether the centrifugal forces can be overcome by the centripetal forces. To paraphrase Pressman and Wildavsky, perhaps we should marvel rather more that projects like Gezhouba and Danjiangkou got built than wonder why there were so many problems. Indeed, the fact that Gezhouba and Danjiangkou were built raises the question "How do we know an implementation success when we see one?" If initial plans were objectively impossible, does their partial realization spell "failure"? For projects designed to achieve multiple purposes, how does one weigh the realization of some objectives against the inability to simultaneously realize others? In the end, to speak of "success" and "failure" is *not* meaningful. Instead, what one can say is that China has urgent problems and that the process of formulating and implementing appropriate and effective responses is painfully slow.

SEVEN

Implementing Energy Policy:
The Rise and Demise of the State
Energy Commission

Thomas Fingar

INTRODUCTION

China's energy policies have evolved in ways that make it impossible to draw a sharp line between formulation and implementation. The salience of energy issues has made it attractive—if not imperative—for myriad special interests to climb on the energy bandwagon.[1] As a result, "energy" policies reflect numerous and often contradictory objectives.[2] Unwilling or unable to rank or integrate multiple goals, post-Mao leaders have left considerable leeway for "flexible" implementation by lower-level officials. Lacking clear guidance, implementing agencies and individuals have responded quite differently. Some have been paralyzed, others have evinced ingenuity and imagination. In response, senior officials have modified and clarified particular aspects of energy policy and issued new instructions to the implementors. The process continues.

How effectively have energy policies been implemented? There is no simple answer to this question. Since formulation and implementation are a continuing process, and attempts to execute energy-related decisions have

Research for this essay was supported, in part, by grants from the Atlantic Richfield Foundation and the Mobil Foundation. Ann Fenwick and Cheng Jiashu provided valuable research assistance, and David M. Lampton, John W. Lewis, and several Chinese friends made helpful comments on earlier drafts. I appreciate their assistance and absolve them of all responsibility for errors of fact or interpretation.

[1] For a more detailed discussion of the mechanisms and consequences of issue linkage, see Thomas Fingar, *Politics and Policy Making in the People's Republic of China, 1954–1955* (Ph.D. dissertation, Stanford University, 1977), and Thomas Fingar, "Introduction: The Quest for Independence," in Thomas Fingar, ed., *China's Quest for Independence: Policy Evolution in the 1970s* (Boulder: Westview, 1980), 8–14.

[2] This is the common phenomenon of "piling on." See, for example, Eugene Bardach, *The Implementation Game* (Cambridge: MIT Press, 1977), chap. 4.

identified problems, generated feedback, and prompted further refinement of national policies, the process seems to be working, albeit with considerable inefficiency. Moreover, despite the many problems outlined below, China has made progress toward some of its energy objectives (e.g., improved efficiency in major consuming industries). The final section of this chapter will argue that many of the achievements to date have been realized despite rather than because of specific energy policies adopted since 1978. Before paving the way for that argument with a description of China's approach to its energy problems it is important to make two points: One is that efforts to formulate and implement energy policies have encountered difficulties everywhere and that many of the problems described below have analogs in other countries.[3] The second point is that China's energy problems were caused by the government. Unlike most other countries, China possesses vast reserves of fossil fuels and untapped hydroelectric potential, but decades of inadequate planning, undervalued fuel and power, and general mismanagement of the economy have led to energy shortages in an energy-rich nation.[4]

Despite three decades of central planning, China had no national energy policy until very recently.[5] As a minor actor in the world energy market, China was not immediately affected by the price increases and energy-related anxieties that rocked most other countries in the mid-1970s. Indeed, until 1977 Chinese officials gloated about their country's energy independence.[6] This situation began to change in early 1977. The increased candor of the

[3] On the problem of formulating and implementing energy policies, see, for example, Crawford D. Goodwin, ed., *Energy Policy in Perspective: Today's Problems, Yesterday's Solutions* (Washington, D.C.: Brookings, 1981); Congressional Quarterly, *Energy Policy, Second Edition* (Washington, D.C., 1981); Peter Auer, ed., *Energy and the Developing Nations* (New York: Pergamon, 1981); Fereidun Fesharaki et al., *Critical Energy Issues in Asia and the Pacific* (Boulder: Westview, 1982); Wilfrid L. Kohl, ed., *After the Second Oil Crisis* (Lexington, Mass.: Lexington Books, 1982); Asian Development Bank, *Asian Energy Problems* (New York: Praeger, 1982), esp. chaps. 6 and 7; and Leslie Dienes and Theodore Shabad, *The Soviet Energy System: Resource Use and Policies* (Washington, D.C.: V. H. Winston and Sons, 1979).

[4] Essential background on China can be found in Vaclav Smil, *China's Energy: Achievements, Problems, Prospects* (New York: Praeger, 1976); Kim Woodard, *The International Energy Relations of China* (Stanford: Stanford University Press, 1980); Kim Woodard, "China in Asia's Energy Development," in Fesharaki et al., 183–226; and Vaclav Smil, "China's Energetics: A System Analysis," in Joint Economic Committee, *Chinese Economy Post-Mao* (Washington, D.C.: U.S. Government Printing Office, 1978), 323–69. On similar problems in the Soviet Union, see Dienes and Shabad, *Soviet Energy System*; Werner Gumpel, *Energiepolitik in der Sowjetunion* (Cologne: Verlag Wissenschaft und Politik, 1970); and Robert W. Campbell, *Soviet Energy Technologies* (Bloomington: Indiana University Press, 1980).

[5] See, for example, Xu Shoubo, "A Proposal for Initiating Scientific Research for An Energy Policy," *Renmin Ribao* (hereafter *RMRB*), Mar. 3, 1980; and the excerpt of Deputy Tu Guanchi's remarks at the Third Session of the Fifth National People's Congress (hereafter Fifth NPC) in *RMRB*, Sept. 15, 1980.

[6] See, for example, Chong Qian, "Behind the So-Called Energy Crisis," *Hong Qi* (hereafter *HQ*), 1974, no. 2:83–86.

post-Mao regime accounts for a portion of this change, but there were other reasons as well. Perhaps the most important reason is that energy problems, specifically shortages of fuel and power, emerged as an early obstacle to the realization of the developmental goals and political strategy of Mao's successors. Though identified as a bottleneck in 1977, energy did not become a salient policy or political issue until the latter part of 1978.[7]

Energy became more salient because shortages and bottlenecks jeopardized not only the economic policies of the post-Mao regime, but the very legitimacy of Party rule. Eager to "get the country moving again" and to restore the credibility and capability of the political system, senior leaders adopted a strategy that tied regime legitimacy to the success of their economic policies.[8]

This strategy was made even riskier in early 1979 by the very policies being adopted to achieve sustained economic growth and increased popular support. Increased information about the outside world, including the economic achievements of Taiwan, South Korea, Hong Kong, and Singapore, invited unfavorable comparisons and unwanted questions about the possible advantages of "capitalist development" and "bourgeois democracy."[9] These questions were further encouraged by official statements on the need to "rely more on the market," to separate the Party from the State, and to strengthen

[7] See "After the Masses Were Informed of Difficulties," *RMRB*, Mar. 11, 1977; Qian Zhengying, "Electric Power Should Play a Pioneering Role," *HQ*, 1977, no. 11:18–23; editorial, "Put the Power Industry at the Forefront," *RMRB*, Nov. 23, 1977; and the Jiangxi Radio report of the meeting of provincial Party secretaries responsible for industry, in Foreign Broadcast Information Service, *Daily Report: China* (hereafter *FBIS*), Sept. 19, 1978, G4–5. On the role of energy at the Party work conference prior to the Third Plenum of the Eleventh Party Congress, see Huang Gudun, "A Look at the CCP Central Committee's Working Conference," *Zheng Ming*, no. 20 (June 1, 1979), in *FBIS*, June 8, 1979, U1–6.

[8] See, for example, editorial, "Let the Whole Party and the Whole Nation Unite with One Heart and Strive to Realize Socialist Modernization," *HQ*, 1979, no. 1:22–26; and Hua Guofeng, "Report on the Work of the Government" (Second Session of the Fifth NPC), *RMRB*, June 26, 1979, in *Beijing Review* (hereafter *BR*), 1979, no. 27 (July 6): 8–9. See also "On Questions of Party History" (Adopted by the Sixth Plenary Session of the Eleventh Central Committee of the Communist Party of China, June 27, 1981), *BR*, 1981, no. 27 (July 6): 10–39, esp. 35–39; Thomas Fingar, "China's Quest for Technology: The Implications for 'Arms Control II,'" in John Barton and Ryukichi Imai, eds., *Arms Control II* (Cambridge: Oelgeschlager, Gunn and Hain, 1981), 239–71. For more general treatment of the risks of rising expectations and politically induced change, see Chandler Morse et al., *Modernization By Design* (Ithaca: Cornell University Press, 1969); and Chalmers Johnson, *Revolutionary Change* (Boston: Little, Brown, 1966).

[9] Commentator, "To Realize the Four Modernizations Requires Upholding the Four Principles," *HQ*, 1979, no. 5:11–15; Gui Shixun, "A Good Analysis Is Highly Beneficial—On How to Understand the Superiority of the Socialist System," *Wenhui Bao*, Apr. 24, 1979, in *FBIS*, May 23, 1979, L2–4; and Zhang Xianyang and Wang Guixiu, "Proletarian Democracy and Bourgeois Democracy," *RMRB*, June 9, 1979.

socialist democracy.[10] One response was a campaign to defend the so-called "Four Principles" (i.e., socialism, dictatorship of the proletariat, Party leadership, and Marxism–Leninism–Mao Zedong Thought) and a crackdown on "Democracy Wall";[11] another was renewed efforts to ensure the success of the strategy for economic growth. Since energy problems jeopardized that strategy, they rose to the top of the political agenda, and for the first time in their history, PRC leaders began to formulate an explicit energy policy.

Although it was not the sole reason for the shift in priorities announced at the Third Plenum of the Eleventh Central Committee in December 1978 and elaborated six months later at the Second Session of the Fifth National People's Congress, energy was—and was stated to be—an important factor.[12] Shortages of fuel and power imperiled the developmental approach adopted in 1977 in two ways. The ambitious modernization effort announced by Hua Guofeng at the First Session of the Fifth NPC in February 1978 was to be financed as well as fueled by the country's energy resources. Exports, primarily of crude oil, were expected to earn sizable amounts of foreign exchange. Revenue from oil sales would, in turn, be used to purchase advanced technologies and complete industrial plants that would enable China to leapfrog across intermediate stages of development to become a "powerful, modern, socialist country" by the end of the century. This strategy had many other problems (e.g., lack of infrastructure and of people with requisite skills made absorption of advanced technologies difficult), but substantial exports of oil were critical to its success.[13] Energy problems also imperiled the purely domestic component of this strategy. Shortages of fuel and power forced en-

[10] See, for example, Hu Qiaomu, "Act in Accordance with Economic Laws, Step up the Four Modernizations," *RMRB*, Oct. 6, 1978; and Xue Muqiao, "How Can We Effect Planned Management of the National Economy," *RMRB*, June 15, 1979. On the separation of Party and state, see Jing Dong, "It Is Impermissible to Replace the Government with the Party," *HQ*, 1980, no. 21:5–8; and Zhang Cheng, "What is Meant by Party Leadership," *RMRB*, Jan. 15, 1979.

[11] Commentator, "Everything Should Proceed from the Basic Interests of the State and People," *RMRB*, Apr. 2, 1979; and Commentator, "A Pressing Topic in Our Present Ideological and Political Work—Gain on Upholding the Four Principles to Promote the Shift of Emphasis of Our Work," *Jiefang Ribao*, Apr. 22, 1979, in *FBIS*, May 18, 1979, O8–15. On the crackdown on "Democracy Wall," see "Official Beijing Circular 'Puts Lid' on Democratic Movement," *Agence France Presse*, March 31, 1979, in *FBIS*, Apr. 2, 1979, L3–4.

[12] See the report on the Central Committee Work Conference prior to the Third Plenum in Huang Gudun (n. 7 above). See also Hua Guofeng "Report" (n. 8 above), 11–12 and 15–16.

[13] Hua Guofeng, "Unite and Strive to Build a Modern, Powerful Socialist Country!" (Report on the Work of the Government delivered at the First Session of the Fifth NPC, Feb. 26, 1978), in *BR*, 1978, no. 10 (Mar. 10): 7–40. See also, Thomas Fingar, "Energy in China: Paradoxes, Policies, and Prospects," in Richard C. Bush, ed., *China Briefing, 1982* (Boulder: Westview, 1983), 49–67; and A. Doak Barnett, *China's Economy in Global Perspective* (Washington, D.C.: Brookings, 1981), esp. 465–78.

terprises, especially those classified as light industries, to operate far below
capacity.[14] As a result, it was impossible to meet the growing demand for
consumer goods at home and in foreign markets, to instill greater worker
discipline, or to reap the benefits of improved management.

This is not the place to review the approach and policies adopted formally
in June 1979,[15] but it is important to note that while energy problems gave
rise to the "eight character policy" of readjustment, reform, consolidation
and improvement, energy was also to play a key role in the implementation
of that policy. Two examples will help to clarify the nature of this double
ends-means linkage.

A major objective of the "eight character policy" was to alleviate energy
shortages and their deleterious economic and political effects.[16] Reform and
consolidation of existing enterprises were supposed to conserve energy
through greater efficiency, but more immediate (and in the short run more
significant) results were to be achieved through readjustment. By achieving a
"better balance" between heavy and light industry (one of the central goals
of readjustment), officials hoped to reduce total demand for energy and to
increase output of high-profit, high-demand products. The logic and explanation were simple and straightforward; light industries require less fuel
and power per unit of output (and per yuan of profit) than do heavy industrial facilities.[17]

The same example can be used to illustrate the use of energy policy to
bring about readjustment, reform, consolidation, and improvement. As a
scarce commodity, energy could be allocated in accordance with previously
determined priorities. In order to bring about readjustment, senior officials

[14] Chen Xi, Huang Zhijie, and Xu Junzhang, "The Effective Use of Energy Is an Important
Issue in Developing the National Economy," *RMRB*, May 13, 1979. An article published the
following year was even more specific: "Because of insufficient motive power, about 30 percent of
industrial productive capacity cannot be brought into play, which has already markedly influenced the development of the national economy. The energy situation is an urgent one." See
Xu Junzhang, Zhang Zhengmin, Yang Zhirong, and Zhu Bin, "On Energy Construction for
China's Modernization," *Ziran Bianzhengfa Tongxun*, 1980, no. 2 (April): 16–22, in *Joint Publications Research Service* (hereafter *JPRS*), no. 76760 (Nov. 5, 1980): 53–62 at 54.

[15] Key documents can be found in *Main Documents of the Second Session of the Fifth National
People's Congress of the People's Republic of China* (Beijing: Foreign Languages Press, 1979). For
analyses, see Robert F. Dernberger, "The Chinese Search for the Path of Self-Sustained Growth
in the 1980's: An Assessment," in Joint Economic Committee, *China Under the Four Modernizations, Part 1* (Washington, D.C.: U.S. Government Printing Office, 1982), 19–26; and Barnett,
China's Economy, 83–108.

[16] Hua Guofeng, "Report," 11–12; and Yu Qiuli, "Report on the Draft of the 1979 National Economic Plan" (Second Session of the Fifth NPC), in *FBIS*, July 2, 1979, L13–28, esp.
L15–22.

[17] Zhou Shulian and Wu Jinglian, "Accord Priority Status to the Development of Light
Industry," *RMRB*, Aug. 31, 1979.

mandated that supplies of fuel and power were to be allocated to light and textile industries on a priority basis, and that allocations to heavy industry were to be reduced.[18] Reform, consolidation, and improvement were to be promoted by distributing more fuel and power to "efficient" enterprises and reducing or terminating supplies to inefficient factories and plants producing low quality goods. As will be shown below, implementation of energy policies was greatly complicated by the fact that they were encumbered with multiple and often conflicting objectives.

Implementation was beset with other problems as well. The remainder of the chapter will focus on the role of the State Energy Commission while considering the character of the policies to be implemented, the capabilities and conflicting interests of other implementing agencies, and the impact of broader contextual factors.

CHINA'S ENERGY POLICY: AN OVERVIEW

Energy policy, like many other programmatic statements issued by PRC leaders, was—and still is—extraordinarily vague. General principles and broad objectives substitute for detailed policy guidelines; "details" are supposed to be worked out in the course of implementation. As a result, agencies and individuals responsible for putting policies into effect enjoy a great deal of flexibility; they are also subject to tremendous pressure.

Policy generality can lead to flexible and effective implementation, but it can also result in confusion and paralysis. Depending on how they respond to real and perceived pressures from higher, lower, or equal levels of the system, executors of policy can improve, obstruct, or distort the "policies" they are supposed to put into effect.[19] This point will be discussed at greater length below. First, however, it will be useful to summarize representative elements of the energy policy adopted in 1978–1979 and, with few exceptions, still in effect today.

Elements of China's Energy Policy

China's overall energy policy emphasizes both production and conservation of energy while giving priority to energy conservation in the immediate future; it regards energy conservation as the primary objective in the technical

[18] Hua Guofeng, "Report," 15; Yu Qiuli, "Report," L18; the *Xinhua* broadcast report of Vice-Minister of the State Economic Commission Ma Yi's speech at the National Conference on Exchanging Experience in Energy Conservation, in *FBIS*, Oct. 31, 1980, L2–3; and Ma Hong, "Economic Readjustment and the Rate of Development," *RMRB*, Dec. 29, 1981.

[19] See, for example, George C. Edwards III and Ira Sharkansky, *The Policy Predicament* (San Francisco: W. F. Freeman, 1978), chap. 10.

transformation and structural reform of the national economy; and it gives priority to the development of coal and hydropower.[20]

As stated, these "policies" are merely broad statements of intent that say nothing about what has been, might be, or will be done to achieve these objectives.[21] Even at this level of abstraction, however, the "policies" have been controversial. For example, does "giving priority to development of coal" mean that more money should be invested in expansion of coal mines than in exploitation of known petroleum reserves? Or does it mean that funds should be used to develop as many and as widely distributed coal fields as possible? Does it mean that coal-fired thermal power plants should have priority over hydro facilities? In all cases or only under certain conditions? What are those conditions? Should priority be given to the development of small, local coal pits or to the opening of major mines with all of the requisite infrastructure? Similarly, does giving priority to conservation mean that more funds should be devoted to increasing the energy efficiency of existing facilities than to developing new sources of supply? Or does it mean building newer, more energy efficient plants? Views on these and countless other questions have differed and continue to be divisive.[22] When policy guidelines are vague, well-intentioned, responsible officials—not to mention ambitious or disgruntled ones—can interpret them in very different ways.[23]

Beijing has adopted more specific energy policies than those summarized above, but they lack the machinery for implementation (e.g., administrative and financial accountability mechanisms, sources of funds, clear lines of

[20] For a much more detailed exposition of energy policy, see Gao Yangwen (Minister of Coal), "On the Issue of China's Energy Policy," in *Meitan Kexuejishu*, 1981, no. 4 (April), translated in *JPRS*, no. 78872 (Aug. 31, 1981): 13–22.

[21] See Jeffrey L. Pressman and Aaron Wildavsky, *Implementation*, 2d ed. (Berkeley and Los Angeles: University of California Press, 1979), xix–xxiii; and Bardach, *Implementation Game* (n. 2 above), chap. 2.

[22] Examples include Li Gengxin, "Important Ways to Solve the Present Urgent Problem of Energy Resources," *Beijing Ribao*, Nov. 23, 1979, in *JPRS*, no. 75003 (Jan. 25, 1980): 9–13; Zuo Hu, "China Should Develop Nuclear Power," *Guangming Ribao* (hereafter *GMRB*), Dec. 12, 1979; Li Rui, "It Is Essential to Develop Hydroelectric Power on a Priority Basis—an Important Question in our Country's Energy Policy," *RMRB*, Mar. 6, 1980; editorial, "China Must Place Primary Emphasis on Coal," *RMRB*, Mar. 20, 1980; Kang Zhaowu and Cao Wenlong, "Manpower Advantage Taken to Expand Limited Mechanization for Coal Extraction," *RMRB*, June 15, 1980; Jin Luzhong, "Energy Transport Methods Require Careful Study," *RMRB*, Sept. 20, 1980; and Zhao Zongyu, "Altering the Composition of Urban and Rural Energy Resources to Control Environmental Pollution," *Huanjing Baohu*, 1981, no. 3:1–5, in *JPRS*, no. 79262 (Oct. 21, 1981): 32–40.

[23] See, for example, Commentator, "Increasing Coal Output Is a Pressing Task," Anhui Radio, Sept. 5, 1981, in *FBIS*, Sept. 8, 1981, O2–3. On the general problem of vague guidelines and the likelihood of "distortion" in the course of implementation, see Edwards and Sharkansky, *Policy Predicament*, chap. 10; and Bardach, *Implementation Game*.

authority and responsibility). To facilitate analysis, illustrative policy guidelines will be subdivided into three broad categories: the allocation of funds; the allocation of energy; and the redistribution of political and economic power.

The Allocation of Funds

Since energy-related expenditures constitute perhaps 20 percent of China's national budget, and fuel and power are distributed by planning agencies instead of markets, every factory manager, local government or Party official, and senior bureaucrat has a stake in the allocation of energy and resources (funds, building materials, engineers, etc.) for the energy sector.[24] As a result, energy policy making resembles the budgetary process elsewhere in two respects: Core allocations remain relatively stable from year to year, producing intense competition for marginal increases in total supply and to effect minor shifts in core allotments. A second similarity is that decisions about the disposition of marginal increases and limited amounts subject to redistribution tend to be made on the basis of political maneuver rather than economic or technical grounds.[25]

Despite the hyperbole used to describe shifts in allotment, budgeting and planned allocations are conservative processes—dramatic changes are quite rare (see chapters 3 and 6 in this volume). However, even though the spoils are marginal, competition for space at the budgetary trough can be intense, costly, and of more lasting importance than the particular decisions reached. Competitors play hard, employ the full range of political instruments (logrolling, compromise, blackmail, side payments, etc.) and carry memories and more tangible fruits into subsequent policy-making rounds.[26]

Although Chinese data preclude detailed analysis and firm conclusions, it

[24] This is an admittedly rough calculation based on the 1982 budget, which allocated 39 billion yuan (or 34 percent of total expenditures) for capital construction. Of this, 18.63 billion (16 percent of the total) was to be directly invested by the state, "mainly for basic construction related to energy and transportation." Counting the heavy investments in railway construction for coal transport as energy investment and adding the administrative cost of energy ministries such as coal and petroleum and investments in "technical transformation" to save energy, bring the total to approximately 20 percent. See Wang Bingqian, "Report on the Draft State Budget for 1982," in *FBIS*, May 7, 1982, K1–7; and Yao Yilin, "Report on the Draft of the 1982 Plan for Economic and Social Development," in *FBIS*, May 10, 1982, K1–12.

[25] Interviews with officials of the State Planning Commission, May and June 1980. Also see Fingar, "Introduction" (n. 1 above). On the general phenomenon, see Aaron Wildavsky, *The Politics of the Budgetary Process*, 3d ed. (Boston: Little, Brown, 1979); and Edwards and Sharkansky, *Policy Predicament*, 267–68. On the politics of redistribution, see Theodore Lowi, "American Business, Public Policy, Case Studies, and Political Theory," *World Politics*, 16, no. 4 (1964): 677–715.

[26] Fingar, *Politics and Policy Making* (n. 1 above).

appears that energy and energy-related allocations have changed relatively little since 1978.[27] But slight shifts have been important politically even though their energy and economic consequences have been minimal. Examples of policies involving the allocation of funds for energy and factors affecting their implementation are summarized below.

Capital construction, the largest item in the Chinese budget, has allocated funds and other scarce resources to the energy sector on a "highest priority" basis since 1979.[28] Since development of oil and gas fields, coal mines, and electric power systems is expensive, the amount of money involved is substantial, and "everyone" has attempted to get a slice of the budgetary pie.[29] Competition became even more intense after 1980, when efforts to shrink budget deficits at the central level and to reduce the number of key projects resulted in decreased total expenditures for capital construction at the same time that a higher proportion of total investment was earmarked for energy development.[30] Concomitant changes in policies governing the retention and disposition of profits retained by enterprises and localities, the conversion of capital construction grants into loans administered by the Construction Bank and the People's Bank, and other reforms extended this competition to new arenas and, unintentionally, reduced the capacity of the central government to implement other policies by manipulating energy allocations. In theory, the decision to allocate more resources to energy "settled" rivalries between the energy ministries (coal, petroleum, and electric power) and other production ministries, but the locus of contention merely shifted from the functional to the areal arena as localities (provinces, counties, and municipalities) competed for funds to develop local energy resources.[31] Since the

[27] Gui Shiyong, "Strive to Consolidate and Develop the Favorable Economic Situation," *RMRB*, July 6, 1983, sec. 2. Also see chapter 3 in this volume.

[28] Hua Guofeng, "Report" (n. 8 above); Zhao Ziyang, "Report on the Work of the Government" (First Session of the Sixth NPC), in *FBIS*, June 23, 1983, K1–26; Yao Yilin, "Report" (n. 24 above); and "The Sixth Five-Year Plan for National Economic and Social Development of the People's Republic of China (1981–1985)," *RMRB*, Dec. 13, 1982, in *FBIS*, Dec. 20, 1982, K5–42.

[29] See, for example, "First Secretary of Yangquan Municipality Has Published an Article in *Shanxi Ribao*: 'If Established as the Energy Base for Shanxi, Yangquan will Make Many Contributions,'" *RMRB*, June 9, 1980; and in the "Excerpts of Speeches by NPC Deputies at Panel Discussions," in *RMRB*, Sept. 6, 1980, and Sept. 7, 1980. See also the excerpts from comments made by deputies attending the Third Session of the Fifth NPC, broadcast by Beijing Radio on Sept. 5, 1980, in *FBIS*, Sept. 8, 1980, L35–37; and Tan Xue's remarks in "Excerpts of Speeches by NPC Deputies at Panel Discussions," *RMRB*, Sept. 9, 1980.

[30] See the *Xinhua* report on the National Electric Power Work Conference in *FBIS*, Jan. 21, 1981, L3; the Beijing Radio report of an interview with three vice-ministers of the Ministry of Power, Feb. 27, 1981, in *FBIS*, Mar. 2, 1981, L13–14; and Li Mengbai, "On Several Problems of Capital Construction," *RMRB*, Oct. 26, 1981.

[31] "First Secretary of Yangquan"; Li Wenyan and Chen Hang, "Efforts Must Also Be Made to Actively Develop Coal Mining in the Five Provinces of Shandong, Anhui, Henan, Guizhou,

factor endowments of localities differed, this competition naturally spilled over into debates about the proper scale of coal mine development, whether to emphasize hydropower rather than thermal generation, and the proper scale of hydroelectric development.[32] In other words, each "decision" merely shifted the locus of contention.[33] These competitions occurred against the background of a tradition of spreading investments widely in the name of equity and in order to secure continued political support (a pork-barrel approach), but they were also shaped by new injunctions to concentrate resources, ensure completion of key projects, and stress efficiency rather than equality.[34]

A second allocation guideline accorded priority to the use of coal. Among other consequences, that decision appears to have made it easier, at least for a time, for the Ministry of Coal to obtain foreign exchange and to negotiate seriously with foreign firms. Conversely, it seems to have had the opposite effect on the Ministries of Petroleum and Electric Power.[35] Despite the forcefulness with which policies emphasizing coal were articulated, they did not go unchallenged. Opponents argued that even though emphasizing coal made sense as a long-term strategy for the nation as a whole, it should not be applied in all circumstances. For example, some argued that it would be foolish to develop coal reserves in places with abundant oil, natural gas, or hydropower resources because coal has more harmful effects on the environ-

---

and Yunnan—On Two Articles Dealing with Development of North China Coal," *RMRB*, Aug. 2, 1979; and Tan Xue, in "Excerpts of Speeches."

[32] Kang Zhaowu and Cao Wenlong, "Manpower Advantage"; the Hubei Radio report on the provincial conference on the coal industry in *JPRS*, no. 76669 (Oct. 21, 1980): 45; editorial, "Pay More Attention to Developing Hydroelectric Power," *RMRB*, Mar. 8, 1982; *Xinhua* Chinese broadcast of June 27, 1983, in *FBIS*, June 28, 1983, R4–5; and "Speed up the Exploitation of Energy Resources in Northeast China, Serve the Four Modernizations," *Ningxia Ribao*, June 10, 1983, in *FBIS*, June 28, 1983, T3.

[33] See E. E. Schattschneider, *The Semisovereign People* (New York: Holt, Rinehart and Winston, 1960), chap. 4.

[34] See chapter 6 in this volume for more on the ethos of respecting allotments to others. On the need to concentrate resources to ensure completion of key projects, see Liu Lixin and Tian Chunsheng, "Conscientiously Control the Scale of Investments in Fixed Assets," *RMRB*, Feb. 21, 1983; and editorial, "Concentrate Funds to Ensure Completion of Key Capital Construction Projects," *RMRB*, Oct. 5, 1982.

[35] This is speculation based partially on anecdotal evidence from foreign businessmen with considerable experience negotiating with officials from the three ministries. Also, see Christopher M. Clarke, "China's Energy Plan for the 80's," *China Business Review* 8, no. 3 (May–June 1981): 48–51. Whether as cause or effect—or both—of the decision to emphasize coal, the Ministry of Petroleum and the so-called "Petroleum Clique" were subjected to criticism in mid-1980. See, for example, "A View of the Work Style of the Leadership of the Ministry of Petroleum Industry in Light of the Bohai No. 2 Accident," *RMRB*, Aug. 24, 1980; Song Zhenming's Self-Criticism Report and the Text of the State Council Decision of August 25, 1980, removing Song from his post and giving Kang Shien a "demerit, first grade" can be found in

ment, requires more costly infrastructures, and is not as versatile.[36] Such calls for adjusting policies to suit the exigencies of specific cases were often linked to argumentation on the need for a "scientific" energy policy and constituted a serious criticism of existing priorities and investment criteria.[37]

Allocations for energy conservation also spawned controversy and competition that impeded implementation of energy and other policies. In 1981 the Center earmarked funds for the "technical transformation" of facilities to make them more energy efficient.[38] Naturally, there was a scramble for the additional (and, from the perspective of enterprises and localities, extrabudgetary) funds. Though originally intended to provide money to modernize the most wasteful equipment in enterprises that consumed the largest amounts of energy (e.g., large enterprises in the metallurgical, chemical, pulp and paper, and electric power industries), general calls to conserve energy, reduce waste (as a criterion for avoiding closure or consolidation— see below), and perceptions of a new free good prompted factory managers, local officials, and local Party representatives to pursue the newly allocated funds with a vengeance. Complaints in the media about inappropriate use of such funds illustrate the ingenuity of lower-level cadres and the lack of real controls. Examples include use of such funds to "replace" capital construction allocations that had been disapproved by higher levels and to expand capacity without assured supplies of energy.[39]

A fourth and final example in this category concerns the priority assigned to the importation of equipment and technologies for the energy sector. Beginning in 1979, as part of the broader effort to rationalize and bring under

RMRB, Aug. 26, 1980. See also the speculative articles by Luo Bing on "Yu Qiuli Deprived of His Power," *Zheng Ming*, no. 33 (July 1980), in *FBIS*, July 9, 1980, U3–6; and "The Petroleum Kingdom," in *Zheng Ming*, no. 34 (Aug. 1, 1980): 5–8, in *FBIS*, Aug. 6, 1980, U2–6.

[36] Examples include Wu Zhonghua (chairman, CAS Energy Committee), "The Way to Solve the Energy Crisis as Seen from Energy Science and Technology," *HQ*, 1980, no. 17, 31–43; Xu Junzhang, Zhang Zhengmin, Yang Zhirong, and Zhu Bin, "On Energy Construction" (n. 14 above); and Zhao Zongyu, "Altering Energy Resources" (n. 22 above).

[37] See, for example, Xu Shoubo, "Proposal for an Energy Policy" (n. 5 above); Shi Xican, Cai Ansi, and Lin Xiangyue, "The Problems of Making Dynamic and Economic Comparisons of Hydroelectric and Thermal Power Stations," *Shuili Fadian*, 1981, no. 3:7–11, in *JPRS*, no. 78818 (Aug. 25, 1981): 13–22.

[38] See *Xinhua* broadcast on the National Forum on Industrial and Communications Work, Sept. 3, 1981, in *FBIS*, Sept. 8, 1981, K12–13; editorial, "Carry out Technical Transformation and Equipment Renewal," *RMRB*, Oct. 11, 1981; editorial, "To Promote the Machine Building Industry, Science and Technology Must Be Developed First," *RMRB*, Oct. 17, 1981; Liu Lixin and Tian Chunsheng, "Strengthen Planned Guidance over Renewal and Transformation of Enterprises," *RMRB*, June 11, 1982; and editorial, "Proceed with Technical Transformation Selectively and Methodically," *RMRB*, Sept. 20, 1982.

[39] Zhao Tianzuo and Huang Jiasheng, "A Second Front Not to Be Ignored," *Jiefang Ribao*, Feb. 3, 1981, in *FBIS*, Feb. 5, 1981, O4; and editorial, "Technical Transformation Is a Major Policy," *RMRB*, Jan. 29, 1982.

greater central control the importation of expensive plant and equipment, officials stated that energy-related technologies would be given priority in the selection of items to be imported.[40] If implemented, this policy would have an immediate and profound effect on the development strategies and prospects of many ministries, industries, enterprises, and localities. For example, light industrial centers such as Shanghai and Tianjin were to have priority in importing equipment that would conserve energy, and regions with major deposits of coal (Shanxi) or oil (Heilongjiang) would be able to import equipment more easily than would most others.[41] This policy made sense in the abstract, but, like many others, it was rife with difficulties when it came to translating general principles into specific policy decisions.

The Allocation of Fuel and Power

As a scarce and essential resource, energy has value far beyond the nominal prices assigned by the State Planning Commission. However, when considering ways to encourage conservation, a shift from oil to coal, and other changes envisioned by their emerging energy policy, PRC leaders rejected the idea of relying primarily on the use of higher energy prices.[42] The only partial exception to this general decision was to reaffirm a series of two-tiered prices whereby above-quota production of coal, oil, and so forth, could be sold at a fixed but higher price, and above-quota purchases of fuel and power would be at prices fixed somewhat higher than those for within-quota purchases.[43] However, even this mechanism appears to have been diluted by crosscutting policies affecting the allocation of fuel and power to certain industries and enterprises.[44]

[40] On general principles guiding technology imports, see Liang Yuan, "The Nine Principles of Importing Technology and Equipment into the PRC," *Qishi Niandai*, 1979, no. 109 (February), in *FBIS*, Feb. 27, 1979, N5–6. See also the *Xinhua* interview with Gu Mu in *FBIS*, Oct. 22, 1981, K3–4; the *Xinhua* release of Oct. 22, 1981, in *FBIS*, Oct. 23, 1981, K9–10; and Denis Fred Simon, "China's Capacity to Assimilate Foreign Technology: An Assessment," Joint Economic Committee, *China Under the Four Modernizations, Part I* (Washington, D.C.: U.S. Government Printing Office, 1982), 514–552.

[41] "State Economic Commission Issues Main Points for This Year's Work in Industry and Communications," *Gongren Ribao*, Feb. 2, 1982, in *JPRS*, no. 80241 (Mar. 4, 1982): 1–6, lists cities to have priority in technology imports for energy conservation.

[42] Xue Muqiao, *China's Socialist Economy* (Beijing: Foreign Languages Press, 1981), 152–53; and He Jianzhang and Zhang Zhuoyuan, "Some Ideas on Price System Reform," *Jiage Lilun Yu Shijian*, 1982, no. 3 (May), in *FBIS*, Aug. 6, 1982, K9–12. On price policy more generally, see chapter 4 in this volume.

[43] Interviews with energy officials, Sept. 6, 1982, and Sept. 10, 1983.

[44] Examples include the State Council Circular on Year End Financial Work reported in *FBIS*, Nov. 5, 1980, L2–4; Yu Qiuli, "Report" (n. 16 above); Kang Shien's speech at the Beijing rally for "Energy Conservation Month," reported by Beijing Radio, Oct. 31, 1979, in *FBIS*, Nov. 1, 1979, L12–18 at L17; and the regulation for the distribution of electric power reported by Beijing Radio on May 24, 1982, in *FBIS*, May 27, 1982, K4–6.

Having rejected price increases as a vehicle for achieving desired changes in energy production and consumption, officials decided to exert greater direct control over the allocation of commercial energy. Allotments of fuel and power were to be used to promote conservation and efficiency, but they were also supposed to facilitate realization of many other goals announced during and after the Second Session of the Fifth NPC in June 1979. As is true of all energy policies adopted since 1978, officials were attempting to achieve multiple and at times contradictory objectives.

One objective, only tangentially related to energy, is to maintain central control despite considerable decentralization of economic authority. Although the Communique of the Third Plenum had called for devolution of economic authority (and Xue Muqiao's ideas about using market forces were highly publicized), it appears that there was considerable uncertainty and disagreement about how far China could or should go in the direction of adopting market mechanisms and transferring authority to lower levels.[45] Faith in the continued efficacy of central planning, especially in areas deemed critical to the success of the economy and the post-Mao economic program, was expressed in commentaries on the "Four Principles," and in reaffirmations of the advantages of socialist development.[46] Amidst a general call for decentralization and the use of market forces, there was a contradictory call for the central allocation of energy. This did not facilitate effective implementation.[47]

For example, the light and textile industries were to receive guaranteed supplies of fuel and power.[48] If enforced, this would mean that electricity could not be diverted from light industrial plants to ensure that other enterprises would meet their output quotas, and that light industrial and textile factories would avoid the fuel shortages and electrical blackouts that had forced them to operate below capacity.[49] Ensuring that such plants operated at full capacity would, in turn, help satisfy the demand for consumer goods, increase State revenues which could be reinvested in the economy, and help provide more jobs at a time when unemployment was a major concern.[50]

[45] Xue Muqiao, "How Can We Effect Planned Management" (n. 10 above); Xue Muqiao, "Some Opinions on Reforming the Economic System," *RMRB*, June 10, 1980; "State Council Directive on Market Controls," *FBIS*, Jan. 16, 1981, L7–9; and editorial, "Strive to Accomplish the Task of Readjusting the National Economy," *HQ*, 1981, no. 1:2–5.

[46] Zhang Zhuoyuan and Xing Junfang, "Develop the Superiority of Socialist Planned Economy," *Jingji Yanjiu*, 1981, no. 9, in *JPRS*, no. 79521 (Nov. 24, 1981): 31–44.

[47] See Thomas Fingar, "Energy and Development: China's Strategy for the 1980's," in Auer, *Energy and the Developing Nations* (n. 3 above), 418–45.

[48] Yu Qiuli, "Report" (n. 16 above), at L16; and the *Xinhua* broadcast report on the National Conference to Exchange Experience on Energy Conservation, in *FBIS*, Nov. 4, 1980, L1–2.

[49] This is why the politics of energy policy in China resemble, in certain respects, Lowi's description of redistributive policies and politics in the United States (see n. 25 above).

[50] Editorial, "Light Industry Must Develop More Rapidly," *RMRB*, Feb. 20, 1979; and editorial, "Light Industry Must Grow by a Relatively Big Margin," *RMRB*, Dec. 3, 1979.

These benefits, however, were achieved at the cost of insulating light industry from market forces and reducing the incentive to conserve energy.

A closely related policy required that fuel and power be provided on a priority basis to those industries producing goods for export.[51] Though this could apply to heavy as well as light industrial enterprises, in fact it meant that those light and textile factories producing for export could obtain all the energy they needed. This, in turn, would enable the central government and local jurisdictions to increase foreign exchange earnings. One consequence of this policy was that factory managers, supported by local government and Party officials, sought to secure overseas markets for their goods in ways that were condemned for undercutting factories and localities elsewhere in China.[52] In other words, the scramble for energy was expressed, in part, as a scramble for foreign markets and foreign exchange.

By 1979 allocation guidelines also required cutting off the supply of fuel and power to wasteful enterprises, especially inefficient heavy industrial facilities.[53] Since heavy industries consumed far more energy in total and per unit of output, much energy could be "conserved" by closing or cutting supplies to inefficient factories.[54] Two very different criteria were mentioned as the basis for determining whether or not supplies should be cut. One was technical efficiency: If an energy audit revealed that a factory was wasting energy, its supply would be reduced until corrective measures were taken.[55] Thus, energy would be used to encourage improved management and technical upgrading of existing facilities. The second criterion was profitability: Enterprises that failed to earn profits would have their supplies of fuel and power reduced until they improved their balance sheets.[56]

[51] See the State Economic Commission Circular to Industrial and Transportation Departments (Dec. 2, 1979), in *FBIS*, Dec. 13, 1979, L4–7. On trade and readjustment, see editorial, "Economic and Trade Relations with Foreign Countries Must Serve the Readjustment of the National Economy," *RMRB*, Feb. 25, 1981.

[52] Xue Muqiao at the Hangzhou Symposium on the World Economy cosponsored by the Institute of World Economy and SRI International, Mar. 24, 1981; and Zhao Ziyang, "Several Questions on Current Economic Work," *HQ*, 1982, no. 7:2–10.

[53] Yu Qiuli, "Report" (n. 16 above); and State Economic Commission Circular (n. 51 above).

[54] Commentator, "The Direction of Developing the Chemical Industry," *RMRB*, Mar. 2, 1980; Yao Yilin, "Report on Readjustment of the 1981 National Economic Plan and State Revenue and Expenditures" (17th Session of Fifth NPC Standing Committee, Feb. 25, 1981), in *FBIS*, Mar. 9 1981, K6–18 at K12; Gao Yangwen (n. 20 above), 17; Ma Hong, "Economic Readjustment" (n. 18 above); and Ma Yi's speech (n. 18 above). For a different approach to the importance of heavy industry to energy conservation, see Qi Jian, "Enliven Heavy Industry and Strive for a Certain Speed of Development," *RMRB*, Oct. 16, 1981.

[55] Kang Shien's speech (n. 44 above) at L16.

[56] State Economic Commission Circular (n. 51 above); Ma Yi (n. 18 above); Zhao Ziyang, "Report" (n. 28 above) at K12; and "Xiao Han, Deputy Chairman of the State Economic Commission, Talks About China's Current Situation in Energy Conservation and the Tasks of the Coming Year," *Jingji Daobao* (Economic Reporter, Hong Kong), no. 47 (Nov. 26, 1980), in *JPRS*, no. 77615 (Mar. 18, 1981): 18–23.

This measure makes sense up to a point, but it does not take adequate account of the irrational price structure (factories that are energy efficient can operate at a loss simply because the fixed prices of their outputs are too low) or the fact that energy costs typically constitute only a small percentage of total production costs (because energy is underpriced).[57] One result is that Party and state officials, eager to maximize the amount of money available to them as a consequence of policy changes that provided for greater profit retention at the enterprise and local level, pressed factories to produce as many high-profit items as possible without regard to the energy consequences (or to associated shortages of necessary but low profit items).[58]

The provision in this policy with the greatest potential impact was the requirement that supplies of fuel and power be reduced if enterprises failed to meet certain (but largely unspecified) criteria. Unquestionably, China could reap substantial economic and energy benefits from closing inefficient plants and redirecting inputs to more efficient facilities, but the roughly 25 percent of the state-owned enterprises operating at a loss perform an important social or welfare function—they are very important to local economies and governments.[59] Even though everyone could agree with the principle that inefficient, energy-wasting factories should be closed, no manager or political leader was eager to take such drastic measures in his or her own district.[60] Closing surplus military bases in the United States and the character of opposition to such measures provides an appropriate analog.

Redistribution of Political and Economic Power

Both the allocation of funds and the allocation of energy generated competition for scarce resources of a kind familiar to all societies. These allocations altered the power balances among different ministries, regions, and cities as well as relationships within and among their subunits. Shifts in the power of individuals and institutions was further altered by other aspects of the energy policy that has been in place since 1979. Concern about being "overextended on the capital construction front" and injunctions to concentrate on the completion of key projects so that they could be brought on line more quickly had important energy and political consequences. As was noted above, projects

---

[57] Xue Muqiao, *China's Socialist Economy* (n. 42 above), 142–46; and editorial, "Enhance the Sense of Urgency and Responsibility for Conserving Energy," *RMRB*, June 29, 1983.

[58] Editorial, "Enhance the Sense of Urgency"; Xu Dixin, "Questions Concerning the System of Economic Responsibility in State Enterprises," *Jingji Yanjiu*, 1981, no. 12, in *JPRS*, no. 79935 (Jan. 25, 1982): 1–11 at 5; Luo Jingfen, "Reform of the Price and Taxation System Is the Key Link in Reforming the Economic System," *Jingji Guanli*, 1980, no. 9:27–30.

[59] Hua Guofeng, "Report" (n. 8 above), 13. Three years later Zhao Ziyang reported that nearly 30 percent of state-owned enterprises incur losses. See Zhao Ziyang, "Report on the Sixth Five-Year Plan," (Fifth Session of the Fifth NPC), in *FBIS*, Dec. 14, 1982, K1–34 at K21.

[60] Interviews with Chinese economist, May 13, 1983, and with energy officials, Sept. 10, 1983.

that would increase the supply of fuel and power were assigned high priority and thereby commanded a substantial share of capital construction funding and other resources. A related policy specified that no new projects were to be undertaken without prior determination that adequate supplies of energy would be available.[61] This power was vested in local planning bureaus and agencies of local government.[62] One consequence of this provision was a reduction in the authority of factory managers and workers to exercise their recently obtained power to decide how to use retained earnings. Another was that enterprises, ministries, and local jurisdictions were placed in direct competition with one another for present and future supplies of fuel and power. Since these decisions are made first within ministries or administrative jurisdictions and then by municipal, provincial, and ultimately national planning authorities, it strengthened some preexisting special relationships and undermined others.[63] If investment funds and the number of projects were reduced, some areas would gain the benefits of new construction; others would have to wait and might lose out entirely.

In mid-1979 and repeatedly thereafter, officials called for enforcement of strict quotas on the consumption and distribution of fuel and power.[64] Presumably this was to involve calculation of the "appropriate" amount of energy needed per unit of production, as well as fixed quotas for the distribution of energy to individual enterprises. Officials and agencies with the power to set such quotas would, in theory, be very powerful; but they would also be subjected to intense pressure from competing interests. The scope for political maneuver was limitless, especially since there were virtually no reliable data on energy consumption. For there to be effective implementation, superiors must be able to measure compliance. To measure, one must have a yardstick.

Efforts to control and manage better the consumption and distribution of energy led to ever greater centralization of authority at a time when decentralization was the dominant trend. This produced friction between local

---

[61] Yu Qiuli, "Report" (n. 16 above), L20.

[62] Interviews with officials of the State Planning Commission, April 1980, and with officials of the State Economic Commission, Sept. 6, 1982.

[63] Such relationships included regularized contacts among individuals and institutions, recurring rivalries the outcome of which had been shaped by the old "rules of the game," contacts forged during earlier periods such as the First Five-Year Plan or the Cultural Revolution, and myriad patron-client ties. In early 1982 the Chinese began to call attention to relationships of this sort and to decry the pernicious consequences of *guanxixue* and *guanxihu* (use of special relationships). Commentators on the "problem" ignored the beneficial role such ties played as the grease and glue that kept the system functioning and prevented it from flying apart in times of great stress. See John W. Lewis, *Political Networks and the Policy Process in China* (Stanford: Northeast Asia–United States Forum on International Policy, 1986).

[64] Kang Shien, Speech (n. 44 above), L16; "State Economic Commission Issues Main Points" (n. 41 above), 2; and editorial, "Put Energy Conservation in a Priority Position," *RMRB*, Oct. 30, 1982.

officials, including local Party officials, and those at the Center; between enterprises and planning agencies; between ministries and planning agencies;
and between enterprises located in the same areal jurisdiction.[65] One example of the trend toward greater concentration of authority in the energy sector
is the decision, in 1982, to transfer authority over local and regional electric-
power grids to the central government (specifically the Ministry of Power).[66]
This shift in authority gave the ministry the capacity to decide which enterprises would receive additional or reduced supplies of power, how much electricity would be available for distribution at any given time, and what new
facilities would be built. Competition for scarce resources was an inescapable
consequence.

Most of these (and several other) energy "policies" were on the books
before the State Energy Commission was established in August 1980. Predictably, given the conflicts and logical inconsistencies identified above, they
were not being implemented as was anticipated or hoped by senior leaders.[67]
To ensure better implementation—and to achieve other objectives at the same
time—the State Energy Commission (SEC) was established in 1980. Since
the ability of officials to implement energy decisions was significantly affected
by the context from which the SEC emerged and in which it operated, the
following section will examine the origins of the Energy Commission.

ORIGINS OF THE STATE ENERGY COMMISSION

The State Energy Commission was established with little fanfare on August
26, 1980.[68] Less than two years later, on May 4, 1982, it was abolished and
its functions were reassigned to other agencies of the central government.[69]
During its brief existence, the SEC was, theoretically, the principal respon-

[65] *Xinhua* broadcast of Jan. 15, 1981, in *FBIS*, Jan. 19, 1981, L15–16; Xu Yaozhong, "If You
Stand on the Rostrum of Tiananmen Square," *Xinhua* broadcast of Feb. 12, 1981, in *FBIS*, Feb.
13, 1981, L3–4; editorial, "Hold the Scale of Capital Construction Under Strict Control,"
RMRB, May 8, 1981; and the *Xinhua* broadcast of June 24, 1983, in *FBIS*, June 28, 1983, O4–5.

[66] *Xinhua* broadcast, Feb. 1, 1982, in *FBIS*, Feb. 2, 1982, K4–5.

[67] See Deng Xiaoping, "The Reform of the Party and State Leadership System" (Aug. 18,
1980), *RMRB*, July 2, 1983, in *FBIS*, July 6, 1983, K1–16.

[68] See the two-line announcement entitled "NPC Standing Committee Decision Establishing
the State Energy Commission," *RMRB*, Aug. 27, 1980. It is noteworthy that the Energy Commission was established without fanfare (i.e., by the Standing Committee of the Fifth NPC
rather than by the Third Session of the full Congress, which opened just four days later) and
with virtually no coverage by China's media.

[69] "NPC Standing Committee Decision on the Proposal to Reform Ministries, Commissions
and Other Agencies Under the State Council," *RMRB*, May 5, 1982. Interviews with officials of
the State Planning Commission, State Economic Commission, and the Energy Research Institute (then subordinate to the Energy Commission and the Chinese Academy of Sciences) in
March 1982 suggested that the Energy Commission would be reorganized as a bureau of the
State Economic Commission. That did not happen; its responsibilities and personnel were re-

sible agency in the energy field. As a supraministerial agency, it might have coordinated, even dictated, the activities of subordinate ministries. Headed by Vice-Premier Yu Qiuli, a member of the Politburo Standing Committee, it might have been expected to have sufficient political muscle to implement any policy it chose. Considerable doubt exists as to whether it was ever seriously expected to implement policies already on the books (see below), but, assuming that it was supposed to put into effect the policies outlined above, it probably could not have done so. To understand why it did not do so and why energy policies proved so difficult to implement, it is necessary to consider both the responsibilities and capabilities of the SEC and the broader organizational and political context in which it operated.

Throughout its existence the Energy Commission was something of an enigma to outside observers and, more important, to bureaucratic functionaries inside China.[70] Its creation qualifies as one of the major nonevents of 1980. Given the fact that energy had been at or near the top of the policy-making agenda for more than two years and that, for nearly a year, authoritative commentaries had called for the formulation of specific energy policies and establishment of a new agency to administer those policies, it is surprising that the new agency received virtually no attention in PRC media.[71] This situation is striking on at least two counts. The first is that senior officials seldom pass up opportunities to demonstrate that they are on top of matters and are acting decisively to meet challenges facing the country. Second, the SEC was created at a time when positive statements about leadership on the energy front would have been expected; instead, officials and the media focused on the so-called Bohai Incident and the punishment of those responsible.[72] This is not the place to review that incident and the way it was handled, but it is worth noting that negative publicity about key energy ad-

---

assigned to several different bureaus of the Economic Commission. Interviews with officials of the Economic Commission and the Energy Research Institute in September 1983 confirmed that many people had returned to the posts they had held prior to formation of the Energy Commission.

[70] Interviews with leading energy officials on Mar. 20 and Sept. 6–10, 1982; Feb. 7–9, Mar. 28, and Sept. 8, 1983. A common theme running through these interviews was that the Energy Commission lacked exclusive or final jurisdiction over any matter of substance and that previously existing agencies continued to operate much as they had in the past. The Commission had seven bureaus: Conservation, Planning, Production, Science and Technology, Foreign Affairs, Laws and Regulations, and Administration and Personnel.

[71] A *Xinhua* English broadcast on Nov. 18, 1979, reported that a "spokesman for the State Economic Commission" had said that China would establish a national energy control body, in *FBIS*, Nov. 19, 1979, L14–15. On energy as a serious problem, see Chen Xi, Huang Zhijie, and Xu Junzhang, "Effective Use of Energy" (n. 14 above).

[72] Editorial, "A Profound Lesson," *RMRB*, Aug. 27, 1980; *Xinhua* broadcast report by Wen Xieyang and Huang Fengchu, Aug. 30, 1980, in *FBIS*, Sept. 3, 1980, L10–12; and sources cited in note 35.

ministrators (the "Petroleum Clique") almost certainly affected the implementation of policy.[73]

The Energy Commission was created in the midst of shifting goals, strategies, and political coalitions; its fate is inseparable from that broader context. Originally envisioned as part of a fundamental restructuring of the bureaucracy that would have transformed most ministries into corporations (possibly similar to the way the former Sixth Ministry of Machine Building was changed into the new Shipbuilding Corporation) coordinated by overarching commissions, the SEC lost a major part of its raison d'être when this plan was abandoned.[74] Indeed, that particular organizational reform might have been abandoned during the interval between the November 1979 announcement that China would create a national energy control body and the August 1980 meeting of the NPC Standing Committee that authorized its establishment. But the SEC was created for reasons that go considerably beyond the requirements of the stillborn restructuring of the state bureaucracy.

One reason was symbolic: Senior leaders needed to demonstrate that they were taking concrete measures to overcome the increasingly obvious and detrimental problems caused by shortages of fuel and power, and that they were acting decisively to overcome the energy-related mistakes enumerated and decried by many delegates to the Third Session of the Fifth NPC.[75] Creating a new agency would not solve those problems, but it would demonstrate resolve and perhaps buy a bit more time for the leaders and their programs. Given the skepticism and loss of confidence on the part of the public and many cadres, this was an important objective.[76]

Another and closely related reason for creating the SEC was to provide

[73] Articles critical of the energy officials and their decisions became more common after the Bohai Incident was publicized in August 1980. See, for example, *Xinhua* broadcast of Sept. 11, 1980, criticizing the Ministry of Petroleum for a misguided natural gas project, in *FBIS*, Sept. 16, 1980, L31–32; Guangdong Radio, Oct. 4, 1980, on a dispute over ownership of an oil pumping station, in *FBIS*, Oct. 6, 1980, P1; Wen Xieyong and Huang Fengchu, above; and the articles summarized and cited in *China Aktuell*, Oct. 1980, 883.

[74] On the proposed transformation of ministries into enterprises coordinated by new commissions, see Liu Yu, "A Big Reorganization Is Brewing in the State Council," *Zheng Ming*, 1980, no. 38 (December), in *FBIS*, Dec. 2, 1980, U1–2. On the transformation of the former Sixth Ministry of Machine Building, see editorial, "An Important Experiment in the Reform of the Economic System," *RMRB*, May 7, 1982. Interviews with an official in the Chinese Academy of Social Sciences and other Chinese citizens in March and April 1983 revealed that they remembered the discussion of this possibility but were not certain about how much consideration was given to the proposal or when and why it had been abandoned.

[75] For a selection of NPC delegates' comments on the country's energy problems and policies, see "Excerpts of Speeches by NPC Deputies at Panel Discussions," in *RMRB*, Sept. 6, 7, and 8, 1980.

[76] See Xu Junhua, "Destroying Superstition and Believing in Marxism," *Xinhua Ribao* (Nanjing), May 19, 1981, in *FBIS*, June 4, 1981, O1–4; and sources cited in note 8.

guidance to lower-level officials faced with the task of interpreting and implementing multiple and often contradictory policies. Creation of the SEC seemed to say, in effect, if you are forced to choose among alternative courses of action, all of which are sanctioned by broad policy statements, select the one that will do the most to conserve or produce energy. In other words, the symbolic importance of the commission probably outweighed its functional significance. The mere fact that it existed made it more likely that energy measures already on the books would be implemented.

According to Yu Qiuli, the commission was supposed to do more than merely exist; it was entrusted with responsibility to "study and formulate principles, policies, laws, and regulations for energy in China."[77] Although the SEC did issue a number of regulations, these fell short of what was needed, as is evidenced by the call to "Make a Serious Effort to Formulate an Energy Law," published in *Renmin Ribao*, just one week after the Energy Commission was abolished.[78]

A third and closely related objective in creating the SEC was to overcome bureaucratic obstacles to policy implementation. It should be recalled that the Energy Commission was established during one of China's recurring campaigns against the evils of bureaucratism and departmentalism.[79] Inertia, entrenched interests, bureaucratic rivalries, parochialism, and incompetence were decried as major obstacles to realizing the four modernizations and, just as important, to realizing the advantages of socialism.[80] These maladies imperiled the developmental plans of Mao's successors at a time when it was particularly important to demonstrate that Party leadership, central planning, and "socialism" could enable China to develop more rapidly and with fewer adverse effects than had the United States, Japan, or even Taiwan. Like the subsequent efforts to restore Party discipline, attempts to overcome or at least ameliorate the effects of bureaucratism and departmentalism were high on the agenda of Deng and his supporters. As a new agency, the SEC presumably would be free of many of the constraints that reduced the responsiveness and effectiveness of other institutions;[81] as a su-

[77] *Xinhua* broadcast of Aug. 26, 1980, reporting the list of State Energy Commission tasks enumerated by Yu Qiuli, *FBIS*, Aug. 26, 1980, L1–2. Calls for detailed rules and energy laws date from at least mid-1979. See Chen Xi, Huang Zhijie, and Xu Junzhang, "Effective Use of Energy" (n. 14 above); and Hua Guofeng, "Report" (n. 8 above), 16.

[78] Shi Taiyou and Tao Heqian, "Make a Serious Effort to Formulate an Energy Law," *RMRB*, May 11, 1982. A number of rules and regulations were issued, however. "State Economic Commission" (n. 41 above) refers to 58 energy-conservation measures issued by the Economic Commission, Planning Commission, and the Energy Commission.

[79] Deng Xiaoping, "Reform" (n. 67 above), and Hua Guofeng, "Speech at the Third Session of the Fifth National People's Congress," in *FBIS*, Sept. 23, 1980, Suppl. 49–68, esp. 58–62.

[80] Ibid.; and Commentator, "The Leadership System Must Be Reformed," *HQ*, 1980, no. 17: 2–4.

[81] See Anthony Downs, *Inside Bureaucracy* (Boston: Little, Brown, 1967), esp. chap. 13.

praministerial body with direct access to the State Council and the Politburo, it might have been able to compel subordinate agencies to change their mode of operation. Why then did it have so little impact on bureaucratic practice? Some of the reasons are discussed below.

The Energy Commission may also have been created, in part, to remove Yu Qiuli from his position as Minister in Charge of the State Planning Commission (SPC) without appearing to demote him or to be launching another round of leadership instability. The Third Plenum had officially discarded the ambitious developmental scheme unveiled by Hua Guofeng and Yu earlier in the year.[82] Even though officials were careful not to create scapegoats or to imitate the kind of punitive behavior they ascribed to the Gang of Four, it is inconceivable that mid-level functionaries would not associate Yu and Hua with the erroneous policies of the recent past. Yu's personal responsibility— and political vulnerability—was further underscored by the disastrous Baoshan steel mill project. This is not the place to rehearse the many errors and shortcomings of the Baoshan project; suffice it to say that they were well known by early 1980 and that dozens of NPC delegates had raised sharp questions about the project, and the thinking on which it was based, at the Third Session of the Fifth NPC.[83] As Minister of the SPC, Yu bore formal responsibility not just for the overly ambitious targets repudiated by the Third Plenum, but also for the specific disaster of Baoshan and for China's lagging oil production.[84] To have retained him as Minister in Charge of the Planning Commission in the light of his demonstrated incompetence as a planner would have undermined the credibility and viability of the reform and restructuring policies adopted in early 1979. In short, Yu had to be eased out of office. Placing him in charge of the SEC did not augur well for that organ's future effectiveness.

The creation of the Energy Commission made it possible to move Yu laterally without loss of face. It would probably be wrong, however, to argue that the SEC was never intended as anything more than a paper organization created to ease Yu Qiuli into retirement.[85] Given his long experience and considerable prestige in the energy area (he had been Minister of the Petroleum Industry from 1958 to 1972; despite attacks by Red Guard critics in 1967, he retained his position and was elected to the Central Committee by

[82] On the ambitious targets of 1978, see Hua Guofeng, "Unite and Strive" (n. 13 above). For the repudiation of those targets, see esp. Hua Guofeng, "Speech" (n. 79 above).

[83] See the comments of Beijing deputies to the Third Session of the Fifth NPC in "Excerpts of Speeches by NPC Deputies at Panel Discussions," *RMRB*, Sept. 7, 1980; and "Die Probleme mit dem Stahlwerk Baoshan summieren sich," *China Aktuell*, October 1980, 874–76.

[84] See Luo Bing, "Yu Qiuli Deprived" (n. 35 above); and "Yu Qiuli degradiert," *China Aktuell*, June 1980, 461–62.

[85] After the Energy Commission was abolished, Yu was appointed to the important post of Director of the General Political Department of the People's Liberation Army. See *China Aktuell*, September 1982, 566.

the Ninth Party Congress in 1969), it made sense to place him in charge of the SEC. As a vice-premier (since January 1975), member of the Politburo (since August 1977), and member of the Party Secretariat (since February 1980), Yu had the stature and the positions necessary to give the new commission clout at the top of the political pyramid. It is possible to argue, therefore, that his appointment to the SEC constituted a serious effort to improve policy implementation. It is also possible to argue, however, that since his star seemed to be in eclipse, his appointment foreshadowed the impotence of the Energy Commission.

OBSTACLES TO THE IMPLEMENTATION OF ENERGY POLICY

During the period 1980–1983, which embraces the two-year existence of the State Energy Commission, implementation of national energy policies was spotty and imperfect at best. Four years after Hua Guofeng announced that "the government will enact unified regulations concerning the allocation and supply of electricity, and plans to formulate as soon as possible an energy act," China had yet to do so.[86] It should be remembered, however, that other nations, including the United States, have also required more time than was anticipated to devise politically acceptable regulations (e.g., for deregulating natural gas or rationing gasoline in a crisis). Lack of unified and comprehensive regulations accounts for China's implementation problems in part, but only in part. This section will examine other reasons it has proven difficult for China to implement the energy policies announced in 1979 and reiterated at regular intervals ever since. The relative importance of the many factors involved appears to have changed over time, but all were present, to a greater or lesser degree, throughout the period under study.

As was noted earlier, even Chinese energy officials profess uncertainty about the role or mission of the State Energy Commission.[87] Abandonment of the bureaucratic reform that would have transformed ministries into corporations may have removed the principal function of the SEC and made it a vestigial organization during most of the time it was in existence. It may have been preserved for a time because it performed useful symbolic functions— and since relatively little staff and no permanent facilities had been assigned the Commission, keeping the organization alive imposed no real costs on the system.[88] An organization with no permanent staff or facilities is bound to be

---

[86] Hua Guofeng, "Report" (n. 8 above), 16; and articles cited in note 78.

[87] See note 70 above.

[88] Many people reassigned to the Energy Commission continued to work at their previous places of employment (e.g., the Economic Commission and the Planning Commission), a factor that contributed to their continued interest in and identification with their previous units. The operational base of the Energy Commission was in the Ministry of Petroleum. Interviews with energy officials on Feb. 7 and Sept. 8, 1983. See also Downs, *Inside Bureaucracy*, 220–22.

ineffective, lacking the rewards, coercive resources, and organizational identity which make functionaries want to implement policy.

Implementation of energy policy in China was impeded by myriad cross-cutting factors. For convenience, obstacles to successful implementation have been grouped under three broad headings: the policies; the implementing agencies; and the broader organizational, political, and policy context.

The "Policies" as Problems

The energy policies summarized above are not really policies at all; they are principles or premises.[89] Policies contain detailed guidelines and specifically enumerated tasks to be implemented, but the measures adopted by China's leaders were little more than Delphic pronouncements requiring interpretation and implementation by functionaries at many levels of the system. Without considerable elaboration, these oft-repeated injunctions simply could not be implemented consistently or in ways that made it easy to assess compliance and results.

To stop with a statement that energy policies were not implemented effectively because they were vague and incapable of implementation would beg two important questions: Why did senior leaders issue only vague or general principles if they believed solution of the country's energy problems to be as important as is suggested above? Why did subordinate officials fail to translate general principles into specific guidelines and regulations that could be implemented? Each of these questions will be considered in turn.

Most policy pronouncements in China contain few guidelines or clear prescriptions for attaining announced goals. In this respect, there is nothing exceptional about the energy "policies" adopted by PRC leaders after the death of Mao. One could trace the origin of such pronouncements to the country's imperial past and the personality of Mao Zedong, but there appear to be more proximate and more important factors in this case. One determinant was the particular political context within which the policies were formulated. Briefly, the context was one in which the appearance of consensus and stability was considered essential for the restoration of Party authority and the success of the still-emerging developmental strategy.[90] Promises of policy continuity, reinstitution of collective leadership, and avoidance of open factional struggle shaped the way senior leaders approached all major policy decisions. Even though subsequent developments make it clear that there was tension, debate, and a jockeying for power within the senior elite,

[89]See Giandomenico Majone and Aaron Wildavsky, "Implementation or Evolution," in Pressman and Wildavsky, *Implementation* (n. 21 above), 177–94; and Bardach, *Implementation Game* (n. 2 above), chap. 2.

[90]See Thomas Fingar, "China's Quest for Technology" (n. 8 above), 257–63; and Deng Xiaoping, "The Present Situation and the Tasks Before Us," Jan. 16, 1980, *Selected Works of Deng Xiaoping* (Beijing: Foreign Languages Press, 1984), 224–58, esp. 236–42.

there appears to have been an overriding commitment to minimize disagreements over specific policies and to preserve the fragile consensus and stability that seemed to exist. One consequence is that policy "decisions" and pronouncements were frequently and deliberately vague lest they be divisive, as they were bound to be in the energy area.

A second reason for adopting general pronouncements rather than detailed policies is that energy decisions were being reached in the context of a concerted effort to decentralize authority and to substitute observance of "economic laws" for rule by executive fiat.[91] There was a deliberate effort to avoid dogmatic and restrictive pronouncements so that lower-level officials would be able to adapt policies to suit the exigencies of their own particular situations. Flexibility, in planning and in the execution of policy, was seen as essential for the success of China's current strategy of development.[92] It was thought possible to shift from mandated targets and detailed prescriptions to general guidelines because of continuing efforts to restore Party discipline and to upgrade the quality of administrative organs and personnel.[93] The achievement of these goals is proving to be more difficult and time-consuming than had been envisioned, but the underlying assumptions about flexibility and tailoring policies to fit specific conditions were not unreasonable.

Finally, senior leaders may have been inhibited by awareness that they lacked the information necessary to draft detailed regulations.[94] It seems likely that the desire for flexibility in a time of organizational, policy, and political transition played a role in their decision. China was, and is, in a state of flux—a transition from a now discredited system to an uncertain replacement.

Whatever the reasons, policy was vague and therefore difficult to implement. Why was this so? One reason is technical; subordinate agencies and officials lacked the information and technical ability to translate abstract

[91] Early examples include Hu Qiaomu, "Act in Accordance," and Xue Muqiao, "How Can We Effect Planned Management" (both n. 10 above). See also Xue Muqiao, "Problems to be Solved in Reforming the Economic Management System," *Jingji Yanjiu*, 1982, no. 1 (January): 3–7, in *FBIS*, Feb. 24, 1982, K11–17; and Wang Jiye, "An Important Principle for Planned Management—On Applying Administrative and Economic Measures," *GMRB*, June 6, 1982.

[92] See Xu Yi, Huang Jubo, and Guo Daimo, "We Must Pay Attention to Leaving Adequate Leeway," *RMRB*, May 10, 1979; and editorial, "An Important Principle for Making Plans Is to Leave No Gaps," *RMRB*, June 16, 1980.

[93] On improvements in the state structure, see Zhao Ziyang, "Report on the Restructuring of the State Council's Organization" (22nd Session of the Standing Committee of the Fifth NPC), in *FBIS*, Mar. 9, 1982, K1–7; and Editorial Department, "Restructuring Administrative Organization Is a Revolution," *HQ*, 1982, no. 6:2–5.

[94] Desire for better data prompted the State Council to launch an extensive survey of the economy (interview with planning official, April 1980). See *Xinhua*, Sept. 3, 1979, in *FBIS*, Sept. 4, 1979, L2–4; *Xinhua*, Feb. 19, 1980, in *FBIS*, Feb. 20, 1980, L11; and *Xinhua*, Apr. 10, 1980, in *FBIS*, Apr. 14, 1980, L6–7. See also Majone and Wildavsky, "Implementation or Evolution."

principles into policies that could be implemented.[95] How, for example, was one to determine the relative energy efficiency of different enterprises if one lacked even rudimentary data on consumption of fuel and power?[96] What levels of consumption were normal or reasonable, and how should those levels be codified as a set of standards or regulations? How should the consumption rates and output value of totally different enterprises be compared? What criteria were to be employed in determining the proper site, scale, and schedule for energy-producing and energy-consuming facilities? The list of such questions is without limit. Neither the central organs (commissions and ministries) nor local administrative and planning agencies possessed the requisite data or skilled personnel to make these determinations.

The situation is further complicated by the fact that experts can, and did, disagree on technical issues.[97] Forced to rely on the assessment of questionably qualified experts who were themselves reticent to express firm opinions, Party and state cadres were understandably reluctant to make decisions for which they would be held responsible.[98] Heightened concern about accountability was another aspect of the broader context within which these decisions were to be made. The prudent course was to delay action pending further study.

Important though they were, technical considerations were less significant than political ones. So long as policy pronouncements remained general, all could endorse them; when they became more specific, they became more contentious. The closing of inefficient facilities is a good idea unless the facility to be closed is your own. Lack of clarity with respect to both technical and economic criteria, and the active and potential opposition of deeply entrenched vested interests, made it uncomfortable, if not impossible, for subordinate officials to translate abstract principles into workable policies. The inevitable result was foot-dragging and paralysis.

The position of lower-level bureaucrats was made even more difficult by

[95] See Qi Siyuan, "Concentrate on Training Scientific and Technical Personnel in the Energy Field," *Gongren Ribao*, Jan. 30, 1981, in *JPRS*, no. 77957 (Apr. 29, 1981): 26–27. On the general problem of underqualified officials see, for example, Commentator, "Be Resolved to Sweep Away Formalism," *Beijing Ribao*, Mar. 25, 1981, in *FBIS*, Apr. 6, 1981, K11–14; Commentator, "Pay Close Attention to Selecting and Promoting Middle Aged and Young Cadres, Do a Good Job of Readjusting Leading Groups," *RMRB*, June 26, 1981; and editorial, "Training of Cadres in Rotation Is a Major Construction Measure of Strategic Significance," *RMRB*, May 14, 1982.

[96] Xu Wen, "Speeding Up Formulation of Energy Standards," *Biaojunhua Tongxun*, 1981, no. 5, in *JPRS*, no. 79608 (Dec. 8, 1981): 37–38; "Five Demands for Saving Energy This Year Proposed," *Tianjin Ribao*, Feb. 27, 1980, in *JPRS*, no. 75735 (May 20, 1980): 60–62; and Kang Shien, "Energy Conservation Month" (n. 44 above).

[97] See, for example, Jin Luzhong, "Energy Transport" (n. 22 above); Shi Xican, Cai Ansi, and Lin Xiangyue (n. 37 above); and interview with Wu Zhonghua (chairman, CAS Energy Committee), Sept. 6, 1982.

[98] See, for example, Commentator, "Quickly Raise the Level of Enterprise Management," *RMRB*, July 13, 1978; and "Continue the Battle to Improve Product Quality," *RMRB*, Oct. 11, 1978.

other developments that occurred simultaneously. Policy changes that permitted enterprises and local jurisdictions to retain a large percentage of revenue from profits (and the low cost of energy) encouraged factory managers, local government officials, and local Party committees to emphasize output and profit rather than energy conservation.[99] Balancing a seeming lack of commitment on the part of senior leaders against the demands of their constituents, these officials were understandably reluctant to implement measures that would be unpopular and might actually reduce the amount of money available to them. Moreover, it was easy to persuade oneself that energy savings could and should be achieved first in other jurisdictions.

The situation with respect to the production of energy was equally complex. The availability of capital construction funds for the development of energy-producing facilities led to a scramble for money, building materials, and the ancillary benefits of energy development.[100] Reluctant to delay or disapprove one of two competing construction projects, dams or coal mines, for example, officials were inclined to start both in the expectation that once begun it would be more difficult to cut off funding and supplies than if one or both were still on the drawing board.[101] This inclination was reinforced by the desire to placate constituents, maintain unity, and to take full advantage of the new situation.

The attitudes and objectives of lower-level officials differed depending on where they were in the overall hierarchy, but, as a general rule, it appears that they interpreted policies in ways advantageous to their own organizations.[102] They also were reticent to implement measures that promised to spark conflict and increased competition. The inherently zero-sum character of many policies, coupled with the fact that there were a great many clearance or decision points (see below) meant that even if one official or group of officials attempted to sharpen and execute specific measures, they could easily be thwarted by others in the system. Moreover, the ethos of "not breaking anyone's rice bowl" worked against active implementation.[103] By failing to specify who was responsible for implementation, how policies were to be put into effect, or the penalties for nonimplementation, senior leaders diminished the likelihood that energy policies would be implemented.[104]

[99] Li Shanhai, "Several Relationships to Be Properly Handled in Energy Work," *Tianjin Ribao*, Jan. 27, 1981, in *JPRS*, no. 77930 (Apr. 27, 1981): 16–19. On the problem of multiple goals, see Pressman and Wildavsky, *Implementation* (n. 21 above), 99–101.

[100] See references cited in note 29 above.

[101] On the problem of local authorities promoting duplicate construction, see Shen Liren, "Preventing Duplicate Construction," *RMRB*, July 12, 1982.

[102] Zhao Ziyang, "Several Questions" (n. 52 above), K6–7.

[103] See chapter 6 in this volume and, more generally, Richard H. Solomon, *Mao's Revolution and the Chinese Political Culture* (Berkeley and Los Angeles: University of California Press, 1971).

[104] Kang Shien (n. 44 above) does not call for assignment of specific responsibility; but see, for example, Jiang Wuning in *Tianjin Ribao*, April 1, 1980, in *JPRS*, no. 75888 (June 17, 1980): 91–95.

The Implementing Agents
Obstacles to implementation resulting from the character of the policies were
further aggravated by deficiencies and competing objectives on the part of
the individuals and agencies charged with putting those policies into effect.
Since the State Energy Commission was created after most elements of
China's current energy policy were already on the books, and since one
reason for its creation was to implement those policies, it is appropriate to
begin with a brief analysis of the agents responsible for implementation prior
to the establishment of the SEC.

In a sense, the imperfect implementation of energy policies before August
1980 is a classic case of responsibility being divided among so many different
agents that no one was willing or able to exercise that responsibility.[105] Unwillingness to make and enforce difficult and divisive decisions was the result
of both the inherent character of the policies and preoccupation with other
opportunities and responsibilities. Principal responsibility for implementing
measures to conserve energy appears to have been assigned to the State
Economic Commission. Throughout 1979 and even after the creation of
the Energy Commission, Economic Commission officials, most notably the
minister in charge, Kang Shien, exhorted the public and the bureaucracy to
save energy.[106] In his radio address launching the first "energy conservation
month" in November 1979, Kang decried wasteful practices, compared
China unfavorably with more advanced industrial nations, encouraged
enterprises to compete in the conservation of fuel and power, and called
for investigation of energy use and implementation of better management
systems. Technical training was to be stepped up and new energy sources
were to be promoted. Significantly, Kang also called for strict but fair administration of rewards and punishments and for increased organizational and
individual leadership (responsibility) in the area of energy use.[107] Typically,
the address was long on exhortation and short on specifics. One month later,
however, the State Economic Commission called for curtailment of energy
supplies to inefficient factories; the fuel and power "conserved" thereby was
to be reallocated to more efficient or more "important" enterprises.[108]

Apparently the Economic Commission did establish a special office to
monitor energy conservation activities, but that office, if it in fact existed,
lacked real authority. It could monitor and perhaps recommend certain ac-

[105] Lack of clear functions and responsibilities has been identified by Chinese officials as a
general problem that must be resolved. See, for example, Hua Guofeng, "Speech" (n. 79 above),
esp. sec. 3; and Zhao Ziyang, "Report on the Restructuring" (n. 93 above), esp. K4.
[106] Kang Shien (n. 44 above); *Xinhua*, Sept. 5, 1979, in *FBIS*, Sept. 6, 1979, L6; and *Xinhua*,
Sept. 4, 1979, in *FBIS*, Sept. 10, 1979, S1–2.
[107] Kang Shien, esp. L16–17.
[108] *Xinhua* broadcast report on the State Economic Commission Circular of December 2 to
Industrial and Transportation Departments, *FBIS*, Dec. 13, 1979, L4–7.

tions, but it could not enforce its decisions and appears to have been largely irrelevant to the functioning of the rest of the organization. Functionaries in the Economic Commission were clearly preoccupied with other tasks associated with the "eight character policy" of readjustment, restructuring, consolidation, and improvement. Energy conservation just was not very high on the list of those with day-to-day responsibilities.[109]

Responsibility for implementing production-related policies seems to have been divided among the State Planning Commission, the Capital Construction Commission, relevant ministries (Coal, Petroleum, and Electric Power), the People's Bank, the Construction Bank, and local planning offices. Of these, the Planning Commission (SPC) and the Construction Commission were the most important because they controlled investment and operating funds. To the extent that policies were put into effect, it seems to have been due to the efforts of these commissions. For example, energy allocations (ultimately controlled by the SPC) were redirected from heavy to light industry, and an increased percentage of capital construction funds was allocated to the energy sector. However, the effectiveness of these measures was limited by the nature of the planning process and the relationships it had spawned.

Budget making in China, as elsewhere, seems to be largely an exercise in doing what was done last year plus a few percentage points.[110] A substantial portion of budgeted allocations are fixed—all debate and modification occur at the margins. The fact that most planning decisions have to be made within a very short period, and in a situation in which everyone's resources are demonstrably inadequate, is one reason that most change occurs only at the margins.[111] A second reason is that the smooth functioning of the system depends on predictability.[112]

A further factor contributing to the inertia of the planning process was the

[109] Energy conservation was only one of many high-priority tasks assigned to the underqualified, overworked staff of the Economic Commission. The Economic Commission had primary responsibility for implementing the "eight character policy" adopted at the Second Session of the Fifth NPC, as well as for improving overall economic performance. The observations of Downs, *Inside Bureaucracy* (n. 81 above), and Pressman and Wildavsky, *Implementation*, chap. 5, are relevant and helpful for understanding why the Economic Commission did not do more to implement energy conservation measures.

[110] See, for example, John Creighton Campbell, *Contemporary Japanese Budget Politics* (Berkeley and Los Angeles: University of California Press, 1977), esp. chap. 10.

[111] On the conservatism of the budgetary process, see Wildavsky, *Politics of the Budgetary Process* (n. 25 above). This widely accepted view is challenged, under certain conditions, by contributors to Randall B. Ripley and Grace A. Franklin, eds., *Policy-Making in the Federal Executive Branch* (New York: Free Press, 1975).

[112] This point was made by several informants from the State Planning Commission, the Energy Research Institute, and the Academy of Social Sciences. See also, Commentator, "On the Stability of Policies," *Gongren Ribao*, Feb. 8, 1981, in *FBIS*, Feb. 25, 1981, L6–8; editorial, "Policies Must Be Consistently Stable, Problems Must Be Solved in Real Earnest," *RMRB*, Apr. 3, 1982; and chapter 6 in this volume.

network of personal ties that had developed over the years. Functionaries in various ministries responsible for liaison with the Planning Commission knew their counterparts in relevant bureaus of the SPC and could invoke ties of friendship and mutual trust to protect their vested interests as well as to lobby for additional resources. Ties disrupted by the Cultural Revolution were reforged as veteran cadres returned to their former positions; a shared sense of loyalty to one another and to the planning process as they knew it intensified the situation.[113] All of these factors conspired against implementation of energy policies requiring hard choices and radical change.

The inertial and parochial forces that operated at the apex of the planning system were found in lower levels of the bureaucracy as well. Local planning offices, Party committees, branch banks, and so forth, found it much easier to continue past practices than to take on the onerous task of implementing unpopular energy policies. Moreover, they had other concerns with higher priorities.[114] And besides, in a period of political and policy uncertainty, who wanted to risk one's career by executing policies that would disadvantage certain comrades, create unhappiness and hostility, and possibly be disavowed if the wind changed once again?

The SEC was created with several and shifting objectives, as was noted above. Two of those objectives are particularly germane to the discussion in this and the preceding section, namely, to draft specific policies, rules, and regulations; and to enhance implementation of measures already on the books. The first objective was explicitly listed by Yu Qiuli in his address to the Standing Committee of the Fifth NPC when the Energy Commission was established;[115] the second objective seems probable but was never officially stated to be a goal of the SEC.

Yu's statement notwithstanding, it was never clear precisely what role the SEC was to play in the preparation and adoption of energy laws and regulations. One of its subordinate units, the Energy Research Institute, was to

---

[113] Interview with energy official, Feb. 7, 1983. Also, Michel Oksenberg, "Economic Policy-Making in China: Summer 1981," *China Quarterly*, no. 90 (June 1982): 165–94. With the partial exception of work on factions, China specialists have yet to apply insights from the vast and growing literature on social and political networks to the study of development in the PRC. The existence of issue networks in the United States is discussed in Hugh Heclo, "Issue Networks and the Executive Establishment," in Anthony King, ed., *The New American Political System* (Washington, D.C.: American Enterprise Institute, 1978), 116–24.

[114] A partial list of their other concerns includes implementing the "eight character policy" of readjustment, reform, consolidation, and improvement; enhancing economic performance; implementing the new responsibility system; juggling the demands of combining planning and market forces; reducing the number of units and personnel; promoting younger and better qualified people; and adjusting to new revenue-sharing formulas. On the general phenomenon involved, see Pressman and Wildavsky, *Implementation*, 99–101; and Edwards and Sharkansky, *Policy Predicament* (n. 19 above).

[115] *Xinhua* broadcast of Aug. 26, 1980 (n. 77 above).

collect and analyze data on energy production and utilization in China and abroad and to study the "regulations and experience" of other countries.[116] This information was forwarded to the Laws and Regulations Bureau, which had responsibility for drafting appropriate statutes. However, the Laws and Regulations Bureau did not enjoy exclusive or final responsibility for preparing or issuing regulations; it had to "consult with other relevant agencies."[117] In short, its role was blurred. Was it a consultative body, a coordinating body, a monitoring organ, or a decision-making institution? Without a clear definition of its power, the SEC could not elicit compliance from other agencies.

SEC responsibilities with respect to implementation were even less clear. Public documents and media commentaries are silent on this point, but interviews with former officials of the Energy Commission suggest that the Economic Commission had primary responsibility for implementing energy-related regulations and that the SEC was supposed to monitor the process and "make appropriate recommendations."[118] Despite its formal status as the paramount energy agency, the SEC was unable to ensure that energy policies were put into effect.

In addition to the policy-related problems outlined previously, the inability of the SEC to accomplish its putative mission was the result of three critical failings: it lacked stature, authority, and resources.[119] Quite simply, the way in which it was created—and neglected—deprived it of an organizational stature that might have overcome the inertia and bureaucratic rivalry of the agencies and agents who would ultimately have to implement decisions. Yu Qiuli was, and was perceived to be, in a state of political eclipse. The personalization of authority in China further diminished the clout of the SEC.[120] In the end, the SEC lacked a clear mandate, had few resources, and was led by a political leader widely perceived (mistakenly) to be on the way out. Given the obvious and repeatedly stated importance of energy problems, this situation is puzzling.

In the end, the SEC had neither carrot nor stick. The SEC staff could monitor and recommend, but they could not force other parts of the bureaucracy to comply.[121] Despite its supraministerial status, the energy

---

[116] Interviews with energy official, Mar. 15 and 20, 1982.

[117] Interviews with energy officials, Mar. 15 and 20, 1982, and Sept. 8, 1983.

[118] Ibid.

[119] For a slightly longer list, but one which includes additional problems mentioned elsewhere in this analysis, see Edwards and Sharkansky, chap. 10.

[120] See Lucian W. Pye, *The Dynamics of Chinese Politics* (Cambridge: Oelgeschlager, Gunn and Hain, 1981). The stature of the Energy Commission was also diminished by the fact that Song Zhenming became a vice-minister after he was removed as Minister of Petroleum because of the "Bohai Incident." *Xinhua* English broadcast of Mar. 23, 1983, in *FBIS*, Mar. 24, 1983, K1.

[121] Interviews with energy officials on Feb. 7 and Sept. 8, 1983.

ministries (coal, petroleum, and electric power) were not formally subordinated to the SEC, and it therefore had no authority or capacity to compel the
ministries or their officials to act in accordance with the general principles or
specific interpretations of the country's energy policy. In Chinese parlance,
the SEC did not have *lingdao guanxi* ("leadership connections").[122] Similarly,
creation of the SEC did not reduce the role of either the State Planning Commission or the State Economic Commission. As a result, bureaucratic interests and personal ties antedating formation of the Energy Commission
continued to be more important than guidance from SEC staff.[123] In other
words, the SEC lacked the authority to overcome the inertia and vested interests of preexisting institutions.[124]

Of all the SEC's disabilities, the lack of resources was the most crippling.
Funds for expanding energy-producing facilities or energy conservation were
channeled through other agencies, primarily the SPC and the State Capital
Construction Commission (SCCC).[125] Additional funds (and, subsequently,
funds originally distributed through the SCCC) were allocated in the form of
loans made by the People's Bank and the Capital Construction Bank.[126]
Moreover, other policy changes occurring simultaneously put an increasing
percentage of total revenues under the control of local authorities (see chapter 3). *No* funds were controlled or distributed by the SEC. Why should
enterprises, localities, industries, and ministries change their ways?

Energy policies were entrusted also to a wide and growing variety of other
agencies, all of which lacked real authority. The Energy Research Institute
(originally subordinate to the SEC and the Chinese Academy of Sciences) was
given responsibility for preparing detailed standards and norms for energy
consumption, and for reviewing the energy impact of proposals made to the
SPC. However, its small staff and lack of formal authority deprived it of real
influence.[127] Other actors in the energy-policy game included the Energy
Research Society (subordinate to the China Association of Science and
Technology),[128] the Energy Committee of the CAS,[129] a special study group
convened by the Technical Economic Research Center of the State

---

[122] Interview of Feb. 7, 1983.

[123] Interviews with energy officials, Feb. 9 and Sept. 8, 1983.

[124] See Downs, *Inside Bureaucracy*.

[125] Interviews with energy officials, Mar. 20, 1982, and Feb. 9, 1983.

[126] See Carl Walter, *China's Banking System: Structure and Reform* (Stanford: Northeast Asia–
United States Forum on International Policy, 1983), and the sources cited therein.

[127] Interviews with energy officials, Mar. 15 and Sept. 6–10, 1982, and Mar. 28, 1983.

[128] *Xinhua*, Jan. 9, 1981, in *FBIS*, Jan. 14, 1981, L17; and *Xinhua*, Jan. 13, 1982, in *FBIS*, Jan.
13, 1982, L12–13.

[129] This committee grew out of a work conference sponsored by CAS in early 1980. See "First
Energy Work Conference Convened by the Chinese Academy of Sciences," *GMRB*, Mar. 14,
1980, in *JPRS*, no. 75978 (July 2, 1980): 44–45.

Council,[130] and energy conservation committees at all levels of the functional and administrative hierarchies.[131] In addition, local planning agencies were to review the energy requirements and sources of supply for proposed projects within their jurisdiction and to deny approval and funding to projects without assured sources of fuel and power.[132] There were literally hundreds of actors or clearance points, each with its own objectives and competing responsibilities. Under these circumstances, it is unlikely that even clearly stated and very detailed energy policies could have been implemented fully; the confused and contentious policies described above could not have been put into effect by the agents entrusted with that responsibility.[133]

The Context

Both the SEC and energy policies were inextricably linked to broader economic, political, and social policies which were themselves in a state of transition. Similarly, organizational and personal relationships were undergoing extensive and divisive change (see chapter 2).[134] In this context, willingness to implement unclear, unpopular, and burdensome policies was minimal. Actors throughout the system were preoccupied with other goals and other problems. Coping with—and taking maximum advantage of—the concurrent policies of readjustment, reform, consolidation, and improvement seems to have been more important to enterprise managers and local political and administrative officials than was implementation of energy policies.[135] Reaping the benefits of decentralization, reducing budget deficits, and restoring stability and confidence in the regime were of greater concern to the top leadership than was the implementation of the energy policies it had adopted. Easing Hua Guofeng and other "leftists" from positions of responsibility without destroying the facade of unity, securing powerful positions for supporters of Deng Xiaoping and other "pragmatists," and preserving as

[130] Xie Jun, "Economic and Technical Experts Enter Zhongnanhai—State Council Sets Up Two Research Centers to Absorb Experts as Advisors on Technical and Economic Policies," *GMRB*, Aug. 30, 1981.

[131] Interview with official of the Economic Commission, Sept. 6, 1982. See also, for example, Guangdong Radio, Jan. 7, 1981, in *FBIS*, Jan. 13, 1981, P1.

[132] Yu Qiuli, "Report" (n. 16 above), L20.

[133] See Pressman and Wildavsky, *Implementation*, chap. 5; and Bardach, *Implementation Game* (n. 2 above), chaps. 2–6.

[134] On leadership and organizational change, see Deng Xiaoping, "Reform" (n. 67 above); and Zhao Ziyang, "Report on Restructuring" (n. 93 above). On the broader survey of changes under way, see Hua Guofeng, "Speech" (n. 79 above); and Hu Yaobang, "Create a New Situation in All Fields of Socialist Modernization" (report to the 12th Party Congress, Sept. 1, 1982), in *BR*, 1982, no. 37 (Sept. 13): 11–40.

[135] See, for example, editorial, "Enhance the Sense of Urgency" (n. 57 above); Gui Shiyong (n. 27 above); editorial, "Energy Conservation" (n. 64 above); and Li Shanhai (n. 99 above).

much personal power and perquisites as possible occupied senior leaders from at least 1979 through 1981. Thereafter, the scope, character, and consequences of the major organizational reform announced in December 1981 and undertaken in early 1982 became more salient than the implementation of other policies, including energy policy. In short, the turbulent, transitional nature of the post-Mao period was not conducive to the implementation of energy policies. Parochial, micro-level concerns overwhelmed measures designed to enhance the common good. Complaints by China's leaders about departmentalism, localism, and a small-producer mentality are not without basis. But the elite was also to blame; senior leaders did not do all that they could have—should have—done to ensure implementation.

LESSONS AND IMPLICATIONS

The energy policies adopted by Mao's successors have proven difficult to implement for reasons of both content and context.[136] Generally speaking, policies have been vague, poorly integrated, and divisive. Ambiguity bespeaks and begets administrative caution; senior leaders have eschewed hard choices in favor of consensus and "stability," and lower-level cadres have been unwilling or unable to act without clearer guidance from above. Whenever policies or implementing agents have attempted to alleviate the country's energy problems by redistributing funds, fuel, power, or other limited resources, adversely affected interests have resisted with every means possible.[137]

Since energy policies emerged from essentially the same context as that within which they were to be implemented, it is fruitless to consider questions such as, Had the policies been better, could they have been implemented more successfully? Policies reflect their origins; in the case under study, both policies and implementation were shaped by the broader political, economic, social, and administrative context. Dozens of other problems and goals competed with energy for attention and resources. Underqualified cadres with inadequate information and ill-defined authority were enjoined to implement often incompatible policies. New and frequently changing policies were issued and had to be implemented in the context of political and economic reform, the restructuring of State organs, and tension between the forces of centralization and decentralization. As a result, implementation of energy policy was episodic and uneven.

The foregoing analysis has identified numerous conditions obstructing the implementation of energy policies without assessing their relative impor-

[136] See Merilee S. Grindle, "Policy Content and Context in Implementation," in Merilee S. Grindle, ed., *Politics and Policy Implementation in the Third World* (Princeton: Princeton University Press, 1980), 3–34.

[137] On the politics of redistributive policies, see Lowi, "American Business" (n. 25 above).

tance. Two reasons underlay the decision to adopt that approach: a desire to depict the magnitude of the problems facing Chinese officials and the need to describe the interactive effects of contemporaneous developments. Moreover, Chinese officials seem to have concluded that the "problem" was not one or two discrete conditions, but the system as a whole.

By way of conclusion, however, I want to offer a more parsimonious explanation for the inconsistent and at times indifferent implementation of energy policies: the lack of a champion.[138] A champion is a crusader, "a monomaniac with a mission."[139] The concept of such a doggedly committed advocate comes from the study of American business, but it has analogs in the public sector and, with appropriate qualifications, is useful for studying developments in China. In the sense the term is used here, Chen Yun has been a champion of efforts to improve the efficacy of central planning by reducing its scope, and Wan Li a champion of new systems of production responsibility in agriculture.[140] Energy policy has never had that kind of advocate. As was noted above, Yu Qiuli might have played such a role, but he did not or could not do so. The same is true of Kang Shien.

Given the complex and largely redistributive character of energy policies, it is easy to understand why political leaders would shrink from the role of energy champion—it looks like, and probably is, a no-win situation. Reluctance to grasp the energy tarbaby has afflicted even Deng Xiaoping. Despite his unrivaled stature and authority and his willingness to identify personally with issues ranging from science to the military, he has said very little about energy-related matters.

Without a champion and without clear support of the country's most powerful leader, energy policy is an orphan, just one among several other "urgent matters." No one has really pushed for better policies or more effective implementation; no one has intervened to end bureaucratic squabbling or administrative dalliance. Perhaps the real surprise is that the results have been better than the preceding analysis would lead one to expect. China has improved energy efficiency and made progress toward several other goals noted above.[141] However, the reasons for this apparent success may have little to do with either energy policies or their implementation.

Up to a point, it probably does not matter that energy or other policies are

[138] On champions and their importance in American industry, see Peter Drucker, *Adventures of a Bystander* (New York: Harper and Row, 1979); and Thomas J. Peters and Robert H. Waterman, Jr., *In Search of Excellence: Lessons from America's Best Run Companies* (New York: Warner Books, 1982), esp. chap. 7.

[139] The term is Drucker's (255).

[140] See chapter 9 in this volume.

[141] For example, industrial production increased at an annual rate of 7.2 percent between 1979 and 1982, whereas energy consumption increased by only 1.9 percent per year. See Zhao Ziyang, "Report" (n. 28 above), K3.

vague and difficult to implement. An edict from the central government or
the Communist Party, however general or ambiguous, is certain to command
the attention and at least minimal compliance of lower-level cadres. Thus,
the simple injunction to "save energy" is sufficient to induce first-order conservation efforts. Such an edict focuses attention, temporarily, and people
respond in ways that are relatively easy for them to do. In other words, to
realize one-time, easy, inexpensive, uncontroversial objectives does not
require detailed policy guidelines. Indeed, such guidelines are superfluous.
The problem comes when policies require more than first-order compliance;
it is in moving beyond the first stage that the difficulties and obstacles outlined above come into play. China has realized some of its energy goals for
reasons having nothing to do with its specific energy policies. For example,
the recession of 1980–1982 probably did more to reduce energy consumption
in heavy industry than did measures to retrofit plants, close inefficient facilities, or improve management. Consumption decreased because the economy was weak and orders for capital goods had fallen.[142] This and many
similar "achievements" are more apparent than real. China's energy officials
recognize this and continue to press for more effective implementation of
policies that have been on the books for several years.

Deng Xiaoping, Zhao Ziyang, and other key leaders appear to have concluded that the obstacles impeding implementation of energy policies are
endemic and that the only way to alleviate them is to transform the system.
The organizational reforms of 1982, which included abolition of the SEC and
reassignment of its responsibilities to the Energy Bureau of the State Economic Commission and to the energy ministries, should be seen as part of the
effort to ensure better implementation in the future. So, too, should the attack
on bureaucratism, departmentalism, seniority, and excessive decentralization. Since most of these problems have been around for a long time and
China's leaders have made repeated efforts to solve them, one should not be
overly sanguine about the prospects for success. Nevertheless, there does
seem to be something different, more serious, and more realistic about the
current spate of reforms. Policy implementation could improve in the years
ahead; unless it does, China faces a very difficult future.

[142] Interviews with energy officials, Sept. 11 and 12, 1983.

EIGHT

Obligatory Tree Planting: The Role of Campaigns in Policy Implementation in Post-Mao China

Lester Ross

OVERVIEW

Forestry is one of the most serious environmental issues affecting China. The People's Republic of China (PRC) inherited a woefully depleted resource base,[1] and Beijing has been trying to turn the situation around ever since. Commercial or planned timber consumption averages only $0.07m^3$ per person annually, barely one-tenth the world level.[2] Most of the populace relies on fuel wood, grass, and plant leavings as their primary energy source for household needs, yet almost 40 percent of all households are said to suffer from fuel shortages for three months or longer each year.[3] Finally, widespread deforestation aggravates erosion, desertification, and flooding, which imperil China's prospects for future development.[4]

I wish to thank Fritz Gaenslen and the workshop participants, especially David M. Lampton, for suggesting revisions for the earlier workshop version of this chapter. The work was supported in part by a research grant from the Joint Committee on Chinese Studies of the American Council of Learned Societies and the Social Science Research Council, with funds provided by the Andrew W. Mellon Foundation.

[1] Rhoads Murphey, "Deforestation in Modern China," in Richard P. Tucker and J. F. Richards, eds., *Global Deforestation and the Nineteenth Century World Economy* (Durham: Duke University Press, 1983), 111–28.

[2] Yong Wentao, "Linye Mianlin de Liang Zhong Qushi" (The Two Trends Facing Forestry), *Nongye Jingji Wenti* (hereafter *NJW*), September 1982, 14–17.

[3] The figure rises to almost 60 percent if shorter periods are considered. These shortages of course are concentrated in the countryside. See the Forestry Development Section of the Agricultural Economics Institute of the Academy of Social Sciences, "Woguo Linye Fazhan Zhanlue de Chubu Shexiang" (An Initial Plan of Strategy for China's Forestry Development), *NJW*, May 1983, 34–38.

[4] Vaclav Smil, *The Bad Earth* (Armonk, N.Y.: M. E. Sharpe, 1983); see also chapter 6 in this volume.

Nonetheless, there has been some progress since 1949. China officially reports an increase in forest cover from 8.6 percent of surface area to about 12 percent, as well as a modest rise in timber reserves. Some areas, like the Leizhou Peninsula in Guangdong, are remarkable successes. The most impressive accomplishments have been the building of windbreaks to protect 13 million hectares of farmland, and the planting of many millions of shade and ornamental trees in the cities and along roads.[5]

In general, however, the quality of plantations has been very low, with survival rates averaging no more than 30–40 percent, using even generous measurement techniques. Plantation growth lags far behind the standards achieved in other countries, and growth increments on a nationwide basis lag behind removals and natural losses as demand continues to rise. Many key provinces have suffered major declines in their forest resource inventories.[6]

Given these problems, many of Mao's successors have welcomed new policy initiatives. As I have argued elsewhere,[7] implementation alternatives fall into three broad categories: bureaucratic authoritative, exhortational campaign, and market exchange. Convinced that economic development was hampered by an unwieldy bureaucracy, Deng Xiaoping and his associates have taken extraordinarily large steps to liberalize the economy through material incentives, enterprise autonomy, foreign trade, taxation, and credit, although the bureaucratic aspect remains dominant.

A great deal of research has focused on market-oriented economic reform and readjustment in the post-Mao era, but far less attention has been paid to the role of campaigns. This is a curious omission considering the centrality of campaigns in the Maoist period. Campaigns provided Mao with a ready instrument to circumvent opposition by taking his case directly to lower echelons of authority or the people. Meanwhile, the Party as an organization used campaigns to transform society and the economy in an avowedly socialist direction. Indeed, the first several decades of the PRC are commonly analyzed in terms of a cyclical progression from one campaign to the next—

[5] He Kang, "Jianshe you Zhongguo Tese de Shehuizhuyi Xiandaihua Nongye" (Building Socialist Modernizing Agriculture with Chinese Characteristics), *Hong Qi* (hereafter *HQ*), Oct. 1, 1982, 29.

[6] Lester Ross, "Forest Area in the People's Republic of China: Estimating the Gains and Losses," *China Geographer* 11 (1980): 123–37, and "Forestry in China Today: Implications for the 1980's," in Randolph Barker and Beth Rose, eds., *Agricultural and Rural Development in China Today* (Ithaca: Cornell University Program in International Agriculture, 1983), 27–38; Chen Zhusheng, "Huanjing Baohu he Huanjing Jingjixue de Yanjiu" (Research on Environmental Protection and Environmental Economics), in Yu Guangyuan et al., eds., *Lun Huanjing Guanli* (On Environmental Management) (Taiyuan: Shanxi Renmin Chubanshe, 1980), 110–25.

[7] Lester Ross, "The Implementation of Environmental Policy in China: A Comparative Perspective," *Administration & Society* 15, no. 4 (February 1984): 489–516.

for example, from the Great Leap Forward to the Socialist Education Movement to the Cultural Revolution.[8]

Campaigns clearly are less prominent in the post-Mao era. The current leadership blames China's past misfortunes in part on campaigns that got out of hand and wreaked havoc, the most notable example being the Cultural Revolution. Therefore, they have resolved not to rely on the "decisive struggle" (*da huizhan*) approach to economic development and the "big criticism" (*da piping*) weapon in literary criticism, two common campaign formats.[9] Nevertheless, there is a persistent tendency to resort to campaigns for implementation albeit under tighter controls and subject to various modifications. A leading example is the Party organizational reform that began in 1983 to revitalize the Party and purge deadwood and the Maoist faithful from the Party rolls. However, this policy has lagged behind schedule, in part because of the leadership's reluctance to unleash the full panoply of campaign weapons, such as "dragging out" bad elements so that they can be criticized and struck down.[10]

If campaigns are distrusted by the post-Mao leadership because they can easily get out of control and create social and economic disorder, why do they persist? The answer rests on a mixture of political and policy factors. The power to organize campaigns is not distributed equally among the elite but rather is concentrated at the peak of the system and among those involved in Party affairs and ideology rather than in economic management.[11] Although the power of the propaganda apparatus has been greatly reduced in the post-Mao era, as is stressed elsewhere in this book, the ideologues continue to actively seek opportunities to enhance their influence through campaigns. Such opportunities no longer are commonplace, as they were when the radicals ruled, and are only infrequently made available by the reformers, who prefer to rely on material incentives. However, conservatives within the leadership are apt to prefer the comfortable ideological trappings of cam-

---

[8]Charles P. Cell, *Revolution at Work: Mobilization Campaigns in China* (New York: Academic Press, 1977); Gordon Bennett, *Yundong: Mass Campaigns in Chinese Communist Leadership* (Berkeley: University of California Center for Chinese Studies 1976); G. William Skinner and Edwin Winckler, "Compliance Succession in Rural Communist China," in Amitai Etzioni, ed., *A Sociological Reader on Complex Organizations*, 2d ed. (New York: Holt, Rinehart and Winston, 1969), 410–38.

[9]Tian Xueyuan and Cai Jianguo, "'Da Huizhan' Shi Zuzhi Jingji Jianshe de Hao Xingshi Ma?" (Is the 'Decisive Battle' A Good Way to Build the Economy?), *Guangming Ribao* (hereafter *GR*), Oct. 29, 1980; Deng Xiaoping, "The Present Situation and the Tasks Before Us," Jan. 16, 1980, 236, in *Selected Works of Deng Xiaoping* (Beijing: Foreign Languages Press, 1983), 224–58.

[10]Xiao Yu, "It Is Better 'Not to Satisfy Addiction,'" *Renmin Ribao* (hereafter *RR*), Dec. 8, 1984.

[11]John H. Kautsky, "Revolutionary and Managerial Elites in Modernizing Regimes," *Comparative Politics* 1, no. 4 (July 1969): 441–67.

paigns, particularly when the conservatives are in the minority and have to cultivate a broader base of support for their views.

Campaigns can also serve the interests of any leadership group when it is faced with particular kinds of policy problems. On the one hand, when a group lacks the resources to advance a policy initiative through the normal bureaucratic route, it can organize a campaign to highlight an issue and try to win additional funds or materiel, as in energy conservation campaigns. Campaigns are particularly attractive in this regard because they themselves are low-cost, off-budget affairs operating outside otherwise pervasive budgetary constraints. On the other hand, campaigns are particularly suited to policies whose success depends on a change in the otherwise prevailing value structure which ordinarily would be hard to obtain through material incentives. This is particularly true in a country where political authority traditionally relied heavily on moral suasion. The leading example is birth control, discussed in chapter 10. Finally, campaigns sometimes can serve as largely symbolic exercises designed to convey an impression of activity without actually making a commitment of resources sufficient to resolve a problem.

In this chapter I will analyze forestry policy through the prism of a campaign that originated in 1981, three years after the momentous Third Plenum, which marked the consolidation of power by the pragmatists. This case is theoretically significant in that it illuminates the political, policy, and symbolic dimensions of campaigns. Unfortunately, however, it will also be revealed that the haste, imbalance, and episodic nature of campaigns is largely incompatible with success in a complex policy like forestry, with its long lead time.

INTRODUCTION

This chapter analyzes policy implementation through campaigns that are short-term or intermittent organizations with flat hierarchies and a simple division of labor, led by the Communist Party and its affiliated mass organizations, and rely largely upon normative incentives reinforced by latent or overt coercion. The Obligatory Tree Planting (OTP) program was adopted by the National People's Congress (NPC) on December 13, 1981. The resolution directed all physically able citizens to plant trees in the interest of society and future generations without personal material reward. The program was initiated with great fanfare befitting an undertaking that promised to greatly accelerate afforestation through the organized yet self-motivated efforts of hundreds of millions of people. Normative exhortation is a hallmark of campaigns, but formal legislative enactment and the threat of legal sanctions in cases of noncompliance were new to the Chinese process of policy implementation. The novel marriage of legal obligations and moral suasion into an instrument of implementation, in accord with the legalization flavor of the post-Mao era, by itself accords theoretical interest to OTP.[12]

Yet the arrival of OTP was not in total harmony with the temper of the time. Following the rise to power of the pragmatists at the Third Plenum in 1978, the prevailing analysis of problems in forestry policy focused on policy fluctuations, vague and uncertain property rights, artificially depressed producer-prices, and a general lack of material incentives. Many Chinese argued that forestry needed stability, clear and legally protected property rights, and higher returns for producers in order to expand the resource base—features seldom associated with a campaign predicated on expanding the commons.

Several reforms were introduced in this light within the prevailing context of unleashing peasant production power, as is discussed in chapter 9 with regard to farming. Forest ownership was decentralized, enterprises were given wider autonomy, procurement prices were raised for collectively pro-duced timber and many other forest products, and the unified planning and distribution system was relaxed, leading to the opening of rural markets for timber and bamboo. These reforms promised an expansion of the resource base in the medium to long term, given stability, further price reforms, and the provision of additional infrastructural supports.

In the short term, however, widespread deforestation resulted because enormous pent-up demand attracted more wood into the market, yet the producers lacked the confidence necessary to invest in resource management for the future. In addition, structural inadequacies, such as the lack of effec-tive law enforcement and a shortage of investment capital, reduced the potential for entrepreneurial investments in forestry. Revelations about ille-gal and ill-conceived logging (*luan kan lan fa*), a major factor in the reported reduction of forest cover from 12.7 percent of surface area to 12 percent in the late 1970s, were widely reported in the press.[13] They coincided with widening differences within the post-Mao leadership over the direction, scope, and pace of economic reform. Beginning in the winter of 1980–1981, a coalition of conservatives and middle-of-the-roaders emerged with sufficient power to slow the pace of reform and reestablish the primacy of plan over market.[14]

Nevertheless, with the exception of the closure of free markets and the

[12]Christopher S. Wren, "China Embarks on Plan to Halt Loss of Forests," *New York Times* (hereafter *NYT*), Dec. 13, 1981; *Zhongguo Qingnian Bao* (hereafter *ZQB*), Mar. 11, 1982.

[13]*RR*, Aug. 6, 1979; Sept. 24 and 28, 1980; Dec. 8 and 13, 1980; and Jan. 3, 1981. The decline in forest cover was reported in *Jingji Ribao*, Apr. 26, 1984, trans. in *JPRS*, CAG 84–025 (Sept. 20, 1984): 8–9.

[14]Dorothy J. Solinger, "The Fifth National People's Congress and the Process of Policy Making: Reform, Readjustment, and the Opposition," *Asian Survey* (hereafter *AS*) 22, no. 12 (December 1982): 1238–75; and chapter 2 in this volume.

return to unified planning and distribution for timber,[15] most steps taken were basically compatible with a market approach and an emphasis on material incentives. The new measures were labeled the "three fixes," which referred to the clarification and stabilization of property rights, the extension of the concept of private plots to woodlots, and the establishment of a production-responsibility system for forestry.[16] The reconstitution of a somewhat weakened unified production and distribution system strengthened the bureaucratic hand of the Ministry of Forestry, which traditionally had distrusted market mechanisms. However, the "three fixes," if carefully carried out, would result in a system of decentralized property rights in which both environmental protection and economic development would be fostered under a system of household initiative motivated by material incentives. Thus, key elements of the post-Mao reforms in forestry remained intact even after the Central Work Conference in December 1980 when Chen Yun's views concerning the primacy of planning were reasserted, indicating how hard it was to halt the reform momentum.

In this context of competition between market and bureaucracy for dominance among implementation modes, OTP suddenly appeared in late 1981, representing a revival of the campaign mode. Several questions arise: Since planners and the Ministry of Forestry supported the bureaucratic approach while economic reformers backed the market, who favored the return of campaigns? To what extent did OTP represent a campaign in the customary sense, or did it amount to something new and more suited to the post-Mao era? Why did OTP appear in the winter of 1981–1982, and how effective did it prove to be? Let us first look at the origins of OTP.

FORMULATION AND LEGITIMATION

Deng Xiaoping was personally credited with proposing OTP.[17] The idea is said to have originated in the immediate aftermath of the floods that struck

---

[15] "Emergency Circular of the State Council Regarding the Absolute Prohibition of Reckless and Illegal Felling of Forests" (in Chinese), Dec. 5, 1980, in *Zhonghua Renmin Gongheguo Guowuyuan Gongbao* (hereafter *ZRGGYG*) 346 (Dec. 25, 1980): 591–92.

[16] "The Ministry of Forestry's Report on the Stabilization of Property Rights and Putting the Production Responsibility System into Effect" (in Chinese), June 30, 1981, in *ZRGGYG* 363 (Sept. 25, 1981): 499–502; "Instructions by the Party Center and State Council Concerning the Large Scale Unfolding of Tree Planting and Afforestation" (in Chinese), Mar. 5, 1980, in *ZRGGYG* 330 (May 15, 1980): 73–78; "Decisions of the Party Center and State Council Regarding Some Problems in Forest Protection and Forestry Development" (in Chinese), Mar. 8, 1981, in *ZRGGYG* 352 (May 15, 1981): 135–42; Yang Furong et al., eds., *Linye Shengchan Jingji Zeren Zhi* (An Economic Responsibility System for Forestry Production) (Beijing: Zhongguo Linye Chubanshe, 1981).

[17] Li Changjian, "Zaofu Zisun Houdai de Qianqiu Daye" (A Great Everlasting Enterprise to Build Prosperity for Our Descendants), *Zhongguo Linye* (hereafter *ZL*), January 1982, 3–5.

the Yangtze and Yellow river valleys in the summer of 1981. Tan Qilong, CCP leader in Sichuan, the most affected province, toured the afflicted areas and quickly concluded that deforestation and excessive logging had aggravated his province's vulnerability to flooding.[18] Vice-Premier Wan Li, a member of the Politburo, was sympathetic to Tan's analysis and brought it to the attention of Deng. The latter concurred and in September recommended a compulsory tree-planting program to help solve China's forestry problems, including flooding. Deng's proposal called for participation without pay by everyone aged eleven or older, with sanctions to be imposed against shirkers. By late September Wan publicly outlined the program.[19]

According to this account, China's policy implementation process consists of leading officials closely monitoring affairs and then proposing prompt policy responses to problems. This is fully in accord with the hallowed image of the decisive yet benevolent cadre. Actually, in the face of a crisis, Chinese leaders, like their counterparts elsewhere, are inclined to embrace available "solutions" regardless of how well these correspond to the problem. I have argued elsewhere that forestry-development proposals were pending when the floods struck and therefore received increased leadership support. Like the "garbage can" model of decision making, problems and solutions come together randomly rather than in rationally planned association. In this case, forestry was supported, even though there is little evidence that it can control floods in large river valleys like the Yangtze.[20]

Although the summer floods supplied a critical impetus to OTP, the groundwork had been set earlier. The idea of large-scale organized tree planting by the people was not new. Seasonal planting campaigns had long been the norm, although their role gradually had been reduced over time in favor of more specialized forest farms and work units. Of more direct relevance was an unpublicized pilot project resembling OTP, which began in 1980 under central auspices in Changping Xian in the hills just north of Beijing.[21]

Months before Deng became personally involved, a central directive

---

[18] James P. Sterba, "Chinese Say Deforestation Caused Flood Damage in Sichuan," *NYT*, Aug. 22, 1981; *RR*, Aug. 19, 1981; Tan Qilong, "Xiqu Hongzai Jiaoxun, Zhenxing Sichuan Linye" (Absorb the Lesson of the Floods, Promote Forestry in Sichuan), *ZL*, November 1981, 5–7.

[19] *RR*, Sept. 23, 1981.

[20] Lester Ross, "Flood Control Policy in China: The Policy Consequences of Natural Disasters," *Journal of Public Policy* 3, no. 2 (May 1983): 209–32; Michael Cohen and James G. March, "The Garbage Can Model of Organizational Choice," *Administrative Science Quarterly* 17, no. 1 (March 1972): 1–25.

[21] Changping Xian Greenification Committee, "Peihe Shi Qu Dagao Yiwu Zhishu" (Do OTP in a Big Way in Conjunction With the Urban Districts), *ZL*, February 1983, 20; Central Greenification Commission, *Obligatory Tree Planting by the Whole People* (Beijing: Zhongguo Linye Chubanshe, 1982), 139–49.

issued in the spring of 1981 on forestry conservation and forestry development declared that all able-bodied citizens had the duty to participate in
afforestation. However, this reference constituted but one paragraph in a
lengthy document of twenty-five articles issued belatedly during the spring
planting season and largely devoted to other subjects. The directive also
offered no clues about how this section was to be interpreted, in particular
how tree planting in terms of a citizen's duty was to be coordinated with
regular afforestation projects. There was no provision for implementation
regarding site selection, planting stock, technical advice, or enforcement.[22]
The Ministry of Forestry always had placed highest priority on planned
afforestation while rightfully complaining about a shortage of funds.[23] Since
no additional resources were provided in 1981 for obligatory forestry work,
afforestation in 1981 proceeded without regard for this provision.

Thus, it appears that Deng's contribution to OTP was more in the role of
godfather reviving an extant but moribund idea, rather than the natural
father of a new program. In this respect the policy implementation process is
highly centralized yet sluggish, with lower-level officials awaiting signals of
personal commitment by top leaders before becoming galvanized into action.
It should be noted, however, that the then minister of forestry personally
credited Deng with including the element of rewards and sanctions to increase the likelihood of compliance.[24]

Nevertheless, the question remains: Why was OTP revived at this time?
The answer appears to be a combination of political repression and symbolic
politics under changed circumstances, resulting in the modification of a
familiar policy instrument. The selfless-sacrifice aspect of OTP was linked to
the rising unease within the Party over what was perceived to be a breakdown of social order and faith in communism. Although the Party's loss of
prestige and the increase in unapproved behavior were at first formally attributed exclusively to the after effects of the Cultural Revolution and the
machinations of the Gang of Four, conservative elements blamed the post-
Mao reforms. Deng Xiaoping for his part had already, in 1979, declared
defense of the "four cardinal principles" (the socialist road, the dictatorship
of the proletariat, leadership by the Communist Party, and Marxism–
Leninism–Mao Zedong Thought) to be an essential accompaniment of the
"four modernizations." However, committed reformers fought to keep their
programs alive.

In the Maoist era, an outbreak of political nonconformity would likely
have been met by vigorous mass campaigns. The campaigns would have
promoted desired moral attributes while condemning objectionable items,
often by targeting helpless individuals for severe criticism and even life-

---

[22] The second paragraph in Article 19 of "Decisions of the Party Center and State Council
Regarding Some Problems in Forest Protection and Forestry Development" (n. 16 above).

[23] Yong Wentao, "Linye" (n. 2 above).

[24] *GR*, Dec. 8, 1981.

threatening punishment. Because such measures created fear and uncertainty among the populace and would have aborted the ongoing reforms, Deng and his associates resolved that future campaigns must avoid "ultraleftist" excesses. Even the term *yundong* ("campaign" or "movement") was deliberately avoided in many instances to soothe people's minds.

Consequently, protocampaigns that emerged at the initiative of conservatives were at first resisted by reformers. When the current was too strong, however, the reformers strove to direct the campaigns along relatively innocuous channels. This was the case with "socialist spiritual civilization," a term apparently first introduced by Ye Jianying in 1979 in an effort to curtail the subversive effects of the four modernizations. Socialist spiritual civilization was defined in terms of an ethic of disciplined selflessness accompanying a high level of intellectual competence.[25] This distinction between spiritual and material civilization echoes the nineteenth-century quest for "Chinese civilization as the essence, Western learning for practical application," as well as the Marxist ideal of combining redness and expertise.

As Hamrin shows, the socialist spiritual civilization campaign did not get off the ground until after the Central Work Conference in December 1980, during which Chen Yun's insistence on the need for economic retrenchment was accepted.[26] Even then, however, its scope was limited. Although Deng conceded the need for a stronger effort in propaganda, he continued to define the task in terms of emancipating the mind, seeking truth from facts, and uprooting feudal influences alongside upholding the four cardinal principles and combatting "bourgeois liberalization."[27] Taken together with a pronounced reluctance to unleash the destructive force of campaigns, Deng's halfhearted endorsement explains why socialist spiritual civilization was largely confined to moral education in the form of the "five stresses and four points of beauty," later expanded to include the "three patriotisms."[28] Activity was concentrated in March, which was designated spiritual civilization month, just as November became energy conservation month. In this fashion, a potentially major campaign was scaled back to the status of a secular holiday.[29]

[25] Yan Ming, "Wuzhi Wenming yu Jingshen Wenming de Guanxi, Neng Fou Deng Tong yu Zhexue Shang de Wuzhi yu Jingshen Guanxi?" (Can the Relationship Between Material and Spiritual Civilizations Be Equated with the Philosophical Relationship Between Matter and Spirit?), *HQ* 423 (June 1, 1983): 18–19; Zhou Jinwei, "On Spiritual Civilization," *Beijing Review* (hereafter *BR*) 24, no. 10 (Mar. 9, 1981): 18–20.

[26] See also Arif Dirlik, "Spiritual Solutions to Material Problems, the 'Socialist Ethics and Courtesy Month' in China," *South Atlantic Quarterly* 81, no. 4 (Autumn 1982): 359–75.

[27] Carol Lee Hamrin, "Competing 'Policy Packages' in Post-Mao China," *AS* 24, no. 5 (May 1984): 508.

[28] Deng Xiaoping, "Implement the Policy of Readjustment, Ensure Stability and Unity," Dec. 25, 1980, in *Selected Works*, 344–50.

[29] Guan Xin, "Tichang 'Wu Jiang' 'Si Mei,' Jianshe Jingshen Wenming" (Promote the Five Stresses and Four Beauties, Build A Spiritual Civilization), *HQ* 370 (Mar. 17, 1981): 27–29.

Forestry's connection with these cosmic issues may seem tenuous, but in fact it was both direct and opportunistic. Forestry was considered capable of contributing to modernization not only in an economic sense but also spiritually through physical labor in the public interest. Tree planting was included among "beautification of the environment" activities organized under the "five stresses and four points of beauty." It was said that tree planting without pay could help to create a Communist ethic of service to the people, build patriotism and collectivism, combine theory and intellectual awareness with practice and physical labor, and inculcate a spirit of arduous struggle rather than passive dependence on government funds.[30] Forestry might also occupy idle youth and build good work habits, as the proposed Young Adult Conservation Corps in the United States seeks to do. Wan Li also expressed a very strong personal commitment to the environment which transcended ideology.[31]

In addition, OTP was a symbolic gesture on the part of the regime to express its concern about the flood danger without making substantial fiscal or other commitments, which would have been difficult in the context of an already sizable budget deficit. The low cost of OTP was particularly attractive amidst urgent efforts to balance the budget by slashing spending for capital construction, including water conservancy. Although the Ministry of Forestry argued in favor of increased support for ongoing programs, any additional funds would have been at the expense of other claimants. The Ministry's case may have been handicapped also by a widespread judgment among reformers that the bureaucratic approach was ineffective and therefore not worthy of additional appropriations.

Policy formulation proceeded very quickly once the leadership's preferences had been reaffirmed. The Ministry of Forestry's Party branch researched and submitted draft documents. Within a month three drafts were ready: a report on Deng's views regarding forestry, a resolution for action by the National People's Congress, and a set of instructions to be issued by the State Council.

Two points should be noted here. First, the ministry's Party branch, rather than the Afforestation Bureau or some other regular administrative component, provided the staffing for OTP. The Party branch's dominant role may well be an exception rather than the norm. To be sure, CCP branches have independent communications with the Central Committee outside formal government channels and can make decisions binding on the government and nongovernment agencies in which they are situated. How-

---

[30] RR, Mar. 15, 1981, and Jan. 10, 1982; Central Greenification Commission, Obligatory, 25–31 (n. 21 above).

[31] Wan Li, "Tigao Renshi Jiachang Lingdao, Zhazha Shishi Gaohao Yiwu Zhishu" (Elevate Our Understanding and Strengthen Leadership, Resolutely Do OTP Well), ZL, February 1983, 3–5.

ever, Party influence in administrative matters has been sharply curtailed in the post-Mao era in order to promote professional management. In this case, the Party branch's prominence is probably due to OTP's largely political rather than professional nature. It would have made little sense to distract regular staff departments with a mobilization assignment at a time when the regime's chief goal was "steady rule through professional bureaucracy, not campaigns."[32] In the process, however, the ministry's regular staff may have been deterred from offering professional advice on OTP's feasibility at early stages of the decision-making process.

Second, Deng in particular insisted that OTP be formalized by an NPC resolution. It was not that he wanted independent input from the NPC—the nominally supreme legislature already had reverted to its traditionally supine role of a rubber stamp in 1981, after having exercised some occasionally vigorous oversight of the government at its 1979 and 1980 sessions.[33] Rather, legitimation by the NPC was considered desirable as part of the post-Mao effort to create a "socialist" legal system, and especially because exhortational campaigns had suffered a decline in their ability to mobilize the populace.

The Ministry of Forestry's Party branch quickly drafted the three requested documents, and then solicited the comments of provincial officials who were already in Beijing attending a national agricultural work conference. The latter unanimously endorsed Deng's idea for OTP while making unspecified suggestions for improvements. Then on October 17 the ministry's Party branch submitted its exposition of Deng's earlier remarks to the Central Party Secretariat. The Secretariat, led by Hu Yaobang, endorsed OTP as an environmental and socialist spiritual civilization measure, stressing OTP's ideological nature while adding the need to focus primarily on urban areas and to select sixty cities and counties as key points for demonstration purposes.

The urban focus of OTP illustrates the random nature of a "garbage can" policy process. The immediate stimulus for OTP was the flooding that originated in remote rural areas. However, the ideological aspects of OTP, coupled with Hu Yaobang's support for market measures in the rural areas, dictated an urban focus of no particular benefit to flood control. In a curious fashion, problems involving rural ecology and urban youth had become joined in a solution well suited to neither.

During the next three weeks the ministry's Party branch met with the General Administration for Urban Construction, the Communist Youth

[32] Michel Oksenberg, "Economic Policy-Making in China: Summer 1981," *China Quarterly* 90 (June 1982): 165–94.

[33] Martin Weil, "The Baoshan Steel Mill: A Symbol of Change in China's Industrial Development Strategy," in Joint Economic Committee (JEC), *China Under the Four Modernizations* (Washington, D.C.: U.S. Government Printing Office, 1983) 1:383–85.

League, the General Political Department and the General Rear Services Department of the armed forces, and several provincial and municipal forestry and parks departments to get their ideas on implementation. The Ministry of Forestry's regular bureaus notably remained on the periphery.[34]

The ministry's Party branch submitted its draft NPC and State Council documents to the Secretariat in the first week of November. On November 9 the Secretariat approved these documents with Hu Yaobang presiding. The Secretariat stressed that OTP would be a mass movement (*qunzhong yundong*) requiring extensive propaganda to publicize successes and to criticize the laggard. Everyone, especially young people, would have to contribute to (*gongxian*) greenification. Even the physically handicapped and elderly would be expected to participate by offering advice or money. On the practical side, the Secretariat ordered that planting should begin on empty public lots, roadways, and tourist locations in the cities, and that nursery work would have to be the main task in 1982. These provisions would presumably ease potential conflicts over land use, and represented an acknowledgment of the shortage of planting stock.

Following action by the Secretariat, the State Council and the Standing Committee of the NPC approved OTP. The issue then was submitted to the NPC at its annual meeting in December. After several speeches in support by the then Minister of Forestry, Yong Wentao, and other deputies, OTP became law at 4:00 P.M. on December 13, 1981.[35]

Nine months had elapsed since OTP was first authorized in a central directive, including a period of four months during which the program was actively supervised by the Central Secretariat. With the exception of the belatedly perceived need for the imprimatur of an NPC resolution, the delay was not due to procedural requirements, public comment under the rubric of the "mass line," or even negotiations with concerned agencies. The final product was very similar to its earlier version. Rather, the slowdown was due to the lack of direct personal intervention by the higher leadership until after the summer floods. Nevertheless, the whole process was still completed three months before Arbor Day (March 12), thus enabling some advance preparations to be made. How then did implementation proceed?

IMPLEMENTATION

For the most part implementation closely resembled the process for past campaigns. Publicity accompanied the parceling out of tasks to subordinate units under Party leadership. Basic-level units then made arrangements for individual citizens. The armed forces and mass organizations, especially the

---

[34] Li Changjian, "Zaofu" (n. 17 above).
[35] The resolution was published in *RR*, Dec. 16, 1981.

Communist Youth League (CYL), played major roles in OTP, though activists were to be recruited from all units.[36] Because this was the new program's first year, some localities were permitted to occupy themselves temporarily in preparatory tasks, especially nursery expansion, until they were ready to plant trees. However, as is frequently the case, tree planting began on a nationwide basis at the same time as the ostensibly experimental key points, whose number in the meantime had grown from sixty to a hundred.[37] Predictably, the impatience to get under way diluted the experimental value of the nonrandomly selected key points.[38]

However, two adjustments were made with regard to implementation. First, a hierarchy of greenification commissions was established from the national level down to counties and municipalities. These commissions were chaired by senior officials, Wan Li in the case of the Central Commission, and frequently by governors at the provincial level. They were composed of representatives of the major agencies involved in greenification, especially the Ministry of Forestry, the State General Administration of Urban Construction, the People's Liberation Army (PLA) (particularly its Rear Services and Political departments), and the CYL. Staffing was to be provided by the forestry and parks departments.

The commissions' tasks were to organize the campaign and coordinate associated activities. Although established with specific reference to OTP, the commissions were expected to coordinate other afforestation programs as well. Although not as prestigious as a cabinet-level agency, such as the State Family Planning Commission, the greenification commissions differed from past ad hoc campaign leadership organs in two respects: the commissions were established on an ongoing basis to convene conferences and review performance rather than to emerge only in peak activity times and disappear in off periods;[39] and there was a strong effort to include all relevant agencies directly rather than treat forestry as merely the responsibility of a single ministry. These changes were made to widen participation by nonforestry agencies and increase attention to arboriculture on a year-round basis. Thus the greenification commissions, like the Gezhouba Dam Technical Committee discussed in chapter 6, are indicative of a central element of the Chinese system: for implementation to succeed when a policy overlaps multiple bureaucratic or territorial boundaries, there must be an arena where these

[36] *RR*, Mar. 4, 1982; *ZQB*, Mar. 11, 1982; Wang Ping, "Zhishu Zaolin, Luhua Yingqu" (Plant Trees and Afforest, Greenify Military Compounds), *ZL*, February 1982, 2–3; Wang Jiangong, "Qingxiao Nian Yingdai Zhan Zai Quanmin Yiwu Zhishu de Zui Qianlie" (Youth Should Stand At the Forefront of OTP), *ZL*, February 1982, 4–5.

[37] *GR*, Dec. 8, 1981; *RR*, May 17, 1982.

[38] S. Lee Travers, "Bias in Chinese Economic Statistics: The Case of the Typical Sample Investigation," *China Quarterly* 91 (September 1982): 478–85.

[39] *RR*, June 3, 1982, and Jan. 13, 1983.

diverse entities can be brought together. Unfortunately, we still know very little about how these coordinating bodies make and enforce decisions, in part because they publish little in the way of journals or other documents.

Second, OTP was given a symbolic boost when March was designated as Socialist Ethics and Courtesy Month with forestry included among the Five Stresses and Four Points of Beauty, which were the focus of the month's activities. As the first month of spring, March symbolizes yearly renewal. Several ceremonial months have been designated in recent years, including January as family-planning month and April as safety month. However, concern has been expressed that people may forget about the goals once the month has ended.[40]

On the whole, however, these adjustments were quite modest considering that past afforestation campaigns had suffered from severe problems of quality. The new policy's incorporation of social behavior goals was unlikely to be of help. The impediments to implementation were severe, and may be grouped into three categories: the basis for compliance; technical shortcomings; and compliance shortfalls.

IMPEDIMENTS TO IMPLEMENTATION

The Basis for Compliance

Although OTP was created in part to rejuvenate afforestation, it was hampered by a lack of consensus among lower-level officials concerning its operational definition. Afforestation traditionally had been conducted on the basis of centrally assigned planting targets with much of the work performed in seasonal campaigns. How did OTP differ from ostensibly normative (but in fact fairly coercive) "voluntary" (*ziyuan* or *zhiyuan*) campaigns? Where was OTP to fit in a policy sector that increasingly featured contract responsibility and private forestry?[41]

The adjective *yiwu*, as in *yiwu zhishu* (obligatory tree planting), distinguishes OTP. *Yiwu* is of modern origins in the Chinese language and connotes a legal obligation to perform a duty or a service for the state. Failure to perform *yiwu* duties leaves the individual or corporate body liable to legal action to force compliance. However, there is an expectation on the part of the state that legal sanctions will generally prove unnecessary because *yiwu* also has an ethical or moral aspect. The ethical component implies that the individual will voluntarily perform his *yiwu* obligations because the duties entailed are righteous and because, as a member of the community, he too benefits from the services performed. Material compensation for *yiwu* duties

---

[40]Christopher S. Wren, "Don't Push, Litter, or Honk, the Chinese Are Told," *NYT*, Mar. 10, 1982; Dirlik, "Spiritual Solutions" (n. 26 above).

[41]While writing this section I benefited from several conversations with Chen-Shen Yen.

is ruled out by definition, although in practice some compensation may be provided, as in the case of compulsory military service.[42]

Yiwu closely resembles the concept of "obligation" in English. An obligation has the connotation of a requirement with the possibility of civil or criminal legal action in the event of noncompliance. A legal obligation or duty is stronger than the concept of "ought" that applies to actions that are morally desirable but not required. Obligations need not all be imposed by government; they may be voluntarily incurred through contracts, promises, or as a function of one's social or economic roles.[43]

The concept of yiwu has broad application in Taiwan with regard to policies as diverse as school attendance, sanitation, and military service, but until recently it enjoyed much less currency in the PRC. For example, the current state constitution adopted in December 1982 refers to eight separate categories of yiwu obligations in the chapter on rights and duties. Yiwu is mentioned much more frequently in the present constitution than in the three previous editions.[44]

The increased prominence of yiwu or obligation in post-Mao China is largely due to a modified conception of the individual's relationship to society. The concept of obligation has no place in a collective or an organic society in which people are accorded status only as members of society rather than as individuals. In the West the problem of obligation thus arose as a by-product of the spread of liberalism or individualism.[45] By contrast, China under both neo-Confucian and Communist philosophy has tended to stress that the individual cannot exist or obtain fulfillment except as a member of society.[46] Raising the concept of obligation into a prominent position in official doctrine in the PRC represents increased willingness to regard the separate identity and interests of individuals as legitimate, although still attenuated by Western standards.[47] Yiwu became more prominent only in the post-Mao era after the pragmatists had solidified their power and could

[42] Wang Gungwu, "Power, Rights and Duties in Chinese History," Australian Journal of Chinese Affairs 3 (January 1980): 1–26.

[43] Joel Feinberg, "Superogation and Rules," in Joel Feinberg, Doing and Deserving: Essays in the Theory of Responsibility (Princeton: Princeton University Press, 1970), 3–24.

[44] The eight categories of obligatory actions are work; education; family planning; child rearing; supporting the integrity of the state and unity among its nationalities; upholding China's security, honor, and interests; military and militia service; and paying taxes.

[45] Thomas McPherson, Political Obligation (London: Routledge and Kegan Paul, 1967).

[46] Donald J. Munro, "The Concept of 'Interest' in Chinese Thought" (Paper presented at the Workshop on the Pursuit of Political Interest in the People's Republic of China, Ann Arbor, Aug. 10–17, 1977); Wang Gungwu, "Power."

[47] Another terminological indication of this change is the revival of hezuo ("cooperative") in place of jiti ("collective") to describe economic organizations. See Huang Daoxia, "Hezuo Jingji yu Jiti Jingji You Shenmo Qubie?" (What Are the Differences Between a Cooperative and a Collective Economy?), HQ 419 (Apr. 1, 1983): 46–47.

pursue modernization on the basis of a more forthright appeal to self-interest. As we shall see, however, OTP was affected also by limits to the regime's tolerance for self-interest.

Yiwu's enhanced stature also reflects the regime's newly increased respect for the rights of citizens. China traditionally has conceived of rights within a narrow ambit governed by a web of reciprocal moral duties and loyalties. By contrast, Western political philosophy not only has carved out a wider set of rights but also has generally resisted the temptation to marry rights and duties, although their reciprocal relationship is understood.[48]

The PRC in the past was particularly unwilling to grant meaningful rights to citizens lest the Party's power be curtailed and the prospects for state-directed social change be foreclosed. The PRC in the post-Mao era has sought to restore the legal system and the scope of citizen rights, albeit within the derived and instrumental sense of rights as connoted by *quanli*.[49] The regime has acted in the belief that this will foster social order and economic modernization. Greater respect for citizen rights has in turn permitted the regime to make legalistic appeals to citizen duties, as in OTP. Indeed, *quanli* and *yiwu* are often encountered joined together in a four-character phrase.

Confusion about the meaning of obligation was widespread, however, even among translators and editors. Reporting on the adoption of OTP, *Beijing Review* in the very same issue translated *yiwu* as "voluntary" on one page and then later as "obligatory" in Premier Zhao Ziyang's work report.[50] China's leading English language publication remained in a state of lexicographical bewilderment, varying its translation from time to time. "Voluntary" generally was preferred despite the fact that OTP was designed to be a departure from past "voluntary" campaigns.[51]

Far more important was the perplexity among forestry officials. Provincial department heads meeting several weeks after the NPC session still wondered what *yiwu* signified and how it differed from their main concern, the state afforestation plan. They were told that OTP involved citizen duty to state and society without compensation, and therefore was not in conflict with the state plan for afforestation acreage. It was said that OTP differed

[48] Munro, "The Concept of 'Interest'"; Wesley Newcomb Hohfeld, *Fundamental Legal Conceptions as Applied in Judicial Reasoning*, Wheeler Cook, ed. (1919; reprint New Haven: Yale University Press, 1964); Stanley B. Lubman, "Emerging Functions of Formal Legal Institutions in China's Modernization," in JEC, *China Under the Four Modernizations* (n. 33 above) 2:239; Jack Donnelly, "Human Rights and Human Dignity: An Analytic Critique of Non-Western Conceptions of Human Rights," *American Political Science Review* (hereafter *APSR*) 76, no. 2 (June 1982): 304 and 308–9.

[49] Wang Gungwu, "Power."

[50] *BR* 24, no. 51 (Dec. 21, 1981): 5 and 15.

[51] *BR* 25, no. 12 (Mar. 22, 1982): 5–6, and 25, no. 22 (May 31, 1982): 6–7. By contrast, the military conscription law of 1984 distinguished between the draft obligation (*yiwu*) for everyone, and "voluntary" (*zhiyuan*) reenlistment periods for skilled personnel who, it may be inferred, will receive some form of bonus pay.

even more sharply with private forestry, which involved private ownership and benefit and had been given increased prominence in the post-Mao era.[52] In other words, OTP was created as a separate third track for greenification policy.

Despite this seemingly pat explanation, OTP's niche was hardly secure. Planned and private forestry and OTP were all bound to compete for planting stock, a commodity that is often in short supply in terms of both volume and variety. Since OTP promised no direct benefit to the participants, it seems likely that OTP would have been given short shrift with regard to seedlings in comparison with more strictly enforced or potentially more profitable forestry programs. The geographical locus of OTP was also hazy, since it had been established on a universal or nationwide basis out of a particular concern for flood control. However, its emphasis on small numbers of plantings by very large numbers of people suggested an urban orientation of little relevance to flood control or the bulk of the populace.[53]

Although OTP was regarded as a separate program, it was expected to morally guide and inspire the entire afforestation effort. The capacity of OTP to fulfill this role was greatly handicapped by the absence of specially earmarked state funding. Like most campaigns, participating units were expected to finance their efforts largely out of their own resources. Moreover, there was a deep, albeit unacknowledged, gulf between the Communist morality espoused by OTP and other socialist spiritual civilization programs and the revitalized privatistic social mores.[54] For example, OTP in rural areas would be organized largely by communes and brigades, yet these larger collectives were being stripped of much of their power in the post-Mao era. In short, as we have seen throughout this volume, action on some policies can foreclose the prospects for other policies linked together in interdependent relationships.

Technical Aspects

Forestry in China has long suffered from a multitude of technical problems. Some of these, like poor planting stock, are partially scientific in nature, whereas others, including a lack of producer incentives and discontinuous forest management, are more specifically policy based. Technical deficiencies have depressed survival rates to the range of 30–40 percent on average, according to official accounts, and the rates may in fact be much lower.[55]

[52] Hua Lin, "Tantan Quanmin Yiwu Zhishu Wenti" (Let's Talk About National Obligatory Afforestation), *ZL*, February 1982, 6–7; *Key Documents in Forestry Work* 7:74–81, and 8:69–74, (unpublished).

[53] Li Changjian, "Zaofu" (n. 17 above).

[54] *RR*, June 21, 1982; Dirlik, "Spiritual Solutions" (n. 26 above).

[55] Yang Zhong, "Kaichuang Xin Jumian, Keji Shi Guanjian" (Science and Technology Are the Keys to Opening a New Vista), *ZL*, February 1983, 11–14; *RR*, Jan. 14, 1978; *Forestry in China* (Rome: Food and Agriculture Organization of the United Nations, Forestry Paper no. 35,

Because technical shortcomings have been most closely associated with the exhortational campaign style of implementation,[56] a key question confronting OTP was its ability to surmount such problems as poor advance planning and plantation management. The regime was increasingly aware of past failures and on this occasion took some preventive measures. In particular, Hu Yaobang and others realized that OTP could easily overwhelm the nation's supply of planting stock. Therefore, 1982, the first year of the program, was specifically designated as a nursery-work key-point year.[57]

A more fundamental point concerned the essence of the campaign, namely the mobilization of large numbers of untrained people for short bursts of frenetic activity in the pursuit of official goals. Too often in the past the result had been wasted effort followed by demoralization, with harmful effects on future forestry work. In the case of OTP, there are indications that some elements of the policy structure favored an all-out campaign-style assault without regard for practical considerations. *Guangming Ribao* (Bright Daily) adopted a tone reminiscent of the Maoist era in its editorial on OTP of December 16, 1981, stressing the need for large-scale increases in forest cover, in contrast to the prevailing theme of improved management of existing facilities accepted by economists and many foresters. This editorial devoted only a few lines to the need for proper techniques, although its intended readership is the intellectual community. Conceding that big-push afforestation campaigns in the past had often failed, the newspaper insisted that the results would be better this time, thanks to changes in policy bolstered by a massive propaganda barrage.[58]

On the whole, however, the wavelike-assault theme so prominent in earlier campaigns was played down this time. A much briefer editorial the same day in the more authoritative *People's Daily* took a more cautious approach, emphasizing the need to take practical measures to facilitate the program rather than to merely mouth slogans. Subsequent reports in *People's Daily* continued to strike a moderate tone, seeking to curb the tendency for campaigns to attack without preparation (*yi hong er qi*).[59] These cautionary statements reflected the advice of the Ministry of Forestry and were embodied in the State Council's regulations on OTP.[60]

There were in fact some improvements in the campaign style of imple-

1982); Robert C. Kellison et al., "Forest Tree Improvement in the PRC," *Journal of Forestry* 80, no. 10 (October 1982).

[56] Ross, "Implementation" (n. 7 above); cf. Cell, *Revolution* (n. 8 above).

[57] Li Changjian, "Zaofu."

[58] *GR*, Dec. 16, 1981.

[59] *RR*, Dec. 16, 1981, Feb. 22 and Mar. 11, 1982.

[60] State Council, "Basic Regulations Regarding the Unfolding of the OTP Movement" (in Chinese), *ZRGGYG* 379 (1982): 148–50.

mentation during OTP's first year. More attention was devoted to nursery development, contributing to a modest 6 percent expansion of nursery acreage in 1982.[61] Several provinces and counties allocated additional funds for nursery development to assist hard-pressed localities.[62] Frequent warnings were issued against formalism and other chronic pathologies of campaign-style implementation.[63]

Nonetheless, technical problems generally were aggravated. While attention was devoted to the supply of seedlings, other desiderata were given short shrift. Urban development is largely unplanned, so it is not surprising that within a year some plantations on public lots had to be uprooted to enable construction projects to proceed.[64] Falsification of statistics and formalism continued to be noteworthy.[65] Management and protection of the new seedlings were frequently neglected.[66] This was largely attributable to the program's public ownership bias—creating a "tragedy of the commons" effect in which public property was degraded by the acts and omissions of members of the community.[67]

An account by a foreign scholar, resident in Beijing at the time, clearly illustrates the problems associated with OTP. The research institute to which he was attached suspended operations for two days so that all personnel could participate in OTP. One day was for the work itself, and the second day was for "rest" (*xiuxi*), in tune with China's leisurely bureaucratic approach to labor. Because no nearby sites were available, the institute staff had to be bused to a more distant site, extending the operation to a third day. The site itself proved to be hilly and very rocky, requiring people to literally break the stones apart so that they could plant the seedlings supplied by the army. The participants returned to Beijing convinced that the trees had no chance for survival because of the harsh environment and because the local farm population would never bother to water or care for the trees.[68]

Even the planting-stock problem continued to be troublesome, although it had been given special attention. As seedling supply became tighter the quality of planting stock fell, thereby reducing growth prospects.[69] In sum, despite some marginal improvements, it seems that most technical problems affecting forestry were aggravated by OTP. The PRC always has been able to

[61] *GR*, Mar. 12, 1983.

[62] *RR*, June 3, 1982.

[63] Wan Li, "Yao Zhazha Shishi, Chi Zhi Yi Heng, Bu Da Mudi, Jue Bu Baxiu" (We Must Be Resolute and Steadfast, and Not Rest Until Our Goals Are Achieved), *RR*, Jan. 13, 1983.

[64] *RR*, July 29, 1982; *GR*, Mar. 12, 1983.

[65] Wan Li, "Yao."

[66] *RR*, June 3 and 8, 1982.

[67] Garrett Hardin, "The Tragedy of the Commons," *Science* 162 (1968): 1243–48.

[68] Information provided by S. Lee Travers, Oct. 20, 1983.

[69] *RR*, May 17 and June 3, 1982.

TABLE 8.1   Youth Involvement in Forestry Work

Year	Area afforested (thousand mu)	Other trees planted (millions)
1979	10,580	est. 500
1980	9,700	1,400
1981	est. 4,000	est. 500
1982	est. 6,000	2,160
1983	6,000	—
1984	6,000	2,700 (918 OTP)

SOURCES: *ZQB*, Mar. 12, 1981; *RR*, Sept. 23, 1981, Sept. 23, 1982, and Nov. 27, 1984; *ZL*, April 1985, 10. By 1984 less than one-third of trees planted by youth were considered part of OTP.

plant very large numbers of trees. The problem has been high rates of failure and poor quality. The increased stress by OTP on volume of effort heightened existing shortcomings in planting stock, advance preparations, and plantation management.

Compliance Shortcomings

The Obligatory Tree Planting program was established on a universal basis involving everyone eleven and older except the elderly and the handicapped. Universal participation was deemed desirable and even essential because trees were felt to be in everyone's interest.[70] Nevertheless, the brunt of the work was expected to be performed by mass organizations and regular institutions rather than by citizens at large. The CYL and PLA were most prominent in this regard. The CYL had been involved in forestry since 1956 when Hu Yaobang was senior secretary, and had resumed active involvement in 1979 after the long Cultural Revolution hiatus.[71] In fact, the CYL was assigned a vanguard role in OTP because its constituency was young and able, and the CYL was considered the most reliable mobilizing agent of unemployed or otherwise idle youth. Young people were also prone to skepticism about the merits of socialism and therefore in need of socialist ethical education.[72]

However, expectations about the CYL's capacity to serve as a shock force appear to have been inflated. Youth afforestation acreage peaked in 1979 and then declined sharply over the next several years (see table 8.1). This seems to have been due in part to the CYL's long-standing organizational difficulties in afforestation, including low levels of skill and a lack of popular support

[70] Jiao Ruoyu, "Zongjie Jingyan Jiakuai Shoudu Luhua Bufa" (Sum Up Experiences and Speed Up the Process of Greenifying the Capital), *ZL*, July 1982, 2–3.

[71] *FBIS Daily Report: People's Republic of China*, no. 44 (Mar. 5, 1979): E25–26.

[72] *ZQB*, Mar. 11, 1982; *RR*, Aug. 13 and 14, 1983.

for planting expeditions to sometimes remote sites.[73] An additional factor was the post-Mao strengthening of property rights and the creation of contract responsibility systems in the economy. These reforms removed potentially afforestable wasteland from the public domain while increasing incentives for the management of private rather than public property.[74] It also is not clear how strongly the CYL was motivated to participate in OTP. Press coverage in *Zhongguo Qingnian Bao* (Chinese Youth Daily) was sparse, and *Zhongguo Qingnian* (Chinese Youth Magazine) did not publish anything on the subject in 1982. What limited press coverage there was tended to emphasize private or paid tree-planting by youth. It appears that even Youth League branches preferred money-making forestry for profit to OTP.[75]

Finally, as Rosen notes elsewhere, the CYL faced an internal crisis as it tried to entice increasingly cynical and individualistically-minded youth into the organization. With other avenues of mobility now open to them, the CYL no longer was the only road to advancement. In short, the economic and social reforms undertaken in the post-Mao era have reduced the regime's capacity to mobilize the populace through the centrally directed "mass organizations."[76]

The PLA for its part was expected to plant all military compounds and also to assist local communities within a ten-kilometer radius of base perimeters.[77] The PLA appears to have been relatively well equipped for its mission, with a long (albeit frequently exaggerated) history of service to civilian society and as a "backbone" element in the implementation of Party policy. Tree planting and the construction of logging roads and narrow-gauge forest railways are among the military's long-standing civilian-sector missions.

In keeping with the PLA's rising commitment to modernization and professionalism, however, direct support for the civilian economy has been declining for some time and now is very modest (with the exception of outmoded defense plants and construction units, which appear to be in the process of transfer to the civilian sector). The PLA's contribution of five million man-days to OTP in 1982 amounted to 20 percent of the PLA's

[73] Yu Chiqian, "Ba Qunzhong Zhishu Zaolin Yundong Xiang Qian Tuijin Yibu" (Advance the Mass Tree Planting and Afforestation Movement A Step Further), *ZL*, March 1957, 3–4.

[74] *RR*, Feb. 25, 1982.

[75] *ZQB*, Oct. 5 and Nov. 4, 1982, and Jan. 18, 1983.

[76] Stanley Rosen, "Prosperity, Privatization and the Chinese Communist Youth League," *Problems of Communism* (1985); *RR*, Feb. 1, 1983; *JPRS*, no. 82643, CPS 380 (Jan. 14, 1983): 101; Victor C. Falkenheim, "Popular Values and Political Reform: The 'Crisis of Faith' in Contemporary China," in Sidney L. Greenblatt et al., eds., *Social Interaction in Chinese Society* (New York: Praeger, 1982), 237–51.

[77] *RR*, Dec. 22, 1982; "Regulations on Tree Planting, Afforestation, and Forest Management in PLA Compounds" (in Chinese), *ZRGGYG* 396 (Mar. 5, 1983): 5–8.

TABLE 8.2   Military Involvement in Forestry Work

Year	Area afforested (thousand mu)	Other trees planted (millions)
1980	—	53,200
1981	77	19,500
1982	150	75,000 (36,000 OTP)
1983	173	43,500

SOURCES: Yong Wentao, "Ba Luhua" (see n. 78); *RR*, June 10, 1982; *GR*, Jan. 5, 1983; Quarterly Chronicle and Documentation, *China Quarterly* 88:229; Wang Ping, "Zhishu Zaolin, Luhua Yingqu" (Plant Trees and Afforest, Greenify Military Compounds), *ZL*, February 1983, 2–3; *JPRS* CAG 016 (June 8, 1984): 1–2.

average annual service to local industry and agriculture in the four-year period 1979–1982.[78] A sustained expansion in the PLA's forestry program would interfere with military training and other service to the civilian sector. Furthermore, there are indications that logistical shortcomings and property rights disputes have hampered PLA greenification activities outside military compounds.[79] (See table 8.2.)

Ordinary cadres and the populace as a whole may have been even less prepared to comply with OTP. Like all campaigns, its success ultimately depends on a personal commitment by local cadres to organize the populace. Indeed, upwards of 500 million people are reported to have participated. However, a major theme throughout OTP's first year was the unevenness of local support, coupled with the need for follow-up inspections to verify that the work had been completed and that the trees had survived.[80] This indicates that participation often was halfhearted or artificially inflated. The legal system failed to increase compliance despite Deng Xiaoping's personal

[78] Sydney H. Jammes and G. Lawrence Lamborn, "China's Military Strategic Requirements," in JEC (n. 33 above) 1:597–604; editorial, "Jishu Guangrong Chuantong, Fazhan Xinxing de Junzheng Junmin Guanxi" (Continue Our Glorious Tradition, Develop Modern Military-Government and Military-Civilian Relations), *HQ* 415 (Feb. 1, 1983): 6–8; Yong Wentao, "Ba Luhua Zuguo de Weida Qunzhong Yundong Tuixiang Qianjin" (Propel Forward the Great Mass Greenification Movement for Our Motherland), *ZL*, February 1983, 7–10; John Philip Emerson, "The Labor Force of China, 1957–80," in JEC 1:246.

If the history of the American military is any guide, one can expect a decline in the PLA's responsibility for forestry. The conversion of many military reservations into national forests as authorized by the Clarke-McNary Act of 1924 was short lived, as was the Civilian Conservation Corps, whose units were for a time under the command of military officers. Conversion of military bases into national forests proved incompatible with the military's sense of mission, although the military regularly uses some national forests for training exercises.

[79] Yang Shangkun, "Jundui Zai Zhishu Zaolin Zhong Yao Duo Zuo Gongzuo" (The Army Must Make a Bigger Effort in Tree Planting and Afforestation), *ZL*, June 1982, 3; *RR*, Feb. 19, 1982.

[80] Wan Li, "Yao" (n. 63 above).

insistence that sanctions be imposed against shirkers on the basis of law. Even key-point counties and Beijing reported participation rates no higher than 70–80 percent;[81] and participation was undoubtedly lower in ordinary units.

A more serious problem was the nature and organization of the campaign itself. Many people regarded the entire socialist spiritual civilization effort as a "soft" task, far less worthy of their participation than "hard" production tasks.[82] The network of coordinating commissions was established to overcome this reluctance to participate, but their capacity to force compliance was limited. Two strategies were adopted to cope with noncompliance. One involved focusing effort on specific projects, like the creation of urban recreational facilities, instead of a vague mandate to plant trees anywhere and everywhere. These projects were more in the nature of conventional public works than the building of spiritual civilization, involved a larger commitment of government resources, and may have involved compensation of some sort for the reduced number of participants.[83] Such projects may be easier to manage and may provide a greater sense of fulfillment for participants, although their long-term prospects are uncertain.

The second strategy involved attaching a task-responsibility system to OTP. The responsibility concept is a widespread innovation in the post-Mao economy as the regime tries to make individuals and groups accountable for their performance in what remains a basically planned economy. However, OTP does not seem compatible with a responsibility system, because planting is divorced from ownership and post-plantation management. The introduction of responsibility systems is also ironic because OTP was intended to serve as a counterbalance to the calculating, materialistic atmosphere engendered by the post-Mao economic reforms.

EVALUATION

Ostensibly, OTP was designed to enhance Communist ethics and accelerate greenification. After almost two years, OTP cannot claim to have achieved very much in either regard. It simply is implausible to expect that brief bursts of mobilized participation will produce enduring change in values, at least in the absence of strong local leadership and compliance-generating mechanisms. The sheer absence of press reports on this subject suggests that the higher leadership really was only concerned with surface behavioral manifestations of the desired values, although of course a minority of the elite may have been more concerned with the erosion of ideologically approved beliefs.

[81] Yong Wentao, "Ba Luhua."
[82] *JPRS*, no. 82991, CPS 397 (Mar. 2, 1983): 21.
[83] *GR*, Apr. 5, 1983.

TABLE 8.3   Afforestation Area (thousand mu)

Year	Area	Year	Area
1970	58,260	1978	67,450
1971	67,880	1979	67,340
1972	69,540	1980	68,250
1973	74,740	1981	61,650
1974	75,040	1982	67,500
1975	74,610	1983	94,800
1976	73,890	1984	est. 104,000
1977	71,900		

SOURCES: *JPRS*, no. 80270 CAG 192 (Mar. 9, 1982): 39; State Statistical Bureau, *Communiques on Fulfillment of China's National Economic Plans* 1980–1983; *BR*, 1984, no. 52 (Dec. 27): 10.

As for the acceleration of greenification, there was a substantial expansion in acreage in 1982, but it is unlikely that much of the credit can be attributed to OTP, assuming for now that the gains were not the products of statistical manipulation and that the trees genuinely will survive (*baocun*). Afforestation acreage increased by 9.4 percent in 1982 over the previous year. However, as table 8.3 indicates, the 1982 area of 4.5 million hectares was essentially equivalent to the average for the previous five post-Mao years 1977–1981. Thus, 1982 appears to represent a return to normalcy from the unusually low level of 1981, rather than a secular increase.

Furthermore, it should be noted that afforested area in the post-Mao era has been lower than in the early 1970s. The decrease may be a bit surprising in light of rising environmental awareness. However, despite favoring an expansion in China's very low forest-cover, foresters themselves have long advocated that the volume of effort be held down to a sustainable effort to minimize waste and raise quality.[84]

More important, improvements in forestry may be due more to the current regime's strong support for contract responsibility and private production systems in the countryside than to OTP. Those leaders who favor giving wider scope to market forces believe that private households have the potential for substantially expanding China's forest resources. Hu Yaobang, CCP general secretary, has urged that private woodlots be permitted on up to 20 percent of wasteland in hilly areas, higher even than the 15 percent norm for lowland agriculture.[85] A major effort was undertaken in 1982–1983 to

[84] Zhang Kexia, "Jiji Gaibian Woguo Senlin Ziyuan Buzu Xianxiang" (Positively Transform the Situation of a Forest Resources Shortage in Our Country), *ZL*, May 1957, 6–8; Wang Zhangfu, "Peiyu Senlin Ziyuan Ying Zou Yi Neihan Kuoda Zaishengchan Wei Zhu de Daolu" (The Development of Forest Resources Primarily Should Rely on Internal Reproduction), *Jingji Yanjiu*, March 1983, 77–78.

[85] *FBIS*, no. 131 (July 8, 1982): R2. This was subsequently codified in central directives.

resolve property rights disputes among households and enterprises in order to expedite forestry development.[86] These reforms are controversial because they have created opportunities for windfall profits from deforestation, and because smaller production units may affect economies of scale.[87] In general, however, these changes are likely to boost forestry development by increasing producer incentives, and were further extended in 1984 after the conservatives within the elite were weakened by the "combat spiritual pollution" affair.

Since OTP was intended to inspire but be separate from the planned afforestation area program, it is not fair to evaluate OTP on the basis of its effect on afforestation alone. We must also look at the planting of scattered trees outside larger woodlots. These plantings are classified as the "four arounds" (*si pian*), referring to villages, residences, roadways, and bodies of water. Unfortunately, this category, which primarily meets fuel wood and amenity needs, is not always distinguished from afforestation acreage. Some localities lump the two together using a conversion formula, such as 6,000 "four arounds" = 1 hectare afforestation.[88]

Because OTP was designed as an extraplan program, scattered plantings were supposed to be subdivided into two categories, the "four arounds" and OTP. Unfortunately, there are no nationwide figures nor even much provincial data on scattered plantings. However, it was reported in June that 1.1 billion OTP trees and 3 billion "four arounds" trees had already been planted in 1982.[89] Since about 65 percent of afforestation is ordinarily conducted in the spring, we may provisionally estimate annual totals of 1.7 billion OTPs and 4.6 billion "four arounds." This assumes no double counting, which is probably a generous assumption.

On the whole, it thus can be concluded that OTP met its planting goal even though 1982 had been designated as a preparatory year for most localities. Almost half the population participated, planting three trees each on average, which was at the low end of the norm but still impressive.[90] As tables 8.1 and 8.2 show, youth and, particularly, PLA plantings increased substantially.

Despite the large number of plantings, there is reason to doubt OTP's staying force. In part this is because of continued warnings against formalism and counting trees regardless of their chances of survival.[91] Perhaps more important is the locational imbalance in plantings. There were 95 million

[86] *RR*, Apr. 10, 1983.

[87] Editorial, "Zhuajin Zai Jin Dong Ming Chun Gaohao Linye 'San Ding'" (Firmly Do the Forestry Three Fixes Well This Winter and Spring), *ZL*, December 1982, 2.

[88] FAO, 115 (n. 55 above).

[89] *JPRS*, no. 81058, CAG 210 (June 15, 1982): 5.

[90] *GR*, Jan. 5, 1983.

[91] *RR*, Jan. 13, 1983.

trees planted in urban areas under OTP in 1982, less than half the urban proportionate share on a per capita basis.[92] This is due to the limited availability of additional sites in urban areas, thanks in part to previous successes establishing roadside trees. Therefore, OTP is primarily rural in practice, although its original focus was urban. Yet a recent editorial warned that OTP is not suitable for rural areas because it runs counter to the prevailing stress on an economic system based on property rights.[93]

As spatial opportunity for OTP has narrowed, so has its separate identity. Sometimes OTP is still referred to as a long-term program to be conducted for the rest of the century and longer,[94] but by its second year it no longer received extensive press coverage. The press now stresses the theme of integrating OTP with regular afforestation rather than its distinctive spiritual mission.[95] It seems unlikely that OTP will regain the glory it briefly enjoyed in 1981–1982; it is more likely to play a major role only in special urban projects like park development under strong local leadership in pursuit of a specific goal.[96]

CONCLUSIONS

This chapter has analyzed a program that has symbolic as well as substantive significance. The Obligatory Tree Planting program and the broader socialist spiritual civilization campaign were the product of a political backlash by conservative elements of the leadership against the inflation, social disorder, and other social problems that they attributed to the post-Mao reforms. Reform advocates resisted the counterassault until after the Central Work Conference in December 1980, at which point they endeavored to keep the scope and intensity of the campaign within much narrower bounds than was true for many campaigns in the Maoist era. They were reasonably successful in manipulating symbols and preoccupying Party committees and propaganda departments in this regard, and indeed the pace of reform later picked up in 1982 and especially in 1984.

The Obligatory Tree Planting program also had substantive goals in forestry development and environmental amelioration, which were endorsed at a later date by Deng Xiaoping, Hu Yaobang, and Wan Li, who were in a different leadership camp. Their action suggests that the program also served other ends. For one, OTP conveyed determination on the part of the leadership to address the danger of floods. Although OTP itself might have been irrelevant, it was already on the shelf and could quickly be put into action.

[92] *GR*, Jan. 5, 1983.
[93] *GR*, Mar. 12, 1983.
[94] Wan Li, "Tigao" (n. 31 above).
[95] *RR*, Mar. 12, 1983; *ZL*, February 1983, 39.
[96] *GR*, Apr. 5, 1983.

While OTP protected the regime from criticism, it is possible that time might be gained for the tedious process of devising meaningful solutions and rearranging fiscal priorities to improve flood control. Hu Yaobang in fact subsequently led the reformers who favored a privatistic, household-based, small watershed-management program and revegetation to reduce the flood danger, although this may have been due as much to budgetary and bureaucratic constraints on large construction projects as to a changed world view.[97]

This interpretation of a leadership adopting a mass-campaign form of implementation because of its symbolic importance and the budgetary constraints on alternatives highlights a major point made nowhere else in this volume. The decision to adopt a mode of implementation is itself a political act in which political and bureaucratic considerations interact. Sometimes it makes sense for politicians to adopt implementation strategies despite their low prospects for success in order to check the strategy of one's opponents, or to gain time for future innovations. When the costs of inaction exceed the costs of almost any action, it is better to do something rather than nothing. This interpretation may seem cynical. However, Chinese politicians are familiar with the use of symbolic politics to disguise one's true intentions and to divide one's critics.[98] Nevertheless, because of the pragmatists' loss of faith in campaigns, one anticipates a decline in the number and intensity of campaigns as they succeed in cementing their power.

A less cynical approach would be to recognize that pragmatists and radicals alike share an elite culture. This culture has symbols that may not seem rational from an outsider's perspective but that nevertheless reflect faith in their abiding value and help to build unity. March and Olson have argued that the American political elite's predilection for government reorganization is an example of a shared interpretation of the world which may have originated in a commonsense, tinkering approach to life.[99] Thus, even pragmatists may embrace campaigns as an expression of faith in their ideology and culture, although the intrinsic logic of their positions leads China on a different course.

Perhaps more important than the substantive aspects, every campaign tends to legitimize nonrational behavior and increase the power of Party functionaries. These effects run counter to the basically rationalizing thrust of the post-Mao reforms. Campaigns thus tend to heighten the anxiety of intellectuals and other segments of society fearful of a return to the Cultural Revolution era. Deng Xiaoping may conclude that campaigns are necessary instruments of policy, but he also must be wary lest their side effects subvert

[97] Ross, "Flood Control" (n. 20 above); *RR*, July 21, 1983.

[98] Lucian Pye, *The Dynamics of Chinese Politics* (Cambridge: Oelgeschlager, Gunn and Hain, 1981); Murray Edelman, *The Symbolic Uses of Politics* (Urbana: University of Illinois Press, 1964).

[99] James G. March and Johan P. Olson, "What Administrative Reorganization Tells Us About Governing," *APSR* 77, no. 2 (June 1983): 281–96.

his broader goals. Indeed, OTP is notable for the degree to which it was focused and designed to minimize interference with ongoing programs. In short, although the post-Mao era will not witness an end to mass campaigns as an instrument of implementation, they are likely to play a much more subordinate role than they played under Mao.

PART IV

Implementing Rural Sector Policies

Context and Content in Policy Implementation: Household Contracts and Decollectivization, 1977–1983

David Zweig

INTRODUCTION

By the summer of 1983 the shift from collective agriculture, as established in 1962,[1] to a system of household farming with collective land ownership was nearing completion. While other changes, such as increased crop diversification and the commercialization of agriculture, the establishment of village and township governments, thereby separating the political and economic roles of the communes, and the creation of new forms of vertical and horizontal associations among households and cooperative units, continue to unfold, decollectivization and the shift to household farming, by and large, has been completed.[2] The moment, therefore, appears propitious for an in-depth analysis, explanation, and evaluation of this transition from collective to household farming.

   This chapter focuses on the decision-making and implementation process behind the "responsibility system" of household contracting, especially "household contracts with fixed levies" (*bao gan dao hu*) or "comprehensive contracts" (*da bao gan*).[3] These two systems have led to the establishment of a household sharecropping system where individual Chinese households rent land from the state for a fixed levy. Although some of these dispersed, self-

I wish to thank Thomas P. Bernstein, A. Doak Barnett, Ann Anagnost, David Bachman, and especially David M. Lampton for their comments and suggestions. I alone am responsible for the final product.
   [1] "Regulations on Work in the Rural People's Communes (revised draft)" (Sixty Articles), *Issues and Studies* (October and December 1979).
   [2] By July 1983, 93 percent of all teams in China had divided the land among households for farming. *Nongmin Bao* (Peasant Daily), July 21, 1983, 1.
   [3] See Appendix at the end of this chapter.

managed households are merging into new cooperatives or associations,[4] the weakening of the collective management system has caused problems which this study also addresses. What follows is the story of implementing the policy of household farming—the major step in decollectivizing Chinese agriculture.

Much of the literature on policy implementation focuses on policies that have failed. Whether analyzing the United States or Third World countries,[5] these findings suggest that "great expectations in Beijing" should be "dashed at the grass roots." To date, however, the responsibility system has been almost universally implemented, with more and more parts of China adopting household contracts with fixed levies. If "failure" is so common elsewhere, how do we explain the Chinese government's "success" in decollectivizing agriculture? What has the reform group around Deng Xiaoping done right? Numerous studies have analyzed local responses to the responsibility system.[6] Several focus on elite-mass interactions on this issue.[7] Others emphasize opposition to this reform.[8] Below I trace elite and provincial decision making and implementation from 1977 to 1983 to explain this "successful" implementation.[9]

The implementation studies assembled by Grindle focused on both the content and the context of the policy, arguing that policy implementation "is an ongoing process of decision making by a variety of actors, the ultimate outcome of which is determined by the *content* of the program being pursued

[4] Andrew Watson, "Agriculture Looks for 'Shoes that Fit': The Production Responsibility System and Its Applications," *World Development* 11, no. 8 (1983): 705–30.

[5] See Jeffrey L. Pressman and Aaron Wildavsky, *Implementation: How Great Expectations in Washington Are Dashed in Oakland* (Berkeley and Los Angeles: University of California Press, 1973), and Merilee S. Grindle, ed., *Politics and Policy Implementation in the Third World* (Princeton: Princeton University Press, 1980), respectively.

[6] Victor Nee, "Peasant Household Individualism," and David Zweig, "Peasants, Ideology, and New Incentive Systems: Jiangsu Province, 1978–1981," in William L. Parish, ed., *Chinese Rural Development: The Great Transformation* (Armonk, N.Y.: M. E. Sharpe, 1985).

[7] Tang Tsou, Marc Blecher, and Mitch Meisner, "Policy Change at the National Summit and Institutional Transformation at the Local Level: The Case of Tachai and Hsiyang County in the Post-Mao Era," *Select Papers from the Center for Far Eastern Studies*, no. 4 (Chicago: University of Chicago, 1979–1980): 242–392; and David Zweig, "The System of Responsibility: National Policy and Local Implementation" (Paper presented at the Conference on Bureaucracy and Rural Development, SSRC Joint Committee on Contemporary China, Chicago, August 26–30, 1981).

[8] David Zweig, "Opposition to Change in Rural China," *Asian Survey* (July 1983); and Jurgen Domes, "New Policies in the Communes: Notes on Rural Societal Structures in China, 1976–81," *Journal of Asian Studies* 41, no. 2 (February 1982): 253–67.

[9] Provincial reportage and reactions spiraled back to Beijing, affecting policy formation and implementation. This way, outcomes initially dependent on the policy rebounded back to the center, generating new policy directions. See H. Hugo Heclo, "Review Article: Policy Analysis," *British Journal of Political Science* 2, part 1 (January 1972): 92. For a summary on evaluating policy "success" or "failure," see chapter 1 in this volume.

and by the interaction of the decision makers within a given politico-administrative *context*."[10] Given this framework, "successful" implementation of household contracts resulted from the fact that, through long-term sustained attention, the reform group was able both to reengineer the external environment and to alter the policy's content, thereby creating continual convergence between *context* and *content*. Moreover, given many peasants' proclivities, the policy's deregulatory character made it almost self-implementing. (See chapters 1 and 2.)

THE MUTUALLY REINFORCING CHARACTER OF CHANGES IN POLICY CONTENT AND CONTEXT

Socialist systems generally can control the political environment to a greater degree than pluralist or authoritarian regimes can. In post-Mao China, the defeat of the major opposition group in early 1980 (see chapter 2) allowed the reform group to move forward rather rapidly with the responsibility system. Also, by continually undermining lingering central opposition after 1980, the reform group had the time and the flexibility to respond to unintended consequences, which in the heat of an intense factional struggle could have seriously undermined policy implementation. Although opposition persisted throughout the system, and although peasant exuberance for dismantling collective property and for shifting away from grain cultivation temporarily strengthened the arguments of those opposed to the reforms, the reformers used the economic success of each policy change to quell opposition and push for even further changes in the policy's content. Although it is difficult to determine the extent to which the good harvests of 1981–1984 resulted from the responsibility system, the incentives inherent in the responsibility system probably helped increase yields; and lifting restrictions on household sidelines surely boosted peasant incomes. Buoyed by increasing productivity and rising peasant incomes, the reformers pressed on, leaving the opposition little ground on which to attack the policy.

The changing content of the policy was due in part to the evolving perceptions of the elites. Through experiments in Anhui, Sichuan, and Gansu provinces, the reformers constantly tested new responsibility systems that had yet to receive official sanction. Central policy documents and editorials in the national press trailed behind those experiments and the regional reports carried in the *People's Daily* and the provincial press. Once the central political context changed, however, the reform group seized the initiative and promoted these "successful" local experiments.

Moreover, the deregulatory character of the responsibility system was critical. Decollectivization made peasants freer, and their initiatives propelled

[10] Grindle, *Politics*, 5–6.

the policy in directions probably not anticipated even by the reformers. Research teams gathered information on peasants' preferences and successful local innovations, which the reformers incorporated into the evolving policy content. Concisely, the evolving policy content resulted partly from local actions; the reformers, following the best traditions of Yanan and the "mass line," adjusted the policy's content in response to mass demands.

Other rural reforms also affected the content of the responsibility system. The diversification of agriculture and the expansion of household sidelines are particularly important. Both trends could not have occurred without weakening the commune structure. If peasants remained tied to the collective economy, they would be unable to follow their own economic logic and seek the most profitable and productive forms of horizontal cooperation. As the leadership came to believe in 1982 that commercialized farming, based on increased lateral trade among households and associations, offered the best future for Chinese agriculture, the reformers adopted household contracts and comprehensive contracts as the policy's final content.

THE INTRODUCTION AND SPREAD OF THE RESPONSIBILITY SYSTEM: OCTOBER 1977 TO JULY 1981

In 1977 some of China's more pragmatic leaders recognized that without a closer link between work performed and remuneration received, Chinese peasants would not work hard and Chinese agriculture would continue to grow at a sluggish pace. Indeed, there had been virtually no change in per capita grain production between 1956 and 1977. Therefore, following Deng Xiaoping's July rehabilitation and the Eleventh Party Congress of August 1977, reformers called for the reintroduction of material incentives in the rural areas.[11] In November 1977 top provincial secretaries and agricultural experts discussed agricultural problems in Beijing.[12] Some advocated "payment according to labor"; others resisted material incentives and supported the Dazhai work-point system (see the Appendix to this chapter). In December the Party's Agricultural and Forestry Department held a management and administrative symposium with cadres from provincial agricultural departments and called for the reversal of many radical policies of the 1960s and 1970s and the implementation of the 1962 Sixty Articles. A *People's Daily* editorial supported these changes, and although "the leading member of the CC-CCP in charge of agriculture" rejected the meeting's eight suggestions and the *People's Daily* editorial, provincial meetings from December through the spring advocated introducing "payment for work."[13]

In March 1978, Wan Li, Party secretary of Anhui, called for a "respon-

---

[11] *People's Daily*, Aug. 29 and Oct. 22, 1977.

[12] An Gang, Song Cheng, and Huang Yuejin, "There is Hope for the Vigorous Development of Agriculture in China," *People's Daily*, July 9, 1981, in *FBIS*, no. 141 (July 23, 1981): K11–18.

[13] *People's Daily*, Feb. 3 and Mar. 23, 1978.

sibility system" for managing rural labor under which "task rates" would replace Dazhai work points, which beginning in 1968 had been popularized throughout the nation.[14] Although Anhui was experimenting with "household quotas," Wan Li prohibited their use for the official record. Given the strength of the "whatever" group in the Politburo (see chapter 2), the minimal position, an official shift from Dazhai work points to task rates, would do. The maximum position, a return to household quotas, could come later. During the fall of 1978 national and provincial officials voiced support for these reforms. At a Work Conference on Rural Income Distribution convened in October 1978 by the Chinese Academy of Social Sciences in Beijing, two leading economists, Yu Guangyuan and Xue Muqiao, publicly criticized Dazhai work points.[15]

At the same time, provinces began to lobby for fixed quotas that linked income to output.[16] In October and November 1978, *Hebei Daily*[17] and *Henan Daily*[18] revealed that some units in their provinces had been experimenting since the fall of 1977 with "individual" or "group contracts" for cotton. Cash bonuses for any above-quota surplus ranged from 15 to 30 percent. Although the term they employed—"fixed quota management system with a bonus for surplus" (*ding e guanli, chao e jiangli*)—differed only in name from "group contracts" (*bao chan dao zu*), names in Chinese politics mean a great deal. The term "quota" (*ding e*) was becoming acceptable as a form of the responsibility system, while the idea of production contracts (*bao chan*) harkened back to policies criticized during the Cultural Revolution. By using the term "quota" (*ding e*) and merely adding a bonus, the policy would meet less opposition than if the term "contract" (*bao*) were used.[19]

An epistemological debate at this time over the basis of "truth" changed the context of implementation for the responsibility system by altering the criterion of policy evaluation.[20] Unlike the "whatever" group, which insisted that truth be based on Mao's words and his political "line," the reformers, resurrecting Mao's slogan of "seeking truth from facts" (*shi shi qiu shi*), denied that truth was based on any a priori "political line"; only a policy's effects could determine its validity. Units, therefore, could not resist reforms on

[14] Wan Li, "Energetically Carry Out the Party's Rural Economic Policy," *Red Flag*, no. 3 (1978): 92–97.

[15] *FBIS*, no. 209 (Oct. 27, 1978).

[16] A direct link between income and output would improve agricultural yields by giving peasants incentives to be concerned with the entire production cycle rather than only a segment of the cycle. Thanks to Tom Bernstein, who clarified this point.

[17] *Hebei Daily*, Oct. 11, 1978, 1, compiled in *China's People's University Materials Room, Materials Republished from the Press, Agricultural Economics* (Zhongguo renmin daxue shubao ziliao, baokan ziliao, nongye jingji) (hereafter *People's University Materials*), no. 10 (1978): 235.

[18] *Henan Daily*, Nov. 2, 1978, 1, in *People's University Materials*, no. 12 (1978): 121–22.

[19] In 1982 Wan Li admitted that he had avoided using such terms as long as possible. See *People's Daily*, Dec. 23, 1982, in *FBIS*, no. 002 (Jan. 4, 1983): K6.

[20] See Tsou et al., "Policy Change" (n. 7 above).

ideological grounds. Also by making economic outcomes, not political orientation, the key criterion of policy evaluation, the reformers circumvented the responsibility system's political content, which, because of its criticism during the Cultural Revolution, was a sensitive issue.[21]

The issue of linking income to output came to a head at the end of 1978. Although the *People's Daily* failed to support provincial endorsements of output quotas before the December 1978 Third Plenum, that Plenum's two draft documents on agriculture accepted that payment based on output with bonuses for overproduction was within the parameters of the responsibility system.[22] However, the document stated that "fixing output quotas based on the individual household and distributing land to the individual are both prohibited."[23]

After the Third Plenum, the reformers established pilot projects for household contracts, and Anhui's Qu county began to experiment with the more decentralized household contracts with fixed levies.[24] These and other experiments triggered a dispute over how to organize spring planting. On March 1, 1979, the *People's Daily* editor supported a letter from Guangdong province criticizing group contracts. Six days later, on March 7, the *People's Daily* presented the opposing view; in 1978 a team in Qu county, Anhui, had established group contracts with individual responsibility—in essence, individual contracts (*lian chan dao lao*). Although county leaders opposed this, the commune secretary, buoyed by peasant support, refused to change. While the major national-level effort of 1979 was popularizing *group* contracts, in particular localities the responsibility system's content continued to change in the direction of *individual* and even household contracts.

Between the springs of 1979 and 1980 important changes propelled this evolution forward. Deng Xiaoping is reported to have supported individual, group, and household contracts at some conference between the Third Plenum and the spring of 1980.[25] In September 1979, when the Fourth Plenum ratified the Third Plenum documents, the prohibition on household contracts had disappeared; household contracts for remote areas were officially authorized.[26] The removal of the "whatever" group from office at the Fifth Plenum in February 1980 greatly weakened opposition to further evolution. Wan Li, the force behind Anhui's experiments, was given responsibility for agriculture, and Zhao Ziyang, the reformer from Sichuan, as well as Hu

---

[21] If a policy has a nonsensitive political content, it is more likely to be implemented successfully. See Grindle, *Politics* (n. 5 above), 28.

[22] See Point 3 of "Decision on Some Questions Concerning the Acceleration of Agricultural Development," in *Issues and Studies* 15, no. 7 (1979): 102–19, and no. 8 (1979): 91–99.

[23] *Issues and Studies* 15, no. 7 (1979): 111.

[24] *People's Daily*, Sept. 16, 1982, in *FBIS* (Sept. 21, 1982): K15–16, and *Xinhua Yuebao*, no. 11 (1982): 91, respectively.

[25] *People's Daily*, May 20, 1981.

[26] *People's Daily*, Oct. 6, 1979.

Yaobang, joined the Politburo's Standing Committee. Hu also was placed in charge of the revived Secretariat, which increasingly became the locus of policy making in the Party, displacing the Politburo, where more conservative leaders could exert influence.

These changes in the political context facilitated further alterations in the responsibility policy.[27] Soon after the Fifth Plenum, "specialized contracts" (*zhuanye chengbao*) for groups and households, reportedly discovered in Shaanxi province by Zhao Ziyang and introduced into Sichuan after the Fourth Plenum, were introduced to the nation.[28] Since a major problem for the reform group would be persuading wealthy units to link income and output at the household level,[29] specialized contracts, whereby peasants with special expertise accepted responsibility for a quota within a particular field of endeavor, was an important innovation. Adaptable to areas with little land, many people, and a fine division of labor, specialized contracts were particularly appropriate for suburban communes.

On April 2, 1980, a *People's Daily* editorial announced that 80 percent of the teams in the nation had adopted some form of responsibility system, with 20 percent using *group* contracts, which, the editorial admitted, the *People's Daily* had criticized one year earlier. Yet, although the paper discussed specialized contracts in Sichuan on the same day, this *People's Daily* editorial ignored them because in Sichuan they were often signed by *individual* households.[30] But with spring planting rapidly approaching and with 20 percent of rural teams still using Dazhai work points, time was of the essence. At a minimum, these teams had to adopt task rates.

Seven days later, the *People's Daily* further loosened the boundaries of the responsibility system. Whereas in the fall of 1979 *individual* contracts were mentioned but not advocated, the *People's Daily* now supported their controlled application.[31] Nonetheless, resistance to linking income to output persisted through part of 1980. On May 15 the *People's Daily* admitted that the responsibility system linking income to output "has constantly incurred censure from all sides." And although *Economic Research* in June supported individual contracts, the article was still trying to convince units to stop using Dazhai work points.[32]

[27] For changes in Guangdong province, see *People's Daily*, May 20, 1981, and for Anhui province, see *Nongye Jingji Wenti*, no. 5 (1981): 5.

[28] *People's Daily*, Apr. 2, 1980. An informed Nanjing source told me of Zhao's "discovery" of this system.

[29] See Zweig, "Peasants and the New Incentive Systems" (n. 6 above).

[30] Throughout this period, forms of the responsibility system which had not yet received official sanction appeared in the *People's Daily* as regional reports or as letters to the editor.

[31] *People's Daily*, Apr. 9, 1980.

[32] "An Exploratory Discussion of the Reform of the People's Commune's Quota Payment System," *Economic Research* (June 1980). Some parts of rural China, including Jiangsu province, still used Dazhai work points until the fall of 1980.

During the summer of 1980, under increased pressure from the provinces to authorize household contracts for more than just "single households living in remote hilly areas," the Central Committee and the State Agricultural Commission sent out more than a hundred people to collect data on the local situation. These research groups found that fluctuations in local implementation made peasants uneasy and affected production. So in September 1980, before the fall harvest and winter planting, the Party Secretariat convened a work conference in Beijing with first secretaries of all provinces, cities, and autonomous regions to discuss the responsibility system.[33]

The most important contribution of this meeting was its clear recognition that policy implementation would have to be more flexible and take regional and local conditions into account. This point is critical for successful implementation.[34] The conference authorized three responsibility systems: task rates, specialized contracts, and household contracts, including household contracts with fixed levies.[35] Once again, in response to local pressures, the content of the policy had changed. The work conference fully integrated household contracts into the responsibility system by authorizing them for all poor areas; in remote mountainous regions and poor backward areas, peasants who had lost faith in the collective had to be allowed to use household contracts or even household contracts with fixed levies.[36] Average areas (*yiban diqu*) with stable collective economies were to avoid household contracts. Where these were already instituted, they were to be permitted to continue, but over time, through the use of various transitionary procedures, the peasants were to be reorganized.

During the winter of 1980–1981, while Central Document (hereafter C.D.) No. 75 was to be passed down for discussion at local levels, Hu Yaobang and Zhao Ziyang traveled across rural China, with Zhao investigating the responsibility system's progress and Hu looking at the issue of diversifying the rural crop mix (*duo zhong jing ying*). Leading members of the State Agricultural Commission under Wan Li also carried out investigations.[37] But as the spring harvest of 1981 neared, many local leaders failed to disseminate the policy, while others began to backtrack on the

---

[33] Changing the locus of decision making from the Politburo to the Secretariat removed Hua Guofeng, who opposed linking income and output, from the decision-making process. See *Ming Bao* (Hong Kong), in *FBIS*, no. 039 (Feb. 25, 1983): W1–2. For an in-depth discussion of the decision-making process for C.D. (Central Document) No. 75 (1980) and C.D. No. 13 (1981), see *People's Daily*, May 20, 1981.

[34] Peter S. Cleaves, "Implementation Amidst Scarcity and Apathy: Political Power and Policy Design," in Grindle, *Politics*, 284–85.

[35] Both C.D. No. 75 (1980) and C.D. No. 13 (1981) were published in *Ban Yue Tan*, no. 8 (Apr. 25, 1981).

[36] *Ban Yue Tan*, no. 8 (Apr. 25, 1981): 8. See also Yu Guoyao, *Red Flag*, no. 20 (1980): 12–15.

[37] *People's Daily*, May 20, 1981.

TABLE 9.1   Developments in the Responsibility System,
1980–1981

	Jan. 1980	Dec. 1980	June 1981	Oct. 1981
Task rates	55.7	39.0	27.2	16.5
Specialized contracts	—	4.7	7.8	5.9
Group contracts	24.9	23.6	13.8	10.8
Individual contracts	3.1	8.6	14.4	15.8
Household contracts	1.0	9.4	16.9	7.1
Household contracts with fixed levies	0.02	5.0	11.3	38.0
TOTALS	84.7	90.3	94.4	94.1

SOURCE: *Economic Research (Jingji yanjiu)*, 1982, no. 11: 6.

reforms.[38] However, having completed their research, the reformist group was prepared for another offensive.

A *People's Daily* commentary of March 2, 1981, listed several problems: Poor areas had confronted numerous difficulties implementing household contracts; peasants had not fulfilled their contractual obligations, some of them leaving the land fallow; team leaders had abdicated responsibility; and some officials had demanded uniform implementation of household contracts.[39] Yet, while outlining these problems, the *People's Daily* unveiled new trends in the content of the responsibility system.

First, wealthy areas had begun to shift from task rates to specialized contracts, a "developing tendency" that was applauded (see table 9.1). Second, average areas could now establish individual contracts within large paddy fields, particularly where the work was done manually. Having witnessed successful experiments in Henan, Hebei, and Shandong in early January, Zhao Ziyang supported contracting segments of large paddy fields among individuals, in spite of the complicated irrigation problems.[40] Third, the commentary divided the country into three areas with different levels of economic development—wealthy, average, and poor—and suggested that each area corresponded to the three responsibility systems outlined in C.D. No. 75.[41]

On the same day the commentary of March 2 was published, the Eighty-eighth Session of the Secretariat decided, based on Hu Yaobang's winter travels, to take new measures to diversify agricultural production. Their

[38] See letter to the editor in *People's Daily*, Mar. 7, 1983.
[39] See "Summarize Experience, Improve and Stabilize the Agricultural Responsibility System," *People's Daily*, Mar. 2, 1981.
[40] *People's Daily*, May 20, 1981.
[41] Ibid.

deliberations led to C.D. No. 13 (1981), promulgated on March 30, 1981, which was a significant step toward the commercialization of Chinese agriculture. The current emphasis on commercialized agriculture, based on individual households or cooperatives of individual households acting as the production, processing, and marketing units, shows the link between the responsibility system and agricultural diversification.

In April and May the policy's official content continued to evolve. At the end of April, *Ban Yue Tan* published both C.D. No. 75 (1980) and C.D. No. 13 (1981), which demonstrated official acceptance of household contracts with fixed levies.[42] Moreover, people now could see that the commentary of March 2 had advanced the content of the policy by supporting individual contracts for paddy cultivation in average areas, something C.D. No. 75 had not mentioned. Then, on May 20, 1981, there appeared one of the most revealing articles ever published in the *People's Daily*, and when it discussed the responsibility system, the policy's content differed from both C.D. No. 75 and the March 2 commentary.[43] Rich areas, with strong collective economies and yearly increases in production "in the main, should (*ying gai*) carry out the system of specialized contracts and those carrying out group contracts can, of their own volition, form specialized groups." Task rates, acceptable in March, were no longer mentioned.

In the provinces, changes were occurring quickly. On May 24 Shanghai's *Liberation Daily* warned that all units, rich and poor, should link income to output.[44] And on June 12, 1981, *Hebei Daily* referred to "dual contracts" (*shuang bao dao hu* or simply *shuang bao*), a formula that automatically included household contracts with fixed levies with collectively managed household contracts. Although both politically and practically these systems differ greatly, this formula of dual contracts included the more noncollectivist (*bao gan*) system within the fold of already acceptable responsibility systems.[45]

DEVELOPMENT, DISORDER, AND RETRENCHMENT: JULY 1981 TO MARCH 1982

The Sixth Plenum of June 1981 changed decollectivization's political context. With Hu Yaobang, a member of the reform group, replacing Hua

[42] *Ban Yue Tan*, no. 8 (Apr. 25, 1981). On March 7, 1981, the *People's Daily* first referred to this system when it ran a letter from Sichuan showing that household contracts with fixed levies had been in effect there for over a year. At the same time, Sichuan's Provincial Party Committee published a circular advocating household contracts with fixed levies. See *Sichuan Ribao*, July 13, 1981, 2, in *FBIS*, no. 154 (Aug. 11, 1981): Q3.

[43] Entitled "Time to Consider 800 Million Peasants," this article explained much about the decisions behind these two documents.

[44] "Even Shanghai County Can Link Income to Output," *Jiefang Ribao* (Liberation Daily), May 24, 1981.

[45] *Hebei Daily*, June 12, 1981, in *FBIS*, no. 131 (July 9, 1981): R1–7.

Guofeng as Party chairman, opponents of the responsibility system at the middle and local levels could no longer look to the Party chairman for support. The Central Committee's decision on Mao, which attributed agricultural problems of the 1960s and 1970s to his errors,[46] indicated to local cadres that a national consensus recognized that Maoist policies in agriculture following the Great Leap Forward (1958) had been wrong. The reforms, therefore, must continue. Following that meeting, Hu Yaobang finally stated that household contracts with fixed levies were part of the responsibility system.[47] Also, in July, Zhao Ziyang visited Lankao county, where the peasants were using household contracts with fixed levies.[48]

From July through September, propelled by peasants' spontaneous actions, support for household contracts intensified. Some provinces adjusted the relationship between the type of locality and the responsibility system it adopted. *Shaanxi Daily* of July 22, 1981, suggested that average areas could now use household contracts, and five days later admitted that a recent provincial meeting had decided that household contracts for fixed levies could now be expanded to areas not dependent on direct state subsidies. And on September 1, 1981, the *People's Daily* announced important findings. According to this Party report, peasants enthusiastically supported household contracts with fixed levies because this more decentralized system of management stopped cadres from expropriating collective resources for personal benefits and created a stronger incentive for peasants than individual or group contracts, which were based on centralized distribution. As the report found, "the overall situation is that in this reform, *the cadres have been compelled to advance by the masses*" (emphasis added).[49]

The effects of the Sixth Plenum on decollectivization are shown in table 9.1. Between December 1980 and June 1981, the use of other types of household contracts increased from 14.4 to 28.2 percent. However, the largest change occurred from June to October 1981, when the number of units using household contracts with fixed levies jumped from 11.3 to 38.0 percent.

The rapid emergence of household contracts with fixed levies, however, created problems during the summer of 1981. Middle-level officials responded in two ways: Some county and commune officials, fearful that this policy heralded decollectivization, tried to block its emergence by forbidding

[46] See "On Certain Questions in the History of Our Party Since the Founding of the People's Republic of China," *Beijing Review*, no. 27 (July 6, 1981).

[47] See An Gang, Song Cheng, and Huang Yuejin, "There Is Hope for the Vigorous Development of Agriculture in China," *People's Daily*, July 9, 1981, 2, in *FBIS*, no. 141 (July 23, 1981): K11–18.

[48] See *Zhengming Daily*, July 26, 1981, in *FBIS*, no. 143 (July 27, 1981): W6, and *People's Daily*, Sept. 1, 1981.

[49] This joint report by the CC-CCP Administrative Office (*Ban Gong Ting*) and the investigation group of the CC-CCP Party School was based on rural investigations from March 20 to May 30, 1981. See *People's Daily*, Sept. 1, 1981, in *FBIS* (Sept. 9, 1981): K7–15.

propaganda about it and by stopping loans to units implementing it.[50] Other places reacted in an opposite manner. Believing that the policy was unstoppable, these county cadres began to force "uniform" implementation upon local units. Hebei peasants, forbidden to establish household contracts in the spring, were compelled to do so in the fall.[51] In July officials in wealthy brigades in Shanxi, Jiangsu, and Fujian admitted that they were under pressure to shift to individual contracts.[52] A Jiangsu commune official expressed concern.

> The levels above us are pushing this policy hard now but it doesn't sit well here. You can't do water conservation projects. How will you use the sprinklers and the machinery? They are really going back. After so many years of building the collective they are taking it apart. There is strength in the collective because the numbers are big. In Anhui, the policy they are using now is not good for us. We don't want it here.[53]

In many localities the word spread that only by implementing *baogan* could an area show that it had emancipated itself from "leftist" tendencies.[54] By September the *People's Daily* called for an end to pressure for uniformity.[55]

Local officials also responded in two ways. First, they too tried to resist the changes advocated both by the national leaders and by the peasants. Some denied their unit's total dependency on state aid,[56] while others created innovative forms of task rates.[57] Resistance also was easier when supported by middle-level officials. But persistent national and peasant pressures, compounded by evaporating middle-level support, caused many local cadres to throw up their hands and abdicate their responsibilities.[58]

Peasants also overreacted to the expansion of household contracts with fixed levies. After the Cultural Revolution, household contracts had been equated with private farming. So when this policy was implemented in the summer of 1981, some peasants believed decollectivization was at hand; otherwise, why was this policy being implemented? Moreover, with local

---

[50] See *Shijie Jingji Daobao* (World Economic Report), Nov. 2, 1981, in *Da Gong Bao* (Hong Kong), Nov. 8, 1981, and *Sichuan Ribao*, Nov. 7, 1981, in *FBIS*, no. 224 (Nov. 20, 1981).

[51] *People's Daily*, Sept. 22, 1981. The Chinese refer to this demand for policy uniformity as *yi dao qie*, or "cutting all with one knife."

[52] David Zweig, "Chinese Agriculture: Pragmatism Gone Too Far?" *Asian Wall Street Journal*, Aug. 12, 1981. Also see *FBIS*, no. 185 (Sept. 24, 1981).

[53] Interview COYCZ, 1981. The full transcript is available from the author.

[54] *Shanxi Ribao*, Sept. 22, 1981.

[55] *People's Daily*, Sept. 22, 1981.

[56] *Shanxi Ribao*, July 22, 1981, in *FBIS*, no. 161 (Aug. 20, 1981): R1–6.

[57] A brigade secretary in Jiangsu shifted to "long-term task rates" so that peasants would assume responsibility for the entire process but would not have to meet a production quota. Personal interview.

[58] *Hebei Daily*, Aug. 23, 1981, referred to these two responses as first "locking horns" and then taking a "laissez-faire" attitude. *FBIS*, no. 171 (Sept. 3, 1981): K7–9.

cadres withdrawing and Party branches immobilized, no one disabused the peasants of this notion. Consequently, in many areas peasants divided collective property.[59]

In addition, fulfillment of the agricultural plan was jeopardized. Acreage allotted for grain decreased; vegetable supplies in state markets shrank as peasants flocked to the free markets; and increased production of cash crops led to waste as marketing organizations refused to purchase above-plan quantities.

These problems precipitated a flurry of national activity and policy readjustments. The National Symposium on Agricultural Economic Problems, convened in late August by the Chinese Agricultural Economic Society under the auspices of the State Agricultural Commission, reported that agriculture was doing well, which undermined some of the opposition that chaos in the rural areas must have created. But actual policy implementation exceeded the provisions of Central Document No. 75; the masses were running ahead of the elites. Therefore, delegates suggested that a new document be composed to deal with the changing situation and the diversity of fears at all levels of rural society.[60]

In late October 1981 a National Rural Work Conference tried to assuage the aforementioned concerns.[61] Those concerned with decollectivization were informed that collective ownership of both land and the basic means of production would persist. On the other hand, since household contracts for fixed levies were now a form of the *collective* responsibility system, its widescale implementation should not lead to further dismantling of collective property. The conference also addressed the problem of plan fulfillment. Peasants, using the decentralized household contracts with fixed levies, would now sign formal contracts with the collective, binding them to the plan's guidelines.

Following the rural work conference, specialists throughout China descended on the rural areas,[62] and many of them met in Yunnan at the National Meeting on Problems of Agricultural Responsibility Systems, December 8–16. This meeting announced that by the end of October, 45 percent of rural units nationwide were using dual contracts.[63] However, the

[59] See *People's Daily*, Aug. 15, 1981, in *FBIS*, no. 162 (Aug. 21, 1981): K21–22; *Shanxi Daily*, Oct. 3, 1981, in *FBIS* (Oct. 22, 1981): T2–3; *People's Daily*, editorial, Oct. 4, 1981, *FBIS* (Nov. 12, 1981); and *FBIS* (Dec. 31, 1981): O3.

[60] See *Nongye jingji wenti* (Problems in Agricultural Economics), no. 10 (Oct. 28, 1981): 3–6, in *Joint Publications Research Service* (hereafter *JPRS*), no. 79741 (Dec. 24, 1981).

[61] A commentary in *People's Daily* (Oct. 30, 1981), entitled "Uphold Collective Ownership of Land, Uphold the Direction of Collectivization," referred to "the recently called national agricultural work conference." See *FBIS* (Nov. 6, 1981): K1–2.

[62] *People's Daily*, Feb. 6, 1982, 2.

[63] *FBIS*, no. 245 (Dec. 22, 1981): K8. This figure matches table 9.1.

conference also stressed the importance of formal contracts so that peasants using household contracts with fixed levies could manage their day-to-day affairs independently, and the state could still protect its interests.

During most of the winter of 1981–1982 the reformists' program seemed to be in abeyance. Zhejiang province publicly declined to bring pressure on the recalcitrant 30 percent of its teams to link income to output.[64] *Red Flag* criticized slogans which implied that people using task rates were ideologically unliberated.[65] A Hunan Radio commentary on January 29, 1982, stated that "growing crops and raising animals are the fundamental factors for getting rich in the rural areas," a very different position from the reformists' goal of diversifying and commercializing agriculture.[66] Heilongjiang province rejected household contracts with fixed levies, stating that "draft animals and farm implements cannot be divided among commune members,"[67] and on February 19 an editorial in Jiangsu province's *Xinhua Daily* voiced support for task rates. Fujian's Lunghai county reported that 20 percent of its teams' leaders had withdrawn or held power "only in name,"[68] and Hunan outlined numerous problems resulting from household contracts with fixed levies.[69] Of 260,000 Hunan teams using this system, over 17 percent had no unified administration.

In mid-February a fascinating article in *Ban Yue Tan* stated that income could be based on "the quantity *or* the quality" of the work performed, that is, income need not be dependent on output.[70] Although many parts of the article were taken verbatim from the "Minutes of the 1981 Rural Work Conference" (which were not published in the national press until April), minor adjustments in the document's contents suggested a different viewpoint from the original "Minutes." The *Ban Yue Tan* article stated that "*planned* production, *planned* marketing and state *monopoly* for purchasing and marketing had to be stressed" (emphasis added); it played down household production; and it expressed fears about what decollectivization would mean for water conservancy and capital construction.

Although these changes appear minor, in the political context of the winter and spring of 1981–1982 they take on major importance. The central work conference took place in October 1981, but the "Minutes" of the meeting had not been published when this issue of *Ban Yue Tan* went to press.

---

[64] *FBIS* (Nov. 24, 1981): O3–5, and *FBIS* (Dec. 3, 1981): O2–3.

[65] *Red Flag*, no. 1 (1982): 49.

[66] *FBIS* (Feb. 2, 1982): P1–2.

[67] *FBIS* (Feb. 1, 1982): S1–2.

[68] *Fujian Daily*, Apr. 12, 1983, as well as Mar. 26 and Apr. 8, 1983. Cited in John P. Burns, *Political Participation in Rural China* (forthcoming), chap. 2.

[69] *People's Daily*, Feb. 6, 1982, in *FBIS* (Feb. 18, 1982): K12–16.

[70] See "Several Questions Concerning Our Present Work in Agricultural Economics," *Ban Yue Tan*, no. 3 (Feb. 10, 1982).

Moreover, the "Minutes" had not yet been transmitted to most localities.[71] Many people first read the new policies in *Ban Yue Tan*. Moreover, the national political tide had briefly turned against the reform group (see chapter 2). A concomitant change in both policy content and context suggests that the reforms had run into resistance from those who could now point to some of the policy's negative effects.

THE BREAKTHROUGH: APRIL 1982 TO APRIL 1983

After the retrenchment of the winter of 1981–1982, continued rural reform and the expansion of household contracts with fixed levies depended on new initiatives to create a more favorable political context. Zhao Ziyang's early March announcement of a major reform of the State Council, and Deng's speech of April 3, 1982, which supported this structural reform, shifted momentum back to the reformers.[72] Also on April 3, a *People's Daily* editorial, while recognizing the rural problems, stated that "compared to the achievements we have made, these problems are secondary, partial and temporary," and that the efforts of the county Party committees, not policy changes, would overcome the problems.[73] On April 6, 1982, the "Minutes of the National Rural Work Conference" were published on the front page of the *People's Daily*, and three weeks later an investigatory report by the General Office of the Central Committee finally mentioned "comprehensive contracts" (*da bao gan*) in the *People's Daily*.[74]

The publication of the "Minutes" precipitated a major study campaign, the target of which was county and prefectural leaders who continued to resist the reforms.[75] While the education campaign of the winter of 1981–1982 had focused on local cadres, in May 1982 Bai Dongcai, secretary of the Jiangxi Provincial CCP Committee, emphasized that "in particular, the secretaries and standing committee members of the county CCP committees must unify their thinking."[76] Although the majority of cadres understood the

---

[71] In Hebei, meetings for transmitting the "Minutes" were not held until February (*FBIS* [Feb. 24, 1982]: R3–4), and other places did not distribute the "Minutes" until March (*FBIS*, no. 062 [April 8, 1982]: K6–8).

[72] For Zhao's speech, see *New China News Agency*, Mar. 8, 1982, in *FBIS*, no. 46 (Mar. 9, 1982): K1–7. (Thanks to Mike Oksenberg for pointing out this speech.) According to Deng Liqun's speech of Nov. 1, 1982, Deng Xiaoping supported the policy to "restructure the administration and economic setup." See *FBIS* (Nov. 8, 1982): K10.

[73] *People's Daily*, Apr. 3, 1982, in *FBIS*, no. 073 (Apr. 15, 1982): K1–3.

[74] *People's Daily*, Apr. 27, 1982.

[75] *People's Daily*, Apr. 3, 1982. The Central Committee also published a booklet called "Several Issues on Further Strengthening and Improving the Responsibility System in Agricultural Production," to explain the major reforms inherent in the "Minutes." *FBIS*, no. 092 (May 12, 1982): O1–2.

[76] *FBIS*, no. 092 (May 12, 1982): O1–2.

new line in agriculture, "there are some cadres, including some leading cadres *at and above* the county level, who are muddleheaded."[77]

The pace of reform increased at the end of June. According to the *People's Daily*, the rural situation now was magnificent.[78] Two days later the *People's Daily* published another speech by Bai Dongcai, in which he argued that dual contracts had helped, not hindered, Jiangxi province's rural economy. Dual contracting had not precipitated the breakdown of local leadership; the problem was the lack of ideological work by rural leaders, "the pernicious influence of Lin Biao and the Gang of Four," and middle-level cadres from the province down, whose political attitudes were behind the times and the changes demanded by the peasants.[79] And on July 4 *Sichuan Ribao*'s "commentator" reported that a recent provincial CCP committee work conference "took a number of new policy measures for developing the rural economy. Some of these represent *a further relaxation of policies*, some involve handing over more decision-making powers to the grassroots."[80] The Sichuan report heralded the major policy changes that were soon to come.

From the summer of 1982 on, the content of the rural reforms became more comprehensive. As household contracts with fixed levies became more acceptable and widespread, the reformers began to work toward commercializing Chinese agriculture, with the individual households as the producing, processing, and transporting units. To achieve this goal, the reformers had to divide the collective into independently managed household units, which could either recombine voluntarily into new cooperatives or companies, sometimes competing with both collective and state-run agricultural companies, or persist as individual specialized units. In line with these changes, the reformers, as we shall see, began referring to the rural area's *cooperative* rather than *collective* economy. Implementing household contracts with fixed levies and comprehensive contracts had become the linchpin in the reformers' overall scheme.

Representatives from more than ten provinces met at the July Forum on Agriculture to discuss "further relaxing policy restrictions."[81] In light of the *Sichuan Ribao*'s reference above to a "further relaxation of policies," the reformers probably expanded the scope of experimental locations for this liberal policy at this time. In this way, by November Wan Li could argue that practice had outstripped the prevailing guidelines. A *Xinhua* report made it clear that a major new reform was in the works. In an interview, a "responsible comrade of the Henan Provincial CCP Committee" said that

---

[77] Ibid. Emphasis mine.
[78] *People's Daily*, June 27, 1982, in *FBIS*, no. 129 (July 6, 1982): K8–11.
[79] See *FBIS*, no. 129 (July 6, 1982): K11–14.
[80] *FBIS*, no. 132 (July 9, 1982): Q2–3. Emphasis mine.
[81] Wan Li referred to this forum in November. See *People's Daily*, Dec. 23, 1983, 1, 2, 4.

there has appeared the omen of a new breakthrough and development in the rural areas, and we are needed there to *adroitly guide actions according to circumstances*. It will no longer meet the needs of the situation simply to issue a general call to perfect the responsibility system. We must have a new policy decision and take new action in the face of a host of new things.[82] (emphasis added)

Undoubtedly, this Henan official had read a draft policy document, because in November Wan Li would also state that, owing to local changes, cadres would need to "adroitly guide actions according to circumstances."[83]

In anticipation of the Twelfth Party Congress, support for comprehensive contracts and the major restructuring of Chinese agriculture grew. The August issue of *China Reconstructs* carried an in-depth report from Hunan describing a system called "contracting by specialization," which was merely one form of *da bao gan*.[84] By August some "specialized" and "key households" (see Appendix), who signed comprehensive contracts, could now withdraw from agriculture, leave farming to other specialized farming households, and produce commodities for enlivening the rural market.[85] On the eve of the Twelfth Party Congress, *People's Daily* announced that comprehensive contracts were the "typical form" of the "contract system linked to output." And since even wealthy units must use the contract system linked to output, they might as well establish comprehensive contracts.[86]

Finally, the new policy line of the responsibility system was stated at the Twelfth Party Congress by Du Runsheng, director of the newly established Rural Policy Research Office (*nongye zhengce yanjiu shi*) of the Party Secretariat, when he said that the decentralized household contracting system was no longer simply the major form of the responsibility system; it had now become a "developmental stage" in rural China's historical development.[87]

Wan Li, in a major speech to the November 1982 Conference of Agricultural Secretaries in Beijing, said that comprehensive contracts and household contracts with fixed levies were "most cherished by the masses." He announced that the Central Committee officially had named the various forms of the responsibility system the "contract system linked to output," and argued that if peasants in wealthy suburbs demanded the right to use comprehensive contracts, "this demand should no longer be held back."[88]

Premier Zhao Ziyang, in his December speech to the Fifth Session of the Fifth National People's Congress (NPC), supported Wan Li's advocacy for universal use of comprehensive contracts. He said that comprehensive con-

[82] See *Xinhua*, July 25, 1982, in *FBIS*, no. 144 (July 27, 1982): K4–5.
[83] *People's Daily*, Dec. 23, 1983, 1, 2, 4.
[84] *China Reconstructs* 31, no. 8 (August 1982): 52.
[85] *Xinhua* Commentator, Aug. 12, 1982, in *FBIS*, no. 157 (Aug. 13, 1982): K11–12.
[86] *People's Daily*, Aug. 29, 1982, in *FBIS*, no. 171 (Sept. 2, 1982): K24–26.
[87] *Xinhua Yuebao*, no. 9 (1982): 139.
[88] *People's Daily*, Dec. 23, 1982, in *FBIS*, no. 002 (Jan. 4, 1983): K2–20.

tracts have "now become the principal form of the responsibility system in most rural areas, adopted not only by economically backward brigades and teams that engage in one crop farming, but also popularized in turn among economically advanced brigades and teams that have a highly specialized division of labor."[89] Zhao's public policy posture had changed greatly since early 1981, when he argued that regional variations necessitated flexible implementation of various responsibility systems. One must wonder, therefore, if peasant reactions changed his views or whether his 1981 policy was strategically motivated to undercut opposition and mobilize support for formally introducing household contracts into the rural areas.

During late 1982 and early 1983, while the reformers pushed for universal implementation of comprehensive contracts or household contracts with fixed levies, they also composed Central Document No. 1 (1983), which was to lead Chinese agriculture in the direction outlined by Wan and Du. The code word for this overall reform was to "relax policies," and at the end of the December session of the NPC, all responsible officials from all departments, committees, and provinces, were told to implement the reforms.[90] Thus, in early 1983 Hu Yaobang gave what *Da Gong Bao* called "a mobilization order":

> The remarkable success in agricultural reform made the leaders of the CCP who have been determined to carry out reforms understand that the implementation of the system of contracting all-round responsibility (comprehensive contracts), the development of specialized households, the diversified strata of the economy and the use of economic methods in management is the way out for China and is the way for China to launch its social and economic development.[91]

Many provinces convened meetings to implement the new liberal policy. Gansu announced that it would "relax its rural policies" and allow peasants to open mines.[92] Guangdong recognized that the key to rural prosperity lay in "relaxing and revising policies," and accepting the household contract system as the principal form of the responsibility system.[93] In early 1983 Fujian and Hunan put out new regulations for enlivening the rural economy.[94]

Widespread mobilization for the commercialization of agriculture greatly expanded the use of the contract system linked to output. Tianjin began to push all its units to accept, at a minimum, individual contracts, if not house-

---

[89] *FBIS*, no. 240 (Dec. 14, 1982): K31.

[90] *Da Gong Bao* (Hong Kong), Feb. 6, 1983, 1, in *FBIS*, no. 028 (Feb. 9, 1983): W1–2.

[91] Ibid.

[92] *FBIS*, no. 247 (Dec. 23, 1982): T1–5.

[93] *FBIS*, no. 249 (Dec. 28, 1982): P4.

[94] *FBIS*, no. 009 (Jan. 13, 1983): K17, and *People's Daily*, Jan. 22, 1983, editorial, respectively.

hold contracts.[95] According to a report from Gansu, 99 percent of its teams used comprehensive contracts.[96] By the end of January specialized households constituted 10 percent of Chinese rural families,[97] and over 70 percent of rural households used comprehensive contracts.[98] Baotou municipality reported successful use of household contracts for vegetable production.[99] And those who were undermining comprehensive contracts, particularly wealthy localities, were told that if Yixing county, Jiangsu, with its highly diversified economy, and Taoan county, Jilin, where agriculture is highly mechanized, were linking income to output successfully, wealthy areas everywhere should be able to do so.[100]

Other pockets of resistance also caved in. In late February, Chen Zuolin, first Party secretary of Zhejiang province, admitted that the province had seen household contracts as a "question of orientation," and had opposed it, fearing it would undermine the collective economy.[101] But as of August 1982 (after the July Forum and before the Twelfth Party Congress), the province had reaffirmed household contracts with fixed levies, promoting them "in the whole province, including some economically developed areas."[102] Two days later *Ming Bao* reported that Mao Zhiyong, first Party secretary of Hunan, purportedly confessed to having opposed linking income to output, fearing it would lead to private farming. He had reported his concerns to the then Party chairman Hua Guofeng, who said that the system was not applicable to Hunan. So they stuck with task rates, and following the publication of C.D. No. 75, Mao rejected household contracts at a provincial meeting of county Party secretaries.[103] These confessions increased the danger of further opposition.

A major shift to comprehensive contracts occurred between the fall of 1982 and the spring of 1983. The three northeast provinces, which had responded more slowly than much of the rest of the country, made a turnaround over the winter, as is shown in these statistics from *Nongmin Bao* for March 22, 1983: Liaoning increased from 31 percent (October 1982) to 92 percent (March 1983); Jilin increased from 29 percent (October 1982) to 94.5 percent (March 1983); and Heilongjiang increased from 8.7 percent (May 1982) to 73 percent (February 1983). These findings suggest that by

[95] *FBIS*, no. 247 (Dec. 23, 1982): R4–6.

[96] Ibid.

[97] *FBIS*, no. 009 (Jan. 13, 1983): K17.

[98] *People's Daily*, Jan. 22, 1983, editorial.

[99] *People's Daily*, Jan. 13, 1983.

[100] See *People's Daily*, Jan. 23, 1983.

[101] *People's Daily*, Feb. 21, 1983, in *FBIS*, no. 038 (Feb. 24, 1983): 07.

[102] This change of policy and posture may have resulted from provincial political changes, because Tie Ying had been first Party secretary of Zhejiang. Thanks to David Bachman, who pointed out this fact.

[103] *Ming Bao*, Feb. 23, 1983, 5, in *FBIS*, no. 039 (Feb. 25, 1983): W1–2.

March 1983 most nonsuburban teams were reporting use of household contracts with fixed levies. Whether these were in fact merely "formalistic" responses is impossible to measure. But according to official information, from the end of 1982 through July 1983 the number of teams using dual contracts increased by 14 percent to 93 percent of all teams in China.[104] The goal of wide-scale implementation of the link between income and output and household contracts with fixed levies was achieved.

EVALUATING SUCCESS AND THE PROBLEM OF UNANTICIPATED CONSEQUENCES

This case study raises one of this volume's recurrent themes—how does one know "successful" implementation when one sees it? Even if initial policy goals are achieved, as has clearly been the case with responsibility policy, how does one deal with possibly deleterious unanticipated consequences? To evaluate this policy's success or failure, therefore, criteria other than the scope of implementation should be considered. Were elite economic goals of increasing agricultural production attained? What were the effects of unintended policy consequences? And were the reformers able to deal with them? This section looks briefly at changes in agricultural output, agricultural productivity, and living standards, as well as the policy's unanticipated consequences and the leaders' responses to them, to see whether the implementation of household contracts has been a "success."

Since the responsibility system was introduced, agricultural production has increased greatly, particularly since 1981. Table 9.2 presents several indicators showing changes in rural production since 1978. Increases in grain output have been impressive, particularly since grain acreage has decreased. Output of other crops has increased even more dramatically. However, if these increases are the result of organizational reforms, they may be short-lived, with little effect on long-term growth rates. Technical infusions remain the only way to increase growth rates in agricultural production.[105] Indeed, to encourage peasants to invest in land, the period of contracts has been lengthened to fifteen to thirty years.

Many costs are now borne by households rather than collectives, creating incentives for individual peasants to increase productivity. Output of grain per mu increased in 1982 over 1981 by 13 percent, which explains why grain acreage could drop while output rose.[106] From 1978 to 1982 total agricultural

[104] *Nongmin Bao*, July 21, 1983, 1, 3.

[105] See Steven Butler, "The Rural Responsibility System: A Fresh Answer to China's Agricultural Problems?" in David Zweig and Steven Butler, *China's Agricultural Reform: Background and Prospects* (New York: Asia Society, 1985), and Nicholas P. Lardy, *Agriculture in China's Economic Development* (Cambridge: Cambridge University Press, 1984).

[106] *Nongmin Bao*, July 21, 1983.

TABLE 9.2 Indicators of Rural Development, 1978–1984 (in 100,000 tons)

	1978	1979	1980	1981	1982	1983	1984
Grain output	3,047.5	3,321.2	3,205.6	3,250.2	3,534.2	3,872.8	4,070.0
Cotton output	21.7	22.1	27.1	29.7	36.0	46.4	62.5[a]
Oil-bearing crops	52.2	64.4	76.9	102.1	118.2	105.5	118.5
Tea output	2.7	2.8	3.0	3.4	4.0	4.0	4.1
Sugar cane	211.2	215.1	228.1	296.7	368.8	311.4	396.6
Meat production (pork, beef, and lamb)	85.6	106.2	120.6	126.1	135.1	140.2	152.5

SOURCES: 1978–1981, *Ban Yue Tan*, no. 16 (1982): 27.
1982 Statistical Yearbook of China.
1983 *Beijing Review*, 1984, no. 35 (Aug. 27), and State Statistical Bureau Communique, Apr. 29, 1984.
1984 *USDA China Outlook and Situation Report* (United States Department of Agriculture, Economic Research Service, 1985).
[a]Chinese Agricultural Yearbook, 1985, 78.

TABLE 9.3   Peasant Standards of Living, 1978–1983

	1978	1979	1980	1981	1982	1983
Housing (approx.)[a] (million m^2)	100.0	300.0	500.0	600.0	600.0	700.0
Average per capita net income[b]	133.6	160.2	191.3	223.4	270.1	310.0
Average per capita income from collective[c]	88.5	102.0	108.4	116.2	142.8	169.5

SOURCES: All data are from *Ban Yue Tan*, 1982, no. 16: 27, unless otherwise marked.
   [a] 1982 and 1983 figures are from State Statistical Bureau Communique, Apr. 29, 1984.
   [b] Values for 1982 and 1983 need adjustment to compensate for a change in the price used for valuing distribution in kind by the collective sector. According to Fred M. Surls (*China Outlook and Situation Report* [United States Department of Agriculture, Economic Research Service, 1984]), 15, the income level for 1982 should be 257.4; there are no data yet for adjusting the 1983 value.
   [c] Chinese Agricultural Yearbook, 1984.

production costs, excluding labor, as a percentage of total income dropped 5 percent; for every 100 yuan of investment, returns rose from 252 to 288 yuan. Also, since 1978 income has been increasing at a faster rate than costs.[107] In short, decollectivization not only has contributed to increases in production; it has improved the economic efficiency of capital.

Finally, the reformers also sought to improve the peasants' living standard. Many "rehabilitated cadres," including Deng, spent the Cultural Revolution in rural areas. Surprised by the peasants' plight, they may have felt some obligation to resolve extant rural poverty. In any case, without an increase in rural living standards rural productivity and output could not have increased. Table 9.3 shows that from this perspective the reforms have also achieved short-run success. Rural housing construction is booming, and per capita income has more than doubled since 1978. From 1978 to 1983, the increase in per capita income outpaced growth in income from the collective, which suggests that individuals were more able than collectives to find profitable economic endeavors. If true, that is precisely the kind of change that the responsibility system was intended to achieve. From a short-term economic perspective the responsibility system appears to be fulfilling the goals of the reform group. Little wonder, therefore, that implementation has been so widespread.

We should note, however, that it is impossible to specify clearly what proportion of these economic gains is attributable to higher purchase prices, the opening of free markets, exceedingly good weather overall, and decollectivization. Hartford argues that the yearly increase in peasant per capita

[107] The rate of increase in total expenditure as compared with the rate of increase of total income dropped 3.9 percent between 1978 and 1982. See *Nongmin Bao*, Aug. 4, 1983.

income from 1979 to 1981 was due 76 percent to increased procurement prices.[108] In different locales various combinations of factors may have been at work. Nonetheless, there is no question that China's leaders, peasants, and urbanites all believe that the responsibility system has played a major role in recent agricultural successes. And in politics, perception is nine-tenths of the law.

All policies, especially major reforms, cause people to change their behavior. Some changes will be desired and predicted; others are unwelcomed or even unanticipated. If severe or unresolved, these unintended consequences can overshadow policy gains and undermine support for the original policy. It would be astonishing if decollectivization, which weakened collective leadership, had not triggered unintended consequences. Some problem areas include population control, capital formation, social unrest, and inequality.[109]

Chapter 10 in this volume explains the links between the responsibility system and the peasants' desire for more children: (1) allocating land according to family size or number of laborers creates strong incentives for more children; (2) weakening collective leadership hurts the state's ability to promote birth control; (3) weakening collective accumulation decreases the collective's ability to ensure old-age security, causing peasants to want more children; and (4) ending collective distribution destroys the mechanism for sanctioning those who had unauthorized children. These factors increased birthrates in 1982. However, the post-Mao leadership perceived this problem and responded rapidly. Linking the responsibility and birth policies, they introduced a new form of "dual contracts," combining remuneration for agricultural work with a willingness to abide by birth-control guidelines. Time will tell if this technique will succeed.

A second problem with long-term implications is the weakening of collective assets and capital formation. While the proportion of total agricultural income accumulated by collective enterprises from 1978 to 1982 stayed stable at 22 percent, income has been shifting from teams to households. Production-team income as a proportion of total income dropped from 55.4 percent to 45.6 percent while the share accruing to household sidelines rose from 22.4 to 32.1 percent.[110] Moreover, the percentage of team income that is now reinvested and saved for peasant welfare has dropped from 14.2 percent

---

[108] Kathleen J. Hartford, *Once More with Feeling* (New York: Columbia East Asian Institute Monograph, forthcoming).

[109] For a list of problems, see Chen Chung-min and Owen Hagovsky, "Agricultural Responsibility System: An Irresponsible Retreat or a Responsible Readjustment?" (Paper presented at the workshop "Studies in Policy Implementation in the Post-Mao Era," SSRC-ACLS Joint Committee, Columbus, Ohio, June 20–24, 1983.) One important problem not addressed here is water management.

[110] *Nongmin Bao*, Aug. 4, 1983.

TABLE 9.4　Distribution of Rural Households by Per
Capita Income (percentage)

	1978	1979	1980	1981	1982	1983
Income groups (yuan)						
100	33.3	19.3	9.8	4.7	2.7	1.4
100–	31.7	24.2	24.7	14.9	8.1	6.2
150–	17.6	29.0	27.1	23.0	16.0	13.1
200–	15.0	20.4	25.3	34.8	37.0	32.9
300–	0.0	5.0	8.6	14.4	20.8	22.9
400–	2.4	1.5	2.9	5.0	8.7	11.6
500+	0.0	0.6	1.6	3.2	6.7	11.9
Gini coefficient	.28	.26	.25	.23	.22	.22
Sample size	34,961	58,153	88,090	101,998	142,286	165,131

SOURCE: Compiled by William L. Parish; first appeared in Mark Selden "Income Inequality and the State," in William L. Parish, ed., *Chinese Rural Development: The Great Transformation* (Armonk, N.Y.: M. E. Sharpe, 1985), 211.
Gini coefficients estimated from the income figures, which are in *Brilliant 35 Years* (Beijing: China Statistical Publishing House, 1984).

in 1978 to 9 percent in 1982.[111] According to the *People's Daily*, many peasants are consuming too much and investing too little,[112] which will have long-term implications for economic growth, irrigation, rural education, and rural health and welfare.

Social tensions have increased as well.[113] Jealousy toward wealthy peasants has forced them to perform various services for their neighbors for free and to loan money that may not be repaid.[114] In some locations, thefts have increased. Extortion by cadres had become so prevalent that the Public Security Bureau had to draft a directive to all its units to protect rural households that have been getting rich.[115]

However, although some households have become quite prosperous, rural income distribution nationwide has become more, not less, equitable.[116] Table 9.4 shows that whereas in 1978, 82.6 percent of rural households made under 150 yuan, in 1983 only 20.7 percent fell into that category, which today represents the official poverty line. Clearly, this policy has dramatically helped alleviate rural poverty in much of rural China. Moreover, table 9.4

[111] Ibid.
[112] *People's Daily*, Sept. 7, 1983.
[113] David Zweig, "Prosperity and Conflict in Rural China," *China Quarterly*, March 1986.
[114] *Nongmin Bao*, Mar. 6, 1983.
[115] For a report on the extortions, see *People's Daily*, Mar. 10, 1983; for the Public Security Bureau's directive, see *Nongmin Bao*, Mar. 6, 1983.
[116] One survey found that from 1978 to 1982 the income gap between rich and poor in suburban Shanghai had narrowed. See *China Daily*, Oct. 11, 1983, 4.

also shows that the Gini coefficient, a standard measure of inequality, has decreased significantly since 1978. Therefore, the reform group's argument that "everyone is getting rich together" has some validity. Nevertheless, some families are growing quite wealthy while other labor-poor households are running into debt,[117] and whereas equality has increased in the short run, only time will tell if China will be able to continue to follow the pattern of equality with growth as occurred in Taiwan and South Korea.[118] Central Document No. 1 (1984) now allows the hiring of peasant labor and permits peasants to sublet their contract land to more successful farmers, which will lead to the centralization of land management.[119] Moreover, the wealthy may use their money to increase their political and social standing, which in turn could strengthen and expand overall inequality in the countryside.[120]

Final evaluation of the success of decollectivization must await future developments. The growth rates engendered to date by this policy will be difficult to maintain without a major infusion of capital. Whether private household financing of each peasant's own individual plot will suffice, or whether the state will be forced to pour funds into the rural areas remains unclear. The potentially disruptive effects of several seasons of bad weather, especially given the weakened irrigation infrastructure brought on by decollectivization, must be recognized. Expanding inequalities within China's peasant society and the shift from a collective economy offering a protective welfare net to a more unstable economic system replete with household bankruptcies and private financial failures could create a strong basis of support for a partial retrenchment of collective and state authority. Still, in the short run, the fulfillment of the reformers' goals of economic growth, increased productivity, and rising peasant incomes, all the while confronting only limited disruptions, tilts the scales of evaluation heavily in favor of viewing this implementation process as having been highly successful.

CONCLUSION

Successful implementation of household contracts occurred because the reform group was highly flexible and innovative throughout most of the pro-

[117] See "Village Volunteer Youth Groups," *China Reconstructs* 32, no. 11 (November 1983): 4–6.

[118] Li Chengrui of the State Statistical Bureau states that the 1984 Gini coefficient of rural inequality was slightly higher than the 1978 coefficient, which suggests that inequality has begun to expand. See Li Chengrui, "Economic Reform Brings Better Life," *Beijing Review*, no. 29 (July 22, 1985): 22.

[119] See *FBIS* (June 13, 1984): K2.

[120] Educational differences help explain income inequality today. According to *Nongmin Bao*, July 21, 1983, 36.9 percent of specialized households (national average was 13 percent), 40.3 percent of rich households, and 18.2 percent of poor households had lower-middle school education. Clearly, the better educated one is, the more likely one is to make it into the ranks of China's new wealthy peasants.

cess. After establishing their preferences, they adjusted the policy's content according to local responses. They had a sense of where they wanted to go, but they also listened to the rural populace. The shift in policy content from the 1977–1978 stress on task rates to the 1983 emphasis on comprehensive contracts was neither prearranged nor randomly achieved. They adjusted the policy's content flexibly, all the while following their own general policy predilections.

The reform group adjusted the policy's political context in order to increase their power. At the same time, the reformers put opposition leaders off guard by the economic gains achieved by each incremental shift in policy. Each policy change, in itself, was unworthy of a major fight, but the aggregate of changes has produced the decollectivization of Chinese agriculture. The reformers created new political institutions they could control to initiate the policies (see chapter 2), and they relied on various ad hoc meetings to advocate the continuation and evolution of the reforms. From 1978 on, they convened major meetings at the end of every year, at which time they put out major policy documents. In the winter of 1978 they rose to prominence at the Third Plenum and set new directions for rural policy. In the fall of 1979 they ratified the New Sixty Points at the Fourth Plenum, and defeated their major opposition the following February. In the fall of 1980 the newly created Secretariat created C.D. No. 75, which certified the responsibility system and household contracts. In the spring of 1981 the Secretariat published C.D. No. 13 on diversification. Four months after Hua's ouster in July 1981, the reform faction held a Rural Work Conference to maintain momentum during the winter of 1981–1982, although the reforms did slacken during that time. In preparation for the Twelfth Party Congress, they held the July Forum on Agriculture, and following this congress they convened the Conference of Agricultural Secretaries. Then, in early 1983 they published Central Document No. 1 (1983), which ultimately pushed through and defeated the final points of resistance. The consistency of meetings and documents, sustained elite attention, and responsiveness to problems over such a long period of time was a rather remarkable feat and a key ingredient in the successful implementation.

Success also was due to the elite's willingness to allow peasants to experiment locally. According to Cleaves, "the challenge for reformers lies in utilizing the discipline inherent in a closed system to loosen the structure and thus to permit the system to adapt and learn, rather than remain persistently sealed from the social forces in its midst. When this task is accomplished, the resources available for policy implementation are recombined and increased."[121] Through careful manipulation of their political power, the reformers loosened the structure of the system. Then, by appealing to the

[121]Cleaves, "Implementation" (n. 34 above), 301.

peasants' pecuniary interests, they set loose these previously sealed "social forces," which helped propel the reforms. As Mao himself had learned, changes in rural policy are doomed without mass support.

The major problem that plagued this policy's implementation process and that has affected the implementation of so many other rural policies is the disastrous tendency toward uniformity and the refusal to allow variations in policy implementation based on local characteristics. Although the reformers stressed the importance of local conditions throughout 1981 and most of 1982, as of July 1982 they began to demand universal implementation of comprehensive contracts, even in wealthy areas that did not support the policy. In the past, radical elites who desired to impose their utopian view uniformly on society were often the culprits. Middle-level cadres, more concerned with protecting their political careers than developing the economy, always have pushed local leaders to implement unsuitable policies. However, this study shows that pragmatic elites also fall prey to this error, as if uniform implementation validates the correctness of their political line as well.

Most important, however, the reform group delicately matched the content of the policy to their ability to affect its political context. They continually monitored the rural areas and when unforeseen local responses changed that context, they quickly adjusted the content. When confronted by fearful cadres, they offered soothing words to calm them, even as they laid the groundwork for future changes and pressed the cadres to accept new forms of the responsibility system. As soon as the political context again swung their way, they changed the content and forcefully pressed on. Meetings and documents signaled bureaucrats throughout China that the reforms would continue. Each political success created a new political context, allowing the reformers, through salami-type tactics, to change the content of the policy and move the rural areas toward widespread use of household contracts and the decollectivization that we see today.

Appendix

THOSE NOT INCLUDED UNDER THE RESPONSIBILITY SYSTEM

Time rates. Collective officials determined each peasant's work value, primarily on a scale from 6 to 10, which would determine the number of points to be received for a day's labor. The value of each point was based on the collective's year-end income and the total number of work points distributed.

Dazhai work points. Different from task rates in two ways: (1) each peasant's evaluation occurred several times a year in an open forum; and (2) emphasis was placed on political attitudes as much as or more than on labor contributions.

THOSE INCLUDED UNDER THE RESPONSIBILITY SYSTEM

Task rates *(xiao duan bao gong)*. Tasks varying from field construction to parts of the productive process, such as planting, weeding, or harvesting, are assigned to work groups, individuals, or households, and fixed amounts of work points are awarded for a set job. Sometimes a quality criterion is attached to the evaluation process to ensure careful as well as rapid work. This system *does not connect income and output*; those that follow do.

Specialized contracts *(zhuanye chengbao)*. Individuals, households, or groups sign contracts to fulfill a quota for sideline production, such as fishery, forestry, or animal husbandry, under collective supervision. For meeting that quota they receive a fixed number of work points, as well as a bonus for surpassing it, comprising more work points, some of the surplus, or all of it.

Individual or group contracts *(lian chan dao lao, dao zu)*. The collective divides its fields into strips, and individuals or groups contract to meet fixed production quotas. Payment is in work points, with bonuses or fines dependent on output. Groups subdivide the work points among their members according to time rates.

Household contracts *(bao chan dao hu)*. All land is divided among households, who contract with the collective to meet a fixed quota. Peasants are paid by the collective in work points, with bonuses and fines dependent on output.

Household contracts with fixed levies *(bao gan dao hu)*. Land is divided among households, who contract to fulfill obligations previously belonging to the collective. Households pay the state agricultural tax, meet the compulsory sale, and make small contributions to the collective's accumulation and welfare fund. Other obligations, such as a compulsory labor contribution (*yi wu gong*), may be included in the contract. Peasants sell or consume all other produce, and households become the primary unit of account and accumulation. Land, however, remains collective property; peasants can use it or lease it but not sell it.

Comprehensive contracts *(da bao gan)*.   All aspects of rural work are divided among households, including "specialized" and "key households," who take over all aspects of collective sidelines, irrigation, and machinery management, as well as agricultural tasks.

Specialized and key households.   Specialized households take no part in collective labor and draw their total income from sideline work, whereas in "key households" only some members withdraw from the collective and work full time on sideline occupations.

TEN

Implementing the "One-Child-per-Couple" Population Program in Rural China: National Goals and Local Politics

Tyrene White

INTRODUCTION

In September of 1980 the Central Committee of the Chinese Communist Party took the unprecedented step of publishing an "Open Letter" to all Party and Youth League members, calling on them to take the lead in the drive to control population growth. The population program, which limited most couples to one child, allowed a second birth on a case-by-case basis where special circumstances warranted, and prohibited a third or more births,[1] constituted one of the most ambitious regulatory policies China had undertaken. It required a large percentage of the population to alter its behavior in very personal, intimate ways. Verbal compliance and passive acceptance at the group or mass level had to give way to active involvement in family planning by a multitude of discrete individuals, whose number was growing at a rapid rate.[2] Moreover, because 79 percent of the population was rural, meeting the stated goal of holding the population to 1.2 billion by the year 2000 hinged on the capacity of the regime to make the great majority of couples of childbearing age throughout the countryside refrain from having a

I wish to thank A. Doak Barnett, Thomas Bernstein, Merilee S. Grindle, David M. Lampton, and R. William Liddle for their comments and suggestions. Also, a special thanks to Professor Chen Chung-min for his invaluable help and guidance during the spring of 1982 in China.

[1] *Renmin Ribao* (People's Daily), Sept. 25, 1980, 1.

[2] *China Daily* Commentator, Dec. 28, 1982, 4, in Foreign Broadcast Information Service, *Daily Report: China* (hereafter *FBIS*), Dec. 29, 1982, K15.

second or additional child for the duration of their childbearing years. In turn, the fate of the "Four Modernizations" hinged on the success of this strict policy for population control.

During the previous three decades of socialist development, China's economy had suffered the ill effects of unbridled population growth. For example, grain production is estimated to have increased at an average annual rate of 2.3 percent between 1957 and 1978, but per capita consumption increased only slightly, from 306 to 318 kilograms. Urban housing space increased by 493 million square meters, but per capita housing was down from 4.5 square meters in the early 1950s to 3.6 in 1983. Perhaps most distressing of all, arable land per capita fell from .2 hectares in 1949 to .1 hectares in 1983, an amount less than one-third the world average.[3]

Thus, a leadership that had staked its legitimacy on the promise of improving the livelihood of Chinese citizens could see all too clearly the implications of failing to clamp down on population growth. During the 1970s efforts had been made to encourage the use of birth control and family planning, resulting in a significant decline in the population growth rate (see table 10.1). Because of the demographic composition of the population, however, China faced another baby boom in the 1980s, which if left unchecked would place an unbearable burden on an already taxed economy and doom the Four Modernizations drive to failure. Given the weight of their concerns, it seemed a small but necessary step to move from "encouraging" only one child per couple to "promoting" and "advocating" it. In practice, however, the policy distance traveled between 1977 and 1980 was great. The pressure on rural couples rose dramatically, threatening long-held views on, and motives for, childbearing that were incompatible with a one-child household. The decentralized regulatory process that had worked well previously was now strained by demands for new regulations and, more important, the resources to enforce them. The administrative apparatus and technical delivery system that had been adequate for less ambitious family-planning goals were now strained under the weight of strict quotas and increasing demand for contraceptive services. And finally, these problems were compounded by the very success of the ongoing process of agricultural reform, which had a negative impact on the enforcement of population control.

Although China's leadership acknowledged that a successful population policy was the cornerstone of its modernization effort, its implementation posed several dilemmas. Foremost among these was the disjuncture between long- and short-term priorities. The control of population growth was the unquestioned prerequisite for the long-term success of the Four Modernizations,

---

[3] Frederick M. Surls and Francis C. Tuan, "China's Agriculture in the 1980's," in *China under the Four Modernizations,* Joint Economic Committee (Washington, D.C.: U.S. Government Printing Office, 1982), 422; Lu Baifu, "The Way for Agriculture," *Beijing Review,* 1983, no. 4 (Jan. 24): 14; *Xinhua,* Jan. 11, 1983, in *FBIS,* Jan. 13, 1983, K14–15.

TABLE 10.1   Rates of Birth, Mortality, and Natural
Increase in Population Growth for the People's Republic
of China, 1949–1983 (per 1,000 population)

Year	Birth rate	Mortality rate	Natural increase in population
1949	36.00	20.00	16.00
1950	37.00	18.00	19.00
1951	37.80	17.80	20.00
1952	37.00	17.00	20.00
1953	37.00	14.00	23.00
1954	37.97	13.18	24.79
1955	32.60	12.28	20.32
1956	31.90	11.40	20.50
1957	34.03	10.80	23.23
1958	29.22	11.98	17.24
1959	24.78	14.59	10.19
1960	20.86	25.43	−4.57
1961	18.02	14.24	3.78
1962	37.01	10.02	26.99
1963	43.37	10.04	33.33
1964	39.14	11.50	27.64
1965	37.88	9.50	28.38
1966	35.05	8.83	26.22
1967	33.96	8.43	25.53
1968	35.59	8.21	27.38
1969	34.11	8.03	26.08
1970	33.43	7.60	25.83
1971	30.65	7.32	23.33
1972	29.77	7.61	22.16
1973	27.93	7.04	20.89
1974	24.82	7.34	17.48
1975	23.01	7.32	15.69
1976	19.91	7.25	12.66
1977	18.93	6.87	12.06
1978	18.25	6.25	12.00
1979	17.82	6.21	11.61
1980	—	—	12.00
1981	20.91	6.36	14.55
1982	21.09	6.60	14.49
1983	18.62	7.08	11.54

SOURCES: For all years except 1980 and 1983, *Zhongguo Tongji Nianjian, 1983* (China Statistical Yearbook) (Beijing: State Statistical Bureau, 1983), 105. For 1980, see State Statistical Bureau, "Communique on Fulfilment of China's National Economic Plan," *Beijing Review*, 1981, no. 20 (May 18): 20. For 1983, see *1984 Zhongguo Jingji Nianjian* (1984 Economic Yearbook of China) (Beijing: Economic Management Publishers, 1984), IV–60.

even among those who were concerned over the severity of the one child policy. As important as this goal was, however, the short-term goal of transforming rural economic structures was of much higher priority. Because the agrarian reform program represented not just a policy debate but also the focus of elite struggle, it was on this issue that political resources were mobilized and expended. Taking their cues from the Center, provincial and local Party leaders left family-planning work, as much as possible, to female comrades, who had always been responsible for this aspect of "women's work," while they concentrated their attention on a rapidly changing rural environment. Only after the Open Letter signaled the importance attached to family planning by central Party leaders did local cadres reassess the priority of this work.

By that time, however, a second dilemma had become apparent: the economic and organizational consequences of agricultural reforms were detrimental to the conduct of a strict policy of population control. This regulatory policy, stressing controlled uniformity in childbearing behavior, stood in sharp contrast to the general thrust of rural economic and administrative reforms. In those areas the watchwords were decentralization of decision making, reduction of administrative oversight, and economic diversification of households, groups, and teams based on local conditions. This dramatic dismantling of the collective system of agriculture was viewed as either desirable or threatening, depending on individual political and economic interests. Thus, at precisely the time when a demographic crisis loomed, deregulatory policies were under way which had polarized rural communities. Advocates and opponents of rural reform coalesced in their opposition to family planning, however, with pro-reform elements blaming "leftists" for the one-child policy, and opponents blaming the "rightists" and their neo-Malthusian population theories for the draconian policy.

It was against this backdrop that central policy makers groped for a strategy to deal with a changing rural context and local opposition or indifference. The result was a strategy of regularized, decentralized administration punctuated by periods of mobilization and the veiled use of economic and sometimes physical coercion. It was augmented by the use of economic incentives to gain compliance, a preferred policy technique of the post-Mao reformist leadership.

This chapter will examine the difficult task faced by China's leadership in its attempts to dictate household size in the rural areas. Drawing on archival materials and data from extended field research in Hubei province,[4] I will

---

[4] Interviews cited below were conducted in three phases in 1982 and 1984. From March through May 1982, fieldwork was conducted with Professor Chen Chung-min of Ohio State University's Department of Anthropology. The interview schedule was jointly developed to meet the needs of our separate research projects, and Chen conducted the interviews in the field. I wish to express my deep appreciation to Dr. Chen, whose willingness to collaborate and

demonstrate that four sets of factors loom large in accounting for problems of implementation: traditional attitudes and values, the decentralized regulatory process, administrative arrangements and the delivery system for family-planning services, and the environment of rural reform in which population policy is being enforced.

Taken together, these factors pose a number of important obstacles to policy implementation. Binding them together is the common theme of low levels of compliance on the part of peasants and cadres in some localities. Although many measures have been put forward by the state to redress problems in the implementation process, they have fallen short of their goal because they fail to solve this central difficulty.

IMPLEMENTING CHINA'S POPULATION PROGRAM: IMPEDIMENTS

The Impact of Traditional Values on Rural Childbearing Preferences

Since implementing the one-child-per-couple program, a campaign has been waged against what is termed "the resurgence of feudal ideas" in the countryside.[5] These "feudal ideas" come in the form of age-old sayings, such as "the more children, the more wealth," "regarding men as superior to women," "raise sons to protect against old age," and "carry on the ancestral line." That these ideas remain in contemporary China is indicative of the difficulty of altering the traditional values and preferences of a rural populace. More important, it is also indicative of the failure of the regime to alter sufficiently the economic environment that fosters them.

A 1981 survey of fifteen production brigades in five counties of Hubei province confirms the importance of traditional values and economic considerations in shaping preferences for household size.[6] Of 728 women of childbearing age (20–49) surveyed, only 5% wanted only one child, 51% wanted two children, 28% wanted three, and 15% wanted four. In what the author

---

share his field notes, intellectual insights, and interview techniques worked to my great advantage. During phase two, October–December 1982, the author continued fieldwork independently, conducting interviews at Hua Shan commune and with district family-planning officials. The opportunity for research was provided by Ohio State University through the OSU-Wuhan University Exchange Program. A third phase of fieldwork and interviewing in the spring of 1984 was undertaken as a Graduate Fellow in the National Program for Advanced Study and Research in China, administered by the Committee on Scholarly Communication with the People's Republic of China, National Academy of Sciences.

[5] Renmin Ribao editorial, "Give First Priority to Propaganda and Education in the Work of Family Planning," Sept. 29, 1981, 1; Xinhua, Jan. 10, 1983, in FBIS, Jan. 13, 1983, K15; Guangming Ribao, Jan. 12, 1983, in FBIS, Jan. 19, 1983, K22; Xinhua Commentator, Jan. 19, 1983, in FBIS, Jan. 25, 1983, K21.

[6] Cheng Du, "Hubei Sheng Nongcun Shengyu Lü Diaocha" (An Investigation of Rural Birth Rates in Hubei Province), Renkou Yanjiu (Population Research), 1982, no. 5: 36–38 and 31.

refers to as "hilly districts where traditional ideology is comparatively dense," however, the numbers climb to 27% wanting two or three children, and nearly 72% wanting four. Asked which sex child they prefer, a sample of 100 women in one brigade responded as follows: only 2.2% wanted a girl, 36.7% wanted a boy, and 61.6% were neutral.[7] In hilly districts, however, the number desiring a male soared to 77%. Asked what they would do if the first child was a girl, 61% said they would want another child. In a separate article based on the same survey, fully one-third of 710 women said they wanted to have a boy even if they already had two girls. Only 2.21% of a sample of 548 said they wanted to have only one girl.[8]

The study concludes that the desire for more children is caused by factors such as the "social economy," "ideology," and "traditional habits." More specifically, 808 people who were asked why they wanted additional children responded as follows: additional labor power, 21%; old-age security, 51%; preserve the ancestral line, 25%; enjoy the pleasure of children, 3%. The problem of old-age security clearly predominates. This category, taken together with those who cited the desire for additional labor power, drew 70% of all responses, demonstrating the role of economic calculations in determining preferences for household size.[9]

The influence of the desire to bear more children, particularly sons, is further evidenced by figures on holders of "only-child certificates" and sterilizations in Hua Shan commune, located in a suburban district of Wuhan municipality, Hubei province. In October 1982 there were 999 couples with only one child. Of these only 42 (4%) had undergone sterilization, and of the 42, only 7 (17%) had girls; 876 had signed "only-child certificates," pledging not to have another child.[10] This certificate rate of 91%, far above the estimated national average of 42%,[11] was achieved by offering short-term, five-year contracts to couples reluctant to sign a permanent agreement. In this way, Hua Shan family-planning workers were able to persuade parents of males and females to sign an agreement, and thus forestall unplanned pregnancies over the short term. It was hoped that after the five-year period, couples with healthy children of either sex would no longer be inclined to have another child.

In one brigade, of 123 single-child couples, 59 (48%) signed the "only-

[7] Cheng's article does not make clear that the size of the sample here is only 100 women, not 728. This information was obtained from personal conversations with another scholar who participated in the investigation. Interview File 2, Nov. 25, 1983.

[8] Cheng Du, "Nongcun Renkoude Zaishengchan—Dui Yige Diaocha Baogaode Fenxi" (The Reproduction of Rural Population—Toward the Analysis of an Investigation Report), *Jingji Yanjiu* (Economic Research), 1982, no. 6:56.

[9] Cheng Du, 31.

[10] Interview File (hereafter IF) 1B-7, 9 (82.10.14).

[11] *Renmin Ribao*, Apr. 10, 1983, 3.

child certificate," 54 (44%) signed a five-year agreement, and 10 (8%) refused to sign altogether. In a second brigade, only the five-year agreement
was in force; 54 of 111 couples (49%) signed and received the "special status" rewards for their child. The other 57 apparently were reluctant to sign,
and eventually agreed only to get a birth certificate for the child; thus, this
group did not get the "special status" rewards. In a third brigade, of the 53
couples with one child, 4 (7%) underwent sterilization procedures after having males, 7 (13%) signed long-term certificates (only 2 of these had girls),
and 25 (47%) signed a short-term contract (17 had girls). Of the remaining
17 who did not fall in any of these categories, it was said that "most of them
have girls." And in a fourth brigade, all 41 single-child couples had either
signed a five-year contract or had an operation, but only 5 of these couples
had girls (12%).[12] According to a commune family-planning cadre, all 81
couples in Hua Shan who had refused to sign an "only-child certificate" have
female children.[13] In short, reluctance to accept having only one child is not
confined to those with one daughter, but parents of females are less inclined
than parents of males to formally agree to limit themselves to one child.

   Is the desire for more children, and particularly more male children, the
product of old ideas or of contemporary economic realities? We already have
seen survey evidence demonstrating the importance of economic factors in
setting preferences for household size. Although the utility of these survey
results admittedly is quite limited, they do suggest that concern for old-age
security is the single most important factor motivating the desire for additional children, particularly males. This reflects a contemporary economic
and social reality: the absence of a universal or even widespread system of
support for the elderly across the countryside.

   In 1980 there were 8,262 "homes of respect for the aged," serving 111,700
people in rural China. Additionally, 4,000 basic accounting units provided
old-age pensions for more than 180,000 people.[14] In 1981, 282 more retirement homes were established, an increase of only 3% over 1980. Assuming
that 5% of the rural population is eligible for such retirement support, these
programs cover only about 1% of those eligible.[15]

   Of the twelve communes in Hong Shan district, where Hua Shan commune is located, in 1982 only one had a retirement home run by the commune. Although the per capita income level of this commune is unknown,
one of its brigades had the single highest per capita collective distributable
income of all brigades in Hong Shan district or the two surburban counties

---

[12] IF 1D-9, 10 (82.5.16); IF 1E-11 (82.5.23); IF 1J-9, 10 (82.11.9); IF 1G-10 (82.10.28).
[13] IF 1B-7 (82.10.14).
[14] *Zhongguo Baike Nianjian, 1981* (Encyclopedia of China) (Beijing: Zhongguo Dabaike Quanshu Chubanshe, 1981), 545.
[15] *Zhongguo Baike Nianjian, 1982* (Beijing: Zhongguo Dabaike Quanshu Chubanshe, 1982),
646.

TABLE 10.2   Comparing Mean Statistics for Xiu Hui
Commune, Zhang Qiu County, Shandong, with Mean
Statistics for Only-Child Households

	Commune	*Only-Child Households*
No. people per household	4.25	4.39
Labor power per household	1.65	2.37
No. persons supported by each laborer	2.57	1.85
1981 collective per capita income (yuan)	123.00	
1981 per capita income from family side-lines (yuan)	30.00	
Total per capita income (yuan)	153.00	240.40
Percentage of total households with per capita income over 500 yuan	1.60	3.80

SOURCE: Zhang Xinxia, "Du Sheng Zi Nu Hu ye you Tiaojian Fufuqilai" (Single-Child Households Also Have the Conditions for Becoming Rich), *Renkou Yanjiu* (Population Research), 1982, no. 5: 32–33.

of Wuhan municipality—817 yuan in 1981.[16] In six other communes, some brigades offered retirement incomes. In the five remaining communes in the district, retirement support from the collective was not offered. Hua Shan, with its 1981 per capita income of 209 yuan, more than double the provincial average, was among the latter group.[17]

Besides old-age insurance, the need for household labor power is another motivating factor for larger households. To counter the idea that wealth and security are strongly associated with household size, several studies have appeared in Chinese journals. Their authors argue that one-child families have higher per capita incomes from collective distribution than multi-child families. A close look at one study, however, reveals that such conclusions have more to do with household size and labor power than with whether it is a one-child household.[18]

A study of Xiu Hui commune in Shandong province compares mean commune statistics on household size, labor power, and income with mean figures for only-child households (see table 10.2). Here, one-child households clearly have higher per capita incomes; but to what is that attributable—childbearing restraint or total household size and labor power? In this case, single-child households are on average slightly larger than the commune

[16] *Changjiang Ribao*, Mar. 19, 1982. IF 1K-7 (82.12.1).

[17] IF 1K-7 (82.12.1). Hubei province's 1981 average income from the collective for commune members was 102 yuan. See *1982 Nian Zhongguo Jingji Nianjian* (1982 Economic Yearbook of China) (Beijing: Jingji Guanli Zazhi She, 1982), VI-123.

[18] Zhang Xinxia, "Du Sheng Zinu Hu ye you Tiaojian Fufuqilai" (Single-Child Households Also Have the Conditions for Becoming Rich), *Renkou Yanjiu*, 1982, no. 5: 32–33 and 43.

average, despite having a single-child couple in the household. More important, average household labor power is also higher. We can conclude only that there is a relationship between labor power and income, since average labor power for the commune is 69 percent of that for single-child households, and income is 65 percent. Thus, a study that seeks to argue for the economic advantages of having only one child actually substantiates peasant assumptions that over the long term, more children are desirable because they bring more labor power to the household.

Not only do peasants remain unconvinced that smaller households generate higher incomes, they also question the argument that females are as economically desirable as males, and for good reason. Traditionally, daughters contributed little or nothing to the family coffers and left the household upon marriage. While they make a substantial contribution in contemporary China, that contribution still shifts to their husband's household at marriage. Moreover, rural wage-earning policies discriminate against women. Where the work-point system remains in force, women typically receive only 70 to 80 percent of what their male counterparts earn.[19] Where land has been contracted to the household, allotments are based on the number of people in the household.[20] Although this eliminates inequalities in the short term, over the longer term single women will leave the household, whereas men will bring a wife into it. Thus, the land distribution formula now in effect under the agricultural responsibility system reinforces traditional attitudes and behavior toward women.

Moreover, in some cases the land-allotment process itself discriminates against women by linking the size of an individual's allotment to his or her previous work-point standard. An example of one team in Hua Shan commune demonstrates the full implications of this distribution system for peasant incomes. When one of Hua Shan's brigades implemented the household-contract responsibility system in 1982, team five had 169 mu of land to distribute among 42 households, 163 people. The land was divided into three grades, each grade having a different quota attached: for grade 1, 1,100 jin of rice per mu (1 jin equals ½ kilogram); for grade 2, 1,000 jin per mu; for grade 3, 900 jin per mu. Of team five's land, 66 percent was grade 1,

[19] Hong Ying, "Women in China Making Headway to Full Equality," *China Daily*, Mar. 6, 1982, 5, in *FBIS*, Mar. 8, 1982, K.15; Wu Naitao, "Rural Women and the New Economic Policies," *Beijing Review*, 1983, no. 10 (Mar. 7): 19. In Hua Shan the same pattern prevailed. IF 5B-13 (82.10.14).

[20] Zhang Huaiyu, "Lun Renkou yu Jingji Jianji Dangqian Nongcun Renkou Kongzhi Wenti" (A Discussion of Population and Economics Concurrently as the Current Problem of Rural Population Control), *Jingji Yanjiu*, 1981, no. 12: 37; Liu Honglian, "Kongzhi Wo Guo Renkou Zengzhang buneng Fangsong" (Do Not Relax Control of Our Country's Population Increase), *Sichuan Caijing Xueyuan Xuebao*, 1982, no. 2:5; Xu Xuehan, "Resolutely Implement the Policy of Rural Population," *Renmin Ribao*, Feb. 5, 1982, 5.

TABLE 10.3   Differential Land Allotments for
Hypothetical Households in One Team of Hua Shan
Commune, Wuhan, Hubei

	"Grain-quota land"	*"Labor land"*	*Totals*
Case 1. Family of 4:			
3 males @ 10 work points (father, 2 sons);	.311 mu × 4 =	(3.36 × 3) + 2.69 =	
1 female @ 8 work points (mother)	1.244 mu	12.77 mu	14.014
Case 2. Family of 4:			
2 males @ 10 work points (father and son);	.311 mu × 4 =	(3.36 × 2) + (2.69 × 2) =	
2 females @ 8 work points (mother and daughter)	1.244 mu	12.1 mu	13.344
Case 3. Family of 4:			
1 male @ 10 work points (father);	.311 mu × 4 =	3.36 + (2.69 × 3) =	
3 females @ 8 work points (mother, two daughters)	1.244 mu	11.43 mu	12.674

23 percent grade two, and 11 percent grade 3. In dividing the land, each household was to receive proportionate amounts of each grade of land.[21]

Step one was to distribute one-third of the average land per capita to each person as "grain-ration land" (*kouliang tian*) to provide for each person's diet. In team five the amount was .311 mu per capita. No distinctions were made based on age, sex, or physical condition. Step two was to distribute "labor land" (*laoli tian*) based on the laborer's previous work-point standard. In team five the standard varied from 10 to 8.5 for men, and 8.5 to 7 for women. Those who had earned 10 work points a day got 3.36 mu, 9 points got 3 mu, and 8 points got 2.69 mu. Thus, table 10.3 shows the total land area to be allotted assuming (1) different household compositions, and (2) consistent work-point standards of 10 for men and 8 for women. As can be seen, a household with two healthy sons would get .67 mu more than if they had two daughters.

How does this difference in land allotment translate into collective income for the household? In team five 25.3 percent of each household's total rice quota had to be sold to the state at the price of 12 yuan per 100 jin. Another 1.3 percent was to be turned over to the team without compensation. After

[21] IF 2G–6–9 (82.11.4).

harvest each household was responsible for paying the agricultural tax of 4 yuan per mu of contracted land and for contributing 3 yuan per mu to the team welfare fund. Finally, brigade cadres estimated that average grain consumption was 600 jin per capita, and that household expenses toward agricultural production averaged 15 yuan per mu of contracted land.[22] If we assume that actual yields are equal to quota levels, that investment and consumption levels are the same for each household, and that all excess production is sold to the state at its above-quota price of 18 yuan per 100 jin, it is possible to calculate household and per capita incomes from rice production alone, assuming different household compositions. The following list gives estimated income from rice production for three hypothetical households in a team in Hua Shan.

	Per Capita Income	Household Income	Household Income as a Percentage of Case 1
Case 1.	415.34	1,661.34	100
Case 2.	390.26	1,561.04	94
Case 3.	365.26	1,461.03	88

We find a spread of 50 yuan in per capita income between families with two sons and families with two daughters, 25 yuan between families with two sons and those with one son and one daughter. For household income, the spread is 200 and 100 yuan respectively. The household income of cases 2 and 3 is shown as a percentage of case 1. The spread of 6% and 12% respectively is slightly wider than under the old system where, assuming that the same number of full labor days is worked by all, families with one daughter and one son would have earned 96% of the income of two-son families, and two-daughter families would have earned 90% of two-son family incomes.

Thus, while the contract system has tended to boost peasant incomes overall, it has *enhanced* the economic value of male offspring relative to female. Moreover, as per-unit yields go up, the value of each additional increment of land increases. In our example, we assumed only that the quota levels for yield per mu were met, whereas the 1981 brigade average yield was 25% higher than the team-five quotas.[23] If 25% higher production levels were used to calculate incomes, the difference of .67 mu between male and female allotments would translate into even wider discrepancies in household income.

The combined weight of traditional values and economic realities, then, is creating strong pressures for more offspring, and especially for more sons. The consequence has been a substantial number of "illicit" births, that is,

---

[22] Ibid.

[23] Brigade rice production in 1981 was 2,810,000 jin. Rice acreage was 2021 mu. Average yield per mu equals 1,390 jin. IF 3G-2–3 (82.11.2).

births outside the plan, and an upsurge in reported cases of abuse of women who give birth to females and of female infanticide.[24]

Underscoring its concern over this phenomenon, *Renmin Ribao*, in April 1983, published birth statistics collected in two counties in Anhui province, which demonstrated a strong bias toward male births. Statistics for four communes in Huaiyuan county show the number of male births as a percentage of the total, ranging from 57.5 to 62.4. In three brigades, the discrepancy between males and females is even higher, with males constituting 77.8 to 90% of all births. Although these figures conceivably could be the result of a naturally occurring pattern of births, two additional cases suggest that it is not. The report notes that one team in the same county had forty cases of female infanticide in 1980 and 1981. In the first three months of 1981, one brigade recorded eight births—three healthy boys and five girls. According to the report, of the five girls three were drowned and two were abandoned.[25] Although the number of reported cases of this kind has been small, many more probably go undetected, particularly cases of infant death through neglect or abandonment. The Chinese press has been vocal in denouncing such behavior, but the phenomenon continues.

The Decentralized Regulatory Process

China's experience with population control is a monumental confirmation of the dilemmas posed by geographic and organizational dispersion in the implementation process.[26] Though based on a centrally directed goal, the implementation of the one-child-per-couple population program is decentralized in two ways: First, it is left to the localities to generate family-planning regulations consistent with central directives and local conditions; second, it is up to the localities to establish and maintain the organizational structure charged with implementing the policy.

China's central directives on family planning instruct cadres to promote only one child per couple, strictly limit second births, eliminate the occurrence of third births, and stress the need for late marriages and late childbirth.[27] To enforce the policy, subordinates are further instructed to establish a system of rewards and penalties designed to encourage compliance. The September 1980 "Open Letter" to all Party and Youth League

[24] *Renmin Ribao*, Mar. 7, 1983, 1; *Guangming Ribao*, Jan. 12, 1983, 1, in *FBIS*, Jan. 19, 1983, K22; Yang Fan, "Save the Baby Girl," in *Zhongguo Qingnian Bao*, Nov. 9, 1982, 3, in *FBIS*, Dec. 7, 1982, K55–56; "Protecting Infant Girls," *Beijing Review*, 1983, no. 5 (Jan. 31): 4; *Renmin Ribao* Apr. 7, 1983, 4.

[25] *Renmin Ribao*, Apr. 7, 1983, 4.

[26] On this generic implementation problem, see, for example, Merilee S. Grindle, "Policy Content and Context in Implementation," in Grindle, ed., *Politics and Policy Implementation in the Third World* (Princeton: Princeton University Press, 1980), 10.

[27] *Renmin Ribao* editorial, "Firmly Adhere to the Scientific and Correct Population Policy," Mar. 14, 1982; *Xinhua*, Mar. 13, 1982, in *FBIS*, Mar. 15, 1982, K4–6.

members outlined several "special considerations" for only-child families: free nursery and school enrollment, medical care, preference in job allocation for the child when it matures, extra housing space for urbanites, and in the rural areas, extra portions of private plot and preference in the allocation of land on which to build houses.[28] Penalties for noncompliance, however, are advocated but not specified, leaving it to the provinces and localities to generate appropriate regulations.

The result of this decentralized approach to family-planning regulations has been some divergence across localities with respect to the provisions in force. In implementing Shaanxi's family-planning regulations, for example, Vice-Governor Tan Weixu stated that the provincial levy for having an un-planned second child, "10 percent of the standard wages or labor income of both husband and wife," conformed with "the standard implemented by all provinces and municipalities." Looking at regulations for Tianjin, Shanghai, Shenyang, and Guizhou, as well as Shaanxi, we see that the 10 percent levy is indeed the common penalty. What varies is the length of time the penalty remains in force. Whereas couples in Tianjin with an unplanned second child would pay the levy for five years, Shanghai violators would pay for only three years. In Shenyang, however, the same couple would have their income docked for fourteen years.[29] In Hua Shan, commune cadres said the penalty was to apply for seven years, in accordance with regulations set by "higher authorities."[30]

Divergence in the regulations does not end at the provincial and munici-pal levels. Lower-level administrative units are responsible for drafting their own regulations. In Tianjin, for example, the family-planning decision of June 1, 1981, states: "In view of the great differences in economic conditions existing in our rural counties, every rural County People's Government may formulate its own stipulations concerning the length and amount of levies in accordance with local conditions and should report its stipulations to the municipal family planning office for the record."[31] This provision grants the five counties under municipal jurisdiction a great deal of autonomy in gener-ating specific regulations governing sanctions for unplanned births.

Why allow local autonomy in the enactment of family-planning regula-tions? Local generation of rules is preferable, it is argued, in order to take into account different economic levels, different types of agricultural arrange-ments, and different demographic characteristics across localities. This

[28] *Xinhua*, Sept. 25, 1980, in *FBIS*, Sept. 26, 1980, L1–4.

[29] Tianjin City Service, Apr. 29, 1981, in *FBIS*, May 8, 1981, R2–3; *Jiefang Ribao*, Aug. 10, 1981, 3, in *FBIS*, Sept. 2, 1981, O3–6; Shenyang Liaoning Provincial Service, Oct. 25, 1981, in *FBIS*, Oct. 28, 1981, S2–3; Guiyang, Guizhou Provincial Service, Nov. 13, 1981, in *FBIS*, Nov. 23, 1981, Q1–2; Xian, Shaanxi Provincial Service, May 3, 1981, in *FBIS*, May 4, 1981, T2–5.

[30] IF 1B-11 (82.10.14).

[31] Tianjin City Service, in *FBIS*, May 8, 1981, R3.

rationale for the voluntary delegation of authority to lower levels, however, masks the structural dilemma—the limited ability of higher levels to compel local administrators to adopt the regulations drafted above, a modified version of them, or any at all. The problem becomes increasingly acute toward the bottom of the administrative system (brigades and teams), for it is there that the rules must finally be enforced, and it is there that the costs of enforcement—material, political, and manpower costs—must be borne.

At the grass roots, teams and brigades must find the funds to provide paid pregnancy leave and "preferential treatments" for single-child households, pay cash bonuses to those who agree to undergo sterilization after having one child, and provide land for those who want to build homes. In addition, they must devise a mechanism to extract penalties from policy offenders, not just once, but for three, five, seven, or fourteen years. The source of funds to reward those who comply with the one-child policy is typically the collective welfare fund, which has been taxed by the new burden placed on it. In some places it has proved inadequate to meet the demands for rewards; thus, promised rewards never materialize.[32] Implementation of the responsibility system has exacerbated this problem, as well as the problem of enforcing penalties. In Guizhou "the necessity to make rewards and penalties stick" was termed by the vice-governor in November 1981 the "current main problem" in family-planning work.[33] Similarly, Jiangsu deputies to the Fourth Session of the Fifth National People's Congress noted that some rural areas "can neither afford to give awards nor do anything as a penalty."[34]

In short, because family-planning regulations are enforced through local funding with local personnel, higher levels cannot force them to be adopted, or if adopted, to be carried out. In Hua Shan commune, for example, there was resistance to the enforcement of economic penalties for those who had violated the birth plan. Only three of six brigades for which information is available had penalties in force in 1982, despite a January 1982 commune meeting encouraging the adoption of stiffer sanctions. Among the three, only one enforced the so-called standard penalty of a 10 percent deduction from the offending couple's combined income for seven years. The two other brigades both opted for a flat fee of 200 yuan for a second birth, and one brigade raised the levy to 300 yuan in the event of a third birth. Where such "flat fee" sanctions are enforced, peasants with rising incomes may increasingly come to view this payment as a good investment for long-term household security.

---

[32] Zhang Yongchen, Cao Jingchun, "Shengchan Zerenzhi yu Kongzhi Nongcun Renkou Zengzhang" (The Production Responsibility System and the Control of Rural Population Increase), *Renkou yu Jingji* (Population and Economics), 1982, no. 1: 13; Zhu Mian, "Nongye Shengchan Zerenzhi yu Nongcunde Jihua Shengyu Gongzuo" (The Agricultural Production Responsibility System and Rural Planned Birth Work), *Renkou Yanjiu*, 1982, no. 5:27.

[33] Guizhou Provincial Service, Nov. 13, 1981, in *FBIS*, Nov. 23, 1981, Q1.

[34] *Xinhua*, Dec. 8, 1981, in *FBIS*, Dec. 10, 1981, K1.

In Hua Shan a brigade women's leader noted that one woman pregnant outside the plan had resisted all efforts at persuasion and threats of a 200 yuan fine by saying that even if she had to pay 500 yuan, she would still have the child.[35]

When asked about the variable enforcement of economic sanctions, the commune family-planning cadre conceded that brigades could not be made to enforce the regulations advocated by the commune.[36] The importance of such sanctions is demonstrated by figures on third births in Hua Shan. Of the five cases of third births which were admitted to have occurred in 1981 and 1982, four were born in brigades that had no penalty in force.

The problems faced by county and commune-level cadres trying to enforce economic sanctions at the local level have been exacerbated by the enactment of structural reforms in the countryside. With the decision to slowly shift political and administrative responsibilities away from the commune to newly established *xiang* governments, the position of commune cadres was called into question and their authority was diminished, in anticipation of the impending structural change, which was scheduled to be completed by the end of 1984.[37] Moreover, in areas where communes were divided into multiple townships, new cadres had to be recruited to carry on all aspects of township work, including family planning. In one Hubei county, however, no county funds were available to pay the salaries of additional family-planning cadres, and the township refused to use collective funds for this purpose. As a result, thirty-one of the fifty-five townships established in early 1984 were still without family-planning cadres six months later.[38]

Thus, commune structural reforms—taken together with the effects of (1) calls for increased exercise of brigade and production team autonomy, (2) a reduction of the number of local-level cadres drawing collective support, and (3) a decrease in the amount of time cadres are willing to spend away from their "responsibility fields" (*zeren tian*) fulfilling administrative duties—are changing the political landscape in the countryside. With the influence of commune-level cadres on the wane, and the formal administrative structure in flux, brigades and teams are becoming increasingly important decisional units in the policy process, particularly when they retain substantial administrative autonomy, as in the case of population policy.

Administrative Structure and the Delivery System for Family-Planning Services
In 1973, Offices for Planned Birth were established at the state, provincial, municipal, and county levels. These offices were charged with overseeing the implementation of population policy, the focus of which was voluntary adop-

---

[35] IF 1C-4 (82.4.6); 1D-8 (82.5.16); 1F-13 (82.10.12); 1H-15 (82.11.4); IF 1J-10 (82.11.9).
[36] IF 1B-11 (82.10.14).
[37] *Renmin Ribao*, Nov. 23, 1983, 1.
[38] Interview File No. 17 (84.6.9), 4.

tion of birth control measures and reduction of family size. In the 1970s this administrative system, combined with a rural delivery system for contraceptive services and supplies, was effective in helping to bring down birthrates.

The system that was adequate for a voluntary family-planning program, however, has been strained by the increasing pressures to limit family size and meet birth quotas. Organizational weaknesses that could be tolerated under a voluntary program have posed severe impediments to implementation of the mandatory one-child-per-couple program. Moreover, new responsibilities have been placed on the administrative and technical cadres, making coordination of activity and high quality performance increasingly difficult at the grass-roots level.

Before discussing the weaknesses in this system, let us first examine more closely one example of how the system works. Hua Shan commune, in early 1982, had a population of approximately 30,600, with 7,100 households and 4,344 couples of childbearing age. Only two individuals at this level are directly involved in daily administration of family planning: the head of the Women's Federation branch, and a staff worker (*ganshi*) in charge of family planning, both of whom began their jobs in January 1981. Before that time the staff position did not exist.[39]

In addition to these cadres who directly administer population policy, the commune director and Party secretary also play a role. These leaders, particularly the local Party secretary, have broad oversight duties in all policy areas; population policy is no exception. Besides being accountable for the results of population-control efforts in the commune, they play an active role by attending meetings on family-planning work. Additionally, they allocate and manage locally generated funds targeted for population work.

Above the commune level is the Hong Shan District Office for Family Planning, the lowest-level office in the formal family-planning structure originating in Beijing. Before the creation of this office in 1979, the district government, the health bureau, and the office for women and children all jointly managed family-planning work. The district office has only 6 people to oversee an area with a population of 364,200, including more than 63,400 women of childbearing age (20–49 years). The staff positions include a director, a vice-director, staff workers for propaganda and professional work, and two staffers handling routine business. The office coordinates laterally with district government and Party officials and reports vertically to the Wuhan Municipal Family Planning Office.[40]

Below the commune level are brigade and team cadres. In Hua Shan brigade administrative committees generally consist of a director, three deputies, and one to four additional committee members. All brigade leaders

---

[39] IF 1A-7 (82.4.6).
[40] IF 1K-1 (82.12.1).

were male, as were the majority of deputies and committee members. However, each brigade committee has one deputy in charge of "women's work" (*funu gongzuo*) called the "brigade women's leader," as is customary. It is this group of women who do the bulk of the daily work in implementing population policy. In Hua Shan they average thirty-eight years of age, have a middle-school level of education, and have been on the job six years. The majority served as team women's leaders before being promoted to the brigade level.[41]

Besides the brigade women's leaders, brigade directors and branch Party secretaries, like their commune-level counterparts, attend meetings, submit reports, and assume general responsibility for fulfilling local population plans. Unlike their superiors, however, they sometimes become more actively involved in policy enforcement, as when they are called on to accompany brigade women's leaders to the homes of recalcitrant couples who do not wish to comply with the birth plan. These cadres also exercise substantial autonomy in the adoption and enforcement of family-planning regulations, and are accountable for brigade performance.

Finally, team-level cadres sit at the bottom of the family-planning administrative structure. Production teams in Hua Shan generally have three administrative cadres, one of whom is the team women's leader. On average, team women's leaders are slightly younger and slightly less well educated and have been in their jobs longer than brigade women's leaders.[42] They are responsible for enforcing the team plan in their own villages, among friends and neighbors with whom they work and live, and for coordinating activity with the brigade women's leader. The team leader plays a role similar to brigade cadres, with one major exception. He does not set the family-planning rules, as brigade cadres do. He does, however, retain substantial influence on the enforcement of them.

Another group of actors involved with population policy are the technical cadres at the commune and brigade levels. In 1982 there were fifty-four barefoot doctors spread among two commune clinics and brigade health stations. Of these, twenty-three had passed qualifying exams to achieve the rank of "country doctor." These individuals, in addition to providing medical services, train brigade and team women's leaders in the use of various birth control devices and offer technical guidance. It is still the women's leaders, however, who actually carry out the routine work of supplying contraceptives and monitoring pregnancies. Commune clinic personnel are responsible only for these technical medical services: (1) providing guidance as to the most appropriate form of birth control for those with special health considerations;

---

[41] These mean characteristics are based on information for all nineteen brigade women's leaders. IF 3A-1–8 (82.4.13).

[42] These mean characteristics are derived from information on team women's leaders in four brigades. IF 3B-14 (82.3.30); IF 1E-6 (82.5.23); IF 3C-7–9 (82.10.26); IF 3D-2–4 (82.11.4).

(2) performing contraceptive procedures; and (3) conducting semiannual check-ups for wearers of intrauterine devices.[43]

How do these personnel coordinate the implementation of population policy? The first task of family-planning cadres is to designate birth quotas. National birthrate targets are set annually by the state, which sets the standard for each province. Once provincial targets are set, lower administrative levels must establish quotas in line with these targets. In Hong Shan district the target is set by government and Party cadres, the district Women's Federation Head, and family-planning-office personnel. According to a district-level family-planning cadre, rather than utilizing a formula based solely on territorial population, such specific factors as the number of couples newly married but childless and the projected number of newlyweds are also considered when local targets are set. Ultimately, however, any specific calculations of this kind must be reduced to a set number of births per 1,000 population. In the case of Hua Shan, the 1982 birth quota was 13.5 per 1,000.[44]

At the brigade level, cadres translate the 13.5 per 1,000 formula into an actual allotment of births for the year. A brigade of 2,000, for example, would plan for 27 births in 1982. In five brigades for which such information is available, three brigade women's leaders further divide the quota to individual teams, while two do not. One cadre noted that rather than subdivide the brigade allotment to the team, she maintained a "unified brigade plan" for births. Because couples usually had a child soon after marriage, she went on, it was better to remain flexible throughout the brigade and allocate birth permits to newlyweds, no matter which team they were from.[45]

In addition to setting birth quotas, brigade cadres also issue birth permits. These permits are the sanction of legitimacy for newborns. In theory, these permits are issued to couples who are entitled to bear a child during that year. In Hua Shan cadres noted that couples who have been married longer and are still childless have first priority. However, birth permits are not issued until after the birth, to avoid having permits illegally transferred to another party. Thus, rather than formally designate who has priority, brigade women's leaders wait to see who becomes pregnant. It is assumed that newlyweds will want to have a child right away; despite national policy, nothing is done to discourage early pregnancy beyond the minimal verbal advocacy of late childbirth by brigade and commune cadres.[46]

A third duty of family-planning cadres is to coordinate the supply and distribution of birth control supplies. Unlike the "top to bottom" process of

---

[43] IF 4A-1–2 (82.4.9).

[44] IF 1K-10–11 (82.12.1); IF 1B-5 (82.10.14).

[45] IF 1E-8 (82.5.23); IF 1F-15 (82.10.12); IF 1G-8 (82.10.28); IF 1H-16 (82.11.14); IF 1J-11 (82.11.9).

[46] IF 1C-4 (82.4.6); IF 1F-14 (82.10.12); IF 1G-11 (82.10.28); IF 1J-11 (82.11.9).

allocating births, the supplying of contraceptives relies on a "bottom to top" reporting system. Brigade and team women's leaders go from door to door gathering information on needed supplies of contraceptives. Their reports are submitted to the commune cadre, who in turn submits a request to the district officer. On the basis of these local reports, annual plans prepared at the district, municipal, and provincial levels flow up the family-planning bureaucracy to Beijing. On the basis of national estimates for needed contraceptive supplies, the State Family Planning Commission coordinates with the State Pharmaceutical Bureau, which is responsible for setting production plans for pharmaceutical companies under its jurisdiction. Thus, in Wuhan municipality the local pharmaceutical company provides the family-planning office with supplies on a monthly schedule, and district-level cadres are responsible for collecting the monthly quota from designated pharmaceutical stations throughout the city. In turn, cadres from lower units must travel to the district office to pick up their monthly allotments and arrange for the distribution to individual households.[47]

The fourth responsibility of local family-planning cadres is to monitor implementation of the birth plan by regularly inspecting the conduct of work at lower levels. According to the commune Women's Federation Head, however, district personnel come to the commune twice a year for formal investigations, and commune family-planning cadres make scheduled visits to each of Hua Shan's nineteen brigades four times a year.[48] Below the commune level, formal, periodic investigations give way to sustained monitoring of village conditions by brigade and team women's leaders.

The fifth task of family-planning cadres is to visit localities or homes at the request of lower-level cadres. When faced with recalcitrant couples who cannot be persuaded to take "remedial measures" to terminate a pregnancy, team or brigade family-planning workers often call in more authoritative personages in their unit (i.e., team or brigade leaders, or Party branch secretaries), or higher-level family-planning cadres, to help persuade them to abort. In line with reports throughout the country, Hong Shan district cadres admit they encounter stiff resistance from those who have a strong aversion to the policy.[49] Nevertheless, couples unwilling to abort a pregnancy, especially a third pregnancy, find themselves under enormous lateral and vertical pressure from those who have complied with the policy and from cadres bent on enforcement.

The sixth job of family-planning cadres is to compile family-planning records. These records, which include data on births, deaths, single-child households, contraceptive methods, abortions, and even menstrual cycles,

[47] IF 1B-9–10 (82.10.14); IF 1K-3 (82.12.1).
[48] IF 1A-8 (82.4.6).
[49] IF 1K-11–12 (82.12.1).

are compiled from the team level up. This process of data compilation has two purposes: First, it enables local and higher authorities to monitor the progress of the population plan. Second, it is necessary to evaluate the performance of each unit against an array of goals (or quotas) set at the start of the year and to reward high achievers. For example, Hua Shan had five family-planning goals in 1982:

Goal	Value
Birthrate: 13.5 per 1,000	40%
"Only-child certificate" rate: 85% of all only-child couples	30%
Late marriage: 90% of marriages	10%
Rate of planned births: 90% of all births	10%
Utilization of birth control: 100% of couples of childbearing age	10%

If the commune achieved 100 percent of its targets, the Party secretary, commune director, and family-planning cadre each received a bonus of 20 yuan. For each target they missed, its value was deducted from this bonus. Brigade cadres who met their quotas each received 30 yuan.[50]

From this review of the multilevel organization for implementing the population program, several conclusions can be drawn. First, there is no question of the efficacy of the organization; penetrating to the team level, the structure is adequate both for the delivery of technical services and for administrative oversight. Second, administrative costs are held down by utilizing available nontechnical personnel to administer the birth plan and to monitor compliance. In the case of Hua Shan only one cadre was added, at state expense, to handle family-planning work. The remaining workers were already holding administrative posts, thus drawing their income from the collective. And third, by supplying birth control supplies directly to the home through this same organization, the state minimizes organizational complexity and competition at the local level and eliminates the need to mobilize couples to acquire contraceptives on their own.

The system also has critical weaknesses, however, which have become more apparent under the strain of increasingly ambitious goals for population control. First, although the co-optation of local cadres as family-planning workers minimizes administrative costs, the result is a specialized family-planning bureaucracy highly dependent on nonspecialized local personnel to enforce the population program. As with rural programs of the past, this one has been plagued by two disruptive responses from local cadres. The first is overzealousness on the part of those eager to overfulfill state plans. This phenomenon was especially common during the early stages of the one-child campaign, the most notorious example occurring in Fujian

[50] IF 1B-12–13 (82.10.14).

province, where it was charged that women were forcefully taken to health clinics for abortions and sterilizations.[51]

In Hong Shan district, too, it was clear that 1979 and 1980 had been periods of mobilization of those with two or more children to undergo sterilizations. Of the 63,400 couples of childbearing age in the district, approximately 10 percent had undergone sterilization procedures by 1982. According to a district family-planning cadre, 80 percent of this total occurred in 1979 alone, and most of these individuals already had two or three children.[52] In Hua Shan commune, data from several brigades also indicate that a disproportionately high number of sterilizations occurred in 1979 and again in 1983. In Yan Jiang brigade, for example, of the total of 170 sterilizations which had been performed by early 1982, 120 occurred in 1979 alone. Here the brigade women's leader proudly stated that she and all team women's leaders had undergone sterilizations to set a good example. Similarly, in Hong Guang brigade 113 out of 166 sterilizations performed by the end of 1983 occurred in 1979, or 68 percent of the total. In 1983, an additional 52 sterilizations occurred, with only one occurring in the intervening three years (1980–82). In Hua Shan and He Dong brigades more than half of the total number of sterilizations performed by the end of 1983 occurred in 1983 alone; in Hua Shan 99 out of 162 (61%) occurred in that year, and in He Dong 34 out of 48 (70%) occurred in 1983.[53] Abortion totals for the commune were also high in the early 1980s, with a ratio in 1980 of 68 abortions for each 100 births, 65 abortions for each 100 births in 1981, and 78 abortions for each 100 births in 1982.[54]

A series of reports out of Guangdong in 1981 on mobilizations for contraceptive surgery also illustrate the consequences of cadre zealousness. In Huiyang prefecture 102,400 operations were carried out in fifty days during May and June 1981, 27,000 in one month in Dongguan county alone.[55] In 1982 provincial leaders announced their intention to carry out two "shock attacks" during the year.[56] National leaders concede that "instances of compulsion" do occur, but that they are "impermissible."[57] As with the case of Guangdong's "shock attacks," however, it may be difficult to judge where persuasion ends and coercion begins.

The other response detrimental to the program has been the complete

[51] Leo A. Orleans, *China's Population Policies and Population Data: Review and Update* (Washington, D.C.: U.S. Government Printing Office, 1981), 18–19.

[52] IF 1K-10 (82.12.1).

[53] IF 1E-9 (82.5.23); Interview File No. 6 (84.3.10), 5, 12; Interview File No. 4 (84.3.3), 14.

[54] IF 1B-10 (82.10.14); Interview File No. 3 (84.2.28), 12.

[55] Guangdong Provincial Service, Aug. 28, 1981, in *FBIS*, Sept. 1, 1981, P5; *Xinhua*, Sept. 11, 1981, in *FBIS*, Sept. 16, 1981, P1.

[56] Guangdong Provincial Service, Feb. 27, 1982, in *FBIS*, Mar. 4, 1982, P5.

[57] See *Xinhua* report on Hua Guofeng's report to the Third Session of the Fifth National People's Congress, Sept. 7, 1980, in *FBIS*, Sept. 8, 1980, L10–11.

neglect of family-planning work. Rural cadres, sympathetic to the plight of labor-poor households and susceptible to the "feudal idea" of preferring male to female offspring, may nominally implement family-planning regulations but be blind to policy infractions.[58] In Hua Shan one brigade women's leader resignedly noted that "people want to have boys; what can we do?"[59] Moreover, some cadres find themselves in the awkward position of enforcing the one-child stricture on relatives or kinsmen in tight-knit or single-lineage villages, as well as exercising childbearing restraint at home.[60]

Higher authorities have limited options for securing the compliance of rural cadres. Threats of demotion, often used against urban cadres, are less potent in villages, where the benefits that accrue from leadership posts do not necessarily outweigh the costs. With respect to material benefits, new agricultural policies reduce the motivations for accepting administrative posts, which reduce the time available for household production but offer little remuneration. Another option, the offer of bonuses for plan fulfillment, may also be of limited utility. Weighing the value of a potential bonus against the time and effort that would have to be expended in order to receive it, local cadres may conclude that the time can be more profitably spent elsewhere.

Another factor affecting cadre enthusiasm and commitment is the lack of remuneration for their efforts.[61] Below the commune level, the bulk of family-planning work falls to brigade and team women's leaders, none of whom receive special compensation for their efforts. Wage scales set in earlier years for brigade women's leaders had not been adjusted by 1982 to account for the added responsibilities. Thus, in Hua Shan, for example, these women received salaries consistently lower than those of other male brigade committee members who hold a lower rank. In three brigades, salaries of brigade women's leaders were from 84 to 91 percent of the salaries of other deputy brigade leaders, and only 87 to 91 percent of the salaries of lower-ranking male administrative committee members.[62] At the team level women's leaders received no administrative salary, and thus were not monetarily compensated for their family-planning work.

[58] Yunnan Provincial Service, Jan. 6, 1980, in *FBIS*, Jan. 14, 1980, Q1; Guangdong Provincial Service, Sept. 5, 1981, in *FBIS*, Sept. 9, 1981, P2; Chen Guomo, "Nongcun Shixing Shengchan Zerenzhi Zemyang ba Jihua Shengyu Baijinqu" (How to Arrange Planned Parenthood Work in Villages Which Implement the Production Responsibility System), *Renkou yu Jingji*, 1982, no. 4: 39.

[59] IF 1F-14 (82.10.12).

[60] Press accounts are replete with examples of errant cadres at all levels who violated the policy or were persuaded to take contraceptive measures. *Guangming Ribao*, Sept. 7, 1979, in *FBIS*, Sept. 19, 1979, Q1–2; Hunan Provincial Service, Sept. 23, 1979, in *FBIS*, Sept. 26, 1979, P2–3; *Renmin Ribao*, Apr. 11, 1980, 4; *Zhongguo Nongmin Bao*, July 4, 1982, 3.

[61] Zhang and Cao (n. 32 above), 13; *Dazhong Ribao*, Sept. 29, 1981, in *FBIS*, Oct. 19, 1981, O1–2; Henan Provincial Service, Feb. 19, 1982, in *FBIS*, Feb. 22, 1982, P3–4.

[62] IF 5B-8 (82.3.30); IF 5E-8 (82.10.8); IF 5D-8 (82.5.11).

A third problem to emerge has been abuse of family-planning workers. Not only are these individuals subject to verbal abuse, there have been reports of violence against them.[63] The threat of violence, taken together with the other factors discussed above, is a powerful disincentive to actively pursue defiant couples.

A second major weakness in the organization is the system of reporting. Statistics are gathered and maintained by family-planning and Party cadres at each level of administration. Although higher cadres go to localities periodically to investigate, it is impossible to get independent verification of local records, short of a house-to-house survey. Thus, district cadres must accept the statistics provided by commune cadres who, in turn, have relied on the reports from brigade cadres. This system of in-house verification leaves a wide margin for tampering with figures to fulfill the local plan. Errors, intentional or accidental, may be passed up through the administrative network undetected. Equally important, higher cadres overseeing family planning have little or no incentive to seek out errors, with bonuses and commendations at stake. With no independent auditing mechanism, then, errors in the reporting system are likely to multiply.[64]

A related problem is the manipulation of registration records. In many localities, households have been denied registration for unplanned births. Additionally, reports have circulated concerning manipulation of the system by people who go to the city or another village to have a child and then return to their rural or urban homes.[65] There, cadres are told that the baby was born to relatives and is registered elsewhere. Because the child is actually not registered in either location, and because sympathetic cadres have no incentive to uncover the deception, it goes unreported.

Two additional weaknesses are found in the delivery system for family-planning services. The first is the quality of medical services available. In some localities, low-quality medical procedures have caused patient injuries.[66] Moreover, those who suffer such injuries are sometimes denied

[63] Tonghua County Family Planning Office, "Cong Yingebu Gongshe Lishugou Daduide Gongzuo Chengguo Tantao Jihua Shengyude Gongzuo Fangfa" (From the Work Achievements of Yingebu Commune's Lishugou Brigade Discuss the Work Methods of Planned Parenthood), *Renkouxue Kan* (Demography Journal), 1982, no. 2: 53; Zong Xin, Bai Jian, "Shilun Nongcun Shengchan Zerenzhi yu Jihua Shengyu" (Exploratory Discussion of the Rural Production Responsibility System and Planned Parenthood), *Renkouxue Kan*, 1982, no. 1: 10; *Hubei Ribao*, Apr. 12, 1982, 2; *Hubei Ribao*, Nov. 12, 1982, 2.

[64] Beginning in 1980, Chinese sources admitted that population statistics were among the types of data subject to falsification at the local level. See John Aird, "Recent Demographic Data from China: Problems and Prospects," in *China Under the Four Modernizations* (n. 3 above), 202–3.

[65] Changshan County Family Planning Office, "Lun Nongcun yi sheng Liangtai Yuling Fufu Ying Shixing Jiezha" (Rural Couples of Childbearing Age with Two Children Should Undergo Operations), *Zhejiang Renkou Tongxun* (Zhejiang Population Bulletin), 1983, no. 2: 34.

[66] Evidence on medical "accidents" is implied through press accounts that refer to the need to improve the quality of technical services and reduce the number of accidents. *Xinhua*, Jan. 10, 1983, in *FBIS*, Jan. 13, 1983, K15; *China Daily*, Jan. 4, 1983, 1.

medical treatment for them.[67] Also common is the improper installation of intrauterine devices, with some localities reporting IUD failure rates of as high as 20 percent of all wearers.[68] To improve the quality of medical services, some localities are offering bonuses to doctors who perform consistently without any "accidents."[69] Though the technique of offering bonuses is seen as a positive incentive to reduce errors and improve medical quality, it may also encourage medical personnel to perform the maximum number of procedures possible, even to the detriment of women's health. The second problem with the delivery system for family-planning services is the provision of contraceptive supplies. As with many other commodities, the supply and distribution system for contraceptives is flawed. Shortages afflict major cities like Beijing, as well as rural areas, disrupting family-planning efforts.[70]

To summarize, the organization for family planning suffers from administrative and technical weaknesses. The administrative weaknesses derive from the dependency of the system on local cadres, especially brigade and team cadres, to carry out family-planning work. Because these individuals are sympathetic to peasant desires for larger families, because the work is hard and the payoff small, and because there is no independent oversight of their performance, those who choose to ignore or loosen the policy run little risk in doing so. Technically, the system suffers from problems of supply and quality of service, further impeding progress toward the goal of one child per couple.

The Impact of the Agricultural Responsibility System

A fourth impediment to implementing the population program has been the policy environment. Agricultural reforms, and particularly the agricultural responsibility system (ARS), have posed major obstacles to family-planning work. In its most liberal form, the ARS allows households or individuals to contract for a specific production quota. Land is parceled out for use by a household, for example, which is responsible for supplying and utilizing the inputs necessary to reach the assigned quota. Households or individuals bear

---

[67] For example, Shaanxi's regulations on family planning include the stipulation that "medical units should improve the quality of surgery and ensure safety. They must provide treatment for accidents and illness caused by this surgery," Shaanxi Provincial Service, May 3, 1981, in *FBIS*, May 4, 1981, T5.

[68] Zhang Xinxia, "Qian Tan Yuling Funu Qingkuangde Xin Bianhua" (Discuss the New Changes in the Conditions of Childbearing Age Women), *Renkou yu Jingji*, 1982, no. 3: 47. In Hong Shan district, cadres estimate that about 20 percent of all IUD wearers have problems with it, such as slippage and expulsion; of these, it was said that "many" get pregnant. IF 1K-11 (82.12.1).

[69] *Jiefang Ribao*, Aug. 10, 1981, 3, in *FBIS*, Sept. 2, 1981, O5; Xin Dan, Peng Zhiliang, "Sichuan Sheng Peng Xian Shixing Jieyu Jishu Zerenzhide Jingyan" (The Experience of Sichuan Province's Peng County in Carrying Out a Birth Control Technical Responsibility System), *Renkou Yanjiu*, 1982, no. 6: 29–31.

[70] Beijing City Service, Aug. 24, 1981, in *FBIS*, Sept. 4, 1981, R1; Beijing Domestic Service, Feb. 25, 1981, in *FBIS*, Feb. 26, 1981, L2–3; Zong Xin, Bai Jian (n. 63 above), 13.

all responsibility for meeting quotas, and income is tied directly to their own production. In short, the basic accounting unit reverts to the household, with team or brigade units acting mainly as agents for the household in the marketing process.

This system of full responsibility (*da bao gan*) has been detrimental to the population plan in four ways. First, as was discussed above, division of land generally has been based on the amount of household labor power, with the result that labor-rich households receive more land, often boosting their incomes faster than their labor-poor neighbors can. This pattern of distribution sets a negative example for young couples already influenced by traditional values and family pressures.

Second, under *da bao gan*, brigade cadres receive parcels of land along with other peasants, and are assigned production quotas. Whereas they formerly drew administrative salaries from the collective, under this system all or a part of their income from the collective comes from cultivating their allotment of land. In three Hua Shan brigades, for example, two brigade leaders got land allotments 50 percent the size given to a full-time male laborer, and one got 30 percent of the allotment. Other brigade cadres also got 50 percent allotments, and team-level cadres got 50 percent or more.[71] As a result, cadres have tended to neglect administrative duties of all types, including family-planning work, preferring to busy themselves on their assigned plots of land in an effort to boost their income from production.[72]

Another effect of the ARS has been to diminish or deplete local welfare funds, from which benefits are paid to holders of one-child certificates. Under the old system, collective income was distributed after the team had siphoned off funds for the welfare fund and various expenses. Now individuals and households are entitled to receive directly all the income from their production, from which they must pay the agricultural tax and contribute to the welfare fund. As a result, the fund sometimes has less money than before, since the team no longer has the discretionary power to set the annual contribution levels. At the same time, a heavier burden has been placed on the fund to provide for the medical and educational costs and other rewards promised to single-child couples. The result, in some instances, has been depletion of the fund without providing all the promised rewards.[73] In Hua Shan, data from two brigades does demonstrate that collective welfare funds have diminished since 1979. In one brigade the fund was cut in half between 1979 and 1981, dipping from 12,000 to 6,000 yuan. In a second brigade, the 1981 welfare fund of 4,648 yuan was only 36 percent of the 1979 level of

---

[71] IF 6E-12 (82.10.8); IF 6G-10 (82.11.4); IF 6H-6 (82.11.9).

[72] Liaoning Provincial Service, Oct. 25, 1981, in *FBIS*, Oct. 28, 1981, S3; Zhu Mian (n. 32 above), 27, 29; Cui Fengyuan, "Guanyu Wo Guo Nongcun Funu Shengyu Lü Wenti" (On the Question of Our Country's Rural Women's Birth Rate), *Renkou yu Jingji*, 1982, no. 2:50.

[73] Zhang and Cao (n. 32 above), 13; Zhu Mian, 27.

12,974 yuan. In both cases, the dramatic drop occurred in 1980 when the responsibility system was introduced into the area.[74]

The responsibility system has also posed problems for the enforcement of penalties. Where the work-point system remains in effect, teams can deduct a percentage of work points earned from those who violate the policy. However, where this system has been abolished, as under *da bao gan*, taking deductions from salaries becomes more problematic, since income flows directly to the peasants.[75] Moreover, as peasants begin to utilize private supply and marketing cooperatives, now being encouraged by the state, local cadres will have no basis for determining household income beyond the value of contractually stipulated quotas. Since "within-quota" income will constitute an increasingly lower percentage of total household income, cadres who do persist in enforcement may find that such penalties fail to deter offenders.

In short, the responsibility system, by its very success, added to the difficulty of population-control work. It demonstrated the economic value inherent in labor power, further undermined the commitment of local cadres to family-planning work, and disrupted the system of rewards and penalties on which compliance largely depends. Thus, as the *da bao gan* system spread across China between 1980 and 1983 (see chapter 9), population growth rates rose to a peak of 14.55 per 1,000 in 1981 and remained high at 14.49 in 1982. Moreover, as the contract system stabilized in 1983 and emphasis was placed on extended contracts, single-child households who had not benefited under the initial land-division process were told that no further readjustments of landholding would be made. In Hua Shan one brigade women's leader conceded that the failure to provide extra allotments of land was a primary cause of the poor state of family-planning work in her village.[76]

TOWARD IMPROVING THE IMPLEMENTATION OF POPULATION POLICY

Faced with this intricate mix of implementation problems, the regime has attempted or proposed several concrete solutions: (1) the drafting of a family-planning law; (2) the provision of retirement insurance; (3) the enforcement of a "dual contract" system linking family planning with agricultural production; and (4) conducting family-planning propaganda and mobilization campaigns.

In an effort to enforce uniform national guidelines, a family-planning law

[74] This drop cannot be attributed to decreases in the overall solvency of the brigades. In both cases, total production value, net income, and per capita income all increased between 1979 and 1981. IF 7E-8–9 (82.10.12); IF 7G-8–9 (82.11.2).

[75] Zhang and Cao, 13; Zhang Huaiyu (n. 20 above), 37.

[76] Interview File No. 6 (84.3.10), 10, 15.

was drafted by the Family Planning Office of the State Council and submitted for discussion by the Commission on Legislative Affairs of the
Fifth National People's Congress. According to a report by Peng Zhen, vice-
chairman of the NPC Standing Committee, the draft went through several
revisions between June 1979 and September 1980, and was originally scheduled to be submitted for approval at the Third Session of the Fifth NPC in
September 1980. In explaining why it was not submitted, Peng noted that
some "unresolved problems" remained and that "the draft is not the result of
consensus of all quarters."[77]

A number of factors probably contributed to the failure to adopt a family-
planning law. First, according to a *Xinhua* report in July 1979 during the
Second Session of the Fifth NPC, the draft law included specific regulations
concerning the rewards to be given to single-child families in both urban and
rural settings. Such specificity would have required localities with widely
differing economic and demographic characteristics to adopt uniform regulations, even if these were inappropriate to local conditions.

Second, the imposition of a national law that specified the obligations of
localities to provide special incentives for single-child couples, while making
no provision for financial compensation, could hardly have been welcomed
by delegates to the NPC sessions. As early as 1980 a report from Guangdong
referred to "the impossibility of implementing the policy of rewards and
punishments due to a lack of funds."[78] Moreover, this issue had been discussed at an earlier October 1979 State Council meeting. According to Li
Xiuzhen, then deputy director of the State Council's Family Planning Leading Group, the vice-premiers present agreed that the State Council should
allot "some money" (*yibufen qian*) for the purpose of providing rewards to
single-child couples. The issue was not resolved, however, but held over for
"additional research."[79] In short, although it was easy to agree in principle
to state subsidization of the costs of a family-planning-incentive program, the
politics of budgetary allocation precluded any immediate solution.

Third, there continued to be numerous concerns about the imposition of a
one-child policy, if not outright opposition. Most prominent were concerns
about (1) an aging of the population (*laohua*), (2) a reduction in the size of the
labor force and the pool of eligible military recruits, and (3) the increasing
numbers of elderly people dependent on state welfare subsidies.[80] Although

[77] *FBIS*, Supplement No. 76, Sept. 23, 1980, 35.
[78] *FBIS*, May 20, 1980, P2.
[79] Li Xiuzhen, "Dangqian Jihua Shengyu Gongzuode Xingshi he Renwu" (The Current
Situation and Tasks in Family Planning Work), *Renkou Yanjiu*, 1980, no. 1:4.
[80] *Xinhua*, Dec. 22, 1979, in *FBIS*, Dec. 28, 1979, L8–9; *Xinhua*, Feb. 13, 1980, in *FBIS*, Feb.
15, 1980, L12–13; Chang Wen and Xin Hai, "Nongye Baochan dao Zu hou Jihua Shengyu
Gongzuo Ruhe Kaizhan—Sichuan Sheng Mianzhu Xian Jihua Shengyu Gongzuo Diaocha"
(How to Do Family Planning Work After Output Quotas Were Assigned to Groups in

such arguments were countered in the press, they continued to provide a concrete rationale for all who opposed the stringency of the one-child program. In the end, no family-planning law was passed; instead, the new constitution adopted in December 1982 contained a much milder provision making family planning an obligatory practice.[81]

Concern over the welfare of the elderly was especially serious among the rural population. For the present, however, the state has no remedy for the crucial problem of peasants' old-age security. It advocates the establishment of retirement pensions or "homes of respect for the aged," but the implementation and funding of these programs is left to the localities. Consequently, most rural villages do not have either retirement homes or pensions.[82] As of 1981 less than 1 percent of the rural elderly were covered by pensions or housed in retirement homes, and average income from pensions was only 10 to 15 yuan a month.[83] At that rate, pensions for the approximately 40 million elderly in the rural areas would cost the state about 5 billion yuan a year.

Proposed alternatives to direct state subsidies include the levying of a supplemental agricultural tax to provide for long-term social security needs,[84] or joint contributions from the state, collectives, and individuals, creating a fund to be administered by the family-planning departments or by a specially created organ.[85] Although plausible in theory, in practice such schemes would present a host of organizational, management, and distribution problems to those charged with implementation, and would require substantial outlays of state funds, above and beyond monies targeted for old-age support, to support the bureaucracy that would inevitably be created. Moreover, the establishment of a system of old-age support cannot be expected to bring immediate returns in terms of fewer rural births. Its reliability could only be proven after many years of uninterrupted payments to peasants, who in the meantime may be hedging their bets by having a second or third child.

Moreover, with the current emphasis on reducing peasants' financial burdens, including their contribution to such programs as family planning and

---

Agriculture—An Investigation of the Family Planning Work in Mianzhu County, Sichuan Province), in *Zhongguo Renkou Kexue Lunji* (Symposium of Chinese Population Science), edited by The Institute of Population Economics, Beijing College of Economics (Beijing: China Academic Publishers, 1981), 189.

[81] *Zhonghua Renmin Gongheguo Xianfa, 1982* (The Constitution of the People's Republic of China) (Beijing: People's Publishers, 1982), 27.

[82] *Zhongguo Baike Nianjian, 1982,* 646.

[83] *Zhongguo Baike Nianjian, 1981,* 545.

[84] Cheng Du (n. 8 above), 56.

[85] Zhou Shigang, "Dui Nongcun Du Sheng Zinu Jiating Shixing Laonian Shehui Baoxian Tantao" (An Inquiry into the Implementation of Old-Age Social Insurance in the Villages), *Renkou Yanjiu,* 1983, no. 5:55.

old-age insurance, it is unlikely that either the wide-scale establishment of state-local cooperative insurance programs or locally funded programs will occur in the near future. A circular issued by the Agricultural Research Office of the CPC Secretariat in November 1983 advocates the establishment of homes for the elderly (*jinglaoyuan*) only where local conditions permit, and only by decision of the local populace.[86] Left with the choice of contributing to the maintenance of retirement homes or supporting a second or third child, peasants will undoubtedly continue to prefer the economic potential of additional children to the state's promise of a stable welfare system in the future.

Neither a State Family Planning Law nor a comprehensive rural system of retirement support addresses the short-term problem of gaining the compliance of rural cadres and of couples of childbearing age. With the family-planning structure disrupted at the local level by the spread of household contracting in 1981 and 1982, China's leaders became increasingly vocal supporters of the "dual contract" (*shuang bao*) system, linking agricultural production quotas with family-planning quotas.[87] The first national publicity for such a system came in 1981, when *People's Daily* reported on the experience of an Anhui prefecture with the new system. Localities in Sichuan and Jilin also began experimenting with this approach in late 1980 and early 1981.[88]

The "dual contract" system requires that household or individual contracts for agricultural production include a clause for family planning, committing the signatory to uphold the local birth plan by not having an unplanned child. The contract also specifies the consequences for failing to comply, whether they be cash penalties, higher state quotas, or in more extreme cases, forfeiting one's right to contract land for production.[89] Typically, commune, brigade, and team cadres are also required to sign contracts with their superiors committing themselves to meet specified family-planning goals. Unlike peasants who forfeit part of their income if found in violation of the policy, however, cadres generally have at stake only bonuses, not their basic income.[90]

According to Hong Shan district family-planning officials, this system began to be implemented in 1982. Demonstrating the policy autonomy of lower units, however, Hua Shan officials were totally unfamiliar with the term

[86] *Zhongguo Nongmin Bao*, Nov. 17, 1983, 1.

[87] See, for example, the comments of Qian Xinzhong in *China Daily*, Jan. 4, 1983, 1, in *FBIS*, Jan. 5, 1983, K24.

[88] On Anhui, see *Renmin Ribao*, June 16, 1981; also, *Renmin Ribao*, Aug. 18, 1981, 4; Chen Guomo (n. 58 above), 39 and 38.

[89] For specific examples of contracts in force, see Zhu Mian, 29, and Zhang and Cao, 14–15 (n. 32 above); Chen Guomo, 39 and 38.

[90] IF 1K-6 (82.12.1).

shuang bao as late as October 1982.[91] Explaining this, district officials said that three communes in the district had taken the lead in implementing this program, with 90 percent of commune members operating under it. Of the remaining communes, eight had adopted the system, which covered 80 percent of their members. Only Hua Shan was said to have failed to adopt the system.

By June 1984, however, the same officials indicated that the provisions of the "dual contract" system, where implemented, were no different than the local regulations had been before the contracts were enforced. In other words, the contracts did not link production quotas or landholding to family planning. Instead, they simply specified the same rewards and penalties already in effect. Moreover, these officials noted that the "dual contract" system was also weakened because of failure to coordinate with legal departments to ensure that the family-planning contract was legally binding. As a result, it was judged an ineffective measure in that district.[92]

Thus, where the "dual contract" system was strictly enforced, the effect may have been to reduce substantially the incidence of unplanned births. However, adoption and enforcement of the "dual contract" system, like other regulations, also rested with local cadres, many of whom apparently chose not to adopt it or, if pushed from above to adopt it, not to enforce it. Cadres sympathetic to peasant concerns undoubtedly took little pleasure in inflicting higher state quotas on offending households, much less denying them the right to contract for "responsibility fields."

Although the overall effectiveness of the "dual contract" system is difficult to judge, it is clear that the 1982 population growth rate was only marginally lower than the 1981 rate, both of which were far in excess of national targets. By August 1982, participants in a family-planning work conference were well aware that work was suffering under the combined influence of "feudal" childbearing attitudes and agricultural reforms.[93] Thus, plans were made to launch a Family Planning Propaganda Month in early 1983 to popularize (*puji*) family-planning policy, birth control knowledge, physiology, hygiene, and eugenics.[94]

This meeting was followed in November by a Family Planning Propaganda Work Meeting, which outlined plans for the campaign extending from January 1, 1983, through Spring Festival in February. Armed with the alarming results of the July 1982 census,[95] Family Planning Commission director Qian Xinzhong made clear in his remarks to the meeting that the

[91] IF 1F-14 (82.10.12).

[92] Interview File No. 16 (84.6.6), 3.

[93] Beijing Domestic Service, Aug. 16, 1982, in *FBIS*, Aug. 24, 1982, K14.

[94] Peng Zhiliang, "Ba Jihua Shengyu Gongzuo Tigao dao yige Xin Shuiping" (Raise Family Planning Work to a New Level), *Renkou Yanjiu*, 1982, no. 6:22.

[95] *Renmin Ribao*, Oct. 28, 1982, 1, 4.

"propaganda" month would combine talk with action—that is, require couples of childbearing age with two or more children to undergo sterilization.[96] Faced with the intransigence of rural couples who violated the population policy by having a second child, and lacking any effective means of dealing with them, the state shifted its emphasis to the continuing problem of multiple births (*duotai*). With third or additional births still comprising 28 percent of all births in 1981 and 24 percent in 1982 despite the official policy of strict prohibition, it was determined that significant improvements could be made in the birth rate and population growth rate in 1983 by concentrating resources on this offending group.[97] Moreover, reducing the number of multiple births would make possible an increase in the number of second births which could be permitted under state plans.

Thus, Family Planning Propaganda Month was a peak mobilization period. According to a January 1983 *Xinhua* report, "1.37 million propaganda workers" and "over 138,000 medical workers" were trained in fourteen provinces, municipalities, and autonomous regions to carry out the month's activities, and in ten provinces approximately 226,000 sterilizations were performed between December 1982 and January 10, 1983. By the end of February "incomplete statistics" indicated that 8.86 million "birth control operations" had been performed nationally.[98] Although the total number of sterilizations performed nation wide during the campaign is unclear, its impact can be seen in statistics from Hubei province, where one million sterilizations occurred during 1983, constituting almost one-third of the cumulative provincial total of 3,020,000.[99] In Wuhan alone, one million yuan drawn from the municipal finance department was spent on this extraordinary effort, dwarfing the annual family-planning budget of 600,000 yuan.[100] Nevertheless, faced with a hostile rural population, an inability to eliminate the occurrence of third or more births, and a high incidence of abortions—costly in both human and economic terms—family-planning officials concluded that "persuading" all those with two or more children to undergo sterilization was the most effective and economical alternative

[96]Qian Xinzhong, "Nuli Kaichuang Jihua Shengyu Xuanchuan Jiaoyu Gongzuo Xin Jumian—Zai Chuanguo Jihua Shengyu Xuanchuan Gongzuo Huiyishangde Jianghua" (Make Great Efforts to Initiate a New Phase in Family Planning Propaganda and Education Work—Speech delivered at the National Family Planning Propaganda Work Conference), *Renkouxue Kan*, 1983, no. 1:9. See also, *Beijing Review*, 1983, no. 7 (Feb. 14): 23.

[97]For the 1981 figure on multiple births, see Qian Xinzhong, "Evolution of China's Population Policy," *Beijing Review*, 1984, no. 3 (Jan. 16): 19. For 1982, see Liang Jimin, Peng Zhiliang, "Quanmian Zhunquede Lijie he Zhixing Dangde Jihua Shengyu Fangzhen Zhengce" (Understand and Implement the Party's Family Planning Policies in an All-Round and Accurate Way), *Renkou Yanjiu*, 1984, no. 3:12.

[98]*FBIS*, Jan. 13, 1983, K13–14; *FBIS*, Mar. 3, 1983, K11.

[99]Interview File No. 14 (84.6.8), 8.

[100]Interview File No. 15 (84.6.7), 9–10.

available. Although this mobilizational technique was no panacea for the myriad problems of local-level implementation, the sustained emphasis on sterilization throughout 1983 and 1984 undoubtedly contributed to a reduction of the annual population growth rates to an estimated 11.54 per 1,000 in 1983 and 10.8 per 1,000 in 1984.[101]

CONCLUSIONS

In any look at China's efforts with population control in the rural areas, the capacity of the regime to enforce changed behavior patterns, and in this case, childbearing behavior patterns, should not be underestimated. Indeed, compared with the lack of connection between government and village throughout much of the world, Beijing's penetration to the household is awesome. In 1979, mobilization campaigns for "voluntary" sterilizations, abortions, and adoption of contraceptive measures were widespread, and the fine line between persuasion and coercion was crossed frequently.

Despite the growing desire of the central leadership to move away from this method of implementation, in 1979 mobilization was the only mechanism available for ensuring the rapid exposure of the rural population to birth control education and their adoption of birth control methods. Provincial-level regulations were being issued, but months would go by before rural localities actively began to enforce them. In addition, Party-directed mobilization was the only means by which to cut through the bureaucracy and compel propaganda, health, family-planning, pharmaceutical, and financial departments to cooperate in the provision of the requisite human and material resources. Local-level cadres, placed under familiar pressures, reacted in familiar ways, assuming that their performance would be judged first and foremost on the achievement of numerical quotas, and that this campaign, like others before it, would peak, wane, and end.

Instead, central leaders, still lacking the organization for administrative enforcement, upped the ante by formalizing the one-child policy in 1980 and firmly extending it to the rural areas. This time, however, Party cadres at all levels would themselves resist being the vehicle of implementation, because of (1) a lack of support for the policy; (2) an impatience with a policy viewed by many as a nuisance; (3) a tendency to view family planning as a women's issue, and thus, of low priority; and (4) a preoccupation with the ongoing agricultural reform process.

With rural Party discipline thus weakened, and with the penetration of

[101] *1984 Zhongguo Jingji Nianjian* (1984 Economic Yearbook of China) (Beijing: Economic Management Publishers, 1984), IV–60; State Statistical Bureau, "Communique on Fulfillment of China's 1984 Economic and Social Development Plan," *Beijing Review*, 1985, no. 12 (March 25): VIII.

the state family-planning bureaucracy dependent on these same personnel, central leaders were compelled to modify the content of population policy in the short term while building a reliable and professional family-planning organization over the long term. Thus, some peasant complaints were addressed by increasing the number of categories in which it was acceptable to have a second child. Simultaneously, however, all those with two or more children were to be persuaded to undergo sterilization. Although this mobilizational technique was at odds with the policy preferences of China's leadership, its use was preferable to program failure, an outcome all too conceivable from the vantage point of mid-1982. In addition, the mobilization campaign had the advantage, as always, of generating local-level compliance as a result of increased pressure from above. Moreover, with work teams composed of family-planning and medical personnel descending on rural villages, cadres were obliged to facilitate their work.

Thus, in 1983 China's population growth rate dropped to 11.54 per 1,000, the first significant drop since 1979. In the intervening years the growth rate had risen, despite monumental efforts to lower it. The failure to do so was partly the result of the demographic composition of the population, of course, as well as the passage of a new marriage law in 1981 that produced a spurt of new marriages that year. More fundamentally, however, it was the result of the gap between program goals and organizational capabilities, a gap which was greatly exacerbated by the ongoing rural reform process. In that environment, the effectiveness of both administrative methods and mobilizational techniques were impaired. Similarly, the decline in 1983's growth rate was due not only to the passing of the most acute phase of the demographic crisis, but also to the most effective use of the combined techniques of regulation and mobilization since the dramatic introduction of the one-child policy in 1979.

In light of the declining population growth rates in 1983 and 1984, should the implementation of population policy be viewed as a success? Despite these more recent achievements, China failed to achieve its targeted rates of population growth in the early 1980s, and the prospect for holding the population to 1.2 billion by the year 2000 is dimming. Using these specific criteria to evaluate performance, then, one is led to conclude that implementation of the one-child-per-couple policy has been less than successful. However, if one's standard of evaluation is not the attainment of specific numerical goals, but is rather the impact of China's population-control drive in increasing the number of one-child households and dramatically reducing the number of third or more births, providing increasingly reliable family-planning services at the grass roots, and sustaining an extensive family-planning propaganda effort geared toward altering traditional childbearing attitudes and preferences, then the process of policy implementation must be considered a success. An important caveat, however, is that these achievements have come at the cost of serious negative side effects—female infanticide, the use of coercion, and violence against family-planning cadres.

Ultimately, judgment of the success or failure of population control in China must be made in light of the enormity of the task at hand: attempting to restrict most couples of childbearing age to only one child, enforcing the policy for a time span of at least two decades, and making the attempt in a developing country with a rural population of eight hundred million. From this perspective, China's failure to attain exceedingly ambitious short-term goals appears less important than the substantial gains that have been made in depressing the rate of population growth to a level much lower than would otherwise be expected. Indeed, viewed against the backdrop of a rapidly changing rural environment, one in which the mechanisms of political and economic control were destabilized and local authority patterns disrupted, these "limited" achievements are phenomenal. In short, given the myriad of generic problems in enforcing family planning, and the specific obstacles to implementation in the Chinese context, a qualified success is perhaps the best that could be expected.

PART V

Education and Science Policy

ELEVEN

Restoring Key Secondary Schools in Post-Mao China: The Politics of Competition and Educational Quality

Stanley Rosen

At present our country lacks talented personnel and is backward culturally. This has already become a great obstacle to carrying out the four modernizations. We must quickly change this situation. In order to speed up the training of qualified personnel and raise the level of education as a whole, we must consider the need to concentrate forces and strengthen the key universities and secondary and primary schools so as to raise their level and the quality of teaching as quickly as possible.—Speech at the National Education Work Conference, April 22, 1978, by Deng Xiaoping.

Education in post-1949 China has been expected both to raise standards (quality) and to achieve popularization (quantity or equality). Throughout the Communist period, educational policy has changed, reflecting the interplay between these basic goals. If the balance had favored the raising of standards in the early 1960s, the so-called Cultural Revolution Decade (1966–1976) reversed these priorities mightily in favor of popularization. With the death of Mao Zedong in September 1976 and the purge of some of his radical associates a month later, China's new leadership began to institute far-reaching changes. Since radical control had been particularly pronounced in the field of education, this policy arena came in for particularly close scrutiny. By the mid-1970s, senior high education had been universalized in large cities like Beijing and Shanghai, tracking within the educational system had been virtually abandoned, and the role of examinations as a criterion for promotion to higher levels of schooling had been greatly restricted. In the new leadership's view, this had seriously compromised educational standards and set back economic growth.[1]

[1] For a discussion of the Cultural Revolution reforms in education, see Suzanne Pepper, "Education and Revolution: The 'Chinese Model' Revised," *Asian Survey* 18, no. 9 (September

Moderate leaders, led by Deng Xiaoping, were forceful advocates for a swing away from the goals of the Cultural Revolution Decade, a position that was welcomed by many segments of society, particularly by intellectuals. The moderates and their intellectual supporters sought to build a high-quality education system that would select and train the best students to provide the brainpower for the future modern China.

Fortuitously, there was an existing model that seemed to meet the need—the system of key schools. This system had a long and eventful history, and had been an important feature of secondary education in the days prior to the Cultural Revolution. During the Cultural Revolution the key-school system—which concentrated limited resources in a relatively small number of schools in order to cultivate outstanding students—was vehemently attacked, even though Mao had fathered these schools in a 1953 directive.[2]

When key schools were abolished during the Cultural Revolution, some of the most vitriolic invective was reserved for the "little treasure pagodas" at the top of the pyramid in each province. Ironically, precisely because the key-school system had been so vilified as symbolic of the unequal educational opportunities in pre–Cultural Revolution China, the support for the restoration of these schools would be the clearest signal that quality rather than quantity was essential. The decision to restore the key-school system was taken in 1977, and by early 1978 the most notorious of the treasure pagodas were being praised in print for their pre–Cultural Revolution achievements.[3] The study that follows is a clear example of how a policy drafted by a divided leadership, in an atmosphere dictating urgency, containing compromises that guarantee a broad base of political and popular support, will inevitably be transformed in the process of implementation as built-in policy contradictions lead to unforeseen costs and erode the initial base of support.

DETERMINING SUCCESSFUL IMPLEMENTATION

The resurrection of China's key schools was intended to produce a rapid restoration of educational quality. However, the original policy guidelines were drafted less than a year after Mao's death, at a time when the Chairman's legacy was far from settled. The publication of the "authoritative

---

1978): 847–90, and Jonathan Unger, *Education Under Mao: Class and Competition in Canton Schools, 1960–1980* (New York: Columbia University Press, 1982), 139–205.

[2] For a detailed discussion of the three stages in the development of key middle schools in post-1949 China, see *Zhongguo Jiaoyu Nianjian 1949–1981* (China Education Yearbook) (Beijing: Zhongguo Dabaike Quanshu Chubanshe, 1984), 167–70.

[3] As examples see *Beijing Review*, 1978, no. 5 (Feb. 3): 18–19; Joint Publications Research Service (*JPRS*), no. 72861 (Feb. 26, 1979): 31–43 (*Beijing Shifan Daxue Xuebao*, no. 5, Oct. 20, 1978); *Guangming Ribao*, Mar. 10, 1978, 4; *Liaoning Jiaoyu*, 1978, no. 4 (April): 24.

assessment" of Mao, the Cultural Revolution, and post-1949 Party history was still four years away. The universal repudiation of the Cultural Revolution reforms was still to come. At the apex of the political system was a leadership far from united over basic developmental strategy. To oversimplify somewhat, we can discern two major groups. On one side was Deng Xiaoping and his adherents, drawing their greatest strength from the "rehabilitated cadres"; on the other side was the then Party chairman and premier, Hua Guofeng, with a potent following among those who had benefited from the Cultural Revolution and those who remained loyal to many of Mao's egalitarian ideas. As early as May 1977 Deng had made clear his commitment to a system of quality education. Arguing that education was the key to achieving modernization, he pressed for the introduction of strict examinations and the concentration of outstanding students in key secondary schools and universities. He further called for the selection of the best talents in science and technology, who would have "conditions created for them to engage in research work with single-minded devotion."[4]

In contrast to Deng's stress on the training of a relatively small core of talented intellectuals isolated from society at large, Hua Guofeng's views explicitly criticized such an "elitist" orientation:

> The modernization of science and technology should not be regarded as a matter only for scientific and technological organizations, nor should it be left to a few people in research institutions or universities. The most powerful base and inexhaustible source of strength for the modernization of science and technology in our country are the masses of the people in their hundreds of millions who, fired with enthusiasm, are determined to . . . exert themselves in study and work.[5]

The earliest public statements on the restoration of the key-school system—including the Ministry of Education notice on the trial plan to run key schools—openly reflected the divergence between Hua and Deng over educational strategy. As the notice stated it, "We must conscientiously implement Chairman Mao's instruction to run key middle schools, fulfill wise leader Chairman Hua's militant call to truly make a success of the revolution in education and carry out Vice-Chairman Deng's directive of successfully running a number of key schools."[6] This divergence extended even to the choice of twenty schools to be run directly by the ministry. Alongside some of

[4] Deng Xiaoping, "Respect Knowledge, Respect Talent," Foreign Broadcast Information Service, Daily Report: China (hereafter *Daily Report*), July 8, 1983, K12–13 (Radio Zhengzhou, July 5).

[5] *Beijing Review*, 1978, no. 13 (Mar. 31): 6–14, at 9. For Deng's own speech at the opening ceremony of the conference, see *Beijing Review*, 1978, no. 12 (Mar. 24): 9–18.

[6] *Renmin Ribao* (People's Daily), Jan. 25, 1978, 1. For a translation of this and 33 other relevant articles, see Stanley Rosen, ed., "China's Keypoint School Controversy, 1978–1983," *Chinese Education* 17, no. 2 (Summer 1984).

the most academically famous pre–Cultural Revolution schools, whose fame had turned to notoriety through Cultural Revolution vilification, such as Jingshan School in Beijing and Nankai Middle School in Tianjin, one found schools linked to model units associated with radical Maoist educational reforms, such as the Dazhai School in Xiyang county, Shanxi, the Daqing Iron Man School in Heilongjiang and the "July 30" School Attached to the Main School of Jiangxi Communist Labor University.[7]

The chosen schools were responsible for *both* popularization and the raising of standards. The successful operation of key schools was to lead to the development and improvement of ordinary schools. Drafted during a period of leadership transition, before the views of Deng and the "reformers" in the Party had emerged victorious, the original key-school program was clearly a compromise, crippled by a fundamental contradiction. The more successful these schools might be in elevating educational quality, the further they would become removed from the ordinary schools. Was the goal to strive for the highest world-class standards in a limited number of schools as Deng had suggested in 1977? Or was it to promote close cooperation between key and ordinary schools so that the advances in the former could be popularized and rapidly brought to the latter, as Hua and his followers suggested? Moreover, how was one to judge a school's success in carrying out the "revolution in education"? The earliest guidelines unequivocally stated that "class struggle must be taken as the main course all the way from elementary schools up to colleges and universities" and that "first place must consistently be given to ideological remolding of the students and resistance to the erosion of bourgeois ideas," a far cry from the priorities of Deng and his followers.[8]

The triumph of Deng's conception of the revolution in education over Hua's is of course inseparable from Deng's political triumph. The gap in quality between the key and the ordinary schools—indeed, the gap within the key-school system—which had been quite narrow in 1978, has become very wide today. Rather than expanding the ranks of key schools, the number of anointed schools has been strikingly diminished. This shrinkage, in turn, has been a response to the harmful competitive logic that arose in the course of policy implementation. The combination of negative outcomes, as the price of competition became clear, and the shrinkage in the number of key schools has somewhat eroded popular and elite support for continued implementation.

The data presented in this extended case study preclude a definitive answer regarding the success of policy implementation. While the top schools *have* been restored to pride of place, and quality education—for some—has returned, the benefits of Deng's revolution in education have been spread

---

[7] Ibid.

[8] *Guangming Ribao* (Bright Daily), Jan. 13, 1978, 1.

rather thin. For example, while China has been investing heavily in "culti-vating talent" through the keypoint schools and the training of scholars abroad, the number of illiterates and semi-illiterates still stands at more than 235 million, almost one in four. Dropout and failure rates in ordinary pri-mary and secondary schools have reached what some consider alarming proportions. Policy readjustments have already begun.

Rather than unequivocally asserting the policy's success or failure, it is more useful to examine what this case study reveals about implementation in China and, more generally, about the Chinese political system. Three points, to be elaborated in the body of the chapter, stand out. First, as was already suggested, goal conflict is endemic in a political system committed to socialist norms of equity and economic development. A political leadership divided over these priorities, such as existed in China in 1977–1978 when the key-school policy directives were drawn up, makes "successful" policy imple-mentation much more difficult.

Second, Chinese policy makers have always reacted with greatest alacrity to what has been perceived as the "principal contradiction." Secondary con-tradictions have been pushed to one side until they have developed into crit-ical problems. In this manner, the key-school policy first formulated in 1977, and especially as later amplified by Deng and his associates, was more con-cerned with nullifying the effects of the reforms introduced by the radicals. This nullification stage was to be temporary. However, the policy measures introduced during that first stage have created their own constituencies and have produced unintended—albeit not necessarily unanticipated—side effects. For example, because promotion examinations had assumed minimal importance during the Cultural Revolution, with university entrance depen-dent more on subjective recommendations from political authorities, the re-stored system needed a recognized, objective indicator of educational quality to convince all participants that political favoritism had been completely excised. Hence, in this first stage, university promotion depended solely on entrance examination score. Currently, a debate has developed over whether the side effects have become so serious that they have assumed the character of a new principal contradiction. The outcome of this debate may decide the future of the key-school system.

Third, this case study reveals the weakness of the Center in controlling events at the basic levels and, indeed, the similar problems faced by lower administrative levels in controlling individual units such as schools—each level of authority is capable of considerable independent action. Policy deci-sions from the Ministry of Education do not always flow smoothly down to the provincial education bureaus, from which they descend to the municipal education bureaus, then down to the district (county) bureaus, and finally to the schools. There is great pressure (and flexibility) at every level to produce "results." And the pressure is manifested from the bottom up as well as from the top down. The masses have means by which to influence school officials, who have powerful levers with which to control their most promising students. Educational bureaus, faced with structural, personnel, and financial limitations, have difficulty in governing the activities of subordinate units. These weaknesses help account for the ready adoption of simplistic, easily measurable indicators—like promotion rate—to determine the compliance of subordinate units. Overworked, underfinanced, and information-starved leadership frequently measures the "progress" with indicators that create counterproductive behavior at every subordinate level.

In addition to the lack of resources necessary to assure compliance, the Center's own priorities have hindered its control over policy deviations. The Center's overriding concern with discovering and quickly developing the nation's most outstanding students, and the absence of an alternative measure of educational quality to replace promotion rate, has meant that counties or schools that *violate* Ministry of Education or provincial bureau guidelines, by single-mindedly maximizing promotion rates, are nonetheless likely to be praised. Those who follow guidelines from higher levels, but are not successful come examination time, are likely to suffer. Because deviations from policy are merely criticized, whereas sanctions are reserved for the unsuccessful, policy violations have been rational strategies for districts and schools. Below we will examine the stages of the implementation process so that we can more clearly see these processes at work.

IMPLEMENTATION STAGE 1, JANUARY 1978–SUMMER 1980: COMPETITION IN COMMAND

In deciding to restore the key schools the Chinese leadership confronted a series of questions. Most central was how to deal with the changes wrought by the Cultural Revolution. Should the pre–Cultural Revolution system be restored in toto, with the original key schools simply reinstated? Should the universities, which began recruiting on the basis of provincial examinations in December 1977 and national examinations in spring 1978, limit themselves only to current senior high graduates, thus denying graduates in the Cultural Revolution era the right to compete? Events of the previous ten years could not be ignored; the original key schools were not necessarily still the best schools, nor were current high school students the equal of those from the "golden age" of Chinese education, as some began referring to the period from 1961 to 1965.

To understand this decision, it is useful to examine briefly some of the effects of the Cultural Revolution. Until 1965, students upon graduation from junior high had a variety of options open to them, with only those determined to seek university entrance moving on to a regular senior high. For example, in 1965 only 9.1 percent of all secondary school students enrolled were in regular senior highs.[9] However, the Cultural Revolution reforms had greatly altered this structure. Promotion from junior to senior high became common, and in cities that had stressed universalization of senior high schooling, such promotion was nearly automatic. Whereas only 9.1 percent of all secondary school students had been in regular senior high in 1965, by 1977 the equivalent figure was 25.8 percent.

In addition, many of the quality secondary schools had been "raided" during the Cultural Revolution, with some of their best teachers and administrative personnel sent elsewhere, their funding greatly restricted, and their control over enrollments curtailed. This was particularly true of the "attached" middle schools, those run directly by universities. Before the Cultural Revolution these schools were akin to college preparatory schools, with many of their students moving directly to the attached university or to other outstanding colleges. During the years of the Cultural Revolution these university attachments were severed as control devolved to the district education bureaus. Those bureaus committed to the equalization of resources sought to build up weaker schools at the expense of stronger ones. According to informants, teacher transfers began in the late 1960s when universities were still closed and were unable to defend their erstwhile attached schools.[10]

With the defeat of the radical line in education, a wide variety of interested social forces looked expectantly to the Center for policies that would favor them. The pre–Cultural Revolution key schools wanted recognition of their earlier status, the return of their teachers, and proper funding to restore their educational quality. Ordinary schools, including those newly established, felt that policy should begin with current conditions. The Cultural Revolution had been a leveling process; thus, all should start equally and prove themselves on the traditional field of battle: the university entrance exams. And indeed there were many more schools clamoring for attention now; the 18,102 regular high schools of 1965 had mushroomed to the 192,152 schools of 1976.[11]

The universities wanted the return of their attached middle schools and, even more, a guarantee that the revival of the entrance examination system would allow them to improve their quality rapidly by choosing the best stu-

---

[9] Gu Mingyuan, "Lun Zhongdeng Jiaoyu de Renwu he Jiegou" (On the Tasks and Structure of Secondary Education), in *Beijing Shifan Daxue Xuebao* (Beijing Normal University Journal), 1982, no. 5 (Aug. 25): 7. For detailed statistics on enrollment breakdowns for students in various forms of secondary schooling, see Stanley Rosen, "New Directions in Secondary Education," in Ruth Hayhoe, ed., *Contemporary Chinese Education* (London: Croom Helm, 1984), 73.

[10] This paragraph is based on interviews with teachers from Beijing and Shanghai universities. Also see *Beijing Ribao* (Beijing Daily), Aug. 6, 1980, 1, and *Tianjin Ribao* (Tianjin Daily), December 2, 1978, 3, for complaints about this from key middle schools.

[11] *Zhongguo Baike Nianjian 1980*, 536.

dents in the country, wherever they might be discovered. Education districts, for their part, were reluctant to give up the increased influence the Cultural Revolution had given them. Students who had been deprived by the Cultural Revolution of an opportunity to further their schooling, and had engaged in individual study for up to ten years, wanted a second chance.

After approval by the State Council, the decision on key schools was announced by the Ministry of Education on January 11, 1978. Predictably, the policy offered something for everyone, with the obvious exception of those who felt that the Cultural Revolution reforms were being eroded. Deprived of powerful spokesmen at the Center, their resistance to the new emphasis on academic achievement began to surface at provincial education meetings, particularly after the university entrance exams of 1977. Their main objections included charges that the examination system favored urban over rural areas, intellectuals were favored over workers and peasants, and everything depended on one's examination marks. These complaints were dismissed either as "sour grapes" or, more ominously, as ravings by those still under the "pernicious influence of the 'gang of four.'"[12]

The new policy stressed the dual aims of "quality" and "fairness," in the sense that, for a limited time, all had the opportunity to succeed through a demonstration of quality. Thus, for the university entrance examinations of 1977 and 1978, the maximum age limit was extended to thirty, providing an opportunity to those who had lost out because of the Cultural Revolution. In 1979 the age limit was reduced to twenty-eight, with a preferred maximum age of twenty-five. In 1977 and 1978 only 20–30 percent of the college freshmen came directly from secondary schools, but it was made clear that the proportion would be increased until all students did so.

Secondary schools, in effect, were being given a few years to restore their quality. By the autumn of 1979 those older students who had not yet succeeded had lost their chance. The average age of the 67,000 students admitted to key universities that year was under twenty, with 71.79 percent of all university recruits coming directly from senior highs. In 1980 the majority of China's new university students were under the age of eighteen, with only 1 percent above the age of twenty-five.[13]

Quality and fairness extended to the secondary schools as well. To guarantee quality, 20 primary and secondary schools around the country were to be run directly by the Ministry of Education as national key schools. In addition, medium and large cities could run key schools both on an all-

[12] Summary of World Broadcasts (SWB), FE/5852/BII/14–15, June 30, 1978 (Guangzhou, June 23); SWB, FE/5852/BII/11–13, June 30, 1978 (Hofei, June 22). Also see Susan Shirk, "Educational Reform and Political Backlash: Recent Changes in Chinese Educational Policy," *Comparative Education Review* 23, no. 2 (June 1979): 183–217.

[13] *Zhongguo Baike Nianjian 1980* (China Encyclopedia Yearbook), 538, and Stanley Rosen, "Obstacles to Educational Reform in China," *Modern China* 8, no. 1 (January 1982): 23.

city basis and, more narrowly, within their individual districts and suburban counties. Each district was allowed to run 2 or 3 key middle schools, subject to local discretion. Provincial education bureaus were authorized to run key schools on an all-province basis and, more narrowly, within individual prefectures and counties. Prefectures and counties also were allowed to run their own key schools.[14] These overlapping administrative relationships had the potential to be a much more hierarchical system than that of the 1960s. With key schools at county, prefectural, municipal, provincial, and national levels, a much tighter rank order of school quality could be maintained. Moreover, so that no school would feel completely slighted, it was announced that ordinary schools should be run no differently from key schools, with those that were successful to be accepted gradually into the key-school fold.[15] By the end of 1979 there were 5,200 key middle schools in the country, containing 5,200,000 students, about 8.63 percent of all secondary school students.[16]

To enable them to restore educational quality quickly, key schools were provided a number of tangible benefits. In terms of funding, they had larger budgets, the main difference lying in increased allocations for building construction and equipment. One key school in North China reported an allocation of 50,000 yuan in 1978 and another 30,000 in 1979 for the purchase of new equipment. Ordinary schools in the same city were granted only about 5,000 yuan each annually for this same budgetary item. By late 1980, when the nation's best key schools were singled out for priority investment, provincial education bureaus began to list the specific benefits accorded these schools, including the allocation of the most qualified teachers; first priority in the allocation and improvement of a wide range of equipment and facilities; priority in the addition of an extra year of schooling; limitations on the number of classrooms and on classroom size; recruitment of students over a broader geographic area; the right to increase administrative, teaching, or laboring personnel; the employment of additional vice-principals; and a special subsidy each year for educational administrative expenses, which varied according to student-body size.[17]

The essence of the key-school system devised in 1977–1978 was competition. Students in senior highs were to compete with each other and with prior graduates for scarce university places. In 1977, 5.7 million candidates sat for the university entrance examinations, with the number increasing to 6 million in 1978 before it began to drop in 1979. Schools also were to compete. There were enough gradations between ordinary schools at the bottom and

[14] *Guangming Ribao*, Jan. 13 and 25, 1978, both on 1; Suzanne Pepper, "Chinese Education After Mao: Two Steps Forward, Two Steps Back and Begin Again?" *China Quarterly*, no. 31 (March 1980): 35.

[15] *Renmin Ribao*, Jan. 25, 1978, 1.

[16] *Zhongguo Baike Nianjian 1980*, 541.

[17] Rosen, "New Directions in Secondary Education."

national key schools at the top to keep administrators and teachers constantly alert to their ranking.

For educational decision makers at the top, the restoration of quality was paramount. They were well aware that the new system encouraged entrepreneurship and extreme measures. Even before the Cultural Revolution, competition between high schools to recruit promising students and increase their university promotion rates was common.[18] Under the new conditions, however, the possibilities for success seemed greater than ever. The results on the 1977 and 1978 college entrance exams fueled the optimism of the less favored. Even the nation's most renowned schools seemed only marginally better prepared than some second-rate schools. For example, in Number 2 Middle School in Guangzhou, long one of that city's top 3 schools, only 46 students met the university standard in the initial examination in December 1977. By 1979 the number of successful students had only increased to 59. Number 2 had achieved its high promotion rate in the 1960s by strictly controlling the number of junior high graduates allowed to proceed on to senior high. Typically, four graduating junior high classes would be halved to two beginning senior high classes. By keeping the student body limited to about 1,000 students, they could guarantee a high promotion rate. By May 1978, however, enrollment had ballooned to 3,700 students, half in senior high.[19] The situation was similar in other cities.

Fujian province, building on its pre–Cultural Revolution success, by early 1978 had already reestablished 189 key secondary schools, 16 at provincial level, 78 at prefectural and municipal levels, 94 at county level, and one provincial-level agricultural middle school, constituting 15.7 percent of the high schools in the province.[20] Using methods the province had perfected in the 1960s—including a total dedication to the preparation of students for the university entrance exam—Fujian greatly enhanced its national reputation in educational circles by achieving the nation's highest minimum passing score in 1978 and 1979.[21]

[18] For strategies adopted by secondary school administrators in Guangzhou before the Cultural Revolution, to increase their promotion rates, see Stanley Rosen, *Red Guard Factionalism and the Cultural Revolution in Guangzhou* (Boulder: Westview, 1982), chap. 1.

[19] Data from Number 2 Middle School are derived from the following sources: (1) interview conducted at the school by Ezra Vogel, June 1980; (2) interview conducted at the school by Susan Gruneberg, May 6, 1978; (3) interview conducted at the school by Mervyn Seldon, December 1978; (4) my own interview with a 1965 graduate of the school, conducted on July 11, 1976, in Hong Kong; (5) my own interview at the school, conducted in June 1984.

[20] *Zhongxue Jiaoyu Jingyan Xuanbian* (A Selection of Documents on the Educational Experiences of Middle Schools) (Beijing: Renmin Jiaoyu Chubanshe, 1980), 223–29.

[21] The provincial minimum passing score is a statement of the relationship between the provincial quota of college freshmen and the top scores achieved. If the quota for a province is 10,000, the 10,000 candidates with the highest scores will be allowed to pass, regardless of their absolute scores. The minimum passing score is therefore the lowest score achieved by the top

Emulating Fujian, other provinces stepped up their stress on exam preparation, particularly after a national newspaper praised Fujian's inspired use of the "key-school" formula, applying it to individual schools, to individual classrooms within schools, and even within the classroom itself, so that the brightest students would be given special tutoring to enable them "to achieve the level of their capabilities."[22] Local education magazines sought to justify the stress on promotion rates—and the measures used to achieve high rates—in terms of its relation to educational quality. Maintaining that those who objected to the "one-sided seeking after promotion rates" were parroting the "gang of four" line, they responded:

> The question of promotion rate is actually the question of educational quality. In general, schools with high educational quality will often have a high promotion rate. In this sense, schools with a high promotion rate who are sending qualified talent to the next level of schooling are making a contribution to the country. Not only is this not a crime, but it is meritorious. We should diligently raise our promotion rates. . . .
>
> . . . At present, some schools in order to raise the quality of their students adopt appropriate measures. For example, they divide classes on the basis of study achievements, they run a key class . . . strengthen the coaching of the top-notch students. . . . This is definitely not any "one-sided seeking after promotion rates," it is a positive step to speed up the cultivation of talent.[23]

Those provinces that had performed less well than was expected on the university entrance exams made future success a top priority. As it was stated in Guangdong:

> The university entrance exam is a test as to whether the quality of a middle school is high or low. We can see from the results on last year's (1978) exam that the achievement of our province is below what it should be. Moreover, it is far behind advanced provinces and municipalities. This reflects the great distance between our middle school work and the demands of the party and state . . . and the demands of the new situation to accelerate the construction of socialist modernization. Party committees at every level and all education workers should pay attention to this problem, acknowledge and not be satisfied with our backwardness, and drive ourselves to catch up.[24]

During the period 1978–1979 the university promotion rate seemed virtually the only statistic of concern to educators at the secondary school

---

10,000 candidates in the province. On this point and on the "Learning from Fujian" campaign, see Suzanne Pepper, *China's Universities: Post-Mao Enrollment Policies and Their Influence on Secondary Education* (Ann Arbor: University of Michigan Center for Chinese Studies, 1984), chap. 3.

[22] *Guangming Ribao*, Sept. 30, 1978; Pepper, *China's Universities*.

[23] *Liaoning Jiaoyu* (Liaoning Education), 1978, no. 12 (December): 11.

[24] *Guangdong Jiaoyu* (Guangdong Education), 1979, nos. 4–5 (April–May): 1.

level.[25] Each year, after the results of the university entrance exam, municipal education bureaus lavished public praise on successful schools and students at large ceremonies, at the same time inquiring—also in public—why
some of the designated key schools had not met expectations.[26] The pressure
on all schools to succeed was intense. Schools within provinces, municipalities, and counties were ranked in terms of their promotion rates, with education bureaus maintaining the pressure by conducting periodic investigations
and the unified testing of schools under their jurisdiction.

"Learn from Dajing"

If the less well endowed schools felt at times that they faced prohibitive odds
in their quest, there were a few spectacular instances in which the odds had
been overcome. Perhaps the most publicized example was Dajing Middle
School in Shanghai. Dajing had leaped in status from a *minban* (privately
run) school all the way to a municipal key school. A steady stream of visitors
paraded down the school's corridors to "learn from Dajing." Over the course
of a month and a half, six articles appeared in Shanghai's *Liberation Daily*
detailing the school's accomplishments.[27] *Shanghai Education* magazine ran a
special issue on the school, examining Dajing's achievements from every
conceivable angle over the course of nine feature articles, written by such
heavyweight organizations as the District Party Committee.[28] What had
Dajing done and why was it so praiseworthy?

Preparations to establish Dajing began in 1962 during the period of economic readjustment, under the auspices of some staff and workers involved
in spare-time education. Needless to say, the school was lacking in virtually
all aspects. Yet, in 1978, of the 166 graduates, 143 registered for the examinations for university, secondary specialist school, or workers' training school.
Of the 143 applicants, 90 met the required academic standard. In 1979, of
the 145 senior high graduates who applied to the same three types of school,
65 met the standard. These results were among the best in the district. In
1979, when middle schools restored their entrance exams, 163 of the 173 junior
high graduates were able to move on to senior highs (including 43 who en-
tered key senior highs). Dajing's examination results ranked first in the
district.[29]

[25] Education bureaus were also concerned with the juvenile delinquency rate and the employment rate of graduates of the schools under their control, but these seem to have been
secondary concerns.

[26] *Nanfang Ribao* (Southern Daily), Nov. 17, 1978, 3, and *Nanfang Ribao*, Dec. 5, 1978, 3.

[27] *Jiefang Ribao* (Liberation Daily), October 20, 21, 22, and 28, and Dec. 13, 1979; and *Wenhui
Bao* (Wenhui News), Oct. 21, 1979. The formal announcement of municipal key-school status
was made at a report meeting on October 20 and reported in *Jiefang Ribao*, Oct. 21, 1979, 1.

[28] *Shanghai Jiaoyu* (Shanghai Education), 1979, no. 10 (October): 2–22, 25; no. 11 (November): 2–9.

[29] *Shanghai Jiaoyu*, October 1979, 2.

Visitors to the school ranged from administrators at Shanghai's best schools to their counterparts at the worst schools. The principal of one of the city's most elite schools, the attached middle school of Fudan University, a man with thirty years of educational experience, rather shamefacedly told the press on leaving Dajing:

> Setting Dajing up as a model had an effect like a violent shock wave, it hit us like a lash; if a *minban* school can pull itself up, what shouldn't we keypoint schools be capable of? With regard to the more than 400 ordinary schools in the city, the shock is also not a small one, because I don't think there is a school in the city whose conditions are worse than those of Dajing. No one has an excuse not to do a good job of running their school.[30]

Although Dajing administrators frequently assured their disbelieving visitors that teachers were not given material rewards such as bonuses when promotion-rate targets were met, press reports and interviews indicate that this practice seems to have been common in many places. One interviewee from Guangzhou, at one of the best of the ordinary schools, related how he and a colleague had their salaries raised twice because they were successful in teaching the key-school graduating class. Other teachers were upset because these two never took part in political or other school activities and paid no attention to Party leadership. Indeed, this interviewee had been involved in the fledgling democracy movement in 1978–1979, but nonetheless was given a plaque by the school for his outstanding service to socialism. He currently writes articles for the dissident journal *China Spring*, published in New York.[31]

Developing Signs of Opposition

The post–Cultural Revolution emphasis on quality—as measured solely by results on the university entrance examinations—had its opponents from the start, but at first their objections were seldom publicized in the media. However, as the side effects of the policy became clear, opponents became vocal, and resistance surfaced from a wide variety of sources, including administrators at the most prominent key schools, the nouveau riche key schools, and ordinary schools. In addition, teachers and parents registered complaints, often by writing letters to local newspapers and magazines. By 1979–1980, three years of results on the exams had diluted the optimism many ordinary schools had felt in 1977–1978. A few schools had moved up in the rankings, some of the original key schools had moved down, but old pre–Cultural Revolution patterns of success were reappearing, particularly as local education bureaus began to concentrate resources on the most promising institutions.

---

[30] *Jiefang Ribao*, Oct. 28, 1979, 2.
[31] Interviews with C.Q.G., December 1982, and W.M., October 1982.

One teacher at one of the better ordinary schools in a Shanghai district described the changes from 1977 to 1979. In the first university entrance exams of 1977, over thirty students from her school had been successful, a source of pride to all at the school. However, the school was not even chosen as a district key school. Consequently, some of the best students transferred to the two or three newly restored key schools in the district, and the number of university successes dropped to just over twenty in 1978. In 1979 it went down to about ten. Each decline caused a perceptible drop in morale among teachers and students. Within the school, rigid streaming according to ability had also led to strains. For example, two of the ten graduating classes were designated "advanced classes," and all students with any hope of success were concentrated there. The brightest students in these classes were given special tuition outside of class. During the course of the term, students from less-favored classrooms were transferred up, if their work showed sufficient promise. Far from stimulating the teacher or the students left behind to do better, such measures had a depressing effect. One class of students went on a three-day strike to protest such mid-term class division, but to no avail.[32]

Some ordinary schools were more desperate than others. They sought to prevent their best junior middle graduates from applying to key senior highs, telling them: "If you remain at our school next semester for senior high, we'll put you in the key classroom; if you apply to a key school and don't make it, you won't be allowed in the key classroom." Others told those who applied elsewhere that they would not be welcomed back at all if they were unsuccessful.[33] By 1982 this problem had not abated. For example, at one school, said to be not atypical, the top ten junior middle graduates planned to register for provincial or municipal key schools as their first choice for senior high, with their current schools their second choice. The school leadership first sought to persuade them by telling them that if they made their present school their first choice, even if they did poorly on the unified promotion exam, they would be placed in the key classroom. When this did not work, they were told that only those who listed the school as their first choice would be accepted, so that if they failed to get into a key school, they would not be accepted back, even if their exam scores exceeded others who had made the school their first choice. Finally, they threatened to expel them, saying, "We only coach students applying for senior high at our school. If you persist in applying for a key school, beginning from this afternoon, it is not necessary for you to return to school to take part in exam preparation."[34] Apparently this exceeded the outer limits of permissible persuasion, and eventually, after complaints, the students were allowed to return to school.

[32] Ruth Hayhoe, "China's Keypoint Mentality" (unpublished paper), 4–5.
[33] *Nanfang Ribao*, May 24 and June 16, 1980, both on 1.
[34] *Yangcheng Wanbao* (Guangzhou Evening News), July 8, 1982, 1.

Ordinary schools had other means of resisting the inevitable shrinking of their opportunities. In some cities, it was reported, they were so successful in opposing the prescribed plan for transferring their best teachers to the key schools that the plan essentially had to be abandoned. The municipal education bureau simply assigned the best of each year's college graduates to teach in the key schools.[35]

One measure that especially disturbed parents and teachers was the early jettisoning of unpromising students. Those unlikely to succeed on the university exams had their graduation dates moved up by about four months. The remaining students would stay behind to prepare for the coming exams. In this way, schools would seek to rise above their neighbors in the annual rankings. Students who did not perceive the glory of early graduation were persuaded not to take the entrance exams. In more extreme cases, it was necessary to expel particularly recalcitrant students.[36] A related phenomenon existed for junior high graduates. Both key and ordinary schools would recruit many more junior high students than could be accommodated at the senior high level. After three years of junior high, they would "spit out" (*tuchu*) those who had not shown enough potential to be a promising candidate for university entrance. Some key schools were reported to have dropped 50 percent of their students in this manner.[37]

If the unsuccessful ordinary schools were engaged in a futile holding operation, even those who had "succeeded" by becoming key schools were wondering whether the benefits were worth the effort. For example, Beijing's Number 35 Middle School had always been only a little better than average, never attracting much attention. However, because of the equalization policies of the Cultural Revolution, traditionally strong schools in the district had declined in quality. This allowed the less prominent and visible Number 35 to improve relatively.[38] Number 35 generally had about 350 senior high graduates. In 1979, 150 were able to enter a university. Although the school had previously been rather undistinguished, people began to take notice. But the achievement required a herculean effort. The teaching staff put in 12-hour days, including Sundays. The teachers spent most of their time on the 30 percent of the students who were the cream of the crop; the middle group of students were essentially ignored; and the poorer students were disdained. Well in advance of the university entrance exams, all other activity had to stop. As the principal complained, now that Number 35 had reached the

[35] Pepper, *China's Universities*, 27–28.

[36] *Shanxi Jiaoyu* (Shanxi Education), 1979, no. 8 (August): 25; Joint Publications Research Service (hereafter *JPRS*), no. 77861 (Apr. 17, 1981): 40–41; *Liaoning Ribao* (Liaoning Daily), Jan. 5, 1981.

[37] Interview at the Ministry of Education, Aug. 17, 1982; *Nanfang Ribao*, Apr. 2, 1980, 2; *Wenhui Bao*, Dec. 23, 1982, 4; *Guangming Ribao*, Sept. 6, 1984, 2.

[38] Interview with C.Q., December 1982.

position of a district key school, it was necessary to exert a tremendous effort to maintain an acceptable promotion rate. Moreover, despite the school's new prominence, the higher levels had not provided it with any tangible benefits; only the burdens had been increased. Ultimately, he concluded, Number 35 simply did not have the staff, facilities, or quality of students to maintain the pace.[39]

Nor, ironically, were administrators at the most elite secondary schools happy with the policy. Unaccustomed to competition from second-rate schools, they argued that current policy was counterproductive. For example, the principal of the nationally prominent Jingshan School complained that there were now so many key schools that his school was being treated just like any other. If the purpose of key schools was the cultivation of talent, he argued, then there should be a small number of true key schools set up, with appropriate staff and funding. There should also be direct ties between key universities and middle schools, with the universities recruiting their students directly from their associated middle schools. By forcing the many key schools to compete each year as the university entrance exams arrive, very little real learning takes place during a student's last year of senior high.[40]

In the countryside, where there was generally only one key school for each county, success or failure on the university exams was, if anything, watched even more closely by the education bureau and the interested masses. One critical report in a local magazine described how, even before the Cultural Revolution, one county middle school had its senior high section closed down when "it was clipped bald" (tuile guangtou) on the entrance exams. In 1978, when the key school could not distinguish itself in a mathematics competition, the teachers did not dare appear on the streets for many days because of the negative reaction from the masses. But in 1979, when the school's university promotion rate was high, all was forgiven; the masses and the leadership were satisfied.[41]

The objections to the side effects stemming from such open competition were simultaneously being reflected in the national press and education magazines. The suggested solution was a sharpening of distinctions between schools and the creation of a fast track for the very best students, so that they could attend "pagoda summits" from primary school on through university. The best teachers, resources, and facilities would be allocated to these schools, and they would serve as a model for the other key schools, which in turn would be a model for ordinary schools.[42] This was to be a collaborative

[39] *Jiaoyu Yanjiu* (Educational Research), 1980, no. 8 (August): 36–38.
[40] Ibid., 33–35.
[41] *Shanxi Jiaoyu*, 1980, no. 5 (May): 7.
[42] *Guangming Ribao*, June 20, 1980, 2; *Renmin Jiaoyu* (People's Education), 1980, no. 7 (July): 3–5.

effort, with the ordinary schools actively supporting the enrollment of their best students in the key schools.[43]

In fact, this fast track was already being created. In Shanghai, for example, virtually all the municipal key schools and even some of the district key schools had "linkage" (*guagou*) relationships with a key university. Jiaotong University by May 1980 had set up linkages with sixteen of the best key schools in Shanghai.[44] Fudan University, East China Normal University, and Shanghai Normal Institute had special ties to their own attached schools, all of which were municipal key schools, in addition to linkages to other schools in the city. The best universities, such as Fudan and East China Normal, also ran primary schools on campus.

Clearly, in its implementation phase, the policy had deviated rather far from the spirit of the original directive. Cooperation between schools had vanished, as had "ideological remolding." In part, of course, this reflected the stress on quality education in each individual school and the competitive atmosphere between schools, with success ratified by the annual examination results. But there were other reasons as well for the policy deviations. To begin with, the Ministry of Education, whose responsibility it was to monitor the policy's implementation, viewed educational reform in a Dengist light—that is, the raising of standards was paramount. Given the legacy of the Cultural Revolution, the restoration of educational quality was expected to take time. Back in May 1977 Deng had spoken of "bringing about a small change in the schools in five years, a medium change in ten years, and a major change in fifteen to twenty years."[45] With such an extended time frame, short-term deviations could be tolerated so long as the major goal of the policy was being accomplished. Policy implementation had implicitly been divided into stages, with an open competition based on unambiguous, easily measurable indicators considered the surest method of stimulating the drive for educational quality. Once students and educators had reoriented themselves toward the pursuit of excellence, the side effects that had appeared in the initial stage could be addressed subsequently.

Second, the Ministry of Education (in June 1985 the Ministry was super-

[43] *Nanfang Ribao*, June 16, 1980, 1; *JPRS*, no. 76052, July 16, 1980 (Guangzhou radio, June 15).

[44] *Jiefang Ribao*, June 9, 1980, 1; *Shehui Kexue* (Social Sciences) (Shanghai), 1980, no. 5 (October): 37. Beginning in 1984 the country's best universities began to recruit a small number of their students by recommendation combined with examination, further diminishing the chances of those not in key schools. For example, students at the twenty-six municipally run key high schools in Shanghai could be recruited in this manner. In 1985, the Ministry of Education permitted forty-three of the nation's best universities to recruit some students by recommendation alone (*baosong*). See *China Trip Notes*, Sept. 1985; *Jiaoyu Wenzhai* (Education Digest), May 20, 1985, 1, and March 20, 1985, 2; *Heilongjiang Gaojiao Yanjiu* (Heilongjiang Higher Education Research), 1985, no. 1, 144.

[45] *Daily Report*, July 8, 1983, K13 (Radio Zhengzhou, July 5).

seded by the State Education Commission) is limited in its ability to control recalcitrant lower levels of administration. While setting the basic policy guidelines, it is the provincial, municipal, district, and county bureaus that must enforce the guidelines. Part of the problem is financial. According to 1979 estimates, the contribution to education made by local governments, brigades, enterprises, and so forth was 28 percent of the total cost, with another 8 percent contributed by families. Central government expenditure on education as a percentage of its total expenditure was only 6.6 percent, whereas it was 15.1 percent in other less developed countries, and 15.6 percent in developed countries.[46] Although recent increases in educational spending had pushed this figure up to 10 percent by 1982, it is clear that much of the cost of education, particularly at the basic levels, is dependent on local authorities. Moreover, with over 90 percent of ministry funding going to recurrent expenses, such as teacher salaries (which are set by district education bureaus), the Ministry of Education has relatively few convenient financial levers with which to discipline districts or individual schools.

Compounding this problem, beginning in 1980 a formal revenue-sharing system was introduced, which gives greater autonomy to provincial governments. Each province is allowed to retain a fixed proportion of the revenues it collects, which will determine its total expenditure. Within this total the provincial government is given more freedom than hitherto in choosing the composition of its expenditure. Provinces have generally extended these revenue-sharing principles down to the county level.[47]

The impact of this change in the state finance system on ministry control over key-school policy was immediate. As early as August 1979 the ministry announced that administration of the twenty national key primary and secondary schools would devolve to the local levels.[48] According to some informants, financial considerations were not the only reason for this downward transfer of authority. The ministry had relied on the support of local education authorities to administer these schools. However, provincial, municipal, and district bureaus were more concerned with the schools directly under their control. In terms of recruitment of the best local students, transfer of outstanding teachers and administrators, increased funding, and so forth, local bureaus tended to ignore the national key schools, causing them to become isolated from the local educational structure. The only solution was to return them to local control.[49]

[46] World Bank, *China: Socialist Economic Development*, vol. 3, 183 (Washington, D.C., 1983).

[47] Ibid., vol. 1, 152. The impact of these revenue-sharing principles is well described in a series of articles in *Jiaoyu Jingjixue Lunwenji* (A Collection of Articles on the Economics of Education) (Beijing: Jiaoyu Kexue Chubanshe, 1982).

[48] *Zhongguo Baike Nianjian 1980*, 541.

[49] Interview with C.Q., December 1982, and interview at the Ministry of Education, Aug. 17, 1982.

Not only do deviations in the implementation process reflect central weakness, but lower-level educational bureaus also appear to have serious constraints on their ability to enforce guidelines. A revealing 1979 investigative report of educational administration in Beijing pointed out some of the difficulties. District and county education bureaus contain "too many people, too many administrative offices, and too many leading cadres." One district bureau had twenty-nine administrative offices and over 220 cadres, with over 40 cadres at the level of deputy section chief or above. This overloaded bureaucracy was consumed with paperwork and meetings. Even the bureau's Party Standing Committee had as many as eleven members. In spite of so much manpower, responsibilities were not well defined. This was compounded by the fact that education bureaus gradually had taken on a wide variety of other tasks, such as youth work, women's work, family planning, militia work, and so forth. In fact, 70–80 percent of the cadres in the bureau had their primary responsibilities in these other issue areas. Overlapping and ambiguous responsibilities also impeded the relationship between municipal, district, and county bureaus. Furthermore, the distinction between Party and government functions was so hazy that the Party Committee often had to make even the most trivial decisions. Finally, the investigation report complained, the municipal education bureau lacked the authority to compel district and county bureaus to take action. Their opinions were often used solely for "reference."[50] In short, too many people, too much administrative overlap, and too little sustained attention permitted a situation to arise in which unbridled competition subverted the initial implementation of policy. In the context of these local constraints on enforcement, one can also better understand why hard-pressed bureaucrats would welcome such straightforward indicators of success as promotion rates.

IMPLEMENTATION STAGE 2, SUMMER 1980–FALL 1981: RATIFYING THE RESULTS OF COMPETITION

In a series of meetings and decisions from June to October 1980 the implementation of the key-school policy moved into its second stage. Most notable, in a formal sense, were two State Council decisions in October. One decision called for a drastic reduction in the number of keypoints and an increase in their quality. The second decision called for a drastic reduction in the number of regular secondary schools and a gradual increase in the number of specialist, technical, and vocational schools. The impact of each of these decisions will be discussed below. In essence, however, these State Council decisions merely ratified and further legitimized processes already

---

[50] *Beijing Ribao* (Beijing Daily), Apr. 15, 1979, 2. For similar complaints see *Xinwen Zhanxian* (Journalism Front), no. 1, 1978, 71, and *Nanfang Ribao*, Dec. 5, 1978, 3.

under way. As early as June the Central Secretariat had met and agreed to concentrate resources in a smaller number of excellent primary and secondary schools.[51]

An important step in this process was the convening of the national work conference on key secondary schools, which was held from July 23 to August 4. The meeting was called to sum up experiences in running key schools since 1978 and to suggest guidelines for the future. Covered extensively in the press, the conclusions of the meeting stressed the importance of developing first those schools which had the best conditions. The best of the key schools should be aided first, with others being helped as resources permitted. Leading educational officials chided those engaging in the excessive measures fostered by open competition. Specifically, the common practices of ranking schools on the basis of promotion rates; of assigning promotion rates to provinces, prefectures, cities, and schools; of rewarding schools and teachers on the basis of promotion rates; of neglecting physical and moral education; of ignoring or discriminating against the majority of students—all came under criticism.[52]

The response to this meeting was immediate. Local newspapers began to report, in substantial detail, the achievements of their city's best key schools, particularly their successes on the university entrance exams.[53] Complaints from administrators at the nation's elite schools also received substantial coverage. For example, two days after the conference closed, an article at the top of page one of *Beijing Daily* lamented the continued existence of as many as 115 key middle and primary schools in the city, with resources among them spread so thin that none were really "key." Producing extensive data to show that the most outstanding of the pre–Cultural Revolution key schools had not been allowed to recover their preeminence, the article called for the diversion of resources in the form of teachers, funding, equipment, and capital construction so that within three to five years the city could once again boast of housing several of the nation's finest schools.[54]

On October 14 the Ministry of Education issued a six-point directive offering the country's best schools some of what they demanded.[55] The directive called for a concentration of resources in the 700 or so best key middle schools in China, citing the need for better leadership, a stronger

[51] *Shandong Jiaoyu* (Shandong Education), 1982, no. 3 (March): 2.

[52] Among the many reports of this conference, see *Guangming Ribao*, Aug. 2, 5, and 31, 1980, all on 1; *Renmin Jiaoyu*, 1980, no. 9 (September): 3–9; *Jiaoyu Yanjiu*, 1980, no. 5 (October): 16–25; *A Selection of Documents* (n. 20 above), 13–41.

[53] See, for example, these vital statistics for Guangzhou's best three schools in *Yangcheng Wanbao*, Aug. 12, 1980, 1; and details on the province's most successful school in *Nanfang Ribao*, Aug. 6, 1980, 1; and *Yangcheng Wanbao*, Aug. 16, 1980, 1.

[54] *Beijing Ribao*, Aug. 6, 1980, 1.

[55] The directive appears in *Zhongguo Baike Nianjian 1981*, 476.

teaching staff, enhanced ideological education, an additional year of schooling, a limitation on the number and size of classes, and suitable laboratory and library materials for these schools. Increased funding was to be provided.

Over the next several months, provincial education magazines and local newspapers reported on the implementation of this directive and the spirit of the July-August conference that had preceded it.[56] Each province chose the schools to be aided first. In Tianjin this decision had already been made by late July. Twenty-seven of the 66 key middle schools were to be given priority, with the others aided as conditions permitted; 5 of the favored 27 were to be given particularly advantageous treatment as municipally run key schools, allowing them to recruit city wide.[57] Fujian reduced the number of key middle schools from 188 to 87 and key primary schools from 300 to 112. Moreover, top priority was to be given to the best 32 middle and primary schools immediately.[58] In Shanxi only 30 of the 473 key schools were to be given special help, with 23 to be jointly administered by provincial, prefectural, and municipal authority.[59]

The gaps between the ordinary schools, the good schools, the better schools, and the best schools were certain to increase under these conditions. This was further guaranteed by the introduction in the autumn of 1980 of an additional year of senior high schooling for the best schools. In Liaoning province, for example, the best schools were to introduce the three-year program in the autumn, with the rest of the key schools expected to follow suit within the next two years, and the ordinary high schools to join in by 1985.[60] In Guangzhou, Guangya Middle School had already reverted to the three-year program in 1979, with 3 more schools following in 1980 and an additional 10 in 1981.[61]

If administrators and students at the less favored schools were alarmed by these developments, they had little time to reflect. On October 17 the State Council approved a report from the Ministry of Education and the State General Labor Bureau calling for a reform in China's secondary school

[56] See, inter alia, *Yunnan Jiaoyu* (Yunnan Education), 1980, no. 12 (December): 4–5; *Liaoning Jiaoyu*, 1980, no. 10 (October): 2–6; *Zhejiang Jiaoyu* (Zhejiang Education), 1980, no. 10 (October): 1–4; *Liaoning Ribao*, Jan. 2, 1981, 1; *Zhejiang Jiaoyu*, 1981, no. 1 (January): 5–10; *Hubei Jiaoyu* (Hubei Education), 1981, no. 1 (January), 2–5; *Fujian Jiaoyu* (Fujian Education), 1981, no. 1 (January): 2; *Guangdong Jiaoyu*, 1981, no. 2 (February): 2–6; *Shanxi Jiaoyu*, 1980, no. 10 (October): 5–7; *Shanghai Jiaoyu*, 1980, no. 9 (September): 2–3; *Beijing Jiaoyu* (Beijing Education), 1980, no. 12 (December): 2–6.

[57] *Guangming Ribao*, June 21, 1980, 2; *Wenhui Bao*, Oct. 5, 1980, 2.

[58] *Fujian Jiaoyu*, 1981, no. 1 (January): 2.

[59] *Shanxi Jiaoyu*, 1980, no. 8 (August): 4.

[60] SWB, July 10, 1980, FE/6467/BII/15.

[61] *Guangzhou Ribao* (Guangzhou Daily), Nov. 25, 1981, 1.

structure.[62] As early as 1978 the Party leadership had stressed the development of vocational and technical education as part of a general restructuring of secondary education.[63] But progress had been slow. In 1965, 31 percent of all high school students had been in agricultural and vocational schools; in 1980 only 0.8 percent were in such schools.[64] The number of regular high schools had been declining since 1977, but they were not being replaced by alternative forms of schooling. This new decision merely formalized a process already under way. For example, Henan province had 6,566 regular senior highs in 1976; by the end of 1981, only 1,703 such schools were left. From 1977 to 1981 the number of senior high students dropped from 1,270,700 to 606,600. Still, in spite of much negative publicity and various provincial directives, most students continued their efforts to crowd into the diminishing places in senior high. In 1981 there were only 10,000 students in vocational schools, with specialist and technical schools faring even worse.[65] Nationally, the situation was no better. In 1977 there had been 18 million students in regular senior highs (26.3 percent of all secondary school students); by 1983 the number had dropped to just over 6 million (13.5 percent of all secondary school students). Students were simply coming out of junior highs with nowhere to go.[66]

In retrospect, the reforms of autumn 1980 solved some of the problems perceived by Chinese educational authorities; it exacerbated others. While removing some participants from the competition by closing down more schools, it raised the stakes for those still in contention. The sharper hierarchical structure—now legitimized by the open ranking of the schools in a province or municipality—enabled the best schools to resist more effectively the pressure their constituents (i.e., parents and education bureaus) placed on them to produce university students. Less fortunate were schools below the top level, such as the district keypoints and the best of the ordinary schools. They did not have university links and generally were not allowed to expand to a three-year senior high program immediately. They remained vulnerable to pressure from education bureaus because if they did not meet

[62] The text of the report can be found in *Zhonghua Renmin Gongheguo Guowuyuan Gongbao* (Communiques of the State Council of the People's Republic of China), no. 16 (Dec. 1, 1980): 491–96. Excerpts are in *Zhongguo Baike Nianjian 1981*, 467–68.

[63] *Guangming Ribao*, Mar. 30, 1982, 2. See *JPRS*, no. 74165 (Sept. 12, 1979): 78–82 (*Guangming Ribao*, July 19) for a typical report.

[64] "On the Tasks and Structure of Secondary Education" (n. 9 above), and *Zhongguo Baike Nianjian 1981*, 471.

[65] *Jiaoyu Yanjiu*, 1982, no. 12 (December): 7. Some provinces were doing better in transforming their secondary school structure. Liaoning, for example, had developed enough alternatives so that by 1981 there were 2,630,000 students in various kinds of secondary schools, whereas the 1977 figure was 3,760,000. See *Liaoning Jiaoyu*, 1981, no. 12 (December): 2.

[66] Stanley Rosen, "Recentralization, Decentralization and Rationalization: Deng Xiaoping's Bifurcated Educational Policy," *Modern China* 11, no. 3 (July 1985): 301–346.

their quota of university enrollees they could lose their key status or, for the ordinary schools, be transformed into vocational schools, have their senior high sections lopped off, or even be closed down completely. They were under pressure from parents who might transfer their children to another school if they felt such a transfer would improve the likelihood of success. Thus, the large majority of secondary schools remained obsessed with promotion rate competition, streaming was still common, and unpromising students were still ignored.

These schools were engaged in a form of "musical chairs." After the decisions of October, the deputy chief of the Fujian Provincial Education Bureau announced just how many chairs would be removed:

> There are 951 regular middle schools in the province. According to the future developmental plan for middle schools, for about 80,000 students enrolled each year, only 400 schools will be needed. The other some 500 schools will be methodically converted to vocational and technical schools. In our modification of middle schools, the first consideration is how to concentrate manpower, resources, and finances to succeed in key schools in the province, in the prefectures and in the municipalities.[67]

Reports in the press indicate that most schools tried to resist such conversions.

Predictably, widespread student demoralization resulted. By the second year of junior high, before the age of fourteen, students could perceive their chances for educational success.[68] In cities where employment opportunities existed, many students simply dropped out of junior high if they could find a job early.[69] Nor was the problem limited to high schools. The Jiabei district in Shanghai discovered that the rate of students held back increased in fourth-year primary school, and a study was conducted to find the cause. Investigators discovered that primary schools prevented weak but qualified students from progressing to the fifth and last year, in order to elevate the proportion of students moving on to key junior highs relative to the proportion of those held back.[70] Concisely, then, the mid-course correction to the implementation process had perhaps reduced problems but had by no means eliminated them. The impressive aspect of post-Mao policy has been the early recognition of implementation problems and the adjustment of policy in the course of implementation.

---

[67] *JPRS*, no. 77668 (Mar. 25, 1981): 82–83 (*Fujian Ribao*, Nov. 8, 1980).

[68] For the importance of second-year junior high, see *Shanghai Jiaoyu*, 1982, no. 4 (April): 10–12. For the devastating psychological effect of failure to enter a good high school, see *Chinese Education* 18, no. 1 (Spring 1985): 43–48.

[69] *Zhongguo Qingnian Bao* (China Youth Daily), July 1, 1980, 3, describes this situation for Changzhou, Jiangsu province.

[70] For statistics on this point, see *Shanghai Jiaoyu*, 1982, no. 2 (February): 6–7.

IMPLEMENTATION STAGE 3, AUTUMN-WINTER 1981–1982:
THE DEBATE IS REOPENED—LONG LIVE HIERARCHY
AND EGALITARIANISM

The reforms of autumn 1980 were clearly insufficient to deal with the deviations that had developed (indeed been encouraged) during the stage of competition. The concentration of resources in a few outstanding schools, combined with the sometimes desperate attempts of lesser schools to prove their worth, created a great deal of opposition throughout Chinese society. The burden on students and teachers was particularly heavy, with many press reports commenting on the health, vision, and general physical problems of students. Moreover, the competition was beginning to resemble faintly Japan's "examination hell," with the earliest competitors barely out of the cradle. As one local magazine put it: "Now the influence of promotion rate quest already has penetrated to primary schools and kindergartens. Parents do their utmost to get their children into a 'famous kindergarten,' then have them test into a key secondary school and finally into a university. Only then can this phase of the competition be said to have concluded."[71]

In the autumn of 1981 this opposition reached the front pages of China's major national newspapers and magazines.[72] Most of the letters and articles deplored the side effects of the system, particularly the poor academic performance of students in ordinary middle schools. For example, even in well-endowed Beijing, less than 30 percent of the 139,000 junior middle school students in the graduating class were up to the graduation level. Among the 54,000 (38.7%) moving on to senior high, only 35.7 percent had a minimum passing score on the entrance test. In addition, statistics from work-study (i.e., reform) schools revealed that 80–90 percent of the students who had committed mistakes were between the ages of twelve and fifteen, with most under thirteen.[73] The disease was clear; the cure was not.

Perhaps the two most controversial and thoroughly discussed questions were these: Should the key-school system be continued? Was it wrong to seek a high promotion rate? A wide range of views were aired. Those affiliated with less favored schools advocated the abolition of the advantaged key schools in favor of a system in which all schools would be allowed to compete on an equal basis.[74] In addition, they argued that seeking a high promotion

---

[71] *Jiangsu Jiaoyu* (Jiangsu Education), 1982, no. 1 (January): 1. For the pressure on primary schools, see *Jiaoyu Yanjiu*, 1981, no. 11 (November): 16–17. Also see *Xin Guancha*, 1984, no. 18: 14–15.

[72] See, inter alia, *Zhongguo Qingnian Bao*, Sept. 10, 26; Oct. 10, 17, 24, 31; Nov. 7, 14, 21; Dec. 5, 12, 19, 26, 1981, and Jan. 2, 9, 1982; *Zhongguo Qingnian* (China Youth), 1981, nos. 20–24, and 1982, nos. 1 and 2. *Renmin Ribao*, Nov. 12, 15, and 17, 1981, all on 3; and *Guangming Ribao*, Nov. 4, 5, 7, 12, 14, and 29, 1981, all on 1.

[73] *Daily Report*, Nov. 18, 1981, K4–5 (*Renmin Ribao*, Nov. 12), and *Daily Report*, Nov. 19, 1981, K1–2 (*Renmin Ribao*, Nov. 15).

[74] *Zhongguo Qingnian Bao*, Nov. 21, 1981, 2, and Dec. 12, 1981, 2.

rate was not in itself bad, so long as it was not "one-sided" (*pianmian*).[75] Nor was it difficult for school officials to deny that their quest was one-sided, as the following report from Hubei province makes clear:

> Some comrades said that the one-sided quest for (a high) promotion rate was incorrect, but that they were not "one-sidedly" seeking this; they were seeking it in an "all-around" way. Others said that the promotion rate in their area is very low, so how can you speak about the problem of overcoming the one-sided quest for promotion rate. It is in those places where the promotion rate is high that the mistake has to be overcome.[76]

Local and provincial education bureaus were said to be besieged by letters and telephone calls from the public urging the abolition of key primary and secondary schools. Administrators at ordinary schools, perhaps in anticipation of such a development, were putting in requests to the key schools for a retransfer of their best teachers.[77]

It was not just those who stood to gain directly from a dismantling of the key-school system who were critical of current policy. More specialized magazines argued that the emphasis on quality education had gone too far. Using statistical data, one author claimed that if current policy trends continued, China would never be able to train enough manpower to build a modernized nation.[78] Given all these criticisms, openly aired, some feared that further public comment on the emphasis on promotion rates could be expanded to a criticism of "intellectual education in first place," leading to a de-emphasis on academics.[79]

The proper solution, the media argued, was to prevent further discrimination against ordinary middle schools.[80] The reforms undertaken, however, marked in important ways a further move toward hierarchy. Ordinary schools were to be removed from the pressure of competing with key schools for outstanding students and high promotion rates. As one article pointed out, only 24 of the more than 1,000 middle schools in Beijing were key schools. Of the 211,000 middle school students recruited in the city in 1981, only 8,000 (3.8%) went to key schools.[81] Studies in some districts in Beijing showed that 52 percent of senior high students had already given up hope of entering a university.[82] It was therefore irrational and unfair to expect the poorly endowed ordinary schools to perform up to key-school standards. Since many of the unfortunate side effects had developed because these lesser

---

[75] *Zhongguo Qingnian Bao*, Oct. 17 and 31, 1981, 2, and Jan. 9, 1982, 2.

[76] *Hubei Jiaoyu*, 1982, no. 2 (February): 3.

[77] *Renmin Jiaoyu*, 1982, no. 1 (January): 32.

[78] *JPRS*, no. 77745 (Apr. 3, 1981): 43–47 (*Journal of Dialectics of Nature—Ziran bianzhengfa tongxun*, no. 3, June 1980).

[79] *Zhongguo Qingnian*, 1981, nos. 23–24 (December): 8.

[80] *Daily Report*, Nov. 20, 1981, K7–8 (*Renmin Ribao*, Nov. 17).

[81] Ibid.

[82] *Beijing Keji Bao*, Feb. 22, 1982, 1.

schools were under pressure to match the key schools and perhaps become key schools themselves, many provincial education bureaus undertook, through structural change, to clip the wings of those schools and make it more difficult to compete with the favored key schools.

One important change announced by many provinces in the winter of 1981–1982 was the elimination of streaming (dividing students into fast and slow classes) at primary and middle schools.[83] Another change was the abolition of key primary schools in some provinces or the elimination of entrance exams and interneighborhood recruitment for these schools. Some went further and restricted recruitment by junior highs as well.[84] Impressed by the media blitz extolling these reforms and on the basis of interviews with educators in Beijing and Shanghai, Western journalists in China filed stories on the "dismantling" of China's "elitist schools" and the "return to egalitarian education."[85] This was, of course, far from the case. What had happened was that now there was a recognition that many schools simply had failed in the competition.

Local education magazines published case studies of ordinary schools that had desperately sought to increase their promotion rates but had finally realized the hopelessness of such dreams. Number 25 Middle School in Shenyang, Liaoning province, had been completely shut out of the 1980 university entrance exams. A school with thirty classrooms and 1,700 students had not gotten a single senior high graduate into any university! The school was facing a crisis. Should they "try again next year for a 'promotion rate'? No! In the new year they fully carried out the Party's educational program and directed their attention to the student body as a whole. From the 'point of disaster' they discovered how to run well an ordinary middle school."[86]

Reading the accounts of various model schools, one quickly recognizes that their conversion to the Party's educational program and their assigned role within it stemmed not from the conviction of its correctness but from their own inability to succeed in the major leagues. Most seem finally to have abandoned their hopes only under the combined weight of a particularly disastrous performance on the university entrance exams and the new regulations making it difficult for them to concentrate their limited resources on their best students.

[83] For representative reports on this change, see *Guangming Ribao*, Nov. 7, 1981, 1 (Shanghai); *Guangming Ribao*, Nov. 16, 1981, 1 (Liaoning); *Yangcheng Wanbao*, Nov. 23, 1981, 1 (Guangzhou); *Shanxi Jiaoyu*, 1981, no. 12 (December): 13; *Beijing Jiaoyu*, 1982, no. 2 (February): 4.

[84] *Beijing Ribao*, Apr. 13, 1982, 1; *Yangcheng Wanbao*, May 20, 1982, 1; *Guangming Ribao*, Nov. 16, 1981, 1.

[85] See Christopher S. Wren, "Elitist Schools in China Now Being Dismantled," *New York Times*, Dec. 19, 1981, 2, and Michael Parks, "China Returns to Egalitarian Education," *Los Angeles Times*, Dec. 6, 1981, 25–26.

[86] *Liaoning Jiaoyu*, 1981, no. 12 (December): 4–6. For detailed accounts of similar decisions by Beijing and Shanghai schools, see *Beijing Jiaoyu*, 1981, no. 12 (December): 2–5; 1982, no. 1 (January): 4–5; and *Shanghai Jiaoyu*, 1981, no. 11 (November): 7–8.

The conclusion to the debate and a summary statement on the proper direction for middle schools appeared on January 21, 1982, when the Ministry of Education issued a "Notice Concerning Some Current Questions in Middle and Primary School Education."[87] The notice made two basic points: First, it declared that middle and primary school education was basic education and should be directed toward all students, with an emphasis on moral, intellectual, and physical components. Five concrete steps to prevent the single-minded pursuit of promotion rate were suggested: (1) There should be no ranking of schools, issuing of targets, rewards to schools or teachers, or assessment of quality on the basis of promotion rates; (2) students and schools should be liberated from the constant testing to which educational authorities have subjected them; (3) one group of students should not be singled out at the expense of others—for example, graduating classes and senior high sections; (4) the curriculum plan must be adhered to; there should be no early abandonment to engage in exam preparation; (5) it must be guaranteed that each night primary school students sleep ten hours, junior high students nine hours, and senior high students eight hours, with one hour for physical exercise and a proper allocation of vacation time.

Second, the document affirmed both the necessity of running key middle and primary schools in order to cultivate talent for the four modernizations and the further concentration of resources into a small number of keypoints. Key and ordinary schools should mutually assist each other so that the quality of both would be raised. Finally, key primary schools were to recruit on a neighborhood basis without examinations.

The decision seems to have been a compromise and reflected rather similar decisions that had been made at the provincial level. Some of those provincial decisions, along with the rationale for continuing the key-school system, began to appear in the national magazine *People's Education (Renmin Jiaoyu)*.[88] But the issues were far from resolved. The question of streaming, for example, was complicated, particularly at the senior high level. In Beijing the practice was to be continued for senior high students.[89] Indeed, during an interview at the Ministry of Education in the summer of 1982 an official strongly defended the practice because of the wide variance in ability of students in ordinary schools.[90] And although the same official contended that ordinary schools that performed well might still become future key schools, by 1982 it was clear that the nation's best schools had by and large overcome the pressure of competition and reasserted their pride of place.

The public debate on the value of the key-school system had ended. As

[87] See *Renmin Jiaoyu*, 1982, no. 2 (February): 3, for the text.

[88] See "Key-point Middle and Primary Schools Cannot Be Abolished," *Renmin Jiaoyu*, 1982, no. 1 (January): 32–33 (Jilin province), and "Persist in Running Key-point Middle Schools," *Renmin Jiaoyu*, 1982, no. 3 (March): 34–35 (Sichuan province).

[89] *Beijing Jiaoyu*, 1982, no. 2 (February): 4.

[90] Interview on Aug. 17, 1982, Beijing.

one report put it, "The fact that their proportion of graduates entering universities reaches 90 percent and more proves their worth."[91] Provinces were moving toward the establishment of three different kinds of middle schools: key, ordinary schools, and vocational schools, with key schools serving primarily as college preparatory schools. Three separate curriculum plans were drawn up, one for key schools and the best of the ordinary schools, which included 10 percent vocational classes; one for the rest of the ordinary schools, requiring 20 percent vocational curriculum, and one for the newly transformed vocational schools, which called for more than 30 percent of the curriculum to be devoted to vocational courses. As Guangdong's vice-governor put it, under this new framework it would no longer be necessary to use promotion rates to rank schools, issue rewards for success, or announce school standings.[92]

IMPLEMENTATION STAGE 4, BEGINNING FALL 1982: THE FUTURE OF KEY SCHOOLS?

If some educational officials and commentators had hoped that the key-school issue and its attendant controversy over promotion rates could be kept off the front pages, these hopes were forlorn. The argument that the lack of motivation of students with limited academic prospects was a separate issue from key schools and promotion rates was unconvincing. By the autumn of 1982 many provinces were taking bolder steps to prevent the one-sided concern with promotion rates, commonly issuing notices forbidding regular high schools from setting up review classes for former graduates to prepare for the senior high and university entrance exams. Violators were warned that participating students would have their exam registrations cancelled and that key schools which, after criticism, still persisted, could lose their key status. Nevertheless, the advantages of university entrance, the severe cutbacks at the senior high level, and poor job prospects compelled many graduating students to remain in school and prepare for the next year's promotion exams, which sometimes doubled the size of classrooms.[93]

By the end of 1982 the quest for a high promotion rate was being called the greatest curse in the work of regular middle schools, one that had "a hundred harms without a single benefit."[94] Interestingly, the new models in this still-continuing phase have been some of the country's best schools. One example is Yucai Middle School, a municipal key school in Shanghai. A long (more than 8,000 characters) investigative report in *Guangming Daily* traced

---

[91] *Daily Report*, July 8, 1982, K9–10 (*China Daily*, July 7).
[92] *Yangcheng Wanbao*, Jan. 4, 1982, 1; *Guangzhou Ribao*, Jan. 5, 1982, 1.
[93] *Guangming Ribao*, Oct. 7, 1982, 2; Feb. 16, 1983, 1, 4; July 31, 1983, 2.
[94] *Guangming Ribao*, Dec. 29, 1982, 1.

Yucai's recent history and success.[95] Of the 158 senior high graduates in 1982, 3 replaced their parents in the work force, 1 became ill and did not take the university exam, and the remaining 154 were all admitted to a university, with 121 making it to key universities. This report led to a series of articles and letters; the message can be summed up in two statements, the first attributed to the Yucai principal and the second from a parent: "Even if we were clipped bald [on the university exam], I would prefer this to one-sidedly seeking a high promotion rate." "I believe that after my child graduates senior high, no matter whether he is promoted to a higher school or goes to work, he has been given an excellent foundation for both."[96]

This message has been ineffective precisely because success on the university exams *does* matter to school officials and parents. Statements such as those above by the beneficiaries of current policy are likely to be unpersuasive to those being disadvantaged. Schools with good reputations have little difficulty in recruiting students. Because of these reputations they can withstand parental or administrative pressure to concentrate on promotion rate. They are likely to be successful because they have the resources and attract outstanding students. The luxury of indifference is not available to lesser schools.

The situation has changed greatly from the summer of 1980, when educators in Beijing could complain that "key schools are not key enough" because there were few distinctions between them and they were treated only slightly better than ordinary schools. By 1983 the gap between the best key schools and the great majority of "others" had become very wide indeed. An article in *People's Daily* put the new situation as follows:

> Originally, expending efforts to run well a group of key schools so that these schools could gather experience, issue teaching materials, and produce teachers in order to lead and stimulate ordinary schools, with the two kinds of school raising standards and moving forward together, this was a correct leadership method. The problem now is in many places there are artificially created key schools. To use the words of the masses, "the key schools are too key, the ordinary schools are too weak." The ordinary schools cannot learn from the experience of the key schools, so the key schools are isolated from the ordinary. Under these conditions, even if these schools have a very high promotion rate, it has lost its significance.[97]

These sentiments have been echoed by some of China's leading intellectuals. The Chinese People's Political Consultative Conference, on which

[95] *Guangming Ribao*, Dec. 29, 1982, 1–2. An earlier brief report on Yucai's reforms is in *Wenhui Bao*, Nov. 8, 1982, 1.

[96] *Guangming Ribao*, Jan. 11, 2; Jan. 13, 1; Jan. 14, 2; Jan. 15, 1; Jan. 21, 2; Jan. 28, 2; Jan. 31, 2; Feb. 16, 1 and 4, all 1983.

[97] *Renmin Ribao*, Mar. 12, 1983, 3.

many prominent intellectuals serve, passed a motion in 1982, reiterated in 1984, indicting key primary and secondary schools for ten crimes (*zuizhuang*) and calling for their abolition. Although these leading intellectuals have complained that their appeals have gone unheeded, they have periodically been allowed access to the media to press their case.[98] In fact, as of mid-1985, the debate over key schools seemed as contentious as ever, with at least three positions gaining a hearing in the official press. Supporters maintained that the continuing lack of funds, the shortage of qualified primary and middle school teachers, and the urgent requirements of modernization all argued for a concentration of resources where they could be used most effectively. Opponents reiterated their familiar arguments about the negative side effects stemming from the policy. A third group argued, as they had previously, that key schools were fine, so long as they were formed "through the natural process of unrestricted competition," rather than by "squeezing the smaller schools out of the field or by anointing them through the decisions of higher authorities."[99]

CONCLUSION

This extended case study has revealed some of the generic strengths and weaknesses of policy implementation in socialist systems, and it develops two of the major themes in this volume. In the wake of the death of Mao and the removal of his radical supporters, the new leadership was able to initiate bold departures in a number of policy spheres. The widespread bureaucratic and popular consensus that a crisis in education existed lent a sense of urgency that facilitated implementation—crisis, as we have seen in chapter 6, can facilitate implementation by reducing opposition. Moreover, the authoritarian nature of the Chinese regime prevented those still sympathetic to the radical cause from mobilizing opposition to the new education initiatives. On the other hand, contrary to the expectation that authoritarian regimes (being less dependent on broad social coalitions than are competitive political systems) should be able to produce unambiguous policy with clear goals, this study has revealed goal conflict from the start. This can be traced to a general contradiction faced by virtually all socialist societies: the need to foster the rapid development of the productive forces while building a social system

---

[98] *Guangming Ribao*, July 31, 1984, 1; *Dagong Bao* (Impartial Daily), Dec. 6, 1982, 2. For some adjustments in the allocation of goods and services undertaken to benefit ordinary schools, see *Zhongguo Jiaoyu Bao*, Dec. 29, 1983, 1; *Renmin Ribao*, Aug. 10, 1983, 3, and Aug. 30, 1983, 3; State Council Communique of Aug. 10, 1983, in *Guowuyuan Gongbao*, 1983, no. 18 (Sept. 20): 839–44.

[99] *Daily Report*, May 14, 1985, K13–14 (*China Daily*, May 10); *Beijing Review*, 1985, no. 18 (May 6): 9–10; *JPRS-CPS* 85-055 (June 6, 1985): 53–54 (*China Daily*, April 14); *Renmin Jiaoyu*, 1984, no. 12 (December): 24; *Guangming Ribao*, Sept. 6, 1984, 2; *Beijing Ribao*, July 28, 1984, 4; *Xin Guancha*, no. 18, 1984, 14–15.

marked by a high degree of equality. In the Chinese case this contradiction was exacerbated by the balance of political forces in the immediate post-Mao period. The original policy design reflected the views of *both* Deng Xiaoping and Hua Guofeng. One could argue, however, that Deng's "hidden agenda" (expressed rather openly in his speeches) *required* a partial failure of the original policy design. As political influence slipped away from Hua and his supporters, Deng's emphasis on the cultivation of talent faced little opposition at the top of the political system. Today, however, many feel that the swing away from popularization has gone too far. Significantly, some of the most vocal champions for a strengthening of basic education for the masses are well-known intellectuals, not Maoist radicals. The recent increase in educational funding has stimulated a debate within the academic community over the relative merits of investing in a small number of schools to produce the highest quality graduates or of devoting considerably more financial resources to combat illiteracy and guarantee a sound basic education for all. The appropriate balance between the raising of standards and popularization is likely to remain a long-term, contentious issue regardless of individual political personalities at the top.[100] Clear policy objectives do not assure smooth implementation, but goal conflict in policy does assure implementation problems.

Were a shift in the direction of popularization to occur, a decline in the policy deviations described in this chapter would likely follow. Under Deng the Chinese definition of socialism has as its primary goal the development of the productive forces. Initiative at every level is encouraged, with peasants urged to "become rich through labor," and university entrance, overseas study, job placement, and so forth all dependent on examination scores. All forms of "egalitarianism," whether in the distribution of income or in the availability of quality education, have been classified as enemies of socialist development. Deviation in the name of raising educational quality may be criticized, but obedience to national or local directives cannot compensate for failure (measured by low promotion rate).

Operating within this framework, a basic dilemma confronts the State Education Commission. The key-school system and its concomitant competitive environment has created an atmosphere in which talent can be discovered early and nurtured carefully. Although undesirable side effects have also appeared, the commission, in combatting these deviations, must be careful not to compromise one of its primary goals: the cultivation of talent. Governing through education bureaus that have considerable discretionary

---

[100] The debate over educational investment is discussed in Stanley Rosen, "Chinese Education During the World Recession: The Paradox of Expansion," in Grant Harman and Frederick Wirt, *The Political Economy of Education: A Comparative View* (forthcoming); Rosen, "Recentralization" (n. 66 above), and *Chinese Education* 17, no. 3 (Fall 1984).

power, leading commission officials often prod those at lower levels, but punishment for violations of policy guidelines appears to be both rare and mild. There is, in effect, a trade-off in which success in the primary objective leads to a reluctant tolerance of unorthodox methods. For example, the former Minister of Education railed against the excessive stress on promotion rate common at the local levels but assured his questioning audience that this did not mean opposition to promotion generally; still less did it mean opposition to the raising of educational quality.[101]

Although we have argued that major sources of the implementation problems discussed in this chapter are traceable to the inherent conflict over goals that marks socialist systems, to certain imperatives in Deng's developmental strategy, and to weaknesses in bureaucratic enforcement agencies, it should also be clear that the Chinese political system has not been entirely unresponsive to flaws in policy content. Indeed, the detailed chronology of implementation stages develops a principal theme of this entire volume—policy implementation problems have given rise to rather quick alterations in policy content. This chapter and chapter 9 both reveal a responsive policy process in which feedback reaches central decision makers quickly. For example, from the beginning, the lack of sharp distinctions between key and ordinary schools kept both in perpetual competition, concentrating their energies on raising their promotion rates. Thus, one major purpose of the key schools— to serve as models and to pass on their successes to ordinary schools—was impossible, since the former was unwilling to enhance the latter's competitive prospects. More recently there has been a great emphasis in the press on the specific educational tasks of ordinary schools; they are no longer being treated as aspiring key schools.

Similarly, the close relationship between educational success and job allocation has always contributed enormously to the attraction of the key schools. Since only college or secondary specialist school graduates are given state-allocated employment, students and their parents shun vocational and agricultural middle schools, as well as those ordinary schools which, because of low university promotion rates, are slated for transformation into vocational schools.[102] A program is currently being implemented experimentally, in which vocational and ordinary schools sign contracts with work units to send their most qualified graduates on to guaranteed jobs. Preliminary results show that such programs greatly enhance the recruitment potential of participating schools and also raise a student's incentive to study.[103] The

---

[101] *Guangming Ribao,* July 31, 1983, 2.

[102] See the preferences of graduating junior high students in *Beijing Ribao,* July 28, 1982, 1. For recent studies which rank occupations in China, see *Chinese Education* 18, no. 1 (Spring 1985): 62–70; Nan Lin and Wen Xie, "Occupational Prestige in Urban China," June 1985 (manuscript).

[103] Shanghai *Wenhui Bao,* March 31, 1983, 1.

prospects for controlling policy deviations seem to depend primarily on the introduction of structural changes of this type. A continuing reduction of senior highs, the expansion of technical and vocational education, and the guaranteed employment of vocational and ordinary school graduates would all be salutary changes leading to behavioral adjustments.

Finally, not only have we seen a system that has responded quickly to problems that have evolved in the implementation stage, we have witnessed a system in which initial policy problems produced unanticipated outcomes. In this policy area, the deregulatory character of present policy has unleashed competitive forces that continually produce unanticipated consequences. This study reveals that, at least thus far, the Chinese system under Deng Xiaoping has been able to respond to these unanticipated consequences.

TWELVE

Implementing China's S & T Modernization Program

Denis Fred Simon

INTRODUCTION

Studies of policy implementation in both the industrialized and the developing nations show that "successful" implementation is the product of organizational adaptation and evolution.[1] Implementation is best viewed as a process rather than as a discrete event. Analysis must focus on the interplay between organizational strategy, political-economic context, and the formal structures and procedures designated for carrying out policies formulated by decision makers at the national level. Attempts at policy implementation usually pass through several stages, each one conditioning the process and affecting the outcome. Strategy to effect policy may unintentionally undergo considerable change during the course of implementation or in response to the influence of contextual factors beyond the immediate control of the planner or policy administrator. These changes should not necessarily be viewed as an indication of shifting goals or a policy failure, but rather may be seen as part of a building process designed to enhance the attractiveness of and facilitate greater receptivity to a new policy.

Within socialist systems, the problems of developing and adapting a strategy for policy implementation are often compounded by the trade-offs between centralized and decentralized control. With respect to science and technology (S & T), the typical concerns of policy implementors tend to be focused on the imperatives of maintaining order, that is, maintaining their ability to control and coordinate, and if need be, to orchestrate events at lower levels.[2] Yet, for S & T to prosper and advance, there must be room for innovation.[3] Berliner, in his study of industrial innovation in the Soviet

[1] Merilee Grindle, ed., *Politics and Policy Implementation in the Third World* (Princeton: Princeton University Press, 1980).

[2] Charles Lindblom, *Politics and Markets* (New York: Basic Books, 1982).

[3] Roy Rothwell and Walter Zegveld, *Industrial Innovation and Public Policy* (London: Frances Pinter, Ltd., 1981).

Union, has shown that the "imperatives of centralized administrative co-ordination" within a socialist system must at some point in time give way to the forces of the marketplace, since competition rather than administrative decree is frequently needed to promote greater effectiveness and efficiency within both the research and development (R & D) unit and the production enterprise.[4] And, as Weiss and others have suggested, it is the prevailing environment—the domestic institutional, economic, social, and ecological setting as well as the international context—that has as much influence on the evolution of technology and its application as have the activities of the formal technological institutions.[5]

This chapter is concerned with some of the methods adopted by the Chinese to improve the "implementation environment" for S & T policy. It offers two basic themes: First, as China's leaders have come to realize, progress in science and technology is not merely dependent upon increased investment in R & D or specific policies adopted to rectify deficiencies within the research sector. Rather, modernization of the S & T sector depends greatly on policies adopted in the area of economic policy. Without adequate demand for new and more advanced products and production processes, China's R & D organizations and personnel will lack the needed incentives to respond to the nation's economic needs. As the Zweig and Clarke chapters in this volume show, changing the larger socioeconomic and leadership contexts can become a precondition for effective policy implementation.

Second, implementation of China's national science and technology policy is, in many ways, the function of a mixed strategy in which key leaders are seeking to balance central control and some market mechanisms. The major objective of current S & T policy is to make science and technology serve the economy, that is, to get more applied, production-related research.[6] Chinese leaders have taken a holistic approach to this policy objective, linking overall changes in the price system and enterprise management with reform of the S & T system at large. The strategy of implementation, which continues to undergo substantial fine-tuning, is characterized overall by the movement away from the Soviet-style, centrally led form of administration and management that dominated Chinese S & T before the Cultural Revolution in the mid-1960s.[7] Instead of being "pushed" from the Center, the development of

[4]Joseph Berliner, *The Innovation Decision in Soviet Industry* (Cambridge: MIT Press, 1976). Berliner suggests that to better understand the determinants of innovation in socialist systems, we must not merely concentrate on the central bureaucracy but also focus on four additional factors: prices, decision rules, incentives, and organizational structure.

[5]Charles Weiss, "Mobilizing Technology for Developing Countries," *Science*, March 16, 1979, 1083–89.

[6]C. A. Tisdell, *Science and Technology Policy: Priorities of Governments* (London: Chapman and Hall, Ltd., 1981).

[7]Richard P. Suttmeier, *Research and Revolution* (New York: Lexington Books, 1974).

S & T is now to be accomplished, for the most part, by what Sigurdson has termed a "demand-pull" approach.[8]

In this chapter I will discuss this facilitative implementation strategy. Policy implementation is viewed as a series of shifting strategies and dynamic processes occurring simultaneously, each designed to alter not only the environment in which science and technology decisions are made, but also the calculus of decision making among persons responsible for establishing research priorities and accomplishing economic objectives. These shifts come about through the incessant pulling and tugging over control and resources which takes place between local and central authorities. Within such a framework, centralized versus decentralized approaches need be viewed, not necessarily as movements along one implementation continuum, but rather as part of the same "mixed" strategy where the role, function, and responsibilities of various central and local units are constantly redefined to achieve greater responsiveness to the central goal of making science and technology serve production.

THE ROLE OF S & T IN THE FOUR MODERNIZATIONS

The Dilemma of Policy Implementation

In an effort to promote a more rapid and sustainable pattern of economic development, China's post-Mao leaders have taken some bold policy initiatives, covering the spectrum from expanded use of profit incentives in industry to dismemberment of the commune system in the rural areas. Beijing's actions within the realm of science and technology have been dramatic and far-reaching as well. Along with the efforts to improve the operation of the domestic research system, Deng Xiaoping and his allies have opened China's doors to large quantities of foreign technology imports, have encouraged the widespread use of foreign experts, and have sent thousands of students and scholars abroad for technical training. Because of the broad range of institutional and attitudinal changes that have been and will continue to be required to make these efforts pay off, the modernization of science and technology is one of the greatest challenges facing China for the rest of the century. The task confronting Beijing involves more than just the mere reformulation of existing policies for science and technology. Progress in science and technology requires nothing less than a major transformation of the economic and political environment in which research is conducted and technology-related decisions are made.

Implementation of a national program to modernize science and technolo-

---

[8] Jon Sigurdson, *Technology and Science in the People's Republic of China* (Elmsford, N.Y.: Pergamon Books, 1980).

gy has not been an easy task for the Chinese leadership. Faced with a domestic infrastructure in science, technology, and education which was decimated by the political turmoil of the Cultural Revolution, Chinese leaders have been faced with the monumental challenge of rebuilding, almost from scratch, an institutional structure and pool of competent scientists and technicians to move the country forward in the years ahead. As a result of the Cultural Revolution, China's research system stagnated, leaving the Chinese ten to twenty years behind the West and Japan in most critical fields in science and technology. Chinese leaders recognize that without appreciable progress and expanded application of modern technology, China's pattern of economic growth will continue to be erratic and uneven at best.[9]

The key factors that have influenced the implementation process related to science and technology can be grouped under three main headings: political, structural, and external. The political factor is a double-edged sword, which derives from and continues to be fueled by the legacy of the Cultural Revolution and the political reversals of the past thirty years.[10] Party cadres in positions of authority, many of whom earned their credentials and attained their positions as a result of their activism during previous political campaigns, such as the anti-science aspects of the Cultural Revolution, remain reluctant to accept a new system of government administration based on technical rather than ideological criteria. The Chinese press continues to contain numerous reports of obstructionism by "rulers of small kingdoms" who are motivated by a combination of jealousy, prejudice, and plain self-interest.[11] Yet, not all of China's policy problems, implementation related and otherwise, would be resolved if scientists and engineers were given a free rein. Within an environment where the resources in finance, manpower, and equipment are scarce, the costs of granting the scientific community extensive authority in policy circles could be severe if national needs were said to be coterminous with the unfettered scientific quest for knowledge.

Many scientists, particularly those affiliated with the Chinese Academy of Sciences (CAS), refuse to surrender their commitment to basic science and

[9]China's leaders have acknowledged that at least half of the gains toward achieving their goal of quadrupling the gross value of industrial and agricultural output by the year 2000 will depend on expanded application of new technology. See "Create New Wealth Through Relying on Advances in Science and Technology," *Renmin Ribao* (People's Daily), Nov. 7, 1982, trans. in *FBIS-PRC* (Foreign Broadcast Information Service–People's Republic of China), Nov. 10, 1982, K5–12.

[10]For an interesting example of the trials and tribulations of one scientist, see Shi Xiyuan, "Strive for the Right of Scientific Research," *Ziran Bianzhengfa Tongxun* (Journal of the Dialectics of Nature), 1980, no. 1, trans. in *JPRS* (Joint Publications Research Service), no. 78995 (Sept. 16, 1981): 49–58.

[11]"Elimination of Prejudice Against Intellectuals Urged," *Guangming Ribao*, July 11, 1984, trans. in *JPRS-CPS* 84-069 (Oct. 18, 1984): 25–26.

"dirty their hands" in the movement to give greater emphasis to applied research.[12] In the inimitable paraphrased words of one CAS scientist, "for thirty years we have been trying to tell the political authorities in Beijing how important basic research is."[13] Even though younger scientists have begun to appear on the scene, the core members of China's scientific community are well advanced in age.[14] A significant percentage of these have been trained in the West or Japan, and as the door to interaction with the outside has reopened, their "role models" for research-project selection and development have tended to be the advanced nations. A major contributor to this state of affairs has been the large numbers of ethnic Chinese in the upper echelons of the foreign scientific community who act as advisers to China. Some leading scientists apparently believe that the current "pro-science" climate may be their last opportunity to achieve a nationally or internationally recognized scientific accomplishment. This "ivory tower" mentality, which is precisely what got the scientific community in political trouble during the Cultural Revolution, is compounded by continued apprehension about the longevity of the present policies. Though strongly committed to the spirit and direction of present policies, an appreciable percentage of Chinese scientists remain uneasy about the future.

The structural factor is associated with the faults in the basic design and organization of the Chinese research system. In spite of Beijing's rhetoric to the contrary, Chinese science and technology has not been applications-oriented. According to one author, only 10 percent of all research can be translated into production; even in research institutes of the highest caliber the rate is only 30–40 percent.[15] The R & D system has tended to be highly compartmentalized, particularly between the civilian and defense sectors. Connections and communications among researchers *and* between researchers and end-users have tended to be erratic.[16] Research institutes have had

[12] Leo Orleans, "Science, Elitism, and Economic Readjustment in China," *Science*, Jan. 29, 1982, 472–77. See also Sun Cang, "Intellectuals and Getting Cocky," *Renmin Ribao*, Apr. 22, 1983, trans. in *JPRS*, no. 83775 (June 28, 1983): 67–68.

[13] Based on interviews conducted by D. M. Lampton in Beijing, January 1984.

[14] Within the CAS-affiliated Dalian Institute of Chemical Physics, for example, the average age of senior researchers is 56.8 years, whereas the average age of mid-level and junior researchers is 46 years and 39 years respectively. The problem would not be so serious if it were not for the fact that many of those in the mid-level category and below lack in-depth training as a result of the Cultural Revolution. See "Bring Out the Positive Factors of Middle-Aged S & T Personnel," *Guangming Ribao*, Feb. 27, 1982, trans. in *JPRS*, no. 81364 (July 26, 1982): 19.

[15] Xia Yulong and Liu Ji, "It Is Also Necessary to Eliminate Erroneous Leftist Influence on the Science and Technology Front," *Jeifang Ribao* (Liberation Daily), Shanghai, June 2, 1981, trans. in *FBIS-PRC*, June 11, 1981, K8–12.

[16] For an assessment of these problems in the case of Shanghai, see "Ten Problems That Urgently Need to Be Solved in Shanghai At Present," *Kexuexue Yanjiu Lunwen Xuan* (Selected Papers on the Study of the Science of Science), 1980, no. 4: 153–60.

very little incentive to serve the needs of enterprises. And the factory manager, concerned mainly with attaining output quotas, has had little incentive to adopt new product or process innovations, because the firm had no marketing responsibilities and the "sale" of all output, irrespective of quality, was assured. "The current state of affairs in our country is that management is more backward than technology. Some of our technological facilities are not at all inferior to other people's, but the products are very backward in both numbers and quality. The reason is primarily bad management."[17]

A related manifestation of the Chinese system has been the problem of labor allocation and mobility.[18] Because of the highly centralized nature of the personnel system and the scarcity of scientific and technical personnel, many individuals have been forced to remain in jobs for which they do not have the proper skills or for which their skills are obviously redundant. Almost two-thirds of the engineers and the technical personnel are concentrated in the machine-building and metallurgy sectors, whereas the number of similar personnel in light industry is less than 15 percent of the total.[19] In some geographic areas there are too many chemical engineers; in others there are not enough. One cause of this imbalance has been the poor communications among components of the research sector. A more important factor, however, has been the operating "culture" among institute managers. Given the difficulty and uncertainty in securing replacement personnel, particularly in outlying areas, institutes have tended to restrict the movement of their personnel and to retain individuals even though job transfers might benefit both the researcher and the receiving institute.

The last, but perhaps most critical, of the three factors that have defined and influenced the context of policy implementation in science and technology has been the external one. This has been alluded to above concerning the proclivity of some scientists to look abroad as a point of reference in selecting research priorities and goals. There has been a tendency for the scientific community to "pay no heed to the national condition, blindly catching up and overtaking, and actually engaging in 'world science'."[20] These tendencies are reinforced by China's expanded participation in bilateral science and technology cooperation programs with the United States, Japan, and Western Europe. Large numbers of Chinese scientists are sent overseas to visit or

[17] Dan Qin, "Energetically Study and Grasp Modern Scientific Management," *Tianjin Ribao*, May 27, 1980, trans. in *JPRS*, no. 76161 (Aug. 5, 1980): 1–6.

[18] Huang Wei and Zhang Jieyu, "The Structure of China's Scientific and Technical Ranks and Current Measures of Readjustment," *Kexuexue Yu Kexue Guanli Yanjiu* (Scientology and the Management of Science Research), 1982, no. 4 (July 20), trans. in *JPRS*, no. 83240 (Apr. 12, 1983): 230–37.

[19] Tao Kai and Ceng Qing, "On the Question of Directional Flow of Scientific and Technical Personnel," *Guangming Ribao*, July 12, 1982, trans. in *JPRS*, no. 83240 (Apr. 12, 1983): 245–50.

[20] Xia Yulong and Liu Ji, K8–12.

work in comparatively more modern, well-equipped research facilities on expensive projects that would fit into the category of "basic" rather than "applied" research. This has served to exacerbate the gap between what many Chinese scientists feel they want to do and what economic leaders believe should be done. And it has created numerous problems as far as the absorption of the overseas trained individuals are concerned, limiting their impact in many cases.

Moreover, as was previously noted, overseas Chinese scientists have had a strong influence on the structuring of research programs and objectives.[21] Finally, China's selection of technologies and equipment has been influenced by the external environment as well. Many Chinese have been inclined to purchase foreign-made "state-of-the-art" items when more "appropriate" technologies or domestically produced equivalents would have sufficed.[22] For example, since 1978 large numbers of foreign computers have been procured without adequate consideration of software or application.[23]

In short, without changes in economic incentives and alteration in the links between researchers and producers, without changes in institutional personnel policies, and without better management of external forces, the effective implementation of any new S & T policy will be frustrated. The context must be changed before policy and institutional behavior will begin to change.

The Big Push of 1978

The pivotal role to be played by science and technology was most clearly articulated at the time of the March 1978 National Science Conference when China's highest political and scientific leaders noted that "the crux of the four modernizations rests with science and technology development."[24] The comprehensive program announced at the March meeting had been the product of many months of intensive political discussion and negotiation, which had begun as early as late 1976. China's stated goal was to "catch up" with the advanced nations in science and technology by the year 2000.[25]

---

[21] For example, see "Deng Xiaoping Meets Overseas Chinese Scientists," *Xinhua* (New China), June 18, 1983, trans. in *FBIS-PRC*, June 20, 1983, A1–2.

[22] Wang Chiwei and Liu Mingdong, "Import of Foreign Technology and Economic Effectiveness," *Caijing Wenti Yanjiu* (Research on the Problems of Finance), July 1982, trans. in *JPRS*, no. 82364 (December 1982): 23–28.

[23] Wu Weixiong, "On the Information and New Technological Revolution," *Shuliang Jingji Jishu Jingji Yanjiu* (Quantitative and Technical Economics), no. 8 (Aug. 5, 1984), trans. in *CEA* 84-105, (Dec. 21, 1984), 34–40.

[24] Richard P. Suttmeier, *Science, Technology and China's Drive for Modernization* (Stanford: Hoover Institution Press, 1980).

[25] Sigurdson, *Technology and Science* (n. 8 above).

A set of eight priority areas were spelled out for immediate attention.[26] It becomes apparent after looking at the list of priorities that their selection reflected, not one homogeneous viewpoint, but the varying interests of the different institutional groups concerned with the modernization of science and technology. In some cases, as in the selection of energy and materials science, the primary objective was clearly economic. In other cases, as in high-energy physics and genetics, the choices reflected the desire of many leading Chinese scientists, a large percentage of whom were foreign trained, to jump back into the world scientific community, and perhaps even achieve a Nobel Prize.[27] A third group of topics—space, computers and electronics, and lasers—were given attention because of their obvious military as well as economic applications. This is not to deny that within some fields, such as genetics, there were practical applications that were possible; but in many instances projects were not conceived or designed with practical applications in mind.

The heavy emphasis placed on the development of high-energy physics has long been a critical point of discussion among both Chinese and Western scientists. Citing the strong interest exhibited by Chairman Mao Zedong in this field, both Deng Xiaoping and Fang Yi, then vice-premier and head of the State Science and Technology Commission (SSTC), argued that substantial resources and personnel should be devoted to the promotion of Chinese advancements in this field. This tendency was reinforced by a coterie of Chinese-American scientists, many of whom were physicists and felt that advanced research in high-energy physics was a good vehicle for boosting China's scientific capabilities and for Chinese scientists to gain international recognition. This desire for international recognition cannot be underestimated, inasmuch as the Chinese scientific community had been shut off from world research for over two decades. Accordingly, a large-scale program to build a 50-GeV proton synchrotron was begun as part of the program of cooperation in science and technology between China and the United States.[28]

The remarkable aspect of this entire process during the first year after the national science conference was that basic research was allowed to command such significant amounts of human and financial resources. This is not to

[26]The eight priority areas include agriculture, computers and electronics, space, genetics, physics, materials science, energy, and lasers.

[27]This point is also made in "Planting a Tall Tree: Science in China," *Nature* 301 (Jan. 27, 1983): 280–84. See also Wang Zhuxiang, "The Function of High Energy Experiments in the Development of High Energy Physics," *Ziran Bianzhengfa Tongxun* (Journal of the Dialectics of Nature), 1979, no. 3 (July): 67–77, trans. in *JPRS*, no. 76663 (Oct. 21, 1980): 2–7.

[28]This project was ultimately cancelled and replaced by a more modest project to build a +2/−2 electron positron.

suggest that applied research was totally ignored. These priorities signaled the strong influence of the Chinese Academy of Sciences in the formulation and implementation of S & T policy.[29] And these priorities also raised the issue of whether various Chinese leaders actually understood the functional differences between "science" and "technology."

This tendency for Chinese "science" to leap ahead and for technology development to lag behind was compounded by the continued disinterest and, in some cases, reluctance of the industrial sector to seize upon the new opportunities for product and process improvement. In short, not only were the dominant scientists reluctant to emphasize applied S & T, but the economic apparatus was not ready to use S & T even if they were available. Central policy would have to place more emphasis on applied science, *and* the economic system would simultaneously have to become more receptive. Ironically, there was need for stronger central control vis-à-vis S & T priorities and less stifling central control over the economy.

Another important dimension of the 1978 national science plan was the lack of attention paid to reform of the basic structure and design of the domestic S & T system itself. After the downfall of the "Gang of Four," the approach adopted by Chinese leaders was to rehabilitate the system as it existed before the Cultural Revolution rather than to consider fundamental structural change. China's research system had been modeled after the Soviet system—with a three-pronged structure characterized by the sharp division between basic and applied research and by the lack of a strong research capability in universities.[30] The system was managed, in principle, by one overarching organization, the State Science and Technology Commission (SSTC).

In 1977, reestablishment of the SSTC after its dismemberment during the Cultural Revolution was one of the first steps taken by the Deng-led regime in its attempts to revitalize China's research sector. However, very little was done at the time to harness the university sector for research purposes. Many Chinese administrators and scientists, some of whom had received extensive training in the Soviet Union, where university research played a minor role, felt no need to change; the Soviet-style system had produced nuclear weapons and other advances.

The initial response to the new stress placed on the modernization of sci-

[29] One merely has to examine the criticisms of the CAS, particularly the comments made at the May 1981 meeting of the Scientific Council, to understand how the CAS had helped set S & T priorities during the initial phase of the S & T modernization program. See *China Examines Science Policy* (Springfield, Va: Foreign Broadcast Information Service, January 1982), 143–72.

[30] Zhang Qiang, "An Important Issue on the Readjustment and Reform of Our Country's Scientific Research System," *Hebei Daxue Xuebao* (Journal of Hebei University), Jan. 25, 1981, trans. in *JPRS*, no. 79432 (Nov. 13, 1981): 26–36.

ence and technology was mixed. In this setting, therefore, there were wide variations in the way in which policies formulated in Beijing were interpreted throughout the country and within individual research units. Cadres within some institutes and enterprises ignored or paid lip service to the call to modernize science and technology. A December 1979 national forum on progress in science and technology acknowledged that "quite a few leading cadres were still accustomed to giving guidance to scientific and technological work by adopting the method of promoting political movements."[31] Moreover, unwilling to relinquish their political positions, they obstructed the call to place persons with technical credentials in positions of authority. Their behavior was primarily motivated by three factors: their lack of technical training, their self-interest, *and* an apprehension that the political winds might once again shift and that a high-profile, "pro-science" position might turn out to be politically dangerous.[32]

In spite of the fact that the majority of scientific and technical personnel received China's renewed emphasis on science and technology positively, a large percentage remained skeptical about the staying power of the new leadership and its policies. Some scientists, fearful of once again being singled out for pursuing their intellectual activities or engaging in a research "failure," viewed the statements coming out of Beijing with some trepidation.[33] This response was antithetical to the research process, which involves an inherent element of risk-taking in order to move ahead. This type of behavior was exhibited by several Chinese scientists who participated in some of the early Sino–U.S. bilateral cooperation projects.[34] Within China this "ongoing fear" produced considerable duplication of research, particularly regarding "successful" projects that had been completed in the West or other parts of China. It was still politically safer to undertake and repeat a proven research experiment than to assume responsibility for a more speculative scientific venture.

In other instances, the response to Beijing's emphasis on science and technology resembled something of a bandwagon effect. Many local officials— some sincere in their efforts to dispel the disdain for science and technology which had been engendered by the Cultural Revolution, others eager to court

---

[31] "National Scientific and Technological Conference in Beijing," *Xinhua*, Dec. 5, 1979, trans. in *FBIS-PRC*, Dec. 6, 1979, L11.

[32] "The Entire Party Should Accord the Proper Importance to Science and Technology," *Guangming Ribao*, Apr. 18, 1981, trans. in *JPRS*, no. 78147 (May 22, 1981): 1–5.

[33] At a forum on scientific achievement held in Beijing in late 1980 a large amount of concern was expressed regarding continued "administrative interference" in research activities. "Forum on Scientific Achievement Held in Beijing," *Xinhua*, Dec. 21, 1980, trans. in *FBIS-PRC*, Dec. 22, 1980, L40.

[34] Interviews by author with various participants in the Sino–U.S. bilateral S & T cooperation programs, 1981–1984.

Beijing's favor—went to extremes in popularizing the value of S & T to peasants and workers. The movement to popularize S & T led to a massive outflow of rather simplistic "scientific and technical publications" and to a proliferation of relatively worthless research institutes.[35] In one province, the number of so-called institutes increased by 153 percent in one year. Many of these institutes came to be called the "three no centers"—having no projects, no equipment, and no personnel.

The difficulties encountered within the realm of the research system itself were compounded by Chinese behavior regarding the acquisition of foreign technology and equipment.[36] Here again the general response to the announcement of the "four modernizations" was to proceed on the basis of the past, with primary emphasis given to the purchase of whole plants and equipment rather than actual technology and know-how. Articles appearing in the Chinese press have suggested that less than 10 percent of the funds expended for "technology imports" actually went for technology.[37] Numerous delegations and buying missions were sent abroad to survey the state-of-the-art in various fields. Many of these missions proceeded to sign contracts for advanced items that China could not possibly use.

The situation concerning computer imports was particularly serious.[38] Many medium and large, high-speed computers acquired from abroad were severely underutilized or poorly maintained.[39] And in some instances the computers were never unpacked from their original shipping crates. Stress was placed on the level of sophistication rather than on the appropriateness of the technology or the maintenance capacity.[40] Contracts were signed by overenthusiastic technical delegations when in fact they had little authority

[35] The circulation of popular scientific magazines and journals has increased tenfold since 1966. There are 109 scientific journals with an overall circulation of 16.5 million, and 34 national/local S & T newspapers with a circulation of almost 5 million. See *China Daily*, Aug. 7, 1981, 3.

[36] Denis Fred Simon, "China's Capacity to Assimilate Foreign Technology," United States, Joint Economic Committee, *China Under the Four Modernizations*, 97th Congress, 2nd Session (Aug. 13, 1982), 514–52.

[37] Guo Xinchang and Yang Haitian, "China's Unfavorable Position in International Technology Transfer Should Be Changed As Quickly As Possible," *Caimao Jingji* (Finance, Trade and Economics), 1982, no. 1 (Jan. 10), trans. in *JPRS*, no. 80736 (May 5, 1982): 31–37.

[38] "On the Requirement That Technology Be Advanced and the Problem of Economic Rationality," *Jingji Yanjiu* (Economic Research), Nov. 20, 1980, trans. in *JPRS*, no. 77285 (Jan. 30, 1981): 34–43.

[39] By May 1979, 332 computers had been imported at a cost of almost 500 million yuan. Less than a third were used as many as ten hours per day; out of 24 computers in Anhui only 3 were used more than eight hours per day. See Guan Weiyuan, "Formulate Scientific Programs in Accordance with the Demands of the National Economy," *Ziran Bianzhengfa Tongxun*, 1981, no. 2, trans. in *JPRS*, no. 79115 (Oct. 1, 1981): 36–45.

[40] Wang Chiwei and Liu Mingdong, "Import of Foreign Technology and Economic Effectiveness" (n. 22 above).

to commit scarce Chinese foreign exchange for these purchases.[41] In addition, feasibility studies and project assessments generally were not conducted beforehand, resulting in inefficient use of both imported items and domestic resources. For example, the ancillary equipment and infrastructure to make the whole-plant and equipment purchases worthwhile were frequently lacking. The results, such as in the case of the multibillion-dollar Baoshan steel mill, turned out to be disastrous, with very little actual transfer of technology taking place.[42]

These problems, though evident by the Third Plenum of the Eleventh Central Committee in December 1978, were not seriously addressed until 1981. Instead, at the Third Plenum, a program of economic readjustment was announced in response to the appearance of a series of domestic budgetary and trade deficits—the largest in the history of the Communist regime. The program, which constituted a major retrenchment, consumed the full attention of both economic and political leaders. At the Second and Third Sessions of the Fifth National People's Congress (June 1979 and September 1980, respectively), several large scientific projects were cut back, and scientists were encouraged to assist with the economic modernization program. High-energy physics, for example, was a prime target for these cutbacks. From an overall perspective, however, the critical shortcomings of the research system were addressed only implicitly. The readjustment program would have important implications for science and technology, particularly with respect to the relationship between research and the economy.[43] However, not until the essential signals underlying the economic readjustment program were in place could Beijing expect any change in the behavior toward the development and use of science and technology.[44]

ECONOMIC READJUSTMENT AND READJUSTMENT OF S & T

Rethinking S & T Modernization

Although the details are scarce, a national science and technology meeting to review the problems and revise the strategy for S & T modernization was

[41] "Problems in Technology Imports Analyzed," *Shijie Jingji Daobao* (World Economic Herald), Feb. 28, 1983, trans. in *JPRS*, no. 83413 (May 5, 1983): 88–89.

[42] For a discussion of the Baoshan steel project, see Martin Weil, "The Baoshan Steel Mill: A Symbol of Change in China's Industrial Development Strategy," in *China Under the Four Modernizations*, 365–93.

[43] According to a speech by Fang Yi in December 1979, "to implement the principle of readjustment, restructuring, consolidating and improving the national economy, scientific and technological work should not be weakened but strengthened." See "National Scientific and Technological Conference in Beijing," *Xinhua*, Dec. 5, 1979, trans. in *FBIS-PRC*, Dec. 6, 1979, L10.

[44] A short discussion of the situation as it existed prior to readjustment is provided in "Factories Apply New Technology in Production," *FBIS-PRC*, Sept. 19, 1980, L26.

held in December 1980.[45] The meeting set the stage for an outpouring of statements regarding the appropriate role of science and technology. These various statements indicate that in early 1981 the stage was being set for a major revision in the approach for stimulating S & T advance.[46]

The new approach was described in two interviews, one with Yang Jike, then vice-governor of Anhui province and a member of the faculty at the Chinese University of Science and Technology, and the other with Tong Dalin, then vice-minister of the SSTC. Yang indicated that applied research would be stressed and that no more than 5 percent of available S & T funds should be devoted to basic research. According to Yang, "the past practice of devoting much manpower and money to isolated sophisticated topics without regard for economic results must change."[47] Tong highlighted five new principles to guide all science and technology work: (1) S & T will be coordinated with the growth of the economy; (2) production technologies and their application will be the key focus of research activity; (3) enterprises should expand their research efforts and strive to popularize research findings; (4) continued efforts should be made to study foreign S & T developments; and (5) basic research should not be ignored, but should grow at a steady but gradual pace.[48] Tong went on to note that the future development of S & T and the success of readjustment of the economy are closely linked.

The fullest expression of the new policy came in a *Renmin Ribao* editorial on April 7.[49] Summarizing further the results of the December 1980 S & T meeting, the editorial noted that the time had come to move away from only "paying attention to advanced science and technology, ignoring production, and reaching for what is beyond one's grasp and of blindly catching up with and surpassing others." The editorial suggested two reasons for China's poor performance with respect to the development of key production technologies: a lack of competition, which has fostered a disregard for economic results, and the tendency to rely principally on increased capital construction rather than on new technology to expand production output.

> What is the aim of scientific research? Some say that it is to probe the unknown. Others say that it is to catch up and surpass world levels. Still others say that it is to achieve good results and train competent personnel. There are grounds for

[45] "Scientists Urged To Contribute to Production," *Xinhua*, Feb. 26, 1981, trans. in *FBIS-PRC*, Feb. 27, 1981, L10.

[46] "Beijing Radio Stresses the Use of Science in the Economy," translated in *China Examines Science Policy* (Springfield, Va.: Foreign Broadcast Information Service, January 1982), 1–2.

[47] "Applied Science to Be Emphasized," *Xinhua*, Jan. 29, 1981, trans. in *FBIS-PRC*, Feb. 5, 1981, L8–9.

[48] "Xinhua Interviews Science and Technology Official," trans. in *China Examines Science Policy*, 11.

[49] "Further Clarify the Policy for the Development of Science and Technology," *Renmin Ribao*, Apr. 7, 1981, trans. in *China Examines Science Policy*, 16–19.

all these sayings. However, what does all this finally boil down to? *To increase the forces of production.* If we deviate from this fundamental aim, it will be difficult to avoid tendencies such as scientific research for its own sake, catching up with and surpassing others for the sake of doing so and achieving good results just for the sake of achieving them, and in the end, production cannot be benefitted and it will be difficult to develop the economy and go on with scientific research.[50]

A more severe criticism of ongoing practices within the S & T sector was presented in a June 1981 editorial in the Shanghai-based *Liberation Daily*. The article, which blamed many of China's problems in the S & T realm on the continued influence of leftist elements, pointed to five problems that had affected the implementation of the program for S & T modernization: (1) placing too much emphasis on blindly catching up with the West; (2) failure to pay adequate attention to the quality of research; (3) impatience for success; (4) continued duplication of research; and (5) neglecting the links between science and technology and the economy.

As the article implied, the last problem was the key: there are insufficient institutional linkages between those responsible for determining economic needs and objectives, on the one hand, and those responsible for setting research priorities, on the other. Consultation and coordination between members of the SSTC and their counterparts in the State Planning and Economic Commissions were rare.

All of the problems cited in the *Liberation Daily*, in one way or another, existed because of Beijing's inability to effectively monitor the implementation process and to ensure adherence to central policies. The State Science and Technology Commission, which had been given the mandate to oversee the rehabilitation and revitalization of the S & T system, had proven itself relatively ineffective at managing national science and technology activities. Public criticism of the SSTC emerged at both the Third and the Fourth Session of the Fifth National People's Congress.[51] Criticism of the SSTC was particularly strong at the Fourth Session in December 1981 when CAS vice-president, Li Xun, seized the opportunity to castigate the SSTC. Even though Li's comments were motivated partly by the traditional rivalries between the SSTC and the CAS, his point that the SSTC had failed to unify research and that institutes were scrambling for research projects without overall coordination was an accurate one.[52]

[50] "Further Clarify the Policy for the Development of Science and Technology."

[51] For a description of the events at the Third Session of the Fifth NPC, see Howard Klein, "National People's Congress Meets in Beijing," *China Exchange News* 8, nos. 5–6 (October–December 1980): 2–3.

[52] Klein, "National People's Congress Meets in Beijing." During this period Chinese scientists in the CAS were unhappy about the efforts of the SSTC to diminish funds for basic research. CAS personnel were distressed by the actions of the SSTC because, they claimed, that organization was staffed not by scientists but by administrators who did not fully understand the nature of scientific inquiry.

The implementation of science and technology policies in the provinces was even more unsettled. The SSTC, acting through its provincial counterparts, continued to be unable to bring about desired changes in personnel policy and the setting of research priorities. Howard Klein documents the basic inconsistencies between the policies coming out of Beijing and the way these policies were being handled at the local level.[53] In a select number of provinces, such as Sichuan, local officials, in conjunction with the provincial branch of the Communist Party, responded in a positive fashion to Beijing's policies.[54] However, in a large percentage of the provinces—Hebei, for example—there was a persistent unevenness in the acceptance and promotion of central policies.[55]

Altering the Implementation Environment

In order to reorient attention toward the development and application of production technologies, fundamental changes in the style and substance of economic management were essential. Discussions about how best to effect these changes were central to the leadership's internal debates concerning the essence of readjustment and economic reform.[56] Beginning in mid-1981, the discourse coming out of Beijing reached a new level of sophistication, with debate focusing on the proper relationship between the plan and the market.[57] One group of decision makers, perhaps led by Chen Yun, viewed the plan as the inviolable principle of economic management.[58] Another group, supported by Xue Muqiao and apparently by Zhao Ziyang, was convinced that overcentralization of decision making was a major source of China's economic stagnation.[59] They advocated relaxation of the plan so

[53] Howard Klein, "An Assessment of Provincial Science Organizations: Current Status and Future Trends," China Consulting Associates (May 1983), unpublished manuscript.

[54] "Sichuan Province Decides to Reform Further the Present System of Scientific Research," *Guangming Ribao*, Sept. 23, 1980, trans. in *China Examines Science Policy*, 123–24.

[55] Li Naiyi, "Place Emphasis on Solving the Question of S & T Work Lagging Behind the New Situation," *Hebei Ribao*, Apr. 26, 1984, trans. in *JPRS-CST* 84–031 (Oct. 15, 1984): 152–54.

[56] See Jack Gray and Gordon White, eds., *China's New Development Strategy* (London: Academic Press, 1982). In many ways, the goals of readjustment and reform contradicted one another. See Wang Jiye and Wu Kaitai, "Resolutely Implement the Strategic Policy of Readjustment," *Renmin Ribao*, Dec. 23, 1980, trans. in *FBIS-PRC*, Jan. 6, 1981, L18–24.

[57] Premier Zhao Ziyang's report to the Fourth Session of the Fifth NPC brought the debates into full swing. In his speech Zhao not only addressed the issue of improving economic results but also commented on the all-encompassing role of the centrally directed economic plan. See "Text of Zhao Ziyang Government Work Report," *FBIS-PRC*, Dec. 16, 1981, K1–35. See also Xu Dixin, "The Current Problem of Economic Readjustment," *Jingji Yanjiu*, June 20, 1981, trans. in *JPRS*, no. 78880 (Sept. 21, 1981): 3–12.

[58] Fang Weizhong, "An Inviolable Basic Principle—Some Understanding on Upholding the Policy of Relying Mainly on the Planned Economy and Supplementing It with Regulation by Market Mechanism," *Hongqi*, May 1, 1982, trans. in *JPRS*, no. 81379 (July 28, 1982): 20–31.

[59] Dorothy Solinger, ed., *Three Visions of Chinese Socialism* (Boulder: Westview Press, 1984).

that market forces could be allowed to determine economic behavior. China's leaders were eager to develop a formula that would harness the "enthusiasm" of the enterprises and, at the same time, prevent a loss of central control over such an important area as capital construction.

One of the key mechanisms adopted to facilitate these changes was the introduction of the economic responsibility system into the industrial sector. As was shown in chapter 9, the response of the peasants in the rural areas to the agricultural responsibility system had been quite positive, though there were some undesirable side effects. Indications that the responsibility system would be widely applied in the industrial sector first appeared at a national conference on industry and transport held in Shanghai in April 1981.[60] The regime's intention to move forward with an even more comprehensive industrial reform was reconfirmed in Premier Zhao Ziyang's remarks at the Third Plenum of the Twelfth Central Committee meeting in late 1984. Reliance on the notion of economic responsibility at the level of the factory would mean that enterprise managers (and workers) would have a material interest in the productivity of their respective firms.[61] Moreover, it would also mean that the basic operating criteria of the past—meeting output quotas—could no longer be the sole consideration in the minds of workers or managers. Instead, a contract system and series of tax reforms were gradually introduced, giving the factory manager, the factory workers, and the factory's suppliers and buyers a financial stake in improving productivity and a legal obligation to meet their commercial obligations.

Introduction of the economic responsibility system was accompanied by several other changes in economic policy, many of which had important implications for science and technology. Most important was the shift in industrial policy from "extensive" to "intensive" development. No longer would productivity increases be sought through the construction of new plants or the importation of whole plants from abroad.[62] Rather, the key to desired increases in productivity would be factory renovation and technological upgrading.[63] Efforts would be made to rationalize plant layout, upgrade

[60] "Industrial Production and Transport Conference Opens," *Xinhua*, Apr. 15, 1981, trans. in *FBIS-PRC*, Apr. 16, 1981, K1–3.

[61] According to Yuan Baohua, deputy head of the State Economic Commission, the economic responsibility system in industry would allow retention of profits and accountability for losses by large and medium enterprises and also provide greater managerial autonomy. See "Industrial Production and Transport Conference Opens."

[62] The new emphasis in technology imports was on the acquisition of know-how and design information rather than large quantities of equipment. Even though decentralization of decision making had posed some problems in 1978–1979, it was believed that the addition of greater local accountability would alleviate some of the problems of waste that had occurred in the past.

[63] According to one study, 60 percent of the equipment in Chinese industry dates back to the 1940s and 1950s, 35 percent from the 1960s, and only 5 percent from the 1970s. See Ding Changqing, "The Machine-Building Industry and Technology Transfer in the National Economy," *Jingji Yanjiu*, July 20, 1982, trans. in *JPRS*, no. 81724 (Sept. 8, 1982): 1–10.

management, and modernize manufacturing techniques. The achievement of significant improvements in energy efficiency also assumed a high priority (see chapter 7 in this volume). In short, the expanded application of science and technology to the existent capital base was policy.[64]

In order to assist with the financing of plant-renovation efforts, the central authorities increased the availability of bank loans and other forms of credit to help pay for acquisition of new items (see chapter 3 in this volume).[65] In addition, a major controversy developed over the existing rate of depreciation in China's industrial plants.[66] Many economists, led by Sun Yefang, claimed that China's depreciation rate was inadequate in comparison with most of the industrialized nations, and that the leadership could not expect modernization of plant and facilities to occur if the period of depreciation remained so long and the rate so low.[67] While Sun's point was well taken, more generous depreciation would increase locally retained funds, possibly providing the financial wherewithal for localities to further subvert central government priorities in areas such as capital construction (as is so clearly shown in chapter 3 above).[68]

Discussion over finances also engendered significant debate over the issue of prices, perhaps the most politically sensitive issue in the realm of Chinese economic policy. Although the leadership was unable, if not unwilling, to

[64] In some cases because of the restrictions applied on further capital construction, several enterprises used the guise of technical transformation as a means to undertake the building of new plants. See "A Second Front Not to Be Ignored," *Jiefang Ribao*, Feb. 3, 1981, trans. in *FBIS-PRC*, Feb. 5, 1981, O5.

[65] "Using Science and Technology to Improve Recovery," *Renmin Ribao*, Nov. 7, 1982, trans. in *FBIS-PRC*, Nov. 10, 1982, K5–12. According to a *Xinhua* report in late 1982, the China Construction Bank provided 1.2 billion yuan in 1982 and 2.0 billion yuan in 1983 in loans for technical transformation of enterprises. See *FBIS-PRC*, Dec. 29, 1982, K20. These funds were supplemented by 11.47 billion yuan in foreign exchange loans provided by the Bank of China between 1979 and 1982. The Bank of China also provided 1.259 billion yuan in *renminbi* loans for domestic production of parts and equipment for imported items—all of which was to be used for technical renovation. See "Loans Used for Technology," *China Daily*, Dec. 20, 1982, 2.

[66] Liu Guoliang, "Reform of Fixed Assets Depreciation System," *Caizheng* (Finance), Dec. 5, 1981, trans. in *JPRS*, no. 80050 (Feb. 8, 1982): 26–27. See also Meng Lian, "Views on Improving the Management of Depreciation Funds of Fixed Assets," *Jingji Yanjiu*, May 20, 1982, trans. in *JPRS*, no. 81215 (July 6, 1982): 34–39.

[67] According to one assessment, China's depreciation rate is only 4.2 percent; the depreciation rate of fixed assets in China includes factory buildings and other utilities beyond production equipment. If it were adjusted to accord more with the Western definition, i.e., to include only production equipment, the rate would still be less than 6 percent—still on the low side. See Sun Shangqing, "Exploration on Technical Transformation," *Jingji Yanjiu*, Feb. 20, 1982, trans. in *JPRS*, no. 80512 (Apr. 7, 1982): 22–35.

[68] In 1982, for example, even though state investment in capital construction declined to 49.8 percent from 56.8 percent in 1981, overall outlays for capital construction increased by 11.2 billion yuan as a result of the enlarging of local autonomy. See Xu Ming, "Ten Billion Yuan: A Warning Mark for Capital Investment," *China Daily*, July 16, 1983, 2.

come to any agreement on when and where to begin, there was a general consensus that major price adjustments would be a necessary prerequisite to achieving significant improvements in plant operation and efficiency. Accordingly, a major step toward price reform materialized at the Third Plenum of the Twelfth Central Committee when Chinese leaders announced a program to remove state-set prices over a large number of goods and services.

Second, new emphasis was placed on improving product quality.[69] Chinese leaders initiated several procedures, including a system of product licensing. Additionally, through this product-licensing mechanism, the State Economic Commission assumed part of the responsibility for making certain that the past practice of producing and overstocking useless goods was abolished. With the introduction of profit and loss within Chinese enterprises, factory managers presumably would become more concerned about the marketability of their products. The availability of alternative goods and the presence of competitors would alter enterprise behavior and enhance the incentives to adopt new technologies and processes—at least that was the hope.

Third, there was a movement toward consolidation of enterprises. This was being encouraged to close down many of the small and inefficient plants that repeatedly lost money. One good example of a successful effort is the television industry in Shanghai. By combining a large number of component producers into a single, large, operating entity, Shanghai leaders have improved efficiency, created greater standardization, and increased overall productivity.[70] One of the central government's aims appears to have been to confront the "small producers" mentality that has been so pervasive in Chinese industry. Now, factories that had pursued the practice of "small and complete" were encouraged to become more specialized. Likewise, factories with many geographically dispersed components were told to bring their various plants under one roof or within closer proximity of one another.

A fourth move to strengthen productivity was embodied in the effort to break down the barriers between the civilian and the defense industrial sectors. China's defense sector has been favored in resource allocation during the last thirty years. According to a report by China's Ministry of Ordnance, the military sector has had appreciably more and higher-quality manpower, manufacturing and testing equipment, and greater financial and political support. To better utilize the unused production capacity in the defense sector, the leadership has encouraged greater cooperation with civilian institutions. Previously, central tasking had been the major vehicle for

---

[69] "Quality Controllers Congress Opens in Beijing," *Xinhua*, Sept. 22, 1982, trans. in *FBIS-PRC*, Sept. 23, 1982, K9–10.

[70] Information supplied from interview in Shanghai by Professor William Fischer, University of North Carolina, 1983.

achieving cooperation between the two sectors. Now, within the bounds of security considerations, the scope and timing of cooperation would be left to the individual components themselves.[71]

Support for the building of bridges between civilian and military industries has come from the highest levels in the Chinese leadership. Zhang Aiping, minister of national defense and former head of China's National Defense Science and Technology Commission, has viewed the development of a civilian R & D capability as an integral part of the overall national modernization drive.[72] He has argued that defense and civilian industries should share information and resources.[73] In early 1983 Zhang stressed that China cannot rely on other nations for acquisition of desired technologies, and he emphasized the need to strengthen the country's scientific and technological research base.[74] Computer and electronics development appears to be one specific area where this bridge-building is being emphasized.[75]

Freeing Up S & T Resources

The various economic reforms mentioned above, by changing the context of implementation, have had important implications for the effectiveness of the S & T reforms themselves. Among the initiatives aimed directly at the S & T system itself, several are critical. Most important has been the initiation of a formal contract system. Factories and research institutes are now encouraged to sign agreements for the exchange of services. Each contract specifies a certain formula for compensating the research institute for its contributions. This emphasis on contract-related research is part of an effort to encourage greater cost-consciousness within the research unit and also to assist the research sector in obtaining funds that cannot be supplied by the central government. Institutes within the CAS, as well as those attached to industrial ministries, have been engendered to depend on the contract approach.

Three forms of contracting appear to predominate: (1) the institute sells its rights to a new technology directly to the factory and receives a fee; (2) the institute signs a contract with a factory to provide technical assistance and receives a percentage of the profit at an annually decreasing rate; and (3) an

---

[71] "Institute Urges Combining Military and Civilian Research," *Keyan Guanli* (Scientific Research Management), July 1982, trans. in *JPRS*, no. 82108 (Oct. 28, 1982): 53–63.

[72] In mid-1982, the National Defense S & T Commission and the National Defense Industries Office were combined to form the National Defense Science, Technology and Industries Commission (NDSTIC), led by Chen Bin.

[73] "Zhang Aiping Stresses PLA's Modernization," *Xinhua*, Dec. 26, 1982, trans. in *FBIS-PRC*, Dec. 27, 1982, K4.

[74] "Zhang Aiping on National Defense Modernization," *Zhongguo Xinwen She* (China News Service), Feb. 28, 1983, trans. in *FBIS-PRC*, Mar. 1, 1983, K8–9.

[75] "Zhang Aiping Hails Electronics Industry Role," *Xinhua*, Mar. 2, 1983, trans. in *FBIS-PRC*, Mar. 4, 1983, K14–15.

institute provides technology to a factory and receives a percentage of sales as compensation, once again at a decreasing rate. These types of arrangements link the productivity of the factory to the utility of the research, and vice versa. In addition, it also serves as a vehicle for "capitalizing" technology— something the Chinese system lacked before the introduction of the research contract system.[76]

Where enterprises and research units have sought to go beyond the limited, short-term features of the contract, they have formed cooperative ventures called alliances, brain trusts, research-production unions, and coalitions.[77] The distinguishing feature of these new organizational forms is that they involve cutting across various administrative boundaries—though the member organizations do not relinquish their formal institutional affiliation. They are structured to facilitate both the joint planning and the selection of projects. The research that occurs is production-oriented, involving both horizontal and vertical integration. Profits and losses are jointly shared, once again providing both partners with a vested interest in a successful venture.

Another innovation designed to promote the implementation of policies for science and technology deals with the new provisions for labor mobility and consulting.[78] In an attempt to expand the availability of technical expertise both to enterprises and to government agencies, scientists and engineers have been given the opportunity to sell their services on a fee-for-service basis. Research units have been instructed to allow their personnel, after completion of their regular jobs, to serve as consultants on a part-time basis.[79] In addition, research societies under organizations such as the China Association for Science and Technology can perform a technical advisory role. This role was formalized in early 1983 with the formation of the China Science and Technology Consultative Service Center in Beijing.[80] The center will serve as a mechanism for bringing together multidisciplinary teams of experts to advise on technical and economic matters on a fee-for-service basis.[81]

[76] Wang Cailiang, "A Number of Problems in Managing Industrial Research with Economic Methods," *Kexuexue Yu Kexue Jishu Guanli*, 1982, no. 1, trans. in *JPRS*, no. 81724 (Sept. 8, 1982): 49–53. Some reservations were expressed at the time regarding the possibility for excesses if adequate political work did not accompany the new emphasis on economic rewards.

[77] Zhou Jinquan, "Bright Future for Implementing Joint Ventures in Scientific Research and Production," *Kexuexue Yanjiu Lunwen Xuan*, 1981, no. 2: 49–55.

[78] "Consultancy," trans. in *Summary of World Broadcasts—Far East*, FE/W1198/A, Aug. 18, 1982, 12.

[79] "Organization and Leadership in Scientific and Technical Consulting Services," *Wen Hui Bao*, Dec. 3, 1981, trans. in *JPRS*, no. 80479 (Apr. 2, 1982): 5–8.

[80] "Scientific Consultancy Service Expanded," *Xinhua*, Jan. 28, 1983, translated in *FBIS-PRC*, Jan. 30, 1983, K6–7.

[81] See also "Fang Yi at Opening of Scientific Service Center," trans. in *FBIS-PRC*, Mar. 22, 1983, K6–7.

These new policies are all designed to stimulate research units to make a sustained effort to insure that their projects have some economic purpose. By encouraging the commercialization of research and at the same time promoting the economic responsibility system in industry and facilitating cooperation between civilian and defense units, the leadership has introduced several new dimensions to the research-production interface previously absent in the Chinese system. So far, as the experience in such provinces as Liaoning indicates, the results have been appreciable, with various new amalgams of research and production units being formed regularly.[82] In addition, municipalities with a strong scientific and technical base such as Shanghai have taken to offering technical guidance and expertise to other geographic areas throughout the country.[83]

These efforts to "deregulate" the research system have been complemented by a program to build a strong research capability within the university system and to link that capability with the technology needs of various enterprises.[84] Faced with a shortage of funds to acquire new equipment and to modernize existing facilities, educational institutions, such as Jiaotong University in Shanghai, have started providing consulting services as a means of raising needed monies. In 1982 the Department of Technical Services at Jiaotong earned over 1.5 million yuan from consulting activities.[85] Faculty can earn 10 percent of the overall profits as a bonus for engaging in these activities. Other universities, such as Fudan and Qinghua, also have attempted to take advantage of the contract research system that is emerging, embarking on similar programs with industry, particularly with respect to electronics and computers. And, toward this end, in late 1984 it was announced that the Chinese Academy of Sciences, in all likelihood, would partially divest itself of control over some of its institutes, moving them over to universities as part of the effort to build university-based research capabilities.

One other current effort being pushed by the current leadership to assure more effective policy implementation is the placing of persons with technical credentials in positions of power and authority. In May 1981 the Chinese Academy of Sciences held a major election in which many management positions were restaffed with scientists rather than administrators. Fang Yi, form-

[82] Zheng Shen, "Cooperation with Research Units Raises Production," *China Daily*, May 2, 1983, 2.

[83] "National Economic Meeting Opens," *Xinhua*, Jan. 27, 1983, trans. in *FBIS-PRC*, Jan. 28, 1983, K7–10. Over 17 provinces are cooperating with Shanghai. In 1982 over 105 technical delegations from around China visited Shanghai to discuss possible technical exchanges.

[84] Lu Dong and You Huadong, "Enterprises Must Develop New Technology in Coordination with Institutes of Higher Education," *Jingji Guanli* (Economic Management), Aug. 15, 1982, trans. in *JPRS*, no. 82045 (Oct. 21, 1982): 12–15.

[85] "University Faculty Receives Bonus for Consulting Work," *China Daily*, Feb. 10, 1983, 3.

er CAS president and former minister-in-charge of the SSTC, but not a scientist, was replaced by Lu Jiaxi, a chemist trained in the West. And in mid-1984, Song Jian, an engineer with extensive experience in China's aeronautics and space programs, replaced Fang Yi as director of the SSTC. Similar changes also have occurred within the local-government apparatus. The number of provincial-level officials with a college education increased from 20 percent in 1978 to 43 percent by mid-1984. In Liaoning, for example, two engineers were named deputy governors.[86] The Communist Party also has been stepping up its efforts to recruit scientists and technicians. Since 1979 the Fujian Provincial Branch of the CCP has admitted almost 10,000 professionals as part of its attempts to dampen the legacy of the Cultural Revolution and to increase leadership competency to make technical decisions.[87]

In spite of the fact that Beijing's new policies have been well received both by factories and by research institutes, implementation of these policies to reengineer the environment in which the shift toward applied science takes place has not always proceeded smoothly. For example, the work environment for intellectuals remains quite difficult.[88]

We should realize that many people are suffering from "short-sightedness." The longstanding leftist ideas of belittling science, culture and the intellectuals, and the pernicious fallacies about the intellectuals spread by the "gang of four" are still affecting the minds of some comrades. Much effort is needed to eliminate this influence. Today, this influence is manifested in: (1) Ideologically and theoretically, some people have not yet truly realized that the great majority of intellectuals are components of the working class who have mastered relatively more knowledge in science and culture. (2) Some people do not really understand that the further we go with modernization, the more we need intellectuals. They even think that "without intellectuals, production will be carried on and houses will be built just the same," and so on. It is high time this kind of prejudice and narrow-mindedness was gotten rid of.[89]

Problems have arisen also with respect to the compensation due scientists and engineers for their consulting activities. In one case, a Shanghai technician was accused of illegal economic dealings when he accepted money for technical assistance he had rendered to a local rubber-product research institute.[90] Although he was later acquitted of the charges, the very fact that such an incident occurred had a chilling effect on others. In another example, in Guangxi province, three technicians were admonished for accepting a

[86] "Technical Experts Appointed to Leading Posts," *Beijing Review*, May 17, 1982, 5. Similar appointments have been made in other provinces and municipalities throughout China.
[87] "Fujian Intellectual Party Members," trans. in *FBIS-PRC*, July 14, 1983, O7.
[88] "Scorn for Intellectuals Is Sign of Backwardness," *China Daily*, Dec. 20, 1982, 4.
[89] "A Major Problem in Implementing the Policy Toward Intellectuals," *Hongqi*, Sept. 1, 1982, trans. in *JPRS*, no. 82121 (Oct. 29, 1982): 22–26.
[90] "Spare-time Work Lands Technician in Trouble," *China Daily*, Dec. 25, 1982, 3.

remuneration of 300 yuan for designing a barge for a local company in Nanning. They were acquitted, but only after severe public ostracism.[91]

The "commercialization" of research has led also to the formation of "technological blockades" in several regions.[92] Spurred on by the potential profitability of developing or possessing various marketable technologies, certain research institutes and enterprises have become reluctant to share their information with their counterparts locally or in other parts of China. And, jurisdictions that are noncompetitive seek to exclude the products of others from their localities. The implementation of a domestic patent law in April 1985 to protect "proprietary" information will, in principle, make the hoarding of technical information less economically rational. Serious questions about the enforcement of the law, however, still remain unanswered.

The ongoing program to increase the efficiency and effectiveness of research units has also encountered obstacles. One source of these problems continues to be administrative and political interference in research.[93] In one example, the work of a research scientist at Shandong Normal University was sabotaged for political reasons by the deputy director of the scientist's research institute.[94] In other instances, under the pressures for "success," scientists themselves have falsified research findings or violated the scientific ethics of the research community.[95] Lastly, the administrative groups within various research institutes have appropriated a "percentage" of the rewards received by some scientists for their research accomplishment, thereby reducing economic incentives for scientists.[96]

Finally, in spite of the efforts to develop and apply science and technology to production through greater reliance on market forces, there has been a parallel effort to further *centralize* decision-making authority. Owing to the continued inability of the SSTC to effectively implement policies for modernizing science and technology, the leadership decided in January 1983 to form a new organization at the supraministerial level to handle the country's major S & T–related matters.[97] This organ is headed by Premier Zhao

[91] "Unjust Punishment of Technicians Criticized," *Guangxi Ribao*, Mar. 10, 1983, trans. in *JPRS*, no. 83145 (Mar. 28, 1983): 27.

[92] Xu Guoquan, "How to View the Keeping of Technical Secrets," *Wen Hui Bao*, Feb. 11, 1981, trans. in *FBIS-PRC*, Feb. 27, 1981, O2–3. See also Shen Junbo et al., "Three Problems in Technical and Economic Cooperation," *Jiefang Ribao*, July 15, 1982, trans. in *JPRS*, no. 81927 (Oct. 5, 1982): 7–10.

[93] Lu Jiaxi, "Several Problems Concerning Current Scientific Research Management," *Keyan Guanli*, July 1982, trans. in *JPRS*, no. 82108 (Oct. 28, 1982): 1–9.

[94] "Conduct Hampering and Sabotaging Scientific Research Definitely Not Allowed," *Renmin Ribao*, Nov. 25, 1982, trans. in *JPRS*, no. 82643 (Jan. 14, 1983): 156–58.

[95] "Ethical Norms for Scientists," *Beijing Review*, Sept. 6, 1982, 24–25, 30.

[96] "Science Awards Cut to Ribbons," *China Daily*, Feb. 19, 1983, 3.

[97] "Zhao Ziyang to Head New Scientific Work Group," *Xinhua*, Jan. 30, 1983, trans. in *FBIS-PRC*, Jan. 31, 1983, K8–9.

Ziyang and is composed of members from all of China's leading civilian and defense organizations, thereby bringing to the S & T front the authoritative stamp of the premier's office on many policy issues.[98]

From one perspective, the emergence of a new centralized body to govern S & T activities stands in direct contradiction to the nature of the reforms described above; this is true. Pressures for recentralization in the S & T area have arisen for two reasons. First, Beijing clearly believes that in certain priority areas direct intervention by the central government is necessary to ensure appropriate levels of coordination and concentration of resources. And second, under a decentralized environment, Beijing lacks the tools to insure consistent adherence to its policies. Within a setting where the financial and personnel resources to advance S & T modernization are scarce, the leadership fears waste and, as in other policy areas, sees its power to set priorities slipping away. In a nutshell, this is the dilemma which the present reform policies pose across the board. The motive for delegation of decision-making authority was efficiency and innovation. However, for delegation to be effective, resources must follow. The provision of resources, in turn, enables lower levels to set priorities that may be at variance with the desires of central planners. It would appear that the leadership can have either more efficiency and innovation or more control, but the experience of the last few years indicates that it is difficult to have both across the board.

PROSPECTS AND CONCLUSIONS

The challenge for reformers ... lies in utilizing the discipline inherent in a closed system to loosen the structure and thus to permit the system to adapt and learn rather than remain persistently sealed from the social forces in its midst.[99]

The literature on policy implementation suggests that environmental context is an important determinant of the success or failure of implementation. Because of the nature of the prevailing economic or political climate, programs identical in content may be implemented differently within various systems. One of the key variables in explaining the different outcomes within alternative environments is the varying degrees of central control. Some regimes opt for a decentralized approach in order to provide the widest flexibility in policy execution. Yet, under these circumstances, national leaders must rely on local leaders, who may act according to the dictates of their local situation or interests rather than central directives.[100]

[98] Since mid-1982 Premier Zhao appears to have taken a more direct interest in the situation regarding science and technology. See Zhao Ziyang, "A Strategic Question on Invigorating the Economy," *Beijing Review*, Nov. 15, 1982, 13–20.

[99] Peter Cleaves, "Implementation Amidst Scarcity and Apathy," in Merilee Grindle, ed. *Politics and Policy Implementation in the Third World* (n. 1 above), 301.

[100] Grindle, *Politics and Policy Implementation in the Third World*, 18–19.

In the Chinese case, a more decentralized approach was initiated in order to overcome the lack of linkage between research and production units. This approach, however, weakened the regime's ability to manage the political dimensions of the implementation problem. By the granting of greater local autonomy, power increasingly devolved into the hands of local officials, some of whom remained committed to the policies and practices of the Maoist era. This weakened Beijing's program for modernizing science and technology. The continued difficulties being experienced by intellectuals throughout China is indicative of the costs incurred by adopting a decentralized approach. This is not to suggest that centralized efforts would have met with any greater success; it is only to highlight the trade-offs when dealing with implementation variables that have different systemic origins.

To overcome the problem of deviation from national priorities, the regime found it necessary to create a high-level S & T body to intervene when and where necessary. Paradoxically, since the May 1982 government reorganization, the move toward decentralization also spawned a proliferation of new organizations responsible for handling high-priority projects that cannot be left to the vagaries of the "unplanned" system. The "leading group for science and technology" has been joined by a "leading group for electronics development" and several other entities at the State Council level, suggesting that Beijing recognizes the need for a "mixed" strategy of implementation. This strategy combines elements of both central guidance and local initiative.

The fact that historically China's most successful technological advances were made in the defense area—where central coordination has been the most extensive—has not gone unnoticed by current leaders. The appointment of Song Jian to direct the affairs of the SSTC, with his defense background and strong advocacy of cybernetics and systems management, confirms that this approach is still valued in the highest echelons of power.

One of the most interesting of the new bodies established at the Center is the Group for Techno-Economic Research. This research and policy-making organization is particularly important because of the oversight role that it plays in the selection and appraisal of national projects. Headed by Ma Hong, who until 1985 also was president of the Chinese Academy of Social Sciences, the group conducts feasibility studies of projects that involve substantial personnel and financial resources. It is composed of natural scientists, engineers, and social scientists, who are charged with providing an interdisciplinary perspective on prospective projects. The need to create and maintain such bodies underlies Beijing's continued apprehension over the "deregulation" of various aspects of the economy.

At the same time, Chinese economic and S & T policy makers continue to speak about technology markets, venture capital, and further expansion of the contract research system. It is hoped that as the overall economy becomes more sensitive to the dynamics of competition, greater attention will be paid to the value of building stronger links between research and production. New awards have been established for individual S & T personnel whose research leads to major advances. Unlike the past practice, when the philosophy of "eating from the same big pot" meant that these awards would be shared, each individual is guaranteed the full amount. In addition, a series of new, locally managed "technology development centers" have been started, each individually or collectively run. As with these other efforts, their main purpose will be to stimulate greater innovativeness and promote the commercialization of R & D.

The focus of this chapter on the "facilitative" aspects of China's implementation strategy highlights the essence of Deng's reform strategy: one cannot implement new policies in an old, inhospitable institutional and economic context. Since authorities in Beijing have not had the power to ensure implementation, contextual reforms, along with continued reaffirmation at the central level of the content of the policy (i.e., S & T serving the economy) have proved to hold the most promising results. This finding supports those described in chapters 2 and 9 in this volume, where it was noted that political leaders can increase the effectiveness of implementation by manipulating either the content of the policy or its political context.

China's experience also highlights the continued tension (particularly in socialist regimes) between the imperatives of control and innovation. The ability to maintain control becomes extremely difficult when external actors are given the resources for independent action. Additionally, as several other essays in this volume indicate, the Chinese case underscores the need to mobilize sufficient political support at all levels to execute a central policy decision successfully. Science and technology as a social activity, unlike economic activity, does not have a readily consumable output that can be utilized by a wide spectrum of the populace. And, in most instances, the output that is produced yields long-term rather than immediate gratification or satisfaction. As a result, the payoffs for expending resources must be made clear from the start. Both China's scientific community and its economic managers have had a different sense of what these payoffs are and should be. The challenge facing Beijing, therefore, will be to create appropriate incentives for innovation without losing at the same time the ability to set priorities and to maintain political support for policies that may have a payoff only in the long run.

PART VI

Political Participation and Elections

THIRTEEN

Leninist Implementation:
The Election Campaign

Barrett L. McCormick

INTRODUCTION

The implementation of reforms in China's system of people's congresses is the subject of this chapter. In June 1979, the National People's Congress passed new laws altering the structure of local government and election procedures. They abolished the revolutionary committees formed during the Cultural Revolution and reinstituted the system of people's congresses and people's governments. They guaranteed various democratic procedures, such as a choice of candidates on ballots, the use of secret ballots, and the right of deputies to submit motions and to query state administrators. For the next eighteen months the Party led a campaign to implement the new laws. The Ministry of Civil Affairs organized and mobilized provincial governments, which mobilized county governments, which mobilized grass-roots units. Despite many reports of delays and malfeasance by lower-level cadres, the nation's 2,757 county-level jurisdictions eventually held direct elections for deputies to local people's congresses and reconstituted people's governments. By examining this "implementation campaign," the kind of resistance it engendered, and the context in which it occurred, this essay will reach conclusions about both implementation in Leninist states and politics in China.

The literature on implementation suggests useful comparisons between China and other countries, and yet the special characteristics of the Chinese political system suggest that such comparisons need to be drawn with caution. In chapter 6 in this volume, "Water: Challenge to a Fragmented Political System," we find many competing organizations with conflicting interests. The tugging and hauling that is described is reminiscent of Pressman and Wildavsky's classic account of bumbling implementation in the United

States.[1] This makes a pluralist interpretation of Chinese politics tempting. However, in the United States the focus of public attention is on policy formation. In China and most of the Third World, the state limits access to policy formulation. This radically changes the context of implementation. As Merilee Grindle writes, "the process of implementing public policies is a focus of political participation and competition."[2] In its classic formulation ("from the masses, to the masses"), the mass line states that the Party will study the interests of the masses, formulate policy, and then allow localities some freedom to determine how the policy will be implemented. The Party asserts an exclusive right to set policy, but localities implement policy according to a multitude of local circumstances. Local circumstances introduce fragmentation and uncertainty to the process of implementation, but they are not the equivalent of American-style pluralism. Bargaining in China between the center and localities is not equivalent to bargaining in the United States among autonomous interest groups and the state.

The comparison between China and the other Third World states provides important insights, and yet China is not the same as other Third World states. China is not a "soft state," to use Gunnar Myrdal's characterization of South Asian states.[3] In China, state organization reaches from central offices in Beijing to each urban neighborhood and rural village. The state owns all major economic enterprises, its economic plan exercises a decisive impact on all other enterprises, and there are no autonomous universities or independent newspapers. China's leaders have been able to alter the land tenure system several times, whereas most authoritarian states have found land reform a daunting task. Population policy, as described in chapter 10 in this volume, is another example of the impressive power of the Chinese state.

Implementation in China occurs in the special context of a Leninist state and patrimonial politics. I will begin by discussing the concept of a "Leninist state," which has several defining characteristics. First, state organization thoroughly penetrates society. Usually one of the first steps in establishing a Leninist state is the extension of political organization from a single center outward to include all political parties, unions, professional associations, firms, and service organizations. Usually this organization is so comprehensive that it reaches all neighborhoods and villages. Second, the state has an hegemonic role in the economy. In some (Stalinist) systems this is accomplished through state ownership of nearly all significant economic

[1] Lampton, this volume; Jeffrey L. Pressman and Aaron Wildavsky, *Implementation: How Great Expectations in Washington Are Dashed in Oakland* (Berkeley and Los Angeles: University of California Press, 1973).
[2] Merilee Grindle, "Policy Content and Context in Implementation," in *Politics and Policy Implementation in the Third World*, ed. M. Grindle (Princeton: Princeton University Press, 1980), 3–34.
[3] Gunnar Myrdal, *Asian Drama: An Inquiry Into the Poverty of Nations* (New York: Twentieth Century Fund, 1968).

organization and command-style economic planning. This results in politics dominating economics. Even those Leninist states that have adopted "market-socialism" have maintained a degree of economic authority far surpassing authoritarian states. In particular, the lack of an autonomous bourgeoisie means that one of the major constraints on the autonomy of most authoritarian states is lacking. Third, Leninist states articulate a relatively formal ideology. This ideology typically states that the party has no "selfish" interests, but that it must adopt a "leading role" in society to achieve an inevitable and comprehensive transformation of society. This "leading role" not only justifies the organizational and economic activities outlined above but also justifies supervision of all public speech. Leninist states sometimes allow brief periods of relative permissiveness, but usually their organization is adequate to insure that nearly all public speech conforms with the current "line," and will resort to coercion when more subtle means fail. In addition to these central characteristics, Leninist states usually practice extensive supervision of personnel matters. Higher levels supervise promotions and appointments at lower levels in political, social, and economic organization—that is, *nomenklatura* in the Soviet Union and "the appointment system" in China. In addition, Leninist states usually maintain an extensive system of secret police coupled with an extensive system of files or dossiers on individual citizens.[4]

In comparative terms, Leninist states are relatively autonomous, and society in a Leninist state lacks relative autonomy. For example, in describing the corporatism of a "bureaucratic-authoritarian state," Guillermo O'Donnell writes that "it contains two components. . . . The first of these is *estatizante* ('statizing'); it consists of the conquest and subordination by the state of organizations of civil society. The other is *privatista* ('privatist'); it consists of the opening of institutional areas of the state to the representation of organized interests of civil society."[5] In practical terms, O'Donnell argues that bureaucratic-authoritarian states "subordinate or destroy" popular organizations such as labor unions while opening the state to serve private bourgeois interests, and that this enables the state to increase the rate of accumulation to "deepen economic growth."

In Leninist states, the "statization" of popular organizations is relatively more thorough. Both types of states intervened in a violent and coercive manner, but Leninist states have been far more successful in building organi-

---

[4] Edward Friedman's "Three Leninist Paths Within a Socialist Conundrum," in *Three Visions of Chinese Socialism*, ed. Dorothy J. Solinger (Boulder: Westview Press, 1984), 11–45, was helpful to me in formulating the central characteristics of a Leninist state, but Professor Friedman is not responsible for the way I use that term.

[5] Guillermo A. O'Donnell, "Corporatism and the Question of the State," in *Authoritarianism and Corporatism in Latin America*, ed. James M. Malloy (Pittsburgh: University of Pittsburgh Press, 1977), 48.

zational structures that perpetuate the subordination of popular interests to the state. Bureaucratic-authoritarian states have been unable to match the network of party cells and neighborhood organizations that define Leninist states. Popular organizations have survived and returned to the forefront of politics in Latin America, but in most Leninist states this seems a remote possibility.[6] Nor have Leninist states opened institutional areas of the state to any private interests (with the possible exception of those of individual state cadres). Whereas the autonomy of bureaucratic-authoritarian states has been limited by a relatively autonomous bourgeoisie, Leninist states have completely destroyed the bourgeoisie as a class.[7] Leninist state power rests not on the support of any social class, but on organizational and economic hegemony. This gives Leninist states a far greater capacity to implement social change than bureaucratic-authoritarian states.

The fragmentation of Leninist states is not equivalent to Western-style pluralism. In contrast to Leninist states, politics in Western liberal democracies involve conflict and compromise among a wide range of relatively autonomous groups and the central authorities. The state and its ranking leaders can influence both the agenda and the outcome of politics but tend to be confined by the culture, institutions, and the relatively autonomous groups around them. The system favors outcomes beneficial to those who already have wealth and power, but the culture and the institutions that sustain the system tend to be reproduced by society and are not dependent on the state.[8] Leninist states are not monolithic in the manner of the totalitarian model, and terms such as Jerry Hough's "institutionalized pluralism" are useful as correctives.[9] However, as Archie Brown argues, citing Robert Dahl's definition of pluralism, a "diffusion of influence" is not the same as "the existence of a plurality of relatively autonomous (independent) organizations (subsystems) within the domain of a state." Brown states: "The crux of the matter is *relative autonomy*."[10] Because Western-style pluralist states are well rooted in society, they tend to be stable, but compared with Leninist states, they lack the autonomy to impose unpopular policies.

For an understanding of the tugging and hauling that does occur in Lenin-

[6]The significant exceptions to this generalization are, first, Czechoslovakia, where in 1968 the leaders of the state decided on their own to reactivate civil society, and Poland, where the autonomous power of the Catholic Church was never effectively subordinated to the state.

[7]For a discussion of the role of the bourgeoisie in limiting the autonomy of even a revolutionary state, see Nora Hamilton, *The Limits of State Autonomy: Post-Revolutionary Mexico* (Princeton: Princeton University Press, 1982), esp. 3–39.

[8]To use Antonio Gramsci's terms, in the United States the bourgeoisie is hegemonic, not merely dominant. See *Prison Notes* (New York: International Publishers, 1971).

[9]Jerry Hough and Merle Fainsod, *How the Soviet Union Is Governed* (Cambridge: Harvard University Press, 1979).

[10]Archie Brown, "Political Power and the Soviet State," in *The State in Socialist Society*, ed. Neil Harding (Albany: State University of New York Press, 1984), 59–60.

ist states, I will discuss the second central concept of this chapter, patrimonial politics. Patrimonialism refers to Weber's ideal type of authority.[11] Guenther Roth distinguishes two kinds of patrimonialism: one based on tradition, and one based on "loyalties that do not require any belief in the ruler's unique personal qualification, but are inextricably linked to material incentives and rewards."[12] In other words, patrimonialism is a system of authority built on networks of patron-client relationships.[13] Weber does not isolate patrimonialism from other forms of authority. In particular, he argues that rational-legal authority, which is bound by rules and bureaucratic organization, and patrimonial authority are *not* mutually exclusive. In Andrew Nathan's words: "The hierarchy and established communications and authority flow of the existing organization provides a kind of trellis upon which the complex faction is able to extend its own informal, personal loyalties and relations."[14]

The strength of formal organization in Leninist states makes extensive patrimonialism *inevitable*.[15] Some Leninist regimes have openly used patrimonialism as a means of recruiting loyal supporters, but the frailty of this kind of legitimacy makes it a strategy of last resort.[16] More often, patrimonialism is an inadvertent result of the structure of the state. The comprehensive hierarchical organization of Leninist states enables the Party to control access to social mobility, including education, employment, and

[11] For Max Weber's discussion of patrimonialism, see Weber, *Economy and Society* (Berkeley and Los Angeles: University of California Press, 1971), 1006–1110.

[12] Guenther Roth, "Personal Rulership, Patrimonialism and Empire Building," in *Scholarship and Partisanship*, ed. R. Bendix and G. Roth (Berkeley and Los Angeles: University of California Press, 1971), 156–69.

[13] Patron-client relationships are usually defined as distinctly personal relationships that involve direct exchanges between participants, which are usually mutually profitable but unequal. For a bibliography of literature on patron-client relations, see S. N. Eisenstadt and Louis Roniger, "Patron-Client Relations as a Model of Structuring Social Exchange," *Comparative Study of Society and History* 22, no. 1 (1980): 42–77.

[14] Andrew Nathan, "A Factional Model for CCP Politics," *China Quarterly*, no. 53: 44.

[15] For evidence of patrimonial politics in the USSR, see Konstantin Simis, *USSR: The Corrupt Society* (New York: Simon & Schuster, 1982); and Wayne DiFranceisco and Zvi Gitelman, "Soviet Political Culture and 'Covert Participation' in Policy Implementation," *American Political Science Review* 78, no. 3 (September, 1984): 603–21. DiFranceisco and Gitelman argue that a substantial majority of Soviet citizens find bribery and "personalized relationships" the most effective means of effecting political outcomes and relate this to the structure of Leninist systems. For Poland, see for example, Andrew Smolar, "The Rich and the Powerful," in *Poland: Genesis of a Revolution*, ed. Abraham Brumberg (New York: Vintage Books, 1983). For an excellent discussion of Romania with broad theoretical implications, see Ken Jowitt, "Soviet Neo-Traditionalism: The Political Corruption of a Leninist Regime," *Soviet Studies* 35, no. 3 (July 1983): 257–97. For a discussion of Bulgaria that contains rich examples of patrimonial politics, see Georgi Markov, *The Truth That Killed* (New York: Ticknor & Fields, 1984).

[16] Many people have pointed out that patron-client relationships can be a means of building legitimacy. However, this type of patronage in China and other Leninist states destroys legitimacy.

promotion. Because Chinese organization limits lateral movement—that is, peasants cannot easily move to a city or even to a more prosperous district, and workers cannot easily look for a job with another factory—most people find themselves dependent on individual supervisors, which inevitably creates opportunities for leaders to use their official authority for personal advantage. In addition, the rigid planning and supply systems mean that surpluses and scarcities abound, with informal interpersonal ties being the only equilibrating mechanism. Finally, although interest groups cannot form autonomous organizations to articulate universalistic political demands, small groups or individuals can present particularistic issues to individual officials in an endless quest for special favors. Considered together, these sources of patrimonialism constitute a passive but powerful and pervasive form of resistance to the state.

Leninist states are caught in a dilemma. They have tremendous political power, but the implementation of policy is defeated by unanticipated consequences and patrimonial resistance. For much of its history, the Chinese Communist Party has been locked in a cycle of fighting corruption by mounting campaigns that generate more corruption. The Yanan Rectification, the Sanfan-Wufan Campaign, the Siqing Campaign, the Cultural Revolution, the Yida-Sanfan Campaign, and since the death of Mao, struggles against "bourgeois liberalism," "spiritual pollution," and the current campaign for Party rectification—all have had the fighting of corruption as a central theme, but patrimonialism remains a pressing problem. "Open" rectification campaigns, like the Cultural Revolution, have aroused popular energies, but have severely weakened institutions, leaving little alternative to personalistic politics. "Closed" campaigns, conducted within the bounds of formal organization and with the goal of strengthening that organization, have resulted in temporary gains, but they leave the structure of organization unchanged. Their future can only be more of the past. In Ken Jowitt's terms, Soviet-style systems are "neo-traditional," endlessly generating rational-legal reforms that are inevitably overcome by a patrimonial environment.[17]

Leninist states institutionalize systems of privilege for ranking cadres, such as restricted shops, special distribution of scarce consumer goods, etc. In Poland, as other bases of legitimacy deteriorated, Gierek made ample use of this kind of patronage to recruit loyal followers (see Smolar). However, this kind of patronage and less-official patronage is available primarily to those who already have power and position. For example, the child of a ranking cadre is far more likely than an ordinary person to have strings to pull to obtain favorable employment and housing. Faced with fundamental inequalities of power and privilege, it is only natural for ordinary people to question the nature of the system and the motives of leaders. *The net result is a deep and widespread cynicism.* Edward Friedman is very good at capturing typical Chinese reaction to patronage, in his article (n. 4 above).

[17] Jowitt, "Soviet Neo-Traditionalism."

THE REFORM PROPOSAL

Against the backdrop of this conceptual framework, this chapter examines the implementation of the Electoral Law for the National People's Congress and the Local People's Congresses of the People's Republic of China (the Electoral Law) and the Organic Law of the Local People's Congresses and the Local People's Governments (the Organic Law), both of which were passed by the Second Session of the Fifth National People's Congress in June 1979. Before presenting the details of the new laws, I will discuss briefly the situation at the time they were promulgated.

Peter Cleaves outlined the pressing problem of implementation in Leninist systems: "In closed systems . . . the state concentrates enormous relative power within its boundaries, but it tends to become blind to the society of which it is a part. . . . A frequent occurrence is that leadership, exhilarated by the reflection of its own power, sponsors highly problematic policies that fail spectacularly."[18] The Great Leap Forward, which probably led to the deaths of tens of millions of Chinese, is a tragic example of how the power and isolation of Leninist states can lead to failure.[19] The Cultural Revolution provided the Chinese with another poignant illustration of the same problem.

After Mao died, many Chinese began to think about the problem of the state, and particularly to think about means of limiting and directing state power. Some youthful critics spoke boldly about the "autonomization of the state organs," the "Asiatic Mode of Production," and the "alienation of power."[20] While not necessarily rejecting Marxism or socialism, these critics called for fundamental changes, such as an end to censorship, an end to the "appointment system," a multiparty system, and the division of executive, legislative, and judicial powers. The group around Deng Xiaoping was equally aware of the problem, but described it in less dramatic terms. Deng lent his prestige to an extensive discussion of "practice."[21] This discussion entailed a criticism of "leftism," "subjectivism," and dogma, all of which Mao had forcefully criticized in his classic essay "On Practice." The central idea of

[18] Peter S. Cleaves, "Implementation Amidst Scarcity and Apathy," in M. Grindle, *Politics and Policy*, 281–303.

[19] Estimates of the number of deaths caused by the Great Leap Forward can be found in Judith Bannister and Samuel H. Preston, "Mortality in China," and Ansley J. Coale, "Population Trends, Population Policy and Population Studies in China," *Population and Development Review* 7, no. 1 (March 1981): 98–110 and 85–97.

[20] See, respectively, Chen Erjian, *Crossroads Socialism*, trans. and ed. Robin Munro (London: Verso, 1984); Wang Xizhe, *Mao Zedong and the Cultural Revolution* (Hong Kong: Plough Publications, 1982); and Li Yanshi, "Commenting on So-Called 'Alienation of Power'," *Nanfang Ribao*, Jan. 30, 1984, trans. Foreign Broadcast Information Service, *China: Daily Report* (hereafter referred to as *FBIS-CHI*) 84-027 (Feb. 8, 1984): P1.

[21] For a sample of that discussion, see *Practice* (Shijian), vols. 1 and 2, ed. the editors of *Zhexue Yanjiu* (Beijing: Zhongguo Shehui Kexue Chubanshe, 1979).

this discussion was that to maintain its grip on reality, *or even to survive*, the state and the Party had to be sensitive to the results of "practice." Practice could only be understood and interpreted in a democratic atmosphere where arbitrary abuses of state power could not be used to suppress unpleasant truths. The party's leading theorists made trenchant public statements criticizing the lack of democracy and calling for prompt reform.[22] In December 1978 the Third Plenum of the Eleventh Party Central Committee called for "strengthening socialist law and socialist democracy."[23]

However, the official definition of democracy incorporated the central features of the Leninist state. Many Chinese and Westerners understood Deng's December 1978 declaration that "democracy wall is good" to indicate an endorsement of the broadest definitions of democracy.[24] Nonetheless, in March 1979 he asserted a traditional Leninist definition of democracy. He stated that the "four cardinal principles" of adherence to the socialist road, insistence on the dictatorship of the proletariat, upholding the leadership of the Party, and sticking rigidly to Marxism-Leninism and Mao Zedong Thought, had to be maintained.[25] At the same time the reform laws were passed, democracy-wall activists were arrested, democracy walls were closed, unofficial publications were suppressed, and intellectuals who had taken part in the wide-ranging debates were silenced. The prosecutor at one activist's trial summed up the official definition of "freedom of speech":

> . . . each citizen's freedom of speech must adhere to the socialist road, insist on the dictatorship of the proletariat, uphold the leadership of the Party and stick rigidly to Marxism-Leninism and Mao Zedong Thought, and these very freedoms alone constitute the Four Basic Principles. There exists no freedom to violate them but only the freedom to uphold them.[26]

Nonetheless, the new laws promulgated shortly thereafter by the National People's Congress promised considerable reform.[27] They defined institutions

---

[22] For example, Wu Jialin wrote: "Our socialist system determines that our socialist democracy should and can be superior to bourgeois democracy. But 'should be' does not mean 'actually is' and 'can' does not denote 'in reality.' It is, to say the least, a naive illusion to think that the system of socialist democracy arises and becomes complete of its own accord without a long period of practice and hard struggle." From "Some Questions Concerning Socialist Democracy," *Beijing Review*, 1979, no. 24 (June 15): 9–13, reprinted in *Chinese Law and Government* 15, nos. 3–4 (Fall–Winter 1982–1983): 99.

[23] The Communique of the Third Plenum is translated in *Beijing Review*, 1978, no. 52 (Dec. 29).

[24] For an account of the impact of this statement, see John Fraser, *The Chinese* (New York: Summit Books, 1980), 230–50.

[25] Deng Xiaoping, "Uphold the Four Cardinal Principles," *Selected Works of Deng Xiaoping* (Beijing: Foreign Languages Press, 1984), 166–91.

[26] "Trial of Wei Jingsheng," *SPEAHRhead*, no. 11 (Autumn 1981): 30.

[27] For a general discussion of the new laws, see Liu Zhuanchen, Pan Bowen, and Cheng

and procedures to strengthen popular supervision of government through the system of people's congresses. China currently has people's congresses at the county, provincial, and national levels, and in some cases at intermediate levels, such as cities under the jurisdiction of a province. At each level of government, people's congresses are theoretically the highest authority, subject only to higher levels of government, except the National People's Congress, which is "the highest organ of state power."[28] The most important provisions stipulated that all deputies to county-level congresses should be directly elected by voters. Previously, deputies to rural county-level congresses were elected by commune-level congresses.[29] Other important reforms included:

1 The new laws guarantee the use of secret ballots. Previously, secret ballots were used in urban areas, but in rural areas, elections often were conducted at mass meetings by a show of hands.

2 The Electoral Law mandates that ballots should always have more candidates than positions. Previously, the number of candidates on the ballot usually equaled the number of positions available.[30]

3 The new law reaffirms the right of citizens to nominate candidates for county-level deputy positions.[31] During the previous decade candidates were usually nominated by the Party.

Jiyou, *Xuanju Fa Zhishi Wenda* (Questions and Answers on Election Law Knowledge) (Shanghai: Shanghai Social Sciences Institute, undated).

[28] *The Constitution of the People's Republic of China* (Beijing: Foreign Languages Press, 1982), 45.

[29] Under present law, deputies to people's congresses above the county level are still elected by the congress at the next lower level, but Minister of Civil Affairs Cheng Zihua has stated that in the future direct election will be extended to higher levels. See Brantly Womack, "The 1980 County-Level Elections in China: Experiment in Democratic Modernization," *Asian Survey* 22, no. 3 (Mar. 3, 1982): 263.

[30] Under the new laws, when county-level deputies are chosen, the number of candidates should exceed the number of positions by 50 to 100 percent, and for higher-level people's congresses, the number of candidates should exceed the number of positions by 20 to 50 percent. One explanation offered for the difference in these ratios is that the deputies to the county-level congresses are elected from election districts each of which elects only a small number of candidates, and therefore the ratio must be higher to insure choice, whereas the deputies to higher-level congresses are elected by lower-level people's congresses, each of which elects a large number of deputies, such that there will be a choice even with a low ratio of candidates to positions. See Tong Ming, "Election with the Same Number of Candidates as Positions and Election with More Candidates Than Positions," *Renmin Ribao*, Feb. 21, 1980, 5, trans. *FBIS-CHI* 80-50 (Mar. 12, 1980): L16.

[31] Actually, nominating is not equivalent to putting a candidate on the ballot. Voters submit nominations to election committees, which, in consultation with voters, establish the actual lists. As Zhang Qingfu and Pi Chunxie argue, the new laws revitalize "democratic consultation" and "integrate the higher with the lower level." See "Revise the Electoral Laws to Institutionalize Democracy," *Renmin Ribao*, May 22, 1979, 3, trans. *FBIS-CHI* 79-103 (May 25, 1979): L5–8.

4   The new laws reaffirm the right of deputies to query state adminis-
    trators and to submit motions to the congresses.[32]
5   The Organic Law empowers county-level people's congresses to estab-
    lish standing committees, a privilege previously restricted to higher-
    level congresses. As full sessions of county-level congresses usually
    occur only once a year for a few days, this theoretically will allow for
    more continuous supervision of local administration.

Despite the insistence on Party leadership and ideological conformity, the
reformers still stated that the reforms would provide many of the benefits
associated with "bourgeois" democracy. In introducing the new laws to the
Second Session of the Fifth National People's Congress, Peng Zhen declared:

> Local revolutionary committees are to be replaced by local people's govern-
> ments. . . . Local people's governments are responsible and accountable to the
> people's congresses at the corresponding levels and to their standing commit-
> tees. As a result of these changes, in localities at or above the county level, the
> people's control and supervision over the local people's governments will be
> substantially strengthened.[33]

The immediate political situation created classic problems of political implementation. First, the aims of the reforms were both hotly contested and
contradictory. Definitions of the democracy China ought to build ranged
from Western parliamentarianism to limited rectification within the Party.
Others, particularly cadres with roots in the Cultural Revolution, rejected
democracy outright. No single reform could accommodate all of these political directions, and the official definitions of the reform incorporated the contradictory proposals of strengthening the Party's leadership of society and
allowing for more popular supervision of government. Second, as Brantly
Womack states, "however popular these democratizing measures are, it was
the support of central leadership rather than popular pressure that led to
their adoption."[34] Concisely, the elite decided to initiate reform, the state
apparatus implemented it, and the elite decided when it had gone far
enough. Moreover, cadres who stood to lose from the reforms would be expected to implement them.

The Leninist vision identifies the party with a moral truth that has the
material force to triumph in history. This relegates conflict to issues of fun-

---

[32] The right to submit motions is not unprecedented. Townsend states that in the 1950s
deputies submitted "fantastic" numbers of motions, just as they do now. See James R. Townsend, *Political Participation in Communist China* (Berkeley and Los Angeles: University of California
Press, 1968), 109.

[33] Peng Zhen, "Explanation of the Seven Draft Laws," in *Main Documents of the Second Session of
the Fifth National People's Congress of the People's Republic of China* (Beijing: Foreign Languages
Press, 1979), 197.

[34] Brantly Womack, "The 1980 County-Level Elections," 162.

damental principle and denies it a positive role in the world of everyday politics. Mao extolled the virtues of conflict, but as Edward Friedman writes, he carried a lighted match, looking for the "forces that would explode and advance egalitarian and communitarian goals."[35] Given the turbulence of the Cultural Revolution and other political campaigns, and the very vivid turmoil of Chinese society throughout the first half of the twentieth century, most Chinese would like to avoid any more explosions. The Western proposition that social conflict strengthens democracy seems absurd in this context. Xu Chongde and Pi Chunxie argue that in capitalist parliaments opposing cliques of monopoly capitalists fight and struggle, but in the people's congresses, deputies represent the common interests of the people and are able to work with "one heart and one mind" to achieve unanimity.[36] Many Chinese can identify with this quest for peace and unanimity. However, confining the reforms within the strictures of a Leninist state raises doubts about the degree to which the people's congresses would provide for popular supervision of government, let alone provide an adequate check on practice. In short, these reforms were implemented in a specific historical, cultural, and institutional context. The definition of democracy was unclear, the dominant political institutions were hostile to it, and many feared the "chaos" that might result.

IMPLEMENTING THE REFORMS

A Leninist strategy of implementation is described in this section. The reformers issued authoritative instructions regarding the content of the reforms and the procedures to be used in adopting them. These statements were publicized in the media and in official state and Party documents. Preexisting government and Party organizations were adapted to implement the reforms. This organization enabled higher levels to mobilize lower levels, culminating in door-to-door canvassing of most of the Chinese citizenry. During the actual process of nominating and voting, election committees at the grass-roots level, in cooperation with other grass-roots organizations, closely monitored all proceedings. This Leninist implementation campaign proved very effective. Besides managing a reform of local government in a reasonably short time, it produced an enormous voter turnout and, with few exceptions, elected what the regime could consider "responsible" deputies.

Through their organization, the Beijing authorities were able to establish and impose an official definition of the reforms despite the general lack of consensus. By Chinese standards the instructions issued to lower levels were

[35] Edward Friedman, "The Innovator," in *Mao Tse-tung in the Scales of History*, ed. Dick Wilson (New York: Cambridge University Press, 1977), 313.

[36] Xu Chongde and Pi Chunxie, *Xuanju Zhidu Wenda* (Questions and Answers on the Election System) (Beijing: Qunzhong Publishing Co., 1980), 158.

precise and public. First and foremost, the reforms were announced and defined in laws publicly promulgated and widely discussed. By Western standards the new laws were imprecisely worded, but in a Chinese context, where there are few laws and where most administrative directives have been and remain "internal" (*neibu*) or secret, these laws were a bold and forceful means of declaring commitment to the reforms. Second, various reports indicate that the state and Party issued other more detailed "internal" instructions to lower levels.[37] Third, the Ministry of Civil Affairs and the General Office for National Direct Election at the County Level produced other, less formal documents explaining the reforms, including at least one widely distributed manual that contains 120 straightforward questions and answers on the elections.[38] Although there were various means of resisting implementation, the organizational force behind these announcements made public criticism difficult.

The campaign for the implementation of election reform began at the national level. Party activities relevant to election work were not widely discussed in the press, but were of crucial importance. At a Party Central Conference on Election Work, it was stated: "The fundamental guarantee for successful elections is to strengthen Party leadership."[39] Election work was formally launched and monitored by the National People's Congress and its Standing Committee. Peng Zhen associated himself with the reforms. A prominent victim of the Cultural Revolution, Peng's visible presence highlighted the regime's commitment to change, but his long-standing commitments to organization, order, and the Party also suggested limits to "democratization." Election work at the national level was conducted by the Ministry of Civil Affairs and the General Office for National Direct Election at the County Level (the General Office). Cheng Zihua served both as minister of civil affairs and director of the General Office. The Ministry of Civil Affairs began by conducting experimental elections in five selected county-level jurisdictions.[40] These experiments established the sequence of procedures used to conduct elections throughout the country: preparation, propaganda, voter registration, nominating candidates, balloting, and convening congresses.

Election work at the provincial level officially began following a resolution adopted by the Standing Committee of the Fifth National People's Congress in February 1980.[41] However, this resolution was something of a formality,

---

[37] See for example, Hefei, Anhui Provincial Service, Feb. 13, 1980, trans. *FBIS-CHI* 80-032 (Feb. 14, 1980): O3–4.

[38] Xu Chongde and Pi Chunxie, *Xuanju Zhidu Wenda*.

[39] Beijing Xinhua Service, Feb. 11, 1980, trans. *FBIS-CHI* 80-031 (Feb. 13, 1980): L6.

[40] Beijing Xinhua Domestic Service, Feb. 11, 1980, trans. *FBIS-CHI* 80-031 (Feb. 13, 1980): L4–6. See also Shenyang, Liaoning Service, Oct. 25, 1979, trans. *FBIS-CHI* 79-210 (Oct. 29, 1979): S2–3.

[41] Beijing Domestic Service, Feb. 12, 1980, trans. *FBIS-CHI* 80-031 (Feb. 13, 1980): L3.

as the central authorities had begun to mobilize provincial-level authorities in December 1979. First, they held a conference attended by provincial leaders, at which the experimental elections were discussed. The ministry also sent work teams staffed by cadres from the General Office to twenty-one provinces to supervise experimental election work.[42] Provincial authorities later supervised further experimental elections.[43] Just as election work at the national level was monitored by the National People's Congress and conducted by the General Office, election work at the provincial level was monitored by provincial people's congresses and conducted by provincial election committees. Provincial election committees generally included approximately twenty leading provincial figures and had a staff to conduct day-to-day business.[44] With the weight of state and Party organizations bearing down from above, provincial cadres were under tremendous pressure to promote implementation of the reforms and to follow Beijing's guidelines. Accordingly, county-level officials were soon mobilized at work conferences convened by provincial authorities.[45]

To follow the process of implementation from the provincial to the grassroots level, this chapter will focus on two districts in the city of Nanjing (Nanking). Because of the limited number of cases, caution must be used in drawing general conclusions from these two cases. Nanjing is the capital of Jiangsu province and has a population of about three and a half million. Administratively, Nanjing resembles a prefecture (*diqu*), being an intermediate level between the province and counties and having jurisdiction over several county-level units. By the time of this writing (December 1983), Nanjing had been enlarged, but at the time of the elections (1980), Nanjing was subdivided into three suburban counties (*xian*) and nine urban districts (*qu*). This portion of the chapter will focus on election work in two of those districts, Baixia and Gulou. Gulou district, with a population of about 300,000, is Nanjing's largest district and is located in the center of the city. Baixia, with a population of about 200,000, is also predominantly urban.

The election campaign reached Nanjing in early June of 1980 when Jiangsu province launched a second wave of trial elections.[46] At that time the Standing Committee and the leading Party Group of the City Revolutionary Committee convened one or more meetings of leading comrades from county

[42] Cheng Zihua, "Cheng Zihua's Report," Beijing Xinhua Domestic Service, Sept. 11, 1981, trans. *FBIS-CHI* 81-177 (Sept. 14, 1981): K2–10.

[43] See for example, Nanchang, Jiangxi Provincial Service, Feb. 25, 1980, trans. *FBIS-CHI* 80-041 (Feb. 28, 1980): O2.

[44] See for example, Changsha, Hunan Provincial Service, Mar. 25, 1980, trans. *FBIS-CHI* 80-066 (Apr. 3, 1980): P6.

[45] See for example, Hefei, Anhui Provincial Service, Mar. 11, 1980, trans. *FBIS-CHI* 80-055 (Mar. 19, 1980): O9.

[46] Nanjing, Jiangsu Provincial Service, Dec. 28, 1980, trans. *FBIS-CHI* 80-252 (Dec. 30, 1980): O1–3.

and district revolutionary committees and civil affairs departments to begin work.[47] Zhou Bopan, an assistant secretary of the City Revolutionary Committee, explained the goals of election work, announced the formation of a Municipal Election Committee, and outlined procedures to be followed. In organizational and procedural matters Zhou closely followed guidelines from above. The Municipal Election Committee was chaired by Zhou Bopan, had approximately twenty members, and was supported by an office staff. Election work was to proceed in four stages: preparation, propaganda and voter registration, nomination of candidates and consultation to determine the official candidates, and voting and convening the congresses. The city's leaders also announced the schedule for subsequent election work in Nanjing. Work on experimental elections in Jiangning county and Baixia district was scheduled to begin immediately, with the goal of convening people's congresses in the first third of September.[48] Other districts and counties were to begin election work on July 1 and to convene congresses by the end of September.

The first stage of election work, preparation, called for extending election organization from the city level down to the grass roots. First, election committees were established at the district level. In both Gulou and Baixia districts, the district election committee was formally under the direct supervision of the District Revolutionary Committee. The Gulou District Election Committee had nineteen members and an office with twenty-seven staff members.[49] According to the higher level's guidelines, election committees were to be composed of people from as many different circles as possible. In both Gulou and Baixia, district election committees were reported to include leading members of the district Party organization, representatives from other democratic parties, and representatives from the worker, women, and youth mass organizations. In addition, the Gulou committee, and probably the Baixia committee, included representatives from the District Public Security, Civil Affairs, and Propaganda Departments.[50]

Second, election work was organized from the district level down to the grass roots. The district election committees divided their districts into election districts (*xuanju qu*) and established an election committee in each.[51]

[47] For a general account of this meeting, see Ling Xuan, "Shi Wei Bushu Xian Qu Xuanju Gongzuo" (City Committee Plans District and County Direct Election Work), *Nanjing Ribao*, June 15, 1980, 1.

[48] "Wo Shi Juti Bushu Xian Qu Zhijie Xuanju Gongzuo" (Our City Makes Concrete Plans for County and District Direct Election Work), *Nanjing Ribao*, June 3, 1980, 1.

[49] Author's interview with election officials at Gulou District Office, Sept. 23, 1980.

[50] Interview at Gulou District Office, and Jun Ji and Jia Hu, "Baixia Qu Zhijie Xuanju Gongzuo Quanmian Zhankai" (Baixia District Direct Election Work Fully Launched), *Nanjing Ribao*, June 21, 1980, 4.

[51] In Gulou district, a population of approximately 300,000 was divided into 173 election districts, each district having from 500 to 8,000 voters and electing from one to twelve representatives, each of whom represented from 500 to 1,500 voters, with an average of about 800.

Election districts could consist of a single unit, an amalgamation of two or more smaller units, or a residential neighborhood. The Baixia District Election Committee convened a meeting of all election-district election committee members to plan further work in early June 1980.[52] Still another layer of election committees was formed at the unit level. All units (except those affiliated with the People's Liberation Army), including lane offices, soon formed election work groups.[53]

The second stage of election work, propaganda, called for a general mobilization. By any standards except those of the Cultural Revolution, this was a major effort in social mobilization. Throughout the city, approximately 74,000 "backbone elements" explained to voters both the procedures and the "significance" of the elections. They used blackboards, materials published by the districts, and the network of loudspeakers in Chinese residential areas, and convened meetings. Throughout Nanjing there were approximately 12,700 meetings held in conjunction with this propaganda effort. The Municipal Election Committee estimated that 80 percent of the city's three and a half million people received education regarding the elections.[54] Gulou district officials claimed to have reached everyone in the district at least once and to have reached many people several times.[55]

Voter registration, conducted by election-district election committees, was also a form of mobilization. Voter registration, as in previous campaigns, involved assessing the political standing of each citizen. However, in past campaigns the emphasis was usually on "ferreting out" counterrevolutionaries. In this campaign the emphasis was on rehabilitating those unjustly accused. In Gulou district nine people were deprived of political rights.[56] Cheng Zihua reported to the Standing Committee of the National People's Congress that political rehabilitations occasioned by the process of voter registration were one of the campaign's major achievements.[57]

The third stage, the nominating process, is supposed to be a cycle of

---

The national average was about 1,250 voters per representative (Cheng Zihua, "Cheng Zihua's Report"). Larger units, such as Nanjing University, were intentionally underrepresented, as their problems and interests were considered distinct from those of the district as a whole. (Interview at Gulou District Office.)

[52] Jun Ji and Jia Hu, "Baixia Qu Zhijie Xuanju Gongzuo Quanmian Zhankai."

[53] "Guanyu Xian [Qu] Zhijie Xuanju Wenti" (On the County [District] Direct Election Question), *Nanjing Ribao,* June 27, 1980, 4.

[54] Ling Xuan, "Wo Shi Xuanju Xuanchuan Quanmian Zhankai Guangda Xuanmin Zhengzhi Reqing Gaozhang" (Our City's Election Propaganda Fully Launched: Vast Numbers of Voters' Political Zeal Runs High), *Nanjing Ribao,* July 25, 1980, 4.

[55] Interview at Gulou District Office, Sept. 23, 1980.

[56] Ibid. Another 218 people were denied the right to vote on the basis of mental incompetency.

[57] Cheng Zihua, "Cheng Zihua's Report."

democratic consultation between voters and cadres. According to the new
election laws, any voter, seconded by three other voters, can nominate the
candidate of their choice. However, in practice the final list of candidates is
established by the election-district election committee "in consultation" with
small groups of voters. The process used in Nanjing (and in most other
places) is known as the "three ups and three downs" (san shang san xia). In
the first round, voters meeting in small groups based on their work group or
their residence, depending on the type of election district they vote in, are
encouraged to make nominations. The election manual urges the selection of
candidates who support the Party and its policies, who are "progressive,"
who are enthusiastic workers, and who enjoy close relations with the
masses.[58] A member of the Election Work Group of Nanjing University set
forth similar criteria for prospective candidates.[59]

The initial round of nominations usually produces a surfeit of nominees.
In Baixia district, the Nanjing Aviation Institute Election District produced
511 nominations for three positions.[60] These initial lists are forwarded to the
election-district election committee, which narrows the field according to its
own dictates. At the Aviation Institute, which was cited as a model, the
entire list, reduced to 269 names by eliminating duplications, was returned to
each small group. The small groups were asked to select the best 5 or 6
candidates from the entire list and to return the short list to the election-
district election committee. The committee in turn narrowed the field to 23
candidates and then held a meeting of representatives from the Party, the
school administration, the union, the youth league, and "all sections of the
masses" to choose the final 5 or 6 candidates.[61] While the new laws allow for
primary elections, officials in Gulou district were aware of only one election
district that had held a primary election, and this was regarded as an unfortunate breakdown of the "three ups and three downs" process. Even in
theory, the nominating process is closely supervised by lower-level cadres
and, as is discussed below, they can easily exert more influence than is
formally permitted.

The fourth stage of the election campaign is voting. The new law is supposed to guarantee voters a choice by putting more candidates on the ballot
than there are positions to be filled. However, the choices are limited. First,

[58] Xu and Pi, Xuanju Zhidu Wenda (n. 36 above), 12.
[59] Author's interview with staffer of Nanjing University Election Work Group, Sept. 25, 1980.
[60] Tan Jiahu, "Nanhang Xuanqu Xuanchu De Daibiao Qunzhong Manyi" (Masses Satisfied
with Deputies Selected in Nanjing Aviation Election District), Nanjing Ribao, July 18, 1980.
[61] Ibid. The exact number of candidates is determined by the election committee during the
"three ups and three downs" process. The laws only stipulate that the number of candidates
appearing on the ballot for county-level deputies should outnumber the number of positions by
50 to 100 percent. Gulou district officials had a preference for keeping the list as short as
possible.

the nominating procedure largely prevents political nonconformists from appearing on the ballot. Second, despite clauses in the electoral law allowing candidates to "campaign," in practice candidates are restricted from making direct overtures to voters. Cheng Zihua has criticized Western-style election campaigns: "In their election campaigns bourgeois candidates often give an extravagant account of what they are going to do and make promises of one kind or another, but after they are elected they often refuse to do what they promised."[62] Other provisions in the Election Law, stipulating that the list of official candidates is to be posted twenty days before the election along with "background data" on the candidates for "repeated discussions and democratic consultations," more closely approximate practice.[63] In their officially endorsed election manual, Xu and Pi state that it is better for election committees to publish materials on behalf of all candidates than for candidates to conduct individual propaganda. In the Nanjing University Election District, campaign literature consisted of a single sheet of paper briefly outlining candidates' biographies and displaying their pictures. The few instances where candidates have conducted their own election campaigns have proved extremely controversial, as is discussed below.

All these procedures result in the election of deputies already endorsed by the Party, such as model workers, Party members, activists, and "backbone elements." In Gulou district, of 339 deputies elected, 164 were model workers, and about the same number were Party members.[64] In the press some commentators have deplored this problem, arguing that while model workers are good people, they may not be the individuals best qualified to actively represent the masses in the congresses.[65] Even official guidelines and ranking leaders have urged election workers to work against the tendency to nominate and elect too many Party members.[66]

The manner in which results of elections are reported indicates that the opinions or platforms of candidates are noncontroversial or taken for granted. In a few isolated instances names of successful candidates are reported, but usually election results are reported only in an aggregate form. For example, cadres in the Gulou district office reported that in Gulou district, of 339 deputies elected, there were 213 men and 126 women and that there were 47 cadres, 37 workers, 18 scientists or technical workers, 53 educators, 38 from the commercial sector, 13 doctors, 46 from organs of the

[62] Cheng Zihua, "Cheng Zihua's Report."

[63] For the relevant codes, see "People's Republic of China Electoral Law for the National People's Congress and Local People's Congresses at All Levels, Article 28." Reprinted in *Chinese Law and Government* 15, nos. 3–4 (Fall–Winter 1982–1983): 201–2.

[64] Interview at Gulou District Office, Sept. 23, 1980.

[65] Li Yuan, "Bring Into Full Play the Role of NPC Deputies," *Guangming Ribao*, Apr. 14, 1981, 3, trans. *FBIS-CHI* 81-082: K2.

[66] See for example, Cheng Zihua, "Cheng Zihua's Report," K8.

government and Party, 11 from the Public Security Department, 56 neighborhood activists, 6 national minorities, and 4 from Taiwan.[67] Exclusive use of this form of reportage implicitly admits the irrelevance of the deputies' own viewpoints. The only reports describing the attitudes of successful candidates emphasize that they are the kind of candidates that the guidelines favor nominating, that is, individuals who support the Party, who are enthusiastic workers, and who enjoy "close relations with the masses." The Party's ability to insure the election of such candidates is strong evidence of its ability to suppress social conflict and gain at least formal popular legitimation for its activities.

The high rate of participation in the elections reveals both the symbolic quality of the elections and the regime's mobilizational capacity. Juan Linz writes that elections in "totalitarian" systems are characterized by "an extraordinary emphasis on participation and involvement of the voter, very often in the pre-electoral process as well as in the election."[68] Cheng Zihua, minister of civil affairs and director of the General Office for National Direct Election, emphasized precisely the high rate of participation:

> Those who actually cast their votes (in 1,925 county-level units holding elections to date) . . . account for 96.56 percent of the registered voters. Never before had there been such a high rate of participation in voting. In this regard, the broad masses said contentedly: "The flowers we grew ourselves are beautiful: the fruit trees we planted ourselves give us sweet fruits."[69]

In this context, voting is not spontaneous and does not express a simple choice among candidates. Linz goes on to state: "Perhaps outside observers are too often tempted to consider the 99.9 percent figure endorsing totalitarian elections as delegitimizing the regime's authority, but for many citizens living under such regimes its total authority can be terribly real."[70]

RATIONAL LEGALISM AND PATRIMONIALISM

The Leninist strategy of policy implementation was considered in the previous section primarily in terms of rational-legal authority, that is, the leaders of the Chinese state made official statements of policy and then made use of extensive formal organization. This strategy has proved a powerful means of implementing state policy, a means more powerful than those available to the leaders of most other kinds of states. However, Leninist states generate a debilitating form of opposition that can be understood in terms of Max

---

[67] Interview at Gulou District Office, Sept. 23, 1980.
[68] Juan Linz, "Non-Competitive Elections in Europe," in *Elections Without Choice*, ed. Guy Hermet, Richard Rose, and Alain Rouquie (New York: John Wiley and Sons, 1978), 44.
[69] Cheng Zihua, "Cheng Zihua's Report," K6.
[70] Linz, "Non-Competitive Elections," 51.

Weber's ideal type of patrimonial authority. As I stated above, patrimonialism refers to authority based on informal and personal relationships.[71] In a purely patrimonial setting, an administrator does not distinguish between his official and his private life; rather, his office is a kind of property he may use for any purpose he sees fit. In comparison with the pure case of rational-legal or bureaucratic authority, this kind of authority is corrupt and arbitrary.[72] China is neither purely bureaucratic nor purely patrimonial. Rather, the two kinds of authority are intertwined in a complex relationship that is at the same time contradictory and symbiotic. The aim of the rest of this essay is to unravel this relationship.

The official state bureaucracy organizes China into functional "units" (*danwei*), which might be, for example, a factory, a farm, or a school. Units are in turn aggregated into hierarchical "systems" (*xitong*). All Chinese belong to a unit. Chinese not only depend on their units to fulfill many basic needs, they cannot transfer to a new unit without their unit's permission. Units and unit leaders are in turn subject to the administrative authority of systems. Promotions usually occur within a single unit or system and seldom involve lateral transfer. As in the Soviet practice of *nomenklatura*, higher levels closely supervise personnel matters at lower levels. This hierarchical and compartmentalized form of organization offers the state tremendous influence over the communication of ideas and the flow of wealth in society. The state controls all the principal links between compartments. It makes nearly impossible any open or formally organized opposition to the state or the current leadership. Without this trellis to support them, campaigns like the election campaign would simply be impossible.

The comprehensive character of Leninist organization inevitably generates extensive networks of informal relationships. The state demands that nearly all significant social interaction should occur within the bounds of its formal organization; there is very little "space" for an autonomous civil

---

[71] Weber defines the "pure type" of traditional authority as follows: "This type of organized rule is, in the simplest case, primarily based on personal loyalty which results from common upbringing. The person exercising authority is not a 'superior,' but a personal master, his administrative staff does not consist mainly of officials but of personal retainers, and the ruled are not 'members' of an association but are either his traditional 'comrades' or his 'subjects.' Personal loyalty, not the official's impersonal duty, determines the relations of the administrative staff to the master" (*Economy and Society*, 226–27).

[72] In Weber's words: "The patrimonial office lacks above all the bureaucratic separation of the 'private' and the 'official' sphere" (ibid., 1028); and referring to patrimonial authority: "There is a wide scope for actual arbitrariness and the expression of purely personal whims on the part of the ruler and the members of his administrative staff. The opening for bribery and corruption, which is simply a matter of the disorganization of an unregulated system of fees, would be the least serious effect of this if it remained a constant quantity, because then it would become calculable in practice. But it tends to be a matter which is settled from case to case with every individual official and thus highly variable" (ibid., 239–40).

society to negotiate formal relationships on its own. On the other hand, the hierarchical and compartmentalized structure of official organization leaves many potentially practical or profitable relationships without official sanction or regulation. Administrators of formal bureaucratic authority perpetually find that official purposes cannot be accomplished within the confines of official organization. They find that they must negotiate informal relationships beyond the state's formal supervision, relationships that in turn open avenues for the pursuit of personal aims.

This relationship between formal and informal organization occurs in many settings; I will outline three typical instances. First, the tremendous authority vested in superiors means that subordinates must account for superiors' personal interests as well as organizational interests. One Chinese commentator wrote:

> Under the conditions of the proletariat having seized political power, to implement the appointment system [i.e., the Chinese version of *nomenklatura*] for a long period of time must give rise to a psychology of lower levels regarding upper levels with awe and finding themselves inferior and some cadres must respond only to upper levels, ignoring the people's interests and aspirations. In this way, bureaucratism can emerge at the present historic period, and even in the proletarian Party and inside the revolutionary ranks, feudal monarch-official or master-servant relations of personal dependence can still be revived.[73]

Second, this form of organization makes formal communication across hierarchical lines very cumbersome. When units from different systems need to make exchanges, it is often more efficient to use informal channels. This leads to the evolution of informal networks outside formal hierarchical organization. These patrimonial networks can be used as a means of resisting the demands of rational-legal organization and bending the power of the state for personal profit. Third, as will be discussed, this system limits the making of political demands to particularistic forms, focusing on individual requests to individual leaders for special consideration for a specific problem, that is, asking for favors. All three of these patterns create a tremendous potential for corruption.[74]

Higher-level cadres responsible for implementing the election reforms left no doubt that many subordinate cadres resisted their implementation. Peng Zhen reported:

[73] Wu Mi, "Guanliaozhuyi Yu Weirenzhi" (Bureaucratism and the Appointment System), *Shanxi Ribao*, Nov. 14, 1980; also *Xinhua Wenzhai*, 1981, no. 1: 10–11.

[74] Corruption has been a focus of concern in the post-Mao press. This has led many to assume that the various "liberal" political and economic reforms have increased the opportunities for corruption. However, neither corruption nor patrimonialism is more prevalent in post-Mao China than it was during previous decades. Exposing and fighting corruption has been a consistent theme in the Chinese press and political campaigns.

At present, quite a number of cadres and other people are not yet familiar with these procedures of socialist democracy [i.e., the reform laws]. This is especially true because the lingering influence of the fascist dictatorship instituted by Lin Biao, Jiang Qing and their ilk still exists *and the vestiges of feudalism are still quite strong.* As a result, some of our cadres, including leading cadres, lacked understanding of socialist democracy and are not accustomed to democratic practices. They are averse to democracy and elections, thinking that they cause too much trouble. *"Elections? What's the point?" they grumble.*[75] [Emphasis added]

Many lower-level cadres failed to follow the provisions of the Electoral Law. They procrastinated in organizing elections, gerrymandered election districts to increase representation of government and Party offices, arbitrarily intervened in the nomination process, failed to place more candidates than positions on the ballot, revoked the credentials of individual deputies lawfully elected but not supported by the local leadership, invalidated entire elections when the results did not please the local leadership, and halted entire county election campaigns in mid-course.[76]

Cadres were *not* resisting the reforms because they threatened to reduce the authority of the Party. Guidelines from higher levels specifically adjured local cadres to "correctly make use of the methods of democratic centralism, concentrate the correct views of the majority of the masses in a timely way and guard against letting things drift."[77] In other words, the reformers at the Center remain Leninists. They have no intention of abandoning the leading role of the Party and have made this amply clear to lower-level cadres.

In fact, the Center claimed that implementation of the Organic Law would increase the legal authority of local governments. Xu Chongde argued that this would give local authorities more control over local administration:

In the past, work departments (offices, bureaus, sections, divisions and so forth) were under so-called dual leadership. However, in actual practice they were more often under the control of the department at the next higher level, so that the people's government at the same level could not give full play to its enthusiasm. Now the organic law stipulates that all work departments should be under the unifed leadership of the local government at the same level.[78]

[75] See for example, Peng Zhen, "Report on the Work of the Standing Committee," in *Main Documents of the Third Session of the Fifth National People's Congress* (Beijing: Foreign Languages Press, 1980), esp. 90–91. A slightly different translation is available in *FBIS-CHI* 80-186, Supplement 076 (Sept. 23, 1980): 29–31.

[76] See for examples, Shijiazhuang, Hebei Provincial Service, in *FBIS-CHI* 81-099 (May 22, 1981): R5; Beijing Xinhua Domestic Service, Sept. 3, 1980, in *FBIS-PRC* 80-173 (Sept. 4, 1980): L12–13; Changchun, Jilin Provincial Service, Sept. 4, 1980, trans. *FBIS-PRC* 80-176 (Sept. 9, 1980): S5; and Peng Zhen, "Report on the Work of the Standing Committee."

[77] *Renmin Ribao*, Aug. 10, 1980, 1, trans. *FBIS-PRC* 80-167 (Aug. 26, 1980): L12–14.

[78] Xu Chongde, "Give Full Scope to the Functions of Local Organs of Power," *Renmin Ribao*, July 17, 1979, trans. *FBIS-CHI* 79-146 (July 27, 1979): L2–7.

However, strengthening rational-legal authority threatened individual cadres if not the Party as a whole. Rational-legal authority creates difficulties for those accustomed to patrimonial or patron-client politics, by restricting the use of personal discretion and opportunities to use official position for personal profit and by enforcing the use of cumbersome procedures. When the leaders of the state acted to strengthen rational-legal authority, lower-level cadres resisted, not because the reforms threatened to diminish either their formal authority or the Party's, but because they threatened to change the basis of authority from patrimonial authority to rational-legal authority—this they feared.

Renmin Ribao reported a case of "sabotaging democratic elections" that provides a glimpse of the struggle between the rational-legal authority of the state and the patrimonial authority of lower-level cadres. According to this account, Neiqiu county of Hebei province has a long history of factional politics centering around the issues of central versus local control and corruption versus reform. Before the Siqing (the "Four Cleans") Campaign of 1964, a faction of local cadres dominated Neiqiu county. During Siqing, the local faction was supplanted by "outsiders." During the Cultural Revolution, the Rebel Faction, led by Li Qingquan, demanded that Neiqiu county be governed by Neiqiu people and "rolled" the outsiders out of the county. Li became a leading figure in the county, paving the way for the pre-Siqing county secretary to return.

Li was removed from office in 1980 and was replaced by Han Jintang, who had been an official in the pre-Siqing administration. Han removed some of Li's Rebel Faction followers, but protected others, who subsequently were accused of various Cultural Revolution brutalities. Han engineered a shake-up of leading cadres throughout the county and down to the commune level. According to *Renmin Ribao*, Han used the shake-up to place "trusted followers" (*qinxin*) in positions of power. Han and his associates stand accused of gross corruption. When the County Party Committee established thirteen serious cases of economic crimes to be investigated, Han and his cronies blocked investigation of all but two. Some of his associates stand accused of embezzlement, and his own family received preferential treatment in obtaining urban residence permits and finding good jobs. It is clear from this account that any reform that would institutionalize elections would have been a threat to this style of politics.[79]

Andrew Walder has systematically analyzed the consequences of these

---

[79] "Neiqiu Xian Difang Zongpaizhuyi Wenti Shoudao Yansu Chuli" (Local Factionalism Problem in Neiqiu County Receives Strict Handling), *Renmin Ribao*, Nov. 8, 1983, 5. Many cases of counties run like Neiqiu have been "exposed" in the media. One of the most famous cases is described in Liu Binyan's "Between Monsters and People," now trans. in Perry Link's *Between Monsters and People* (Bloomington: University of Indiana Press, 1984).

kinds of relations at and below the unit level.[80] Walder points out that employees in the state sector are dependent on their units for housing, medical care, and social security. These are distributed according to a unit or workshop leader's evaluation of the employee's *biaoxian*, or attitude. Walder states that "the ability of superiors to reward employees flexibly, according to subjective evaluations, has provided fertile ground for the growth of pervasive networks of informal social ties based on *personal* loyalties" (Walder's emphasis).[81] Those who seek to gain more must persuade the leadership of both their political "redness" and their personal loyalty. Walder concludes that in this setting, small-group political meetings, such as those where nominations are made, "are imbued with the substance of ritual" and that dissent is not practical.[82] Those who take an active part in political meetings do so in order to improve their standing in the eyes of their leader or their patron and usually participate by defending the Party line and informing on less enthusiastic co-workers.

By making public the nominations procedure, the reform laws created problems for grass-roots cadres. If Walder's argument applies, a position as deputy is a bit of patronage used by leaders to reward activists who have demonstrated personal and political support.[83] Under the prereform nominating procedures, the leader had broad discretion to offer the position to the candidate of his choice. Under the reform rules, ordinary unit members, though unlikely to risk antagonizing their leaders by nominating or voting for "inappropriate" candidates, are witness to a greater portion of the proceedings. The leader now must manage the election process in a public forum presumably subject to the new laws. Moreover, the leader will be put in an unfavorable light with his superiors if problems are conspicuous. The "three ups and three downs" nominations procedures require far more time and effort and expose lower-level cadres to greater risks, regardless of how democratic they are.

Considering patrimonial authority as a basis of resistance helps put into context the kinds of problems encountered in implementing the reforms. The main form of resistance available to lower-level cadres is delay. While outright opposition is risky, they can plead for individual exemptions from established schedules. If county-level officials fail to keep up the pressure, then entire county election campaigns could halt in mid-course. Higher-level

[80] Andrew Walder, "Dependence and Authority in Chinese Industry," *Journal of Asian Studies* 43, no. 1 (November 1983): 51–76.

[81] Ibid., 52.

[82] Ibid.

[83] The profit and loss of becoming a county-level deputy requires further research. At the very least, Chinese people's deputies receive paid vacation for the length of the congress, free transportation to and from the conference, and a few days in relatively pleasant surroundings.

cadres can overcome this problem with enough attention to organization and mobilization, but there are limits to the number of such campaigns that the Center can manage during any given period.

In other cases, cadres formally implement the policy, but covertly subvert its intent. This line of resistance is more feasible if the tacit approval of immediate superiors can be obtained. Instances of this kind of resistance range from using strong-arm tactics during the "three ups and three downs" to violations of major provisions in the new laws. For example, *Nanjing Ribao* reported the case of one cadre who informed voters prior to balloting that although there were five names on the ballot, it would be best if the middle three were elected.[84] Election organizers have been tempted to "gerrymander" on behalf of their own units to maximize their personal influence.[85] On a grander scale, in April 1983 the Standing Committee of the Jiangxi Provincial People's Congress declared that county-level people's congresses in twenty-two jurisdictions in two prefectures (about one-fifth of all jurisdictions electing representatives to the Jiangxi Congress) had failed to have more candidates than positions on the ballot. The credentials of 196 deputies to the provincial people's congress were rejected, and the twenty-two lower-level congresses were ordered to conduct new elections.[86]

Cadres objecting to a policy may implement it in a manner that discredits it. Evidence for the use of this tactic is circumstantial but compelling. For example, in Changsha, at the Hunan Teachers' Training College, faced with the candidacy of a self-proclaimed non-Marxist, the normal nominating process broke down. Unable to secure what they considered an appropriate list of candidates by normal means, the authorities organized a series of primary elections, and still failing to obtain a "suitable" list, arbitrarily placed candidates of their own choosing on the list. This instigated student marches and a fast. The students succeeded in opening a channel of protest to Beijing, but were nonetheless suppressed.[87] Cheng Zihua and other leaders condemned the students.[88]

In a broader perspective, the patrimonial or patron-client environment captured the entire reform project. More generally, Carl Lande argues, "in many developing polities the great bulk of individual self-representation is self-representation pure and simple, without any pretense of a concern for the categorical interest of any collectivity, be it society as a whole or any sub-

---

[84] "Xuanju Bu Neng Ying 'Baojia' Shuping" (Elections Cannot Be "Escorted" with Strong Commentary), *Nanjing Ribao*, Aug. 24, 1980, 4.

[85] Shijiazhuang, Hebei Provincial Service, in *FBIS-CHI* 81-099 (May 22, 1981): R5.

[86] Nanchang, Jiangxi Provincial Service, Apr. 21, 1983, trans. *FBIS-CHI* 83-082 (Apr. 27, 1983): O4–5.

[87] See Shan Zi, "Election in Changsha," *SPEAHRhead*, nos. 12–13 (Winter–Spring 1982): 20–22.

[88] Beijing Xinhua Service, trans. *FBIS-CHI* 81-172 (Sept. 4, 1981): K2.

group within it."[89] Representation in a "civic culture" may involve particularistic issues, but it often concerns broad groups and results in formal rational-legal legislation. Patron-client systems tend to restrict discussion of universalistic issues but allow discussion of particularistic problems on behalf of individuals or narrowly defined groups. Patrimonial solutions are usually informal and ad hoc. In theory, deputies to people's congresses are vested with the authority to raise universalistic demands and to represent broad interests. According to official proclamations, the people's congresses are the final authority at each level of government. Deputies are organized to inspect various aspects of local administration, they have the formal right to query local cadres, they can submit motions in the congresses, and they can elect deputies to the next higher congress and leading officials at their level of government. However, in practice, only the leadership introduces formal legislation dealing with universalistic issues. Deputies seldom do more than call attention to specific problems of immediate concern to their constituency. These problems are usually resolved at the discretion of administrators on a case-by-case basis and rarely are incorporated into formal legislation.

The most significant channel of communication opened by the reforms is the deputies' right to bring their constituents' concerns to the attention of administrators by submitting motions to the people's congress sessions. At most sessions of people's congresses very large numbers of motions are received. The Second Session of the Fifth National People's Congress received 1,890 motions, and the Third Session received 2,300.[90] At the Baixia District Congress, deputies put forward 565 motions.[91] However, motions usually consist of individual problems or vague policy recommendations. For example, one deputy complained that a construction company building a new building failed to finish sidewalks and left residents with muddy walkways. Other deputies at the Baixia Congress submitted motions regarding the failure of night-soil collectors to regularly service public restrooms and the failure of garbage collectors to enter certain lanes or to allow residents enough time to get their garbage to curbside before departing.[92] In Beijing a Moslem deputy succeeded in reopening a Moslem restaurant for his Moslem constituents.[93] Other motions, especially those submitted at the National People's Congress, may involve grander problems, but they still cannot

---

[89] Carl H. Lande, "Networks and Groups in Southeast Asia," in *Friends, Followers and Factions*, ed. Steffen Schmidt et al. (Berkeley and Los Angeles: University of California Press, 1977), 75–99.

[90] Beijing Xinhua Service (July 1, 1979), trans. *FBIS-CHI* 79-129 (July 3, 1979), L5–6, and Beijing Xinhua Service (Sept. 27, 1980), trans. *FBIS-CHI* 80-190 (Sept. 29, 1980), L3.

[91] "Renmin Daibiao Wei Renmin" (People's Deputy for the People), *Nanjing Ribao*, Sept. 3, 1980, 4.

[92] Ibid.

[93] Sun Guiben, "Doncheng Qu Chunxia Fanguan Huifu Yingye" (Dongcheng District Chunxia Moslem Restaurant Back in Business), *Beijing Wanbao*, June 6, 1980, 2.

attain the force of law. Instead, motions are submitted to a motions committee or to the congress presidium. If these bodies find merit in the motion, they forward it to the relevant department. For example, in the case of the complaints related to construction projects, the motion would be forwarded through the hierarchy of local government to the construction company. In this regard, the processing of deputies' motions resembles the handling of letters to the editors of newspapers. Deputies are less vulnerable to reprisals than are letter writers, but they still have limited influence.[94] The only time the congress as a whole reviews the handling of motions occurs when the leadership of the congress makes a general report to the deputies at the succeeding congress session regarding the handling of all the motions submitted at the prior session.

Inspection tours provide another limited opportunity for deputies to offer suggestions to administrators. While on tour, deputies have far greater freedom of information than is usual in China, but the tours nonetheless are organized and guided by administrators or leaders of a congress.[95] Prior to convening the Nanjing Municipal People's Congress, 200 deputies were organized into ten small groups to inspect various aspects of city administration. Accompanied by responsible cadres from the relevant bureaus, deputies inspected the city bus system, city schools, drainage channels, and public restrooms, and various enterprises. Some of the inspection groups effected on-the-spot solutions to problems. For example, one group discovered that a pricing dispute between producers and marketers of padded jackets had left a batch of scarce jackets languishing in a warehouse. The deputies negotiated a compromise that brought the jackets into the stores in time to serve seasonal demand.[96] After the inspection tour in Nanjing, deputies spent a day and a half in conference with the City Party Committee, the City Revolutionary Committee, and responsible cadres from all of the city's departments and bureaus.[97] This produced some informal commitments from the city leadership. For example, as a result of one inspection group's findings, the city announced a plan to remodel forty-three public restrooms and the intention to search for means to keep others in more sanitary conditions.[98] However,

[94] For an account of one reasonable motion that encountered unreasonable delays, see "Ordeal of a Deputy's Motion," *Renmin Ribao*, May 7, 1981, 4, trans. *Chinese Law and Government* 15, nos. 3–4 (Fall–Winter 1982–1983): 191–92.

[95] See for example, Beijing Xinhua Service, May 21, 1981, trans. *FBIS-CHI* 81-099 (May 22, 1981): K1–2.

[96] Ning Fang, "Yipi Mianyi Luxu Ying Shi" (Padded Jackets One After the Other Supply the Market), *Nanjing Ribao*, Dec. 9, 1980, 1.

[97] Tan Jiahu, "Renmin Daibiao Zhengxie Weiyuan Shicha Huodong Jieshu" (People's Deputies and Political Consultative Conference Members Inspection Activities Conclude), *Nanjing Ribao*, Dec. 5, 1980.

[98] Chen Shungeng, "Xin Jian Gaijian Gong Ce 43 Cuo" (Forty-three Public Restrooms to Be Built or Rebuilt), *Nanjing Ribao*, Dec. 9, 1980, 1.

because these tours are organized by higher levels and because the resulting commitments are informal, the inspection tours are simply vehicles for particularistic, not universalistic, demands.

Deputies have the formal right to query officials at their level of government while their congress is in session. At the National People's Congress, deputies' queries have been used to bring up controversial issues and to criticize government boondoggles and tragedies, such as the Bohai oil-rig disaster (an incident where, owing to gross negligence, lives and property were lost at sea).[99] *Nanjing Ribao* urged local deputies to make good use of their right to question authorities and encouraged authorities to provide forthright answers and especially not to blame all problems on the "evil 'gang of four.'"[100] However, even at the Third Session of the Fifth National People's Congress (1980), which was touted for its democratic spirit, deputies dissatisfied with the responses to their queries had no official recourse.[101]

Deputies also have formal authority to elect various local leaders and deputies to the people's congress at the next higher level.[102] However, these elections appear to be more closely supervised than lower-level elections. In Beijing and Shanghai, municipal people's congresses have elected leading cadres recently transferred from leadership positions in other provinces. In Shanghai, Hu Lijiao, former chair of the Henan Provincial People's Congress Standing Committee, was elected chair of the Shanghai Municipal People's Congress Standing Committee within a few months of his transfer from Henan to Shanghai.[103] In Beijing, Jiao Ruoyu was elected mayor of Beijing three months after he arrived in the capital.[104]

These elections, however, had a significant impact on local leadership. In his "Summing Up Report" to the Standing Committee of the National People's Congress, Cheng Zihua listed the election of "fairly good leading bodies" as a main achievement of the elections, noting that the age of the county-level leadership elected by the congresses was 3.4 years younger than the previous group.[105] In Nanjing, elections of county and district leadership by county-level congresses resulted in a 30 percent turnover of county and district magistrates and assistant magistrates. This turnover decreased the average age of this group by four years (with the average age becoming 49.8)

[99] Beijing Xinhua Service, Sept. 5, 1980, trans. *FBIS-CHI* 80-175 (Sept. 8, 1980): L26.

[100] "Ni Zenyang Huida Zhixun" (How Did You Respond to Inquiries?), *Nanjing Ribao*, Sept. 25, 1980.

[101] Li Yuan, "Bring Into Full Play the Role of NPC Deputies" (n. 65 above).

[102] The new laws specify that county-level people's congresses will elect their county's representatives to higher-level people's congresses, members of the standing committee of their congress, leading comrades of the district or county people's government, and the leading cadre of the people's procuracy and leading judges of the district court.

[103] *Beijing Review*, 1981, no. 18 (May 4): 5.

[104] Beijing City Service, Apr. 28, 1981, trans. *FBIS-CHI* 81-091 (May 12, 1981): R1–3.

[105] Cheng Zihua, "Cheng Zihua's Report."

and increased the proportion with high school or higher degrees to one third.[106] This turnover of lower-level cadres aroused great resentment. *Nanjing Ribao* reported that some cadres (erroneously) equated losing elections with being purged in a campaign and argued that they had to accept that the people were the masters of the country.[107]

The ability of the system of people's congresses to confine political demands to particularistic issues indicates the limits of change. To a limited extent, the reforms have strengthened institutions. But the institutions themselves are fundamentally part of the patrimonial system. As it is conducted in public and must keep the appearance of maintaining formal procedures, "institutionalized patronage" is more equitably distributed than informal patronage and offers officials less opportunity for illicit personal profit. However, patronage is still closely rationed and distributed by state officials and not by deputies or ordinary citizens.

It is not just that the channels which voters or deputies can speak through are relatively restricted, but that these channels are a relatively small portion of the system of people's congresses, which is in turn a relatively small part of Chinese politics. The greater part of congress sessions are taken up by lengthy reports delivered by local administrators. The relative influence of people's congresses on the whole system of government can be judged from the brevity and infrequency of their sessions—provincial congresses meet for less than a week to ten days once a year.[108] Despite the reforms, the primary role of the people's congress system remains the mobilizing of lower levels to implement decisions made at higher levels.

Though limited and vulnerable, the reforms are highly significant. One member of the Jiangsu delegation to the Fourth National People's Congress (which was convened during the ascendancy of the Jiang Qing group) reported that his departure to congress sessions had to be kept secret even from his family and that, at the session, deputies were permitted to vote only "yes."[109] The right to speak out, even if not equivalent to the right to shape policy, is very important. In the National People's Congress, the right to speak out is the right to bring up issues like the Bohai oil-rig disaster. In Baixia district it is the right to complain about filthy toilets and muddy walkways. In terms of the ideal of democratic government, these are small matters, but compared with years past, they are a significant step forward.

[106] "Wo Shi Xian Qu Rendaihui Fenbie Xuanchu Xin De Lingdao" (Our City's County and District People's Congresses Each Select New Leadership), *Nanjing Ribao*, Nov. 1, 1980, 1.

[107] Jin Zhong, "Bo Luoxuan 'Hanxin Lun'" (Refute Defeated Candidates' "Bitter Disappointment Theory"), *Nanjing Ribao*, Oct. 5, 1980, 1.

[108] Standing committees of seventeen provincial-level people's congresses met about every two months for an average of four or five days.

[109] "Gaibian Lingdao Zuofeng Wei Qunzhong Mo Fuli" (Transform the Style of Leadership to Work for the Well-being of the Masses), *Nanjing Ribao*, Sept. 27, 1980, 2.

CONCLUSION

Two contradictory themes have been presented in this chapter. First, the Leninist mode of implementation—mobilization and organization—is a powerful tool for promoting political change. The campaign to implement the Election and Organic Laws is evidence of the power of this tool. In particular, reforming the structure of local government in more than 2,757 county-level units in two years and mobilizing over 95 percent of the voters to vote are impressive achievements. Second, extensive patrimonial networks are powerful impediments to the implementation of any reform in China and particularly to reforms that seek to promote rational-legal authority. In the case of the election campaign, the patrimonial authority of lower-level cadres was used to narrow the scope of already limited reforms.

China's Leninist-style organization facilitates both mobilization to implement policies *and* patrimonial resistance to central initiatives. The hierarchy of election-reform offices reaching from ministries in Beijing to the streets of Nanjing could not have been constructed and would not have been effective without the preexisting organizational trellis. Leninist mobilization depends on the ability of cadres at all levels to reward the "correct" participation and to sanction "mistakes." On the other hand, this same organization generates patrimonial opposition. It grants enormous authority to leaders at nodal points in the system without providing an adequate means of supervision, and constrains the making of political demands to particularistic patterns, resulting in widespread use of public office for personal gain.

This essay accounts for patrimonialism with reference to social and political structure rather than to culture. Others could plausibly argue that patrimonialism in China has ancient historical origins and that it is perpetuated by Chinese culture. The current Party line accepts this argument; it defines "feudalism" as corrupt and arbitrary rule founded on the economic base of small-scale peasant production; it acknowledges that "feudalism" persists into the current period and is a threat to socialism. However, the Deng Xiaoping leadership argues that "feudalism" is only a remnant of a previous historical period, which policies such as "promoting socialist law and socialist democracy" and the "four modernizations" will eliminate. While it is undeniably true that Chinese culture has accorded central importance to networks of relationships (*guanxi*) from Confucius to the present, it is also true that both the Party line and cultural interpretations understate the extent to which the current system *itself* recreates patrimonial patterns of authority.

The Leninist strategy of implementation has limits despite its power. These limits are roughly analogous to the limits Alec Nove finds in the Soviet command economy. He argues that in specific sectors where central authorities focus their attention, such as defense, the Soviet economy is able to achieve impressive results, but that on the whole, command economies cannot be as efficient as market economies. This is because central planners have a limited capacity to process information and to issue instructions and consequently must focus their attention on limited policy spheres.[110] In China it is difficult for local authorities to resist implementation of any policy energetically promoted by the Center. However, central authorities are limited both in the span of policies they can attend to at any given time and in the length of time they can devote to any single issue. Consequently, they may achieve fine results in some areas while leaving a legacy of chaos in others.

For example, the county-level election reform was more successfully implemented than lower-level election reform primarily because it was a focus of higher-level attention. Attempts to popularize the election of cadres in factories and in people's communes have failed.[111] The county-level campaign "succeeded" because it became a "flagship" policy. The massive campaign organized for implementing the county-level elections required huge inputs of expertise, time, and money, which were unavailable for organizing lower-level elections. The amount of organization a Leninist campaign requires increases exponentially for each level down the hierarchy which the campaign must reach. In addition, implementation will be most successful where rational-legal authority is strongest and when direct confrontation with patrimonial authority can be avoided. Deputies to county-level congresses are relatively marginal figures and pose little threat to the distribution of power. Conversely, a unit or work-group leader, whether or not the job is pleasant or desirable, has an important role in the further distribution of penalties and rewards and consequently is in a far more controversial position. Ironically, because China is compartmentalized, lower-level jobs can sometimes be more important. Implementing unit-level elections could be extremely disruptive, whereas the county-level elections could occur almost unnoticed.

The patrimonial substructure of Chinese politics has a tremendous capacity to absorb rational-legal reforms instituted by higher levels. Other Leninist states have the same problem—even after considerable economic development. In China the current campaign for Party rectification features attacks on cadres who use their official position for private gain. And yet, inasmuch as that campaign, like the election campaign, was designed to reinforce Leninist organization, and not to fundamentally alter the structure of social organization, it must, like the election campaign, suffer defeat. Some students

---

[110] Alec Nove, *The Soviet Economic System* (London: Allen & Unwin, 1977).

[111] See for example, John Burns, "The Implementation of Sub-Village Elections in South China, 1979–82" (Paper presented at conference, "Implementation in Post-Mao China," Ohio State University, June 1983).

at Nanjing University seem to have expressed a similar skepticism of the election campaign, when, according to a staffer of the Nanjing University Election Work Group, they declined to vote for any of the candidates appearing on the ballot and instead wrote in "the man from Atlantis," the star of a B-grade American TV series then showing on Chinese TV.[112]

[112] Interview at Nanjing University, Sept. 25, 1984.

CONTRIBUTORS

David Bachman, assistant professor of politics, Princeton University, is the author of *Chen Yun and the Chinese Political System*, and his research interests focus on China's political economy and decision making.

Christopher M. Clarke is a China analyst, Bureau of Intelligence and Research, U.S. Department of State. Clarke is former associate director of research at the National Council for U.S.–China Trade, Washington, D.C., and a frequent contributor to *China Business Review*. The views expressed in this article represent solely those of the author and do not necessarily represent the views of the Department of State or the U.S. government.

Thomas Fingar is Chief of the China Division, Office of East Asian and Pacific Affairs, Bureau of Intelligence and Research, United States Department of State. Until January 1986 Fingar was senior research associate in the International Strategic Institute at Stanford University. Work for his contribution to this volume was conducted while at Stanford, and the views expressed in his chapter do not necessarily represent those of the U.S. government. Fingar is the author of *China's Quest for Independence*.

David M. Lampton is associate professor of political science, Ohio State University, and adjunct scholar at the American Enterprise Institute, Washington, D.C. He is the author of numerous books and articles, most recent of which is *Paths to Power: Elite Mobility in Contemporary China*.

Barrett L. McCormick is assistant professor of political science at Marquette University. In 1979–1980 he was at Nanjing University and since then has written about democracy, due process, and patrimonial authority in China's post-Mao political reforms.

Barry Naughton is assistant professor of economics, University of Oregon. His current research interests include industrial policy and planning, urban living standards and income distribution, and the interaction between economic reform and macroeconomic policy in China.

Stanley Rosen is associate professor of political science at the University of Southern California in Los Angeles. He is the author of *Red Guard Factionalism and the Cultural Revolution in Guangzhou* and coeditor of *Policy Conflicts in Contemporary China: A Documentary Survey, with Analysis* (with John P. Burns) and *Socialist Democracy and the Chinese Legal System: The Li Yizhe Debates* (with Anita Chan and Jonathan Unger). He edits the journal *Chinese Education*.

Lester Ross is assistant professor of political science at Purdue University where he specializes in comparative politics and public policy. He has authored numerous articles and a forthcoming book on Chinese resource management and environmental protection policies.

Denis Fred Simon is Ford International assistant professor of management, Sloan School of Management, Massachusetts Institute of Technology. Simon has undertaken extensive research and publication concerning technology transfer with respect to both Taiwan and the People's Republic of China. He presently is undertaking research with respect to the reform of the science and technology system in China. He is author of *Taiwan, Technology Transfer, and Transnationalism*.

Dorothy J. Solinger teaches political science in the School of Social Sciences at the University of California, Irvine. Her most recent publications include *Chinese Business Under Socialism* and an edited volume entitled *Three Visions of Chinese Socialism*. Her current work deals with China's economic readjustment of 1979–1982.

Tyrene White is assistant professor of political science, Swarthmore College. White has undertaken long-term research in Hubei province in the People's Republic of China and is writing on leadership change, policy implementation, and income inequality at the local level.

David Zweig is on the faculty of the Fletcher School of Law and Diplomacy, Tufts University. He also is an associate in research at the Fairbank Center, Harvard University. His most recent articles have appeared in *World Politics* and *China Quarterly*, and he is completing a volume entitled *Agrarian Radicalism in China, 1968–1978*.

INDEX

People's Liberation Army (*continued*)
of, 184; and election work, 397;
General Political Department of,
44, 210n, 236, 237; General Rear
Services Department of, 136, 236,
237; in OTP, 237, 244, 245–46. *See
also* Military sector
Performance evaluation, 7–8, 18–19,
23–24
Persecution, of commodity-price work-
ers, 109–10
Personalistic politics, 20, 388
Personal relationships. *See* Interpersonal
networks
Personnel, 21, 22; educational bureau-
cracy, 339; Leninist states supervis-
ing, 385; reforms in, 9, 25–47, 210,
221–22; S & T, *see* Scientists *and*
Technocrats; tax, 121, 129–31, 153.
See also Leadership.
Petroleum, 65–66, 193. *See also* Bohai oil-
rig disaster; Ministry of Petroleum
"Petroleum Clique," 199n, 208
Physics, high-energy, 361, 365
Pi Chunxie, 391n, 393, 399
PLA. *See* People's Liberation Army
Plan, state, 83, 89, 91, 368–69. *See also*
Five-Year Plan
Planners/Planning, 21, 22, 120, 122; in-
vestment, 51–80; water, 172–73,
177–78
Planning Office (Changban), 177, 183–
84, 185
Plenum (Central Committee): Fourth
(September 1979), 34, 260, 261, 280;
Fifth (February 1980), 34, 260, 261;
Sixth (June 1981), 37, 38, 40, 264–
65. *See also* Third Plenum
Pluralism, 386
Poland, 113, 386n, 388n
Police, 21, 22, 44n, 385
Politburo, 25–26, 34, 40, 41, 211, 262n;
age in, 30; Standing Committee of,
34, 207, 261; State Energy Commis-
sion and, 210
Politics: and economy, 94, 384–85; of
energy policies, 212–13; in S & T

policy, 357, 363, 379; water prob-
lems and, 157, 163, 165, 169–89.
See also Context, implementation;
Patrimonialism
Pollution, water, 164–65, 175
Popularization, 8, 27–28; of education,
321, 324, 351; of S & T, 364, 366
Population: Baixia, 395; Gulou, 395,
396n; Hong Shan, 299; Hua Shan,
299; illiterate and semi-literate, 325;
Nanjing, 395; OTP-participating,
246–47; tax-paying, 131
Population density, water supplies for,
158
Population displacements, in water pro-
jects, 181–83, 187
Population growth. *See* Birthrate
Population policy, 5, 12, 384. *See also*
Birth control
Populist ideology, 8
Port construction, 66
Power division, between central and
local officials, 70–71
"Practice," 389–90
Pragmatists, 221, 228, 251, 281; and for-
estry policy, 229, 239–40; local, 78,
79
Press. *See* Media
Pressman, Jeffrey, 15, 187, 189, 383
Price bureaucracy, 21, 22
Price controls, 11, 81–118
Price indexes, 90
Price reforms, 11, 78, 81–118, 139, 145,
370–71
Prices, 11, 26, 75, 77, 173–74, 204; agri-
cultural, *see* Agricultural products;
cost-benefit analysis with, 173; ener-
gy, 12, 17, 173, 174, 191, 201, 204;
forest products, 229; negotiated, 90,
97, 98, 99, 100, 103, 107, 109; water,
12, 167–68, 174; world commodity,
21. *See also* Inflation; Price reforms
"Principal contradiction," 325
Private ownership: enterprise, 113, 125,
126; farm, 34, 266, 273; forest, 10,
229, 230, 245, 248–49, 250
Privatizing, 385, 386

Designer: Rick Chafian
Compositor: Asco Trade Typesetting Ltd.
Text: 10/12 Baskerville
Display: Baskerville